BEGINNING PERL

T0252293

BEGINNING

Perl

BEGINNING
Perl

Curtis "Ovid" Poe

WILEY

John Wiley & Sons, Inc.

Beginning Perl

Published by
John Wiley & Sons, Inc.
10475 Crosspoint Boulevard
Indianapolis, IN 46256
www.wiley.com

ISBN: 978-1-118-01384-7
ISBN: 978-1-118-22187-7 (ebk)
ISBN: 978-1-118-23563-8 (ebk)
ISBN: 978-1-118-26051-7 (ebk)

Manufactured in the United States of America

10 9 8 7 6 5 4 3 2 1

For general information on our other products and services please contact our Customer Care Department within the United States at (877) 762-2974, outside the United States at (317) 572-3993 or fax (317) 572-4002.

Wiley publishes in a variety of print and electronic formats and by print-on-demand. Some material included with standard print versions of this book may not be included in e-books or in print-on-demand. If this book refers to media such as a CD or DVD that is not included in the version you purchased, you may download this material at http://booksupport.wiley.com. For more information about Wiley products, visit www.wiley.com.

Library of Congress Control Number: 2012944681

This book is dedicated to my wife, Leïla, and our daughter, Lilly-Rose.

When I first had the opportunity to write this book, I was going to turn it down because I had a newborn daughter. Leïla, however, insisted I write it. She knows how much I love writing and was adamant that she would be supportive while I wrote this book. She has been more than supportive: She has kept me going through a long, painful process. Leïla, I love you. And beaucoup. You know what I mean.

CREDITS

Acquisitions Editor
Mary James

Project Editor
Maureen Spears

Technical Editor
chromatic

Production Editor
Christine Mugnolo

Copy Editor
San Dee Phillips

Editorial Manager
Mary Beth Wakefield

Freelancer Editorial Manager
Rosemarie Graham

Associate Director of Marketing
David Mayhew

Marketing Manager
Ashley Zurcher

Business Manager
Amy Knies

Production Manager
Tim Tate

Vice President and Executive Group Publisher
Richard Swadley

Vice President and Executive Publisher
Neil Edde

Associate Publisher
Jim Minatel

Project Coordinator, Cover
Katie Crocker

Proofreader
James Saturnio, Word One New York

Indexer
Robert Swanson

Cover Designer
Ryan Sneed

Cover Image
© RTimages / iStockPhoto

ABOUT THE AUTHOR

CURTIS "OVID" POE started programming back in 1982 and has been programming Perl almost exclusively for 13 years. He currently sits on the Board of Directors for the Perl Foundation, speaks at conferences in many countries, but is most proud of being a husband and father.

ABOUT THE TECHNICAL EDITOR

CHROMATIC is a prolific writer and developer. He is most recently the author of *Modern Perl*, from Onyx Neon Press (http://onyxneon.com/).

ACKNOWLEDGMENTS

AS WITH MANY BOOKS, this one would not have been possible without many people helping me along the way. In particular, I want to thank Michael Rasmussen, my "secret reviewer" who, despite not being one of the official reviewers, nonetheless diligently reviewed every chapter and came back with many helpful comments that made this a far better book.

I also have to thank chromatic, my technical reviewer, who managed to annoy me time and time again by pointing out subtle issues that I should have caught but didn't. He's a better programmer than I am, damn it.

Mary James and Maureen Spears, my primary contacts at Wiley, Wrox imprint, were a joy to work with and really helped keep my spirits up when this book seemed to drag on far longer than I thought. Their senses of humor and help through the editorial process were invaluable. I also have to thank San Dee, whoever the heck she is. Her name kept popping up through the editorial process and her work catching many issues in this book is much appreciated.

I also need to thank Adrian Howard, Ævar Arnfjörð Bjarmason, Alejandro Lopez, Andy Armstrong, Aristotle, Michael Schwern, Ricardo Signes, Sean T Lewis, and Simon Cozens for foolishly agreeing to review a book of this length.

Finally, I'd like to thank the people working on the Open Feedback Publishing System at O'Reilly and for engendering a review community (http://ofps.oreilly.com/titles/9781118013847/) for this book and for all the helpful comments this site generated.

There are far too many to name and I apologize in advance for not mentioning all of you here.

On a personal note, I have to say that many times I've read the comment "and all errors are mine" and I've thought, "But that's what reviewers are for, right?" The reality is far different. When you write a book, the reviewers will catch a huge number of issues, as mine did, but they can't catch all of them. I now realize that in a work of this scope, I have to take responsibility for any flaws. The reviewers are generally not paid for this work and they're not going to sit there, hours every night, months on end, worrying over every paragraph as I did. They caught most issues, but the remaining flaws in this work are mine and mine alone. Mea Culpa.

CONTENTS

INTRODUCTION

"Get a job, hippy!"

That was the subtitle for this book that was sadly, but wisely, rejected. However, it conveys two things about this book that I've tried to focus on: getting a job and having fun while learning the skills you need. Well, as much fun as you can reasonably have while learning how to program.

Although many books aren't explicit in this intent, I'll say it up front: This book is about money. Information Technology (IT) workers are in high demand, even during the current economic downturn, and this book draws not only on your author's 13 years of experience with the Perl programming language, but also on surveys that have been conducted regarding "Perl in the wild." That's why you'll find an astonishing decision in this book: We focus on Perl versions 5.8 and 5.10. They're no longer officially supported, but these are the versions of Perl that most companies still use. Fortunately, the Perl 5 Porters (also known as P5P) strive hard to maintain backward compatibility, so the code in this book still runs on the latest versions of Perl. As a result of this focus, by the time you finish this book, you'll have the skills necessary to accept many Perl jobs.

I first conceived of a Perl book aimed at developing job skills when I was living in Portland, Oregon. Later, I moved to London and made a few inquiries about working on it, but to no avail. Then I moved to Amsterdam and started working with Wrox to create this book. I'm now living in Paris and am finishing this book. The common thread in all those cities is that Perl opened up the door for jobs. With many other excellent dynamic programming languages, such as PHP, Python, and Ruby fighting for the same slice of the pie, some Perl developers moved to other languages, leaving companies in need of developers to maintain their code and build new systems in Perl. Perl developers are in high demand, and this book is about meeting that demand.

Lest you think that Perl is just for maintaining legacy code, I can assure you that plenty of companies, large and small, are still turning to Perl as their first choice of programming language. It's powerful, solid, and the Comprehensive Perl Archive Network (CPAN) is still the largest collection of open source code dedicated to a single language. Many times you'll find that rather than needing to write new code to solve a tricky problem, you can turn to the CPAN and find that someone's already written that code.

I've been paid to program in many languages, including 6809 Assembler (boy, did I just date myself, or what?), BASIC, C, Java, COBOL, FOCUS, JCL (Job Control Language), VBA, and JavaScript, but I keep coming back to Perl. Why? Well, why not? It's a powerful language. If your programming needs are CPU-bound, such as in real-time ray tracing, then Perl may not be the best choice, but otherwise, it's an excellent language. I tend to work on large-scale database-driven applications, and the performance issues there are usually located in the network, the database, or the file system. You'd have the same performance issues regardless of the programming language, so you may as well choose a language that you enjoy.

So what have I done with Perl? Probably the most prominent example is movies. If you read in the paper that your favorite movie made x millions of dollars over the weekend, there's a good chance that I worked on the Perl software that processes those numbers (in real time, I might add) because those numbers are often reported by a single company.

I also worked for several years on the central metadata repository for the BBC, the world's largest broadcaster. When another team in the BBC needs data about programs (if you're in the UK, you may have heard of this little thing called iPlayer), it probably called the Perl software that I worked on.

I also worked for the world's largest online hotel reservation firm. When I started, the firm was busy converting many of its Java programs to Perl because Perl was just so darned useful. Almost all its backend code is written in Perl, which is a large part of its huge success.

I currently work for Weborama, one of the pioneers of online marketing technologies in Europe. I deal with insane amounts of traffic and data, all of which Perl handles quite nicely. In fact, Weborama ditched some other popular programming languages in favor of Perl because, well, Perl just gets the job done.

At the end of the day, Perl is so much fun to use that although I still dabble in other languages (mostly JavaScript, but Erlang is looking particularly interesting right now), I'm happy to keep hacking in Perl. I dash out a quick `bash` script from time to time and then kick myself when I find it's easier to write in Perl as soon as it starts getting complicated. Perl has been very good to me.

WHO THIS BOOK IS FOR

Is this book for you? I've tried hard to ensure that even someone with no programming experience can pick up this book and learn Perl.

If You Have No Programming Experience

However, if you have no programming experience, you're going to want to pay a lot of attention to Chapter 1, where I describe many different resources available to help a new programmer. You'll generally find the Perl community to be a friendly place, always happy to help someone learn. Without a background in computers, you might struggle with Chapter 2, which is about installing Perl code from the CPAN, but just turn back to Chapter 1 for a many excellent resources on where to turn for help (including local user groups where you can meet other Perl programmers). After you get over the learning curve in Chapter 2, you'll find the rest of the book to be as straightforward as a programming book can be.

If You're An Experienced Programmer

If you're an experienced programmer looking for a comprehensive resource into a language, this is that book. Chapter 1 mostly covers where to look for help, but you probably already know how to find programming answers by now. Chapter 2 is about installing Perl modules from the CPAN and that's worth at least skimming, but you're going to want to start paying attention at Chapter 3, where we discuss Perl's variables. Perl doesn't focus much on the *kinds* of data you use, but how you organize that data. Perl makes the assumption that you're competent and know what your data is and makes it easy to organize your data they way you need it.

WHAT THIS BOOK COVERS

Though this will come as a surprise to some, we focus on two unsupported versions of Perl: 5.8 and 5.10. This is because multiple surveys and your author's personal experience working for and consulting with multiple companies show that they're conservative about upgrading programming languages and tend to use older versions. Fortunately, P5P focuses heavily on ensuring that newer versions of Perl are backward compatible, so all of the examples in this book should work on the newest versions of Perl. When appropriate, we do discuss some newer features that you may encounter and clearly indicate when this happens.

We focus on the core of the Perl language, and then move to working with databases, with a focus on web technologies. Why web technologies? Money. This book is about getting a job. If you don't already know SQL or HTML, it will eventually (by Chapter 15) be worth hitting some online tutorials to learn a bit of SQL and HTML. You won't need much to use to use this book, but it will be worth understanding the basics to make some examples easier to understand.

HOW THIS BOOK IS STRUCTURED

This book is written so that each chapter builds on previous chapters.

➤ **Chapters 1 and 2:** The first two chapters of this book (cunningly referred to as Chapters 1 and 2), are mostly background information. They tell you where to look for extra help and how to set up a CPAN client to install additional Perl modules.

➤ **Chapters 3 through 10:** These chapters cover the core of the Perl language. By the time you're done with them, you should find it easy to write Perl to handle many common tasks. They are actually the "Beginning Perl" this book's title refers to.

➤ **Chapters 11 through 13:** These chapters start covering modules (a way to organize your code) and object-oriented programming (a powerful way to create reusable "experts" that can handle common programming tasks).

➤ **Chapter 14:** This chapter covers testing, a subject near and dear to my heart. Many programmers suffer from *fear-driven programming*. This is a problem when you work with large systems and are afraid to change something because you don't know what it will break. Done right, testing can free you from that fear and give you the confidence to make any changes you might need, even on large systems.

➤ **Chapters 15 through 18:** These are somewhat optional, but don't skip them. They're the chapters that can give you a smattering of skills that mid- to high-level Perl programmers need. You learn how easy it is to build websites in Perl, how to work with databases, how to handle many common tasks (such as working with dates), and how to work with command line applications.

➤ **Chapter 19:** This chapter finishes up by summarizing what you've covered and what you still have to learn. You also build a web application to manage multimedia rights data to fight DMCA takedown notices. It's an ambitious task, but you can see how easy it is to do with Perl and the CPAN.

➤ **Appendix:** Each chapter in this book ends with a set of exercises to further sharpen the skills you've learned throughout the chapter. This appendix gives the answers to those exercises. Don't cheat and read them first because that would be, uh, cheating.

WHAT YOU NEED TO USE THIS BOOK

Perl code, fortunately, runs on almost every operating system and often requires no changes when switching from, say, Windows to Linux. The only thing you will need to use the examples in this book is Perl version 5.8 or newer. Later chapters require that you install code from the CPAN, but Chapter 2 covers using the CPAN thoroughly.

CONVENTIONS

To help you get the most from the text and keep track of what's happening, we've used a number of conventions throughout the book.

TRY IT OUT

The *Try It Out* is an exercise you should work through, following the text in the book.

1. They usually consist of a set of steps.

2. Each step has a number.

3. Follow the steps through with your copy of the database.

How It Works

After each *Try It Out*, the code you've typed will be explained in detail.

> **WARNING** *Boxes with a warning icon like this one hold important, not-to-be forgotten information that is directly relevant to the surrounding text.*

> **NOTE** *The pencil icon indicates notes, tips, hints, tricks, or and asides to the current discussion.*

As for styles in the text:

➤ We *highlight* new terms and important words when we introduce them.

➤ We show keyboard strokes like this: Ctrl+A.

➤ We show filenames, URLs, and code within the text like so: `persistence.properties`.

➤ We present code in two different ways:

```
We use a monofont type with no highlighting for most code examples.
```

We use bold to emphasize code that's particularly important in the present context.

SOURCE CODE

As you work through the examples in this book, you may choose either to type in all the code manually or to use the source code files that accompany the book. All the source code used in this book is available for download at `http://www.wrox.com`. A file name is provided for each code snippet or listing presented in the book and this file name corresponds to the source code on the `www.wrox.com` site. When at the site, simply locate the book's title (either by using the Search box or by using one of the title lists) and click the Download Code link on the book's detail page to obtain all the source code for the book.

> **NOTE** *Because many books have similar titles, you may find it easiest to search by ISBN; this book's ISBN is 978-1-118-01384-7.*

After you download the code, just decompress it with your favorite compression tool. Alternatively, you can go to the main Wrox code download page at `http://www.wrox.com/dynamic/books/download.aspx` to see the code available for this book and all other Wrox books.

ERRATA

We make every effort to ensure that there are no errors in the text or in the code. However, no one is perfect, and mistakes do occur. If you find an error in one of our books, like a spelling mistake or faulty piece of code, we would be grateful for your feedback. By sending in errata you may save another reader hours of frustration and at the same time you can help us provide even higher quality information.

To find the errata page for this book, go to `http://www.wrox.com` and locate the title using the Search box or one of the title lists. Then, on the book details page, click the Book Errata link. On this page you can view all errata that has been submitted for this book and posted by Wrox editors. A complete book list including links to each book's errata is also available at `http://www.wrox.com/misc-pages/booklist.shtml`.

If you don't spot "your" error on the Book Errata page, go to `http://www.wrox.com/contact/techsupport.shtml` and complete the form there to send us the error you have found. We'll check the information and, if appropriate, post a message to the book's errata page and fix the problem in subsequent editions of the book.

P2P.WROX.COM

For author and peer discussion, join the P2P forums at `p2p.wrox.com`. The forums are a web-based system for you to post messages relating to Wrox books and related technologies and interact with other readers and technology users. The forums offer a subscription feature to e-mail you topics of interest of your choosing when new posts are made to the forums. Wrox authors, editors, other industry experts, and your fellow readers are present on these forums.

At `http://p2p.wrox.com` you can find a number of different forums to help you not only as you read this book, but also as you develop your own applications. To join the forums, just follow these steps:

1. Go to `p2p.wrox.com` and click the Register link.

2. Read the terms of use and click Agree.

3. Complete the required information to join as well as any optional information you want to provide, and click Submit.

4. You will receive an e-mail with information describing how to verify your account and complete the joining process.

> **NOTE** You can read messages in the forums without joining P2P but to post your own messages, you must join.

After you join, you can post new messages and respond to messages other users post. You can read messages at any time on the web. If you want new messages from a particular forum e-mailed to you, click the Subscribe to this Forum icon by the forum name in the forum listing.

For more information about how to use the Wrox P2P, be sure to read the P2P FAQs for answers to questions about how the forum software works as well as many common questions specific to P2P and Wrox books. To read the FAQs, click the FAQ link on any P2P page.

For Instructors: Classroom and training support material are available for this book.

1

What Is Perl?

WHAT YOU WILL LEARN IN THIS CHAPTER:

➤ Getting Perl

➤ Learning about the community

➤ Understanding the Perl documentation

➤ Using a terminal

➤ Writing your first Hello, World! program

My goodness, where to start? To even begin to cover a language with such a rich history and huge influence over the world of computing and the web is a daunting task, so this chapter just touches on the highlights.

By the time you finish with this chapter, you'll have a good understanding of the history of Perl and where to go to get more help when you need to know more than this book offers. Learning how to find the answers to your questions is probably one of the most valuable skills you can develop.

Before you install Perl, a word about Perl terminology — information that you need to know to converse intelligently with other Perl users.

The name of the language is Perl. It is not PERL. Larry Wall, the creator of Perl, originally wanted a name with positive connotations and named the language Pearl, but before its release, he discovered another programming language named Pearl, so he shortened the name to Perl.

The name of the language causes a bit of confusion. When people write *Perl* (uppercase), they are referring to the programming language you learn in this book. When people write `perl` (lowercase), they are referring to the binary executable used to run Perl, the language.

So perl is the binary and Perl is the language. The former parses and runs the latter: perl parses and runs Perl. If someone writes PERL, you know immediately that they're not familiar with the Perl language. This is why sometimes you see experienced programmers use PERL to refer to poorly written Perl programs.

Due to the wording of the original documentation that shipped with Perl, many programmers assume that PERL is an acronym for *Practical Extraction and Report Language.* However perlfaq1 — the documentation that shipped with Perl — sets the record straight:

```
... never write "PERL", because perl is not an acronym, apocryphal
   folklore and post-facto expansions notwithstanding.
```

Remember, there is no such thing as PERL. It's Perl, the language, or perl, the executable.

DYNAMIC PROGRAMMING LANGUAGES

Perl, Python, Ruby, and PHP are all examples of *dynamic programming languages.* In contrast to languages such as Java, C++, and other *static programming languages,* the dynamic languages often delay certain things until run time that static languages might decide at compile time, such as determining which class a method will dispatch to. Without going into detail beyond the scope of this book, dynamic languages tend to be rapid to develop in, but have certain kinds of errors that are less common in static languages.

Discussions about dynamic and static typing are about type theory, and the terms are poorly defined. However, there is one solid rule you should remember: Computer *scientists* have reasonable disagreements about type theory, whereas computer *programmers* have unreasonable ones. If you get into "static versus dynamic languages" debates, and you don't understand type theory, you're going to sound like a fool to those who do. So don't do that.

PERL TODAY

Today, Perl is widely used throughout the world. It comes standard on every major operating system apart from Windows and is still extensively used in web development, thus driving many websites. New startups choose Perl as their language of choice for data processing, system administration, web development, and other uses.

As of this writing, Ricardo Signes, a long time Perl hacker, is overseeing the development of Perl. Perl 6, a new language with roots in Perl 5, is being actively worked on with several interesting implementations, including a Niecza, which runs on Mono/.NET.

PERL JOB OPPORTUNITIES

A quick search of many job sites shows plenty of opportunities, but there are fewer competent developers vying for these roles. If a career in Perl interests you, you can also check out http://jobs.perl.org/ for a website dedicated to listing jobs that have Perl as their major technology, compared to jobs where Perl is merely used incidentally.

This book mostly focuses on 5.8.*x* and 5.10.*x* versions of Perl, even though support for both of these has officially been discontinued. Why? This was a difficult decision to make, but there were several reasons for this decision. An important consideration is that surveys show most businesses still run these versions of Perl. It's a strange thing for a book author to stand up and say, "This book targets an unsupported version of the language," but you go to war with the Perl you have, not the Perl you want.

Fortunately, this choice isn't as bad as it might sound. The Perl 5 Porters (known as "P5P") work hard to keep new releases of Perl backward compatible. Perl 5.14.2 ships with almost half a million tests (455,832, to be exact) to ensure that Perl works exactly as intended. Thus, what you learn to write throughout this book generally works unmodified on later versions of Perl.

GETTING PERL

Obviously, it's difficult to program Perl if you don't have it installed on your computer; this section covers several methods for doing this. Even if you already have Perl installed, you should to read this section anyway because if your system depends on your Perl installation, you might want to install a separate version to avoid changing behavior that your system requires.

So how do you get Perl? Well, you're in luck. Almost every major operating system aside from Windows ships with Perl by default. This is often referred to as the *system Perl*. You can test whether you already have Perl installed by opening up a terminal and typing **perl -v** at the command line. Currently, on my MacBook Pro, this prints the following:

```
$ perl -v
This is perl 5, version 14, subversion 2 (v5.14.2) built for darwin-2level
Copyright 1987-2011, Larry Wall
Perl may be copied only under the terms of either the Artistic License or the
GNU General Public License, which may be found in the Perl 5 source kit.
Complete documentation for Perl, including FAQ lists, should be found on
this system using "man perl" or "perldoc perl". If you have access to the
Internet, point your browser at http://www.perl.org/, the Perl Home Page.
```

Perl is supported on more than 100 platforms — did you even know there were that many? If you want a different version of Perl than what you already have installed, go to http://www.perl.org/get.html.

> **NOTE** If you use OS X, you already have Perl installed. However, you will eventually build modules or install other modules. To do this, you need to install the Developer Tools found on your OS X install DVD or in Apple's AppStore. Only the UNIX Development Support tools are required, but there's no harm (other than disk space) in installing all of them. Why Apple built a wonderful computer for developers and made the development tools optional is one of life's many inscrutable mysteries.

Working with Non-Windows Platforms: perlbrew

If you do not run Windows, check out `perlbrew` (http://www.perlbrew.pl/). This tool enables you to install multiple and run different versions of Perl.

Running different Perl installations is important because there's a good chance that some of your operating system depends on the behavior of the system Perl. Therefore, using `perlbrew` to install your own versions of Perl not only ensures that you don't need to worry about breaking your system Perl, but you also can play with different versions.

That being said, so long as you're not overwriting any modules that your system Perl uses, it's fine to use your system Perl for learning Perl. It's also usually fine to upgrade your system modules, but it's not recommended. If a core module your system depends on changes in an incompatible way, the results are unpredictable. Windows does not have this problem because it does not depend on Perl.

If your system has both `bash` and `curl` installed, you can try to install `perlbrew` with the following command-line command:

```
curl -kL http://xrl.us/perlbrewinstall | bash
```

If you don't have `curl` installed but you do have `wget`, you can install `perlbrew` with this:

```
wget --no-check-certificate -O - http://install.perlbrew.pl | bash
```

If that works on your system, it should enable you to easily install multiple versions of Perl without superuser (root, or administrator) permissions. It's then easy to switch between those versions. This has many benefits, including the following:

➤   It's easy to try new versions of Perl.

➤   You don't risk breaking your system's Perl.

➤   You don't need superuser permission to install *Comprehensive Perl Archive Network* (CPAN) modules.

➤   You can test production code on newer versions of Perl.

To install and use Perl version 5.14.2, type the following (but see the `perlbrew available` command below):

```
perlbrew install perl-5.14.2
perlbrew switch perl-5.14.2
```

The installation takes a while because `perlbrew` needs to download and build the version of Perl you're asking for.

After `perlbrew` installs, you can use the following commands:

➤ **perlbrew help:** Typing **perlbrew help** shows you how to use `perlbrew`. It's quite easy.

➤ **Installing an older Perl version:** If you want to install an older version of Perl, you can run the following:

```
perlbrew install perl-5.8.3
```

➤ **Switching versions:** You can run `perlbrew list` to see which versions of Perl you have installed and can switch to a different version. Following is the author's setup:

```
$ perlbrew list
  perl-5.10.1
  perl-5.12.3
  perl-5.14.0
* perl-5.14.2
  perl-5.8.3
```

The asterisk before the version indicates which version of Perl you're running at the moment.

➤ **Testing code:** To test your code against different versions of Perl, use the following:

```
perlbrew exec myprogram.pl
```

The author used this command extensively while writing this book because it's extremely useful when you want to find out if your code is compatible with different versions of Perl.

➤ **Available versions:** As of this writing, following are the Perl versions available to install on the author's computer. The `perlbrew available` command lists all available versions:

```
$ perlbrew available
  perl-5.15.4
i perl-5.14.2
  perl-5.12.4
i perl-5.10.1
  perl-5.8.9
  perl-5.6.2
  perl5.005_04
  perl5.004_05
  perl5.003_07
```

The leading i indicates which versions of Perl you have installed, and the list of available versions will grow over time.

If you can use `perlbrew`, it will make your programming life much more pleasant.

> **NOTE** Using `perlbrew` is great, but it requires that you already have Perl 5.8 or newer installed on your system. However, as because version 5.8 was released in July of 2002 (see as shown in Table 1-1), this is generally not a problem.

Using Windows

Windows is one of the few operating systems that does not include Perl by default. This makes things a bit more difficult, but you have a wide variety of options here. Your author recommends Strawberry Perl, but ActivePerl is also an excellent choice. Cygwin is only recommended only if you want a Linux emulation layer.

Strawberry Perl

Strawberry Perl (`http://strawberryperl.com`) is the newest option for Windows, but it's the one many developers prefer today. It's also free and it's the choice of Perl that Larry Wall utilizes when he uses Windows. Strawberry Perl does not offer commercial support. Like many open source projects, support is excellent — but on a volunteer basis.

When you install Strawberry Perl, the following software is installed with it:

➤ Mingw GCC C/C++ compiler

➤ `dmake` make tool

➤ `ExtUtils::CBuilder` and `ExtUtils::ParseXS`

➤ `Bundle::CPAN`

➤ `Bundle::LWP` (which provides more reliable HTTP CPAN repository support)

➤ `XML::Parser` and `XML::LibXML`, which enables most CPAN XML modules

➤ DBI and DBD drivers for SQLite, ODBC, MySQL, and Postgres

➤ Additional minor modules to enhance the stability of Win32 Perl.

Don't worry about what all this means for now. As you move further along in the book, these items will start to make sense. Just know that they make Perl on Windows easy enough to use that it rivals Perl on Linux for many tasks. Unless you have a particular reason to use another version of Perl, the author recommends Strawberry Perl. Some things to remember with Strawberry Perl follow:

➤ **Pros:** Strawberry Perl "just works." Almost everything you need to develop Perl is bundled with it, including many tools that are usually mandatory in a work environment.

➤ **Cons:** It's relatively new and companies that rely on Windows are sometimes uncomfortable with software that lacks commercial support.

ActiveState Perl

Another strong alternative for Windows is ActivePerl (`http://www.activestate.com/activeperl`). It's free, but commercial support is provided. ActivePerl has been available for more than a decade and is probably the most popular Perl for Windows. When considering ActivePerl, remember the following:

➤ **Pros:** ActivePerl has been around for more than a decade, and it is maintained by a company with a strong history of supporting Perl and dynamic languages. It's also often updated faster than Strawberry Perl. Additionally, some binary packages are easier to install with ActiveState than with Strawberry Perl.

➤ **Cons:** ActivePerl does not ship with the full set of tools with which Strawberry Perl ships. Further, it contains some non-open source utilities and, unlike Strawberry Perl, it cannot be embedded in other open source projects.

Cygwin

One way to run Perl on Windows is to install Cygwin, a free Linux emulator for Windows. You can download Cygwin from `http://www.cygwin.com/`. Click the Install Cygwin link for instructions.

By default, Cygwin does not install Perl. You can easily find instructions on the web for installing and running Perl under Cygwin, including many useful YouTube videos. If you go this route, make sure that when you install Cygwin, you select both Perl and the GCC/C++ packages from Development menu when you're given a choice on which packages to install. However, to get the most out of Perl on Cygwin, make sure you have the following packages installed:

➤ `perl`

➤ `gcc/C++`

➤ `gnupg`

➤ `gzip`

➤ `lynx`

➤ `make`

➤ `ncftp`

➤ `ncftpget`

➤ `tar`

➤ `unzip`

➤ `wget`

This list should cover most of what you need. Keep the following in mind:

➤ **Pros:** With Cygwin, you get a Linux environment, which means that most Perl programs can run unchanged.

➤ **Cons:** As an emulation layer, it tends to be a bit slow. It's also a bit difficult to install everything correctly if you're not used to it.

> **NOTE** *If you have issues getting Perl to run on Windows, go to* `http://win32` `.perl.org/`. *Your easiest (and best) options are to go with the ActiveState or Strawberry Perl options, but* `win32.perl.org` *gives you plenty of answers to questions you may encounter.*

THE PERL COMMUNITY

You didn't read detailed instructions on how to install Perl for Windows or how to install alternative versions of Perl on your operating system of choice. As mentioned previously, Perl is supported on more than 100 platforms, and although the author has tried writing instructions on how to do this in the past, the impossibility of handling that obscure error that someone inevitably has makes this difficult. Fortunately, Perl is easy to install on Windows, and the language has a strong community supporting it; this community can help you work through even the most unusual issues.

Because the Wrox "Programmer to Programmer" series targets experienced developers looking to expand their skills, you, the developer, will likely be familiar with software installation. If you're new to programming, you might need a bit more help. Either way, the following sections discuss a variety of resources to help you start.

> **NOTE** *Consult these sources regularly when you get stuck on a particular problem. This is one of the lovely things about the open source community: Quality help is widely available, and it's free. There's no need to struggle on your own when so many people can help you learn Perl.*

IRC

Internet Relay Chat (IRC) has been around since 1988, and it's often a great way to get questions answered "in real time." With IRC, you have several options:

➤ mIRC (`http://www.mirc.net/`): For Windows, this is probably the most popular IRC client, but it's shareware, and you can use it only for 30 days before paying.

➤ KVIrc (`http://www.kvirc.net/`): This is a good, free choice for a graphical IRC client, and it's available for most platforms.

➤ Colloquy (`http://colloquy.info/`): For OS X, the author uses this.

➤ Chatzilla (`http://chatzilla.hacksrus.com/`): If you use the Firefox browser, it has the capable Chatzilla add-on, which this should work regardless of which operating system you choose.

➤ freenode: You can also access `freenode` with any browser via `http://webchat.freenode` `.net/`.

Actually, any IRC client you're comfortable with is fine.

When you get on IRC, connect to the `irc.freenode.net` server and join #perl. The #perl channel generally has plenty of users, and you can get many Perl questions answered quickly and easily — or at least get told where to RTFM, which stands for *Read The Manual.* (the "F" is silent.)

If you're not familiar with IRC, hit you favorite search engine and search for **list of IRC commands**. You can also consult the Wikipedia page for IRC (`http://en.wikipedia.org/wiki/Irc`) for more information, including lists of other IRC clients.

PerlMonks

PerlMonks (`http://www.perlmonks.org/`) is a fantastically useful Perl site that's been around for more than a decade. Your author joined in 2000, unsurprisingly as "Ovid," and has been a regular contributor for years.

In the top right corner of the site, you see many useful links. Seekers of Perl Wisdom is probably the most useful when you need an answer to a problem. When you first post a question, it shows in Newest Nodes, and many people follow that to try to help answer the new questions. Fortunately, the regular users at PerlMonks generally don't suffer as much from the "first post" silliness you often find at other sites.

In addition to answering questions, PerlMonks has book reviews, *Meditations* (a section for people who just want to muse about Perl-related things), tutorials, Perl news, site discussion, and a *chatterbox* for those who just want casual conversation or have a quick question.

If you're serious about learning Perl, PerlMonks is a good place to start. Many of the top minds in Perl hang out there, and it's a good resource with plenty of history to search through. PerlMonks is "all Perl, all the time." Joe Bob says, "Check it out."

Perl Mongers

For those who like a bit of real-life interaction (and who doesn't?), there's also Perl Mongers (`http://www.pm.org/`). Founded by `brian d foy` in 1997, Perl Mongers is an organization of Perl hackers in different cities who meet periodically to, well, do whatever they want. Your author ran the Perl Mongers group in Portland, Oregon (`Portland.pm`) for several years, and has attended Perl Mongers meetings in a number of countries.

The local Perl Mongers user groups are Perl enthusiasts who enjoy hanging out together and talking about stuff. Sometimes that stuff is Perl. The `Portland.pm` group generally schedules technical talks followed by a "social" at a local pub, often the excellent Lucky Lab in Portland, Oregon. If you ever visit Portland, check out that pub.

There are Perl Mongers groups on every continent except Antarctica, but there was discussion of an Antarctica group starting up when Mongers found out there was a Perl programmer there. If you live near a major city, there's a good chance there's a Perl Mongers group close to you. If not, create one!

StackOverflow

StackOverflow (`http://stackoverflow.com/`) was created in 2008 by Joel Spolsky and Jeff Atwood as an "open" site for anyone to ask programming-related questions. It has spun off numerous related sites and has become extremely popular as the site where you can ask just about any technology question.

Perl questions are answered quickly with solid information, and you can easily see the "rating" of the users who respond to your questions. Because of how questions are tagged, it's easy to quickly drill down to questions that might be relevant to your situation.

LEARNING HOW TO ASK EFFECTIVE QUESTIONS

Quite often on PerlMonks, StackOverflow, or other sites, you see a question like "I tried to use module XYZ, but when I tried to print with it, it didn't work. What am I doing wrong?"

That's it. "Didn't work" isn't explained. No code sample is provided. Nothing.

Here's how to ask an effective question:

1. State what you're trying to do.

2. Explain how you tried to do it.

3. Explain what result you expected.

4. Explain what result you had instead.

"How you tried to do it" often involves posting a minimal code sample. Posting no code is just as bad as posting 500 lines of code. Just give people an idea of what you're trying to do, and answer any follow-up questions they have (if any).

It's also a good idea to indicate how you already tried to find an answer. People are often more helpful if it looks like you've already tried to find an answer to a basic question.

TRY IT OUT   **Register for a Free Account at PerlMonks**

Every chapter, has "Try It Out" sections, but for this first chapter, there's not much to "try out." After the "Try It Out" sections, there is usually a "How It Works" section explaining what you've just done, but this first one is self-explanatory, so "How It Works" is skipped this time. Instead, this Try It Out is to nudge you to PerlMonks and get you started on your journey to Perl. Just do the following:

1. Go to `http://www.perlmonks.org/` and click Create a New User. (The link is on the right, below the login box.)

2. Read some of the useful information, such as "Don't create a username people can't type."

3. Fill out the small form and wait for your confirmation e-mail.

I encourage you to click the Newest Nodes or Seekers of Perl Wisdom links and read through some of the material there. Much, if not most, of the information might seem foreign to you, but by the time you finish this book, you'll be answering questions for newcomers. Or you should be: Answering questions is one of the best ways to learn new material.

USING PERLDOC

Now that you've installed Perl, the first thing you should do is get acquainted with the extensive Perl documentation that ships with the language. As this book covers various topics, a `perldoc` tip often prefixes sections, like this:

```
perldoc perlnumber
```

If you type **perldoc perlnumber** into your terminal, you receive an introduction to how numbers are used in Perl. If you prefer a web browser, go to `http://perldoc.perl.org/`, select your Perl version, and then go to: `http://perldoc.perl.org/perlnumber.html`.

By constantly reinforcing `perldoc` throughout this text, you get the tools to find answers to most questions yourself. This is one bit of advice the author would have liked to received when starting his Perl journey in the '90s. You don't need to memorize the material in the documentation, but as you become more familiar with it, you'll find it easier to remember where to look it up later.

Understanding the Structure of perldoc

The Perl documentation is written in POD, short for *Plain Old Documentation*. POD is an easy-to-learn markup language for documenting Perl. It's easy enough to learn (and you will in Chapter 11), but flexible enough, that many authors write their books in POD.

When you type **perldoc <documentation name>**, the program searches through parts of your system where it thinks the documentation may be found, looking for a file with a `.pod` or `.pm` extension. The `.pod` extension is preferred, and `.pm` is used if the file with the `.pm` extension has embedded POD and the `.pod` extension is not found. The program then formats the POD and displays it. For earlier versions of `perldoc`, you could add the `-v` switch to see where the `perldoc` command is looking for your POD:

```
perldoc -v perldoc
```

If your version of `perldoc` supports (see `perldoc perldoc`) this, use the `-D` switch to see where `perldoc` is looking for the documentation. The `-v` switch now displays the description of Perl's built-in variables:

```
perldoc -v '$_'
perldoc -v '@ARGV'
```

You can also type **perldoc perlvar** to see all of Perl's built-in variables.

You can read `perldoc perldoc` for more information about how to customize `perldoc` output or to see what other command-line switches it supports.

Getting Started with perldoc

The first thing you want to do is type **perldoc perl**. This gives you a brief description of some of what Perl can do and quickly directs you to

```
perldoc perlintro
```

That's a gentle introduction to Perl. If you're dedicated, you could start there and not buy this or any other Perl book. That approach works if you have lots of time and patience. This book presents what you need to know most, including where to get more information.

The `perlintro` is clear but terse. It assumes that you already know how to program and rushes through the basic features of the language. As a result, there are many bits and pieces you should be aware of but won't be. So to follow up on the `perlintro`, you'll want:

```
perldoc perltoc
```

As you might expect, that's the *Table of Contents* for the Perl documentation. For Perl 5.14.2, that Table of Contents is more than 20,000 lines! That's a huge amount of documentation. It's longer than many of the chapters in this book, and your author hopes his publisher doesn't notice. In contrast, Perl 5.8.3's Table of Contents weighs in at a measly 11,911 lines. However, this book mostly focuses on 5.8 and 5.10, and it won't actually talk (much) about what's in those newer documents.

Using Tutorials and FAQs

Perl comes bundled with many tutorials you can read with `perldoc`. Table 1-1 lists the tutorials that are some of the popular ones included in Perl version 5.8.3. You can type **`perldoc <tutorialname>`** to read these tutorials.

TABLE 1-1: perldoc Tutorials

TUTORIAL	DESCRIPTION
perlreftut	Tutorial on references
perldsc	Data structures cookbook
perllol	Data structures: arrays of arrays
perlrequick	Regular expression quickstart
perlretut	Regular expression tutorial
perlboot	Object Oriented (OO) Perl for beginners
perltoot	OO tutorial, part 1
perltooc	OO tutorial, part 2
perlbot	OO tricks and examples
perlstyle	Style guide
perlcheat	Cheat sheet
perltrap	Traps for the unwary
perldebtut	Debugger tutorial

> **NOTE** *The object oriented (OO) Perl documentation which ships with Perl 5.8 and 5.10 was very useful in its day but is now considered to be rather out of date. Its examples and recommended practices should be considered suspect. We'll be covering OO starting in chapter 12.*

Because the author had so much fun cutting and pasting from the documentation and padding the page count, Table 1-2 lists the Frequently Asked Questions (FAQs) that ship with Perl.

TABLE 1-2: perlfaq

FAQ	DESCRIPTION
perlfaq	Perl FAQs
perlfaq1	General questions about Perl
perlfaq2	Obtaining and learning about Perl
perlfaq3	Programming tools
perlfaq4	Data manipulation
perlfaq5	Files and formats
perlfaq6	Regexes (regular expressions)
perlfaq7	Perl language issues
perlfaq8	System interaction
perlfaq9	Networking

These FAQs are extensive. For example, the following are some of the questions addressed in perlfaq2:

➤ What machines support Perl? Where do I get Perl?

➤ How can I get a binary version of Perl?

➤ I don't have a C compiler on my system. How can I compile Perl?

➤ I copied the Perl binary from one machine to another, but scripts don't work. Why?

What's nice is that for any of these questions, you can type **perldoc -q "something I'm looking for"** and perldoc will spit out the sections from any FAQ that matches the term you give it. (Actually, perldoc matches against *regular expressions*, which aren't covering until Chapter 8, so pretend you didn't read that bit.)

A full reference manual also ships with the Perl documentation along with extensive information about the internals of Perl (not for the faint of heart), linking Perl to C and C++ programs, platform-specific information, and other things that aren't covered in this book.

Using the perldoc -f function

One of the most useful `perldoc` commands is `perldoc -f`. When you type **perldoc -f**, followed by a function name, you can see a complete description of the function in question and quite possibly far more than you ever need to know. For example, `perldoc -f my` displays the following:

```
my EXPR
my TYPE EXPR
my EXPR : ATTRS
my TYPE EXPR : ATTRS
        A "my" declares the listed variables to be local (lexically) to
        the enclosing block, file, or "eval".  If more than one value
        is listed, the list must be placed in parentheses.
        The exact semantics and interface of TYPE and ATTRS are still
        evolving.  TYPE is currently bound to the use of the "fields"
        pragma, and attributes are handled using the "attributes"
        pragma, or starting from Perl 5.8.0 also via the
        "Attribute::Handlers" module.  See "Private Variables via my()"
        in perlsub for details, and fields, attributes, and
        Attribute::Handlers.
```

It starts with the grammar for the function and then a brief (and sometimes verbose) explanation of that function. In the preceding example, the grammar could represent any of the following:

```
my $dog;
my Dog $spot;
my $dog : HasSpots;
my Dog $spot : HasSpots;
```

> **NOTE** In real-world Perl, you almost always see the first form from the previous code, `my $dog`, and not the three that follow it. The semantics of the last three forms were never well defined and caused confusion, so people don't use them. This is an example where the docs show you what you can do, not what you should do.

USING A TERMINAL WINDOW

You can skip this section if you already know how to use a terminal window. Otherwise, this section will explain the absolute minimum you need to know about opening and using a terminal window. As with a number of other languages, if you want to program in Perl, much of your professional life will be spent in a terminal window.

Using the Command Line

Perl comes from a UNIX background and, as a result, is often run from a terminal window. Unlike many graphical user interface (GUI) systems, terminals enable you to type commands directly into the system rather than clicking an icon on a screen or selecting items from menus. Getting used to the command line not only gives you all the power of a GUI system, but also leverages the considerable power of the command line. If you're not familiar with this method, hit your favorite search engine for how to use the command line on your system, but for now, this section concentrates on getting a terminal window open.

This isn't difficult, but ask a geek friend for help if you get stuck.

Working with the Terminal Window in Linux

If you're familiar with Linux, you probably already know about the terminal window. Unfortunately, because there are more than 100 Linux distributions and many different window managers, it's impossible to tell you how to do this on your system. However, following are some general tips:

1. Look for an icon on your desktop that looks like a computer screen. It may say Terminal or Console next to it. Try double-clicking that. You can also often right-click your desktop and look for open terminal or something similar.

2. In the menu system under the System folder, you may also find the Konsole or Gnome Terminal program.

3. Search your desktop menu for the words **terminal** or **console**. Many Linux systems have icons on their menus, and you may see a terminal icon there.

Working with the Terminal Window in Mac OS X

If you're on a Mac, you can follow these steps:

1. Go to your desktop and press Command-Shift-G (in other words, hit all those keys at the same time). This brings up a *Go to folder* dialog.

2. Type **/Applications/Utilities** in the text window, and click Go.

3. Scroll through the applications until you see the Terminal icon.

4. Drag this to the dock. You'll use the terminal a lot in this book, so you want to have this handy.

A quick check of a search engine for **mac command line** or **learning os x terminal** should bring you up to speed on some of the basic commands. When you use the Mac command line, you'll find that most standard UNIX/Linux commands operate the same way.

> **NOTE** *Alternatively, go to iTerm2 (*http://www.iterm2.com/*) to download their free terminal application. The author uses iTerm2, which is an excellent replacement for* Terminal.app *that is included with OS X.*

Working with the Terminal Window in Windows

For Windows, you have a couple options:

➤   If you've installed Cygwin, you can double-click the Cygwin desktop icon (not the installer!) and you'll automatically be at a command-line prompt ready to go.

➤   Press the Windows key and r at the same time. This should bring up a Run dialog box. Type **cmd** (short for command) into the box, click OK, and a terminal window pops up.

➤   You can bring up the Run dialog box by clicking Start; then you should see Run as one of the menu items. Click that and it's the same procedure: type **cmd** into that box and click OK.

If you don't like the standard terminal on Windows, some people prefer `console`, available via free download at `http://sourceforge.net/projects/console/`.

For Windows, the terminal window is sometimes referred to as a *DOS window*. DOS stands for *Disk Operating System* and earlier versions of Windows were based on DOS with a Window manager on top. Today, Windows is a GUI system, and the DOS window is an emulation layer, but the commands have not changed much over time.

If you're unfamiliar with the Windows command line, search the Internet for **list of DOS commands** to learn more about this environment.

Creating a Work Directory

Now that you have a terminal window open, you might want to find out where you are on your system. To see the current directory you are in, you can type **pwd** (print working directory) on Linux or OS X, or **cd** (with no arguments) on Windows. You can type **ls** on Linux or OS X to see a list of files in the current directory or **dir** if you're on Windows.

> **NOTE** *A folder in Windows or OS X is what most other operating systems refer to as a directory. This text says directory.*

Create a folder named `wroxperl` and change to it. For most major operating systems, type this:

```
mkdir wroxperl
cd wroxperl
```

You should now be in an empty directory, suitable for creating your sample programs. When you create them, make them in separate directories named `chapter1`, `chapter2`, and so on. This makes it easier to organize and refer back to them. So go ahead and create a `chapter1` directory now and change to it:

```
mkdir chapter1
cd chapter1
```

You won't need this until you get to the "Hello, World!" section (it's a law that all programming books start with this), but stay in the terminal for now to get used to the `perldoc` command.

INSTALLING THE PERLDOC COMMAND

You probably have `perldoc` installed. You can verify this by typing `perldoc -h` to bring up a help page for `perldoc`. Annoyingly enough, some systems that include Perl by default don't include the `perldoc` command even though it is installed by default when you install Perl manually. If your system uses `apt`, you can install `perldoc` with:

```
sudo apt-get install perl-doc
```

Unfortunately, that won't work on systems that don't use `apt`, and because Perl is available on more than 100 platforms, this book can't cover them all. Thus, in the event that you don't have `perldoc` installed, try hitting IRC, PerlMonks, StackOverflow, or your favorite search engine to find out how to install `perldoc`. Or ask your geek friend to do it for you. Pizza is a great payment.

TRY IT OUT   Getting Used to perldoc

You don't want to just read about the command line; you must get used to it, too. You'll see a lot of Perl's internal documentation here. You don't actually have to read it right now, but you should be familiar enough with seeing it to know where to look for more information.

1. Open a terminal. Actually, you should already have one open by this time. To navigate, try the following commands by typing the following:

➤ **q:** To exit (quit) `perldoc`

➤ **Spacebar or the down arrow:** This enables you to scroll through the pages

➤ **Forward slash (/) and some letters:** Enables you to search through the documentation

Unfortunately, most of those commands depend on you having a sane pager program, such as `less`. You can set the `PAGER` environment variable to your desired pager or just play around with your `perldoc` to see which commands it accepts.

2. See which `perldoc` version you're using.

```
perldoc -V
```

3. Read about what the `perldoc` command can do on your version of Perl.

```
perldoc perldoc
```

4.   Read (skim) about Perl.

```
perldoc perl
```

5.   Read the Table of Contents. (Actually, there's probably too much here to read).

```
perldoc perltoc
```

6.   Search for information in the FAQs, which provide a wealth of information.

```
perldoc -q variable
perldoc -q file
```

7.   Read about some Perl functions.

```
perldoc -f print
perldoc -f map
```

8.   If your Perl is new enough (5.12 or better), you can read about some built-in Perl variables. Older versions of Perl use the -v to "verbosely" show you where perldoc is searching for your documentation. Newer versions of Perl use the -D switch for this.

```
perldoc -v '$_'
perldoc -v '@ARGV'
```

How It Works

The perldoc command searches all places where it thinks Perl documentation may be living and reads likely files it finds to determine if they contain the information you need. If you are curious to know, you can run the following command to see for yourself where it's (mostly) searching:

```
perl -le 'print join "\n", @INC, map {split /:/} @ENV{qw/PERL5LIB PATH/}'
```

If you understand that command and what it's doing, there's a good chance you don't need this book. By the time you're done with this book, you'll understand it.

CREATING HELLO, WORLD!

Now that you've read far too much documentation (who am I kidding? You skimmed it), it is time for that traditional rite (write?) of passage, "Hello, World!" As one friend explained to me, he was proud that he could write "Hello, World!" in 15 programming languages — though he could program in none. Try to avoid that, okay?

Writing Your First Program

First, open your terminal and type this:

```
perl -e 'print "Hello, Wrox!\n"'
```

Oh, wait. Sorry Windows people. You have to type this:

```
perl -e "print \"Hello, Wrox!\n\""
```

Except that it might not work, depending on your version of Windows. See `perldoc perlfaq3` and read the section "Why don't Perl one-liners work on my DOS/Mac/VMS system?" to understand why your life is difficult. If you have a Mac, the "Mac" section likely does not apply to you because OS X handles Perl and the command line quite well, thank you.

Aside from your author blatantly patronizing the publisher, the "Hello, Wrox!" snippet shows something common about Perl: running Perl from the command line. This won't be covered much in the book, but as you get more familiar with Perl, you'll see people doing things like this:

```
perl -pi.bak -e 's/version = 13/version = 14/' <list of files>
```

That changes all strings in `<list of files>` matching "version = 13" to "version = 14" and create backups of all those files with a `.bak` extension. That's more or less equivalent to the following Perl program that is also listed in `perldoc perlrun`. (Although it's been cleaned up to be "safer.")

```
#!/usr/bin/perl
my $extension = '.bak';
my $oldargv;
LINE: while (<>) {
    if ($ARGV ne $oldargv) {
        my $backup;
        if ($extension !~ /\*/) {
            $backup = $ARGV . $extension;
        }
        else {
            ($backup = $extension) =~ s/\*/$ARGV/g;
        }
        rename($ARGV, $backup);
        open(ARGVOUT, ">", $ARGV)
          or die "Cannot open '$ARGV' for writing: $!";;
        select(ARGVOUT);
        $oldargv = $ARGV;
    }
    s/version = 13/version = 14/;
}
continue {
    print;  # this prints to original filename
}
select(STDOUT);
```

As you can see, using Perl on the command line effectively gives you a lot of power to get things done quickly. You can read `perldoc perlrun` to understand some of this, but search for `perl` **one-liners** online to see what you can do if you're interested in this area.

Getting back to "Hello, World!", the general way you write a Perl program is to save a file with the program code and then type **perl <programname>**. The first line of the program is often the *shebang line,* which you learn more about in a bit. After that is your program text. All you need to do to get a basic Perl program running is to type up your program, save it (usually with a .pl extension), and then type **perl <*programname*>.**

Listing 1-1 is a short Perl program that shows how a simple program may look. You learn more about the strict, warnings, and diagnostics in Chapter 3.

LISTING 1-1: Hello, World!

```
#!perl
use strict;
use warnings;
use diagnostics;
# this is a comment
print "Hello, World!\n"; # so is this
```

TRY IT OUT   **Your First Perl Program**

This is a simple example to demonstrate writing a Perl program, saving it, and running it.

1. Type the following code into your favorite editor, and save it as bonjour.pl.

```
#!/usr/bin/perl
# "Hello world!, in French
print "Bonjour, tout le monde!\n";
```

2. From the command line type **cd** (change directory) into the directory where you saved your program, and type **perl bonjour.pl.** You should see this output:

```
Bonjour, tout le monde!
```

How It Works

On the command line, when you type perl followed by the name of a file containing a Perl program, Perl reads that file, parses the code, and executes it. The sharp (#) begins a comment. It can be on its own line or embedded in a line after some code.

> **NOTE** *People sometimes mistakenly refer to Perl as an interpreted language, but it's not quite a compiled one, either. Like many modern languages, it falls somewhere in between the two. When you run a program with* perl programname.pl, *Perl first compiles your Perl down to a set of opcodes and then executes those. Because there is generally no complicated compile/link phase for executing a Perl program, it's very easy to quickly make and test changes to programs.*

WINDOWS AND THE .PL EXTENSION

On Windows, when you install Perl, you'll often find that the .pl extension is associated with Perl in the registry. New Perl programmers on Windows often double-click a Perl program icon and then wonder why they see a brief flash of a console before it disappears, taking their program output with it. That's because Perl is usually run from the command line. One trick to work around this is to add the following code as the last line of your program:

```
<STDIN>;
```

That causes Perl to hang, waiting for you to enter some input, leaving the console up. Just pressing Enter makes the console disappear. This is explained more when you cover user interaction in Chapter 17, but for now do not use this trick. Get used to running Perl from the command line.

Shebang Lines

The first line of a Perl program often starts with a *shebang line*. A shebang line starts with "sharp" (#) and an exclamation point, also known as a "bang" (!), hence the term shebang. The line is followed by a path telling the shell where to find the interpreter that is used to execute the program.

On a system that understands the chmod command, you can type **chmod +x *programname*** to make the program directly executable. If it's in your path, you can then type ***programname*** to run the program. Otherwise, you can type the full or relative path to the program to execute it.

For example, if you're in /Users/ovid/wroxperl/chapter1 and you create a program called runme in that directory, you could run it like this:

```
$ ./runme
$ /Users/ovid/wroxperl/chapter1/runme
```

For now, you can just type **perl *programname*** to run the programs.

The shebang line might take one of a number of different forms. On a Linux system, this often looks like one of the following:

```
#!/usr/bin/perl
#!/usr/local/bin/perl
#!/usr/bin/perl -w
#!/usr/bin/env perl
```

The first two lines point directly to the Perl executable that should run the program. The third line, with the -w switch, tells Perl to run the program with global warnings. The final line tells Perl to use the env program to find out which perl is currently set as the default perl for your system. This is useful if you have different versions of Perl installed and want your program to always run with the Perl you're currently using.

Some people just do the following:

```
#!/perl
```

And that generally does what you want.

On Windows you might see the following:

```
#!C:\Perl\bin\perl.exe
#!C:\strawberry\perl\bin\perl.exe
```

The first line is often found when running with ActiveState Perl. The line version is found when running with Strawberry Perl.

When perl sees the shebang line, it attempts to run your program using whatever it finds after the #!. Generally, this isn't a problem, but if you want to run the script on more than one machine, even with the same architecture, you could have a problem if someone installs Perl in a different location.

Fortunately, there is one simple trick you can follow to ensure you don't have problems with shebang lines: Don't install modules and scripts by hand. Instead, package them as proper distributions and install them with the standard Perl toolchain (such as cpan or cpanm). You learn module installation in Chapter 2 and module writing in Chapter 11.

For the Perl code that can be downloaded with this book, you will not be using shebang lines because they tend not to be portable. You will need to run the programs by explicitly typing **perl programname**.

SUMMARY

By this time you've learned a bit about the history of Perl, where to go to get more information, installing Perl, and running a simple Perl program. This isn't a huge amount of information, but it's the foundation you need to progress in Perl.

▶ **WHAT YOU LEARNED IN THIS CHAPTER**

TOPIC	KEY CONCEPTS
History	The basic history of the Perl language, its releases, and common use.
Getting Perl	About system Perl and `perlbrew` for those who use UNIX-style systems. Cygwin, ActivePerl, and Strawberry Perl are compared as options for Windows users.
Community	Perlmonks, IRC, Perl Mongers, and StackOverflow are all valuable resources for learning Perl.
`perldoc`	Perl comes with extensive documentation. You learned the basic structure of the docs and how to look up basic information.
Using a terminal	You use a terminal extensively when programming Perl. You learned how to launch a terminal and run a program from the command line.

Understanding the CPAN

WHAT YOU WILL LEARN IN THIS CHAPTER:

➤ Understanding the CPAN

➤ Using CPAN clients to install modules

This is the end of Chapter 10. Or it was. Many Perl books, if they include information about the *Comprehensive Perl Archive Network* (CPAN), mention it almost as an afterthought, just as your author was going to. However, CPAN is the soul of Perl. Its use is so common that your author repeatedly found it hard to create compelling examples of Perl without duplicating code already on the CPAN. Thus, the CPAN is now not only near the front of the book, it has an entire chapter all to itself. You cannot be a real Perl programmer without understanding the CPAN.

It's been said that the best way to make a technology popular is to release a killer app that requires it. VisiCalc, a precursor to spreadsheets, made the Apple II computer popular. Ruby on Rails is the killer app that made the Ruby programming language famous.

Perl has the CPAN. Though many have tried, nothing compares to the CPAN.

THE HISTORY OF THE CPAN

In 1994, on the Perl-packrats mailing list, an idea was born. The idea was simple: Make a single place for Perl authors to upload their modules and for others to download them. That idea became the Comprehensive Perl Archive Network (CPAN) and was launched in 1995. Since then, it has grown to an enormous size. By October of 2011, the CPAN had this to say for itself http://www.cpan.org/

> *The Comprehensive Perl Archive Network (CPAN) currently has 100,649 Perl modules in 23,600 distributions, written by 9,282 authors, mirrored on 269 servers.*

The breadth of modules available on the CPAN is amazing. Following is an overview of what's available:

➤ **Many popular Web frameworks:** Including `Catalyst`, `Dancer`, and `Mojolicious`.

➤ **`DBI`, the standard database interface:** Or if you prefer ORMs (Object-Relational Mappers).

➤ **`DBIx::Class` and `Rose::DB`:** These classes make working with databases much easier.

➤ **Artificial intelligence modules in the `AI::` namespace:** You can find out about namespaces a bit more in Chapter 3, "Variables."

➤ **More testing modules than you can imagine in the `Test::` namespace:** They're great for testing your code to make sure it's not misbehaving.

➤ **An entire `bioperl` distribution:** This is available because Perl is used heavily in biology research.

➤ **An `Acme::` namespace:** This is where people upload humorous modules just for fun.

The author has more than 40 modules on the CPAN at `http://search.cpan.org/~ovid/`; although, many of them are for rather obscure problems.

That's part of what makes the CPAN so great. When you have a relatively obscure problem, there's a good chance there's a CPAN module for it. Today, many are surprised when they have a problem and there's *not* a CPAN module for it. Whenever possible, don't reinvent the wheel. Look for a solution on the CPAN to see if you can save a lot of time and effort by using someone else's code. That's why it's there.

Oh, and did I mention that most code on the CPAN is both free and open source?

> **WARNING** *You see many differences between Windows and other operating systems. That's unfortunate, but those differences are minimized as much as possible. The short description: Use the automated tools recommend (for CPAN clients, for example) and don't try to do this stuff manually. You'll probably get it wrong until you understand what's happening here. Fortunately, this is probably your biggest hurdle if you use Windows.*

CPAN AND METACPAN

The following are two main websites (and many mirrors) that Perl developers currently use to find modules:

➤ **`http://search.cpan.org/`:** The search interface to the original CPAN and currently the one that most people think of when they think of the CPAN website. It enables you to browse distributions, search distributions, check test results on modules, and read reviews of said modules.

➤ **http://www.cpan.org/:** When writing a book, you always face a danger in describing new technology because it may change or cease to exist by the time the book is printed, but this site has enough developers working on it and seems stable enough that it's worth including in this book. It has a search engine with autocomplete driven by the excellent ElasticSearch search engine (http://www.elasticsearch.org/). In addition to offering everything that cpan.org offers, it also has an API where you can write your own CPAN tools. You can sign up for a free account with metacpan and add modules as favorites, link other accounts to your metacpan account, and even accept PayPal donations by e-mail address. In short, it's social networking for the CPAN. Add the API on top of it, and the author expects that metacpan is the future of the CPAN. (Your author has also been wrong before.)

➤ **http://kobesearch.cpan.org** and **http://cpan.uwinnipeg.ca:** Alternatively, some people like these sites, but they're less popular.

> **NOTE** Sadly, the maintainer of http://kobesearch.cpan.org and http://cpan.uwinnipeg.ca, Randy Kobes, has passed away. The future of these sites is uncertain. Our condolences to his family and friends.

In 1994, on the Perl-packrats mailing list, an idea was born. The idea was simple: Make a single place for Perl authors to upload their modules and for others to download them. "That idea became the CPAN". You won't actually use much of this information when you first start learning Perl, but the further you go in your Perl journey, the more crucial CPAN will be. You will repeatedly face a hard problem and then find that someone else has done the work for you and has uploaded it to the CPAN.

Finding and Evaluating Modules

For http://www.cpan.org, you can browse the modules at http://www.cpan.org/modules/index.html. You can browse by author, module name, recent modules, and so on. However, many people look for modules to handle a problem they need to solve, not for a particular author or module name. Given the size of the CPAN, browsing is somewhat impractical. You want to search for a module and not just browse them. For that, you want to use http://search.cpan.org/.

The front page of http://search.cpan.org has a list of module categories you can browse through, but given the size of the CPAN, this list is not well maintained. Instead, use the search box. Say you need to write some software that displays the weather forecast. Searching for **weather** brings up something like this:

➤ weather

➤ Weather::Bug::Weather

➤ App::Dataninja::Bot::Plugin::Weather

➤ Weather::Com::Base

➤ Geo::Weather

➤ Yahoo::Weather

➤ Weather::Com

➤ Weather::Google

➤ Weather::Underground

➤ Weather::Bug::CompactWeather

And that's just the first page of search results!

Each result actually has a bit more detail. For example, the Weather::Google module has this:

```
Weather::Google
Perl interface to Google's Weather API
Weather-Google-0.05 (2 Reviews) - 26 Jan 2010 - Daniel LeWarne
```

The first line is the name of the module and also a link to the module documentation. After that is a short description, its current distribution name, a link to reviews (if any), the date of its release, and the author name. As you get more familiar with the CPAN and the Perl community, you can recognize author names, which may help you decide whether a given distribution is worth looking at.

If you click the Weather::Google link, you see a page, as shown in Figure 2-1.

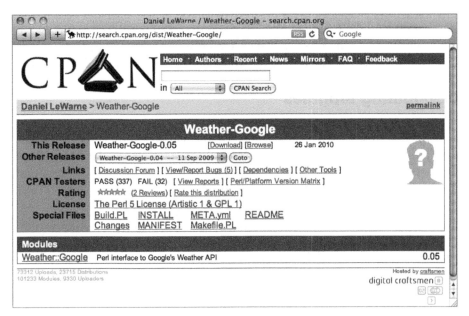

FIGURE 2-1

There's a lot of information on this page, so the following list just covers the highlights.

➤ **Standard format:** In reading through the documentation, you can see that most Perl modules have a standard format with sections for NAME, SYNOPSIS, DESCRIPTION, and so on. Reading through those three sections should tell you if the module in question satisfies your needs.

➤ **Weather::Google link:** Clicking this link, which is found in the Modules section on the bottom of the page, shows you the main documentation for the module. Larger modules, such as DBIx::Class, often have many modules bundled together, so read through the list carefully to understand which ones give you the most useful information. You might even find a Documentation section below the Modules section.

➤ **CPAN Testers:** Refer to Figure 2-1 to see that Weather::Google has a CPAN Testers section with PASS (337) FAIL (32). When users upload a module to the CPAN (well, to PAUSE, that isn't covered), many people download that module and attempt to build it on their system. As you can see, Weather::Google fails to build on approximately 10 percent of the systems. This is a rather high failure rate, so you might want to click the [View Reports] link and browse through some of the test failures to find out what's going on.

➤ **Rating:** Most modules do not have user ratings attached, but in Figure 2-1, you see that there are two five-star (good) ratings. You can click through to read what the ratings say.

There is, of course, much more information available on this page, and you should play around with it to try to learn a bit more about it.

Downloading and Installing

You've searched for a module, found one you want, and now you want to install it. That's usually fairly simple after you do it one or two times, but getting to that first module to install can be problematic if you're on Windows.

Following is an explanation of how to do this manually because, you need to know this when you eventually start writing your own modules. Later, you learn how to use various CPAN tools, which make most of this automatic. After you've read about manual installation, you'll be grateful that there's an automatic procedure that does all of this work for you. However, you'll sometimes find that you need to install modules by hand, or maybe you're just a masochist and like doing things the hard way. It's up to you.

To download and install a module, follow these steps:

1. **Click the download link next to the module name to download the distribution.** For example, for the Weather::Google distribution (see Figure 2-1), you'll download a file named Weather-Google-0.05.tar.gz.

Most CPAN distributions (exceptions tend to be old distributions) end in with .tar.gz or .tgz. These are tarred, gzipped files. There's some old UNIX history going on behind the names, but you can ignore that.

2. **Unpack the distribution.** How you do this depends on your platform:

➤ **If you're a OS X or Linux user:** You can unpack the distribution with this command:

```
tar zxf Weather-Google-0.05.tar.gz
```

> **WARNING** *If you have the tar command, you can type* **man** **tar** *for more infor-*
> *mation about the* tar *command. Warning: it's a long, complicated page and if*
> *you're unfamiliar with man output, it can be daunting. A web search may prove*
> *more useful.*

> ➤ **If you're a Windows user:** You'll generally find a WinZip or other zip program that
> enables you to unpack .tar.gz and .tgz files. If you don't have a command line
> interface, double-click the distribution icon to unpack it. Make sure it's unpacked
> into the correct directory. The distribution might come with a .zip extension. If
> your tar command is new, you should be able to just use tar zxf filename.zip.
> Otherwise, use a zip program to handle it. You won't find these distributions often,
> and they're usually from Windows users.

3. **When unpackaged, change to the directory that's created and list the files.** If you're on
   Windows, use the dir command instead of ls.

```
cd Weather-Google-0.05/
ls
```

You should see a list of files like the following:

```
Build.PL
Changes
INSTALL
MANIFEST
META.yml
Makefile.PL
README
lib
t
```

You can ignore most of those for now. The README file usually contains instructions for installing,
but in this case, it's merely a copy of the documentation that ships with the distribution. That's fine.
What you are interested in are two files:

```
Build.PL
Makefile.PL
```

> ➤ If you see Build.PL you can build, test, and install your distribution with this:

> ```
> perl Build.PL
> ./Build
> ./Build test
> ./Build install
> ```

> ➤ For a Makefile.PL, you can do this:

> ```
> perl Makefile.PL
> make
> make test
> make install
> ```

Read the output of each of those steps carefully to make sure they're doing what you want. In this case, when you run `./Build` (or `perl Build`) it has output similar to the following:

```
$ perl Build.PL
Checking prerequisites...
  requires:
    !  XML::Simple is not installed
  build_requires:
    !  Test::Pod is not installed
ERRORS/WARNINGS FOUND IN PREREQUISITES.  You may wish to install the versions
of the modules indicated above before proceeding with this installation
Run 'Build installdeps' to install missing prerequisites.
Created MYMETA.yml and MYMETA.json
Creating new 'Build' script for 'Weather-Google' version '0.05'
```

This means you need:

```
$ perl Build installdeps
```

And hope all the dependencies install correctly. This may fail due to not having sufficient permissions or simply because some dependencies fail their tests. If your module has a `Makefile.PL` and no `Build.PL`, it might not even allow you to automatically install these dependencies (it depends on how the `Makefile.PL` is written), thus forcing you to download and install all dependencies by hand, possibly repeating this procedure over and over.

The `./Build test` or make test steps are completely optional. They merely run any tests included with the distribution. If you run this, you'll see similar output:

```
$ ./Build test
t/00-load.t ................ 1/1 # Testing Weather::Google 0.05
t/00-load.t ................ ok
t/01init.t ................. ok
t/02current_conditions.t .... ok
t/03forecast_conditions.t ... ok
t/04forecast_information.t .. ok
t/05language.t ............. ok
t/pod-coverage.t ........... ok
t/pod.t .................... ok
All tests successful.
Files=8, Tests=388,  4 wallclock secs
Result: PASS
```

> **NOTE** `Weather::Google` *requires an Internet connection for the tests to run. This is not surprising because it contacts Google for the results, but it's problematic because you won't always have an Internet connection when running tests. It's one of many subtle issues that can occur when testing.*

There's also a problem with the `./Build install` and `make install` commands. They often require root access and must be run like this:

```
sudo ./Build install
sudo make install
```

(If you're a Windows user, this probably won't apply because you'll probably have Administrator access to your box.)

That's because the default installation is usually in a directory that your regular user accounts won't have access to. You can install your modules to some place you do have access to if you want:

```
perl ./Build.pl --install_base /path/to/install/modules
#or
perl Makefile.PL INSTALL_BASE=/path/to/your/home/dir
```

WHY ARE BOTH BUILD.PL AND MAKEFILE.PL REQUIRED TO BUILD PERL MODULES?

A long time ago, in a garage far, far away, `Makefile.PL` was created to allow creation of a `Makefile` to build your Perl module. Unfortunately, with more than 100 supported platforms and many different and conflicting `make` programs, it was difficult to write portable makefiles. Plus, some systems don't support make at all!

Thus, `Build.PL` was created. `Makefile.PL` relies on `ExtUtils::MakeMaker` to create makefiles. `Build.PL` relies only on Perl to install itself. Because Perl is far more portable than `make`, it was considered by some to be a better solution. `ExtUtils::MakeMaker` turns out to be far too difficult to extend for new features. Unfortunately, `Module::Build` has historically had a few bugs and many developers rejected it. It offers more features, but some of the same features needed to be implemented differently.

The battle between the two formats rages to this day and you're rather stuck with the mess.

Now you need to understand a lot about how to tell Perl where to find these modules, which can get annoying if you're not familiar with Perl. If you don't use Windows, use `perlbrew` if possible. You'll install the modules in a subdirectory off your home directory, and `perlbrew` can magically handle making sure that Perl knows where your modules are.

If you do use Windows, you might want to use Strawberry Perl because the CPAN module (and thus, module installation) magically works out-of-the-box. However, if you prefer to use ActivePerl, read the `ppm` section later in this chapter. Fortunately, ActiveState Perl has been updated to make using the CPAN much easier. Make sure you use a recent version of ActiveState Perl version 5.10.1 or better. The CPAN client bundled with it is preconfigured, and when you first run it, it notes that you're missing dmake and a compiler and downloads, builds, and installs them for you. You see a message similar to the following when you first run cpan:

```
C:\>cpan
It looks like you don't have a C compiler and make utility installed. Trying
to install dmake and the MinGW gcc compiler using the Perl Package Manager.
This may take a few minutes...
```

Then just wait a few minutes while it handles downloads and installs everything. After that is done, everywhere that you see instructions to run the make command, type dmake.

Or you can install Strawberry Perl, which is not an issue because it comes bundled with everything you need.

And now to have you really hate your author: all of the above can mostly be ignored unless you're debugging why a module didn't install correctly. That's because CPAN clients will take care of all of that for you.

CPAN CLIENTS

Have you been scared enough to not do install modules on your own? To be fair, so far this book has skimmed the surface of things that can go wrong if you try to install modules manually. The author has been doing this for years and is quite used to it, but prefers the clients. Essentially, when you want to install a module, clients take care of finding that module, downloading and building its dependencies along with the module itself, and then installing the module where your Perl code can find it. Because this is automated, it's much faster and easier than doing it by hand.

Using the CPAN.pm Client

The CPAN.pm module that comes bundled with Perl is the oldest of the CPAN clients. To run it, type **cpan**, which puts you in the CPAN shell. If you use Strawberry Perl for Windows (sense a theme here?), the CPAN client is configured for you already. Otherwise, when you first run cpan, it prompts you for basic information. The prompt message may vary. Older versions ask the following:

```
Are you ready for manual configuration? [yes]
```

Newer versions ask the following:

```
Would you like to configure as much as possible automatically? [yes]
```

The sense of the question has been reversed. If you're asked to configure as much as possible automatically, press Enter, and cpan sets everything up for you, except for your urllist. The urllist tells the client where to find and download CPAN modules from CPAN mirrors all over the world. Follow the instructions carefully, choosing the continent you're on, then your country, and finally a few mirrors that are hopefully close to you. Don't stress too much about getting these mirrors perfect; newer CPAN clients ask you if you want it to automatically pick the mirrors for you, making this much easier than it used to be. Starting with a CPAN client is a breeze compared to what it used to be.

If you choose to go the manual configuration route, you will be asked many questions about the CPAN build and cache directory, the cache size, what you want to cache, terminal settings, whether to follow prerequisites, where various programs are installed, and so on. Most of these questions have defaults, and if you don't understand the question, pressing Enter and accepting the default is usually fine.

After configuring the CPAN, you probably want to install `Bundle::CPAN` to ensure that your CPAN is updated to the latest version. To install a module, type `install module::name` at the cpan prompt.

```
cpan > install Bundle::CPAN
```

This takes a while for the first time, but it updates your CPAN client to the latest version. It also adds a few extra features, such as readline support, that are not available by default due to license issues.

For the `Weather::Google` module discussed earlier in the chapter (refer to Figure 2-1), you use this code:

```
cpan > install Weather::Google
```

When you do this, the client

➤ Finds the latest version of the module

➤ Downloads it

➤ Unpacks it

➤ Builds it

➤ Follows dependencies (optional)

➤ Tests it

➤ Installs it

If any dependencies exist, the CPAN client either prompts you if you want to install them, or if you've configured it to follow dependencies automatically, it goes through its find, download, unpack, build, follow, test, and install steps for every dependency. For `Weather::Google`, you have dependencies on both `LWP::Simple` and `XML::Simple` (both, in turn, having other dependencies). Having your client do all this automatically for you is a huge timesaver and means it's more likely to get it right than you will.

> **NOTE** *If any tests fail, the client does not install the module. You can either choose a different module, or if you've investigated the tests and don't think they apply to you, you can force the module to install anyway:*
>
> ```
> cpan > force install Weather::Google
> ```

To better understand what you can do with your cpan client, a small amount of help is available.

```
cpan> help
```

The output varies considerably depending on the CPAN version you installed.

> **NOTE** *If you use a Linux/OS X computer and you decided to install modules in directories to which your regular user does not have access, you may need to type* sudo cpan *to allow your modules to install. If feasible, you should install it as a non-root user. Otherwise, rather than having the entire package download and configuration running as root, you may elect to only have* sudo *run during the installation. You can do this by altering the* make_install_make_command *in the CPAN client. You type* o conf make_install_make_command *to see the current value.*
>
> ```
> cpan[2]> o conf make_install_make_command
>     make_install_make_command [/usr/bin/make]
> ```
>
> *And you type the same command, followed by its new value, in quotes. You prefix the value with* sudo *to ensure that the CPAN client will only prompt you for your password during module installation.*
>
> ```
> cpan[3]> o conf make_install_make_command 'sudo /usr/bin/make'
>     make_install_make_command [sudo /usr/bin/make]
> ```
>
> *If you do this, you will want to do the same for the* Module::Build *install command:*
>
> ```
> o conf mbuild_install_build_command 'sudo ./Build'
> ```
>
> *You will need to type* o conf commit *to save this change. Otherwise it will only be in effect for your current CPAN session.*

Using the Cpanm Client

A new and popular CPAN client is cpanm, also known as App::cpanminus. It's fast, requires no configuration, and has no dependencies on other modules. This makes it easy to install. If you use a package management system such as Debian, FreeBSD ports, and so on, search for cpanminus and attempt to install it that way.

You can also install it using the following steps:

1. Type this option:

```
curl -L http://cpanmin.us | perl - --sudo App::cpanminus
```

2. If you use `perlbrew`, `local::lib`, or some other method to ensure your Perl modules do not require root access to install, you can omit the `--sudo` switch:

    ```
    curl -L http://cpanmin.us | perl - App::cpanminus
    ```

3. Click the download link at `http://search.cpan.org/dist/App-cpanminus/` and install it manually, as explained previously.

    ```
    tar zxf App-cpanminus-1.5004.tar.gz
    cd App-cpanminus-1.5004/
    perl Makefile.PL
    make
    make test
    make install
    ```

As previously mentioned, the `make install` step may need to be changed to `sudo make install`.

If you're on Windows and using `nmake`, change the last three lines:

```
nmake
nmake test
nmake install
```

4. To install a module, type `cpanm module`. The `cpanm` program attempts to install the module for you, quickly and easily. It produces little output beyond "downloading this, configuring that," and related messages. Many modules ask questions such as "Do you want to install X?" `cpanm` attempts to do the right thing without bothering you. Large, complicated modules with many dependencies can be a hassle to install even with the `cpan` client; `cpanm` usually makes it easy.

PPM

If you use ActivePerl, you're probably on Windows, and if you have trouble with a CPAN client, you can use `ppm` or the Perl Package Manager that ships with ActivePerl. This uses a large set of prebuilt modules that work. Want to install `Text::CSV_XS`?

```
ppm install Text::CSV_XS
```

If you run `ppm` without any arguments, a GUI launches and you can browse installed packages or upgrade, remove, or install new packages. The GUI enables you to do anything the command-line version of `ppm` does, and you may find it a more comfortable environment to work in. However, you cannot upgrade core modules (modules that ship with Perl) with `ppm`. As a result, you cannot install any module that requires a core module to be upgraded.

CPAN::Mini

`CPAN::Mini` isn't actually a client, but it's so useful that you need to know about it. Sometimes you'll find that you want to install a CPAN module, but you have no Internet connection or a slow Internet connection. `CPAN::Mini` enables you to create a "mini" CPAN mirror on your computer, complete with the latest versions of all modules.

To use CPAN::Mini, follow these steps:

1. Open your favorite text editor, and type the following:

```
local: ~/minicpan/
remote: http://cpan.pair.com/pub/CPAN/
```

2. Save this in your home directory as .minicpanrc.

3. The local: key should point to where you want your miniature copy of CPAN to be store. If you prefer, you can use a full path to a particular directory:

```
local: C:\home\users\ovid
```

> **NOTE** Windows uses a backslash instead of a forward slash for directory separators, but Perl is smart enough to do the right thing, even if you use forward slashes instead:
>
> ```
> local: C:/home/users/ovid
> ```

4. The remote: key should point to a close CPAN mirror. You can see a list of CPAN mirrors at http://www.cpan.org/SITES.html.

5. Then install CPAN::Mini:

```
cpanm CPAN::Mini
```

6. From there run the minicpan command periodically to update your local copy.

> **NOTE** The first time you run this command, it takes a long time because it needs to fetch the latest version of every CPAN module. If you run it regularly, subsequent updates are much faster.

7. To install modules from your local CPAN::Mini mirror, configure your CPAN client to use this mirror:

```
$ cpan
cpan shell -- CPAN exploration and modules installation (v1.9800)
Enter 'h' for help.
cpan> o conf urllist unshift file:///Users/ovid/minicpan
Please use 'o conf commit' to make the config permanent!
```

As noted in the output, use o conf commit if you want this change to be permanent.

When this is done and when you attempt to install a module, the module is fetched from your local mirror instead of using the Internet.

8. You can tell `cpanm` to only look for modules in your mirror and only the mirror:

```
cpanm --mirror ~/minicpan/ --mirror-only Weather::Google
```

9. If you make heavy use of shell aliases, add the following to your list of aliases:

```
alias minicpanm='cpanm --mirror ~/minicpan/ --mirror-only'
```

10. When you're without an Internet connection, use the following code:

```
minicpanm Weather::Google
```

TRY IT OUT   **Configure a CPAN Client and Install File::Find::Rule**

You're now going to configure a CPAN client and install `File::Find::Rule`. Once this is done, you'll find it easy to download and install new modules from the CPAN.

This example requires an Internet connection. This example will use `App::cpanminus` because it's one of the easiest ways to install Perl modules. `App::cpanminus` also has no dependencies, which makes it easy to install. Install it manually because this is the most portable option.

1. Point your Web browser to `http://search.cpan.org/dist/App-cpanminus/` and click the download link.

2. Unpack, build, and install the application:

```
tar zxf App-cpanminus-1.5004.tar.gz
cd App-cpanminus-1.5004/
perl Makefile.PL
make
make test
make install
```

Remember, if you're on Windows, you may need to type **nmake** instead of **make**.

Alternatively, if you have the curl executable installed, you can try to install `App::cpanminus` with one of the following commands:

```
curl -L http://cpanmin.us | perl - App::cpanminus
curl -L http://cpanmin.us | perl - --sudo App::cpanminus
```

The first time you install `App::cpanminus`, it may take a while because it downloads, builds, and installs a number of useful modules.

3. Install the `File::Find::Rule` module.

```
cpanm File::Find::Rule
```

You'll likely get output similar to the following:

```
$ cpanm File::Find::Rule
--> Working on File::Find::Rule
Fetching authors/id/R/RC/RCLAMP/File-Find-Rule-0.33.tar.gz ... OK
Configuring File-Find-Rule-0.33 ... OK
==> Found dependencies: Text::Glob, Number::Compare
--> Working on Text::Glob
Fetching authors/id/R/RC/RCLAMP/Text-Glob-0.09.tar.gz ... OK
Configuring Text-Glob-0.09 ... OK
Building and testing Text-Glob-0.09 ... OK
Successfully installed Text-Glob-0.09
--> Working on Number::Compare
Fetching authors/id/R/RC/RCLAMP/Number-Compare-0.03.tar.gz ... OK
Configuring Number-Compare-0.03 ... OK
Building and testing Number-Compare-0.03 ... OK
Successfully installed Number-Compare-0.03
Building and testing File-Find-Rule-0.33 ... OK
Successfully installed File-Find-Rule-0.33
3 distributions installed
```

If you previously installed `File::Find::Rule`, it may say that the module is up to date, or it may tell you that it's upgraded from a previous version.

How It Works

When you try to install a module, `cpanm` inspects the package to figure out if the module depends on other modules being installed. According to the `Makefile.PL` that ships with `File::Find::Rule`, this module depends on five other modules:

➤   `File::Spec`

➤   `File::Find`

➤   `Test::More`

➤   `Number::Compare`

➤   `Text::Glob`

The first three modules, `File::Spec`, `File::Find`, and `Test::More` are included with Perl. The `Number::Compare` and `Text::Glob` modules, however, need to be downloaded, unpacked, built, and installed. The `cpanm` installer does this for you. Because those two modules require only `Test::More` as a dependency, they do not require more modules to be downloaded and built.

After those are built and installed, `File::Find::Rule` is then built and installed for you.

SUMMARY

Congratulations! You now know how to find and install modules from the CPAN! In this chapter you learned about the CPAN, the world's largest collection of open source code dedicated to a single programming language. You learned the `cpan` and `cpanm` clients, how to create a miniature CPAN mirror, and you installed your first module, `File::Find::Rule`.

▶ **WHAT YOU LEARNED IN THIS CHAPTER**

TOPIC	KEY CONCEPTS
CPAN	The world's largest collection of open source code for a single language. This makes it very easy to find code you need rather than writing it yourself.
`http://www.cpan` `.org`	The website for the CPAN. Use this to search for modules that solve problems you face.
`CPAN.pm`	The original client program for downloading and installing CPAN modules
`App::cpanminus`	A new and excellent alternative to `CPAN.pm`. It is much less verbose than the origina CPAN client.
PPM	The CPAN client bundled with ActivePerl.
`CPAN::Mini`	How to create a local CPAN mirror. It's useful when installing modules when you don't have an internet connection.

3

Variables

WHAT YOU WILL LEARN IN THIS CHAPTER:

➤ Understanding programming in Perl

➤ General things to remember as you work with variables

➤ Understanding scalars

➤ Using data in arrays and hashes

➤ Working with array and hash slices

➤ Implementing scalar and list content

➤ Understanding the scope of variables

➤ Working with strict, warnings, and diagnostics

➤ Using Perl's context feature

WROX.COM CODE DOWNLOADS FOR THIS CHAPTER

The wrox.com code downloads for this chapterare found at `http://www.wrox.com/remtitle`
`.cgi?isbn=1118013840` on the Download Code tab. The code for this chapter is divided into
the following major examples:

➤ `example_3_1_variable.pl`

➤ `example_3_2_diagnostics.pl`

➤ `exercise_3_2a_array.pl`

➤   `exercise_3_2b_array.pl`

➤   `exercise_3_3_fruit.pl`

➤   `listing_3_1_scope.pl`

➤   `listing_3_2_vars.pl`

➤   `listing_3_3_our.pl`

➤   `listing_3_4_diagnostics.pl`

➤   `listing_3_5_hello.pl`

This chapter examines the three primary data types of Perl: scalars, arrays, and hashes. Unlike many other languages that focus on things such as strings, integers, floats, and so on, Perl's types focus on how you organize your data, rather than what the data is. It's an approach to data types that is unusual to those who think of "types" as restricting data to certain values, but in practice, it's a robust, powerful approach that many other programming languages follow.

Don't worry about the size of this chapter because you won't need to memorize it. Most of this information will be reinforced in subsequent chapters. Primarily, you need to understand how to create and assign values to Perl's three primary data types (scalars, arrays, and hashes). You also need to ensure that you understand context because it will come up repeatedly in your career as a Perl programmer. Many inexperienced Perl programmers struggle to understand bugs in context because it's often treated as an afterthought.

WHAT IS PROGRAMMING?

You've already received quite a bit of background about Perl, but now is the time to start programming. For those new to programming, a Perl program is a file — often many files — of text instructions telling the computer what to do with some data. For example, pretend that the following is a program to send cucumber recipes to a cucumber fetish mailing list. This program uses *pseudocode*, a made-up language designed to explain programming ideas.

```
email_addresses = read_list_of_email_addresses()
cuke_recipe     = read_new_recipe()

for each address in email_addresses
    email_to(address, cuke_recipe)
```

Even if you have never programmed before, you can probably guess what each line in this "program" does. At its core, there's nothing mysterious about programming. *Take some data and do something with it.*

But where is this data? Usually, when you have data in a program, you keep it in a *variable*, a named container for data, and variables are the little beasties everyone loves and hates. They're the things you always get wrong but you must get oh so right. As you program, many of your errors will be the wrong data in the wrong variable. Have fun!

A FEW THINGS TO NOTE BEFORE GETTING STARTED

The following sections discuss a few general concepts that make this chapter much easier to follow. We're going to explain a few things that you will see throughout this book, such as making your programs safer and how to recognize variables. You'll want to be familiar with these concepts as you will use them extensively in your career.

strict, warnings, and diagnostics

You learn more detail about this later, but for now, assume that every code snippet begins like this:

```
use strict;
use warnings;
use diagnostics;
```

Those three statements can save you a lot of pain. They force you to properly declare most variables and subroutines, and warn you when you're doing silly things. And if you include the use diagnostics line, they actually give you an extended description of what you did wrong, along with suggestions on how to fix it. Experienced programmers generally omit diagnostics, but when you start, they're invaluable.

> **NOTE** These three lines won't be listed for every code snippet because it would just be useless noise. When you don't see them, assume they're there unless you are told otherwise, although they will be slipped in from time to time as a reminder.

Next, look at a few variables:

```
my $nick_name = 'Ovid';
my @cats      = ( 'Valentin', 'Arthur' );
my $nick      = $nick_name;

print $nick;
```

That example assigns values to some variables. The statement in the third line copies the string Ovid from the variable $nick_name to the variable $nick. The print statement prints the word Ovid to your console.

If you're an experienced programmer, you already understand much of what's going on here, and you can probably guess a lot more. But for now, let's cover some common ground that applies to most variables you work with in Perl.

The my Function

Each variable in the preceding code is declared with the my function. When you *declare* a variable, you're telling Perl "hey, we have a variable we're going to start using." This makes Perl happy. The my function in Perl is the most common way to declare a variable, and it also makes the variable visible only to the current scope (which is covered later in this chapter) to hide it from other parts of your program. That's important to ensure that a distant part of your program doesn't silently change your data.

> **NOTE** *For more information, see* `perldoc -f my`. *(Remember that the* `-f` *switch is used to list functions.)*

You can declare variables inother ways; actually, the variable declaration is sometimes optional. You'll learn more about that in the "Scope" section in this chapter, but for now, be sure to declare your variables with `my`, as shown here:

```
my $nick_name = 'Ovid';
```

This protects this part of your program from being accidentally changed by another part where you used the same variable name. That kind of self-inflicted bug is too easy to create and extremely difficult to find and fix. Use `my` and you can make your programming life easier.

> **NOTE** *Even experienced Perl programmers object to describing* `my` *as a function. However, Perl's distinction between functions, operators, and keywords is a bit fuzzy at times; it's understandable that this is a point of disagreement for some people. The key takeaway here is simple: Don't get hung up on terminology.*

Sigils

Moving a bit further to the right in the sample code presented at the beginning of this discussion, you see punctuation before each variable name — in this case the dollar sign, `$`, as shown here:

```
my $nick_name = 'Ovid';
```

In Perl, this leading punctuation is called a *sigil* because, like the word *scalar*, it is a common word that has been repurposed. A sigil was originally a carved or painted symbol of great power. So, in Perl, a *sigil* is a punctuation symbol that tells you something about the variable you use.

Getting back to that dollar sign sigil, in Perl, when you see a variable beginning with a dollar sign, you know that you're accessing a $calar value. The "S" shape of the dollar sign is a (theoretically) handy mnemonic for scalar. Or maybe it's a handy mnemonic for $ingle value.

Note the phrase, "You're accessing a $calar value." That does not read, "contains a scalar value." When you learn about arrays and hashes (or containers that can contain multiple values), the leading "$" shows you when you're accessing a $ingle value of the array or hash, instead of multiple values. You learn more that when you discover arrays and hashes.

> **NOTE** *For more information, see* `perldoc perldata`.

Identifiers

Variables usually have names. Actually, many things in Perl have names, also called *identifiers*. These are things such as subroutines (discussed in Chapter 7), file handles (discussed in Chapter 9), packages (discussed in Chapter 11), and a few others. Just about anything you can pick a name for in Perl follows fairly simple naming rules.

> **NOTE** *For more information, see* `perldoc perlglossary`.

Perl names must start with a leading letter or underscore. You can optionally follow that with one or more letters, numbers, or underscores. The following are all valid variable names:

```
my $x;
my $foo;
my $_some_1;
my $DontMakeVariableNamesLikeThis;
my $make_names_like_this_instead;
my $item_3;
my $verily_I_say_unto_you_the_number_of_the_tr_tag_shall_be;
```

(The author used that last one in anger in a project several years ago, and somewhere out there is a maintenance programmer who wants to kill him.)

As a matter of style in Perl (yes, Perl has a style, as you can see at `perldoc perlstyle`), don't use `camelCaseWords`. Instead, use `words_separated_by_underscores`. This is because the latter is easier to read, particularly for those who do not speak English as a first language. The practice of using camelCase is merely a holdover from older programming languages that didn't allow underscores in identifiers. Perl programmers are not down with arbitrary limitations imposed by archaic programming conventions. They have enough arbitrary limitations already, thank you.

The following are not valid variable names:

```
my $answer-to-life;
my $~destructor;
my $3rd_times_the_charm;
```

As with all things in life and Perl, there are some caveats, the biggest of which is that Perl is allowed to violate the rules it sets for you. So, in Perl programs, you sometimes see things the following:

```
my $host      = $1;
my $this_perl = $^X;
my $taint_mode = ${^TAINT};
```

You can read about these and other special variables in `perldoc perlvar`. the most common ones are covered in this book as they appear.

> **NOTE** *All the previous names use ASCII characters. Although it is generally not recommended, you can use UTF8 characters in your identifiers by including* use utf 8 *in your program as shown here:*
>
> ```
> use utf8;
> my $cédille = 'French letter';
> print $cédille;
> ```
>
> *Even though you can do this, you shouldn't, given that many programmers cannot type these characters.*

SCALARS

In Perl, a *scalar* is merely a single value. The following are some scalars:

```
my $celsius_temp = 37;
my $nick_name    = 'Ovid';
```

A scalar can be a number, a string, or a reference. (You learn more about references in Chapter 6). If you have a math or physics background, forget that you might know another definition for scalar. In Perl, it just means a single value.

> **NOTE** *For more information, see* perldoc intro.

In the previous example, `my` is a function declaring the variable, followed by the variable itself, followed by the assignment operator (=), followed by a numeric literal (37) or a string literal (`'Ovid'`).

> **NOTE** *A literal is a hard-coded value in a program, as opposed to a variable containing that value. See* perldoc perlglossary *for this and other terms you may be unfamiliar with.*

If you don't assign anything to the variable, it has a special value called `undef`.

```
my $var; # its value is undef
```

As you progress through this book, you'll see that a variable with an `undef` value often causes "uninitialized" warnings in your code. You'll see some of those warnings later and you'll discover tips on how to avoid them.

BEING SELECTIVE WITH VARIABLE NAMES

Unlike some other programming languages, Perl enables you to assign just about any kind of data to a variable. Perl focuses on making data structures easy and expects you to know what kind of data you're working with. Many programmers who prefer "bondage and discipline" languages are keen to disagree, in the hands of an experienced programmer, you tend not to get the type of data wrong as often as you might think. Sadly, this is more a matter of experience than proof, so it's time to pull the "appeal to authority" fallacy out of the hat and say "Trust me on this."

This means that you can do the following, but it's not a good idea:

```
my $celsius_temp = 37;
my $nick_name    = 'Ovid';
$celsius_temp    = $nick_name;
```

Picking intelligent variable names can help you realize when you've done something silly.

If you prefer, you can declare several scalars at once by putting parentheses around them, as shown here:

```
my ( $celsius_temp, $nick_name );
```

And you can even assign values to them when you declare them by putting parentheses around the right side, as shown here:

```
my ( $celsius_temp, $nick_name ) = ( 37, 'Ovid' );
```

As you might expect, that assigns 37 to `$celsius_temp` and "Ovid" to `$nick_name`.

Strings

Assigning a string to a scalar is simple:

```
my $person = 'Leila';
my $wife   = "lovely";
```

Both these lines of code are valid ways to assign a string to a scalar. When using single quotes, what you see inside of the quotes is generally exactly what you get. However, when you use double quotes, you can use escape characters ("\n" for newline, "\t" for tab, and so on) and interpolate (embed) other variables in the string. Following is an example that prints out "lovely Leila" with a newline at the end:

```
my $person = 'Leila';
my $wife   = "lovely $person";
print "$wife\n";
```

Sometimes you need to include quotes in your quotes. You can escape the quotes or use a different set of quotes, as shown here:

```
my $city = 'R\'lyeh';
my $city = "R'lyeh";
print $city;
```

Quotes and Quote Operators

Sometimes, though, you must interpolate something and use double quotes at the same time, as shown here:

```
my $reviewer = 'Adrian';
my $review   = "$reviewer wrote \"This book is awful\"";
```

That can be painful and confusing to read, so Perl provides rich quotelike- operators. (See `perldoc perlop` and search for "Quote-like Operators"). The `q{}` replaces single quotes and `qq{}` replaces double-quotes. This can eliminate much painful escaping.

```
my $reviewer = 'Adrian';
my $review   = qq{$reviewer wrote "This book is wonderful"};
```

Also, the actual delimiter used with `q` and `qq` does not need to be curly braces (`{}`). It could be almost any pair of delimiters you choose, such as shown in the following examples:

```
my $review   = qq!$reviewer wrote "This book is awful"!;
my $review   = qq<$reviewer wrote "This book is awful">;
my $review   = qq[$reviewer wrote "This book is awful"];
my $review   = qq($reviewer wrote "This book is awful");
my $review   = qq@$reviewer wrote "This book is awful"@;
```

You can even use quotes over multiple lines, as shown here:

```
my $letter = qq{
Dear $editor,

I really liked the subtitle that you rejected and beg you to reconsider.
It was brilliant and perfectly conveyed the tone of this book. In case
you want to reconsider, it's:
```

```
    "Get a job, hippy!"

Sincerely,
Ovid
};
```

However, if you go that route, it's generally considered better to use "here-docs." These types of strings require a << followed by a string literal of your choosing. All following text will be included in the string until the string literal is found again:

```
my $letter = <<"END_APOLOGY";
Dear $editor,

I'm very sorry for mocking you in the last email. I promise it won't
happen again. Can I still get paid?

Sincerely,
Ovid
END_APOLOGY
```

You can use just about any string literal.

```
my $get_customers_with_orders = <<"SQL";
SELECT c.id
  FROM customers c
  JOIN orders o ON c.id = o.customer_id
SQL
```

Just be sure to pick a descriptive literal (END is a popular one) for the here-doc. Yes, you can use a single dot (.) or even an empty string, but this is considered bad style, which can lead to confusing code or even strange errors.

> **WARNING** *The final string literal in a here-doc must have a newline at the end of it, or Perl won't see it, and you'll get an error like this:*
>
> ```
> Can't find string terminator "END_APOLOGY" anywhere before EOF.
> ```
>
> *It's a confusing thing that trips up a few people.*

> **NOTE** *You can also use here-docs with single quotes, in which case nothing inside of the here-doc will be interpolated.*

Escape Sequences

Many times when creating strings you come across characters that can be awkward to type. The full list can be seen with `perldoc perlop`, but Table 3-1 shows the main escape sequences you'll encounter.

TABLE 3-1: Main Escape Sequences

SEQUENCE	DESCRIPTION
\t	Tab
\n	Newline
\r	Carriage return
\x{263a}	Wide hex character
\N{name}	Named Unicode character

Now consider the following:

```
print "I mean it!\nI'm really sorry for mocking you!\n";
```

This line of code prints the following:

```
I mean it!
I'm really sorry for mocking you!
```

Table 3-2 shows a few special escape sequences that are less common but are sometimes used to control the "case" of characters.

TABLE 3-2: Special Escape Sequences

SEQUENCE	DESCRIPTION
\l	Lowercase next character
\u	Uppercase next character
\L	Lowercase until \E
\U	Uppercase until \E
\E	End case modification

You can use these just as you would other escape characters. For example, the following prints "`E.E. Cummings`" and offends your literature professor:

```
print "\Ue.e. c\Eummings\n";
```

Numbers

Manipulating strings is fine, but much of your work as a programmer will deal with numbers such as integers, floating point numbers, hexadecimal numbers and other beasties. It's not very useful to have a programming language that doesn't do math, so this section shows you several ways of declaring numbers in Perl.

Integers and Floats

Scalars can hold numbers, too. Just assign the numbers to them:

```
my $answer = 42;
my $body_temp_fahrenheit = 98.6;
```

You can use integers or floats as needed. Internally, Perl stores these numbers; however, the C compiler that built Perl supports them.

Integers are represented exactly, but as with other programming languages, floating point numbers are only an approximation because of how computers store numbers internally. For example, the `int` function takes the integer value of a number, but this can lead to unpleasant surprises:

```
print int(4.39 * 100);
```

Depending on your Perl, that will likely print 438 instead of 439. That's because 4.39 is represented internally as something like 4.3899999999999 and when you multiply it by 100 and drop the decimal part, you get 438. This is a general limitation with programming languages, not just Perl.

WHY PERL DOESN'T REPRESENT FLOATING POINT NUMBERS CORRECTLY

The reason Perl often doesn't represent floating point numbers correctly is because not all numbers can be stored in a finite amount of memory. For example, 1/3 is .3333... (with an infinite number of 3s after it). Internally, a floating point number is actually stored as the number and a "floating point" that explains where the decimal should be.

The number is stored in binary (ones and zeros) format. Each binary digit covers a base two fraction such as 1/2, 1/4, 1/8 ... 1/number of bits. All fractions whose binary digit corresponds to 1 are added together. For example, a standard floating point number is 32 bits long and the number .75 can be represented exactly as 110 00000000000000000000000000000. The first two digits mean that .75 is considered to be 1/2 + 1/4 (in this case, an exact match).

continues

(*continued*)

However, the number 1/3 can only be approximated as 01010101010101010101010
101010101. That is 1/4 + 1/16 + ... + 1/4294967296 (yes, we skipped many
numbers). This means that with a 4 byte (32 bit) float, the closest approximation of
1/3 is 0.333333333255723.

If you want to explore this more, the following program will print out the
fractions, the binary number and something close to the internal equivalent of the
$num that you have chosen. You can alter $bits to change the number of bits of
representation of the number to better see how these approximations change.

```perl
use strict;
use warnings;

my $num  = .3;
my $bits = 32;

# don't touch anything below this line
my $accumulator = 0;
my $bitstring   = '';

my @fractions;
for ( 1 .. $bits ) {
    my $denominator = 2 ** $_;
    my $fraction = 1 / $denominator;
    if ( $accumulator + $fraction <= $num ) {
        push @fractions, "1/$denominator";
        $bitstring .= "1";
        $accumulator += $fraction;
    }
    else {
        $bitstring .= "0";
    }
}

my $fractions = join " + ", @fractions;
print <<"END";
Fractions: $fractions
Bits:      $bitstring
Result:    $accumulator
END
```

Note that this is not a perfect description of what's going on, but it's gives you the
general idea. By the end of chapter 5, you should understand that entire program.

Octal, Hex, and Exponential Notation

If you need to, you can designate integer numbers (and only integer numbers) as octal or hex by
prepending them with a 0 or 0x respectively:

```
my $answer     = 052;   # 42 in decimal
my $hex_number = 0xFF;  # 255 in decimal
my $hex_number = 0xff;  # also 255 in decimal
```

You can also use exponential notation if needed, and like many other languages, Perl is rather flexible about how you write it. The following are all equivalent:

```
my $number_of_stars_in_universe = 3e23;
my $number_of_stars_in_universe = 3E+23;
my $number_of_stars_in_universe = 3.0e+23;
```

Naturally, you can represent small numbers with this, too.

```
my $electron_mass = 9.1093822e-31;
```

Perl doesn't "remember" the format of the number you used, so if you assign a hex or octal value to a number, Perl prints the integer equivalent, but if you print a number using an exponential format, Perl will printonly the integer equivalent if it can be represented without exponential notation (in other words, when it's small enough).

You see more about working with numbers in Chapter 4.

> **NOTE** *For more information, see* `perldoc perlnumber` *and* `perldoc perlfaq4` *(Date Manipulation).*

ARRAYS

In Perl, an *array* is an ordered list of scalars. The following is how you might assign a few numbers to an array:

```
my @even = ( 2, 4, 6, 8, 10 );
```

> **NOTE** *For more information, see* `perldoc perlintro`.

For an array, the variable is preceded by an @ (at) sign, so the mnemonic for this is an "@rray." And when you have a list of items, separate them with a comma and use parentheses () around them. For now, just take my word for it. In Chapter 4, you learn more about this in detail when you discover precedence.

So, the preceding code has an array on the left and a list on the right, and you're assigning the list to the array.

Of course, just as with scalars, you can use any kind of data you need to use. You can even assign lists with a mix of strings or other scalars to an array:

```
my $nine = 9;
my @stuff = ( 7, 'of', $nine );
```

If you just print the array as shown in the following example, what happens?

```
my $nine = 9;
my @stuff = ( 7, 'of', $nine );
print @stuff, "\n";
print "@stuff\n";
```

Although there are ways you can tweak this, the code just presented will probably print the following:

```
7of9
7 of 9
```

Breaking Down the Code

In the previous example, the `print` function takes a list of arguments. Consider the first `print` statement in the example:

```
print @stuff, "\n";
```

This tells Perl to dutifully print every item in the list, one after another, with the newline being printed last. Because no item in the list contains a space, they run together as they're being printed.

The second version has the array being interpolated into a string:

```
print "@stuff\n";
```

When an array is interpolated into a string, the individual elements are, by default, separated with a single space, generating the "7 of 9" output.

> **NOTE** Although an array interpolated into a string is separated by default by a single space, this is actually controlled by the value of the $" special variable. Read `perldoc perlvar` to understand this better. Some sloppy programmers like to abuse that variable, and you'll see it in code from time to time.

The array `@stuff` has two integers and one string. Because Perl is more focused on data structures than strict limitations on the kinds of data they contain, you can generally use whatever kinds of data you want.

Accessing Elements

Now printing out an array is all fine and dandy, but often when you're working with an array, you are trying to work with one element of the array or all elements. (Sometimes you work with a few elements called a *slice*, and you'll learn more about that in a bit.)

You may remember earlier in this chapter the discussion said that, "in Perl, when you see a variable beginning with a dollar sign, you know that you're accessing a $calar value." It's the same with arrays. Arrays are indexed by numbers, with the first element of the array being indexed by 0 (zero). Getting that first element looks like this:

```
my @words = ("and", "another", "thing");
print $words[0];
```

Remember that the sigil before the variable name indicates how you're accessing it, not the type of variable. This is a frequent source of confusion for newer Perl programmers, so you need to pay careful attention to this.

On the right side of the variable name, square brackets appear around the index. When you're using square brackets in Perl, it usually means you're dealing with an array.

Naturally, if you want to access all the elements, you can do this:

```
my @words  = ( "and", "another", "thing" );
my $first  = $words[0];
my $second = $words[1];
my $third  = $words[2];
```

As you might expect, you can also assign to individual elements of the array this way:

```
$words[1] = "one more";
print "@words\n";
```

That prints and one more thing.

When accessing an individual element of an array, you have a dollar sign on the left and square brackets on the right. This will be repeated quite a bit. It's one of the classic stumbling blocks for new Perl programmers. If your eyes glaze over and you stop reading about the sigils and things like that, it's your own darn fault when you get them wrong!

Sometimes you'll find that you want some trailing elements of an array, but you're not sure of the length. It's easy to find out the length of the array, but there's actually an interesting trick here. If you access an array with a negative number, you access array elements from the end of the list going backward, starting with –1 (because 0 would be the first element).

```
my @words = ( "and", "another", "thing" );
my $last  = $words[-1];
print $last;
```

That prints thing. Of course, $words[-2] would be another and $words[-3] would be and.

LENGTHS OF ARRAYS

In Perl, arrays are not of a fixed size. Consider the following array:

```
use strict;
use warnings;
use diagnostics;
my @words;
my $word = $words[8];
```

Perl will allow you to try to access an element beyond the end of the array, and it will not issue any sort of warning. When you try to do something with the $words variable, you'll probably get a warning about using an "uninitialized" value. And if you're not careful, you'll have a hard time trying to track it down because the warning will occur when you use the variable even though the actual problem stems from the actual assignment.

Naturally, this also means that you can access array elements with nonexistent negative elements, as shown here:

```
my @words = ("this", "that");
my $no_such_word = $words[-17];
```

Again, no warning occurs unless you do something with $no_such_word, which causes an uninitialized warning.

When you do this you don't actually change the length of the array. It still has the same number of elements. However, if you assign past the end of the array, any uninitialized elements up to that assignment will have the undef value.

```
use strict;
use warnings;
use diagnostics;
my @words = ("this", "that");
$words[5] =  "bad idea";
```

With this code, you now have an array with six elements:

```
'this', 'that', undef, undef, undef, 'bad idea'
```

The only safety you get here is if you try to assign to a nonexistent negative element, as shown here:

```
use strict;
use warnings;
use diagnostics;
my @words = ("this", "that");
$words[-5] =  "bad idea";
```

That generates the following output:

```
Modification of non-creatable array value attempted, subscript -5
at bad.pl line 5 (#1)
(F) You tried to make an array value spring into existence, and the
subscript was probably negative, even counting from end of the array
backwards.
Uncaught exception from user code:
Modification of non-creatable array value attempted, subscript -5
at bad.pl line 5.
```

Needless to say, this is one area you want to be careful with. Pay attention to your data.

As a handy shortcut, so long as you assign literals to the array and not variables, you can use the qw() operator (as in "q"uote "w"ords) like this:

```
my @odds = qw( 1 3 5 charlie );
```

The qw() operator takes a string and automatically separates it on whitespace, so this line of code is equivalent to the following:

```
my @odds = ( 1, 3, 5, 'charlie' );
```

Sometimes you see something like this:

```
my @odds = qw( 1, 3, 5, 'charlie' );
```

That's probably not what you want, and if you have warnings on, it will warn about a "Possible attempt to separate words with commas." Because the string in the qw() operator is separated by whitespace, the commas will be included in the values and not be used as a list separator.

As with the qq() operator, qw() enables just about any pair of balanced delimiters. Some common ones include the following:

```
my @odds = qw! 1 3 5 charlie !;
my @odds = qw<1 3 5 charlie >;
my @odds = qw{ 1 3 5 charlie };
my @odds = qw[ 1 3 5 charlie ];
```

Those are useful cases when one of the words in the string might contain a delimiter, as shown here:

```
my @punctuation = qw[ . ; ! ( ) { } ];
```

Iterating over Arrays

Naturally, you don't want to always access array data by assigning the value of different elements to different variables. You often want to iterate over the elements and do something with them. The following is one way to do this (Chapter 5 goes into more detail during a discussion of control flow):

```
my @array = ( 'this', 'is', 'an', 'array' );
for my $element (@array) {
    print "$element\n";
}
```

That should print the following:

```
this
is
an
array
```

HASHES

One of the reasons Perl is so popular is because of how easy it is to sling data around. Hashes are a perfect example of this. A *hash* is similar to an array, except that instead of indexing into the hash using integers, you use strings. You refer to the strings you index into the hash as *keys*, and the values they return are, well, *values*.

The following is a hash with three keys and their values:

```
my %people = (
    "Alice",    1,
    "Bob",      2,
    "Ovid",     "idiot",
);
print $people{'Alice'};
```

You could simulate that with an array, but it would be clumsy and require many almost useless variable declarations:

```
my @people = ( 1, 2, 'idiot' );
my $alice  = 0;
my $bob    = 1;
my $ovid   = 2;
print $people[$alice];
```

> **NOTE** *Please refer to* `perldoc perlintro` *for more information.*

Accessing Elements

As you have already seen, accessing data in a hash is simple:

```
my %people = (
    "Alice",    1,
    "Bob",      2,
    "Ovid",     "idiot",
);

my $number = $people{'Bob'};
print "Bob = $number\n";
print "Bob = $people{'Bob'}\n";
```

You'll immediately notice a few things here. First, you can see that to access an individual element of the hash, you have a dollar sign for the sigil (see a pattern?) and *curly brackets* (*curly braces*, *curlies*, *squiggly braces*, or whatever you call 'em) around the index.

Second, as mentioned, the "keys" of the hash correspond to an array's numeric indices. You could do that if you wanted to like this:

```
my %french_word_for = (
    1, 'un',
    2, 'deux',
    3, 'trois',
);
print "The French word for '3' is $french_word_for{3}\n";
```

That can be confusing, and you probably just want an array itself, although sometimes a hash might be a good choice if the integers are widely separated (which would otherwise be a *sparse array* with many empty elements).

You can also note that you retrieved the hash value without quoting the key:

```
my $french_word = $silly_example{3};
my $other_data  = $another_example{some_key};
```

When accessing a single value, you are not required to quote the key, so long as it follows the rule of an identifier. So, this is wrong, and you must quote the key:

```
my $other_data  = $another_example{-some_key};
```

> **NOTE** *Autoquoting hash keys even applies if the key appears to be a builtin or subroutine name.*

Iterating Over Hashes

Iterating over a hash is fairly simple. One way to do this is to use the `keys` function. This returns the list of keys from the hash, as shown in the following example:

```
my %people = (
    "Alice", 1,
    "Bob",   2,
    "Ovid",  "idiot",
);
for my $name ( keys %people ) {
    print "$name is $people{$name}\n";
}
```

That might print something like this:

```
Ovid is idiot
Bob is 2
Alice is 1
```

The order of the hash keys is effectively random, so there's no guarantee that your version of Perl will print those lines in this order. It's actually not random, but the reasons for that are beyond the scope of this book. Just remember that you should never rely on hash order. However, you'll learn more about that in Chapter 10 during a discussion of sorting.

There is a corresponding `values` function that returns the values of the hash — again without any predictable order.

Adding Data to Hashes

To add a new value to a hash, simply assign the new value to a key:

```
$people{Austen} = 'Jane';
```

That adds a new value to the hash or overwrites the value for the key `Austen` if it exists.

You can add multiple key/value pairs by assigning the hash and a list:

```
%people = ( %people, Austen => 'Jane', Lincoln => 'Abraham' );
```

If any of the keys in the list match keys in the original hash, the original values is replaced with the new ones.

IDIOMATIC PERL

When you write Perl code, it's generally considered nice to follow the `perlstyle` document (`perldoc perlstyle`), but not everything is contained in there. This section provides some tips to write hashes in a "Perlish" way.

The way the hashes were written before builds more or less on your previous knowledge. But in Perl code you'll usually find hashes written like this:

```
my %people = (
    Alice => 1,
    Bob   => 2,
    Ovid  => "idiot",
);
```

Or you may find them written like this:

```
my %people = (
    'Alice' => 1,
    'Bob'   => 2,
    'Ovid'  => "idiot",
);
```

Those last two hash declarations are the same thing. The => operator in Perl is sometimes known as the "fat comma" (no "fat comma" jokes, please). It generally acts just like a normal comma, but it has the side benefit of automatically quoting whatever is on the left side of the fat comma, but only if it matches the rules of an identifier. The following is a syntax error because 2Bob would not be a valid identifier (because it begins with a digit):

```
my %people = (
    Alice => 1,
    2Bob  => 2,
    Ovid  => "idiot",
);
```

You are not required to use the fat comma in hashes, but they're a common way of writing a hash because they make the key/value pairs more obvious. For example, compare the following two hashes and think about which one is easier to read:

```
my %vegetables = ( 'celery' => 'yuck', 'spinach' => 'delicious' );
my %vegetables = ( 'celery', 'yuck', 'spinach', 'delicious' );
```

As you might imagine, if you declare a large hash, the fat comma can tremendously improve readability.

Also, the trailing comma after the last key/value is not required, but it makes is easier to avoid syntax errors if you decide to re-order how you wrote the hash, or if you add more key/value pairs. It's difficult to forget a comma you've already added.

There is no requirement to line up the key/value pairs when declaring a hash because whitespace is usually not significant. However, it's generally considered good style because it is easier to read.

SLICES

Sometimes you'll get a data structure with a lot of data, but you don't want all of it. In Perl, a *slice* is a way to select a few elements of an array, list, or hash instead of the entire set of data.

Array Slices

You've already learned that "the sigil that starts the variable indicates how you're accessing it," so as you might guess, to take several elements out of an array at once, you use the @ sign at the front. The following is an example:

```
my @names = ('Alice', 'Bill', 'Cathy', 'Doug');
my @men   = @names[ 1, 3 ]; # Bill and Doug
my @women = @names[ 0, 2 ]; # Alice and Cathy
```

> **NOTE** For more information, see `perldoc perlintro`.

It's the square brackets (`[ ]`) that tell you what type of variable you're indexing into (an array, in this case), not the leading sigil. Again, this is a concept you need to get used to because it's core to understanding the Perl language. And, yes, this drum is being beaten repeatedly because everyone gets it wrong sooner or later.

Generally, it doesn't make sense to take a single-element slice. So, if you do this, you get a warning (if you have warnings enabled, which you learn more about in a bit).

```
use warnings;
my @stuff = ('bits', 'and', 'bobs');
my $item = @stuff[1];
print $item;
```

That issues the following warning:

```
Scalar value @stuff[1] better written as $stuff[1] at stuff.pl line 3.
```

Make that recommended change and the warning goes away.

Hash Slices

Naturally, you can take a slice of a hash. Because you use the leading sigil to indicate how you're accessing the variable, you use the @ sign again, but with curly braces. The following is an example:

```
my %nationality_of = (
    'Ovid'          => 'Greek',
    'John Davidson' => 'Scottish',
    'Tennyson'      => 'English',
    'Poe'           => 'Tacky',    # Geek?
);

my @nationalities = @nationality_of{ 'Ovid', 'Tennyson' };
print "@nationalities";
```

That prints "Greek English," despite the fact that Ovid was actually a Roman poet. Garbage in, garbage out.

CONTEXT

Context is one of the more useful features of Perl. *Context* means an expression can change its value based on what the calling code expects to receive. This sounds strange, and some new programmers — not you, of course — get confused by it. When you get used to it, you'll find it easy and natural. Take care to understand this concept because you'll see it constantly in Perl programs.

> **NOTE** *For more information, see* `perldoc perlglossary`.

There are three main types of context: *scalar*, *list*, and *void*. They often mean "what the left side of an expression wants to get." Rather than belabor this, the following are some examples of this beautiful craziness.

Scalar Context

This is an example of scalar context:

```
my $number_of_things = @things_in_common;
my $number_of_things = scalar @things_in_common;
my $number_of_things = ( 'liars', 'fools', 'certain politicians' );
my $number_of_things = %hash_example;
```

When dealing with assigning values to variables, what you have on the left side of the = determines the "context" on which you're evaluating the right side. So, if you have a scalar on the left, you have scalar context.

Arrays in Scalar Context

Following is an example of an array in scalar context:

```
my @things_in_common = ( 'liars', 'fools', 'certain politicians' );
my $number_of_things = @things_in_common;
```

As you might guess from the variable name, $number_of_things is equal to 3, the number of elements in @things_in_common. That's because the scalar context value of an array returns the number of elements in that array.

If you want to force scalar context, you can use the scalar keyword, as shown here:

```
my @things_in_common = ( 'liars', 'fools', 'certain politicians' );
my $number_of_things = scalar @things_in_common;
```

That last line has exactly the same meaning with or without the scalar keyword, but it does make it explicit that you meant scalar context and weren't trying to assign an element of the array to $number_of_things.

The `scalar` keyword is also essential when you want to force scalar context and not list context. So, the following is probably not correct:

```
my @things_in_common = ( 'liars', 'fools', 'certain politicians' );
my %count_for = ( useless_things => @things_in_common );
print $count_for{useless_things};
```

With a comma operator, whether you deal with the regular comma or the fat comma (=>), you are using list context, so you can fix the previous snippet with the `scalar` keyword, as shown here:

```
my @things_in_common = ( 'liars', 'fools', 'certain politicians' );
my %count_for = ( useless_things => scalar @things_in_common );
print $count_for{useless_things};
```

> **NOTE** See `perldoc -f scalar` *for more information.*

Lists in Scalar Context

If you force scalar context with a list (again, an array is a container for a list), whatever is on the left side of each comma is evaluated, the result is thrown away, and the right side is evaluated. That leads to common errors like this:

```
my $number_of_things = ( 'liars', 'fools', 'certain politicians' );
print $number_of_things;
```

That prints `certain politicians` instead of the number 3. Thus, you usually don't want to use a list in scalar context; use an array instead.

Hashes in Scalar Context

Naturally, you can also use scalar context with a hash, as shown here:

```
my %hash = ( 1 => 2 );
print scalar %hash;
```

However, that's probably going to print something like `1/8`, and that's about as useful as an ashtray on a motorcycle. In scalar context, you're actually seeing a bit about the internal structure of the hash. It has its uses, but they won't be covered here.

List Context

You have list context when the left-side value expects a list. Here's how to copy an array to another array:

```
my @copy = @old_array;
```

This is a "shallow" copy in that you're copying only the top-level elements. Later, when you learn about references (Chapter 6), you learn about this in more detail.

If you want, you can also assign a hash to an array, as shown here:

```
my %order_totals = (
    Charles    => 13.2,
    Valerie    => 17.9,
    'Billy Bob' => 0,
);
my @flattened = %order_totals;
```

That "flattens" the key/value pairs in the hash into a list. If you print the resulting array, you might get something like this:

```
Billy Bob 0 Charles 13.2 Valerie 17.9
```

Again, this is because a hash is not ordered. If you need to retrieve the elements of a hash in order, see Chapter 10, which explores sorting.

One of the nice things about list context is that you can force it with parentheses. For example, if you want to assign the first element of an array to a scalar, just put parentheses around the scalar, as shown here:

```
my @swords = ( 'katana', 'wakizashi' );

my $number_of_swords = @swords;
my ($left_hand)      = @swords;
```

However, you aren't limited to a single scalar. You can assign several scalars at the same time, as shown here:

```
my ( $left_hand, $right_hand ) = @swords;
```

This can come in extremely handy when you learn more about subroutines in Perl.

This has an interesting side effect. When you're facing down Toshiro Mifune and you realize that your katana and wakizashi swords are in the wrong hands, you're in trouble. Here's how you might do that in C:

```
other_hand = left_hand;
left_hand = right_hand;
right_hand = other_hand;
```

Too bad. You're dead.

In Perl, because you can use list context with those scalars, you can do this to swap those values:

```
( $right_hand, $left_hand ) = ( $left_hand, $right_hand );
```

Pretty handy, eh?

You can mix scalars and other variables with this:

```
my ( $first, @extra ) = ( 1, 2, 3, 4 );
```

$first will have the value of 1 and @extra will be 2, 3, and 4. However, the scalars must come first!

```
my ( @extra, $last ) = ( 1, 2, 3, 4 );
```

That doesn't do what you want because @extra slurped up all the values and $last will be undefined.

Now it's time for you to get some experience actually working with these variables.

TRY IT OUT   **Printing Scalars, Arrays, and Hashes**

This chapter has covered a lot of ground, so now get your hands a bit dirty to see how this works. All the code for this Try It Out can be found in code file example_3-1_variables.pl.

1. Type the following program into your favorite editor, and save it as example_3_1_variables.pl:

```
use strict;
use warnings;
use diagnostics;

my $hero = 'Ovid';
my $fool = $hero;
print "$hero isn't that much of a hero. $fool is a fool.\n";

$hero = 'anybody else';
print "$hero is probably more of a hero than $fool.\n";

my %snacks = (
    stinky   => 'limburger',
    yummy    => 'brie',
    surprise => 'soap slices',
);
my @cheese_tray = values %snacks;
print "Our cheese tray will have: ";
for my $cheese (@cheese_tray) {
    print "'$cheese' ";
}
print "\n";
```

2. Now that you've saved it, run it with perl example_3_1_variables.pl. It will probably print something similar to the following:

```
Ovid isn't that much of a hero. Ovid is a fool.
anybody else is probably more of a hero than Ovid.
Our cheese tray will have: 'havarti' 'soap slices' 'brie'
```

If it didn't, the inclusion of strict, warnings, and diagnostics will provide clues to where you mistyped.

How It Works

Now skip the `strict`, `warnings`, and `diagnostics` because you'll learn more about those in the cleverly named "strict, warnings, and diagnostics" section of this chapter. For now, just know that they make writing correct code much easier. Instead, look at the first assignments:

```
my $hero = 'Ovid';
my $fool = $hero;
print "$hero isn't that much of a hero. $fool is a fool.\n";

$hero = 'anybody else';
print "$hero is probably more of a hero than $fool.\n";
```

That should be clear by now, but with the second assignment to the `$hero` variable, you can see that it does not change the value of `$fool`. You're copying the values of these variables, not the variables themselves.

For the rest, the only new thing here is the use of the `values` keyword. This was mentioned earlier, but this example shows it in action:

```
my @cheese_tray = values %snacks;
print "@cheese_tray\n";
```

That prints `limburger brie soap slices` and guarantees that you have a memorable (if unpopular) party.

SCOPE

Now it's time to talk about scope. No, this is not about the mouthwash, but rather the *scope* of variables, or "where you can see them from." Using scope is a way of ensuring that variables declared in one part of your program are not available in other portions of the program. This helps to prevent unrelated code from accidentally changing those values.

> **NOTE** *For more information about scope, see* `perldoc perlintro`*.*

my Variables

Variables declared with `my` are referred to as *lexically scoped*. This means that they do not exist outside of the scope in which they are declared. This generally means *file scoped* or *block scoped*.

File scoped means that any `my` variable declared outside of a block is visible from that point on to the end of the file in which it is declared. This also means that if you have several packages in a file (which you learn about in Chapter 11), the `my` variable in question will be visible to all packages in that file. You generally want to avoid that.

However, if they are declared inside of a block, they remain scoped to that block. In Perl, a *block scope* is simply one or more Perl statements delimited by curly braces. For example, the following is a bare block:

```
my $answer = 42;
{
    my $answer = 'forty-two';
    print "$answer\n";
}
print "$answer\n";
```

That prints the following:

```
forty-two
42
```

This is because the my declaration inside of the block "hides" the variable from the scope outside of the block.

> **NOTE** *You cannot declare Perl's built-in variables like this, with one exception. Prior to version 5.10, you were not allowed to do the following, even though it appeared to obey the rules:*
>
> ```
> my $_;
> ```
>
> *That was not allowed because $\_ is one of Perl's built-in special variables, which you learn about in* Perl's Built-In Variables *section later in this chapter. As of version 5.10 and after, this restriction was lifted, and you are now allowed to use* my *$_, but not for the other built-ins. See* perldoc perl5100delta *and search for* **Lexical $_** *for more information.*

Listing 3-1 (code file listing_3_1_scope.pl) provides a more real-world example with a block in a for loop.

LISTING 3-1: Variable Scoping in Blocks

```
use strict;
use warnings;
use diagnostics;

my @numbers = ( 1, 2, 3, 4, 5 );
for my $number (@numbers) {
    my $reciprocal = 1 / $number;
    print "The reciprocal of $number is $reciprocal\n";
}
print $number;
print $reciprocal;
```

The program in Listing 3-1 will not run. Instead, you'll get a bunch of errors similar to the following:

```
Global symbol "$number" requires explicit package name at numbers.pl line 11.
Global symbol "$reciprocal" requires explicit package name at numbers.pl line 12.
Execution of /var/tmp/eval_NAV1.pl aborted due to compilation errors (#1)

(F) You've said "use strict" or "use strict vars", which indicates
that all variables must either be lexically scoped (using "my" or "state"),
declared beforehand using "our", or explicitly qualified to say
which package the global variable is in (using "::").

Uncaught exception from user code:
Global symbol "$number" requires explicit package name at numbers.pl line 11.
Global symbol "$reciprocal" requires explicit package name at numbers.pl line 12.
Execution of $numbers.pl aborted due to compilation errors.
```

The @numbers variable does not appear in the error message because it's file scoped and thus visible everywhere in this file. The error occurs because the $reciprocal and $number variables are declared with my inside of the block and are not available outside of it. Note that the $number variable is also lexically scoped to that block, even though it might appear to be outside of it. That's just how for loops work.

To make the broken code run, simply delete the two print statements after the for loop.

But you may have noted the "requires explicit package name" error highlighted in the previous error message. What exactly does that mean?

Package Variables

In Perl, a *package* is just a namespace to keep variables, subroutines, and other things organized. By default, things live in the package main. You declare what package (namespace) you're in with the package keyword. You learn about this more indepth in Chapter 11, but for now, when you write simple programs, you need to knowonly the basics.

Generally, you'll find that package variables are *globally scoped*. A globally scoped variable is available anywhere in your program.

> **NOTE** *A namespace is just a place where any names used won't show up in another namespace. They're a convenient way to organize your code. You'll find more in-depth coverage of this in Chapter 11.*

Consider the following code:

```
package main;
use strict;
use warnings;
```

Here, the `package main;` statement isn't required because `main` is the default package. However, sometimes you see code written like this:

```
package MyCompany::Stuff;

use strict;
use warnings;

%MyCompany::Stuff::department_number_for = (
    finance     => 13,
    programming => 2,
    janitorial  => 17,
    executive   => 0,
);
```

And later, other code can reference this with the following:

```
my $department_number = $MyCompany::Stuff::department_number_for{finance};
```

It doesn't matter if that code is in the same package, or even a different file, so long as the `MyCompany::Stuff` package has been loaded. When addressing a package variable with the full package name included in it, this is known as a *fully qualified variable*. However, typing `$MyCompany::Stuff::department_number_for{finance}` can be annoying. It's also error-prone because the following is legal but probably not what you intended (note the misspelling of "Sutff"):

```
my $department_number = $MyCompany::Sutff::department_number_for{finance};
```

Thus, you have several options to deal with this. One is to not use the `strict` pragma. (A *pragma* is a special module, the name of which is usually written in all lowercase letters, which alters the compile or runtime behavior of your program.) Any variable referenced without the `my` function is automatically a variable in the current package.

```
package main;
$answer = 42
print "$anwser\n";
```

That's legal Perl, but you can see how easy it is to misspell variable names, so you shouldn't forget `strict` because that way lies madness.

The vars Pragma

Moving along, prior to Perl 5.6.0, you had the `vars` pragma that looked like Listing 3-2 (code file `listing_3_2_vars.pl`).

LISTING 3-2: The vars Pragma

```
package MyCompany::Stuff;

use strict;
use warnings;
```

```
use vars (
    '%department_number_for',
    '$some_other_package_variable',
);

%department_number_for = (
    finance      => 13,
    programming  => 2,
    janitorial   => 17,
    executive    => 0,
);
$some_other_package_variable = 42;
print $department_number_for{finance};
```

Outside of the package, you would still need to refer to those variables by the fully qualified variable names, and run the risk of typos, but it saves typing inside of the package.

Declaring Package Variables with our

Starting with version 5.6.0, Perl introduced the our function. Unlike the my function that says "this variable is mine," the our variable says "this variable is ours." In other words, it's like any other package variable, but it has a cleaner syntax.

Listing 3-3 (code file listing_3_3_our.pl) shows an example with the our function.

LISTING 3-3: Declaring Variables with our

```
package MyCompany::Stuff;

use strict;
use warnings;

our %department_number_for;
our $some_other_package_variable;

%department_number_for = (
    finance      => 13,
    programming  => 2,
    janitorial   => 17,
    executive    => 0,
);
$some_other_package_variable = 42;
print $department_number_for{finance};
```

Many people have a habit of declaring variables with the vars pragma or with the our function. Do not do this unless you need to share that variable outside of your package. When someone else's code changes that variable's value and breaks your code, it can be difficult to track down.

Using Local Variables

Of course, sometimes you want to limit the scope of your package variables. You can't use the my keyword to declare them, but you can use local to make it clear that they're "localized" to a given scope. They'll retain their value in the outer scope but you're free to change them in the inner scope, if needed. Here is an example:

```
our $answer = 42;
{
    local $answer = 57;
    print "$answer\n";
}
print "$answer\n";
```

That prints the following:

```
57
42
```

Whenever you need to temporarily change the value of a package variable, use the `local` function. Of course, you can do this with fully qualified variable names, too, as shown here:

```
local $MyCompany::Stuff;
```

That ensures that you can do just about anything you want with $MyCompany::Stuff in your local scope without causing problems for others who rely on the original value.

If you need to keep the original value and change it, assign it to itself with `local`, as shown here:

```
our $answer = 42;
{
    local $answer = $answer;
    print "$answer\n";
    $answer = $answer + 2;
    print "$answer\n";
}
print "$answer\n";
```

That prints the following:

```
42
44
42
```

Be sure you understand why that works because it's a common idiom in Perl.

STRICT, WARNINGS, AND DIAGNOSTICS

Before going much further, we need to stop for a word from our sponsors: `strict`, `warnings`, and `diagnostics`.

Strictly speaking you don't need the `my` in front of a variable declaration. Or perhaps that should read "unstrictly" speaking. For most experienced Perl programmers, you'll see the following two lines at the top of virtually all their Perl programs:

```
use strict;
use warnings;
```

And when you're new to Perl, adding the following line is also recommended:

```
use diagnostics;
```

`strict`, `warnings`, and `diagnostics` are pragmas. As mentioned earlier, in Perl, a pragma is a special module, the name of which is usually written in all lowercase letters, which alters the compile or runtime behavior of your program.

Of course, you can leave these pragmas out when writing your software, but it's a bad idea, and many Perl developers will not help you if you omit these things. Why? Because they save so much development by protecting you from silly mistakes, you'd be insane to not use them. You're not insane, are you? (Hmm, you are learning Perl, though).

If you actually need to, you can turn these off, as shown here:

```
no strict;
no warnings;
```

However, if you do so, it's recommended that you do so only with two conditions:

➤   It's a limited scope.

➤   You turn off only the bits you need.

```
{
    no warnings 'uninitialized';
    $total = $total + $some_value;
}
```

In the preceding code, $total might be accumulating some of your order total, but sometimes $some_value might be allowed to be undefined. In that case, you might decide it's okay to turn off "uninitialized" warnings in that scope. (Good luck spelling "uninitialized" correctly the first time, by the way.)

> **NOTE** *You should read* `perldoc strict` *and* `perldoc warnings` *to better understand how they work and what bits you can turn off.* `perldoc perllexwarn` *goes into extensive detail about how the* `warnings` *pragma is structured.*

You see more examples later in the book, but there's no point in covering them in depth now. By the time you understand them, you'll be better prepared to understand why to do this.

Now let's look at the individual pragmas to see the basics.

strict

For `strict`, you could actually write the following:

```
use strict 'vars';
use strict 'subs';
use strict 'refs';
```

However, you usually just want to write this (which means the same thing):

```
use strict;
```

The vast majority of the time, `strict` means "declare your variables." If you forget to do so, your program will not run. For example, say that you try to do this:

```
my $name = 'Danny';
my $nick = $naem;
```

You get a compile-time error because you misspelled $name (unless you created my $naem for some reason).

warnings

For `warnings`, things are a bit different. They're generally just warning you about bad things your program is doing. But, in reality, these things might be okay. Your program will run, but warnings are printed when your code thinks you're doing something dodgy. You should look at the warnings closely to find out what they actually mean. For example, if you have warnings enabled, the following code generates a warning about an uninitialized value in addition:

```
use warnings;
my $x;
my $y = $x + 2;
```

For versions of Perl prior to 5.6.0 (and sometimes after, for backward compatibility), you often see the `-w` switch (see `perldoc perlrun`) on the shebang line instead:

```
#!/usr/bin/perl -w
use strict;
```

This is because the `warnings` pragma was introduced in version 5.6.0. If you have the misfortune to work with an older version of Perl, be aware that 5.6.0 came out in 2000. In terms of technology, it's ancient, and is no longer supported.

THE DIFFERENCE BETWEEN -W AND WARNINGS

One important difference between the –w switch and warnings is that –w has a global effect (yes, it will even effect code in other files you've loaded), and warnings affects only the scope in which it is declared. Consider this example:

```
#!/usr/bin/perl
use strict;
my $x;
{
    use warnings;
    my $y;
    print $y;
}
print $x;
```

In this code, you get a warning about the use of an uninitialized value for $y but not for $x because in this example the warnings pragma affects only the block in which it is used. To fix this, declare warnings at the top of the file, like so:

```
#!/usr/bin/perl
use strict;
use warnings;

my $x;
{
    my $y;
    print $y;
}
print $x;
```

diagnostics

If you're relatively new to Perl, you should also use the diagnostics pragma, as shown in Listing 3-4 (code file `Listing 3-4 diagnostics.pl`). This gives long-winded explanations of why you've been so naughty. The masochists will love it.

LISTING 3-4: Using diagnostics

```
use strict;
use warnings;
use diagnostics;

my $x;
my $y = $x + 2;
```

The program shown in Listing 3-4 prints out a much longer diagnostic method to help you understand not only what went wrong, but also why. Reading through these diagnostic messages is a great way to understand what Perl is doing. The following is an example:

```
Use of uninitialized value $x in addition (+) at diag.pl line 5 (#1)

(W uninitialized) An undefined value was used as if it were already
defined.  It was interpreted as a "" or a 0, but maybe it was a mistake.
To suppress this warning assign a defined value to your variables.

To help you figure out what was undefined, perl will try to tell you the
name of the variable (if any) that was undefined. In some cases it cannot
do this, so it also tells you what operation you used the undefined value
in.  Note, however, that perl optimizes your program and the operation
displayed in the warning may not necessarily appear literally in your
program.  For example, "that $foo" is usually optimized into "that "
. $foo, and the warning will refer to the concatenation (.) operator,
even though there is no . in your program.
```

As you can see, the diagnostic information is fairly good. If you (unlike the vast majority of programmers out there) actually read your errors and warnings carefully, you'll have no problem understanding what happened.

> **WARNING** *Unfortunately, for versions of Perl prior to 5.10.0, you won't see the name of the variable in this warning. This meant that warnings from long strings with many interpolated variables were a nightmare. Now they're just an annoyance.*

Working Without a Net

You might think that strict and warnings aren't that important, but consider the following example:

```
$disarm_nuclear_weapon = true;
```

Without strict, a *bareword* (a string literal without quotes) is just a string. That snippet might assign the string true to $disarm_nuclear_weapon. However, some terrorist programmer who has read Chapter 7 on subroutines might add this above that line:

```
sub true { 0 }
```

And now you've assigned a false value (see Chapter 5) to $disarm_nuclear_weapon and started World War III. Thanks a lot, buddy! Just use strict and warnings, and keep the world safe from terrorism!

Now let's get some hands-on experience with uninitialized variables.

TRY IT OUT   Understanding Uninitialized Variables

This example is simple, but sometimes seeing the warnings in action enables you to be more comfortable with them when you encounter real-world code. All the code in this Try It Out can be found in code file example_3_2_diagnositcs.pl.

1. In your favorite text editor, enter the following code, and save as example_3_2_diagnostics.pl:

```
use strict;
use warnings;
use diagnostics;
my $x;
print 3 / $x;
```

2. Now type perl example_3_2_diagnostics.pl from the command line. You should see something similar to the following.

```
Use of uninitialized value $x in division (/) at diag.pl line 5 (#1)
  (W uninitialized) An undefined value was used as if it were already
defined.  It was interpreted as a "" or a 0, but maybe it was a mistake.
To suppress this warning assign a defined value to your variables.

To help you figure out what was undefined, perl will try to tell you the
name of the variable (if any) that was undefined. In some cases it cannot
do this, so it also tells you what operation you used the undefined value
in.  Note, however, that perl optimizes your program and the operation
displayed in the warning may not necessarily appear literally in your
program.  For example, "that $foo" is usually optimized into "that "
. $foo, and the warning will refer to the concatenation (.) operator,
even though there is no . in your program.

Illegal division by zero at diag.pl line 5 (#2)
  (F) You tried to divide a number by 0.  Either something was wrong in
your logic, or you need to put a conditional in to guard against
meaningless input.

Uncaught exception from user code:
Illegal division by zero at diag.pl line 5.
```

How It Works

If you removed the three pragmas of strict, warnings, and diagnostics (actually, removing strict would not alter this), you'd just see the following output:

```
Illegal division by zero at diag.pl line 5.
```

An experienced programmer can immediately understand the problem and fix it. However, with warnings, you'd also get an additional error message:

```
Use of uninitialized value $x in division (/) at diag.pl line 5
```

This tells you not that $x is 0, but that you forgot to initialize it. When Perl does math, uninitialized values are treated as a zero, and you get a warning if you have warnings enabled.

However, as mentioned previously, the `diagnostics` pragma gives you much more information about what the problem is, and often gives you recommendations on how to resolve the problem, such as the following:

```
(F) You tried to divide a number by 0.  Either something was wrong in
your logic, or you need to put a conditional in to guard against
meaningless input.
```

The `(F)` means it's a trappable, fatal error. *Trappable* means that you can catch the error, handle it, and try to continue running the program. You learn more about error handling in Chapter 7.

The rest of the diagnostic information informs you that you have a logic error, or perhaps that value is expected, and you need to check for that value before trying to divide with it. You learn how to do that in Chapter 5.

Over time, you'll get used to the various error messages that Perl outputs, and you can stop using `diagnostics`. You should try deleting the `use diagnostics` line in the code and running it again to see the difference.

PERL'S BUILT-IN VARIABLES

Perl has many special built-in variables that are global in scope. Though the number of these variables can seem bewildering at first, the common built-in variables are easy to memorize and can be used to make your life simpler, including handling some common tasks that other languages might require a library or extra code to handle. We will generally introduce these special variable as the need arises, but a few deserve special mention upfront.

$_

One of the most common special variables is the `$_` variable, sometimes referred to as *dollar underscore*. This is the "default" variable and many functions automatically operate on this.

> **NOTE** For more information about `$_`, see `perldoc perlvar`.

For example, when iterating over an array, you can do this:

```
for my $element (@array) {
    print $element;
}
```

Or you can do this:

```
for (@array) {
    print "$_\n";
}
```

That's because, when you use a for loop and you don't create a variable to assign the elements to, the $_ variable is automatically populated with the value. the print function, by default, prints the $_ variable if it doesn't have any arguments, as shown here:

```
for (@array) {
    print;
}
```

That prints all the elements on a single line, and you probably don't want that. Instead, if you use Perl 5.10 or newer, you can use the feature pragma to import the say function. say is just like print, but it automatically adds a newline to whatever you print. Like print, it automatically uses the value of $_ as an argument if no arguments are provided.

```
use feature 'say';
for (@array) {
    say;
}
```

%ENV

The global %ENV hash contains environment variables. These are variables generally set *outside* your program, but your program can read them to modify its behavior. For example, the $ENV{HOME} environment variable, on most operating systems, contains the home directory of the current user who is running the program.

Setting an environment variable in your program will not cause your operating system to see the new value, but all other parts of your program will see it. Because this is a global variable, use with care.

@ARGV

Another useful built-in variable is @ARGV. This built-in array contains the arguments passed in on the command line. Listing 3-5 (code file Listing 3-5 hello.pl) shows a way you can rewrite "Hello, World!" but take the arguments from the command line:

LISTING 3-5: Rewriting "Hello, World!" with @ARGV

```
use strict; # yes, I use these even for short programs
use warnings;

print "Hello, @ARGV";
```

Save that as `hello.pl` and type this on the command line:

```
perl hello.pl John Q. Public
```

That should print out `Hello, John Q. Public`.

> **NOTE** *If you pass no argumentsto the* `hello.pl` *program, you won't get an uninitialized warning because empty arrays are simply empty. There are no uninitialized values present.*

There are plenty of other special variables in Perl, and you learn about some of them as this book progresses. For now, you can read through `perldoc perlvar` and weep or laugh. Fortunately, you won't encounter most of them.

Other Special Variables

As mentioned, Perl has many special variables built in to the language. Table 3-3 lists a few of them. Don't worry about their meaning for now; just be aware they exist. New ones will show up from time to time throughout the book.

TABLE 3-3: Common Special Variables

VARIABLE	DESCRIPTION
@_	Parameters passed to a subroutine
$0	The name of your program
$a, $b	Special global variables used in `sort` subroutines
%ENV	Hash containing your environment variables
@INC	Contains paths to look for files loaded with `do`, `require`, or `use`
%INC	Contains entries for every file loaded with `do`, `require`, or `use`
$^V	The current Perl version (Perl 5.6.0 or later)
$^X	The executable used to execute your program
$1, $2, ...	Subpatterns extracted from regular expressions (Chapter 8)
$!	Value of system error calls
$@	Perl syntax error trapped by `eval`

> **NOTE** *You should read* `perldoc perlvar` *for more information.*

SUMMARY

This chapter covered Perl's three primary data types: scalars, arrays and hashes. You learned that Perl tends to focus on how you organize your data rather than the kind of data you have. You've learned the basics of declaring new variables and assigning data to them. You've learned how to iterate over arrays and hashes. You've also been introduced to context, one of the key ideas of how data is handled in Perl. You've also been introduced to the idea of scope, a concept used to limit what parts of your program can see which variables.

EXERCISES

1. What are some differences between `strict` and `warnings`?

2. Create an array with the values "Andrew," "Andy," and "Kaufman" (without the quotes). Write a program that prints `Andrew "Andy" Kaufman`.

3. Create a hash with the keys being names of fruits and the values being their normal color. Print every key/value pair as a separate line similar to `bananas are yellow`.

▶ **WHAT YOU LEARNED IN THIS CHAPTER**

TOPIC	KEY CONCEPTS
Scalars	A container for a single value.
Arrays	A container for a list of values.
Hashes	An unordered container for key/value pairs.
Slices	Extracting a subset of data from arrays and hashes.
Scope	Where you can "see" variables.
Lexical variables	Variables restricted to a given scope.
Package variables	Variables associated with a given package.
Built-in variables	Special variables built into the language.
Context	How a given expression is evaluated.
`strict`	A pragma to require variable declaration. Also used to prevent certain unsafe behaviors with references and subroutines.
`warnings`	A pragma to warn about unsafe behaviors.
`diagnostics`	A pragma to provide verbose explanations of errors and warnings.

Working with Data

WHAT YOU WILL LEARN IN THIS CHAPTER:

➤ Working with scalars

➤ Working with arrays

➤ Working with hashes

WROX.COM CODE DOWNLOADS FOR THIS CHAPTER

The wrox.com code downloads for this chapter are found at `http://www.wrox.com/remtitle .cgi?isbn=1118013840` on the Download Code tab. The code for this chapter is divided into the following major examples:

➤ `example_4_1_names.pl`

This chapter shows you much of the basic data manipulation available in Perl to help you Get Stuff Done. Quite frankly, this chapter is boring. It serves more as a reference chapter that you can conveniently flip back to when you want to understand how to manipulate data in a particular way. If you like, you can think of it as an appendix slipped into the front of the book. The builtins described here are not an exhaustive list. They're the ones you're most likely to encounter in your daily work.

For many languages there is a strong distinction between operators and functions. This distinction is less clear in Perl. Some things that look like functions are sometimes referred to as *named unary operators* (see `perldoc perlop`). To sidestep the inherent ambiguity, many Perl developers refer to operators and functions as *built-ins* (sometimes spelled *builtins*, as is done here). This book often uses these terms interchangeably. A builtin, in this context, means an operator or function built in to the Perl language.

> **NOTE** *Subroutines and functions are considered distinct in some languages. If you refer to a function as a subroutine, invariably some AD&D rules lawyer turned programmer will come along and imperiously state, "No, no. That's a subroutine," even if it has no bearing on the discussion at hand. Because Perl is designed to be a working language, you don't get bogged down in terminology. That's why sometimes you might see* `my` *described as a function (as it is in* `perldoc perlfunc`*), even though it's clearly not behaving like normal functions. The* `print()` *function is sometimes described as a named unary operator when it's used with parentheses. Don't be a rules lawyer and get bogged down in terminology.*

Because Perl's type system focuses more on how you organize your data than what kind of data that you have, many string, numeric, bitwise, and boolean operators work on just about any kind of data you have. Most of the time this "just works," but you still have a responsibility as a programmer to understand what type of data you have.

> **NOTE** *The parentheses are optional on most builtins. Your author tends to omit parentheses because he views them as visual clutter, but other developers prefer to be explicit. Just choose the style you prefer, and stick with it for consistency. This chapter skips back and forth to get you used to each. However, when a function name is mentioned in the body of the text, the parentheses are usually included to avoid confusion.*
>
> *Also, many of these functions and operators are prefix, infix, or postfix.*
>
> ➤ **prefix:** *Placed before their operand (*`! $var`*)*
>
> ➤ **infix:** *Placed between two operands (*`$var + $var`*)*
>
> ➤ **postfix:** *Placed after their operand (*`$var++`*)*
>
> *Sometimes an operator's meaning may change slightly if you use it as a prefix operator instead of as an infix operator. I'll describe these conditions as they arise. They're actually natural to use this way.*

USING SCALARS

In Chapter 2, you learned that a *scalar* is a variable that contains a single value. Perl actually doesn't care what kind of data you have in that value, so stuff anything in there that you need:

```
my $answer     = 'forty two';
my $num_answer = 42;
```

Clearly `'forty two'` is a string and `42` is an integer, but Perl expects you (mostly) to handle them with care and not mix them up. If you try to use `42` as a string, Perl treats it as a string composed of the characters '4' and '2'. If you try to treat 'forty two' as a number, Perl treats it as the number 0, and if you have warnings enabled, Perl usually complains loudly when you try to use it as a number.

This section starts with many of the string builtins first, listed mostly in alphabetical order with "operators" coming after. Many of these functions automatically operate on the $_ variable if no variable is specified. In Chapter 5, when you learn about control flow, you see many operations that set the $_ variable if no variable is declared. This may sound strange, but it becomes clearer when you see examples. You also see $_ being set in the map() and grep() functions, which are introduced in this chapter.

Builtins are introduced with a snippet of "grammar" that shows more or less how to use it. The grammar deliberately does not always match what you see in perlfunc. This is to avoid less common use cases (as with the my() builtin) or to just make builtins a bit easier to read and see common usage.

> **NOTE** *Remember, you can read more about all the builtins that are "words"* (print(), chomp(), *and so on) by using* perldoc -f *builtin:*
>
> ```
> perldoc -f chomp
> perldoc -f ucfirst
> ```
>
> *For the operator-like builtins such as* +, ==, << *and so on, you just have to read the gory details in* perldoc perlop.

Working with Strings

In Perl, just about anything can be coerced into a string merely by treating it as a string. The following sections are a list of various functions and their usage in alphabetical order.

chop() and chomp()

```
chop (defauls to $_)
chop VARIABLE
chop( LIST )
chomp (defaults to $_)
chomp VARIABLE
chomp( LIST )
```

The chop() builtin removes the last character from a string and returns it.

```
my $name = 'Ovid';
my $last = chop $name;
```

$last is now set to 'd' and $name is 'Ovi'. The chop() function was primarily used to remove the newline from strings, but for that you now use the chomp() function.

`chomp()` removes newlines from the end of strings. It's particularly useful when you read lines from a file and want to remove the newline from each record.

> **NOTE** Actually, `chomp()` removes whatever is stored in the $/ variable, also known as the input record separator. Most of the time, $/ is equal to a newline, but sometimes people set it to a different value when they want to change how to read records from a file. You learn more about this in Chapter 9. Read `perldoc perlvar` and look for $INPUT_RECORD_SEPARATOR if you can't wait.

You can also use both `chop()` and `chomp()` with lists, arrays and hashes, but this usage is less commonly seen in production code. For lists (and arrays), both `chop()` and `chomp()` work their magic on each individual element, but for hashes they affect only the values of the hash and not its keys.

Both `chop()` and `chomp()` modify the variable directly. However, `chop()` returns whatever character was removed from the string, and `chomp()` returns the number of characters removed, if any. As a general rule, it's recommended that you not use `chop()`.

chr() and ord()

```
chr (defaults to $_)
chr NUMBER
ord (defaults to $_)
ord  STRING
```

`chr()` accepts a number and returns the character associated with that number. For example, the following code assigns the string "Ovid" to the variable $name. The dot operator (.) is used in Perl for string concatenation.

```
my $name = chr(79).chr(118).chr(105).chr(100);
```

If the number is greater than 255, `chr()` returns the corresponding Unicode character.

The `ord()` function does the reverse: It returns the numeric value of the first character in the string passed to it.

```
my @values = ( ord('O'), ord('v'), ord('i'), ord('d') );
```

`@values` now contains (79, 118, 105, 100).

Although the characters represented by the values 128 through 255 are not ASCII, Perl's `chr()` function does not return Unicode values for them to maintain backward compatibility.

index() and rindex()

```
index STR,SUBSTR,POSITION
index STR,SUBSTR
rindex STR,SUBSTR,POSITION
rindex STR,SUBSTR
```

Given a string, index() lets you find the first occurrence of a substring within it, with indexing starting at 0. If the substring is not found, it returns -1. You can also supply a starting position from which to search. The rindex() function is identical the index() function, but it finds the last occurrence of the string.

So when the word "miminypiminy" springs to your lips as the perfect description of something (it means "delicate, mincing, or dainty," but you knew that), you naturally wonder where the substring iminy may be found within said word.

```
#                    012345678901
my $word     = 'miminypiminy';
my $first    = index  $word, 'iminy';
my $second   = index  $word, 'iminy', $first + 1;
my $last     = rindex $word, 'iminy';
my $not_last = rindex $word, 'iminy', $last - 1;

print "First:    $first\n";
print "Second:   $second\n";
print "Last:     $last\n";
print "Not last: $not_last\n";
```

And that prints out:

```
First:    1
Second:   7
Last:     7
Not last: 1
```

Now you can tell your friends you're an expert in miminypiminy, but don't be surprised when they laugh.

lc(), lcfirst(), uc(), and ucfirst()

```
lc (defaults to $_)
lc      EXPR
lcfirst (defaults to $_)
lcfirst EXPR
uc (defaults to $_)
uc      EXPR
ucfirst (defaults to $_)
ucfirst EXPR
```

These handy little functions are part of the useful suite of tools that Perl provides for manipulating data. The lc() function forces an entire string to lowercase. The uc() function forces the string to uppercase. The lcfirst() and ucfirst() functions do the same thing, but only on the first character. Naturally you can combine all of these functions.

Following is one way to print Perl, for example:

```
print ucfirst lc 'PERL';
```

All these functions respect locale settings. You'll see more in Chapter 9 when we discuss Unicode.

length()

```
length (defaults to $_)
length EXPR
```

The `length()` function returns the number of characters in a string. Due to Unicode, this is not necessarily the same as the number of bytes. So the following code prints 6, as you would expect:

```
print length('danger');
```

But the following code prints 9 when it tries to figure out the length of Japan when it's written in Japanese:

```
print length('日本国');
```

That's because each of those characters is composed of 3 octets (*bytes*, but see the Unicode section in Chapter 9), and Perl doesn't know that you have Unicode in your source code. To handle it correctly, use the `utf8` pragma. The following correctly prints 3:

```
use utf8;
print length('日本国');
```

Many people mistakenly use the `length()` function to try to determine the length of an array or hash. Use `scalar(@array)` or `scalar(keys(%hash))` for this, not the `length()` function. That's not what it's for.

pack() and unpack()

```
pack   TEMPLATE, LIST
unpack TEMPLATE, VARIABLE
unpack TEMPLATE
```

The `pack()` and `unpack()` builtins are two functions that nobody remembers or understands, even though conceptually they're simple.

The `pack()` function accepts a template and a list of values, "packing" that list of values into a single value according to the template. The `unpack()` function does the reverse by taking the same template and "unpacks" a scalar value into a list of values. Unlike `pack()`, `unpack()` defaults to the `$_` variable.

Read `perldoc -f pack` and `perldoc -f unpack` to understand the templates. They're not covered much in this book because they're not terribly common in production code, but the following code gives a quick example of reading fixed-length data quickly. The code uses dots in the comment to show you where each field in the record ends.

```
#                  .        .     .  .
my $record = '20080417john     39552027';
my ( $hired, $user, $emp_number, $dept ) = unpack 'A8A8A5A3', $record;
print "Hired: $hired\nUser:  $user\nEmp#:  $emp_number\nDept:  $dept\n";
```

The preceding code prints out:

```
Hired: 20080417
User:  john
Emp#:  39552
Dept:  027
```

And that's probably the last you'll see of these two functions in this book. Just be aware they exist.

> **NOTE** *If you want to know more about* `pack()` *and* `unpack()`, *see* `perldoc`
> `perlpacktut`.

print()

```
print (defaults to $_)
print FILEHANDLE LIST
print LIST
```

This book uses `print()` quite a bit and you've seen examples in Chapter 3, but it's worth covering a few things here. First, `print()` takes a list. With `print()`, you can think of a scalar variable as a list with one element, which is why `print($name)` works.

```
my $customer = 'Alex';
print "Customer: $customer\n";
```

This raises the obvious question of where you're printing to and that's where filehandles come in.

The optional FILEHANDLE argument is something covered more in Chapter 9, which discusses files. For now be aware that a filehandle is usually (not always) one of three things:

➤   A "handle" to an actual file.

➤   STDOUT: The default place where a program writes normal output.

➤   STDERR: The default place where a program writes error output.

If you don't specify a filehandle, `print()` defaults to printing to STDOUT. The following two `print()` statements are identical:

```
print $name;
print STDOUT $name;
```

WARNING *No comma appears after the filehandle argument. If it did, Perl would assume that the filehandle is one of the list arguments you're trying to print:*

```
print STDOUT, $name; # probably not what you wanted
```

This code prints something like

```
No comma allowed after filehandle at myprogram.pl line 1.
```

However, a filehandle can be stored in a scalar, and then Perl can't determine what you mean:

```
use strict;
use warnings;
my $name = 'foo';
open my $fh, '>', 'somefile.txt'
   or die "Can't open somefile.txt for reading: $!";
print $fh, $name;
```

In the previous example, Perl tries to print the filehandle and $name *to* STDOUT *instead of what you probably want:*

```
GLOB(0x100802eb8)foo
```

Again, Chapter 9 covers filehandles in more detail.

STDOUT, short for *standard output*, generally goes to your terminal, but you have ways to redirect it to files, sockets, or other places. Not all of this is covered in this book as it's a bit advanced. Just remember that generally STDOUT is the "normal" printed stuff you see.

STDERR, short for *standard error*, also tends to show up on your terminal, but you can also redirect it to other locations. Error handling functions like die() and warn() direct their output to STDERR. You learn more about error handling in Chapter 7 when you deal with subroutines. For now, just be aware that when you run a Perl program from the terminal, you usually see both STDOUT and STDERR output written there.

sprintf() and printf()

```
sprintf FORMAT, LIST
printf  FILEHANDLE FORMAT, LIST
printf  FORMAT, LIST
```

The sprintf() and printf() functions format data according to the printf() function of the underlying C libraries. They are extremely useful for reporting. The sprintf() function formats and *returns* the string whereas printf() formats and *prints* the string and the common formatting codes are explained in Table 4-1. Any "extra" values in the list are ignored:

```
my @musketeers = qw( Aramis Athos Portos );
printf "%s,%s\n", @musketeers; # prints "Aramis,Athos"
my $two_musketeers = sprintf "%s,%s", @musketeers;
# $two_musketeers is now "Aramis,Athos"
```

TABLE 4-1: Common printf() Formats

FORMAT	MEANING
%%	Percent sign
%c	Character
%s	String
%d	Signed integer, in decimal
%u	Unsigned integer, in decimal
%o	Unsigned integer, in octal
%x	Unsigned integer, in hexadecimal
%e	Floating-point number, in scientific notation
%f	Floating-point number, in fixed decimal notation
%g	Floating-point number, in %e or %f notation

In addition to the common formats, Perl also supports several commonly accepted formats that are not part of the standard list of printf() formats. (See Table 4-2).

TABLE 4-2: Perl-Specific printf() Formats

FORMAT	MEANING
%X	Like %x, but using uppercase letters
%E	Like %e, but using an uppercase "E"
%G	Like %g, but with an uppercase "E" (if applicable)
%b	An unsigned integer, in binary
%p	A pointer (outputs the Perl value's address in hexadecimal)
%n	Special: stores the number of characters output so far into the next variable in the parameter list

When using `sprintf()` formats, you have a percent sign and a format letter. However, you can control the output by inserting attributes, also known as *flags*, between them. For example, inserting an integer controls the default minimum width:

```
my $formatted = sprintf "%20s", 'some name';
print "<$formatted>\n";
```

This code prints <   some name> because the `%20s` format forces a string to be 20 characters long. That's equivalent to:

```
printf "<%20s>\n", 'some name';
```

To left-justify the string, insert a - (hyphen) after the leading `%` symbol:

```
my $formatted = sprintf "%-20s", 'some name';
print "<$formatted>\n";
# <some name            >
```

Conversely, if you want to enforce a maximum width, use a dot followed by a number:

```
printf "%.7s", 'some name';
```

That prints `some na`. You can also combine them, if you want:

```
printf "%5.10s", $some_string;
```

The previous code ensures that you print a minimum of 5 characters (padding with spaces, if needed), and a maximum of 10. To force every string to be the same length — useful for reporting — set the minimum and maximum to the same value:

```
printf "%10.10s", $some_string;
```

You can also use the `printf()` formats to control numeric output, but that's covered a bit later in the chapter when you learn about numeric builtins.

Table 4-3 lists some of the common flags used with `printf()` formats.

TABLE 4-3: Common printf() Flags

FLAG	MEANING
Space	Prefix non-negative number with a space.
+	Prefix non-negative number with a plus sign.
–	Left-justify within the field.
0	Use zeros, not spaces, to right-justify.
#	Include a leading zero for octal, prefix nonzero hexadecimal with 0x or 0X, and prefix nonzero binary with 0b or 0B.

> **NOTE** See `perldoc -f sprintf` for a full description of the format options.

substr()

```
substr EXPR,OFFSET,LENGTH,REPLACEMENT
substr EXPR,OFFSET,LENGTH
substr EXPR,OFFSET
```

The `substr()` function takes an expression (usually a string) and an offset and returns the substring of the string, starting at the offset. Like the `index()` and `rindex()` functions, the offset starts at 0, not 1. The following code prints `hearted`:

```
my $string = 'halfhearted';
my $substr = substr $string, 4;
print $substr;
```

You can also specify an optional length argument after the offset. This limits the returned substring no more than the specified length. The following code prints `heart`:

```
my $string = 'halfhearted';
my $substr = substr $string, 4, 5;
print $substr;
```

An underappreciated use of `substr()` is its lvalue property. In Perl, an *lvalue* is something to which you can assign. The "l" stands for "left" and is found on the left side of an expression. For `substr()`, you can supply a replacement string for the string you return:

```
my $string = 'halfhearted';
my $substr = substr $string, 0, 4, 'hard';
print "$substr\n$string\n";
```

The previous code prints:

```
half
hardhearted
```

The `substr()` function is useful, but it's often overlooked in favor of regular expressions, something covered in Chapter 8.

tr/// and y///

```
VARIABLE =~ tr/SEARCHLIST/REPLACEMENTLIST/cds
VARIABLE =~ y/SEARCHLIST/REPLACEMENTLIST/cds
```

The `tr///` and `y///` operators are identical. The `y///` variant is exactly equivalent to `tr///` but is provided for those who use Perl as a replacement for `sed`, a stream editor utility provided in UNIX-like environments.

The `tr///` builtin takes a list of characters on the left side and replaces it with the corresponding list of characters on the right side. It returns the number of characters replaced. The string being altered must be followed by the binding operator (`=~`). The binding operator is generally seen when using regular expressions. (Refer to Chapter 8.)

This might sound strange, so some examples are in order.

To replace all commas in a string with tabs, use the following code:

```
my $string = "Aramis,Athos,Portos";
$string =~ tr/,/\t/;
print $string;
```

If, for some reason, you want to make all vowels lowercase use:

```
$string =~ tr/AEIOU/aeiou/;
```

You can also specify a range by adding a hyphen. To make all letters lowercase (though obviously the `lc()` function would be clearer here) use:

```
$string =~ tr/A-Z/a-z/;
```

The `tr///` builtin also accepts several switches, `c`, `d`, and `s`, but you probably won't see them much in day-to-day usage unless you do a heavy amount of text munging (the act of making several incremental changes to an item that combine to destroy it). Read `perldoc perlop` and see the `Quote` and `Quote-like Operators` section.

Using String Operators

As mentioned, the difference between Perl's functions and operators is a bit vague at times, but for convenience, the punctuation bits are referred to as operators.

Repetition Operator: x

```
STRING    x INTEGER
(STRING)  x INTEGER
```

The x operator is for repetition. It's often used to repeat a string several times:

```
my $santa_says = 'ho' x 3.7;
print $santa_says;
```

The previous code assigns `hohoho` to `$santa_says`.

Sometimes you'll want to assign a single value multiple times to a list. Just put the string in parentheses to force list context:

```
my $ho = 'ho';
my @santa_says = ($ho) x 3;
```

`@santa_says` now contains the three strings `ho`, `ho`, and `ho`.

> **NOTE** *In many places where Perl expects an integer, a floating-point number is fine. Perl acts as if you've called the* int() *function on the number. This includes using floating-point numbers with the* x *operator, or even accessing array elements.*

Concatenation Operator: .

```
STRING . STRING
```

Unlike many other languages, the dot operator (.) is used for string concatenation instead of the + operator. Not only is this visually distinctive, but also it tells Perl to treat the data as strings instead of numbers.

```
my $first   = 1;
my $second  = 2;
my $string  = $first . $second;
my $answer  = $first + $second;
print "$string - $answer";
```

The previous code prints 12 - 3. This is because the concatenation operator considers the 1 and 2 to be strings and concatenates (joins) them. The addition operator, +, expects numbers and adds the 1 and 2 together, giving the answer of 3.

You can also "chain" together multiple concatenation operators. The following code shows one way to join two strings with a space:

```
my $full_name = $first_name . ' ' . $last_name;
```

Autoincrement and Autodecrement Operators: ++ and --

```
++VARIABLE
--VARIABLE
VARIABLE++
VARIABLE--
```

The ++ and -- operators are for autoincrement and autodecrement. They return the value of the variable and increase or decrease the variables value by one. They seem rather strange for strings, but they return the next or previous letter. If they're used as a prefix operator (++$var), they change the value *before* returning it. If they're used as a postfix operator ($var++), they change the value *after* returning it. So if you want to find the next character after 'f', you can do this with the following code:

```
my $letter = 'f';
$letter++;
print $letter;
```

When you get past the 'z', the letters double. If $letter is 'z' and then you call $letter++, the $letter is now 'aa'. You won't see this often in code, but your author has seen it used to create the prefix letters in code that automatically generated outlines.

In the faint hope of making this clearer, the following code shows exactly what `perldoc perlop` has to say on this subject:

> If, however, the variable has been used in only string contexts
> since it was set, and has a value that is not the empty string
> and matches the pattern "/^[a-zA-Z]*[0-9]*\z/", the increment is
> done as a string, preserving each character within its range,
> with carry:

```
        print ++($foo = '99');        # prints '100'
        print ++($foo = 'a0');        # prints 'a1'
        print ++($foo = 'Az');        # prints 'Ba'
        print ++($foo = 'zz');        # prints 'aaa'
```

The "pattern" mentioned in the previous code is a *regular expression*, covered in Chapter 8. For now, understand that `/^[a-zA-Z]*[0-9]*\z/` means that the string must match zero or more letters, followed by zero or more numbers.

> **NOTE** For the pedants in the audience, yes, the regular expression described for autoincrement/autodecrement matching can match a string consisting of zero letters and zero numbers, but the correct way to write it would have been a bit more cumbersome and probably obscured this even more:
>
> ```
> /^(?:[a-zA-Z]*[0-9]+|[a-zA-Z]+[0-9]*)\z/
> ```

The main reason I mention autoincrement and autodecrement operators for strings is to introduce the range operators. Understanding that some operators are used with both numbers and strings is essential to understanding some of the unusual aspects of Perl.

> **NOTE** Be careful when using the ++ and -- operators. `perldoc perlop` has this to say on the subject:
>
> > Note that just as in C, Perl doesn't define when the variable
> > is incremented or decremented. You just know it will be done
> > sometime before or after the value is returned. This also
> > means that modifying a variable twice in the same statement
> > will lead to undefined behaviour. Avoid statements like:
> > $i = $i ++;
> >   print ++ $i + $i ++;
> > Perl will not guarantee what the result of the above statements is.
>
> To use these operators safely, don't use them more than once with the same variable in the same expression. It's often safer to place them on a line by themselves because they modify the variable in place, and you don't need to use the return value:
>
> ```
> my $i = 7;
> $i++;
> # more code here
> ```

The "Whatever" Operator

```
STRING .. STRING
```

The double dots, `..`, are the range operator. Although the range operator is usually used for numbers, it can also be used for letters. Here's how to assign the lowercase letters 'a' through 'z' to an array:

```
my @alphabet = ( 'a' .. 'z' );
```

Of course, you can do this with uppercase letters, too:

```
my @alphabet = ( 'A' .. 'Z' );
```

If the left string is greater than the right string, nothing is returned.

Internally, when used with strings, the range operator uses the special autoincrement behavior discussed with ++ and --.

> **NOTE** *The range operators actually have a tremendous amount of power and are useful in many more ways than shown here. Read the "Range Operators" section of* `perldoc perlop` *to learn more about them.*

Scalar::Util

In Perl 5.7.3, the `Scalar::Util` module was included in the Perl core. This module implements a number of useful functions. The two most common are `blessed()` and `looks_like_number()`. The `blessed()` function is useful to determine if a scalar is actually an object (see Chapter 12) and the `looks_like_number()` function returns a boolean (true or false) value indicating whether a string, well, looks like a number. To use these functions, you must explicitly import them as follows:

```
use Scalar::Util 'blessed';
# or
use Scalar::Util 'looks_like_number';
# or both
use Scalar::Util qw(blessed looks_like_number);
my $is_number = looks_like_number('3fred'); # false
my $is_number = looks_like_number('3e7');   # true!
```

Chapter 5 covers boolean values in more detail and discusses conditionals.

> **NOTE** *As usual, type* `perldoc Scalar::Util` *for more information. If you use a version of Perl before 5.7.3, you may need to install this module from the CPAN.*

Numeric Builtins

Naturally, Perl has plenty of numeric functions. It wouldn't be much of a programming language if it didn't! Many of the functions are the basic arithmetic operators you're familiar with.

Arithmetic Operators: +, -, *, /, and **

```
NUMBER + NUMBER
NUMBER - NUMBER
NUMBER * NUMBER
NUMBER / NUMBER
NUMBER ** NUMBER
```

The +, -, *, and / operators are for addition, subtraction, multiplication, and division, respectively. In terms of precedence, multiplication and division are calculated first, left to right, and addition and subtraction are calculated last, left to right. The following code prints 11:

```
my $answer = 8 + 6 / 4 * 2;
print $answer;
```

Although your author generally avoids parentheses to prevent visual clutter, they are strongly recommended when you're doing math to avert confusion. The previous code is equivalent to:

```
my $answer = 8 + ( ( 6 / 4 ) * 2 );
print $answer;
```

If you want the addition first, followed by the multiplication and then division, just use parentheses to group things logically:

```
my $answer = ( 8 + 6 ) / ( 4 * 2 );
print $answer;
```

Now you have 1.75 as the answer instead.

Exponentiation is handled with the ** operator. To calculate the cube of 25, use the following code:

```
print 25 ** 3;
```

That prints 15625.

> **NOTE** The arithmetic operators are infix operators. This means that they are placed in between a left and right operand. They have no meaning as postfix operators, but the + and – operators are special.
>
> You can use the - operator to reverse the sign of a number:
>
> ```
> my $num1 = -17;
> print -$num1;
> my $num2 = 42;
> print -$num2;
> ```

> *Those two* `print()` *statements print* 17 *and* −42, *respectively.*
>
> *A prefix plus (referred to as a* unary plus*) has no distinct meaning, but it is sometimes placed after a function name and before parentheses to indicate grouping. For example, the following code doesn't do what you want; it prints* 3 *and throws away the* 4*:*
>
> ```
> print (1 + 2) * 4;
> ```
>
> *Perl will interpret that as:*
>
> ```
> print(3) * 4;
> ```
>
> *Instead, use a unary plus to make it clear to Perl that the parentheses are for grouping and not for the function call.*
>
> ```
> print +( 1 + 2 ) * 4;
> ```

The Modulus Operator: %

```
INTEGER % INTEGER
```

The % is the modulus operator. It returns the remainder of the division between the left and right operands. Like many operators and functions that take integers, if floating-point numbers are used, their integer value (see the `int()` function later in this chapter) is used. Thus, because 25 divided by 9 is 2 with a remainder of 7, this means that 25 modulus 9 is 7.

```
print 25 % 9; # prints 7
```

abs()

```
abs (defaults to $_)
abs NUMBER
```

The `abs()` function returns the absolute value for a number. Thus, if the number is greater or equal to zero, you get the number back. If it's less than zero, you get the number multiplied by −1.

exp()

```
exp (defaults to $_)
exp NUMBER
```

The `exp()` function returns e (approximately 2.718281828) to the power of the number passed to it. See also: `log()` (later in this chapter).

hex() and oct()

```
hex (defaults to $_)
hex STRING
oct (defaults to $_)
oct STRING
```

Given a string, `hex()` attempts to interpret the string as a hexadecimal value and to print the base 10 value. For example, the following two lines are equivalent and each prints the decimal number 2363.

```
print hex("0x93B");
print hex "93B"; # same thing
```

This works on strings, not numbers. The following code prints 9059:

```
print hex 0x93B;
```

Why does it print that? Because 0x93B is a hexadecimal number, and it's evaluated as 2363. The `hex()` function then sees it as the string 2363, which, if interpreted as a hexadecimal number, is 9059.

The `oct()` function is almost identical, but it expects strings that it considers to be octal numbers instead of hexadecimal numbers. This means that each of the following lines print the decimal number 63:

```
print oct("77");
print oct("077");
```

> **NOTE** *If you need to go from decimal to either hexadecimal or octal, use the* %h *or* %o *format for* `sprintf()` *and* `printf()`, *respectively:*
>
> ```
> printf "%x", 2363;
> printf "%o", 63;
> ```
>
> *To format the hexadecimal number with a leading* 0x, *just add it to the string before the* % *character:*
>
> ```
> printf "0x%x", 2363;
> # 0x93b
> ```
>
> *To format the octal number with a leading* 0, *use the* # *flag after the* % *character:*
>
> ```
> printf "%#o", 63;
> # 077
> ```

int()

```
int (defaults to $_)
int NUMBER
```

The `int()` function returns the integer value of the number. In other words, it truncates everything after a decimal point.

```
print int(73.2); # prints 73
```

For some programming languages, if all numbers in a mathematical operation are integers, an integer result is returned. For example, in Ruby, the following code prints 3 instead of 3.5:

```
print 7/2;
```

Perl assumes that you don't want do discard this extra information, so it prints 3.5, as expected. To force an integer response, you can use the `int()` function:

```
print int(7/2); # prints 3
```

> **NOTE** To force integer math, you can also use the `integer` pragma. See
> `perldoc integer` for more information.

log()

```
log (defaults to $_)
log NUMBER
```

The `log()` function, as with most programming languages, returns the natural logarithm of NUMBER (the number raised to the power of e). See also `exp()` (later in this chapter).

rand() and srand()

```
rand NUMBER
srand NUMBER
```

The `rand()` function returns a random fractional number between 0 and the number passed to it. If no number is passed, it assumes 1. If you prefer integer numbers, use the `int()` function with it. Thus, to simulate the roll of a six-sided die, you could do this:

```
print 1 + int(rand(6));
```

Adding 1 to it is necessary because if you don't, you get numbers between 0 and 5.

The `srand()` function is used to set the seed for the random number generator. As of Perl version 5.004 (released in 1997), Perl calls `srand()` for you the first time that `rand()` is called. You want to set only the seed if you want to generate predictable "random" results for testing or debugging. As of Perl 5.10, `srand()` also returns the seed used.

> **NOTE** *The* `rand()` *function is for convenience, but it's not strong enough for cryptography. The CPAN lists several useful modules, including* `Math::Random::Secure`, `Math::Random::MT::Perl`, *and* `Math::TrulyRandom` *that are intended for this purpose. Your author has no background in cryptography, so he can't comment on their effectiveness.*

sprintf() and printf()

```
sprintf FORMAT, LIST
printf  FILEHANDLE FORMAT, LIST
printf  FORMAT, LIST
```

You've already seen the `sprintf()` function in relation to strings and seen that it can be used to format numbers, but you should know that it can also round numbers when you use it with the `%f` template. You merely specify how many digits (optional) you want before the decimal point and how many digits you want after. Some examples follow:

```
printf "%1.0f", 5.2;    # prints 5
printf "%1.0f", 5.7;    # prints 6
printf "%.2f",  6.248; # prints 6.25
```

Often you see people recommending that you add `.5` to a number and call the `int()` function to round off, but this fails with negative numbers. Just use `printf()` or `sprintf()`.

sqrt()

```
sqrt (defaults to $_)
sqrt NUMBER
```

The preceding code returns the positive square root of the number, which does not work with negative numbers unless the `Math::Complex` module is loaded.

```
use Math::Complex;
print sqrt(-25);
```

That prints `5i`. If you are not familiar with imaginary numbers, you will probably never need (or want) the `Math::Complex` module.

Trigonometric Function: atan2(), cos(), and sin()

```
atan2 (defaults to $_);
atan2 NUMBER
cos (defaults to $_)
cos NUMBER
sin (defaults to $_)
sin NUMBER
```

The atan2(), cos(), and sin() functions return the arcus tangent, cosine, and sine of a number, respectively. If you need other trigonometric functions, see the Math::Trig or POSIX modules.

Bitwise Operators

As you might expect, Perl also provides a variety of bitwise operators. Bitwise operators don't work directly on the values, but they allow you to manipulate individual bits within those values. We don't cover them in this book, but we include them here for completeness.

Table 4-4 explains these operators.

TABLE 4-4: Common printf() Flags

OPERATORS	TYPE	GRAMMAR	DESCRIPTION
&	Infix	NUMBER & NUMBER	Bitwise "and"
|	Infix	NUMBER | NUMBER	Bitwise "or"
^	Infix	NUMBER ^ NUMBER	Bitwise "xor"
~	Prefix	~NUMBER	Bitwise negation
<<	Infix	NUMBER << NUMBER	Left shift operator
>>	Infix	NUMBER >> NUMBER	Right shift operator

If you're familiar with bitwise operators, these behave as you would expect. For example, a quick check to see if a number is even follows:

```
print "Even\n" if 0 == ($number & 1);
```

This is identical to the following modulus check:

```
print "Even\n" if 0 == ($number % 2);
```

> **NOTE** See Bitwise String Operators in perldoc perlop if you need to do bit manipulation. You may also use bitwise operators on strings.

Understanding Booleans

You use boolean operators to determine if a value or expression is true or false. Because Perl lets you assign strings and numbers to variables, the boolean operators are separated into string and numeric versions. You learn the string versions first.

Although their use is covered in Chapter 5, you see the if/else statement now just so you can understand how they work.

The `if` statement takes an expression in parentheses and, if it evaluates as true, executes the code in the block following it. If an `else` block follows the `if` block, the `else` block executes only if the if expression evaluates as false. For example:

```
my ( $num1, $num2 ) = ( 7, 5 );
if ( $num1 < $num2 ) {
    print "$num1 is less than $num2\n";
}
else {
    print "$num1 is not less than $num2\n";
}
```

That code prints `7 is not less than 5`. The < boolean operator is the boolean "less than" operator and returns true if the left operand is less than the right operand.

Now that you have this small example out of the way, the following sections discuss the boolean operators.

eq, ne, lt, le, gt, ge, and cmp

All these are *infix* operators. They are "spelled out" in Perl to make it clear that they are for strings. Table 4-5 explains them.

TABLE 4-5: Boolean String Operators

OPERATOR	MEANING
eq	Equal
ne	Not equal
lt	Less than
le	Less than or equal to
gt	Greater than
ge	Greater than or equal to
cmp	String compare

A string is considered "less than" another string if, depending on your current locale settings, an alphabetical sorting of that string causes it to come before another string. This means that a comes before b, punctuation tends to come before and numbers and numbers come before letters. Also, zzz comes before zzza because the first three letters of each match, but zzz is shorter than zzza. This also means that 100 comes *before* 99 when doing a string compare because 1 comes before 9. It's a frequent trap that inexperienced Perl programmers fall into.

For example, the following prints yes because a comes before bb:

```
if ( 'a' le 'bb' ) {
    print 'yes';
}
else {
    print 'no';
}
```

The special cmp infix operator returns -1 if the left operand is less than the right operand. It returns 0 if the two operands are equal, and it returns 1 if the left operand is greater than the right operand. The following, for example, prints -1:

```
print 'a' cmp 'b'
```

This seems strange, but it comes in handy when you sort lists. Chapter 10 discusses sorting issues in more detail, but for now be aware that you can sort a list alphabetically with the following code:

```
my @sorted = sort { $a cmp $b } @words;
```

Actually, the sort() function defaults to sorting alphabetically, so that's equivalent to this:

```
my @sorted = sort @words;
```

Naturally, all these have numeric equivalents, as detailed in Table 4-6.

TABLE 4-6: Boolean Numeric Operators

OPERATOR	MEANING
==	Equal
!=	Not equal
<	Less than
<=	Less than or equal to
>	Greater than
>=	Greater than or equal to
<=>	Numeric compare

The operators in Table 4-6 all behave as you expect. The numeric compare operator, <=> (sometimes affectionately referred to as the *spaceship operator*), has the same rules as the cmp operator but does numeric sorting rather than alphabetical sorting. So to sort a list of numbers in ascending order:

```
my @sorted = sort { $a <=> $b } @numbers;
```

> **NOTE** *You can sort numbers in reverse order by reversing the* $a *and* $b:
>
> ```
> my @descending = sort { $b <=> $a } @numbers;
> ```

Finally, you have the boolean operators which do not compare strings or numbers but simply return true or false. Table 4-7 explains them:

TABLE 4-7: Boolean Operators

OPERATOR	TYPE	MEANING
!	Prefix	Equal
&&	Infix	And
||	Infix	Or
//	Infix	Defined or
not	Infix	Not
and	Infix	And
or	Infix	Or
xor	Infix	Exclusive or

WHAT IS "TRUTH"?

Sometimes people get confused about true/false values in Perl. It's actually quite simple. The following scalar values are all false in Perl:

➤ undef

➤ "" (the empty string)

➤ 0

➤ 0.0

➤ "0" (the "string" zero)

Any other scalar value is true.

These operators return true or false depending on the true and false values of their operands. The following code gives some examples that should make their meaning clear:

```
if ( ! $value ) {
    print "$value is false";
}
```

```
if ( $value1 && $value2 ) {
    print "both values are true";
}
if ( $value1 || $value2 ) {
    print "One or both of the values are true";
}
if ( $value1 // $value2 ) {
    print "One or both of the values are defined";
}
if ( $value1 xor $value2 ) {
    print "Either $value1 or $value2 is true, but not both";
}
```

The not, and, and or operators are the equivalent of the corresponding !, &&, and || operators, but they have a lower precedence. See the section on "Precedence and Associativity" for more information.

> **NOTE** The // operator is a bit special. Introduced in Perl version 5.10.0, it's the defined or operator. The || operator evaluates the left operand to see if it's true. The // operator evaluates the left operand to see if it's defined (that is, if it has a value assigned to it) and if the left operand has any value, including one that is ordinarily considered to be false; then it is returned. Otherwise, the right operand is returned.
>
> It avoids many bugs where you would ordinarily use the || operator but might accidentally ignore a valid value that happens to evaluate as false.
>
> This feature is not available prior to version 5.10.0.

One useful feature is that boolean operators all return the first value evaluated that allows Perl to determine the condition is satisfied. For example, the && operator returns the left operand if it's false. Otherwise, it returns the right operand.

```
my $zero  = 0;
my $two   = 2;
my $three = 3;
my $x = $zero  && $two;   # $x is 0
my $y = $three && $zero;  # $y is 0
my $z = $two   && $three; # $z is 3
```

However, this is more commonly used with the || and // operators (remember, // is only available on Perl version 5.10.0 and up) by assigning the first value that is not false (or not defined, in the case of the // operator):

```
use 5.10.0; # tell Perl we want the // operator
my $zero  = 0;
my $two   = 2;
my $three = 3;
```

```
my $undef;
my $w = $zero  || $two;   # $w is 2
my $x = $undef || $zero;  # $x is 0
my $y = $zero  // $two;   # $y is 0!
my $z = $undef // $three; # $z is 3
```

Assignment Operators

Perl offers a wide variety of assignment operators, including many shortcut operators to handle common tasks. Table 4-8 lists these operators. The lvalue is the left hand side of the operator and the rvalue is the expression on the right.

TABLE 4-8: Assignment Operators

OPERATOR	EQUIVALENT EXPRESSION
=	Assign rvalue to lvalue
+=	lvalue = lvalue + rvalue
-=	lvalue = lvalue - rvalue
*=	lvalue = lvalue * rvalue
/=	lvalue = lvalue / rvalue
||=	lvalue = rvalue if ! lvalue
//=	lvalue = rvalue if ! defined lvalue
&&=	lvalue = lvalue && rvalue
|=	lvalue = lvalue l rvalue
&=	lvalue = lvalue & rvalue
**=	lvalue = lvalue ** rvalue
x=	lvalue = lvalue x rvalue
<<=	lvalue = lvalue << rvalue
>>=	lvalue = lvalue >> rvalue
^=	lvalue = lvalue ^ rvalue

You've already seen the = assignment operator. It just tells Perl to evaluate the expression on the right and assign the resulting value to the variable or variables on the left. However, there are many shortcut assignment operators available. These operators save you a bit of typing. They're in the form of 'operator' and the equals sign (=), and they tell Perl to treat the operator like an infix operator with the value you assign to be the left operand, the value on the right to be the right operand, and assign the results to the left operand.

The following examples all have the equivalent expression in the comment after the assignment.

```
$x += 4;        # $x = $x + 4;
$y .= "foo";    # $y = $y . "foo";
$z x= 4;        # $z = $z x 4;
```

Precedence and Associativity

What does the following code do?

```
print -4**.5;
```

If you remember your math, raising a number to .5 is equivalent to take the square root of the number. If Perl evaluates the infix exponentiation operator (**) first, it means the following:

```
print -sqrt(4);
```

If Perl evaluates the prefix negation operator (-) first, it means this:

```
print sqrt(-4);
```

The first version prints -2, but the second version, depending on how you wrote it and which version of Perl you use, prints something like Can't take the sqrt of -4, or perhaps nan (which means "not a number").

In this case, the exponentiation operator has a higher precedence than the prefix negation operator and thus is evaluated first.

The main precedence rules that you need to remember are that math operations generally have the same precedence you learned in math class. Thus, multiplication and division (* and /) have a higher precedence than addition and subtraction (+ and -). So the following assigns 13 to $x, not 25.

```
my $x = 3 + 2 * 5;
```

But what happens when you have several of the same operator in the same expression? That's when associativity kicks in. *Associativity* is the side from which the operations are first evaluated. For example, subtraction has left associativity, meaning that the leftmost operations are evaluated first. So 20 - 5 - 2 means 15 - 2, not 20 - 3.

On the other hand, exponentiation is right associative. The following code prints 512 (2 raised to the 9th power), and not 64 (8 squared).

```
my $x = 2 ** 3 ** 2;
print $x;
```

If you actually want to print 64, use parentheses to force the precedence. Parenthesized items always have the highest precedence.

```
my $x = ( 2 ** 3 ) ** 2;
```

Table 4-9 lists the associativity of various operators, in descending order of precedence. Operators are separated by spaces rather than commas to avoid confusion with the comma operator.

TABLE 4-9: Operator Associativity

OPERATOR	ASSOCIATIVITY
Terms and list operators	Left
`->`	Left
`++ --`	Nonassoc
`**`	Right
`! ~ \ and unary + and -`	Right
`=~ !~`	Left
`* / % x`	Left
`+ - .`	Left
`<< >>`	Left
Named unary operators	Nonassoc
`< > <= >= lt gt le gr`	Nonassoc
`== != <=> eq ne cmp ~~`	Nonassoc
`&`	Left
`| ^`	Left
`&&`	Left
`|| //`	Left
`.. ...`	Nonassoc
`?:`	Right
`= += -= *= and so on`	Right
`, =>`	Left
List operators (rightward)	Nonassoc
`not`	Right
`and`	Left
`or xor`	left

The first item, "Terms and list operators," might sound strange. Terms are variables, quotes and quote-like operators, anything in parentheses, and functions that enclose their arguments in parentheses.

> **NOTE** *If you're familiar with C, operators found in C retain the same precedence in Perl, making them a bit easier to learn.*

Table 4-9 is a daunting list, and memorizing it might seem like a scary proposition. Many programmers recommend memorizing it. That's not a bad idea, but there are a couple of issues with memorizing precedence levels:

➤ You may simply forget the precedence levels.

➤ When the maintenance programmer behind you sees you abusing precedence and associativity, she's not going to be happy to stumble across the following:

```
print 8**2 / 7 ^ 2 + 3 | 4;
```

Using parentheses can clarify this code. The following means exactly the same thing:

```
print( ( ( ( 8**2 ) / 7 ) ^ ( 2 + 3 ) ) | 4 );
```

(Both of those lines print 12, by the way).

No, I'm not advocating making such a complicated bit of code, but even for simple expressions, it can come in handy to make it clearer exactly what you intended.

ARRAY AND LIST FUNCTIONS

Arrays and lists have a variety of useful functions that make them easy to manipulate. Because Perl focuses more on data structures than the kinds of data you have, it's very important to have a rich variety of tools to make manipulating these data structures as easy as possible.

Built-in Array Functions

Many years ago your author was asked if Perl supports linked lists (a type of data structure that makes it easy to manipulate lists). I replied "of course it does, but we rarely need them." This is because Perl has a wide variety of builtins for array manipulation.

pop() and push()

```
pop (defaults to @_)
pop  ARRAY
push ARRAY, LIST
```

The `pop()` function pops and returns the last value off the end of an array. The array length is shortened by one element.

```
my $last_element = pop @array;
```

The `push()` function pushes one or more values onto the end of an array, making it longer.

```
my @array = ( 1 .. 5 );
push @array, ( 6 .. 10 );
```

In the preceding example, `@array` now contains ten elements, the numbers 1 through 10, in the correct order.

> **NOTE** The `@_` special variable hasn't been covered yet. It contains the arguments to subroutines, which are explained more in Chapter 7.

shift() and unshift()

```
shift (defaults to @_)
shift   ARRAY
unshift ARRAY, LIST
```

The `shift()` and `unshift()` functions behave like the `pop()` and `push()` functions, but they operate on the beginning of the list.

splice()

```
splice ARRAY,OFFSET,LENGTH,LIST
splice ARRAY,OFFSET,LENGTH
splice ARRAY,OFFSET
splice ARRAY
```

The `splice()` function allows you to remove and return items from a list, starting with the OFFSET. If LENGTH is supplied, only LENGTH elements are removed. If a LIST is supplied, the removed elements are replaced with the LIST (possibly changing the length of the array). As usual, OFFSET, starting with 0, is the first element of the list.

```
my @writers = qw( Horace Ovid Virgil Asimov Heinlein Dante );
my @contemporary = splice @writers, 3, 2;
```

The preceding example assigns Asimov and Heinlein to `@contemporary` and leaves Horace, Ovid, Virgil, and Dante in `@writers`.

If you do not specify an offset, the `splice()` function removes all elements from the array.

There are also a variety of list functions, some of which are covered in far more depth in Chapter 10, when you learn about `sort`, `grep`, and `map` in greater detail. Some basics appear a little later in this chapter, though.

join() and split()

```
join STRING, LIST
split PATTERN, STRING
split PATTERN, STRING, LIMIT
```

The `join()` builtin takes a string and a list and joins every element in the list into a single string, with each element separated by the string value.

```
my $result = join "-", ( 'this', 'that', 'other' );
```

> **NOTE** *Don't be confused by the differences between arrays and lists in Perl. A list is either a list of values literally defined in the code, using the comma opera-tor, or the return value of something evaluated in list context.*
>
> *Here, you have an array on the left and a list on the right:*
>
> ```
> my @words = ( 'this', 'that', 'other' );
> ```
>
> *And here is the* `split` *function splitting a string into a list and assigning it to an array:*
>
> ```
> my @array = split '-', $string;
> ```
>
> *This sounds silly and pedantic, but as Larry Wall himself has said, "There is no general rule for converting a list into a scalar." However, you can safely use sca-lar context with arrays.*
>
> *Further more, lists are immutable (they cannot be changed), but arrays are.*

This assigns `this-that-other` to `$result`. As you might expect, you can use an array for the list. The following is identical behavior:

```
my @array = qw( this that other );
my $result = join '-', @list;
```

The opposite of `join()` is `split()`. However, the first argument to split is a regular expression pat-tern, and you won't be covering those until Chapter 8, so the following just gives you a quick (and incomplete) example of splitting a string on tabs:

```
my @fields = split /\t/, @string;
```

The previous code takes a string, splits it on the tabs (discarding the tab characters), and returns the individual fields into the `@fields` array. The `split()` function is powerful due to the power of regu-lar expressions, but it has traps for the unwary, so it's not covered for now.

reverse()

```
reverse LIST
```

Does what it says on the tin: It reverses a list. However, in scalar context it concatenates the list elements and prints the reverse of the resulting string. The latter behavior can be confusing in some cases.

```
my @array    = ( 7, 8, 9 );
my @reversed = reverse @array;
my $scalar   = reverse @array;
```

In the preceding example, although the @reversed array now contains 9, 8, and 7 (in that order), the $scalar variable now contains the string 987. However, this behavior is useful if you want to reverse a single word:

```
my $desserts = reverse 'stressed';
```

Or if you prefer to be explicit:

```
my $desserts = scalar reverse 'stressed';
```

sort()

```
sort LIST
```

Although this chapter briefly touched on sort() earlier, it's covered it more in-depth in Chapter 10, but following are a few examples to get your started. In these examples, an optional block occurs after the sort() function. As the sort function walks through the list, the special variables $a and $b contain the two elements to be compared while sorting. If you reverse them ($b, then $a), then the sort occurs in the reverse order than normal.

```
# sorting alphabetically
my @sorted = sort @array;
# sorting alphabetically in reverse order
my @sorted = sort { $b <=> $a } @array;
# sorting numerically
my @sorted = sort { $a <=> $b } @array;
# sorting numerically in reverse order
my @sorted = sort { $b <=> $a } @array;
```

Reversing the $a and $b to reverse the sort looks strange, and you might be tempted to do this to sort a list in reverse alphabetical order:

```
my @sorted_descending = reverse sort @array;
```

That works and it's easy to read, but it must sort the entire list and then iterate over the list again to reverse it (note that this has been fixed in Perl versions 5.10.0 and newer). It's not as efficient, particularly for huge lists. That being said, it may not be a big deal. If your program runs fast enough with the "reverse sort" construct, don't sweat it. Making your programs easy to read is a good thing.

grep()

```
grep EXPR,  LIST
grep BLOCK, LIST
```

The grep() function filters a list of values according to whatever is in the BLOCK or EXPR (EXPRESSION). The name comes from an old UNIX command of the same name, but it operates a bit differently in Perl. It's covered more in Chapter 10, but the basic usage is simple. Each item in the list is aliased to $_ and you can compare $_ to a value to determine if you want the selected value. For example, to get all values greater than 5:

```
my @list = grep { $_ > 5 } @array;
```

You can use this to rewrite an array in place. To remove all values less than 100, use this code:

```
@array = grep { $_ < 100 } @array;
```

The grep() function is extremely powerful, but I'll wait until you know more about Perl to show you the full power of this tool. The preceding syntax is the most common syntax for grep(), but it's not the only syntax.

map()

```
map EXPR,  LIST
map BLOCK, LIST
```

The map() function, like the grep() function, takes a list and creates a new list. However, unlike the grep() function, it doesn't filter a list; it applies a function to each element of a list, returning the result of the function. It aliases each element in a list to $_. To multiply every value in a list by 2, use this code:

```
my @doubled = map { $_ * 2 } @array;
```

Or to uppercase every element in a list, use this:

```
my @upper = map { uc($_) } @array;
```

If you remember the uc() function, you know it defaults to operate on $_, so the preceding can be written as follows:

```
my @upper = map { uc } @array;
```

The map() and grep() functions can also be chained. If you want to take the square root of all values in a list that are greater than zero, just use map() and grep() together:

```
my @roots = map { sqrt } grep { $_ > 0 } @numbers;
```

Many programmers like to put the map() and grep() on separate lines based on the theory that it makes the code easier to read. This is true, particularly if your map() and grep() blocks are complicated.

```
my @roots = map  { sqrt }
            grep { $_ > 0 }
            @numbers;
```

Like grep(), there's a huge amount of power here that I've barely touched upon and will cover more in Chapter 10.

The map() and grep() functions are often confusing to new Perl programmers, but they are core to the power of Perl. You must take the time to understand them and know completely how they work.

One caveat about map() and grep(): They operate on every element of a list. If you need to operate only on a few of the elements or if your map() and grep() statements are complicated, it's better to use a for loop with the array. Chapter 5 covers these.

List::Util

Starting with Perl 5.8.0 (released in March 2002), the List::Util module was bundled with Perl. This module includes many list functions that provide even more power when you deal with lists and arrays. For example, to sum all elements in a list together, you can use the following code:

```
use List::Util 'sum';
my $total = sum @numbers;
```

Because sum() accepts lists and not just a single array, you can use multiple arrays as follows:

```
my $total = sum @weight_supplies, @weights_food;
```

See perldoc List::Util for a full list of useful functions. There's also the List::MoreUtils module, but you need to install that from the CPAN.

BUILT-IN HASH FUNCTIONS

Hashes, of course, also have useful functions to help you work with them. A *hash* is often called a *dictionary* in other languages. Instead of looking up values with numeric indices, you look them up with strings.

delete()

```
delete KEY
```

The delete() function removes a key/value pair from a hash.

```
my %birth_year_for = (
    Virgil                      => '70 BCE',
    Shakespeare                 => '1564 CE',
    'Elizabeth Barrett Browning' => '1806 CE',
    'Carrot Top'                => '1965 CE',
);
delete $birth_year_for{'Carrot Top'};
```

That, thankfully, removes Carrot Top from your list of birth years.

exists()

```
exists KEY
```

But how do you know that you actually deleted a given key/value pair in a hash? You can check it with the exists() function. The following code prints Carrot Top not found! because the string Carrot Top does not exist as a hash key:

```
my %birth_year_for;
if ( exists $birth_year_for{'Carrot Top'} ) {
    print "Carrot Top not expurgated!";
}
else {
    print "Carrot Top not found!";
}
```

keys()

```
keys HASH
```

Sometimes you just want to iterate over all the keys to the hash. This is easy with the keys() function:

```
for my $key (keys %hash) {
    if ( $hash{$key} < 10 ) {
        delete $hash{$key};
    }
}
```

values()

```
values HASH
```

Or if you want to just inspect the values of a hash, use the values() function:

```
my @large_enough = grep { $_ >= 10 } values %hash;
```

each()

```
each HASH
```

If you prefer, you can iterate over the keys and values at the same time using the each() function and a while loop. You'll learn while loops in Chapter 5, but for now, just know that it looks like the following code:

```
while ( my ( $key, $value ) = each %hash ) {
    print "$key: $value\n";
}
```

In the previous example with keys(), you saw how to delete items from the hash. It is generally okay to do this even when using the each() function, but do not add key/value pairs to the hash. This breaks the each() function, and you'll get unpredictable results. Also, don't call the each function if you call other code at the same time (typically via a subroutine — discussed in Chapter 7) if you can't guarantee that it won't also try to iterate over the same hash. This is because calling each() twice on the same hash at the same time means that the each() function cannot figure out what you meant to do. When in doubt, just use keys().

```
# this is always safe
for my $key (keys %hash) {
    my $value = $hash{$key};
}
```

TRY IT OUT **Printing Your Name in Various Cases**

This is a good time to take a break and see how some of the builtins you've learned work in actual code. In this Try It Out, you combine a couple things you learned to build more powerful structures. In this case, you take uppercase and lowercase versions of a name and both lowercase, but with an uppercase (initial-capped) first letter. For example, PUBLIUS OVIDIUS NASO should convert to Publius Ovidius Naso. All the code in this Try It Out can be found in code file example_4_1_names.pl.

1. In your wrox/chapter4/ directory, enter the following program, and save it as example_4_1_names.pl:

```
#!perl

use strict;
use warnings;
use diagnostics;

my @upper = qw(PUBLIUS OVIDIUS NASO);
my @lower = qw(publius ovidius naso);

print join " ", map { ucfirst lc } @upper;
print "\n";

my $name = join ' ', map( ucfirst( lc($_) ), @lower );
$name .= "\n";
print $name;
```

2. Run the program with perl example_4_1_names.pl. You should see the following output:

```
$ perl example_4_1_names.pl
Publius Ovidius Naso
Publius Ovidius Naso
```

How It Works

Although the `@upper` and `@lower` arrays are different, you have virtually identical code manipulating arrays into the wanted output. You can also see how Perl combines many simple functions together to make this task easy. The author has deliberately used slighting different syntax with each to show you different styles of Perl.

As you've seen, the `map()` function applies its changes to every element of a list, returning a new list. In this example, you can see the code first applying `lc()` to every element, but in the first argument, you don't even specify the `$_` because `lc()` defaults to operating on `$_`.

The `ucfirst()` function is applied to the value returned by `lc()`. Finally, you use `join()` to join the resulting values with a space for printing. The second version uses the `.=` to show appending the new-line to a variable.

If you are more familiar with lower-level languages such as C, or static languages such as Java, this code might seem strange, but it shows how to pack a lot of power into a single line of code. When you get comfortable with the language, you'll find it easy to read this code and appreciate its power.

SCOPING KEYWORDS

A variety of keywords in Perl can affect the scope of variables or are related to scoping issues. You've already seen some of these, but this section covers them for completeness.

my()

```
my VARIABLE
my (LIST OF VARIABLES)
```

The `my()` builtin declares a new variable or list of variables. They are locally scoped to the file, block, or `eval` in which they are declared. *Scoped* means that code outside of the given file, block or eval cannot see those variables.

local()

```
local VARIABLE
local (LIST OF VARIABLES)
```

The `local()` builtin scopes the value of a package variable or list of package variables to the current file, block, or `eval`. Any changes made to "localized" variables inside of that scope are forgotten outside of that scope.

```
$Foo::bar = 3;
{
    local $Foo::bar = 5;
    print $Foo::bar;       # prints 5
}
print $Foo::bar;           # prints 3
```

As of Perl version 5.10.0, you can use `local()` to safely make changes hash values and they'll be reverted to their original value when the scope ends. Prior to 5.10.0, there were a few bugs with this feature (namely when using variables as hash keys).

As a general rule, you want to minimize your use of `local()`, but it's important to use it when working with Perl's global variables, filehandles, globs, or package variables. It's useful when you want to temporarily override a value and ensure that called subroutines see your new value, or to make sure that you don't accidentally change a global value. You'll see more of this in subsequent chapters, particularly the chapter on subroutines, Chapter 7.

our()

```
our VARIABLE
our (LIST OF VARIABLES)
```

The `our()` builtin allows you to declare package variables in the current package without needing to use the full package name. The following code declares the package variable `$Foo::manchu`:

```
package Foo;
our $manchu = 'Computer Criminal';
```

You could do the following, but note how the author accidentally misspelled the package name:

```
package Foo;
$Fu::manchu = 'Computer Criminal';
```

The `our` builtin makes package variables safer to use because accidentally misspelling the variable name will result in a compile time error when you use `strict`. Be aware that code outside of the package containing the `our` variable can still access that variable if it uses the fully qualified package name.

Many developers use the `our` keyword to declare package variables at the top of a package. This is a bad habit. The use of `our` should be discouraged unless you absolutely need to share a variable value outside of your package. Even then, it's better to do this through a subroutine to preserve encapsulation and help avoid typos. Chapter 11 describes packages and modules in more details.

state()

```
state VARIABLE
```

Beginning with Perl version 5.10.0, you could declare state variables. These are like declaring variables with `my()`, but they are initialized only once and retain their value. For example, writing a subroutine (refer to Chapter 7) that tracks how many times it's been called is easy:

```
sub counter {
    state $counter = 1;
    print "This sub was called $counter times\n";
    $counter++;
}
for (1..10) { counter() }
```

Prior to version 5.10.0, you would have had to write that subroutine like the following:

```
{
    my $counter = 1;
    sub counter {
        print "This sub was called $counter times\n";
        $counter++;
    }
}
for (1..10) { counter() }
```

That's ugly and can obscure the intent of what's going on. The `state()` builtin makes this clear.

For reasons of backward compatibility, you cannot use the `state()` builtin unless you ask for it:

```
use feature 'state';
```

Or you specify a minimum version of Perl:

```
use 5.10.0;
```

The latter syntax asserts that your code can use all features available in that version of Perl.

State variables are generally used in subroutines, so we'll cover them in Chapter 7.

SUMMARY

In this chapter, you've learned the basics of manipulating data in Perl. You've learned more about the three primary data types: scalars, arrays and hashes. You've seen the most common functions and operators used to manipulate those data types. You've also learned the basics of precedence — the order in which Perl evaluates parts of an expression — and associativity — the order in which multiple uses of a single operator are evaluated. You've also saw how variables get aliased to other variables, causing changes in one variable to affect the other.

EXERCISES

1.   Which of the following variables evaluate to true?

```
my $first  = undef;
my $second = ' ';      # a single space
my $third  = 0.0;
my $fourth = '0.0';
my $fifth  = 0;
my $sixth  = 'false';
```

2.   Given the following array of Fahrenheit values, create a new array, @celsius, containing the Fahrenheit temperatures converted to Celsius. Remember that to convert Fahrenheit to Celsius, you must first subtract 32 and then multiply the number by 5/9.

```
my @fahrenheit = ( 0, 32, 65, 80, 212 );
my @celsius    = ...
```

3.   Given an array called @ids, create a new array called @upper containing only the values in @ids that were all uppercase to begin with.

```
my @ids   = qw(AAA bbb Ccc ddD EEE);
my @upper = ...
```

When you finish, @upper should have only the values AAA and EEE.

4.   What values do $answer1, $answer2, and $answer3 contain after all these statements have been executed?

```
my $answer1 = 3 + 5 * 5;
my $answer2 = 9 - 2 - 1;
my $answer3 = 10 - $answer2++;
```

▶ WHAT YOU LEARNED IN THIS CHAPTER

TOPIC	KEY CONCEPTS
String/Numeric builtins	Core data manipulation.
Bitwise operators	Manipulating binary data.
Boolean operators	How "truth" works in Perl.
Assignment operators	How to assign data to variables.
Precedence	The order in which builtins are evaluated.
Associativity	The direction in which identical operators are evaluated.
Array and list functions	Manipulating arrays and lists.
Hash functions	Manipulating hashes.

5

Control Flow

WHAT YOU WILL LEARN IN THIS CHAPTER:

➤ Working with `if`/`elsif`/`else` expressions

➤ What are and when to use `for`/`foreach` loops

➤ Understanding and working with `while`/`until` loops

➤ Understanding the various statement modifiers and how to use `do while`/`do until`

➤ What are `given`/`when` statements and statement modifiers and when to use them

WROX.COM CODE DOWNLOADS FOR THIS CHAPTER

The wrox.com code downloads for this chapter are found at http://www.wrox.com/remtitle .cgi?isbn=1118013840 on the Download Code tab. The code for this chapter is divided into the following major examples:

➤ `Example_5_1_unique.pl`

➤ `Example_5_2_arrays.pl`

From previous chapters, you now understand some of the basics of Perl, but now you get closer to the heart of programming. When you program, you constantly make decisions loop over data based on those decisions. That's what this chapter is all about: how Perl makes decisions and looping over data.

USING THE IF STATEMENT

This section starts with boolean logic. As explained in Chapter 4, the following values are considered "false" in Perl:

➤   `undef`

➤   `""` (the empty string)

➤   `0`

➤   `0.0`

➤   `"0"` (the "string" zero)

Some languages have specific boolean objects, or TRUE and FALSE identifiers. Perl does things a little differently. As you work through the examples, try to see what Perl does and why. If you have experience with programming languages that have a different approach, consider the strengths and weaknesses of the different approaches; then you can appreciate what Perl does and why.

Understanding Basic Conditionals

Conditionals are statements that make decisions. You use these statements in real life, for example: "If I have lemons, make lemonade" and "while I have lemonade, drink it."

We'll start with the `if` statement. A basic `if` statement looks like `if ( EXPRESSION ) BLOCK`:

```
if ( EXPRESSION ) {
    # 0 or more statements
}
```

An expression might have a simple boolean operation in there. The following code guarantees that `$y` will be greater than `$x` by swapping their values if `$x < $y` evaluates as true.

```
if ( $x < $y ) {
    ( $y, $x ) = ( $x, $y );
}
```

You can even put compound conditionals in there if you like:

```
if ( $x < $y && $y > 10 ) {
    # do something
}
```

The previous code works because the < and > operators have a higher precedence than the && operator (refer to Chapter 4). However, many programmers prefer parentheses to be explicit:

```
if ( ( $x < $y ) && ( $y > 10 ) ) {
    # do something
}
```

Optionally, you can use the and, or, xor, and not forms of various boolean operations because those have the lowest precedence of all operations, and you don't need to memorize the precedence order:

```
if ( $x < $y and $y > 10 ) {
    # do something
}
```

It reads nicer, too. Just remember the golden rule of precedence: When in doubt, consider using parentheses to force precedence. Even if you get it right, another programmer reading your code might not.

CURLY BRACES AND THE IF STATEMENT

Some programmers familiar with other languages ask why Perl requires curly braces around the body of code associated with the if statement. For some programming languages, the curly braces are optional if only a single statement is executed:

```
if ( x == y )
    x++;
```

For Perl, the curly braces are always required. A common source of bugs in programming languages such as C is when a developer tries to add an extra statement to an if block, not noticing that no curly braces are delimiting the block:

```
if ( x == y )
    x++;
    y++;
```

Never again will you try to add an extra statement to an if block and wonder why your code is broken.

Because this is Perl, you're not limited to simple boolean constructs in if statements. The expression inside of the parentheses in the if statement is evaluated in scalar context, and the result is then evaluated as true or false, This is sometimes referred to as *boolean context*. Consider the following:

```
if (@names) {
    # do something
}
```

As you may recall, an array evaluated in scalar context returns the number of elements in the array. In the case of if (@names) BLOCK, if the @names array is empty, the if block does not execute. This works for hashes, too:

```
if (%names) {
    # will not execute if %names is empty
}
```

> **NOTE** The `if (%names) { ... }` construct is a bit weird. Internally, a hash creates buckets *used to determine where a given key's values are to be found. In scalar context, a hash returns a string with the number of buckets used, followed by a forward slash, and then followed by the number of buckets allocated for that hash. This is sometimes useful for debugging hash problems but otherwise has little practical use.*
>
> *However, if the hash is empty, it returns* `0` *(zero) in scalar context, allowing the* `if (%names) { ... }` *construct to work. The following prints* `3/8` *and* `0` *and should make it clear what's happening:*
>
> ```
>     my %hash1 = ( foo => 1, bar => 2, baz => 3 );
>     my %hash2;
>     my $scalar1 = %hash1;
>     my $scalar2 = %hash2;
>     print "$scalar1 and $scalar2";
> ```
>
> *You can also use the* `if` *statement with assignment. The following evaluates to false if no customer is returned:*
>
> ```
>     if ( my $customer = get_customer($id) ) {
>         # only executed if $customer evaluates to true
>     }
> ```

else/elsif/unless

Sometimes, you want to take a different action depending on whether a value is true or false. You can follow the `if` block with an `else` block.

```
if ( $temperature > 0 ) {
    print "The temperature is above freezing: $temperature\n";
}
else {
    print "The temperature is not above freezing. Exiting the program.";
    exit;
}
```

Or if you want to test other conditions if the first `if` fails, you can use an `elsif` block.

```
if ( $temperature >= 100 ) {
    print "It's boiling in here!\n";
    cool_things_down($temperature);
}
elsif ( $temperature < 0 ) {
    print "It's freezing in here!. Exiting.\n";
    exit;
}
elsif ( $temperature > 13 and $temperature < 21 ) {
    print "It's perfect weather for outdoor exercise.  Impromptu holiday!\n";
    exit;
}
else {
    print "The temperature is acceptable. Proceed.\n";
}
```

The final `else` is optional:

```
if ( $customer_is_male ) {
    redirect_to_male_apparel();
}
elsif ( $customer_is_female ) {
    redirect_to_female_apparel();
}
```

Many (including your author) recommend that a final `else` block be supplied — even if it does nothing — to make it clear to other programmers who work on your code that you did not make a mistake and overlook a condition. Adding a comment to that else block makes it even more clear.

```
if ($customer_is_adult) {
    redirect_to_adult_apparel();
}
elsif ($customer_is_teen) {
    redirect_to_teen_apparel();
}
else {
    # TODO:  implement redirect_to_preteen_apparel()
}
```

You can also use multiple `elsif` statements:

```
if ( !$color ) {
    print "No color found";
}
elsif ( 'blue' eq $color ) {
    print "#0000FF";
}
elsif ( 'green' eq $color ) {
    print "#00FF00";
}
elsif ( 'red' eq $color ) {
    print "#FF0000";
}
else {
   print "I don't know what to do with color ($color)";
}
```

Long `if`/`elsif`/`else` chains should be avoided, if possible, because they start to make to code harder to read. For example, with the previous code it's better to use a hash:

```
my %color_code_for = (
    blue  => '#0000FF',
    green => '#00FF00',
    red   => '#FF0000',
);
if ( !$color ) {
    print "No color found";
}
elsif ( my $code = $color_code_for{$color} ) {
    print $code;
}
```

```
else {
    print "I don't have a code for the color '$color'";
}
```

Using the hash, if you want to support new color codes, you can just add a new entry to the hash rather than create new elsif blocks for every color.

```
my %color_code_for = (
    black => '#000000',
    blue  => '#0000FF',
    green => '#00FF00',
    red   => '#FF0000',
    white => '#FFFFFF',
);
if ( !$color ) {
    print "No color found";
}
elsif ( my $code = $color_code_for{$color} ) {
    print $code;
}
else {
    # print "I don't know what to do with color ($color)";
    print "I don't have a code for color ($color)";
}
```

> **NOTE** *As with many languages, the whitespace is not particularly significant. Your author prefers* uncuddled else *statements because he finds them easier to read. Others prefer a more compact format:*
>
> ```
> if ( $temperature >= 100 ) {
>     print "It's boiling in here!\n";
>     cool_things_down($temperature);
> } elsif ( $temperature > 0 ) {
>     print "The temperature is acceptable. Proceed.\n";
> } else {
>     print "It's freezing in here!. Exiting.\n";
>     exit;
> }
> ```
>
> *Still others prefer all braces to be aligned vertically:*
>
> ```
> if ( $temperature > 0 )
> {
>     print "The temperature is above freezing: $temperature\n";
> }
> else
> {
>     print "The temperature is not above freezing. Exiting.";
>     exit;
> }
> ```
>
> *All these are perfectly acceptable, and arguments for or against one notwithstanding, don't stress about it. Just pick one style and stick with it.*

Of course, as already seen, you can also reverse the sense of a condition with the ! or not operators:

```perl
if ( !$allowed ) {
    print "You can't do that!";
}
if ( not $found ) {
    print "I didn't find it!";
}
```

Perl also has a rather curious unless statement. It's the opposite of the if statement. The previous statements can be rewritten as follows:

```perl
unless ( $allowed ) {
    print "You can't do that!";
}
unless ( $found ) {
    print "I didn't find it!";
}
```

As with the if statement, you can use elsif and else, but as you might imagine, it can be confusing:

```perl
unless ($condition) {
    # ...
}
elsif ( $some_other_condition ) {
    # ...
}
else {
    # ...
}
```

The use of the unless check is sometimes discouraged. The logic can be confusing, and many developers cheerfully fantasize about using pliers to extract your fingernails if you abuse the unless statement.

The Ternary Operator ?:

As with many other programming languages, Perl also provides a ternary operator as a "shortcut" for an if/else statement. The ternary operator's syntax looks like the following:

```perl
VALUE = CONDITION ? IFTRUE : IFFALSE
```

You can write this:

```perl
my $max = ( $num1 < $num2 ) ? $num2 : $num1;
```

That's the same as writing:

```perl
my $max;
if ( $num1 < $num2 ) {
```

```
        $max = $num2;
    }
    else {
        $max = $num1;
    }
```

But as you can see, the ternary operator is much more compact. With the ternary operator, you don't need to predeclare the $max variable because the ternary operator does not introduce a new scope.

You can also chain ternary operators:

```
my $max = ( $num1 < $num3 and $num2 < $num3 ) ? $num3
        : ( $num1 < $num2 )                    ? $num2
        :                                        $num1;
```

With good formatting this construct is easy to read and has the advantage of the final `else` being required, which is a syntax error if you omit it. The only caution is to be careful about abusing ternary operators because said abuse can be hard to read. For example:

```
my %has_thirty_days = (
    4  => 1,
    6  => 1,
    9  => 1,
    11 => 1,
);

my $days_in_month = 2 == $month ? $year % 100 ? 29
                                : $year % 400 ? 28
                                :               29
                  : $has_thirty_days{$month} ? 30
                  :                             31;
```

Does that work or not? Yes it does (with major caveats about Gregorian and Julian calendars), but do you really want to maintain that? Don't write code like that. We only show this to make it clear that ternary operators are hard to read if you're not careful.

FOR/FOREACH LOOPS

Often, you need to go through each element in a data structure and decide to do something with that element. You often use loops to do this, and in Perl you accomplish it in a variety of ways, using a lot of tips and tricks. This section starts by looking at `for/foreach` loops with arrays and lists.

Arrays

A `for` loop iterates over every element in an array or list. A basic `for` loop in Perl looks like the following:

```
for my $number (@numbers) {
    print "$number\n";
}
```

There's also a `foreach` version:

```
foreach my $number (@numbers) {
    print "$number\n";
}
```

In Perl, `for` and `foreach` are identical. There is no difference aside from the spelling. Your author likes `foreach` because he feels it reads better, but it's a matter of personal preference.

> **NOTE** *If you read* `perldoc perlintro` *and* `perldoc perlsyn` *on this subject, there's a strong implication that* `for` *and* `foreach` *loops are somehow different. The docs generally describe* `for` *as being used with C-style for loops (covered later) and* `foreach` *loops for lists. Unfortunately, the documentation is misleading on this point (this has been fixed in the documentation for 5.16.0). There is no difference between the two.*

The `for`/`foreach` loop is one builtin that assigns to the `$_` by default. If you don't specify a variable name, `$_` is assumed. The following code prints the numbers 5, 6, and 7.

```
my @numbers = ( 5, 6, 7 );
foreach (@numbers) {
    print "$_\n";
}
```

When you combine the loop with builtins, which operate on `$_` by default, you can shorten your code a bit. The following code removes newlines from each element and if the element evaluates as true prints the element.

```
foreach (@names) {
    chomp;
    if ($_) {
        print;
    }
}
```

By contrast, the following is the same code using a named variable (remember that the `foreach` here could be written as `for`):

```
foreach my $name (@names) {
    chomp $name;
    if ($name) {
        print $name;
    }
}
```

Whichever method you prefer, just be aware that it's common to see experienced Perl developers know when to use the $_ variable and take advantage of this fact. If you are not familiar with the builtins that default to assigning a value to $_, you will find some Perl code harder to read.

One important thing to remember about for loops is that the variable you use to designate each element, whether it's $_ or a named variable, is an alias to the element in question. This allows you to modify an array in place. For example, if you want all elements in an array that are less than zero to be set to zero, you can take advantage of aliasing:

```perl
my @numbers = ( -7, -5, -1, 0, 3, 6, 29 );
foreach my $number (@numbers) {
    if ( $number < 0 ) {
        $number = 0;
    }
}
print join ',', @numbers;
```

The previous code snippet prints 0,0,0,0,3,6,29. If you want to manipulate the value but not change the original array, just assign the element to a new variable. This is one case in which the $_ default can be clearer.

```perl
my @numbers = ( -7, -5, -1, 0, 3, 6, 29 );
foreach (@numbers) {
    my $number = $_; # don't use an alias
    if ( $number < 0 ) {
        $number = 0;
    }
}
print join ',', @numbers;
```

Running the previous code shows you that the array has escaped unchanged.

> **WARNING** A subtle trap occurs with for loops when you forget that the list elements are aliased:
>
> ```perl
> for my $number (1,2,3) {
>     $number++;
> }
> ```
>
> While appearing to be legal Perl, the previous code, generates the following error at run time:
>
> ```
> Modification of a read-only value attempted at ...
> ```
>
> Because for loops alias the elements in a list to a variable ($number, in this case), any changes to that variable effect the list elements themselves. The numbers 1, 2, and 3 in the list above are hard-coded verbatim values and they cannot be changed, hence the error message.

Lists

The `for` loop is useful for arrays, but you can use them with anything that returns a list.

```perl
my %economic_description = (
    libertarians => 'Anarchists with jobs',
    anarchists   => 'Libertarians without jobs',
    randroids    => 'Closet libertarians',
    democrats    => 'the tax and spend party',
    republicans  => 'the tax cut and spend party',
);
foreach (sort keys %economic_description) {
    my $description = lc $economic_description{$_};
    $_              = ucfirst;
    print "$_ are $description.\n";
}
```

And that allows you to offend just about everyone by printing:

```
Anarchists are libertarians without jobs.
Democrats are the tax and spend party.
Libertarians are anarchists with jobs.
Randroids are closet libertarians.
Republicans are the tax cut and spend party.
```

Even though you have the `$_ = ucfirst` line in there, this code does not change the hash keys; although the `for` loop aliases its arguments. This is because `keys()` (like the `sort()` function in the loop) returns a new list.

Range operators, when used in list context, also return a list.

```perl
for my $number ( -10 .. 10 ) {
    $number++;
    print $number;
}
```

The previous code prints the numbers from -9 to 11. Although it may appear that you have numeric literals here and thus `$number++` should throw a `Modification of read-only value` error, you don't have that problem. This is because the range operator returns a list. If the values of the list are not assigned to anything, they are anonymous variables. This means that you can change them like any other variable, even if it looks strange.

USING THE DEVEL::PEEK MODULE TO PEEK INTO A SCALAR

Okay; for those who must understand why the range operator works even when modifying the variable, following is some advanced magic.

```perl
perl -MDevel::Peek -e 'Dump(1)'
```

The previous code should output something similar to:

continues

(continued)

```
SV = IV(0x100827d10) at 0x100827d20
  REFCNT = 1
  FLAGS = (IOK,READONLY,pIOK)
  IV = 1
```

The `Devel::Peek` module was released with Perl in version 5.6.0. It exports a `Dump()` function that enables you to "peek" into a scalar to see what it looks like to Perl. In this case, you call `Dump()` on the literal value 1 and you can notice on the FLAGS line that it says READONLY.

Now try this again with 1..1. This range operator returns a 1 element list containing the number one. The code is as follows:

```
perl -MDevel::Peek -e 'Dump(1..1)'
```

And here's the output:

```
SV = IV(0x100802f98) at 0x100802fa8
  REFCNT = 1
  FLAGS = (IOK,pIOK)
  IV = 1
```

FLAGS does not contain READONLY and thus can be modified. See `perldoc Devel::Peek` for more information.

C-Style

Of course, there's also the C-style `for` loop (how `for` loops would be written the C language), with the syntax:

```
for (EXPRESSION ; EXPRESSION ; EXPRESSION) BLOCK
```

This, for example, prints the numbers 0 through 9:

```
for ( my $i = 0; $i < 10; $i++ ) {
    print "$i\n";
}
```

For those not familiar with this style of loop, the three semicolon separated expressions correspond to loop initialization, the loop test, and the loop change.

All three of these expressions are optional. The following code is almost equivalent to the previous code, except that the `$i` variable is no longer lexically scoped to the `for` loop.

```
my $i = 0;
for ( ;$i < 10; ) {
    $i++;
    print "$i\n";
}
```

You can even omit that loop test with a `last()` command, which you will learn about in this chapter in the section "last/next/redo/continue."

C-style `for` loops are not popular in Perl and often not needed. For example, sometimes you need the index of an array, so you do the following:

```
for ( my $i = 0; $i < @array; $i++ ) {
    print "$i: $array[$i]\n";
}
```

But you can write the previous code cleaner, which is more commonly seen like the following:

```
for my $i ( 0 .. $#array ) {
    print "$i: $array[$i]\n";
}
```

The special `$#` syntax at the front of the array name means "the index of the last element of an array." So if an array has four elements, `$#array` returns 3.

> **WARNING** You should use the `$#some_array` only for iterating over the indexes of an array, as shown previously. Inexperienced Perl programmers sometimes write code like the following and wonder why it seems to randomly fail.
>
> ```
> if ( $#array ) {
>     # do something with array
> }
> ```
>
> The `$#array` syntax returns a true value (–1) if there are no elements in the array; a false value (0) if there is one element in the array; and a true value (1 or greater) if there is more than one element in the array. The following example should make this clear:
>
> ```
> #!perl -l
> print "$#array\n";
> @array = ('fail!');
> print "$#array\n";
> push @array, 'not fail!';
> print "$#array\n";
> ```
>
> That prints –1, 0, and 1. If you want to know if an array is empty, just use the array in scalar context:
>
> ```
> if (@array) { ... }
> ```

An example of a handy C-style `for` loop is when you must iterate over a range of numbers not easily generated by the range operator. The following code prints a vertical sine wave in your terminal:

```
for ( my $i = 0 ; $i <= 25 ; $i += .25 ) {
    my $amplitude = int( 40 + 35 * sin($i) );
```

```
        print " " x $amplitude;
        print ".\n";
    }
```

You can write the previous code without the C-style `for` loop, but you might find it harder to understand.

```
for my $i ( 0 .. 100 ) {
    $i = $i / 4;
    my $amplitude = int( 40 + 35 * sin($i) );
    print " " x $amplitude;
    print ".\n";
}
```

Or perhaps the variable increment is set within the program:

```
for ( my $i = 7; $i < 10; $i += $user_choice ) {
    print "$i\n";
}
```

Which you prefer in any context is just a matter of preference.

TRY IT OUT Finding Duplicate Array Elements

Sometimes, an array has repeated elements you want to remove, and preserving the order of the array is important. Using a hash and a `for` loop makes this easy. The following is a simple trick to find unique elements when you don't care about the order. All the code in this Try It Out is found in code file `example_5_1_unique.pl`.

1. Type the following program into your editor as `example_5_1_unique.pl`:

```
#!/usr/bin/perl
use strict;
use warnings;
use diagnostics;

my @array = ( 3, 4, 1, 4, 7, 7, 4, 1, 3, 8 );
my %unordered;
@unordered{@array} = undef;

foreach my $key (keys %unordered) {
    print "Unordered: $key\n";
}

my %seen;
my @ordered;

foreach my $element (@array) {
    if ( not $seen{$element}++ ) {
        push @ordered, $element;
    }
}
```

```
    foreach my $element (@ordered) {
        print "Ordered: $element\n";
    }
```

2. Run the program with `perl example_5_1_unique.pl` and you should see something similar to the following:

```
    Unordered: 8
    Unordered: 1
    Unordered: 4
    Unordered: 3
    Unordered: 7
    Ordered: 3
    Ordered: 4
    Ordered: 1
    Ordered: 7
    Ordered: 8
```

How It Works

Look at the unordered code first because it may look a bit strange.

```
    my @array = ( 3, 4, 1, 4, 7, 7, 4, 1, 3, 8 );
    my %unordered;
    @unordered{@array} = undef;

    foreach my $key (keys %unordered) {
        print "Unordered: $key\n";
    }
```

The line `@unordered{@array} = undef` uses a hash slice as described in Chapter 3. Because you don't care about the values and because hashes cannot have unique keys, the right side of the assignment operator is not important. You now have an array with the keys 1, 3, 4, 7, and 8. However, because hashes do not have an order, printing the keys shows an apparent random order.

You can, of course, sort the keys:

```
    foreach my $key ( sort { $a <=> $b } keys %unordered ) {
        print "Unordered: $key\n";
    }
```

But that merely prints the keys in ascending numeric order, not in the order of the original array. You can see how to do that next. The following code puts together many of the concepts you've already learned.

```
    my %seen;
    my @ordered;

    foreach my $element (@array) {
```

```
      if ( not $seen{$element}++ ) {
          push @ordered, $element;
      }
  }

  foreach my $element (@ordered) {
      print "Ordered: $element\n";
  }
```

The key to this is the not $seen{$element}++ expression. The $seen{$element} when first encountered has an undefined value. Perl interprets this value as 0 and the ++ postfix operator increments it by
1. However, because it's the postfix ++ and not the prefix ++, the increment operation happens *after* the
value is returned, thus ensuring that not $seen{$element}++ is effectively not 0, which evaluates as
true. The next time that $element has a previously seen value, the $seen{$element} already has
a value of 1 or higher, thus causing the not $seen{$element}++ to be the equivalent of not 1
(or a higher number). Because not 1 evaluates as false, the if block does not execute after the first
time the $element appears.

This is a common idiom in Perl and is worth studying and practicing.

DISABLING UNINITIALIZED WARNINGS

You might wonder why $seen{$element}++ does not issue a warning about incre-
menting an uninitialized value. The following three statements have identical behavior, but only the last one issues an uninitialized warning:

```
$seen{$element}++;
$seen{$element} += 1;
$seen{$element} = $seen{$element} + 1;
```

The first two do not issue a warning as described in the Declarations section of
perldoc perlsyn:

```
If you enable warnings, you'll be notified of an uninitialized value
whenever you treat undef as a string or a number.  Well, usually.
Boolean contexts, such as:
    my $a;
    if ($a) {}
are exempt from warnings (because they care about truth rather than
definedness).  Operators such as "++", "--", "+=", "-=", and ".=",
that operate on undefined left values such as:
    my $a;
    $a++;
are also always exempt from such warnings.
```

If you must use a statement that might issue a warning and you do not want that
warning, you can do the following:

```
    {
        no warnings 'uninitialized';
        $seen{$element} = $seen{$element} + 1;
    }
```

The `no warnings 'uninitialized'` statement disables uninitialized warnings in the scope of that block. You can deliberately use a block here to ensure that you don't suppress other uninitialized warnings that you care about. You could also do this:

```
    $seen{$element} ||= 0;
    $seen{$element} = $seen{$element} + 1;
```

In Perl, there are usually multiple ways to get the job done.

TRY IT OUT   Splitting an Array

Sometimes, you want to split up an array into separate arrays based on the data in the array. This Try It Out code walks through an array of numbers, creating two new arrays with positive and negative numbers and skipping zero. All the code in this Try It Out is found in code file `example_5_2_arrays.pl`.

1. First, type the following program and save it as `example_5_2_arrays.pl`:

```
#!perl
use strict;
use warnings;
use diagnostics;

my @numbers = ( -1, 3, 8, -17, 42, 0, 13, -3 );
my ( @negative, @positive );

foreach my $number (@numbers) {
    if ( $number < 0 ) {
        push @negative, $number;
    }
    elsif ( $number > 0 ) {
        push @positive, $number;
    }
    else {
        # skip zero
    }
}

print "Negative: @negative\nPositive: @positive\n";
```

2. Run the code with `perl example_5_2_arrays.pl`. You should have the following output:

```
Negative: -1 -17 -3
Positive: 3 8 42 13
```

How It Works

At this point, things should be fairly clear. You walk through the `@numbers` array and push each element on the corresponding `@negative` or `@positive` array, depending on whether it is negative or positive. The trailing `else` block is not required, but it is a nice hint to future programmers that you did not accidentally skip the number zero.

> **NOTE**   *What's a future programmer? It might be the person the company hires after they promote you for having the foresight to read this book. However, that future programmer might be you! Just because the code is clear now doesn't mean it'll be clear six months from now. This means that your code should be as clear as possible, and you should try to avoid clever tricks in your code. Many of the best programmers write code that looks simple because they know that reading code is just as important as writing it.*

USING WHILE/UNTIL LOOPS

The `while` statement has the general syntax of `while ( EXPRESSION ) BLOCK`. The block is executed while the EXPRESSION is true.

```perl
my $i = 10;

while ( $i > 0 ) {
    if ( rand(3) > 2 ) {
        $i++;
    }
    else {
        $i--;
    }
    print $i,$/;
}
```

The previous code gradually lowers the value of `$i` until the expression `$i > 0` evaluates as false.

The main difference between `while` loops and `for` loops is that `while` loops iterate until a condition is false, whereas `for` loops iterate over a list.

You commonly use the `while` loop in Perl with iterators. The one you know now is the `each()` iterator for hashes.

```perl
my %odd_couples = (
    'Abbott' => 'Costello',
    'Martin' => 'Lewis',
    'Lemmon' => 'Matthau',
);
```

```
while ( my ( $star1, $star2 ) = each %odd_couples ) {
    print "$star1: $star2\n";
}
```

You'll see more of `while` loops as you go through the book. Chapter 9 covers iterating over lines in a file, and you'll see other forms of iterators as you work through various examples.

The opposite of the `while` loop is the `until` loop. The syntax is the same, replacing `while` with `until`. The `while` loop iterates while its condition is true and the `until` loop iterates while its condition is false. The following code computes the factorial of the number 5 (5 * 4 * 3 * 2 * 1):

```
my $factorial = 1;
my $counter   = 1;

until ( $counter > 5 ) {
    $factorial *= $counter++;
}

print $factorial;
```

Like the `unless` statement, you should use the `until` statement cautiously because of the potential to confuse programmers. The previous code is probably better written as:

```
my $factorial = 1;
my $counter   = 1;

while ( $counter <= 5 ) {
    $factorial *= $counter++;
}

print $factorial;
```

Lists

Programmers often try to use `while` or `until` loops with lists instead of iterators or boolean conditions. You can do this but it is fraught with danger and should be avoided. The following are several ways you can fail spectacularly:

```
my $total = 0;
while ( my $price = shift @orders ) {
    $total += $price;
}
print $total;
```

Most of the time, the previous code works just fine until you have a sale item with a price of zero.

```
my @orders = (5,5,0,5);
my $total = 0;
```

```
while ( my $price = shift @orders ) {
    $total += $price;
}
print $total;
```

The previous code prints 10 instead of the (probably) wanted 15. So you decide to get clever to ensure the price is defined:

```
my @orders = ( 5, 5, 0, undef, 5 );
my $total = 0;
while ( defined( my $price = shift @orders ) ) {
    $total += $price;
}
print $total;
```

This previous code is also going to fail because you've managed to sneak an undefined value into the array. If you need to use a while loop here, do it like this:

```
my @orders = ( 5, 5, 0, undef, 5 );
my $total = 0;
while (@orders) {
    my $price = shift @orders;
    $total += $price;
}
print $total;
```

If you insist on using a while/until loop here (perhaps because you want the array empty at the end), you should still consider rewriting with a for loop.

```
my $total = 0;
for my $price (@orders) {
    $total += $price;
}
@orders = ();
```

As you can see, the for loop is shorter and easier to read.

last/next/redo/continue

When you work with loops, it's often useful to have fine-grained control over how the loops behave. The last(), next(), redo(), and continue() builtins help with this.

Using last ()

The last() builtin automatically exits a loop. For example, to find the first perfect square (a square number that is the square of an integer) in an array, you could do the following:

```
my @numbers = ( 3, 7, 9, 99, 25 );
my $first;
for my $number (@numbers) {
    my $root = sqrt($number);
```

```
        if ( int($root) == $root ) {
            $first = $number;
            last;
        }
    }
    if ( defined $first ) {
        print "The first perfect square in the array is $first\n";
    }
    else {
        print "No perfect square found in array\n";
    }
```

The previous code exits the loop when $number equals 9 and prints the following:

```
    The first perfect square in the array is 9
```

The last builtin is handy when you want to process a loop until you reach a wanted condition and then terminate the loop.

Using next()

The next() statement is useful when you want to skip the processing of some elements. You can use this to rewrite the previous code to find all perfect squares in a loop:

```
    my @numbers = ( 3, 7, 9, 99, 25 );
    my @perfect_squares;

    for my $number (@numbers) {
        my $root = sqrt($number);

        if ( int($root) != $root ) {
            next;    # skip the rest of the loop BLOCK
        }

        print "Found perfect square: $number\n";
        push @perfect_squares, $number;
    }
```

Using the continue Statement

The continue statement is not common, but it's useful if you have a block of code that must be executed every time through a loop, before the loop check occurs again. The syntax looks like this:

```
    for    (EXPRESSION) BLOCK continue BLOCK
    while (EXPRESSION) BLOCK continue BLOCK
```

Regardless of a next or last statement in the loop body, the continue always executes after the last statement in the loop body executes:

```
    use strict;
    use warnings;
```

```perl
my @numbers = ( 3, 7, 9, 99, 25 );
my @perfect_squares;

for my $number (@numbers) {
    my $root = sqrt($number);

    if ( int($root) != $root ) {
        next;     # skip the rest of the loop BLOCK
    }

    print "Found perfect square: $number\n";
    push @perfect_squares, $number;
}
continue {
    print "Processed $number\n";
}
```

The previous example prints the following:

```
Processed 3
Processed 7
Found perfect square: 9
Processed 9
Processed 99
Found perfect square: 25
Processed 25
```

Using the redo Statement

The `redo` statement is even less common. What it does is `redo` the body of the loop without testing the condition or executing the `continue` block. It's a bit confusing to people, and even the `perldoc -f redo` documentation sheds little light on the matter. It's used seldom enough that I won't mention further, aside from using it in one of the exercises at the end of this chapter.

Labels

When I listed examples of the for/foreach/while/until syntax, I omitted labels. Labels can be useful for cleaning up code. A *label* is a bare identifier followed by a colon. The `next`, `last`, and `redo` builtins take an optional label as an argument. If that label is present, control jumps to that label. Labels can be used to make your code a bit more self-documenting:

```perl
NUMBER: foreach my $number (@numbers) {
    # lots of code
    if ($some_condition) {
        next NUMBER;
    }
    # more code
}
```

However, the real power of labels lies in controlling the behavior of `next`, `last`, and `redo` when you use nested loops. Say that you have two arrays of strings, @strings1 and @strings2, and you want to find any strings in the first array that are substrings of any strings in the second array. The following code shows one way to write that:

```
my @strings1 = qw( aa bb cc dd ee );
my @strings2 = qw(
  an
  intelligent
  robber
  needs
  a
  good
  ladder
);

my @found;

DOUBLED_LETTER: foreach my $double (@strings1) {
    foreach my $word (@strings2) {
        if ( index($word, $double) != -1 ) {
            push @found, $double;
            next DOUBLED_LETTER;
        }
    }
}

print "@found";
```

The previous code prints bb dd ee. If the next DOUBLED_LETTER; statement were not present, the code would continue searching for words containing the double letter, even if the double letter were already found. If your arrays were large, this could be extremely inefficient by processing more data than is needed.

STATEMENT MODIFIERS

As an alternative to the previously described if/while/for blocks, you can add the if/while/for to the end of a single statement:

```
print "We can haz cheez" if $trite;
```

You may find them a bit cleaner:

```
if ($trite) {
    print "We can haz cheez";
}
```

Types of Statement Modifiers

The allowed modifiers follow:

```
STATEMENT if      EXPRESSION;
STATEMENT unless  EXPRESSION;
```

```
STATEMENT while    EXPRESSION;
STATEMENT until    EXPRESSION;
STATEMENT for      LIST;
STATEMENT foreach LIST;
```

Unlike the block form of these keywords that you've already seen, parentheses are optional around the EXPRESSION or LIST, for example:

```
print "We have a valid user: $user\n" if $user;
```

When using a for/foreach loop, $_ is aliased to the variable. The following code prints the numbers 1 through 5 on successive lines.

```
my @array = ( 1 .. 5 );
print "$_\n" foreach @array;
```

The while and until loops behave similarly. The EXPRESSION is evaluated before the statement. Thus, the following code prints 9 through 0, not 10 to 1.

```
my $countdown = 10;
print "$countdown\n" while $countdown--;
```

The STATEMENT may be a compound statement. The example from perldoc perlsyn follows:

```
go_outside() and play() unless $is_raining;
```

The previous code reads nicely, but it does have a subtle trap. The play() subroutine is not called if go_outside() returns false. You can replace the and with a comma if you want to avoid this:

```
go_outside(), play() unless $is_raining;
```

Statement modifiers should be used sparingly. It's recommended that you use them when the emphasis is to be placed on the statement and not on the modifier.

```
print "Using config data" if $config;
```

For the preceding code, printing Using config data is the expected behavior and is what the programmer should focus on when skimming code. The if $config modifier is easily overlooked. If if $config is a normal condition that the programmer should be more aware of, avoid using the modifier.

```
if ($config) {
    print "Using config data";
}
```

Use of keyword (EXPRESSION or LIST) BLOCK versus a statement modifier is largely a matter of preference, but if you have a compound statement or the condition is what needs the emphasis, avoid the statement modifier.

do while/do until

The `do` builtin (`perldoc -f do`) isn't covered much in this book because the common uses for it belongs to Perl version 4, which should have been put to death when Perl 5 was released in 1994, but there is one form of the `do` builtin that is still in use:

```
do BLOCK
```

This form of `do` executes the statements in the BLOCK and returns the value of the last executed EXPRESSION. You most commonly use this form with a `while` or `until` statement modifier. The grammar looks like this:

```
do BLOCK while EXPRESSION;
do BLOCK until EXPRESSION;
```

For example:

```
my $factorial = 1;
my $counter   = 1;
do {
    $factorial *= $counter++;
} while $counter <= 5;
print $factorial;
```

The do/while, do/until syntax has two major differences between `while` and `until` statements. First, it guarantees that the BLOCK executes at least once. Second, it's not actually a loop. Many people mistakenly think it's a loop, but it's just a standard `do BLOCK` statement followed by a statement modifier. As a result, `next`, `last`, `redo`, and `continue` statements do not apply.

TRY IT OUT   **while versus do {} while**

The `while` versus `do {} while` difference is subtle; the following small program shows how the difference can trip you up.

1.   Save the following as `example_5_3_while.pl`.

```
use strict;
use warnings;

my $number = 0; # a deliberately false value

while ($number > 0) {
    print "You should never see this\n";
}
do {
    print "Unfortunately, you do see this\n";
} while $number > 0;
```

2.   Run the program with `perl example_5_3_while.pl`. You should see the following:

```
Unfortunately, you do see this
```

How It Works

The `while (EXPRESSION) BLOCK` tests the `EXPRESSION` prior to executing the block. However, the `do BLOCK while EXPRESSION` version always executes the block at least once. Thus, subtle logic errors can creep into your code if you are not careful. Combine that with the fact that `do BLOCK while EXPRESSION` is not actually a loop, and you can get more errors. Consider this `while` loop:

```
while (1) {
    last if $counter < 0;
    if ( rand() < .5 ) {
        $counter--;
    }
}
```

The `while (1) BLOCK` is sometimes used to create an *infinite* loop; using a `last()` in the previous code gives you a chance to break out of that loop. However, you can't use `last` with a `do/while` block:

```
use strict;
use warnings;
my $counter = 2;
do {
    last if $counter < 0;
    # do something else
    $counter--;
} while 1;
```

The previous code results in a fatal and confusing error because it's not actually a loop:

```
Can't "last" outside a loop block at program.pl line 6 (#1)
```

If you add `use diagnostics`, you get the following extended error message:

```
(F) A "last" statement was executed to break out of the current block,
except that there's this itty bitty problem called there isn't a current
block.  Note that an "if" or "else" block doesn't count as a "loopish"
block, as doesn't a block given to sort(), map() or grep().  You can
usually double the curlies to get the same effect though, because the
inner curlies will be considered a block that loops once.  See
perlfunc/last.
```

The mention of "double curlies" is unfortunate. It suggests that you can do something like the following code:

```
use strict;
use warnings;
my $counter = 2;
do {{
    last if $counter < 0;
    # do something else
    $counter--;
    print $counter,$/1
}} while 1;
```

Except that actually *is* an infinite loop because the `last` affects the innermost block, but the `while 1` is still looping forever over the outermost block. Allowing doubled curly braces to be abused like this is like pouring a 20-year-old single malt whisky into cola: Just because you can doesn't mean you should.

If you're tempted to use double curly braces with `last`, use a subroutine (Chapter 7) and a `return` statement instead.

GIVEN/WHEN

Many languages offer a `switch` statement. These statements are used to easily choose one or more of several alternatives. A `switch` statement tends to look like the following:

```
switch(number) {
    case(0):
        printf("The number is 0");
        break;
    case(1):
        printf("The number is 1");
        break;
    case(2):
        printf("The number is 2");
        break;
    default:
        printf("The number is unexpected");
}
```

There are a number of historical reasons why a switch statement tends to be written in this manner, but I'll skip over those and go straight to Perl's `given`/`when` statement, which is available in Perl version 5.10.0 or better.

Basic Syntax

The syntax of `given`/`when` looks like the following code:

```
given (EXPRESSION) BLOCK
```

And BLOCK is composed of zero or more `when` statements:

```
when (EXPRESSION) BLOCK
```

Those statements can be followed by a default BLOCK statement. The previous switch statement can be written in Perl as follows:

```
use 5.10.0;
my $number = 1;
given ($number) {
```

```
      when(0) { print "The number is 0"; }
      when(1) { print "The number is 1"; }
      when(2) { print "The number is 2"; }
      default { print "The number is unexpected"; }
  }
```

If you read the code aloud, it actually reads much better than the switch version. For some languages, the switch statement can operate only on integers (part of a historical discussion I am sidestepping). In Perl, the given keyword assigns the value of EXPRESSION to $_ and the EXPRESSION in when (EXPRESSION) BLOCK tests the value of $_. Thus, you can do things like the following code:

```
given ($number) {
    when ($_ < 0) {
        print "The number is negative";
    }
    when ($_ > 0) {
        print "The number is positive";
    }
    default {
        print "The number is 0";
    }
}
```

> **WARNING** Like say and state, the given/when construct is new for Perl version 5.10.0. To use it, you must explicitly state your minimum required Perl version number:
>
> ```
>     use 5.10.0;
> ```
>
> Or use the feature pragma:
>
> ```
>     use feature ":5.10";   # all new features
>     use feature "switch";  # or only given/when
> ```
>
> Why it's use feature "switch" and not use feature "given" is one of life's little mysteries.

If you actually want the when statement to test subsequent when statements, you can use the continue keyword:

```
given ($word) {
    when ( lc $_ eq scalar reverse $_ ) {
        print "'$word' is a palindrome\n";
        continue;
    }
    when ( length($_) > 10 ) {
        print "The length of '$word' is greater than 10 characters\n";
    }
}
```

> **WARNING** *Without going into too much detail, you should be cautious about using* given/when *for the time being. The following blog post explains more (though it's probably a bit advanced for you at this point):* http://blogs.perl .org/users/komarov/2011/09/givenwhen-and-lexical.html.
>
> *If you want to avoid bugs, you can usually replace the* when *with a* for *and it works just fine:*
>
> ```
> for ($number) {
>     when ($_ < 0) {
>         print "The number is negative";
>     }
>     when ($_ > 0) {
>         print "The number is positive";
>     }
>     default {
>         print "The number is 0";
>     }
> }
> ```
>
> *Just make sure that you don't use a variable name with the* for *loop to ensure you're setting the* $_ *variable.*
>
> *To understand more about* given/when, *you can read* perldoc persyn *if you have version 5.10.0 or better. Also, if you want to use* given/when *without the other useful features of newer versions of Perl, see* perldoc feature.

The Switch Module

Don't use this module.

Added in Perl version 5.7.2 and removed in Perl version 5.13.1, the Switch module allowed you to write switch statements in Perl:

```
use Switch;
switch ($val) {
    case 1         { print "number 1" }
    case "a"       { print "string a" }
    case [1..10,42] { print "number in list" }
    case (\@array) { print "number in list" }
    case /\w+/     { print "pattern" }
    case qr/\w+/   { print "pattern" }
    case (\%hash)  { print "entry in hash" }
    case (\&sub)   { print "arg to subroutine" }
    else           { print "previous case not true" }
}
```

Unfortunately, this was implemented as something known as a *source filter*. Source filters rewrite your code before it's compiled, but due to the heuristic nature of Perl's parser, they're considered extremely unreliable. In fact, the `Switch` module, though useful, has a variety of bugs and limitations that, although obscure, are nonetheless difficult to work around.

`Switch` was eventually removed from the Perl core because its functionality is replaced with the `given`/`when` statement. Your author strongly recommends that you do not use the `Switch` module.

SUMMARY

In this chapter you learned the basics of control flow in Perl. The `if` statement and `for` and `while` loops make up the bulk of control flow for Perl; although, many variations exist. Control flow enables your programs to make decisions about what to do and how to do it.

EXERCISES

1. What does the following line of code do? How might you improve it?

```
print for 1..10;
```

2. The following code has a syntax error. Fix it.

```
my $temperature = 22;
print $temperature < 15? "Too cold!\n"
    : $temperature > 35? "Too hot!\n";
```

3. Create an array called `@numbers` and assign some numbers to it. Write the code to print the average value of the numbers.

4. Developers new to Perl who have experience with languages such as Java or C might write the following bit of code. However, it has a logic error. Explain what the logic error is and what the programmer might have done to see the logic error when running the code. Then rewrite the code in a simpler format.

```
my @array = qw( fee fie foe fum );
    my $num_elements = @array;

    foreach ( my $i = 0; $i <= $num_elements; $i++ ) {
        print "$array[$i]\n";
    }
```

5. You're writing a game and want to randomly generate a character's statistics for strength, intelligence, and dexterity. Each statistic is determined by summing the values of two rolls of a six-sided die. For example, if you determine the character's strength and roll the die twice and get the values 2 and 6, the characters strength is 8 (2 + 6). Write the code to generate a new character. Remember that the code to simulate one roll of a six-sided die is `1 + int(rand(6))` (from Chapter 4). You use a "heredoc" (see Chapter 3) to print the character's statistics.

```
my %stat_for = (
  strength     => undef,
  intelligence => undef,
  dexterity    => undef,
);

# add your code here

print <<"END_CHARACTER";
Strength:      $stat_for{strength}
Intelligence:  $stat_for{intelligence}
Dexterity:     $stat_for{dexterity}
END_CHARACTER
```

6. For extra credit, imagine that the character is considered "exceptional" and you don't want to allow any statistic with a value less than 6. Hint: This is one case in which a `redo()` statement can come in handy.

▶ **WHAT YOU LEARNED IN THIS CHAPTER**

TOPIC	KEY CONCEPTS
`if/elsif/else`	Do different things based on whether or not something is true or false.
`?:`	The ternary operator is a shortcut for `if/else` that some programmers use.
`foreach`	Used to iterate over a list.
`while/until`	Used for looping while some expression is true or until some expression is false.
`last/next/redo/continue`	Used to control restarting or exiting loops.
Statement modifiers	`if/foreach/while` expressions put after a statement to modify its behavior.
`given/when`	A clean way of picking one or more statements to execute, based on a particular condition.

6

References

WHAT YOU WILL LEARN IN THIS CHAPTER:

➤ Creating and understanding array, hash, anonymous, and other references

➤ Manipulating references

WROX.COM CODE DOWNLOADS FOR THIS CHAPTER

The wrox.com code downloads for this chapter are found at `http://www.wrox.com/remtitle.cgi?isbn=1118013840` on the Download Code tab. The code for this chapter is divided into the following major examples:

➤ `example_6_1_complex.pl`

➤ `listing_6_1_sales.pl`

➤ `listing_6_2_dclone.pl`

In Perl, you tend to care more about how you organize your data than the kinds of data you have. As a result, Perl enables rich, complex data structures and imposes few limits on how you can organize your data. When you get used to the syntax, you may be pleasantly surprised. Memory management is handled for you; there is no pointer math to get wrong; and there are no external libraries to choose from and load. You just use the references.

REFERENCES 101

In some languages, complex data structures are built up via *pointers* (something that "points" to a variable's location in memory) stored in other data structures, with perhaps pointers to those data structures, in turn, stored in other data structures. Then you can have fun with pointer math, memory management, and obscure compiler errors.

Some languages, on the other hand, offer a bewildering array of different classes to implement a variety of different data structures, depending on what you need and how much time you have to spend reading obscure documentation.

Perl makes it simple. Put any kind of data in any kind of data structure. You, the programmer, are expected to know what to do with it, and Perl (usually) handles the garbage collection and pointer math for you. Like many things in Perl, it *just works*. A reference in Perl doesn't directly contain data; it is just a scalar variable that tells Perl where some data is kept. To access that data, you need to dereference it.

There are two ways of creating a reference in Perl. You can take a reference to an existing variable by putting a backslash, \, in front of it. The other way is to create an anonymous reference and assign it to a variable.

> **NOTE** There's actually a third way to take a reference. It's called the `*foo{THING}` syntax. (Apparently because Perl doesn't have enough weird names for things.) It accesses the value of a typeglob, which isn't discussed here because it's somewhat advanced magic. See `perldoc perlref`. Typeglobs should not be confused with the `glob()` function (Chapter 9).

Array References

As you recall, an array is just a container for a list. To assign a reference to that array to a scalar, prepend it with a backslash:

```
my @fools = qw(jester clown motley);
my $fools = \@fools;
```

The `$fools` variable now contains a reference to the `@fools` array. You can copy the values to another array by prepending it with the @ sign (the array sigil).

```
my @copy_of_fools = @$fools;
```

To access individual elements of the `$fools` array reference, you use the same syntax as you would to access the original array, but you use the dereferencing operator, `->`, between the array name and the square brackets. The following prints `jester - motley`:

```
my @fools      = qw(jester clown motley);
my $aref       = \@fools;
my $first_fool = $aref->[0];
my $last_fool  = $aref->[2];
print "$first_fool - $last_fool";
```

> **NOTE** *You often see Perl programmers refer to array references as* arefs. *Hash references are* hrefs. *Subroutines (Chapter 7) are* subrefs *or* coderefs. *Sometimes you can just say* ref *when you are talking about references in general. Hence, the* `$aref` *and* `$href` *variable names are used in some of this book's examples. Although these are not great variable names, the following is often considered worse:*
>
> ```
> my $fools = \@fools;
> ```
>
> *It's okay in Perl to have multiple variables named* `$fools`, `@fools`, *and* `%fools`, *but it's confusing and should be avoided whenever possible.*

Naturally, you can iterate over an array reference just like you would an array:

```
foreach my $fool ( @$aref ) {
    print "$fool\n";
}
```

And if you need to iterate over the indexes, use the $# syntax in front of the array reference. The following code does the same thing as the previous code;

```
my @fools = qw(jester clown motley);
my $fools = \@fools;
foreach my $i ( 0 .. $#$fools ) {
    my $fool = $fools->[$i];
    print "$fool\n";
}
```

Although your author generally does not recommend the following (it can be confusing), be aware that you can dereference the value and interpolate it into a string just as you would a regular scalar:

```
foreach my $i ( 0 .. $#$fools ) {
    print "$fools->[$i]\n";
}
```

Hash References

You take a reference to a hash the same way you take a reference to an array. Like an array reference, you access individual elements using the dereference operator after the variable name.

```
my %words = (
    dog   => 'chien',
    eat   => 'manger',
    clown => 'clown',
);
my $english_to_french = \%words;
my %copy = %$english_to_french;
my $eat = $english_to_french->{eat};
while ( my ( $english, $french ) = each %$english_to_french ) {
    print "The french word for '$english' is '$french'\n";
}
```

The previous code snippet should print something like this:

```
The french word for 'eat' is 'manger'
The french word for 'clown' is 'clown'
The french word for 'dog' is 'chien'
```

> **NOTE** *Although it's been stated that the proper way to access elements in a reference is to use the dereferencing operator, it's not the only way. You can prepend a $ sign to the variable and skip the dereferencing operator, optionally wrapping the variable in curly braces:*
>
> ```
> $foo->[7];
> $$foo[7];                  # same thing
> ${$foo}[7];                # same thing
> $word_for->{laughter};
> $$word_for{laughter};      # same thing
> ${$word_for}{laughter};    # same thing
> ```
>
> *You might notice the lack of the dereferencing operators. With these alternative ways to dereference, Perl can be much harder to read, particularly if the maintenance programmer is not familiar with this syntax or fails to note that something is dereferenced.*
>
> *It's recommended that you limit your use of this syntax to those cases in which it's absolutely needed (as with reference slices, explained in the "Slices" section later in this chapter).*

Anonymous References

Anonymous references are commonly used to create rich data structures in Perl. They seem strange at first, but they're easy to use.

When you access an individual array or hash element, you wrap the index value in [] or {} respectively. Those braces are also used to construct anonymous hashes and arrays:

```
my $stuff = [ 'foo', 'bar', 'baz' ];
my $colors = { red => '#FF0000', green => '#00FF00', blue => '#0000FF' };
```

However, it doesn't make much sense to construct an anonymous array or hash and assign it directly to a scalar just so you can dereference it again. Instead, they are powerful when you use them inside of other data structures.

Anonymous Arrays

The following is an array of arrays (sometimes referred to as an AoA). The formatting, as usual, is optional and used primarily to make these easier to read:

```
my @results = (
    [ 12, 19, 4      ],
    [ 454, 2, 42     ],
    [ 6,   9, 13, 44 ],
);
```

An array can contain three anonymous arrays, the last of which has four elements instead of three. Accessing each of these array references is as easy as you might expect:

```
my $aref1 = $results[0];
my $aref2 = $results[1];
my $aref3 = $results[2];
```

And then you can access individual elements with the normal dereferencing syntax:

```
my $number = $aref2->[2];
```

By this time, $number should contain 42. However, you can directly access that variable from the @results array by simply dereferencing it directly:

```
my @results = (
    [ 12, 19, 4      ],
    [ 454, 2, 42     ],
    [ 6,   9, 13, 44 ],
);
my $number = $results[1]->[2]; # number is now 42
my $results = \@results;
```

If you have an array of arrays of arrays (AoAoA), you would repeat this:

```
my $number = $aoaoa[3]->[1]->[0];
```

As a shortcut, Perl enables you to omit the dereferencing operator if you're already accessing an individual element in a data structure:

```
my $number = $aoaoa[3]->[1]->[0];
my $number = $aoaoa[3][1][0];       # same thing
```

The latter syntax is more common than the former, but be wary of creating data structures too complex because they're often difficult to read.

When using normal data manipulation builtins, just dereference the array and use it as you normally would:

```
push @$array, $value;
```

If you have a more complex data structure, use curly braces to tell Perl exactly what you're dereferencing:

```
push @{ $some_array[3][0] }, $some_value;
```

Anonymous Hashes

Anonymous hashes work the same way, but you use curly braces instead of square brackets. The following is a hash of hashes (HoH), but you can make the top-level hash an anonymous hash assigned to a scalar:

```
my $sales = {
    monday    => { jim => 2, mary => 1 },
    tuesday   => { jim => 3, mary => 5 },
    wednesday => { jim => 7, mary => 3 },
    thursday  => { jim => 4, mary => 5 },
    friday    => { jim => 1, mary => 2 },
};
```

As you might expect, these are easier to read. What are Mary's sales for Friday?

```
my $num_sales = $sales->{friday}{mary};
```

You must use the dereference operator on the first element, but subsequent elements no longer require said dereferencing. Of course, you can use the dereference operator multiple times, if you prefer:

```
my $num_sales = $sales->{friday}->{mary};
```

Mixing and matching anonymous data structures enable you to create powerful data structures. Listing 6-1 (code file listing_6_1_sales.pl) is a smaller version of the previously shown $sales data structure, but instead of showing the number of sales for Jim and Mary, you can provide anonymous array references showing the commission per sale.

LISTING 6-1: Working with Data Structures

```
use strict;
use warnings;
use diagnostics;

my $sales = {
    monday  => {
        jim  => [ 3, 4 ],
        mary => [ 4 ],
```

```
        },
        tuesday => {
            jim   => [ 3, 5, 1 ],
            mary  => [ 1, 1, 1, 1, 9 ],
        },
};

my $commissions = $sales->{tuesday}{jim};
my $num_sales   = @$commissions;
my $total       = 0;

foreach (@$commissions) {
    $total += $_;
}

print "Jim made $num_sales sales on Tuesday and earned \$$total commission\n";
```

That tells you that Jim isn't earning a lot of money.

```
Jim made 3 sales on Tuesday and earned $9 commission
```

You can escape the first dollar sign on `$total` to tell Perl not to interpolate that dollar sign as part of a variable, but merely print it.

As with arrays, data manipulation builtins behave as normal, so long as you dereference the item first.

```
my @days_of_the_week = keys %$sales;
my @sales_people     = keys %{ $sales->{monday} };
```

Other References

Arrays and hashes are the two most common types of references, but there are a variety of other references that can prove useful from time to time. The most popular is a subroutine reference. The following prints the number 9:

```
my $add_two = sub {
    my $number = shift;
    return $number + 2;
};
print $add_two->(7);
```

Don't worry about how that works for now. Chapter 7 covers subroutine references, but it's included it here for completeness.

Naturally, you can take a reference to a scalar. The following prints `Ovid`:

```
my $name = 'Ovid';
my $ref  = \$name;
print $$ref;
```

Scalar references might seem odd, but they do have uses at times.

TRY IT OUT   **Walking Complex Data Structures**

You haven't had many pages to read, but you covered a lot of ground. Now this Try It Out walks through a compound data structure to make a simple report. You want to print a report showing the top salesperson per day. All the code in this Try It Out is found in code file `example_6_1_complex.pl`.

1. Save the following code as `example_6_1_complex.pl`:

```
use strict;
use warnings;
use diagnostics;

my @day_of_week = qw(
  monday
  tuesday
  wednesday
  thursday
  friday
);

my @sales = (
    { jim   => 2, john      => 7, mary   => 1 },
    { alice => 4, jim       => 3, mary   => 5 },
    { jim   => 7, mary      => 3, pablo => 10 },
    { jim   => 4, mary      => 5 },
    { jim   => 1, katherine => 4, mary   => 2 },
);

print "Top sales per day report\n\n";
printf "%10s   %10s  %s\n", 'Weekday', 'Person', 'Num sales';

# get the name of the day and sales for that day
foreach my $i ( 0 .. $#day_of_week ) {
    my $day        = ucfirst $day_of_week[$i];
    my $daily_sales = $sales[$i];

    # find top salesperson for the current day
    my $top_sales = 0;
    my $top_person;
    while ( my ( $salesperson, $num_sales ) = each %$daily_sales ) {
        if ( $num_sales > $top_sales ) {
            $top_sales  = $num_sales;
            $top_person = $salesperson;
        }
    }
    printf "%10s:  %10s  %-3d\n", $day, $top_person, $top_sales;
}
```

2. Run the code with `perl example_6_1_complex.pl`, and if you've copied it correctly, it should output the following:

```
Top sales per day report
   Weekday      Person  Num sales
   Monday:        john  7
```

```
    Tuesday:        mary  5
  Wednesday:       pablo  10
   Thursday:        mary  5
     Friday:   katherine  4
```

How It Works

All things considered, this is actually a fairly simple data structure (they're so easy in Perl that people often create far more complicated ones), but look at the top two arrays.

```perl
my @day_of_week = qw(
  monday
  tuesday
  wednesday
  thursday
  friday
);
my @sales = (
    { jim   => 2, john       => 7, mary   => 1 },
    { alice => 4, jim        => 3, mary   => 5 },
    { jim   => 7, mary       => 3, pablo => 10 },
    { jim   => 4, mary       => 5 },
    { jim   => 1, katherine => 4, mary   => 2 },
);
```

You can write this example in many ways, but in this case, assume that the @sales in the second array are for Monday, Tuesday, Wednesday, Thursday, and Friday. Each entry in @sales is a hashref with the first name of the salesperson as the key and the number of sales as the value.

The next two lines print out the top of your report:

```perl
print "Top sales per day report\n\n";
printf "%10s   %10s  %s\n", 'Weekday', 'Person', 'Num sales';
```

The printf() formats were carefully chosen to match the printf() formats for each day's entry on the report.

Now you have a strange bit at the top of the for loop:

```perl
# get the name of the day and sales for that day
foreach my $i ( 0 .. $#day_of_week ) {
    my $day        = ucfirst $day_of_week[$i];
    my $daily_sales = $sales[$i];
```

The reason you use the $i variable and assign values from 0 to $#day_of_week (remember, that's the value of the last index in that array) is that by using this index, you can fetch the name of the day from @day_of_week and fetch the daily sales in the @sales array.

Next, use a while loop to iterates over the $daily_sales hash reference:

```perl
# find top salesperson for the current day
my $top_sales = 0;
my $top_person;
```

```
    while ( my ( $salesperson, $num_sales ) = each %$daily_sales ) {
        if ( $num_sales > $top_sales ) {
            $top_sales  = $num_sales;
            $top_person = $salesperson;
        }
    }
    printf "%10s:  %10s  %-3d\n", $day, $top_person, $top_sales;
}
```

Simply keep track of the highest sale for that day and the name of the sales person associated with it. At the end of the `while` loop, print that information out.

Of course, you can write the preceding code in many different ways. It's also not robust. What if more than one salesperson makes the same number of sales? What if the length of the `@day_of_week` and `@sales` arrays do not match? (Refer to the subroutines discussing in Chapter 7.)

WORKING WITH REFERENCES

Knowing how to create references and fetch data out of them is one thing. However, many times you need to copy all or part of a reference without changing the original reference. Or perhaps you can't figure out why you're not getting the right data, so you need to debug your reference. The next sections cover several ways to handle these issues.

Debugging

In the first Try It Out in this chapter, you saw how to work with references and even print them out. However, sometimes they're a bit confusing, and you're not sure what you have. For example, say you have the following line as line 23 of your program:

```
print $aref->[0]{sales};
```

And your program dies with the error message:

```
Not a HASH reference at some_program.pl line 23.
```

Now you want to know what you actually have in the `$aref` variable.

One way to handle this is to just print `$aref->[0]`. In this case, it might print something such as `ARRAY(0xc51220)`. When you print a reference, you see the type of reference (`ARRAY` in this case) followed by its hexadecimal address in memory.

Another way to deal with this is the `ref()` function:

```
print ref $aref->[0];
```

For something that is not a reference, `ref()` returns the empty string. The following is a handy little program that shows various reference types. You won't understand all these yet, but that's okay. When you're done with the book, this will be clear:

```
use strict;
use warnings;
use CGI;

my $foo;
sub handler {}

my $scalar    = ref $foo;
my $scalarref = ref \$foo;
my $arrayref  = ref \@ARGV;
my $hashref   = ref \%ENV;
my $coderef   = ref \&handler;
my $globref   = ref \*foo;
my $regexref  = ref qr//;
my $objectref = ref CGI->new;

print <<"END_REFERENCES";
Scalar:        $scalar
Scalar ref:    $scalarref
Array ref:     $arrayref
Hash ref:      $hashref
Code ref:      $coderef
Glob ref:      $globref
Regex ref:     $regexref
Object ref:    $objectref
END_REFERENCES
```

And that prints:

```
Name "main::foo" used only once: possible typo at refs.pl line 10.
Scalar:
Scalar ref:    SCALAR
Array ref:     ARRAY
Hash ref:      HASH
Code ref:      CODE
Glob ref:      GLOB
Regex ref:     Regexp
Object ref:    CGI
```

You see nothing printed for `$scalar` because `ref()` returns the empty string if called with an argument that is not a reference. The strange `main::foo` warning happens because you take the reference to something called a typeglob. We won't cover them much in this book, but you can read `perldoc perldata` for more information if you're curious.

The rest of the names should be straightforward, even though we've not covered all the types yet. Chapter 9 covers globs (slightly), and Chapter 8, covers regular expressions (the `$regexref`). Calling `ref()` on an object (Chapter 12) merely returns the name of the object's class.

> **WARNING** *All the references used in this chapter have been* hard references. *Hard references tell Perl where to find some data. However, there's also a* soft reference, *sometimes referred to as a* symbolic reference. *Rather than telling Perl where some data is kept, it contains the name of a variable or subroutine that Perl can then access or call to get the data you want. Soft references are considered dangerous because they're easy to get wrong. As a result, they are illegal when you use* strict, *which isn't discussed further in this book. See* perldoc strict *and* perldoc perlref *for more information.*

For large data structures, you might find it frustrating to keep printing individual elements to find out what they are. This is where the useful Data::Dumper module comes in handy. Data::Dumper has been shipped with Perl since version 5.005 (released July 1998).

You can add the following before the offending line to see what you have:

```
use Data::Dumper;
print Dumper($aref);
```

That might print out something like this:

```
$VAR1 = [
             [
                 1,
                 3
             ],
             [
                 2,
                 5
             ]
         ];
```

As you can see by reading this data structure, you have an array ref of array refs, not an array ref of hashrefs. Data::Dumper is an invaluable debugging tool when trying to figure out just what went wrong with your code. See perldoc Data::Dumper to understand how to customize its output.

If you want to print out the values of arrays and hashes that are not references, you must pass them by reference to Data::Dumper and your output may look confusing:

```
use Data::Dumper;
my @words = qw( this that other );
print Dumper(@words);
```

That prints out:

```
$VAR1 = 'this';
$VAR2 = 'that';
$VAR3 = 'other';
```

However, when you pass the array by reference, you get a cleaner output, so long as you understand references:

```
print Dumper(\@words);
$VAR1 = [
            'this',
            'that',
            'other'
          ];
```

Copying

Sometimes you need to copy a data structure. For example, you might want to change some data in a data structure, but leave the original data structure unchanged. Ordinarily you can copy a variable like this:

```
my $x = 3;
my $y = $x;
$y    = 4;
print "$x - $y";
```

That prints 3 - 4. This is because the assignment operator copies the value from one expression to a variable (or variables). However, what happens when that value is a reference?

```
use Data::Dumper;
my $aref1   = [ 1, 3, 7 ];
my $aref2   = $aref1;
$aref2->[0] = 9;
print Dumper($aref1, $aref2);
```

That prints:

```
$VAR1 = [
            9,
            3,
            7
          ];
$VAR2 = $VAR1;
```

But how can the two variables be the same? You only changed the first value of the second array reference.

That's because when you did $aref2 = $aref1, you copied the reference (not the data!) from $aref1 to $aref2. In Perl, copying a reference is automatically a shallow copy. A *shallow copy* copies only top-level values. The data any references point to will be shared between the variables. To do a *deep copy* of an array reference and not share the values, you must dereference the array. In this case, dereference the array and use [] to create a new array reference.

```
use Data::Dumper;
my $aref1   = [ 1, 3, 7 ];
my $aref2   = [ @$aref1 ];
$aref2->[0] = 9;
print Dumper($aref1, $aref2);
```

That prints:

```
$VAR1 = [
            1,
            3,
            7
          ];
$VAR2 = [
            9,
            3,
            7
          ];
```

And as you can see, the two variables no longer share the same array reference.

This can particularly confuse programmers who are not aware of this. The following is some broken code attempting to copy a data structure and clear out the sales in the new structures:

```perl
use Data::Dumper;

my %old_sales = (
    monday    => { jim => 2, mary => 1 },
    tuesday   => { jim => 3, mary => 5 },
    wednesday => { jim => 7, mary => 3 },
    thursday  => { jim => 4, mary => 5 },
    friday    => { jim => 1, mary => 2 },
);

my %new_sales = %old_sales;
while ( my ( $day, $sales ) = each %new_sales ) {
    $sales->{jim}  = 0;
    $sales->{mary} = 0;
}
print Dumper(\%old_sales, \%new_sales);
```

And that prints (reformatted for clarity):

```
$VAR1 = {
  'monday'    => { 'jim' => 0, 'mary' => 0 }
  'tuesday'   => { 'jim' => 0, 'mary' => 0 },
  'wednesday' => { 'jim' => 0, 'mary' => 0 },
  'thursday'  => { 'jim' => 0, 'mary' => 0 },
  'friday'    => { 'jim' => 0, 'mary' => 0 },
};
$VAR2 = {
  'monday'    => $VAR1->{'monday'},
  'tuesday'   => $VAR1->{'tuesday'}
  'wednesday' => $VAR1->{'wednesday'},
  'thursday'  => $VAR1->{'thursday'},
  'friday'    => $VAR1->{'friday'},
};
```

As you can see, you have overwritten the values in the `%old_sales` hash. It would be tedious to dereference each hashref and take a reference to each hash, but it's also error prone. A much simpler way to handle this is to use the `Storable` `'dclone'` (deep clone) function. It does a deep copy of a reference. Listing 6-2 (code file `listing_6_2_dclone.pl`) shows how it's done.

LISTING 6-2: Using dclone to Deep Copy Data Structures

```
use strict;
use warnings;
use diagnostics;
use Data::Dumper;
use Storable 'dclone';

my %old_sales = (
    monday    => { jim => 2, mary => 1 },
    tuesday   => { jim => 3, mary => 5 },
    wednesday => { jim => 7, mary => 3 },
    thursday  => { jim => 4, mary => 5 },
    friday    => { jim => 1, mary => 2 },
);

my %new_sales = %{ dclone(\%old_sales) };
while ( my ( $day, $sales ) = each %new_sales ) {
    $sales->{jim}  = 0;
    $sales->{mary} = 0;
}
print Dumper(\%old_sales, \%new_sales);
```

And running `listing_6_1_dclone.pl` shows that you have the wanted result (again, reformatted for clarity);

```
$VAR1 = {
  'monday'    => { 'jim' => 2, 'mary' => 1 }
  'tuesday'   => { 'jim' => 3, 'mary' => 5 },
  'wednesday' => { 'jim' => 7, 'mary' => 3 },
  'thursday'  => { 'jim' => 4, 'mary' => 5 },
  'friday'    => { 'jim' => 1, 'mary' => 2 },
};
$VAR2 = {
  'monday'    => { 'jim' => 0, 'mary' => 0 }
  'tuesday'   => { 'jim' => 0, 'mary' => 0 },
  'wednesday' => { 'jim' => 0, 'mary' => 0 },
  'thursday'  => { 'jim' => 0, 'mary' => 0 },
  'friday'    => { 'jim' => 0, 'mary' => 0 },
};
```

Remember, when copying references, if it's a flat data structure like an array or hash, you can just dereference and assign the values (optionally creating a new reference):

```
my $acopy = [ @$aref ];
my %hcopy = %$href;
```

But if there are references in there, you have a shallow copy and possibly unwanted side effects.

Slices

When working with arrays and hashes, you sometimes want to fetch several items from the array or hash at once. For example, if you have an array with sales for each day of the month and you only want sales for the first seven days, you don't need the rest of the array. You might recall that the syntax is to prefix the variable name with an @ (array) symbol and provide two or more indexes/keys.

```
# array slice
my @array = qw(foo bar baz quux);
my ( $var1, $var2 ) = @array[ 1, 2 ];

# hash slice
my %hash = (
    this    => 'is',
    another => 'boring',
    example => 'innit?'
);

my ( $first, $second ) = @hash{ 'another', 'example' };
print "$var1, $var2\n";
print "$first, $second\n";
```

And that prints:

```
bar, baz
boring, innit?
```

When you have references, you must, as expected, dereference the variables first. The following code prints the same output as the previous code. You dereference the variables to get the slices:

```
# array slice
my $arrayref = [ qw(foo bar baz quux) ];
my ( $var1, $var2 ) = @$arrayref[ 1, 2 ];
# hash slice
my $hashref = {
    this    => 'is',
    another => 'boring',
    example => 'innit'
};
my ( $first, $second ) = @$hashref{ 'another', 'example' };
print "$var1, $var2\n";
print "$first, $second\n";
```

However, if you want to take a slice of a complex data structure, you must use curly braces to make it clear what you take a slice of:

```
my ( $jim, $mary, $alice )
    = @{ $sales->[12]{tuesday} }{qw/ jim mary alice /};
```

Yes, the syntax is painful and ugly. Taking slices from references is something that often confuses newer programmers. You may want to avoid this feature.

SUMMARY

References are Perl's answer to pointers. Instead of containing data, they tell Perl where the data is contained. The syntax is a bit different from using a normal variable, but it's clear what's going on after you get used to it. References are also the key to building up complex data structures. If you want to know far more than you ever wanted to know about references, you can read the following docs included with Perl:

➤ References: `perldoc perlref`

➤ Reference tutorial: `perldoc perlreftut`

➤ Data structures cookbook: `perldoc perldsc`

➤ Lists of lists: `perldoc perllol`

EXERCISES

1. Create an array called `@first` and assign several values to it. Take a reference to that array, and then dereference it into an array named `@second`. Print both arrays to ensure that you've copied it correctly.

2. Write the code to find the individual number of sales Jim made on Friday and the total number of the sales he made on Friday. Assume each number is the total for an individual sale.

```
my $sales = {
    monday    => { jim => [ 2       ], mary => [ 1, 3, 7       ] },
    tuesday   => { jim => [ 3, 8    ], mary => [ 5, 5          ] },
    wednesday => { jim => [ 7, 0    ], mary => [ 3             ] },
    thursday  => { jim => [ 4       ], mary => [ 5, 7, 2, 5, 2 ] },
    friday    => { jim => [ 1, 1, 5 ], mary => [ 2             ] },
};
```

3. You want to print out the score for Jim and Mary, but the following code is wrong. What's wrong with it? Show two ways to fix it.

```
my $score_for = {
    jim   => 89,
    mary  => 73,
    alice => 100,
    bob   => 83.
};
my ( $jim, $mary ) = %$score_for{ qw{jim mary} };
print "$jim $mary";
```

▶ **WHAT YOU LEARNED IN THIS CHAPTER**

TOPIC	KEY CONCEPTS
Basic References	A shared data structure, which is Perl's answer to pointers.
Anonymous References	The building blocks of complex data structures.
Data::Dumper	A powerful debugging tool to examine variables.
Copying	How to safely copy a reference.
Slices	How to retrieve a subset of items from a reference.

7

Subroutines

WHAT YOU WILL LEARN IN THIS CHAPTER:

➤ Declaringa subroutine

➤ Passing data to subroutines

➤ Returning data from subroutines

➤ Using prototypes

➤ Using subroutine references

➤ Understanding recursion

➤ Implementing error checking

WROX.COM CODE DOWNLOADS FOR THIS CHAPTER

The wrox.com code downloads for this chapter are found at `http://www.wrox.com/remtitle` `.cgi?isbn=1118013840` on the Download Code tab. The code for this chapter is divided into the following major examples:

➤ `example_7_1_running_total.pl`

➤ `example_7_2_length.pl`

➤ `example_7_3_zip.pl`

➤ `example_7_4_maze.pl`

➤ `listing_7_1_fibonacci.pl`

➤ `listing_7_2_binary_search.pl`

A subroutine is just a way of providing a "name" to a piece of code. This is useful when you need to execute the same piece of code in several different places in your program, but you don't want to just "cut-n-drool" the same code all over the place.

Even if you don't want to reuse a piece of code, applying a name is useful. Compare the following two lines of code:

```
my $result = 1 + int( rand(6) );
my $result = random_die_roll();
```

Just by intelligently naming a subroutine, you can see that the second line of code much clearer than the first. Thus, you can use subroutines to make your code more self-documenting. As an added benefit, the name of a subroutine is documentation that you don't forget to add.

SUBROUTINE SYNTAX

A basic subroutine (often just called a *sub*) is declared with the syntax of

```
sub IDENTIFIER BLOCK
```

IDENTIFIER is the name of the subroutine, and BLOCK is the block of code that is executed. So if you want to write a subroutine that simulates the roll of one six-sided die, you can write it like this:

```
sub random_die_roll {
    return 1 + int( rand(6) );
}
```

The return() builtin is used to return data from a subroutine.

Now that you have assigned a name to that block of code, you can use it more or less like any Perl builtin. This code prints a random number from 1 to 6:

```
my $result = random_die_roll();
print $result;

sub random_die_roll {
    return 1 + int( rand(6) );
}
```

> **NOTE** In Perl, there is no formal distinction between a subroutine and a function. In some programming languages, a function and a subroutine are the same, but a function returns a value and a subroutine does not. There is no such distinction in Perl. As a result, people sometimes refer to subroutines as functions. Again, don't get hung up on terminology. Functionality (pun probably not intended) is what you should pay attention to.

Argument Handling

Subroutines are often used when you want to reuse some code but with different data. The data you pass to subroutines is an argument. For example, whereas six-sided dice are the most common, many games have dice with a different number of sides. So you might want to pass to `random_die_roll()` the number of sides of the die you want to roll:

```
my $result = random_die_roll(10);
```

The arguments to a subroutine are stored in the special `@_` array. The following is how to write the sub that enables you to optionally pass the number of sides of the die you want to roll:

```
sub random_die_roll {
    my ($number_of_sides) = @_;
    # have a useful default if called with no arguments
    $number_of_sides ||= 6;
    return 1 + int( rand($number_of_sides) );
}
```

> **WARNING** *Use parentheses around the variables you assign the subroutine arguments to. This is just normal Perl syntax for force-list context. The following code is a common mistake many Perl beginners make:*
>
> ```
> sub random_die_roll {
>     my $number_of_sides = @_;
>     # ... more code
> }
> ```
>
> *That evaluates the `@_` array in scalar context, setting `$number_of_sides` to the number of elements in `@_`. That's probably not what you want.*

If you prefer, you can also write the argument handling like this:

```
sub random_die_roll {
    my $number_of_sides = shift;
    # ... more code here
}
```

The `shift()` builtin (and the `pop()` builtin), when used in a subroutine and called with no arguments, default to shifting off the first value of `@_`. You can be explicit if you prefer:

```
my $number_of_sides = shift @_;
```

Sometimes you see subroutine calls prefixed with an ampersand:

```
my $result = &random_die_roll();
```

Although valid, this is an older form of subroutine syntax the author recommends you do not use except in one special case:

```
my $result = &random_die_roll;
```

You called `&random_die_roll` without parentheses. When you do that, the current value of `@_`, if any, is passed to the new subroutine. This is sometimes useful, but it's confusing because it looks like you called the subroutine without any arguments.

Multiple Arguments

Sometimes you want to roll a die more than once and add up the value of each die roll. Passing multiple arguments to an array is simple. The following is how to roll a six-sided die three times and print the result:

```
sub random_die_roll {
    my ( $number_of_sides, $number_of_rolls ) = @_;

  # have a useful default if called with no arguments
    $number_of_sides ||= 6;

    # the number of times to roll the die defaults to 1
    $number_of_rolls ||= 1;
    my $total = 0;
    for ( 1 .. $number_of_rolls ) {
        $total += 1 + int( rand($number_of_sides) );
    }
    return $total;
}

print random_die_roll( 6, 3 );
```

Because there is more than one way to do it, you can handle the arguments like this:

```
my $number_of_sides = shift;
my $number_of_rolls = shift;
```

Or if you prefer to be explicit:

```
my $number_of_sides = shift @_;
my $number_of_rolls = shift @_;
```

Subroutines in Perl are *variadic*. That means they can take a variable number of arguments. So if you pass too many arguments to a subroutine, Perl usually ignores the extra arguments. The following prints a random number from 1 to 10 and ignores the second argument:

```
sub random_die_roll {
    my ($number_of_sides) = @_;
    # have a useful default if called with no arguments
    $number_of_sides ||= 6;
```

```
        return 1 + int( rand($number_of_sides) );
    }
    print random_die_roll( 10, 3 );
```

You can pass as many arguments as you like and Perl still happily ignores them:

```
    print random_die_roll( 10, 3, $some_val, @foobar );
```

This is a legacy of Perl's roots that you still have today. There are modules such as `Params::Validate` to help deal with this, but Perl programmers usually just read the documentation and know how they're supposed to call the subroutines.

Named Arguments

When you start passing multiple arguments to a subroutine, it can be confusing to know what the arguments mean. Is the following telling you to roll a six-sided die four times or a four-sided die six times?

```
    print random_die_roll( 6, 4 );
```

One way to do that is to use named arguments. In Perl, you handle this by passing a hash:

```
    print random_die_roll(
        number_of_sides => 6,
        number_of_rolls => 4,
    );

    sub random_die_roll {
        my %arg_for = @_;

        # assign useful defaults
        my $number_of_sides = $arg_for{number_of_sides} || 6;
        my $number_of_rolls = $arg_for{number_of_rolls} || 1;
        my $total = 0;

        for ( 1 .. $number_of_rolls ) {
            $total += ( 1 + int( rand($number_of_sides) ) );
        }
        return $total;
    }
```

This is useful because not only is it more self-documenting, but it also makes it easy for any argument to be optional. When you called `random_die_roll(6,3)`, what if you want the default number of sides but to have it rolled three times? You'd have to write something like the following:

```
    my $result = random_die_roll(undef, 3);
    # or
    my $result = random_die_roll(0, 3);
```

Both of those can be confusing because their intent may not be clear. Instead, you can write the following:

```
    print random_die_roll( number_of_rolls => 4 );
```

There is a slight problem with this, though. What if someone doesn't read your documentation (you write documentation, don't you?) and they try to call it like this?

```
print random_die_roll(2);
sub random_die_roll {
    my %arg_for = @_;

    # assign useful defaults
    my $number_of_sides = $arg_for{number_of_sides} || 6;
    my $number_of_rolls = $arg_for{number_of_rolls} || 1;
    my $total = 0;

    for ( 1 .. $number_of_rolls ) {
        $total += ( 1 + int( rand($number_of_sides) ) );
    }
    return $total;
}
```

Enabled warnings warn about `Odd number of elements in hash assignment`. You also get the default values for the `$number_of_sides` and `$number_of_rolls`. Quite often programmers overlook warnings, forget to enable them, or have so many other warnings that they miss simple ones like this. A better way to handle named arguments is to pass a hash reference instead.

```
print random_die_roll(
    {
        number_of_sides => 6,
        number_of_rolls => 4,
    }
);

sub random_die_roll {
    my ($arg_for) = @_;

    # assign useful defaults
    my $number_of_sides = $arg_for->{number_of_sides} || 6;
    my $number_of_rolls = $arg_for->{number_of_rolls} || 1;
    my $total = 0;

for ( 1 .. $number_of_rolls ) {
        $total += ( 1 + int( rand($number_of_sides) ) );
    }
    return $total;
}
```

With this code, if you use `strict` (and you should), then calling `random_die_roll(6)` results in the following fatal error:

```
Can't use string ("6") as a HASH ref while "strict refs" in use
```

It's far better to have your program die horribly than to return bad data.

Aliasing

One thing to be aware of when using subroutines is that the @_ array aliases its arguments, just like we saw with foreach loops in Chapter 6. Thus, you can write the following:

```
my $number = 40;
inc_by_two($number);
print $number;
sub inc_by_two {
    $_[0] += 2;
}
```

That modifies the $number variable in place and prints 42. However, if you call it like this:

```
inc_by_two(40);
```

That generates the following error:

```
Modification of a read-only value attempted at ...
```

Naturally, the aliasing cascades, so this throws the same error:

```
inc_list(3,2,1);

sub inc_list {
    foreach (@_) {
        $_++;
    }
}
```

As a general rule, subroutines are safest when they don't have side effects like this. Instead of trying to rely on aliasing to change variables in place, you should generally assign @_ to new variables and return new values.

```
sub inc_list {
    my @numbers = @_;
    foreach (@numbers) {
        $_++;
    }
    return @numbers;
}
```

State Variables (Pre- and Post-5.10)

When you call a subroutine, variables declared in that sub are reinitialized every time you call the subroutine. However, sometimes you only want to initialize the variable once and have it retain its value between subroutine invocations. If you use Perl version 5.10.0 or better, you can declare a state variable. The following is a subroutine that tracks the number of times it has been called:

```
use 5.010;

sub how_many {
    state $count = 0; # this is initialized only once
    $count++;
    print "I have been called $count time(s)\n";
}

how_many() for 1 .. 5;
```

That prints:

```
I have been called 1 time(s)
I have been called 2 time(s)
I have been called 3 time(s)
I have been called 4 time(s)
I have been called 5 time(s)
```

On versions of Perl older than 5.10.0, you can still do this, but you wrap the subroutine in a block and declare the $count variable in that block, but outside of the subroutine:

```
{
    my $count = 0;

    sub how_many {
        $count++;
        print "I have been called $count time(s)\n";
    }
}
how_many() for 1 .. 5;
```

That prints the same thing.

The reason it works is because the subroutine is in the block in which the $count variable has been declared. It is said to "close over" the scope of that variable and is thus known as a *closure*. Closures are common in Perl but are usually used with anonymous subroutines, as discussed in the "Closures" section of this chapter.

The $count variable doesn't need to be declared in a block like that, but if you don't, other sections of code might see the $count variable and accidentally change its value. The block is just there to safely restrict the scope of $count.

> **WARNING** It's generally a bad idea to have a subroutine referring to variables not explicitly passed to the subroutine. This is because if some other code changes those variables in the way the subroutine does not expect, it can be difficult to find out which part of the code is responsible for making that change. This is why for older Perl's you put the $count variable in a limited scope to make sure that other code can't touch it.

However, this style to make state variables is clumsy and error prone. Consider a subroutine that ensures it's never called with the same argument twice in a row:

```
use strict;
use warnings;

do_stuff($_) for 1 .. 5;

{
    my $last = 0;
    sub do_stuff {
        my $arg = shift;
        if ( $arg == $last ) {
            print "You called me twice in a row with $arg\n";
        }
        $last = $arg;
    }
}
```

That code generates the following warning:

```
Use of uninitialized value $last in numeric eq (==) at ...
```

Why? Variable declaration happens at compile time before the code is run. However, variable assignment happens at runtime and the assignment of 0 to $last doesn't happen until after the calls to do_stuff(). Thus, the first time do_stuff() is called, $last is declared but has no value assigned to it! This is not an issue with state variables:

```
use strict;
use warnings;

do_stuff($_) for 1 .. 5;

sub do_stuff {
    state $last = 0;
    my $arg = shift;
    if ( $arg == $last ) {
        print "You called me twice in a row with $arg\n";
    }
    $last = $arg;
}
```

That doesn't have the warning because at compile time $last is declared, but the first time you enter the do_stuff() subroutine, the $last = 0 assignment happens.

> **NOTE** See perldoc feature and perldoc -f state for more information about using state variables.

Passing a List, Hash, or Hashref?

This section isn't actually about Perl but about good coding style. You can skip it if you want, but if you're new to programming, it's worth reading.

Many times when writing a subroutine, you must decide if you want to pass single arguments, multiple arguments, references, and so on. this section offers a few good rules to consider.

If you have more than two arguments to pass to a subroutine, consider using a hash reference to use named arguments, especially if some of the arguments are optional. Consider the following subroutine call where the account number may be optional. If the customer has only one account, the subroutine might default to that account. If you want to check the balance and there is no amount to $debit, that might also be optional. Named arguments are warranted here:

```
# probably bad
my $balance = get_balance( $customer, $account_number, $debit );

# better
my $balance = get_balance({
    account_number => $account_number,
    customer       => $customer,
    debit          => $debit,
});
```

With that, you can omit the account_number and debit and still have code that is easy to read. Plus, the order of the arguments becomes irrelevant.

But you might think that passing a hash reference is overkill here. It's perfectly easy to read with good variable names, right? Well, you may find yourself in a section of your code where the variable names are not so clear:

```
my $balance = get_balance({
    account_number => $acct,
    customer       => $co,
});
```

Well-chosen named arguments make code much easier to read. So is there ever a reason to pass a list to a subroutine? Sure! If you pass only one or two items, or if every item in the list is conceptually the same, passing a list is fine:

```
sub sum {
    my @numbers = @_;
    my $total = 0;
    $total += $_ foreach @numbers;
    return $total;
}
print sum(4, 7, 2, 100);
```

In this case, using named arguments would be silly because you're just summing a list of numbers.

Sometimes passing a list would be a bad idea. Imagine if the numbers you passed into sum() were two million order totals you've just read from a CSV file. When you pass the list to sum(), Perl must copy every value, and this might eat up a lot of memory. Instead, you can pass a reference, and Perl copies only the single value of the reference:

```
sub sum {
    my $numbers = @_;
    my $total = 0;
    $total += $_ foreach @$numbers;
    return $total;
}
print sum(\@two_million_numbers);
```

Sometimes you might want to pass a hash to a sub, but as explained previously, there is nothing to stop one from passing something that isn't a hash. As a result, hard-to-find bugs can creep into your code. Using a hashref when you want a hash is much safer.

TRY IT OUT   Writing a running_total() Subroutine

Imagine that you're reading a bunch of data and need to sum the results of some data, but do this repeatedly while keeping a running total. You might just write a sum() subroutine and keep the running total of the results, or you might have a running_total() subroutine that does this for you. In this Try It Out, you write such a subroutine to see how it works. This example requires Perl version 5.10 or better, but you'll also see how to rewrite it with Perl 5.8. All the code in this Try It Out uses example_7_1_running_total.pl

1. Type in the following program, and save it as example_7_1_running_total.pl:

```
use strict;
use warnings;
use diagnostics;
use 5.010;

my @numbers = (
    [ 3, 1, 4, 9, 32 ],      # total 49
    [ 5, 200 ],              # total 205
    [ 22, 75, 100, -3 ],     # total 194
);

foreach my $group (@numbers) {
    my ( $total, $running_total ) = _running_total($group);
    print "Total is $total and running total is $running_total\n";
}

sub _running_total {
    state $running_total = 0;
    my $numbers = shift;
    my $total    = 0;
    $total += $_ for @$numbers;
    $running_total += $total;
    return $total, $running_total;
}
```

2. Run the program with perl example_7_1_running_total.pl. You should see the following output:

```
Total is 49 and running total is 49
Total is 205 and running total is 254
Total is 194 and running total is 448
```

How It Works

This one is straightforward, but it has a quirk. There is nothing unusual about this, but the subroutine name is prefixed with an underscore (_). This it a Perl convention that says, "This subroutine is private and you can't use it." This is important because if other code were to call this subroutine, the running total would increase for all areas of the code that called it, and there's a good chance you didn't want that.

The use 5.010 statement is what tells Perl that it can use all syntactic constructs available in Perl 5.10. (Yes; the version number is annoying.)

If you use a version of Perl less that version 5.10, you could write the running total subroutine like this:

```
{
    my $running_total = 0;

    sub _running_total {
        my $numbers = shift;
        my $total   = 0;
        $total += $_ for @$numbers;
        $running_total += $total;
        return $total, $running_total;
    }
}
```

The extra block around the variable and subroutine is to ensure that no code outside of the subroutine can accidentally change the $running_total value. That's ugly because of the extra block, but it gets the job done.

RETURNING DATA

When writing subroutines, it's not helpful if you can't return data. The following section explains many of the ways to do this that you'll encounter in real code. The clearest way to do this is to use the return builtin.

Returning True/False

Many of the most basic subroutines return a true or false value. The following is one way to write an is_palindrome() subroutine, ignoring the case of the word:

```
sub is_palindrome {
    my $word = lc shift;
    if ( $word eq scalar reverse $word ) {
        return 1;
    }
    else {
        # a bare return returns an empty list which evaluates to false
        return;
    }
}
```

```
for my $word (qw/Abba abba notabba/) {
    # remember that the ternary ?: operator is a shortcut for if/else
    my $maybe = is_palindrome($word) ? "" : "not";
    print "$word is $maybe a palindrome\n";
}
```

And that prints:

```
Abba is   a palindrome
abba is   a palindrome
notabba is not a palindrome
```

Unlike some other languages, you can put a `return` statement anywhere in the body of the subroutine. However, you can make this subroutine even simpler:

```
sub is_palindrome {
    my $word = lc shift;
    return $word eq scalar reverse $word;
}
```

If you don't include an explicit return statement in a subroutine, the subroutine returns the result of the last expression to be evaluated, allowing you to write `is_palindrome()` as follows:

```
sub is_palindrome {
    my $word = lc shift;
    $word eq scalar reverse $word;
}
```

It's strongly recommended that you use an explicit return on all but the simplest subroutines because in a complicated subroutine, explicit return statements clarify flow control.

WARNING *Some developers prefer to return* `undef`, *an empty string or a zero for false.*

```
sub is_palindrome {
    my $word = lc shift;
    return $word eq scalar reverse $word ? 1 : 0;
}
```

That's okay, but consider the following:

```
if ( my @result = is_palindrome($word) ) {
    # do something
}
```

That's a silly example, but if you return an empty string or a zero for false, then `@result` *will now be a one-element array and evaluate to true! This can cause strange bugs in your code if you don't consider this.*

> **NOTE** *If you need a review of true and false values, see "Using the If Statement"*
> *section in Chapter 5.*

Returning Single and Multiple Values

As you might guess from the preceding examples, returning a single value is as simple as returning `$some_value`:

```
use constant PI => 3.1415927;
sub area_of_circle {
    my $radius = shift;
    return PI * ( $radius ** 2 );
}
print area_of_circle(3);
```

The previous code prints `28.2743343`, the area of a circle with a radius of 3 (of whatever units you use).

Returning multiple values is simple. Just return them!

```
return ( $first, $second, $third );
```

Be aware, though, that if you return an array or hash, its data is flattened into a list:

```
sub double_it {
    my @array = @_;
    $_ *= 2 for @array;
    return @array;
}
```

This code returns a new list with the values doubled. However, if you want to return two arrays, or two hashes, or an array and a hash, and so on, you want to return references:

```
sub some_function {
    my @args = @_;
    # do stuff
    return \@array1, \@array2;
}
my ( $arrayref1, $arrayref2 ) = some_function(@some_data);
```

Be careful with returning multiple values. Many languages allowonly a single value to be returned from a subroutine. This is actually not a bad idea. If you try to return too much from a single subroutine, it's often a sign that the subroutine is trying to do too much.

RETURNING A LIST WITHOUT PARENTHESES

You may have noticed the last line of the _running_total subroutine you used earlier:

```perl
sub _running_total {
    state $running_total = 0;

    my $numbers = shift;
    my $total   = 0;

    $total += $_ for @$numbers;
    $running_total += $total;
    return $total, $running_total;
}
```

Note that this returns a list of values but you're not using parentheses around the list. In Perl, it's fine to return a list like this. The comma operator is what defines a list (not the parentheses, like many people believe) and because return has a fairly low precedence (Chapter 4), there is no need to wrap the list in parentheses. However, many people feel more comfortable with using parentheses here, and that's fine:

```perl
return ( $total, $running_total );
```

With or without parentheses, returning a list this way is the same thing. Just remember that you need the parentheses when assigning the values to variables:

```perl
my ( $total, $running_total ) = _running_total(\@numbers);
```

wantarray

The wantarray builtin (perldoc -f wantarray) gives you some information about how the subroutine was called. It returns undef if you don't use the return value, 0 if you use it in scalar context, and 1 if you expect a list. The following should make this clear:

```perl
sub how_was_i_called {
    if ( not defined wantarray ) {
        # no return value expected
        print "I was called in void context\n";
    }
    elsif ( not wantarray ) {
        # one return value expected
        print "I was called in scalar context\n";
    }
    else {
        # a list is expected
        print "I was called in list context\n";
    }
}
```

```
how_was_i_called();
my $foo               = how_was_i_called();
my ($foo)             = how_was_i_called();
my @bar               = how_was_i_called();
my ( $this, $that ) = how_was_i_called();
my %corned_beef       = how_was_i_called();
```

The previous code prints:

```
I was called in void context
I was called in scalar context
I was called in list context
I was called in list context
I was called in list context
I was called in list context
```

Note the following about the previous code:

➤   The first `how_was_i_called()` did not assign the result to any values, so it's in "void" context.

➤   The second `how_was_i_called()` assigns to `my $foo` and results in a scalar context.

➤   The `my ($foo)` results in a list context because the parentheses force a list context. Also, the `my @bar`, `my ( $this, $that )`, and `my %corned_beef` result in the subroutine being called in list context.

There are a variety of uses for `wantarray`, but it is usually used for returning a reference when called in scalar context:

```
sub double_it {
    my @array = @_;
    $_ *= 2 for @array;
    return wantarray ?  @array : \@array;
}
```

With that, if you call `double_it()` in scalar context, you get an array reference back.

Use of the `wantarray` builtin is controversial, and many programmers recommend against it because it can lead to surprising code when developers are not expecting the subroutine to behave differently just because they're calling it with a different context.

FAIL!

Subroutines never know how they're going to be called (or at least, they shouldn't), but they should handle problems. The following is a great example of a problem:

```
sub reciprocal {
    my $number = shift;
    return 1 / $number;
}
```

As you may recall from math class, the reciprocal of a number is 1 divided by that number (or that number raised to the power of –1). However, what happens when you pass a zero to your reciprocal subroutine? Your program dies with an `Illegal division by zero` error. Or what happens if you pass a reference instead of a number? Or maybe you passed a string? That's where you want to check the error and handle it appropriately.

"Wake Up! Time to Die!"

Sometimes you need your program to die rather than spit out bad data. You can use the `die` builtin for this. The `die` builtin optionally accepts a string. It prints that string to STDERR (refer to Chapter 4) and halts the programs execution at that point. (Although you can trap this with `eval {...}` as you see in the "eval" section of this chapter.) So, say you have a program that should be executed via the command line as follows:

```
perl count_to.pl 7
```

And that should count from 1 to the number supplied. You want that number to look like a number and to be greater than 0. Otherwise, you want the program to die. Arguments to programs are passed via the @ARGV variable. (Chapter 18 covers command=line handling.) You also use the `looks_like_number()` subroutine exported from the standard `Scalar::Util` module.

```
use strict;
use warnings;
use Scalar::Util 'looks_like_number';
my $number = $ARGV[0];
if ( not @ARGV or not looks_like_number($number) or $number < 1 ) {
    die "Usage: $0 positivenumber"}
print "$_\n" for 1 .. $number;
```

If you run that without any arguments, with an argument that doesn't look like a number, or with a number less than 1, the program dies with the following error message:

```
Usage: count_to.pl positivenumber at count_to.pl line 8
```

> **NOTE** *The* $0 *variable contains the name of the program you're currently running. See* `perldoc perlvar` *for more information.*

That's a handy way to stop a program before serious problems occur and let the user know what the problem is.

If a problem is worth a warning but not worth stopping the program, you can `warn` instead:

```
unless ($config_file) {
    warn "No config file supplied. Using default config";
    $config_file = $default_config_file;
}
```

It works the same, but your program keeps running.

carp and croak

Calling `die` is useful, but you might notice that it prints the line number of where it died. Quite often that's a problem because you don't want to know where the code died, but the line number of the calling code. This is where the `carp()` and `croak()` subroutines come in. These are exported automatically by the standard `Carp` module with a `use Carp;` statement, but your author likes to be explicit about what functions he's importing.

```
use Carp 'croak';
sub reciprocal {
    my $number = shift;
    if ( 0 == $number ) {
        croak "Argument to reciprocal must not be 0";
    }
    return 1 / $number;
}
reciprocal(0);
```

And that prints something like:

```
Argument to reciprocal must not be 0 at reciprocal.pl line 5
main::reciprocal(0) called at reciprocal.pl line 11
```

It tells you where the error occurred (line 5) and where it was called from (line 11). In this simple example, it's not that important, but in larger programs where `reciprocal()` can be called from multiple locations, it's vital information to track down the error.

If you don't want to stop the program but you need a warning, there's also the `carp()` subroutine that is like `croak()`, but for `warn` instead of `die`.

```
use Carp qw(croak carp);
unless ($config_file) {
    carp "No config file supplied. Using default config";
    $config_file = $default_config_file;
}
```

The `Carp` module also exports `confess()` and `cluck()`. These are like `croak()` and `carp()`, but they also provide full stack traces.

eval

Sometimes you want to try to run some code that might fail but handle the failure gracefully, rather than killing the program. This is where the `eval()` builtin comes in handy. There are two types of eval: string and block.

String eval

The first form of eval takes a string as its argument. The Perl interpreter is used to interpret the expression and, if it succeeds, the code is then executed in the current lexical scope. This form of eval is often used to delay loading code until runtime or to allow a developer to fall back to an alternative solution to a problem. The special $@ variable is set if there are errors.

Consider trying to debug the following example, shown earlier in the chapter:

```
use Data::Dumper;
$Data::Dumper::Indent = 0;
my @numbers = ( 1, 2, 3 );
my @new     = map { $_++ } @numbers;
print Dumper(\@numbers, \@new);
```

That printed something like this:

```
$VAR1 = [2,3,4];$VAR2 = [1,2,3];
```

However, the $VAR1 and $VAR2 variables can be confusing, particularly when you try to figure out what went wrong with your program. Data::Dumper offers a syntax that enables you to "name" these variables:

```
print Data::Dumper->Dump(
    [\@numbers, \@new],
    [qw/*numbers *new/],
);
```

And that prints a much more "friendly":

```
@numbers = (2,3,4);@new = (1,2,3);
```

However, the syntax is cumbersome. As a result, your author has released Data::Dumper::Names. It behaves like Data::Dumper but tries to provide the names of the variables. Simply change Data::Dumper to Data::Dumper::Names and you should get the preceding output. But what if you don't have that installed? You can use a string eval to fall back to Data::Dumper:

```
eval "use Data::Dumper::Names";

if ( my $error = $@ ) {
    warn "Could not load Data::Dumper::Names: $error";
    # delay loading until runtime. This is a standard module
    # included with Perl
    eval "use Data::Dumper";
}
$Data::Dumper::Indent = 0;

my @numbers = ( 1, 2, 3 );
my @new     = map { $_++ } @numbers;
print Dumper(\@numbers, \@new);
```

With this code, regardless of whether you could successfully load Data::Dumper::Names, you still get sensible output; although, you get a large warning message to boot.

Block eval

The block form of eval traps the error with code that might fail. This is similar to try/catch with other languages; although it has some issues as you'll soon see.

```
sub reciprocal { return 1/shift }

for (0 .. 3) {
    my $reciprocal;
    eval {
        $reciprocal = reciprocal($_);
    };  # the trailing semicolon is required

    if ( my $error = $@ ) {
        print "Could not calculate the reciprocal of $_: $error\n";
    }
    else {
        print "The reciprocal of $_ is $reciprocal\n";
    }
}
```

And that prints:

```
Could not calculate the reciprocal of 0: Illegal division
  by zero at recip.pl line 1.
The reciprocal of 1 is 1
The reciprocal of 2 is 0.5
The reciprocal of 3 is 0.333333333333333
```

As you can see, the block form of eval is very useful. Unfortunately, it's also tricky to use safely. Now look at a few of the problems and their solutions.

evalGotchas

You probably noticed that after the block eval, you should immediately save the error into a variable:

```
eval { ... };
if ( my $error = $@ ) {
    handle_error($error);
}
```

Why is that? Because in the previous example, if handle_error() itself has an eval, it may reset $@, causing you to lose your error message.

Another common mistake is this:

```
if ( my $result = eval { some_code() } ) {
    # do something with $result
}
else {
    warn "Could not calculate result: $@";
}
```

As you might guess, if some_code() is allowed to return a false value (zero, the empty string, undef, and so on), you might think you have an error when you actually don't. A better way to write the preceding code is this:

```
my $result;
my $ok = eval { $result = some_code(); 1 };
if ($ok) {
    # do something with $result
}
else {
    my $error = $@;
    warn "Could not calculate result: $error";
}
```

The eval block has a bare 1 as the last expression. The block returns the value of the last expression, and if some_code() does not generate an error, $ok is set to 1 and $result has the return value of some_code(). Otherwise, $ok is set to undef.

But there's *still* a problem with the previous code! If you work on a large system, it's entirely possible that your eval() might be called from code that is also wrapped in an eval. When you call eval(), you've clobbered the outer code's $@. So you need to rewrite this again, localizing the $@ variable!

```
my $result;
my $ok = do {
    local $@;
    eval { $result = some_code(); 1 };
};
```

That's starting to get tedious, but it's fairly safe. You now know about the problems with eval, which you will probably encounter in older code. The author strongly recommends that you install the excellent Try::Tiny module from the CPAN.

Try::Tiny

The Try::Tiny module provides a try/catch/finally system for Perl. Now rewrite your reciprocal code using it.

```
use Try::Tiny;

sub reciprocal { return 1/shift }

for my $number (0 .. 3) {
    my $reciprocal;

    try {
        $reciprocal = reciprocal($number);
        print "The reciprocal of $number is $reciprocal\n";
    }
    catch {
        my $error = $_;
        print "Could not calculate the reciprocal of $_: $error\n";
    };
}
```

This behaves exactly like your previous eval solution, but it does not clobber the $@ variable. Also, any error is now contained in $_ instead of $@, which is why you now name the number as $number to avoid confusion.

The catch block executes only if the try block trapped an error.

You can also provide an optional finally block that always executes, error or not:

```
try {
    $reciprocal = reciprocal($number);
    print "The reciprocal of $number is $reciprocal\n";
}
catch {
    my $error = $_;
    print "Could not calculate the reciprocal of $_: $error\n";
}
finally {
print "We tried to calculate the reciprocal of $number\n";
};
```

Install Try::Tiny from the CPAN, and read the documentation for more information about this excellent module. You also want to read its source code (perldoc -m Try::Tiny) to learn more about the effective use of prototypes (explained in the section "Prototypes Summary" later in this chapter); although some of the code is advanced.

SUBROUTINE REFERENCES

One lovely and powerful feature about Perl is the capability to take references to subroutines. This seems strange, but if you're familiar with this feature, you can do strange and wonderful things. You can take references to existing subroutines or create anonymous subroutine references.

Existing Subroutines

The use of a leading ampersand to call a subroutine was previously mentioned. Just as $, @, and % are the sigils for scalars, arrays, and hashes, the & is the sigil for subroutines; although it's not seen as often. Thus, taking a reference to an existing subroutine results in the following:

```
sub reciprocal { return 1 / shift }

my $reciprocal = \&reciprocal;
```

And there are two ways of calling this:

```
my $result = &$reciprocal(4);
print $result;

my $result = $reciprocal->(4);
print $result;
```

The first method, using &$reciprocal(4), is dereferencing the subroutine with the & sigil and calling with arguments like usual. However, the author recommends the second form, $reciprocal->(4), using the standard -> dereferencing operator. This is easier to read (you're less likely to miss that leading &) and it's more consistent in your code if you consistently use the dereferencing operator.

Anonymous Subroutines

Just as you can have anonymous arrays and hashes (among other things), you can also have anonymous subroutines by omitting the subroutine name identifier and assigning the result to a variable:

```
my $reciprocal = sub { return 1 / shift };
print $reciprocal->(4);
```

Closures

So far, taking references to subroutines seems interesting, but how do you use this? One way is to use a closure. A *closure* is a subroutine that refers to variables defined outside of its block. It is said to *close over* these variables. These have a variety of uses; although they won't be covered extensively. Check out the book *Higher Order Perl* by Mark Jason Dominus if you truly want to have your mind twisted by their power.

> **NOTE** *Although a closure does not need to be an anonymous subroutine, it's usually implemented as such.*

Closures are often used for iterators and lazy evaluation. Say you want to periodically fetch the next Fibonacci number. In mathematics, Fibonacci numbers are in the form:

```
F(0) = 0
F(1) = 1
F(n) = F(n-1) + F(n-2)
```

So you end up with an infinite list like this:

```
0, 1, 1, 2, 3, 5, 8, 13, 21 ...
```

Obviously computing an infinite list all at once is not feasible, so you can use a closure to create an iterator that generates these numbers one at a time, as shown in code file `listing_7_1_fibonacci.pl`.

LISTING 7-1: Computing the FibonacciSequence

```
use strict;
use warnings;
use diagnostics;

sub make_fibonacci {
    my ( $current, $next ) = ( 0, 1 );
    return sub {
        my $fibonacci = $current;
        ( $current, $next ) = ( $next, $current + $next );
        return $fibonacci;
    };
}

my $iterator = make_fibonacci();
```

continues

LISTING 7-1 *(continued)*

```
for ( 1 .. 10 ) {
    my $fibonacci = $iterator->();
    print "$fibonacci\n";
}
```

The `make_fibonacci()` subroutine returns an anonymous subroutine that references the `$current` and `$next` variables declared in the `make_fibonacci()` subroutine, but outside of the anonymous subroutine. The `$iterator` variable contains a reference to this anonymous subroutine, and it "remembers" the values of the `$current` and `$next` variables. Every time it is invoked, it updates the values of `$current` and `$next` and returns the next Fibonacci number. Eventually, you get to the `for` loop that prints the first 10 Fibonacci numbers. You can pass the `$iterator` variable to other subroutines just like any other variable, and it still remembers its state.

You can create several iterators with this same subroutine, and each will have a separate copy of `$current` and `$next`.

TRY IT OUT   Writing a Dispatch Table

As you may recall from Chapter 4, the length builtin works only with scalars. For arrays and hashes, you use scalar and scalar keys, respectively. This Try It Outwrites a `mylength()` subroutine that uses a dispatch table with anonymous subroutines to handle this differently. All the code in this Try It Out uses the code file `example_7_2_length.pl`.

1.   Type in the following program, and save it as `example_7_2_length.pl`:

```
use strict;
use warnings;
use diagnostics;
use Carp 'croak';

my %length_for = (
    SCALAR => sub { return length ${ $_[0] } },
    ARRAY  => sub { return scalar @{ $_[0] } },
    HASH   => \&_hash_length,
);

sub _hash_length { return scalar keys %{ $_[0] } }

sub mylength {
    my $reference = shift;
    my $length    = $length_for{ ref $reference }
        || croak "Don't know how to handle $reference";
    return $length->($reference);
}

my $name    = 'John Q. Public';
my @things  = qw(this that and the other);
my %cheeses = (
    good => 'Havarti',
    bad  => 'Mimolette',
);
print mylength( \$name ),    "\n";
print mylength( \@things ),  "\n";
```

```
print mylength( \%cheeses ), "\n";
print mylength($name), "\n";
```

2. Run the code with `perl example_7_2_length.pl`. It prints out the following:

```
14
5
2
Uncaught exception from user code:
Don't know how to handle John Q. Public at ...
```

The exception might be printed before, after, or in the middle of the list of numbers. That's because STDERR and STDOUT are handled separately by your operating system, and you cannot guarantee that they will be printed in sequence.

How It Works

When you first call `mylength()`, Perl calls the `ref` builtin on your argument and attempts to fetch the subroutine reference from the `%length_for` hash. If that subref is not found, you `croak` with an error. The SCALAR and ARRAY keys have anonymous references inlined as the values, while showing the HASH key pointing to a reference to an existing subroutine, just to make the syntax clear. When you call `$length->($reference)`, you pass `$reference` as an argument to the subroutine reference you fetched from `%length_for` hash.

This type of code is called a *dispatch table* because it enables you to dispatch to different code paths based on a particular condition, and you have a table (the `%length_for` hash) containing those code paths.

> **NOTE** *Many beginning Perl programmers try to do something like this:*
>
> ```
> sub foo {
>     my $foo_arg = shift @_;
>     sub bar {
>         my $bar_arg = shift @_;
>         # do something
>     }
>     bar($foo_arg);
> }
> ```
>
> *While that's a silly and useless example, some developers think they can "nest" subroutines like that to hide the inner subroutine from the outside world. The syntax is legal, but the inner subroutine is not hidden and can be called like any other. Use an anonymous subroutine if you ever need to do this:*
>
> ```
> sub foo {
>     my $foo_arg = shift @_;
>     my $bar = sub {
>         my $bar_arg = shift @_;
>         # do something
>     };
>     $bar->($foo_arg);
> }
> ```

PROTOTYPES

A *prototype* is a simple compile time argument check for subroutines. After the subroutine name but before the opening curly brace of the block, you can include a prototype in parentheses. The syntax looks like this:

```
sub sreverse($) {
    my $string = shift;
    return scalar reverse $string;
}
my $raboof = sreverse 'foobar';
print $raboof;
print sreverse 'foobar', 'foobar';
```

And that prints `raboof`, the reverse of `foobar`. (You may recall that reverse takes a list and does not reverse a string unless called in scalar context.)

Argument Coercion

With a prototype using the scalar sigil $, you can force scalar context on the argument to `sreverse()`. Because only one sigil is used in the prototype, you also guarantee that only one variable is used as the argument.

So you can write this:

```
sub sreverse($) {
    my $string = shift;
    return scalar reverse $string;
}
print sreverse("this", "that");
```

And Perl fails at compile time, telling you that you have passed too many arguments to the subroutine:

```
Too many arguments for main::sreverse at proto.pl line 5, near ""that")"
Execution of proto.pl aborted due to compilation errors.
```

You don't even need `strict` or `warnings` for this error to stop your program from compiling.

You can also use @ or % for a prototype. This slurps in all remaining arguments in list context.

```
sub foo(@) {
    my @args = @_;
    ...
}
```

That might seem silly, but it means you can combine it with another prototype character:

```
sub random_die_rolls($@) {
    my ( $number_of_rolls, @number_of_sides ) = @_;
    my @results;
    foreach my $num_sides (@number_of_sides) {
        my $total = 0;
        $total += int( 1 + rand($num_sides) ) for 1 .. $number_of_rolls;
        push @results, $total;
    }
    return @results;
}
my @rolls = random_die_rolls 3;
print join "\n", @rolls;
```

That might print something like:

```
8
26
31
```

It simulates three rolls of each of the subsequent die with the requisite number of sides. In this particular case, the prototype offers no particular advantage.

So far there's nothing terribly exciting here, but you can start to do interesting things if you put a backslash in front of a sigil. When you do this, you can pass the variable, and it is accepted as a reference. The following is a subroutine that attempts to lowercase all hash values that are not references.

```
use Data::Dumper;
$Data::Dumper::Sortkeys = 1;

sub my_lc(\%) {
    my $hashref = shift;
    foreach my $key (keys %$hashref) {
        next if ref $hashref->{$key};
        $hashref->{$key} = lc $hashref->{$key};
    }
}

my $name = 'Ovid';
my %hash = (
    UPPER => 'CASE',
    Camel => 'Case',
);

# hey, no backslash required!
my_lc %hash;
print Dumper(\%hash);
```

And that prints out:

```
$VAR1 = {
          'Camel' => 'case',
          'UPPER' => 'case'
        };
```

Because the hash is passed as a reference, it's modified in place. Just copy the hash and return it if you don't want this behavior:

```
sub my_lc(\%) {
    my $hashref = shift;
    my %hash = %$hashref;
    foreach my $key (keys %hash) {
        next if ref $hash{$key};
        $hash{$key} = lc $hash{$key};
    }
    return %hash;
}
my %lc_hash = my_lc %hash;
```

More Prototype Tricks

There's a lot more you can do with prototypes, but your author generally doesn't recommend them if you don't know what you're doing. They don't specify what type of variable you're passing in. They tend to specify the context of the variable you're passing in and this mimics Perl builtins. For example, say you want to write your own `length()` subroutine. In Perl, the `length()` builtin is only for scalars. It's not for arrays and hashes. Here's a lovely little example, borrowed from a long Tom Christiansen e-mail to the Perl 5 Porters list (and republished at `http://www.perlmonks` `.org/?node_id=861966`).

For some reason, you decide that you want to write a wrapper around the `length()` builtin because you want it to handles arrays and hashes. You've already shown how to handle this with a dispatch table, but try to handle this with prototypes.

```
sub mylength($) {
    my $arg = shift;
    return
        'ARRAY' eq ref $arg ? scalar @$arg
      : 'HASH'  eq ref $arg ? scalar keys %$arg
      :                              length $arg;
}

my $scalar = "whee!";
print mylength($scalar), "\n";

my @array = ( 1, 18, 9 );
print mylength(@array), "\n";

my %hash = ( foo => 'bar' );
print mylength(%hash), "\n";
```

You can probably already guess that something is wrong because even though you haven't covered how to use prototypes with different kinds of arguments, this looks, well, strange. Except that it's stranger than you think. This prints out:

```
5
1
3
```

You can understand why it prints 5 for whee!, but why 1 for the array and 3 for the hash? The mylength() with a $ prototype prints 1 for the array with three elements because the $ prototype forces scalar context, so $arg contains the number of elements in the array, not the array itself! Thus, you wind up returning the value of length(3) and the string "3" is only one character long, thus returning 1.

The hash is even stranger. In the previous example, that prints 3 on some implementations. This is because that hash in scalar context probably evaluates to something such as 1/8, as described in Chapter 3. The string "1/8" has a length of 3. An empty hash in scalar context evaluates to 0, which has a string length of 1.

> **WARNING** *If the output of* mylength() *seems strange to you, be aware that Perl's* length() *builtin behaves the same way. See* perldoc -f length*.*

You can fix that by wrapping the three primary data type sigils in the \[] prototype syntax. This tells Perl to pass a single scalar *or* array *or* hash as a reference to the subroutine.

```perl
sub mylength(\[$@%]) {
    my $arg = shift;
    return
          'ARRAY' eq ref $arg ? scalar @$arg
        : 'HASH'  eq ref $arg ? scalar keys %$arg
        :                              length $$arg;
}
my $scalar = "whee!";
print mylength($scalar), "\n";
my @array = ( 1, 18, 9 );
print mylength(@array), "\n";
my %hash = ( foo => 'bar' );
print mylength(%hash), "\n";
```

That prints the expected:

```
5
3
1
```

You don't need to test for an invalid reference type, such as a subroutine reference, being passed to mylength() because Perl tries to check that at compile-time.

> **WARNING** *Parentheses are required with the* mylength() *subroutine because otherwise you get an error about* Too many arguments for main::mylength*. Why do you need parentheses here and not for the* sreverse() *subroutine earlier? This is because of a known bug in Perl that has been fixed in version 5.14. You can read the gory details at* https://rt.perl.org/rt3/Public/Bug/Display.html?id=75904 *if you're curious.*

Mimicking Builtins

The `mylength()` subroutine mimicked the behavior of the `length` builtin, but customized for your own needs. We'll look a bit more at mimicking builtins. A backslash before a sigil tells Perl that you want that variable to be accepted as a reference. So you can rewrite `push` like this:

```
sub mypush(\@@) {
    my ( $array, @args ) = @_;
    @$array = ( @$array, @args );
}
mypush @some_array, $foo, $bar, $baz;
mypush @some_array, @some_other_array;
```

This works because the `@` sigil in a prototype tells Perl to slurp in the rest of the arguments as a list. You can use a `%` sigil in a prototype, but it's useless unless you use a backslash to force a reference.

You can also separate optional arguments with a semicolon.

```
sub mytime(;$) {
    my $real_time = shift;
    if ($real_time) {
        return scalar localtime;
    }
    else {
        return "It's happy hour!";
    }
}
```

This `mytime()` subroutine usually lies to you and tells you it's fine for a drink, but if you pass it a true value, it return a string representing a human-readable version of the current local time.

```
Sat Dec 24 11:11:26 2011
```

One nifty trick with prototypes is to use an ampersand (`&`) as the first argument. Say you want to increment every element in a list by one. You might write this:

```
use Data::Dumper;
my @numbers = ( 1, 2, 3 );
my @new     = map { $_++ } @numbers;
print Dumper(\@numbers, \@new);
```

That prints out:

```
$VAR1 = [
          2,
          3,
          4
        ];
$VAR2 = [
          1,
          2,
          3
        ];
```

If you look at that carefully, you realize that you've incremented all the values of the original list but not the new one! Why is that? Chapter 4 briefly explains the map builtin. In that explanation, $_ is aliased to every element in the original list. Because $_++ uses the post-increment operator, you successfully modified the original value of $_ in the @numbers list but returned $_ to @new before you incremented it!

You can use a clever subroutine prototype to create an apply() subroutine that applies an anonymous subroutine to every element in a list and returns a new list. This leaves your old list intact and successfully creates the new list:

```
sub apply (&@) {
    my $action = shift;
    my @shallow_copy = @_;
    foreach (@shallow_copy) {
        $action->();
    }
    return @shallow_copy;
}
use Data::Dumper;
my @numbers = ( 1, 2, 3 );
my @new     = apply { $_++ } @numbers;
print Dumper(\@numbers, \@new);
```

And this prints the desired result:

```
$VAR1 = [
          1,
          2,
          3
        ];
$VAR2 = [
          2,
          3,
          4
        ];
```

The & as the first symbol in the prototype enables a subroutine to accept a block as the first argument, and this block is considered to be an anonymous subroutine. You are not allowed to use a comma after it. The @ enables you to pass a list after the anonymous subroutine.

In the apply() subroutine, you copy @_ to @shallow_copy and then iterate over @shallow_copy. Because the loop aliases $_ to each variable in the new array, the $action anonymous subroutine doesn't touch the original array and lets it "do the right thing."

Of course, being a shallow copy, this now breaks:

```
my @munged = apply { $_->[0]++ } @list;
```

The dclone() subroutine from Storable (described in Chapter 6) enables you to do a deep copy, if needed.

Forward Declarations

A forward declaration is a subroutine declaration without a subroutine body. It's just a way to tell Perl "Hey, I'm going to define this subroutine later." Some programmers like predeclaring their subroutines because it solves certain parsing problems in Perl. You author won't cover it in-depth but will explain one case where it can prevent compile errors.

> **NOTE** There's a saying that only `perl` (lowercase) can parse Perl (uppercase). This is true. Many languages have extremely well-defined grammars that enable you to unambiguously declare the semantics of a given expression. For a variety of reasons, this is not possible with Perl. That's why the Perl parse is heuristic in nature — that is to say "it usually guesses correctly." Very, very seldom will you have issues with this, but for some examples of how the `perl` parser can sometimes get things wrong, see `perldoc -f map`.

When using prototypes, you often get subtle errors if you omit the parentheses. For example, the following is a potential mysterious error:

```
use strict;
use warnings;
use diagnostics;

my $reciprocal = reciprocal 4;

sub reciprocal($) {
    return 1/shift;
}
```

That's going to generate a number of errors, even though the code looks fine. The first one looks like this:

```
Number found where operator expected at recip.pl line 5, near "reciprocal 4" (#1)
    (S syntax) The Perl lexer knows whether to expect a term or an operator.
    If it sees what it knows to be a term when it was expecting to see an
    operator, it gives you this warning.  Usually it indicates that an
    operator or delimiter was omitted, such as a semicolon.
    (Do you need to predeclare reciprocal?)
```

What's happening here? Well, when the Perl parser starts compiling the code down to its internal form, it encounters the `reciprocal 4` construct. Because it has not yet seen the prototype for the `reciprocal` subroutine, it doesn't know that 4 is an argument for a subroutine named `reciprocal()`. You can solve this in one of three ways. One way is to define the `reciprocal()` subroutine before that line of code. That ensures that when Perl gets to `reciprocal 4`, it already knows what it is.

If you prefer your subroutines to be defined after the main body of code, you can use a forward declaration with the correct prototype:

```
use strict;
use warnings;
use diagnostics;

sub reciprocal($);

my $reciprocal = reciprocal 4;

sub reciprocal($) {
    return 1/shift;
}
```

That let's Perl successfully parse `reciprocal` 4 when it gets to it.

Finally, you can use parentheses with the subroutine call and that let's Perl know that you really wanted a subroutine and it's not just a bare word:

```
use strict;
use warnings;
use diagnostics;

my $reciprocal = reciprocal(4);

sub reciprocal($) {
    return 1/shift;
}
```

Prototype Summary

Prototypes can be confusing and complicated, but to top it off, they're also buggy. You've already seen one bug. Another one is that you can declare a number of invalid prototypes, such as (@@).

You can also declare useless prototypes. Consider a prototype of (@$). The @ symbol tells Perl to slurp in all arguments, leaving nothing for the $. Perl does not warn you about this.

Also, when you get to the chapter on objects (Chapter 12), you may be tempted to use prototypes for methods. This does not work because prototypes are checked at compile time, but you don't know what method you will be calling until runtime. For now, just remember that prototypes are a bit of a minefield. They would have been left out of this book entirely, were it not for the fact that a number of programmers use them and often do so incorrectly. You are now warned.

There are far more issues with prototypes, but they're far beyond the scope of this book. If you want to use them, I recommend that you carefully read about them and make sure you know what you're doing.

> **NOTE** *For more information on prototypes, see the Prototypes section* `perldoc perlsub.`

Writing a zip() Subroutine That Takes Two Arrays

Sometimes you have data in several data structures that you want to combine into a single data structure. For example, if you have two arrays with the values of one array corresponding to the values in the second array, you may want to "zip" those two arrays together into a key/value hash.

All the code in this Try It Out uses the code file `example_7_3_zip.pl`.

1. Type in the following program and save it as `example_7_3_zip.pl`:

```perl
use strict;
use warnings;
use diagnostics;
use Carp 'croak';
use Data::Dumper;

sub zip(\@\@;$);

my @names = qw(alice bob charlie);
my @tests = qw(87    72);
my @final = qw(100   53  87);
my %test_grades = zip @names, @tests, 0;
my %final_grades = zip @names, @final;

# uncomment the following line to see how this breaks
#my %blows_up = zip @tests, @final;
print Dumper( \%test_grades, \%final_grades );

sub zip (\@\@;$) {
    my ( $first, $second, $default ) = @_;

    # if we don't have a default, croak if arrays are not
    # the same length
    if ( @_ < 3 and ( @$first != @$second ) ) {
        croak "zip() arrays must be the same length without a default";
    }
    my $max_index = $#$first;
    if ( $#$second > $max_index ) {
        $max_index = $#$second;
    }
    my @zipped;
    for my $i ( 0 .. $max_index ) {
        my $first_value  = $i <= $#$first  ? $first->[$i]  : $default;
        my $second_value = $i <= $#$second ? $second->[$i] : $default;
        push @zipped, $first_value, $second_value;
    }
    return @zipped;
}
```

2. Run the program with `perl example_7_3_zip.pl`. You should see something similar to the following output;

```
$VAR1 = {
          'alice' => '87',
          'charlie' => 0,
```

```
            'bob' => '72'
        };
$VAR2 = {
            'alice' => '100',
            'charlie' => '87',
            'bob' => '53'
        };
```

charlie now has a grade of 0 instead of an undefined value.

How It Works

The main "trick" here is the use of the \@\@;$ prototype. The first two \@ bits tell Perl that you're going to pass in arrays and to accept them as array references. The semicolon tells Perl that any sigils after the semicolon are optional. Then provide a final $ to tell Perl there's an optional final argument.

The @_ < 3 test is where you check to see if you actually have that $default value. You don't want to make the mistake of using defined $default here, because you may want to have an undefined $default padding out your zipped values.

Then, calculate the $max_index because you need to know how many elements you'll be iterating over. Part of the actual magic is in these two lines:

```
my $first_value  = $i <= $#$first  ? $first->[$i]  : $default;
my $second_value = $i <= $#$second ? $second->[$i] : $default;
```

If the current index is less than or equal to the largest index value for the given array references (see the section "Array References" in Chapter 6 if you don't remember the $#$first syntax), then you know that array has a value for that index. Otherwise, use the default value.

If you don't like the $#$ syntax (and many don't), you can use the following:

```
my $first_value  = $i < @$first  ? $first->[$i]  : $default;
my $second_value = $i < @$second ? $second->[$i] : $default;
```

That works, too. Use whichever you feel is easier to read.

RECURSION

A *recursive* subroutine is a subroutine that calls itself. Why might it do this? Because it's often clearer to express something in a recursive form. Also, sometimes it is easier to break a large problem into smaller problems and solve those. This section lets you look at both.

Basic Recursion

Remember that Fibonacci numbers are the following:

```
F(0) = 0
F(1) = 1
F(n) = F(n-1) + F(n-2)
```

To write that as a recursive subroutine for finding the *n*th Fibonacci number, use this code:

```
sub F {
    my $n = shift;
    return 0 if $n == 0;
    return 1 if $n == 1;
    return F($n - 1) + F($n - 2);
}
print F(7);
```

And that correctly prints 13, which closely matches the mathematical definition of Fibonacci numbers.

> **WARNING** *Recursive functions should almost always have one or more statements that return without recursing. This is to prevent infinite loops. If you write a recursive subroutine that never returns, look at your return statements carefully to see if you forgot to have one break out of the recursion.*

Divide and Conquer

Divide and conquer, in computer science, is a way to break a problem down into smaller problems to try to solve each of those, perhaps breaking those down into smaller problems. For example, say you have a sorted list of integers and want to find an integer in that list. One way to do this is to iterate over the list:

```
sub search {
    my ( $numbers, $target ) = @_;
    for my $i ( 0 .. $#$numbers ) {
        return $i if $numbers->[$i] == $target;
    }
    return;
}
```

This code works, but it can be slow. Imagine if you have a list of 1,000 elements. You might have 1,000 iterations before you find the number. Doing this repeatedly could be a performance problem. A better strategy (again, assuming the list of numbers is sorted), is to do a binary search. This search checks to see if your number is less than the midpoint of the list. If so, repeat the process for the first half of the list. If not, repeat for the second half of the list. Repeat until you find the index or run out of list. This means for the first iteration, you have at most 500 numbers to compare, then 250, and then 125, 63, 32, 16, 8, 4, 2, and 1. So you have at most 10 iterations before finding the number. You see how to do this in code file listing_7_2_binary_search.pl

---

LISTING 7-2: Performing a binary search

```
use strict;
use warnings;
```

```
my @numbers = map { $_ * 3 } ( 0 .. 1000 );

sub search {
    my ( $numbers, $target ) = @_;
    return _binary_search( $numbers, $target, 0, $#$numbers );
}

sub _binary_search {
    my ( $numbers, $target, $low, $high ) = @_;
    return if $high < $low;
    # divide array in two
    my $middle = int( ( $low + $high ) / 2 );
    if ( $numbers->[$middle] > $target ) {
        # search the lower half
        return _binary_search( $numbers, $target, $low, $middle - 1 );
    }
    elsif ( $numbers->[$middle] < $target ) {
        # search the upper half
        return _binary_search( $numbers, $target, $middle + 1, $high );
    }
    # found it!
    return $middle;
}

print search(\@numbers, 699),"\n";
print search(\@numbers, 28),"\n";
```

The previous code prints 233 when you search for the number 699, and undef when you search for the number 28. It's also fast. You'll note how the code successfully divided the problem into smaller and smaller steps recursively to find what you were looking for.

Memoization

Recursive subroutines can be expensive in terms of memory. If the subroutine is a pure subroutine, you can *memoize* (cache or "memorize" previous results) it. The Memoize module on the CPAN can help with this.

The memoize subroutine provided by the module enables a subroutine to remember a previous result for a set of arguments. The first time you call a memoized subroutine, it calculates the value. On any subsequent call it returns the cached value.

> **NOTE** *A pure subroutine relies only on the arguments passed to it and always returns the same value for each set of arguments. It's also guaranteed not to have side effects.*

```
use Memoize;

memoize('F');

sub F {
```

```
      my $n = shift;
      return 0 if $n == 0;
      return 1 if $n == 1;
      return F($n - 1) + F($n - 2);
   }
   print F(50);
```

That quickly prints 12586269025, but if you remove the memoize('F') line, it can take several hours to run. That's because the recursive subroutine calls are often calculating the same thing, calling themselves over and over. If you walk through the subroutine several times, you'll understand why this saves so much time.

Of course, everything has a price. The memoize subroutine works by using extra memory to store the computed value. Often, you'll find that trading RAM time for CPU time is a good trade-off.

TRY IT OUT   **Writing a Recursive Maze Generator**

All the code in this Try It Out is included in code file example_7_4_maze.pl.

1.   Type in the following program and save it as example_7_4_maze.pl:

```
use strict;
use warnings;
use diagnostics;

use List::Util 'shuffle';

my ( $WIDTH, $HEIGHT ) = ( 10, 10 );
my %OPPOSITE_OF = (
    north => 'south',
    south => 'north',
    west  => 'east',
    east  => 'west',
);

my @maze;
tunnel( 0, 0, \@maze );
print render_maze( \@maze );
exit;

sub tunnel {
    my ( $x, $y, $maze ) = @_;
    my @directions = shuffle keys %OPPOSITE_OF;
    foreach my $direction (@directions) {
        my ( $new_x, $new_y ) = ( $x, $y );
        if     ( 'east'  eq $direction ) { $new_x += 1; }
        elsif ( 'west'  eq $direction ) { $new_x -= 1; }
        elsif ( 'south' eq $direction ) { $new_y += 1; }
        else                            { $new_y -= 1; }

        # if a previous tunnel() through the maze has not visited
        # the square, go there. This will replace the _ or |
        # character in the map with a space when rendered
```

```perl
        if ( have_not_visited( $new_x, $new_y, $maze ) ) {
            # make a two-way "path" between the squares
            $maze->[$y][$x]{$direction} = 1;
            $maze->[$new_y][$new_x]{$OPPOSITE_OF{$direction}}
              = 1;

            # This program will often recurse more than one
            # hundred levels deep and this is Perl's default
            # recursion depth level prior to issuing warnings.
            # In this case, we're telling Perl that we know
            # that we'll exceed the recursion depth and to
            # not warn us about it
            no warnings 'recursion';
            tunnel( $new_x, $new_y, $maze );
        }
    }

    # if we get to here, all squares surround the current square
    # have been visited or are "out of bounds". When we return,
    # we may return to a previous tunnel() call while we're
    # digging, or we return completely to the first tunnel()
    # call, in which case we've finished generating the maze.
    # This return is not strictly necessary, but it makes it
    # clear what we're doing.

    return;
}

sub have_not_visited {
    my ( $x, $y, $maze ) = @_;

    # the first two lines return false  if we're out of bounds
    return if $x < 0 or $y < 0;
    return if $x > $WIDTH - 1 or $y > $HEIGHT - 1;

    # this returns false if we've already visited this cell
    return if $maze->[$y][$x];

    # return true
    return 1;
}

# creates the ASCII strings that will make up the maze
# when printed
sub render_maze {
    my $maze = shift;

# $as_string is the string representation of the maze
    # start with a row of underscores:
    # _____
    my $as_string = "_" x ( 1 + $WIDTH * 2 );

    $as_string .= "\n";
```

```perl
for my $y ( 0 .. $HEIGHT - 1 ) {

    # add the | vertical border at the left side
    $as_string .= "|";

    for my $x ( 0 .. $WIDTH - 1 ) {
        my $cell = $maze->[$y][$x];

        # if the neighbor is true - we have a path
        $as_string .= $cell->{south} ? " " : "_";
        $as_string .= $cell->{east}  ? " " : "|";
    }
    $as_string .= "\n";
}
return $as_string;
}
```

2. Run the program as `perl example_7_4_maze.pl`. You should see output similar to the following:

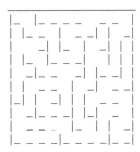

Due to the random nature of this program, your maze will likely not match this one.

How It Works

This is the most complex Try It Out to date, and you should read and run the code a few times to understand how it works.

You start at position 0,0, randomly shuffle the north, south, east, and west directions, and choose the first direction. If that puts you in a square that is not out of bounds (outside of the grid boundaries) and has not yet been visited, then you mark a two-way path between the two squares. Then you move to the new square and repeat the process. This moving to a new square is done recursively by calling `tunnel()` with the new square's coordinates.

When you get to a square surrounded by out of bounds or surrounded by already visited squares, then you return from the `tunnel()` subroutine and the next of the random north, south, east, and west directions is tried for the previous squares.

Eventually, you've tried every north, south, east, and west direction for every square. When that's done, the recursion ends and you render the map. Now, you should look at the successive building of a 3-by-3 map.

```
Y_____
0|_|_|_|
1|_|_|_|
2|_|_|_|
   0 1 2 X
```

As you can see, the upper right-left corner is 0,0; the upper-right is 2,0; the lower-left is 0,2; and the lower-right is 2,2. Because arrays start with 0, the largest index is 2, which is why you refer to $HEIGHT - 1 and $WIDTH - 1 in the code. The code starts in the upper-left corner. Now here's a sample run:

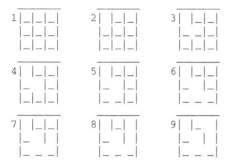

As you can see, the code randomly progresses (tunneles) from 0,0 to 0,1 to 1,1 to 1,2 before ending up at a dead end at 0,2 in the fifth rendition of the maze. What does it do then? It can't go left or down because those are out of bounds. It can't go up because that's a visited square. It can't go right because that's also a visited square. As a result, the tunnel() subroutine returns, but it returns to itself because it calls itself. The code then continues in the for loop for square 1,2. If you play around with this a bit, particularly for larger maps, you can better understand how recursion can draw the entire maze.

The downloadable version available at http://www.Wrox.com is a bit more elaborate. It attempts to redraw the maze at every step to let you see how the maze is built.

THINGS TO WATCH FOR

Writing subroutines allows you to write more maintainable code, but a few guidelines can make your subroutines better. None of these guidelines should be taken as hard-and-fast rules.

Argument Aliasing

Don't forget that the @_ array aliases the arguments to the subroutine. It's easy to forget this and write code that usually works, but breaks when you least expect it. The following is some code that tries to modify an array "in place," but breaks when you pass it hard-coded values:

```
sub fix_names {
    $_ = ucfirst lc $_ foreach @_;
}
fix_names(qw/alice BOB charlie/);
```

That throws a `Modification of a read-only value` error because arguments to `fix_names()` are hard-coded into the program.

Scope Issues

As much as possible, subroutines should rely only on the arguments passed to them and not on variables declared outside of it. You may have noticed that with the exception of one of the `_running_total()` examples (and even that closely encapsulated the state in an outer block), and the "maze" example in this chapter, you've adhered to this rule closely. Why? Take a look at this subroutine:

```
sub withdraw {
    my $amount = shift;
    if ( $customer->{balance} - $amount < $minimum_balance ) {
        croak "$customer->{name} cannot withdraw $amount";
    }
    $customer->{balance} -= $amount;
}
```

Where did `$minimum_balance` come from? Where did `$customer` come from? What happens if something else changes them in a way to make their data invalid? Who changed them? If you move this subroutine somewhere else, are those external variables still in scope?

So why did the `example_7_4_maze.pl` example earlier in this chapter break this rule? It's a trade-off. The opening of the `tunnel()` subroutine looked like this:

```
sub tunnel {
    my ( $x, $y, $maze ) = @_;
```

However, if you pass in all the variables you need (taking into consideration the variables needed in `have_not_visited()`), then it looks like this:

```
sub tunnel {
    my ( $x, $y, $maze, $opposite_of, $height, $width ) = @_;
```

At which point, the argument list starts to get ridiculous, and it's harder to figure out what's going on. For a one-off demonstration, this is okay. In reality, when you need to track this much data, switching to object-oriented programming (Chapter 12) is one strategy to control the chaos.

Doing Too Much

Your author has worked on corporate code with "subroutines" that are thousands of lines long. They're a mess, and it's hard to figure out what's going on.

A subroutine should generally do one thing and do it well. If it needs to do more, it can call other subroutines to help it out. If you try to do too much in a subroutine, not only does the subroutine start to become confusing, but also what happens if something else needs that "extra" behavior you've squeezed into that subroutine? Keep subroutines small and tightly focused.

Too Many Arguments

I've already listed the example of what the `example_7_4_maze.pl tunnel()` function would look like if you passed in all required variables. If you look at the downloadable version, you'd need to pass in even more:

```
my (
    $x,      $y,                     $maze,   $opposite_of, $height, $width,
    $delay, $can_redraw, $delay, $can_redraw,  $clear
) = @_;
```

There are ways to work around this, but this example would have been ridiculous if you passed in that many arguments. When something like this happens, try to rewrite your code in such a way that you need fewer arguments. If you can't, consider switching to named arguments and passing in a hashref; although in this case it would not have helped much.

SUMMARY

You now know far more about subroutines than you probably expected. In Perl, subroutines are powerful and can even be assigned to variables as references and passed around.

Subroutines are a useful way to organize your code with named identifiers to promote code reuse and more readable code.

EXERCISES

1. Write a subroutine named `average()` that, given a list of numbers, returns the average of those numbers. Don't worry about error checking.

2. Take the subroutine `average()` and add error checking to it. Make sure the error is fatal.

   Hint: Try the `looks_like_number()` subroutine from `Scalar::Util`, described earlier in this chapter.

3. Write a subroutine called `make_multiplier()` that takes a number and returns an anonymous subroutine. The returned anonymous subroutine can accept a number and return that number multiplied by the first number. Use your code to make the following print `yes`, twice.
   Hint: Use a closure.

```
my $times_seven = make_multiplier(7);
my $times_five  = make_multiplier(5);
print 21 == $times_seven->(3) ? "yes\n" : "no\n";
print 20 == $times_five->(4)  ? "yes\n" : "no\n";
```

4. Write a `sum()` subroutine that sums its arguments via recursion.

▶ **WHAT YOU LEARNED IN THIS CHAPTER**

TOPIC	KEY CONCEPTS
@_	The subroutine argument array.
return	How to return data from a subroutine.
wantarray	Determine the context in which a subroutine was called.
warn/carp	How to report warnings.
die/croak	How to report problems and stop the program.
eval STRING	Delay the parsing of code until runtime.
eval BLOCK	Trap fatal errors in code.
$@	The default eval error variable.
Try::Tiny	A better way of trapping errors in Perl.
Subroutine refs	How to pass subroutines as variables.
Closures	Subroutines that refer to variables defined in an outer scope.
Prototypes	Sigils added to a subroutine definition to suggest how arguments are passed.
Recursive subroutines	Subroutines that call themselves.
Memoization	Making subroutines faster by using more memory.

8

Regular Expressions

WHAT YOU WILL LEARN IN THIS CHAPTER:

➤ Understanding basic regular expression matching

➤ Understanding substitutions, lookahead/lookbehind anchors and named subexpressions.

➤ Creating useful regular expression modules

WROX.COM CODE DOWNLOADS FOR THIS CHAPTER

The wrox.com code downloads for this chapter are found at `http://www.wrox.com/remtitle .cgi?isbn=1118013840` on the Download Code I've replaced the tabs in the following code with spaces. Please review. The code for this chapter is divided into the following major examples:

➤ `example_8_1_name_and_age.pl`

➤ `example_8_2_dates_pl`

➤ `listing_8_1_data_structure.pl`

➤ `listing 8_2_composed_regexes.pl`

Sometimes instead of exactly matching text, you want to find some text that looks like something you're expecting. This is where Perl's regular expressions come in.

A *regular expression* is a pattern that describes what your text should look like. Regular expressions can get complex, but most of the time they're straightforward when you understand the syntax. Regular expressions are often called *regexes*. (A single regular expression is sometimes called a *regex* or worse, a *regexp*).

An entire book can be (and has been) written on this topic. This chapter focuses on those aspects of regular expressions you're most likely to encounter.

BASIC MATCHING

Say you have a list of strings and want to print all strings containing the letters cat because, like your author, you love cats.

```
my @words = (
    'laphroaig',
    'house cat',
    'catastrophe',
    'cat',
    'is awesome',
);

foreach my $word (@words) {
if ( $word =~ /cat/ ) {
print "$word\n";
    }
}
```

That prints out:

```
house cat
catastrophe
cat
```

The basic syntax of a regular expression match looks like this:

```
STRING =~ REGEX
```

The =~ is known as a binding operator. By default, regular expressions match against the built in $_ variable, but the binding operator binds it to a different string. So you could write the loop like this:

```
foreach (@words) {
if (/cat/) {
print "$_\n";
    }
}
```

There is also a negated form of the binding operator, !~ used to identify strings not matching a given regular expression:

```
foreach my $word (@words) {
if ( $word !~ /cat/ ) {
print "$word\n";
    }
}
```

And that prints the following:

```
laphroaig
is awesome
```

Without the binding operator, use negation like normal:

```
foreach (@words) {
if ( !/cat/ ) {
print "$_\n";
    }
}
```

If you want to match a forward slash (/), you can escape it with a backslash. Alternatively, as with quote-like operators, you can use a different set of delimiters if you precede them with the letter m (for 'm'atch). The following are all equivalent and match the string 1/2.

```
/1\/2/
m"1/2"
m{1/2}
m(1/2)
```

Quantifiers

If you just want to match an exact string, using the index() builtin is faster:

```
my $word = 'dabchick';
if ( index $word, 'abc' >= 0 ) {
print "Found 'abc' in $word\n";
}
```

But sometimes you want to match more or less of a particular string. That's when you use quantifiers in your regular expression. For example, to match the letter a followed by an optional letter b, and then the letter c, use the ? quantifier to show that the b is optional. The following matches both abc and ac:

```
if ( $word =~ /ab?c/ ) { ... }
```

The * shows that you can match zero or more of a given letter:

```
if ( $word =~ /ab*c/ ) { ... }
```

The + shows that you can match one or more of a given letter:

```
if ( $word =~ /ab+c/ ) { ... }
```

This sample code should make this clear. Use the qr() quote-like operator. This enables you to properly quote a regular expression without trying to match it to anything before you're ready.

```perl
my @strings = qw(
abba
abacus
abbba
babble
Barbarella
Yello
);

my @regexes = (
qr/ab?/,
qr/ab*/,
qr/ab+/,
);

foreach my $string (@strings) {
foreach my $regex (@regexes) {
if ( $string =~ $regex ) {
print "'$regex' matches '$string'\n";
        }
    }
}
```

And that prints out the following (the exact syntax of the stringified regex might change depending on your version of Perl):

```
'(?-xism:ab?)' matches 'abba'
'(?-xism:ab*)' matches 'abba'
'(?-xism:ab+)' matches 'abba'
'(?-xism:ab?)' matches 'abacus'
'(?-xism:ab*)' matches 'abacus'
'(?-xism:ab+)' matches 'abacus'
'(?-xism:ab?)' matches 'abbba'
'(?-xism:ab*)' matches 'abbba'
'(?-xism:ab+)' matches 'abbba'
'(?-xism:ab?)' matches 'babble'
'(?-xism:ab*)' matches 'babble'
'(?-xism:ab+)' matches 'babble'
'(?-xism:ab?)' matches 'Barbarella'
'(?-xism:ab*)' matches 'Barbarella'
```

Sadly, nothing matches `Yello`, an excellent music group, but studying the rest of the matches should make it clear what is happening.

However, you may wonder what that bizarre `(?-xism:ab*)` is doing on the regex you printed? Those are regular expression modifiers, which are covered in the "Modifiers and Anchors" section of this chapter.

If you need to be more precise, you can use the `{n,m}` syntax. This tells Perl that you want to match at least *n* times and no more than *m* times. There are three variants of this:

```perl
/ab{3}c/    # 1 a, 3 'b's, 1 c (only "abbbc")
/ab{3,}c/   # 1 a, 3 or more 'b's, 1 c
/ab{3,6}c/  # 1 a, 3 to 6 'b's, 1 c
```

Table 8-1 summarizes the different types of regex quantifiers and their meaning.

TABLE 8-1: Regex Quantifier

QUANTIFIER	MEANING
*	Match 0 or more times.
+	Match 1 or more times.
?	Match 0 or 1 times.
{n}	Match exactly *n* times.
{n,}	Match at least *n* times.
{n,m}	Match at least *n* times but not more than m times.

By default, all quantifiers in Perl are greedy. That means they'll try to match as much as possible. For example, the dot metacharacter (.) means "match anything" except newlines and .* matches the rest of the string up to a newline. In the "Extracting Data" section later in this chapter when you learn to print out just the bits you've matched, you'll discover that for the word cataract, the regular expression a.+a matches atara and not just ata. If you want a quantifier to be lazy (match as little as possible) instead of greedy, just follow it with a question mark:

```
if ( "cataract" =~ /a.+?a/ ) {
    # the first match is now "ata" instead of "atara"
}
```

> **NOTE** By now you've noticed that some characters in regexes have a special meaning. These are called metacharacters. The following are the metacharacters that Perl regular expressions recognize:
>
> {}[]()^$.|*+?\
>
> If you want to match the literal version of any of those characters, you must precede them with a backslash, \. As you go through the chapter, the meaning of these metacharacters will become clear.

Escape Sequences

Sometimes, you want to match a wide variety of different things that are difficult to type, or may match a wide range of characters. Many of the common cases are handled with escape sequences. Table 8-2 explains some of these sequences and we'll give a few practical examples after the table. This is not an exhaustive list, just a list of the more common sequences.

TABLE 8-2 Common Escape Sequences

ESCAPE	MEANING
\A	Beginning of string.
\b	Word boundary.
\c*X*	ASCII control character (for example, CTRL-C is \cC).
\d	Unicode digit.
\D	Not a Unicode digit.
\E	End case (\F, \L, \U) or quotemeta (\Q) translation, only if interpolated.
\e	Escape character (ESC, not the backslash).
\g{*GROUP*}	Named or numbered capture.
\G	End of match of m//g.
\k<*GROUP*>	Named capture.
\l	Lowercase next character only, if interpolated.
\L	Lowercase until \E, if interpolated.
\N{*CHARNAME*}	Named character, alias, or sequence, if interpolated. You must use charnames (see Unicode in Chapter 9).
\n	Newline.
\p{*PROPERTY*}	Character with named Unicode property.
\P{*PROPERTY*}	Character without named Unicode property.
\Q	Ignore metacharacters until \E.
\r	Return character.
\s	Whitespace.
\S	Not whitespace.
\t	Tab.
\u	Uppercase next character only, if interpolated.
\U	Uppercase until \E, if interpolated.
\w	Word character.
a\W	Not word character.
\z	True at end of string only.
\Z	True right before final newline or at end of string.

Of those, the ones you'll most commonly see are \w (word characters), \d (digits), \s (whitespace), and \b (word boundary).

Say you have some strings and you want to find all strings containing phone numbers matching the pattern *XXX-XXX-XXXX* where *X* can be any digit. You might use the following regular expression:

```
for my (@strings) {
if ( /\d{3}-\d{3}-\d{4}/ ) {
print "Phone number found: $string\n";
    }
}
```

And that indeed matches 555-867-5309. Unfortunately, it also matches a string containing 555555555-867-444444444 and that, presumably, is not a phone number. You can deal with this in several ways. If you know the phone number has whitespace on either side, you could try to match whitespace with the \s escape:

```
for my (@strings) {
if ( /\s\d{3}-\d{3}-\d{4}\s/ ) {
print "Phone number found: $string\n";
    }
}
```

Maybe you don't know what is on either side of the phone number. You might make a mistake and try to match non-digits with \D:

```
for my (@strings) {
if ( /\D\d{3}-\d{3}-\d{4}\D/ ) {
print "Phone number found: $string\n";
    }
}
```

That looks reasonable, but try this:

```
print "Phone: 123-456-7890" =~ /\D\d{3}-\d{3}-\d{4}\D/
    ? "Yes"
    : "No";
```

That prints No. Why? Because \D must match something. The first \D matches a space, but the second one has nothing to match. What you want is the \b. That matches a word boundary. A word is matched by \w and that's any alphanumeric character, plus the underscore. A word boundary matches no characters but matches when there is a transition between a word and nonword character. (This means that \w\b\w can never match anything).

```
print "Phone: 123-456-7890" =~ /\b\d{3}-\d{3}-\d{4}\b/
    ? "Yes"
    : "No";
```

That prints Yes because the final \b matches between the final digit and the end of the string.

> **WARNING** The \d matches any Unicode (Chapter 9) character that represents a digit, and there are far more than you probably know about, including a few mistakes that have crept into the Unicode standard. If you want to match only the digits 0 through 9, use the [0-9] character class. See sections "Character Classes" and "Grouping" later in this chapter

Extracting Data

At this point, you're probably thinking "That's nice, but what good is that data if you can't get it?" It's simple: Put parentheses around any data in a regular expression that you want to extract. For every set of capturing parentheses, use a $1, $2, $3, and so on, to access that data.

> **NOTE** These special variables will only be populated if the match succeeds.

```
if ( "Phone: 123-456-7890" =~ /(\b\d{3}-\d{3}-\d{4}\b)/ ) {
my $phone = $1;
print "The phone number is $phone\n";
}
```

And that prints the following:

```
The phone number is 123-456-7890
```

You can use this to populate data structures. Consider the following block of text. You want to create a hash of names and their ages. Listing 8-1 shows (code file listing_8_1_data_structure.pl) an example of this.

LISTING 8-1: Building Data Structures with Regexes

```
use strict;
use warnings;
use diagnostics;
use Data::Dumper;

my $text = <<'END';
Name: Alice Allison Age: 23
Occupation: Spy
Name: Bob Barkely   Age: 45
Occupation: Fry Cook
Name: Carol Carson  Age: 44
Occupation: Manager
Name: Prince        Age: 53
Occupation: World Class Musician
```

```
    END

    my %age_for;

    foreach my $line (split /\n/, $text) {
    if ( $line =~ /Name:\s+(.*?)\s+Age:\s+(\d+)/ ) {
            $age_for{$1} = $2;
        }
    }
    print Dumper(\%age_for);
```

And that prints something like this:

```
    $VAR1 = {
              'Bob Barkely' => '45',
              'Alice Allison' => '23',
              'Carol Carson' => '44',
              'Prince' => '53'
            };
```

> **NOTE** *If captures starting with $1 sound odd, it might be because other indexes in Perl start with 0 and not 1. In this case, $0 is reserved for the name of the program executed.*

If that regular expression is confusing, the following is a way to make it read easier: Put a /x modifier at the end, and all whitespace (unless escaped with a backslash) will be ignored. You can then put comments at the end of each part to explain it.

```
    my $name_and_age = qr{
        Name:
        \s+        # 1 or more whitespace
        (.*?)      # The name in $1
        \s+        # 1 or more whitespace
        Age:
        \s+        # 1 or more whitespace
        (\d+)      # The age in $2
    }x;

    foreach my $line (split /\n/, $text) {
    if ( $line =~ $name_and_age ) {
            $age_for{$1} = $2;
        }
    }
```

That makes regexes much easier to read.

As was explained earlier, the . metacharacter will match anything except newlines, but see the /s modifier in the "Modifiers and Anchors" section of this chapter. So .* means match zero or more of anything. The .* is made lazy by adding a question mark after it. If we didn't do this, it would have matched greedily and pulled in all the whitespace it could before the \s+. The resulting data structure would have looked like this:

```
$VAR1 = {
        'Carol Carson ' => '44',
        'Alice Allison' => '23',
        'Bob Barkely  ' => '45',
        'Prince       ' => '53'
      };
```

> **WARNING** *Be careful when using the . metacharacter. Avoid it you possibly can. Because it matches indiscriminately, it's easy for it to match something you don't intend. It's far better to have a regular expression state explicitly what you want to match. For the* $name_and_age *regex, your author probably would have written* [[:alpha:]]*?, *but this hasn't been covered yet.*

You can also use those digit ($1, $2, and so on) variables in a regular expression. However, you precede them with a backslash. The $1 captured by the first set of parentheses is matched by \1. The following is how you can find double words:

```
print "Four score score and seven years ago" =~ /\b(\w+)\s+\1\b/
    ? "The word ($1) was doubled"
    : "No doubles found";
```

And that prints the following:

```
The word (score) was doubled
```

Use the \b (word boundary) after the \1 to ensure that strings such as the theramin are not reported as doubled words.

Modifiers and Anchors

A regular expression modifier is one or more characters appended to the end of the regular expression that modifies it.

Earlier, when printing a regular expression, you saw (?-xism:ab?). The (?-) syntax shows the modifiers in effect for the regular expression. If the modifying letter is after the minus sign (-), then it does not apply to the regex. For the $name_and_age regular expression used earlier, you can also add an/i modifier at the end of it. When that's added, it makes the regular expression case-insensitive. /name/i matches Name, name, nAMe, and so on.

For the (?-) syntax, if a modifying letter is before the minus sign, it means that it applies to this regex:

```
my $name_and_age = qr{
    Name:
    \s+         # 1 or more whitespace
    (.*?)       # The name in $1
```

```
    \s+        # 1 or more whitespace
    Age:
    \s+        # 1 or more whitespace
    (\d+)      # The age in $2
}xi;
print $name_and_age;
```

And that prints the following:

```
(?ix-sm:
    Name:
    \s+        # 1 or more whitespace
    (.*?)      # The name in $1
    \s+        # 1 or more whitespace
    Age:
    \s+        # 1 or more whitespace
    (\d+)      # The age in $2
)
```

Table 8-3 shows the most common modifiers.

TABLE 8-3: Common Regex Modifiers

MODIFIER	MEANING
/x	Ignore unescaped whitepace.
/i	Case-insensitive match.
/g	Global matching (keep matching until no more matches).
/m	Multiline mode (explained in a bit).
/s	Single line mode (The . metacharacter now matches \n).

You already know about the /x and /i modifiers, so now look at the /g modifier. That enables you to globally match something. For example, to print every non-number in a string, use this code:

```
my $string = '';
while ("a1b2c3dddd444eee66" =~ /(\D+)/g ) {
    $string .= $1;
}
print $string;
```

And that prints abcddddeee, as you expect.

You can also use this to count things, if you're so inclined. Here's how to count every occurrence of a word ending in the letters at.

```
my $silly = 'The fat cat sat on the mat';
my $at_words = 0;
$at_words++ while $silly =~ /\b\w+at/g;
```

The $at_words variable contains the number 4 after that code runs. If you don't like statement modifiers (putting the while at the end of the statement), you can write it this way:

```
while ( $silly =~ /\b\w+at/g ) {
    $at_words++;
}
```

You might recall that while loops are often used with iterators. The /g modifier effectively turns the regular expression in to an iterator.

The /m and /s modifiers look a bit strange, but to discuss those, you need to understand anchor metacharacters first.

Anchor metacharacters are used to "anchor" a regular expression to a particular place in a string. They do not match an actual character. You've already seen one anchor: \b. The ^ is used to match the start of the string, and the $ is used to match the end of the string. They are synonymous with \A and \Z. Both $ and \Z match the end of a string or before a newline. Therefore, if you have a newline in your string, the $ matches immediately before the newline.

```
my $prisoner = <<"END";
I will not be pushed, filed, stamped, indexed, briefed, debriefed or numbered.
My life is my own.
END
print $prisoner =~ /^I/          ? "Yes\n" : "No\n";
print $prisoner =~ /^My/         ? "Yes\n" : "No\n";
print $prisoner =~ /numbered\.$/ ? "Yes\n" : "No\n";
print $prisoner =~ /own\.$/      ? "Yes\n" : "No\n";
That prints:
Yes
No
No
Yes
```

In other words, only /^I/ and /own\.$/ matched. If you want /^My/ and /numbered\.$/ to match, use the /m switch to force a multiline mode. That forces the ^ and $ to match at the beginning and end of every string (separated by newlines) instead of the beginning and end of the entire string.

You also need to know that if the $ is not the last character in the regular expression, Perl assumes that this is the sigil introducing a scalar variable:

```
my $match = "aa";
if ( $some_string =~ /$match/ ) {
    # match words containing aa
}
```

Later, you see how to take advantage of this to build complicated regular expressions that would ordinarily be too difficult to write.

Character Classes

Sometimes, you want to match a few characters as even numbers. You can do this with a character class. You put the characters you want in square brackets, []. Here's a silly way to extract all positive, even, ASCII integers from a string:

```
my $string = '42 85 abcd 8 4ever foobar 666 43';
my @even;
push @even => $1 while $string =~ /\b(\d*[02468])\b/g;
```

That leaves @even containing the numbers 42, 8, and 666. Here's how it works. By now you already know that the \b matches a word boundary, so the 4 in 4ever cannot be matched because not only is that an abomination to the English language, but also there is no "boundary" between the 4 and ever.

The \d*[02468] means "zero or more digits, followed by a 0, 2, 4, 6, or 8" — in other words, a positive even integer.

In a character class, only the -]\^$ characters are considered "special." So a . can match a literal dot, not "any character except newline." If the first character is a caret, ^, then it's a negated character class. This means it can match anything except what's listed in the character class, and you can use this to match odd numbers:

```
my $string = '42 85 abcd 8 4ever foobar 666 43';
my @odd;
push @odd => $1 while $string =~ /\b(\d*[^02468])\b/g;
```

That pushes 85 and 43 onto the @odd array. (Of course, you could have simply used [13579] for the character class.)

The dash (-) if used any place after the first character in a character class tries to create a range. For example, as mentioned earlier \d matches any Unicode character. (Chapter 9 discusses Unicode.) If you want to match only the 0 through 9 ASCII digits, you can use [0-9]. This is generally easier to read than [0123456789]; although, they mean the same thing.

You can have multiple ranges in a character class. [0 9a-fA-F] can match all hexadecimal digits.

Perl also supports POSIX character classes. These have the form [:name:]. Despite the square brackets around them, you must use an additional set of square brackets around them. For example, to match all alphabetical and numeric characters (the same as \w, but without the underscore), you could use [[:alnum:]]. You can combine these, too. To match all digits and punctuation characters, use [[:digit:][:punct:]]. Table 8-4 explains Perl's POSIX-style character classes and their meaning.

TABLE 8-4: POSIX Character Classes

CLASS	MEANING
`[:alpha:]`	Letters (Think "Unicode" — Chapter 9. It's more than you think.)
`[:alnum:]`	`[:alpha:]` plus Unicode digits.
`[:ascii:]`	ASCII only.
`[:cntrl:]`	Control characters.
`[:digit:]`	Unicode digits.
`[:graph:]`	Alphanumeric and punctuation characters.
`[:lower:]`	Lowercase letters.
`[:print:]`	Printable characters (`[:graph:]` plus `[:space:]`).
`[:space:]`	`\s`. In other words, tab, newline, form feed, and carriage return.
`[:upper:]`	Uppercase characters.
`[:xdigit:]`	Hexadecimal digits (`[0-9a-fA-F]`).
`[:word:]`	`\w`.

> **NOTE** *A common, confusing mistake for regular expressions is to try to use POSIX-style regular expressions like this:*
>
> ```
> if ( $string =~ /[:alnum:]/ ) {
>    ...
> }
> ```
>
> *Not only does that not work, but it also doesn't generate an error. This is because Perl sees* `[:alnum:]` *as being a character class matching* :, a, l, n, u, m. *(It's OK to list a character more than once in a character class.) You must write that* `[[:alnum:]]` *for Perl to recognize the regex correctly.*

As a Perl extension to POSIX character classes, you can include a ^ after the `[:` to indicate negation. So to match anything that is not a control character, use `[[:^cntrl:]]`.

Grouping

For a character class, list the types of characters you're looking for. For a group, you can list the types of words you're looking for. To group words (or patterns), put parentheses around them; then you can do all sorts of interesting things, including using quantifiers:

```
# cat, optionally followed by astrophe
/cat(astrophe)?/
```

You can use a | character in the group to alternate between different patterns:

```
# matches catastrophe, cataract and catapult, but not cat
/cat(astrophe|aract|apult)/
```

You've seen parentheses before used when you want to extract data into the $1, $2, and $3 variables and so on. If you want to group but don't want to extract the data (perhaps you're inserting a group into an existing regex and don't want to change all your match variables), use the (?:...) syntax:

```
# matches catastrophe or cataract, but without setting $1
/cat(?:astrophe|aract)/
```

As you've already seen (?-xism:...) earlier, you may wonder if the (?:...) syntax is related — it's the same thing. You can set those modifiers to tell Perl how to behave. For example, make part of a regex case-insensitive. Maybe you're writing code to list everyone who is a volunteer. Unfortunately, the people who typed in the data typed volunteer, Volunteer, and VOLUNTEER.

```
use Data::Dumper;

my $text = <<'END';
Name: Alice Allison  Position: VOLUNTEER
Name: Bob Barkely    Position: Manager
Name: Carol Carson   Position: Volunteer
Name: David Dark     Position: Geek
Name: e.e. cummings Position: Volunteer
name: Fran Francis   Position: volunteer
END

my @volunteers;
foreach my $line (split /\n/, $text) {
if ( $line =~ m<Name:\s+(.*?)\s+Position:\s+(?i-xsm:volunteer)\b> ) {
push @volunteers => $1;
    }
}
print Dumper(\@volunteers);
```

And that prints the following:

```
$VAR1 = [
        'Alice Allison',
        'Carol Carson',
        'e.e. cummings'
      ];
```

You can sneakily put the . in the Name pattern to still match e.e. cummings.

Why didn't it add Fran Francis to that list? Because she has name: in front of her name, but you didn't make that part of the regular expression case-insensitive.

Typing `(?i-xsm:volunteer)` might be a bit cumbersome. If the entire regular expression is not using the `/x`, `/s`, or `/m` modifiers, you don't need the `-xsm` in the group. You need them only if you need to explicitly disable them — and you don't need to list all of them. So you could have written `(?i:volunteer)`, which is cleaner.

TRY IT OUT   **Using /g and [[:alpha:]]**

Earlier you extracted names and ages from a section of text by splitting the text on newlines and matching resulting lines against a regular expression. All the code in this Try It Out uses the `example_8_1_name_and_age.pl` code file.

```
foreach my $line (split /\n/, $text) {
if ( $line =~ /Name:\s+(.*?)\s+Age:\s+(\d+)/ ) {
        $age_for{$1} = $2;
    }
}
```

If `$text` is huge, that's rather inefficient and can better be handled with a while loop and the `/g` modifier. Also, we mentioned earlier that the `(.*?)` should be avoided. Now let's be more precise.

1. Type in the following program, and save it as `example_8_1_name_and_age.pl`:

```
use strict;
use warnings;
use Data::Dumper;

my $text = <<'END';
Name: Alice Allison Age: 23
Occupation: Spy
Name: Bob Barkely   Age: 45
Occupation: Fry Cook
Name: Carol Carson Age: 44
Occupation: Manager
Name: Prince        Age: 53
Occupation: World Class Musician
END

my %age_for;
while ( $text =~ m<Name:\s+([[:alpha:] ]+?)\s+Age:\s+(\d+)>g ) {
    $age_for{$1} = $2;
}
print Dumper(\%age_for);
```

2. Run the program with `perl example_8_1_name_and_age.pl`. You should see the following output:

```
$VAR1 = {
          'Bob Barkely' => '45',
          'Alice Allison' => '23',
          'Carol Carson' => '44',
          'Prince' => '53'
        };
```

How It Works

This works almost the same as the previous version but with some important differences. First, the /g turns the regular expression match into an iterator you can use with the `while` loop. It forces the regular expression to keep matching until no more matches are found.

The example uses `m<...>` for the regular expression — just to remind you that you can use different delimiters.

The `[[:alpha:] ]` matches alphabetic characters plus a space character. Note the space before the trailing square bracket.

In short, there's nothing magical here, but now you can move to some more advanced regular expression techniques.

ADVANCED MATCHING

As you work with regular expressions more, you'll want to do more powerful things with them. Regular expressions are a special-purpose declarative language embedded in Perl. Although they're generally not Turing complete (http://en.wikipedia.org/wiki/Turing_complete), they're still powerful. (Even if they were Turing complete, you'd upset a lot of programmers if you wrote your programs solely in terms of regular expressions.)

Substitutions

Substitutions are the next logical step in your programming journey (although not an "advanced" feature of regexes). They have the following form:

```
s/regular expression/replacement text/
```

You prefer a rare steak to a well-done steak (as you should), so you need to fix this menu item:

```
my $main_course = "A well-done filet mignon";
$main_course =~ s/well-done/rare/;
print $main_course.
```

And that prints `A rare filet mignon`.

As with the normal `m//`, you can use the `/g` modifier to make substitutions global. The following is a (stupid) technique to remove all doubled words from a text:

```
my $text = "a a b b c cat dddd";
$text =~ s/\b(\w+)\s+\1\b/$1/g;
print $text;
```

And that leaves you with `a b c cat dd`.

Now use the `/x` modifier to make this a bit clearer.

```
$text =~ s/
    \b              # word boundary
    (\w+)           # capture to $1
    \s+             # whitespace
    \1              # doubled word (matches $1)
    \b              # word boundary
 /$1/gx;            # replace doubled with $1
```

The left side of the substitution is a regular expression, and the right side is not. Thus, you can use \1 inside the regex and $1 outside the regex.

Lookahead/Lookbehind Anchors

As you know, an anchor matches a particular place in a string without actually matching a character. Lookahead/behind anchors (and their negative counterparts) are primarily used with substitutions (and sometimes split()) to allow fine-grained control over matching. A positive lookahead enables you to match text following a regular expression, but not including it in the regular expression. The positive lookahead syntax is:

```
(?=$regex)
```

For example, if you want to replace all xxx followed by yyy with ---, but not replacing the yyy, you can do this:

```
my $string = 'xxxyyyxxxbbbxxxyyy';
$string =~ s/
xxx       # match xxx
(?=yyy)   # followed by yyy, but not included in the match
  /---/xg;
print $string;
```

And that prints out the following:

```
---yyyxxxbbb ---yyy
```

The negative lookahead syntax is (?!$regex). That enables you to match a regular expression not followed by another regular expression, but the negative lookahead is not included in the match. Say your young child is writing a "compare and contrast" essay about Queen Elizabeth of the United Kingdom and queen bees and ants. She writes this:

```
The queen rules over the United Kingdom and is loved by
her subjects but a queen ant just lays a lot of eggs.
The queen lives in a palace and the queen bee lives
in a hive.
```

Obviously, you are horrified because the queen of the United Kingdom should be referred to as Queen Elizabeth in this context. So you write this:

```
my $childs_essay = <<'END_ESSAY';
The queen rules over the United Kingdom and is loved by
her subjects but a queen ant just lays a lot of eggs.
```

```
The queen lives in a palace and the queen bee lives
in a hive.
END_ESSAY

$childs_essay =~ s/the queen/Queen Elizabeth/gi;
print $childs_essay;
```

And that prints out the following:

```
Queen Elizabeth rules over the United Kingdom and is loved by
her subjects but a queen ant just lays a lot of eggs.
Queen Elizabeth lives in a palace and Queen Elizabeth bee lives
in a hive.
```

Obviously, that's not going to earn your daughter a good grade, so let's use a negative lookahead to replace only those instances of queen not followed by the words ant or bee.

```
my $childs_essay = <<'END_ESSAY';
The queen rules over the United Kingdom and is loved by
her subjects but a queen ant just lays a lot of eggs.
The queen lives in a palace and the queen bee lives
in a hive.
END_ESSAY

$childs_essay =~
s/
the
    \s+
queen
    \s+
    (?!ant|bee)
    /Queen Elizabeth /gxi;

print $childs_essay;
```

And that prints out the desired paragraph:

```
Queen Elizabeth rules over the United Kingdom and is loved by
her subjects but a queen ant just lays a lot of eggs.
Queen Elizabeth lives in a palace and the queen bee lives
in a hive.
```

Your daughter may not get a wonderful grade for the essay, but at least she'll be following proper editorial style.

> **NOTE** *The Queen Elizabeth/queen ant example seems fairly contrived, but it's based on a true story of an online news organization whose computer-driven editorial rules had a news story about ants referring to Queen Elizabeth laying thousands of eggs and having a lifespan of many times that of her workers. We hope Her Majesty was amused.*

Positive lookbehinds are designated with `(?<=$regex)` and negative lookbehinds are written as `(?<!$regex)`. They are identical to their lookahead counterparts with two exceptions:

➤ They match text before the regular expression.

➤ They cannot match a variable-width regex, meaning that `*`, `+`, and `?` quantifiers are not allowed.

Named Subexpressions (5.10)

If you use Perl 5.10 or better, you can also use named subexpressions. Ordinarily, you refer to a captured group in the regex with `\1`, `\2`, and so on. After a successful match, those are `$1`, `$2`, and so on. With named subexpressions you can name them and make things easier to read.

To name a subexpression, use the syntax `(?<name>...)`. To refer to it again inside of the regex, use `\g{name}`. To refer to the match outside of the regex, be aware that it's a key in the special `%+` hash. For example, the double-word stripper would look something like this:

> **NOTE** The `%+` hash is a special variable that contains only entries for the last successfully matched named subexpressions in the current scope. Thus, if a named subexpression fails to match, it will not have an entry in the `%+` hash. There is a corresponding `%-` hash not covered here. See `perldoc perlvar` and `perldoc perlretut` for more information.

```
use v5.10;

my $text = "a a b b c cat dddd";
$text =~
s/
     \b
(?<word>\w+)
     \s+
     \g{word}
     \b
     /$+{word}/gx;

print $text;
```

For a clearer example consider matching dates. You may remember the code to convert a date to the ISO 8601 format. Here you can rewrite it with named subexpressions.

Before:

```
my $provided_date = '28-9-2011';

$provided_date =~ s{
    (\d\d?)       # day
```

```
    [-/]          # - or /
    (\d\d?)        # month
    [-/]          # - or /
    (\d\d\d\d)      # year
}
{
sprintf "$3-%02d-%02d", $2, $1
}ex;

print $provided_date;
```

After:

```
my $provided_date = '28-9-2011';

$provided_date =~ s{
(?<day>\d\d?)
    [-/]
(?<month>\d\d?)
    [-/]
(?<year>\d\d\d\d)
}
{
sprintf "$+{year}-%02d-%02d", $+{month}, $+{day}
}ex;

print $provided_date;
```

This has an added advantage of no longer requiring you to keep track of the number of the capture. Therefore, if you need to switch the day and month around, use this code:

```
s{
(?<month>\d\d?)        # month
        [-/]
(?<day>\d\d?)
        [-/]
(?<year>\d\d\d\d)
    }
    {
sprintf "$+{year}-%02d-%02d", $+{month}, $+{day}
}ex;
```

The regular expression changed, but the substitution did not.

You can also use the named parameters outside of the substitution as long as you're in the same scope, for example:

```
print LOGFILE "converted provided date to ",
sprintf "$+{year}-%02d-%02d", $+{month}, $+{day};
```

TRY IT OUT Converting Date Formats

Substitutions are common and you need to get used to them. Use a simple example converting the U.S. style MM/DD/YYYY dates to the more common (outside the United States) DD/MM/YYYY dates. All the code in this Try It Out uses the example_8_2_dates.pl code file.

1. Type in the following program and save it as example_8_2_dates.pl.

```
use strict;
use warnings;
use Data::Dumper;

my @dates = qw(
    01/23/1987
    11/30/2000
    02/29/1980
);

foreach (@dates) {
s{\A(\d\d)/(\d\d)/}
    {$2/$1/};
}
print Dumper(\@dates);
```

2. Run the program with perlexample_8_1_dates.pl. You should see the following output:

```
$VAR1 = [
         '23/01/1987',
         '30/11/2000',
         '29/02/1980'
       ];
```

How It Works

This simple example has several subtleties you should be aware of because they crop up often in Perl code.

The substitution operator, s///, when the binding operator, =~, is not used, defaults to $_. Further, like the regular expressions you've seen earlier, you're permitted to use alternative delimiters. You didn't use / for the delimiter because that would have forced you to escape the other forward slashes and make the substitution harder to read:

```
s/\A(\d\d)\/(\d\d)\//$2\/$1\//;
```

As a side-effect to using balanced delimiters ([] and <> would also have been nice options), you can put the regular expression and the substitution value on separate lines.

```
s{\A(\d\d)/(\d\d)/}
    {$2/$1/};
```

This is not required, but it can also help improve readability.

Another interesting thing you can do with substitutions is execute code via the /e modifier. When using this modifier, the substitution code is not considered to just be a string; it's Perl code to be evaluated. For example, consider the substitution to change American-style dates:

```
s{\A(\d\d)/(\d\d)/}
    {$2/$1/};
```

What if the U.S. style date had been written 28/2/2011? Well, you know that's February 28th, but your regex doesn't. And maybe it was sometimes entered as 12-12-1999. That's a pain, too. Let's fix that. While we're at it, we'll also convert the data to the ISO 8601 unambiguous date format of YYYY-MM-DD.

```
local $_ = '28-9-2011';
s{
        (\d\d?)      # day
        [-/]         # - or /
        (\d\d?)      # month
        [-/]         # - or /
        (\d\d\d\d)   # year
    }
    {
sprintf "$3-%02d-%02d", $2, $1
}ex;
print;
```

And that correctly prints 2011-09-28. Use the /x modifier to make it easy to read. The /x modifier never applies to the right side of the substitution. Instead, you can use extra whitespace here because the /e modifier turns the right side into Perl code instead of a simple string.

All the other regex modifiers, including the /g, can be used with substitutions.

COMMON REGULAR EXPRESSION ISSUES

While you're messing around with regular expressions, consider a few common issues that can arise. These may seem superfluous to this chapter, but these issues are raised so often that they bear mentioning. The following are a few things you can do with regular expressions, along with a few things you should not do.

Regexp::Common

You know a number might be represented as 2, 2.3, .4, -3e17, and so on. You can legally write a number in a variety of ways, and writing a regular expression for it is hard. So don't write it. When you need a regular expression that you think someone else has already written, look at the Regexp::Common module to see if it's in there. The following is how to match a real number:

```
use Regexp::Common;
print "yes" if '-3e17' =~ $RE{num}{real};
```

The following is how to blank out profanity. (Knowing it would never get through the editorial process, I regretfully omitted the full example).

```
use Regexp::Common;
my $text = 'something awful or amusing';
$text =~ s/($RE{profanity})/'*' x length($1)/eg;
print $text;
```

There's more in this module, so install it and have fun reading the docs.

E-mail Addresses

If you've never read RFC 822 (`http://tools.ietf.org/html/rfc822`), your author recommends that you do. It's a great way to get to sleep. It's also a great way to realize that if you've been trying to validate e-mail addresses with a regular expression, you've been doing it the wrong way.

E-mail addresses can contain comments. The local part of the domain name cannot contain spaces (unless they're in comments), but they can contain dashes. They can even start with dashes. Lots of people with last names such as O'Malley have trouble sending and receiving e-mail because `o'malley@example.com` is a perfectly valid e-mail address, but many e-mail validation tools think that apostrophe is naughty.

So whatever you do, don't do this:

```
if ( $email =~ /^\w+\@(?:\w+\.)+\w$/ ) {
# Congrats. Many good e-mails rejected!
}
```

You see that a lot in code. It doesn't work. You can't use regular expressions to match e-mail addresses. The one your author knows of that is closest to being correct is an almost one-hundred-dred line (beautiful) monstrosity written by Jeffrey Friedl. You can see it in the source code of `Email::Valid`; the module you should use instead follows:

```
use Email::Valid;
print (Email::Valid->address($maybe_email) ? 'yes' : 'no');
```

Actually, `Email::Valid` tells you only if the e-mail address is well-formed. If you ask nicely, it tries to tell you if the host exists. It cannot tell you if the e-mail is valid.

> **NOTE** There is only one way to know if an e-mail is valid: Send an e-mail using that address and hope someone responds. Even then, you may get a false bounce or the mail server might be down. Nothing's perfect.

HTML

Eventually, every programmer hears about people trying to parse HTML with regular expressions. The following is an attempt your author tried to make once:

```
$html =~ s{
            (<a\s(?:[^>](?!href))*href\s*)
            (&(&[^;]+;)?(?:.(?!\3))+(?:\3)?)
            ([^>]+>)
         }
         {$1 .decode_entities($2) .   $4}gsexi;
```

Do you know what that does? Neither do I. I can't remember what I was trying to do, but I don't care because it didn't work. I learned to use a proper HTML parser instead. HTML does not have regular grammar and thus cannot be properly parsed with regular expressions. Even if it did, there are plenty of tricky edge cases. For example, what if you have angle brackets in quotes?

```
<input type="text" name="user" placeholder="<enter name>">
```

Or what it someone uses single quotes? Or no quotes? Or uses capitalized tags? There are many examples of HTML that browsers handle nicely, but you would struggle to parse with regular expressions.

That said, if you use a well-defined subset of HTML and you write small, one-off scripts for extracting data, you can use regexes. Just don't blame anyone but yourself when it breaks. Instead, consider HTML::TreeBuilder, HTML::TokeParser::Simple, or any of a variety of other great HTML parsing modules.

Composing Regular Expressions

Sometimes, a regular expression is complicated. For example, you might want to match an employee number in the format *department-grade-number*, where *department* is one of four different valid department codes for a company, AC, IT, MG, JA, the *grade* is a two-digit number from 00 to 20, and the *number* is any five or six-digit number. The regular expression might look like this:

```
if ( /\b(AC|IT|MG|JA)-([01]\d|20)-(\d{5,6})\b/ ) {
my $dept       = $1;
my $grade      = $2;
my $emp_number = $3;
    ...
}
```

For regular expressions, that one isn't too bad, but maybe you still want it to be a bit easier to read. You can compose regular expressions easily by using variables and the qr// operator.

```
my $depts         = join '|' =>qw(AC IT MG JA);
my $dept_re       = qr/$depts/;
my $grade_re      = qr/[01]\d|20/;
my $emp_number_re = qr/\d{5,6}/;
if ( /\b($dept_re)-($grade_re)-($emp_number_re)\b/ ) {
my $dept       = $1;
my $grade      = $2;
my $emp_number = $3;
    ...
}
```

The qr() operator can "quote" your regular expression and, in some cases, precompile it, leading to significant performance gains when you later use it in a match.

As a more complicated example, your author was writing a preprocessor for Prolog code (Prolog is a programming language) and wanted to match math expressions. The following are all valid math expressions in Prolog (the actual code is more complicated):

```
2 + 3
Var
-3.2e5 % SomeVar / Var
```

The code to match those is presented in Listing 8-2 (code file `listing_8_2_composed_regexes.pl`).

LISTING 8-2: Building Complex Regular Expressions from Smaller Ones

```perl
use strict;
use warnings;
use diagnostics;
useRegexp::Common;
my $num_re = $RE{num}{real};
my $var_re = qr/[[:upper:]][[:alnum:]_]*/;
my $op_re  = qr{[-+*/%]};
my $math_term_re = qr/$num_re|$var_re/;
my $expression_re       = qr/
    $math_term_re
    (?:
        \s*
        $op_re
        \s*
        $math_term_re
    )*
/x;
my @expressions = (
    '2 + 3',
' + 2 - 3',
    'Var',
    '-3.2e5 % SomeVar / Var',
    'not_a_var + 2',
);
foreach my $expression (@expressions) {
if ( $expression =~ /^$expression_re$/ ) {
print "($expression) is a valid expression\n";
    }
else {
print "($expression) is not a valid expression\n";
    }
}
```

And that prints the wanted output:

```
(2 + 3) is a valid expression
( + 2 - 3) is not a valid expression
(Var) is a valid expression
(-3.2e5 % SomeVar / Var) is a valid expression
(not_a_var + 2) is not a valid expression
```

You may think that the regular expression isn't that complicated, but if you print out the entire thing, it looks like this (formatted to fit this page and still be a valid regular expression):

```
/(?x-ism:(?-xism:(?:(?i)(?:[+-]?)(?:(?=[.]?[0123456789])(?:[
0123456789]*)(?:(?:[.])(?:[0123456789]{0,}))?)(?:(?:[
E])(?:(?:[+-]?)(?:[0123456789]+))|))|))|(?-xism:[[:upper:]][
[:alnum:]_]*))(?:\s*(?-xism:[-+*/%])\s*(?-xism:(?:(?i)(?:[
+-]?)(?:(?=[.]?[0123456789])(?:[0123456789]*)(?:(?:[.])
(?:[0123456789]{0,}))?)(?:(?:[E])(?:(?:[+-]?)(?:[0123456789
]+))|))|))|(?-xism:[[:upper:]][[:alnum:]_]*)))*)/x
```

If you want to write that by hand, be my guest, but don't ask anyone (including yourself) to debug it.

SUMMARY

Regular expressions are powerful, and you've skimmed only the surface of what they can do. This chapter focused on what you'll most likely encounter in the real world, but there are many areas of regular expressions you have only seen a small bit of. You should read the following to learn more:

```
perldoc perlre
perldoc perlretut
perldoc perlrequick
perldoc perlreref
```

If you have Perl version 5.12 or above installed, you can also read `perldoc perlrebackslash` and `perldoc perlrecharclass`. You can also read them on `http://perldoc.perl.org/`.

In addition, the excellent book *Mastering Regular Expressions* by Jeffrey Friedl is highly recommended.

By now, you should understand most common uses of regular expressions including matching arbitrary text, making substitutions, and extracting useful data from strings.

EXERCISES

1. In the United States, Social Security numbers are a sequence of three digits, followed by a dash, followed by two digits, followed by another dash, followed by four digits, which can look like this: `123-45-6789`.

   Ignoring that not all combinations of numbers are valid, write a regular expression that matches a U.S. Social Security number.

2. Imagine you have a block of the following text read from a file:

```
my $employee_numbers = <<'END_EMPLOYEES';
alice: 48472
bob:34582
# we need to fire charlie
   charlie : 45824
# denise is a new hire
denise : 34553
END_EMPLOYEES
```

Those are employee login names and their user numbers. Obviously, an admin has been sloppy in keeping these in a text file. Write code that can read that text and create a hash with employee usernames as the keys and employee numbers as the values. There should be no leading or trailing whitespace in either the keys or the values. Ignore empty lines and lines starting with a #.

3. Given the following text with dates embedded in the YYYY-MM-DD format, write code that can rewrite them as $monthname $day, $year. For example, 2011-02-03should become February 3, 2011. Assume the dates are valid (in other words, not January 40th or something stupid like that).

```
my $text = <<'END';
We hired Mark in 2011-02-03. He's working on product
1034-34-345A. He is expected to finish the work on or
before 2012-12-12 because our idiot CEO thinks the world
will end.
END
```

▶ **WHAT YOU LEARNED IN THIS CHAPTER**

TOPIC	KEY CONCEPTS
Regular expressions	Patterns to describe strings.
Quantifiers	Matching a pattern a variable number of times.
Escape sequences	Sequences for controlling matches.
Extracting data	Extracting matched data into variables.
Modifiers	Special trailing characters that later regex behavior.
Anchors	Matching "places" in a string and not characters.
Character classes	Groups of individual characters.
Grouping	Groups of patterns.
Substitutions	Replacing matched text.
Regexp::Common	A module providing many common regular expressions.
Email::Valid	A module to properly validate an e-mail address.
Lookahead/lookbehind anchors	Anchors to match text before and after a regex.
Named subexpressions	A cleaner way to match data.
Composed regexes	Building complex regexes from smaller ones.

Files and Directories

WHAT YOU WILL LEARN IN THIS CHAPTER:

➤ Understanding files handling

➤ Working with directories

➤ Understanding Unicode and Unicode rules

➤ Useful file manipulation modules

Up to this point, except for a brief discussion of @ARGV in Chapter 3, the data in your program has been embedded in the program, which isn't useful. In the real world, we're constantly reading data from files, Web services, databases, and a variety of other sources. This chapter introduces you to the basics of reading and writing to files and directories.

WROX.COM CODE DOWNLOAD FOR THIS CHAPTER

The wrox.com code downloads for this chapter are found at `http://www.wrox.com/remtitle.cgi?isbn=1118013840` on the Download Code tab. The code for this chapter is divided into the following major examples:

➤ `.targets.txt.swp`

➤ `.tree.pl.swo`

➤ `.tree.pl.swp`

➤ `example_9_1_spies.pl`

➤ `example_9_2_tree.pl`

➤   listing_9_1_targets.pl

➤   listing_9_2_reading_from_data.pl

➤   spies1.txt

➤   spies2.txt

➤   spies3.txt

➤   spies4.txt

➤   targets.txt

BASIC FILE HANDLING

As you probably know by now, most common operating systems have their data internally organized around files and directories. Even if the data is stored in a database, it's probably represented as files somewhere. Perl makes it easy to read and write files, and you can see the most common ways to do that.

Opening and Reading a File

For this section, type the following into a file named targets.txt in a directory named chapter_9.

```
James|007|Spy
Number 6|6|Ex-spy
Agent 99|99|Spy with unknown name
Napoleon Solo|11|Uncle spy
# This guy is only rumored to exist. Not everyone believes it.
Unknown|666|Maybe a spy
```

Those are names, case numbers, and bizarre job titles for people your overly optimistic intelligence agency wants to interrogate.

To open a file, use the open() builtin. The two most common forms of open() follow:

```
open FILEHANDLE, MODE, FILENAME
open FILEHANDLE, FILENAME
```

The first preceding syntax is the *three argument open*, and the second is the *two argument open*. The second is an older version of open() and it's generally frowned upon today, but is explained here so that you can understand it if you see it in legacy code. (If someone is still writing using the two argument open today, it's either because they must support a version of Perl prior to version 5.6 or they don't know any better.)

The arguments to open() follow:

➤ **FILEHANDLE:** The identifier you will use elsewhere to read or write to the file

➤ **MODE:** Specifies if you are opening the file to read and/or write to it

➤ **FILENAME:** Mostly, just what it looks like, the name of the file in your system

> **NOTE** *See* `perldoc -f open` *for more information than you expected.* `perldoc opentut` *is good, too. If you need fine-grained control over how to open files (such as* `die`*ing if you try to open for writing a file that already exists), see* `perldoc -f sysopen`*. It's also explained in detail with* `perlopentut`*.*

Reading Files

To open a file in read mode, use the < sign for the mode. The following is what it looks like:

```
my $filename = 'chapter_9/targets.txt';
open my $spies_to_espy, '<', $filename
    or die "Cannot open '$filename' for writing: $!";
```

That is a lot of new stuff at once, so I'll break it down carefully.

The `my $spies_to_espy` variable contains the filehandle that you can use to access the contents of `$filename`. Like variables, a filehandle with a descriptive name leads to clearer code. Filehandle is commonly abbreviated at `$fh`.

The < tells Perl you're going to open the file for reading. If the attempt to open the file fails, the `open()` builtin returns false and sets the special `$!` Variable, which contains a human-readable description of the error. You can print `$!` to provide an error message. If the previous file does not exist, that might print the following:

```
Cannot open 'chapter_9/targets.txt' for writing: No such file or
directory at my_program.pl line 17.
```

When using `open()` and other related functions, always include the `or die` section at the end. Otherwise, Perl may ignore the error and silently Do The Wrong Thing, which would be disappointing. To automate, remember you can install the handy `autodie` module from the CPAN to take care of this for you:

```
use autodie;
my $filename = 'chapter_9/targets.txt';
open my $filehandle, '<', $filename;
```

If `open()` fails, you get a virtually identical error message to the previous one.

The `autodie` module was included with Perl as of version 5.10.1, so if you have that version of Perl or newer, you won't need to install it separately.

> **NOTE** *Windows, and some operating systems, use the backslash, \, as a file-name delimiter. This could be an issue in Perl, which uses the \ to specify characters such as tab, \t, and newline, \n.*
>
> *When you attempt to do something like*
>
> ```
> my $filename = "chapter_9\targets.txt";
> ```
>
> *In a double-quoted string, the \t is the tab character but your filename is probably not* chapter_9<TAB>argets.txt. *You can escape the \ like this:*
>
> ```
> my $filename = "chapter_9\\targets.txt";
> ```
>
> *But that can quickly start to get ugly:*
>
> ```
> my $file = "path\\to\\some\\$file";
> ```
>
> *In a Perl program just use forward slashes, and internally Perl will Do The Right Thing for your operating system.*
>
> ```
> my $file = "path/to/some/$file";
> ```
>
> *Or:*
>
> ```
> my $file = "C:/path/to/some/$file";
> ```
>
> *That's much cleaner.*

Now that you have opened the file, read from it and print the name, case number, and description of each record. Listing 9-1 shows the code to do this (code file `listing_9_1_targets.pl`).

LISTING 9-1: Reading and Parsing a File

```perl
use strict;
use warnings;
use diagnostics;

my $filename = 'chapter_9/targets.txt';

open my $spies_to_espy, '<', $filename
    or die "Cannot open '$filename' for writing: $!";

while ( my $line = <$spies_to_espy> ) {
    next if $line =~ /^\s*#/; # skip comments!
    chomp($line);
    my ( $name, $case_number, $description )
```

```
          = split /\|/, $line;
        print "$name ($case_number): $description\n";
    }
    close $spies_to_espy or die "Could not close '$filename': $!";
```

And that prints out the following:

```
James (007): Spy
Number 6 (6): Ex-spy
Agent 99 (99): Spy with unknown name
Napoleon Solo (11): Uncle spy
Unknown (666): Maybe a spy
```

The following discussion takes this line by line so that you can clearly see what is going on here.

```
while ( my $line = <$spies_to_espy> ) {
```

The angle brackets around the filehandle turn it into an iterator. If you assign it in list context (such as assigning it to an array), it can read in every record in the file, as separated by the value in the $/ variable. If you assign it to a scalar, as shown previously, it acts like an iterator, returning one line at a time, or undef when there is no more input. As you recall from Chapter 5, you usually use while loops with iterators.

> **NOTE** *The sharp-eyed among you may wonder what's going on with using a* while *loop and a filehandle. What if the filehandle just returns an empty string or some other value that evaluates to false? It still Just Works because when reading filehandles in a* while *loop, Perl magically converts it as follows:*
>
> ```
>     while ( my $line = <$fh> ) { ... }
>     # becomes
>     while ( defined ( my $line = <$fh> ) ) { ... }
> ```
>
> *Remember that the assignment,* my $line = <$fh>, *returns the value of the entire expression and the filehandle can return only* undef *at* EOF *(end of the file). Thus, the* while *loop works. This behavior happens because Perl knows that's what you need here. Don't rely on this behavior for other uses of* while.

The $/ variable defaults to whatever the newline character is for your operating system. For Windows, this is the carriage return plus line feed (\r\n). For UNIX-like systems such as Linux, Mac OS X, AIX and so on, it's just the line feed character (\n) and for versions of Mac OS prior to OS X, it's just the carriage return (\r). Other operating systems may use different characters, but Perl takes care of this for you.

NOTE *If you have a file from another operating system, or if the file delimits "records" with a different character, you can assign a different value to the $/ variable to ensure that lines are split correctly. Just be sure to use the* `local()` *builtin with it to avoid having other parts of your system picking up the new value. You can also read an entire file into a scalar by setting $/ to* undef. *This is often referred to as slurp mode. Just using a bare* local $/; *can set $/ to an uninitialized value:*

```
my $file_contents = slurp('chapter_9/targets.txt');
print $file_contents;
sub slurp {
    my $file = shift;
    open my $fh, '<', $file
      or die "Cannot open '$file' for reading: $!";
    local $/;
    my $contents = <$fh>;
    return $contents;
}
```

That's written for clarity. However, you'll often see it written like this:

```
sub slurp {
    my $file = shift;
    open my $fh, '<', $file
      or die "Cannot open '$file' for reading: $!";
    return do { local $/; <$fh> };
}
```

The next line of code should be clear. You can skip comments in the file by preceding them with a # symbol. The \s* allows you to have zero or more spaces in front of the # symbol.

```
next if $line =~ /^\s*#/; # skip comments!
```

Then you have the chomp():

```
chomp($line);
```

As you may recall from Chapter 4, chomp() removes anything matching $/ from the end of the variable. In this case, you don't need to do this because you're adding it back in when you print the data. It is a good habit to get into. You often store data in variables and probably do not want the line separator.

Then you split the line on the pipe character, |. Because split() expects a regular expression as its first argument and the | is used for alternation, you need to escape it to match a literal pipe character.

```
my ( $name, $case_number, $description )
    = split /\|/, $line;
```

And finally you can print your results:

```
print "$name ($case_number): $description\n";
```

The final line closes your filehandle:

```
close $fh or die "Could not close '$filename': $!";
```

If the filehandle falls out of scope, Perl closes the filehandle for you. You'll see many programs take advantage of this feature and not close their filehandles.

The <> operator assigns to $_ by default, so you can omit the my $line = if you prefer:

```
while (<$fh>) {
    next if /^\s*#/; # skip comments!
    chomp;
    my ( $name, $case_number, $description ) = split /\|/, $_;
    print "$name ($case_number): $description\n";
}
```

Reading Files the Wrong Way

For versions of Perl prior to version 5.6 (released over a decade ago!), you often see this syntax:

```
open FH, $filename
  or die "Cannot open '$filename' for reading: $!";
```

Or:

```
open FH, "< $filename"
  or die "Cannot open '$filename' for reading: $!";
```

This combines a few practices that are today considered bad. The FH looks like a bareword and should not be allowed with use strict, but in this instance, it's considered to be a typeglob. You use it like a normal filehandle:

```
while ( my $line = <FH> ) { ... }
```

This is considered bad practice because typeglobs are package globals, and there can be some strange bugs associated with other portions of your program messing with global variables. Imagine trying to debug what's going wrong with this:

```
open FH or die $!;
```

That's perfectly legal, and it might just open a file in read mode, but this monstrosity isn't covered here. (Again, see perlopentut for the gory bits).

You can use the two argument form of open() in this bad example:

```
open FH, $filename;
# and
open FH, "< $filename";
```

For the first, you simply omitted the < mode. If that's left off, Perl assumes read mode. For the second, it's included in the string, along with the filename. That does the same thing. It has to do with making this seem a bit more familiar to UNIX programmers, but suffice it to say that it's strongly discouraged today. If the `$filename` contains user input and a malicious user provides a filename with any mode-specific characters at the start, you will have significant security implications.

Don't do that. Stick with the three argument open.

> **NOTE** *For more information on typeglobs, see "Typeglobs and Filehandles" in* `perldoc perldata`*.*

Writing Files

Writing files has a similar syntax, but you use > to open the file in write mode. If you want to append to a file, use >>. So to add Maxwell Smart as a new target in `targets.txt`, you could write the following:

```
open my $fh, '>>', $filename
    or die "Cannot open '$filename' for appending: $!";
print $fh "Maxwell Smart|86|Definitely a spy\n";
```

And now the file should contain the following (code file `target.txt`):

```
James|007|Spy
Number 6|6|Ex-spy
# This guy is only rumored to exist. Not everyone believes it.
Unknown|666|Maybe a spy
Maxwell Smart|86|Definitely a spy
```

Nothing unusual about this, except for the `print` line:

```
print $fh "Maxwell Smart|86|Definitely a spy\n";
```

There's no comma after the `$fh`. That's what lets Perl know that `$fh` is a file handle it's printing to instead of something to print. So if you see something like this on your screen when you weren't expecting any output:

```
GLOB(0xbfe220)Maxwell Smart|99|Definitely a spy
```

You probably put a comma after the filehandle, telling Perl that it's something to print instead of a filehandle to print to.

If you want, you can rewrite the file by reading it and then writing to it. Now sort the lines of the file and strip the comments from it. Following is one way to do that:

```
my $filename = 'chapter_9/targets.txt';

open my $fh, '<', $filename
    or die "Cannot open '$filename' for reading: $!";
```

```
# each element in @lines gets one line from the file
# remember grep from Chapter 4?
my @lines = sort grep { !/^\s*#/ } <$fh>;
close $fh or die "Cannot close '$filename': $!";

open $fh, '>', $filename
  or die "Cannot open '$filename' for writing $!";
print $fh @lines;
close $fh or die "Cannot close '$filename': $!";
```

Again, this code builds on everything you've learned so far. There's nothing too magical here.

There is another way to rewrite a file. You need four things: `seek()`, `tell()`, `truncate()`, and read-write mode.

To open a file in read-write mode, prepend the mode with a +. In this case, use +< mode. There is a corresponding +> mode, but you should probably never use it because it deletes the contents of your file first. That's probably not helpful. Following is your new program:

```
my $filename = 'chapter_9/targets.txt';
open my $fh, '+<', $filename
  or die "Cannot open '$filename' in read-write mode: $!";

my @lines = sort grep { !/^\s*#/ } <$fh>;

seek $fh, 0, 0
  or die "Cannot seek '$filame', 0, 0: $!";
print $fh @lines;
truncate $fh, tell($fh)
  or die "Cannot truncate '$filename': $!";
close $fh or die "Cannot close $filename: $!";
```

The `seek()` function has the following syntax:

```
seek FILEHANDLE, OFFSET, STARTINGAT
```

The values for STARTINGAT follow:

> ➤ 0: Sets the new position in bytes to OFFSET

> ➤ 1: Sets the new position to the current position plus OFFSET

> ➤ 2: Sets the new position to the end of file plus OFFSET, which is usually a negative value

The `tell()` function returns the position of the filehandle, in bytes. The `truncate()` builtin tells Perl to truncate the file at the given position.

This may seem a bit confusing, but it's what Perl needs to know to handle this. Again, don't forget that you can use `autodie` to make this simpler:

```
use autodie;
my $filename = 'chapter_9/targets.txt';
open my $fh, '+<', $filename;
my @lines = sort grep { !/^\s*#/ } <$fh>;

seek    $fh, 0, 0;
```

```
print     $fh   @lines;
truncate $fh, tell($fh);
close     $fh;
```

Although your author usually uses `autodie`, you can avoid it in examples to constantly remind you to check the success or failure of your system calls. As usual, see `perldoc -f` for the various functions to learn more about them.

File Test Operators

When you work with files or directories, you often want to know things about them first. For example, you might want to see if a file exists before trying to read it. The `-e` file test operator does this. You can also use the `-f` operator to find out if it's a file.

```
my $filename = 'somefile';
if ( -e $filename && -f $filename ) { ... }
```

Every time you use a file test operator, the system makes another `stat()` call (see `perldoc -f stat`) and this can be expensive, so Perl let's you use a special filehandle named `_`. When a file test operator is used, subsequent file test operators can use `_` that contains the results from the last `stat()` call. This is generally much less expensive, particularly if you stack many file test operators:

```
# does it exist? Is it a file? Is it readable?
if ( -e $filename && -f _ && -r _ ) { ... }
```

Also, if you use Perl 5.9.1 or better, you can stack the operators and write the above as follows:

```
if ( -e -f -r $filename ) { ... }
```

There are a great many file test operators, and you won't cover all of them. Just be aware that they're there for you. See Table 9-1 for a list, which is loosely sorted with the most common ones at the top of the table.

TABLE 9-1: File test Operators and Their Meaning

OPERATOR	MEANING
-e	File exists
-f	File is a plain file
-d	A directory
-r	File is readable by effective uid/gid
-w	File is writable by effective uid/gid
-x	File is executable by effective uid/gid
-z	File has zero size (it's empty)

OPERATOR	MEANING
-s	File has nonzero size (returns size in bytes)
-o	File is owned by effective uid
-R	File is readable by real uid/gid
-W	File is writable by real uid/gid
-X	File is executable by real uid/gid
-O	File is owned by real uid
-l	File is a symbolic link
-p	File is a named pipe (FIFO) or filehandle is a pipe
-S	File is a socket
-b	File is a block special file
-c	File is a character special file
-t	Filehandle (often STDOUT) is opened to a tty
-u	File has setuid bit set
-g	File has setgid bit set
-k	File has sticky bit set
-T	File is an ASCII text file (heuristic guess)
-B	File is a "binary" file (opposite of -T)
-M	Script stat time minus file modification time, in days

> **NOTE** In Table 9-1, you see references to real and effective uid and gid. These are UNIX terms indicating the real and effective user and group IDs. Normally you have a real user ID and group ID. (Your user belongs to a group, and this may have different permissions than the user.)
>
> Sometimes programs can run with setuid, and these change your effective user id to something else while preserving your real user ID. This allows programs such as passwd to change the /etc/passwd file, something that only root can do. However, although passwd uses your effective user ID to allow you to change /etc/passwd, it can check your real user ID to make sure that you can't change someone else's password.
>
> Programs that use setuid are inherently dangerous because it's easy to get this wrong and can open up serious security holes.

The Diamond Operator

You've seen the angle brackets, <>, around a filehandle, but if you use them without a filehandle, or with the special ARGV filehandle (not the @ARGV array), they're called the *diamond operator*, and they're useful for certain types of programs. They cause each filename in @ARGV to be opened, in sequence, and read. This is better seen than explained. Consider the following program, myfilter.pl.

```
use strict;
use warnings;
while (<>) {
    next unless /\S/;
    print;
}
```

If you call that with perl myprog.pl file1.txt file2.txt file3.txt, then it prints out every "nonblank" (in other words, containing at least one nonwhitespace character, \S) line from each of those files.

Note that while (<>) is identical to while (defined ($_ = <ARGV>)).

> **NOTE** while (<>) *is the same as* while (defined($_ = <ARGV>)). *But how do you know this? Perl has a handy module named* B::Deparse. *The* B:: *modules are backend modules and let you see some things about Perl normally not visible. In this case, use* B::Deparse *to "deparse" the* while (<>) *construct.*
>
> ```
> perl -MO=Deparse -e 'while (<>) {}'
> ```
>
> *That prints the following:*
>
> ```
> while (defined($_ = <ARGV>)) {
>     ();
> }
> -e syntax OK
> ```
>
> *You can see the changed code that has been neatly formatted.* B::Deparse *has a number of interesting options to help you better understand complicated code. See* perldoc B::Deparse *for more information. The* -M *switch for Perl tells it to load the module requested, in this case the mysteriously named* O. *(That's the letter O, not the number 0). See* perldoc O *to understand how that loads* B::Deparse. *And if you're brave, see* perldoc B *for a better understand of the* B:: *modules, but be warned: it's dense.*

Temporary Files

Sometimes you need to create temporary files that disappear when your program ends. For example, you may want to filter a file but write it out to a tempfile first. Other times, you may want to create a tempfile and feed it to another program. There are several ways to do this, but you can use the File::Temp module because it's fairly common.

```
use File::Temp 'tempfile';
my $fh = tempfile();
# or, if you also need the name:
my ( $fh, $filename ) = tempfile();
If you need a particular suffix for the tempfile:
my ( $fh, $filename ) = tempfile( SUFFIX => '.yaml' );
```

`File::Temp` also has an object-oriented interface and provides a number of features. In this case, just remember that it's a handy module when you want to write out some temporary data.

DATA as a File

Perl has two special tokens: `__END__` and `__DATA__`, which, if on a line by themselves, tell Perl that it's reached the end of the program and to stop compiling. However, the `__DATA__` token also tells Perl that it can read the data after said token (`__END__` can sometimes do this too, but read `perldoc perldata` for the details and pretend you never knew you could do this.).

Listing 9-2 (code file `listing_9_2_reading_from_data.pl`) has an example.

LISTING 9.2: Reading DATA

```
use strict;
use warnings;
use diagnostics;
use Data::Dumper;

my %config;

while (<DATA>) {
    next if      /^\s*#/;              # skip comments
    next unless /(\w+)\s*=\s*(\w+)/;  # key = value

    my ( $key, $value ) = ( $1, $2 );
    if ( exists $config{$key} ) {

        # we've already seen this key, so convert the value to an
        # array reference
        # Does $config{$key} currently store a scalar or an aref?
        if( ! ref $config{$key} ) {
            $config{$key} = [ $config{$key} ];
        }
        push @{ $config{$key} } => $value;
    }
    else {
        $config{$key} = $value;
    }
}
print Dumper(\%config);

__DATA__
# max_tries = 3
max_tries = 2
```

continues

LISTING 9-2 *(continued)*

```
timeout   = 30
# only these people are OK
user = Ovid
user = Sally
user = Bob
```

Running the code in Listing 9-2 prints something similar to the following:

```
$VAR1 = {
           'max_tries' => '2',
           'timeout' => '30',
           'user' => [
                        'Ovid',
                        'Sally',
                        'Bob'
                     ]
        };
```

In this case, you used the DATA section of your code to embed a tiny config file. As a general rule, you can read from only the DATA section once, but if you need to read from it more than once, use the following code:

```
# Find the start of the __DATA__ section
my $data_start = tell DATA;
while ( <DATA> ) {
    # do something
}
# Reset DATA filehandle to start of __DATA__
seek DATA, $data_start, 0;
```

In case you're wondering, yes, you can also write to the DATA section if you have the correct permission, but this is generally a bad idea and is left as an exercise for the foolhardy. (Hint: If you get it wrong, you can overwrite your program.)

> **NOTE** The example of using a DATA section for configuration works, but be aware that this is only to show you how __DATA__ works. There are plenty of useful modules on the CPAN for handling configuration files. Some popular ones are AppConfig, Config::General, Config::Std, and Config::Tiny. You could still keep your config in the DATA section, but you want it to be in a separate file because this is something that others are likely to need to read and edit.

binmode

When working with text files, opening the file and reading and writing to it is generally handled transparently. However, what happens if you open a file written on a Linux system and being read on a Windows system? As explained earlier, the $/ variable defaults to the newline character, but that is \n on Linux and \r\n on Windows. Perl silently translates newline characters the appropriate newline character for your operating system. This means that reading and writing text files (such as XML or YAML documents) works transparently, regardless of the operating system you are on.

What happens if you work with a binary file, such as an image? You don't want Perl to try and "fix" the newlines, so you open the file and use the `binmode` builtin:

```
my $image = 'really_cool.jpg';
open my $fh, '<', $image
    or die "Cannot open '$image' for reading: $!";
binmode $fh; # treat it as a binary file
```

With this code, you don't need to worry about newlines being translated.

> **NOTE** See `perldoc -f binmode` *for more information.*

The `binmode` builtin accepts an optional "layer" description (older versions of Perl referred to this as the "discipline"). The `:raw` layer is the default, so the following two lines are equivalent:

```
binmode $fh;
binmode $fh, ':raw';
```

If you want to tell Perl that the file is UTF-8 (we'll explain this in the Unicode section of this chapter), you can use the `:encoding(UTF-8)` layer:

```
my $kanji_examples = 'kanji.txt';
open my $fh, '<', $kanji_examples
  or die "Cannot open '$kanji_examples' for reading: $!";
binmode $fh, ':encoding(UTF-8)';
```

If you use the three-argument form of `open()` (and you should), you can specify the layer directly in the mode:

```
open my $fh, '<:raw', $some_file
  or die "Cannot open '$some_file' for reading: $!";
```

TRY IT OUT   Writing a Filter

Sometimes you need to take a bunch of files and filter them by some criteria. Imagine, for your intelligence agency, that you have agents all over the world who regularly send files to you via SFTP. These agents are detailed to investigate suspected spies. The files they send contain one or more lines with additional information in the format `name|information|number`. Because your agents are careless, they don't respect the `\d\d\d\d\d` number format, so you need to fix this before you combine their data into one master file. You can write out the data as `name|number|information`. All the code in this Try It Out is found in code file `example_9_1_spies.pl`.

1. Type in the following program and save it as `example_9_1_spies.pl`:

```
use strict;
use warnings;
```

```perl
while (<>) {
    if (/^\s*#/) {
        print;      # keep the comments
        next;
    }
    chomp;
    my ( $name, $description, $number ) = split /\|/, $_;
    if( defined $name ) {
     printf "$name|%05d|$description\n", $number;
    }
}
```

2. Now create four text files, spies1.txt to spies4.txt, with the following contents:

➤   * spies1.txt

James|Definitely a Spy|007

➤   * spies2.txt

Number 6|Won't answer Questions|6

➤   * spies3.txt

This guy is only rumored to exist. Not everyone believes it.

Unknown|Maybe a spy|666

➤   * spies4.txt

Maxwell Smart|Definitely a spy|86

3. Run the program with perl example_9_1_spies.pl spies*.txt. If your operating system does not properly support shell metacharacter expansion, you may need to run the program as follows:

```
perl example_9_1_spies.pl spies1.txt spies2.txt spies3.txt spies4.txt
```

You should see the following output:

```
James|00007|Definitely a Spy
Number 6|00006|Won't answer Questions
# This guy is only rumored to exist. Not everyone believes it.
Unknown|00666|Maybe a spy
Maxwell Smart|00086|Definitely a spy
```

How It Works

The diamond operator, <>, automatically opens in read-mode every file passed in as an argument to the program. Thus, when you run the program with the following command:

```
perl example_9_1_spies.pl spies1.txt spies2.txt spies3.txt spies4.txt
```

The while (<>) will set $_ successively to each line in spies1.txt, spies2.txt, spies3.txt, and spies4.txt, just as if they were all concatenated into one big file.

Unlike the previous `while (<>)` example, you do need the `chomp()` command here because your input is generally in the form `name|description|number` but your output is `name|number|description`. This means you need to remove the newline from the number but add it back in to the end of every line in the `printf()`.

DIRECTORIES

When working with Perl, you'll sometimes need to work with directories. In general, you don't want to do this directly because it's easy to make mistakes. Instead, you can use a number of useful modules (explained later in the "Useful Modules" section), but it's useful to see some of the low-level details in case you work on code that uses them.

Reading Directories

When reading directories, you usually need a directory handle. The `opendir` builtin enables you to create a directory handle, and the `readdir` builtin can read all entries from a directory handle.

```
opendir (my $dh, $directory)
  or die "Cannot open '$directory' for reading: $!";
# get all entries not starting with a dot
my @entries = grep { !/^\./ } readdir($dh);
closedir $dh
  or die "Cannot close '$directory': $!";
```

> **WARNING** Do not be tempted to think that `readdir()` returns only files and directories. Depending on what your operating system supports, it might be a symbolic link (-d), a named piped (-p) or a socket (-S). These are generally not covered in this book, but you should be aware of this because it's a common beginner mistake.

Note that `opendir()` does not have a three-argument form. You do not "write" to directories, although you can certainly create directories and files in them.

Globbing

You can also use the `File::Glob` module to glob directories (using wildcard characters to match a "glob" of files or directories). This uses the common file globbing semantics. For example, `*.txt` matches any file with a `.txt` extension. You can use the `glob()` builtin or the angle brackets for this behavior.

> **NOTE** See `perldoc File::Glob` for more information on `glob()` and `<>`.

The following are three equivalent ways to list all directory entries with a `.txt` extension. Start using `autodie` to make your life simpler.

Using `opendir()`:

```
use strict;
use warnings;
use autodie;
my $dir = 'drafts/';
opendir(my $dh, $dir);
my @txt = grep { /\.txt$/ } readdir($dh);
print join "\n", @txt;
closedir $dh;
```

Using `glob()`:

```
use strict;
use warnings;
use autodie;
my $dir = 'drafts';
my @txt = glob("$dir/*.txt");
print join "\n", @txt;
```

Using `<>`:

```
use strict;
use warnings;
use autodie;
my $dir = 'drafts';
my @txt = <$dir/*.txt>; # no quotes!
print join "\n", @txt;
```

> **NOTE** *Typeglobs and fileglobs are not the same thing. Your author apologizes for the confusion.*

UNICODE

When Perl is processing data, it needs to know what character set it is encoded as. As the world becomes more interconnected, it's increasingly important that different systems communicate correctly.

This is introduced now because as you're reading and writing files; it's increasingly common to find that those files are not ASCII or Latin-1, as many developers assume. (Or more correctly, many developers aren't aware of the issues.)

> **WARNING** *Any version of Perl prior to 5.6 is broken by default for Unicode. 5.12 is sometimes considered the minimum "safe" version, and 5.14 offers a level of Unicode support that few other languages can equal.*

What Is Unicode?

In the good ol' days of programming (arbitrarily defined as "when your author was growing up"), aspiring programmers were typing game programs directly from the BASIC listing in programming magazines. These programs were written in ASCII, the American Standard Code for Information Interchange. Back then, characters tended to be represented by 7 or 8 bits of data. ASCII characters took 7 bits of data, with values ranging from 0 to 128. Eight-bit numbers could use characters from 129 to 255. Different systems often represented the 129 to 255 numbers in different ways and were sometimes referred to as extended ASCII. You might have had interesting graphic figures or you may have had accented characters. But what did the Japanese do when they wanted to write 日本国? Clearly having only 255 characters is not enough for many writing systems.

The Unicode standard is a way to describe every character in every writing system with a single number. This number is called a code point and it's composed of one or more octets. We use the word octet to refer to 8 bits, so all characters that can be represented by the numbers 0 to 255 take up 1 octet of space. Your author's wife is French, and her first name is Leïla. The ï in Leïla is represented as the code point U+00EF. (The 00EF is hexadecimal.) The letters A and a are U+0041 and U+0061, respectively, and 国 is U+56FD. However, a code point describes a character, but it doesn't describe the encoding of that character. The EF in code point U+00EF is the decimal number 239. That number can be described in 8 bits as 11101111. Some encodings, such as UTF-8 and UTF-16, encode that in 16 bits (2 octets). UTF-32 encodes that in 32 bits (4 octets).

> **NOTE** A bit is a single 0, or 1. 8 bits forms an octet. Many people refer to 8 bits as 1 byte, but in reality, a byte's length is dependent on the machine you're running it on, so use the word octet to avoid ambiguity.

The code point associated with a character has no relation to the encoding. Any given character encoding (such as UTF-8, UTF-32, and so on) is free to encode any code point in any way it wants, so long as the encoding is unambiguous.

UTF-8 has an advantage over many other encodings because ASCII characters are represented identically in ASCII and UTF-8, making it backward compatible with ASCII. This is why UTF-8 tends to be the dominant encoding for Unicode. If you send ASCII to a system that is expecting UTF-8, it often works just fine.

That doesn't tell you, however, how to use Unicode.

Two Simple Rules

A typical workflow for a program follows:

➤ Initialization

➤ Input

➤ Calculation

➤ Output

The two simple rules are to decode all your text input and encode all your text output. With this, you can ensure that inside of your Perl program, you work with Perl's internal string format and don't have to worry about errors that occur when you try to concatenate strings in different encodings.

Decoding Your Data

Decoding your data means "decode your data to Perl's internal format." What is Perl's internal format? It doesn't matter. If Perl ever needs to change that internal format, you should not rely on knowing the details. Suffice it to say that Perl generally treats your text data as binary data instead of characters until you decode it and write it out somewhere. This is the hard part. You must find out what the encoding of your source data is! So if your data is in 7bit-jis (a Japanese pre-Unicode encoding), you could use the Encode::decode() function to transform it into Perl's internal format:

```
use Encode qw(encode decode);
my $string = decode('7bit-jis', $byte_string);
```

And now Perl can happily handle this for you, including reporting its length correctly.

However, it's better to not need to decode strings on a string-by-string basis. It's better to decode them at the source, if possible (thus making it harder to forget). You can use Perl's IO layers to handle that. One way is to specify the layer with binmode():

```
open my $fh, '<', $some_file or die $!;
binmode $fh, ':7bit-jis';
```

Or better still, specify it with the mode because it's harder to miss:

```
open my $fh, '<:7bit-jis', $some_file or die $!;
```

If you don't know the encoding of your source data, ask the person who sent you the data. If that fails, Encode (first shipped with Perl 5.7.3) includes the Encode::Guess module. It's not a bad module, but it's a "guess" at the encoding. Read the documentation carefully, and be aware that it guesses wrong from time to time.

Encoding Your Data

Now that you've decoded your data and done fun things with it, you need to encode it back to its original format before you send it along. Not surprisingly, the encode() function from Encode does this for you:

```
use Encode qw(encode decode);
my $encoded = encode('7bit-jis', $string);
```

Or again, use the IO layers:

```
open my $fh, '>:7bit-jis', $some_file or die $!;
```

Then, when you write the data out to the console, a file or some other data sink, it will be encoded correctly.

A Typical Unicode Nightmare

So decode your input and encode your output. Not too bad, right? Well, that's until you try it. First, look at this code snippet.

```
my $string = '日本国';
my $length = length($string);
print "$string has $length characters\n";
```

And that prints out (assuming you have the correct font installed):

```
日本国 has 9 characters
```

Of course, that's not true. It has 9 octets, but it clearly has 3 characters. So the first thing that many people do is this:

```
use utf8;
my $string = '日本国';
my $length = length($string);
print "$string has $length characters\n";
```

Many people assume that use utf8 means "magically make everything UTF-8," but that's not correct. You get the following output:

```
Wide character in print at /var/tmp/eval_Yrhm.pl line 4.
日本国 has 3 characters
```

> **NOTE** You can cut-and-paste 日本国 from http://en.wikipedia.org/wiki/
> Japan because you are unlikely to type those characters directly.

Note the strange Wide character in print warning, but you now have the correct length. The use utf8 pragma tells Perl only that your source code is UTF-8. It doesn't tell Perl that your output is UTF-8, so Perl is expecting a binary output to the STDOUT filehandle, but you've sent UTF-8, so fix that.

```
use utf8;

my $string = '日本国';
my $length = length($string);
binmode STDOUT, ':encoding(UTF-8)';

print "$string has $length characters\n";
```

And that gives you the correct output with no warnings. (The `Wide Character in Print` warning occurs even if you don't `use warnings`).

Alternatively, if you don't want to apply that encoding layer to all of STDOUT you could just encode the string from Perl's internal format to UTF-8, which also makes the warning go away:

```
use utf8;
use Encode qw(encode decode);

my $string = '日本国';
my $length = length($string);
$string    = encode('UTF-8', $string);

print "$string has $length characters\n";
```

But you're still not quite sure where you want to be in understanding this. The use `utf8` pragma tells Perl that your source code is UTF-8, but it doesn't tell Perl that your input is UTF-8. Try this:

```
use utf8;
use Encode qw(encode decode);

my $string = shift @ARGV;
my $length = length($string);
$string    = encode('UTF-8', $string);

print "$string has $length characters\n";
```

If you save that as `length.pl` and run that with `perl length.pl` 日本国, you will get output similar to this:

```
æ¥æ¬å½ has 9 characters
```

You won't even get a warning. Why? Because you haven't decoded the data and Perl assumes it's Latin-1 data (ISO-8859-1) that it already knows how to deal with. When you explicitly decode the data, everything works as expected:

```
use utf8;
use Encode qw(encode decode);

my $string = decode('UTF-8', shift);
my $length = length($string);
$string    = encode('UTF-8', $string);

print "$string has $length characters\n";
```

If you are unsure of what encodings your system provides, the following one-liner will print all of them for you:

```
perl -MEncode -e 'print join "\n" => Encode->encodings(":all")'
```

> **WARNING** Be careful when using the UTF-8 layer. Many Perl references will tell you to do something like this:
>
> ```
> binmode STDOUT, ':utf8';
> ```
>
> Or this:
>
> ```
> open my $fh, '<:utf8', $filename;
> ```
>
> This is extremely bad because :utf8 is not the same as :encoding(UTF-8). The :encoding(UTF-8) layer says "this filehandle is guaranteed to be UTF-8" and it will die if you feed it invalid data. The :utf8 layer says "this filehandle is in UTF-8," but it doesn't verify that this is true. As a result, programs that use the :utf8 layer can be deliberately fed invalid data, and this is a security hole. Do not use the :utf8 layer.
>
> Read http://www.perlmonks.org/?node_id=644786 for more information.

> **NOTE** Just because your source code is UTF-8 doesn't mean that your text editor or IDE is set to recognize or save your source code as UTF-8. Consult your editor's documentation on how to do this.
>
> Also, your terminal program may not default to UTF-8. Check how to set your terminal's preferences for displaying UTF-8 data correctly. This is often in a preference titled "Character Encoding" or something similar. If your terminal cannot handle UTF-8 data, use a modern terminal program.
>
> In the event that your terminal and editor/IDE both claim to handle UTF-8 data correctly and you still see garbage on the screen, you may need to ensure you have the correct fonts installed. You need to consult your operating system's documentation for how to do this.

Lots of Complicated Rules

Before going further, read the following:

```
perldoc perlunitut
perldoc perlunifaq
perldoc perlunicode
perldoc perluniintro
perldoc Encode
```

Unfortunately, although the two simple rules cover general cases, they won't cover all cases because they can't, but we're going to cover a few issues to be aware of.

Case Folding

Case folding is converting all the characters in a string to uppercase or lowercase. This is useful when you want to make case-insensitive comparisons. It's also often a dangerous thing to do with Unicode. Consider the following program:

```
use utf8;
binmode(STDOUT, ":encoding(UTF-8)");
print uc("σ"), "\n";    # Greek small letter sigma
print uc("ς"), "\n";    # Greek small final letter sigma
```

That prints out the same letter twice, an uppercase sigma character:

Σ
Σ

The σ and ς characters are the same lowercase sigma character, but the latter is used at the end of the word. When you call uc() on them, they both resolve to an uppercase sigma, Σ. This leads to this problem:

```
use utf8;
binmode(STDOUT, ":encoding(UTF-8)");
print lc(uc("σ")), "\n";    # Greek small letter sigma
print lc(uc("ς")), "\n";    # Greek small final letter sigma
```

That prints σ twice, meaning that case-folding is not round-trip safe in Unicode.

In earlier versions of Perl, in some cases, characters in the range 128 to 255 would often have strange behavior when you tried to use lc, uc, ucfirst, and so on. When used as characters, they would sometimes be considered Unicode code points, and when used as bytes, they could be considered "unassigned characters" and not match \w in regular expressions. The solution is simple:

```
use feature 'unicode_strings';
```

Unfortunately, that feature was not added until Perl 5.11.3 (a development release). So today it's argued that you should use Perl 5.12 or better (preferably 5.14) if you want to be "Unicode safe."

Converting Between Encodings

You need to convert between UTF-16 and ISO-8859-1 (Latin-1). To do this, you must convert from one encoding to Perl's internal format and then convert to the desired format:

```
my $string = decode('UTF-16', $utf16_data);
my $latin1 = encode('iso-8859-1', $string);
```

However, ISO-8859-1 is a subset of UTF-16, so you may lose data.

Wide Character in Print

You'll see this warning a lot when you work with character encodings and you're not being careful. When this happens, it's because you haven't specified your encoding layer. Perl then assumes your data is ISO-8859-1 (for backward compatibility) and tries to output UTF-8. Any data that doesn't fit in the ISO-8859-1 range emits this warning. That's why you got this warning with this code snippet used earlier:

```
use utf8;
my $string = '日本国';
my $length = length($string);
print "$string has $length characters\n";
```

Assuming Everything Is UTF-8

The input data may be read from files, the command line, sockets, and other data sources. The output data may be written to STDOUT, files, or other data sinks. To tell Perl that all input and output data is UTF-8, you can set the PERL_UNICODE environment variable to AS. The A and S letter combination is described in the -C section of perldoc perlrun.

Unfortunately, it's not as simple as setting the environment variable in your code. You must set this before you run your program. On a Linux style system, you can do this:

```
PERL_UNICODE=AS perl program.pl
```

Or you can export the variable, and it will be set for all programs:

```
export PERL_UNICODE=AS
```

On Windows, the syntax is:

```
set PERL_UNICODE=AS
```

This can be a hassle to do every time, and it may very well be the wrong thing to do if you have non-UTF-8 data.

is_utf8()

Sometimes you see this in code:

```
use Encode 'is_utf8';
if ( is_utf8($string) ) {
    # wrong!
}
```

Or the identical:

```
if ( utf8::is_utf8($string) ) {
    # wrong!
}
```

This does not work as you think it does. The is_utf8() function is used internally to determine if Perl should treat a string as Latin-1 or UTF-8. However, just because the UTF-8 flag is set does not mean that the string is actually UTF-8. Like the Encode::Guess module, it's just a guess (for you) and you explicitly set your encoding layers as described earlier.

A UTF-8 Shortcut

If you want a shortcut for assuming that @ARGV, your filehandles, and your source code are all UTF-8, you can install the utf8::all module from the CPAN.

```
use utf8::all;
```

You may recall this program from earlier:

```
use utf8;

use Encode qw(encode decode);
my $string = decode('UTF-8', shift);
my $length = length($string);
$string    = encode('UTF-8', $string);

print "$string has $length characters\n";
```

With the utf8::all pragma, this becomes:

```
use utf8::all;
my $string = shift @ARGV;
my $length = length($string);
print "$string has $length characters\n";
```

In other words, it makes it easier to write programs with UTF-8 data. It's not perfect, but it's a good start.

Printing Unicode

By now you already know how to open your STDOUT to handle printing Unicode, but what about typing those funny characters? Well, you don't have to. One way to avoid this is with the charnames pragma:

```
use utf8::all;
use charnames ':short';

# note that double-quoted strings are required
print "\N{greek:Sigma} is an upper-case sigma.\n";
```

And that prints the following (with no warning due to utf8::all):

```
Σ is an upper-case sigma.
```

The \N{} construct with charnames is resolved at compile time, so you cannot use variables there.

You can also use the Unicode full names:

```
use utf8::all;
use charnames ':full';
print "\N{GREEK SMALL LETTER ETA WITH DASIA AND PERISPOMENI}\n";
```

Which prints ἥ.

If you know the code point but not the name, you can use \N{U+codepoint}. Again, remember this is done at compile time. Thus, the code point for the smiley face character is U+263A, so you can print it with this:

```
use utf8::all;
print "\N{U+263A}\n";
```

Or you can just fall back to the chr() function:

```
print chr(0x263a);
```

See http://unicode.org/charts/ for a list of the appropriate names you may want to print.

Unicode Character Properties and Regular Expressions

The character ἥ is a Greek letter, but is it uppercase or lowercase? You can try Unicode character properties to find out:

```
use utf8::all;
my $character ='ἥ';
if ( $character =~ /\p{Lowercase}/ ) {
    print "$character is lower case\n";
}
if ( $character =~ /\p{Uppercase}/ ) {
    print "$character is upper case\n";
}
```

That correctly prints ἥ, which is lowercase.

Unicode properties are properties about characters that describe something about it. They might describe the case of the letter, the script used, whether it's a math symbol or punctuation, and so on. Unicode is so all-encompassing — and it must be because it is trying to handle all writing systems — that you can find many strange things in Unicode land. Here's one of them:

```
use utf8::all;
# latin capital letter d with small letter z
my $character = "\N{U+01F2}";
if ( $character =~ /\p{Lowercase}/ ) {
    print "$character is lower case\n";
}
if ( $character =~ /\p{Uppercase}/ ) {
    print "$character is upper case\n";
}
if ( $character =~ /\p{Titlecase_Letter}/ ) {
    print "$character is title case\n";
}
```

And that prints this:

```
ǲ is title case
```

This is because the *Latin capital letter d with small letter z* is considered a *Titlecase* character and is not uppercase or lowercase. Fun, eh?

> **NOTE** *See* `perldoc perluniprop` *for a full list of Unicode properties supported and how to use them. See also Chapter 4 of the Unicode version 6 standard:* `http://www.unicode.org/versions/Unicode6.0.0/ch04.pdf.` `perldoc` `perlunicode` *also has a list of common properties in the "Unicode Character Properties" section.*

Further Reading

You can spend a long time understanding Unicode, and this section of the book is far too short, but the following are a couple good starting points for understanding Unicode and some of the associated issues.

First, read Joel Spolsky's famous "The Absolute Minimum Every Software Developer Absolutely, Positively Must Know About Unicode and Character Sets (No Excuses!)" article at `http://www.joelonsoftware.com/articles/Unicode.html`

Second, read this: `http://stackoverflow.com/questions/6162484/` `why-does-modern-perl-avoid-utf-8-by-default`

In that link, Tom Christiansen explains, in depth, many of the traps to be aware of. It's mind-bending, but it begins to give you an idea of what you're up against.

Also, `http://en.wikipedia.org/wiki/Free_software_Unicode_typefaces` has a list of Free Unicode fonts you can install if you're tired of seeing broken characters when you try to print Unicode.

USEFUL MODULES

If you start working frequently with the filesystem, you'll be happy to know that many Perl modules are available to take away the drudgery. Further, as they get new features added and bugs fixed, they'll correctly handle issues that you don't want to have to worry about.

File::Find

The `File::Find` module was released with Perl 5 and is useful for walking through directory structures and finding files and directories matching the criteria you're looking for. It's a great module that, unfortunately, is showing its age. You'll often find when working with Perl that older modules are stable, powerful, and have difficult interfaces. This is because when Perl 5 was released, many people were still experimenting with all its features and trying to figure out the best way to work with them. `File::Find` is a module from that era and its interface is clumsy, but it works well. It has a variety of options, but you must do most of the work. The following is one way to delete all empty text files in a directory and its subdirectories:

```
use File::Find;
find( \&wanted, 'some_directory/' );
sub wanted {
    if ( /\.txt$/ && -f $_ && -z _ ) {
        # only delete empty text files
        unlink $_ or die "Could not unlink '$File::Find::name': $!";
    }
}
```

You could also have written that as the following (but this is a touch clumsy):

```
use File::Find;
find( sub {
        if ( /\.txt$/ && -f $_ && -z _ ) {
            unlink $_ or die "Could not unlink '$File::Find::name': $!";
        }
    },
    'some_directory',
);
```

From the documentation:

```
find(\&wanted,  @directories);
find(\%options, @directories);
```

The `find()` function does a depth-first search over the given `@directories` in the order they are given. For each file or directory found, it calls the `wanted()` subroutine. (The details on how to use the `wanted()` function are upcoming). In addition, for each directory found, it will `chdir()` (change directory) into that directory and continue the search, invoking the `wanted()` function on each file or subdirectory in the directory.

Every time the `wanted()` function is called, the following three variables will be set:

➤   `$File::Find::name`: The full path to the file or directory found

➤   `$File::Find::dir`: The full path to the current directory found

➤   `$_`: The short name of the file or directory found

In this case, the *full path* is relative to the starting directory.

When you start a Perl program, its "current directory" is generally the directory you were in when you started the program. However, you can call `chdir($some_directory)` and Perl will attempt to change its current directory to that directory. Thus, the `$_` variable is relative to the current directory that the `File::Find::find()` function is in at the time.

In other words, if you write the following:

```
find sub { print "$_ -> $File::Find::name\n" }, 'notes/' );
```

If there is a file named `notes/some_file.txt`, the following variables will be set when that file is reached:

➤ `$File::Find::name` — `notes/some_file.txt`

➤ `$File::Find::dir` — `notes/`

➤ `$_` — `some_file.txt`

Because the `find()` function changes into the directory it's searching at the time, file test operators and functions such as open and unlink should operate on `$_` instead of `$File::Find::name`. However, the latter is useful if you need to do error reporting:

```
# the $_ is optional with unlink as it default to $_
unlink $_ or die "Could not unlink '$File::Find::name': $!";
```

It's also useful if you need to collect the names for later use:

```
find (\&html_documents, @directories);
my @html_docs;
sub html_documents {
    push @html_docs, $File::Find::name
        if /\.html?$/;
}
```

When the `find()` function is finished, your Perl program's current directory becomes the one you started with, so working with the `@html_docs` array needs the full paths relative to the current directory and not just the short name in `$_`.

> **NOTE** See `perldoc File::Find` for many more options for this module.

File::Path

`File::Path` was released with Perl 5.001 and lets you manipulate file paths and not just individual files and directories.

```
use autodie ':all';
use File::Path qw(make_path remove_tree);
make_path('path/to/create/', 'another/path/to/create');
remove_tree('path/to/remove');
```

Those should be self-explanatory. The latter removes a "tree" because `path/to/remove/` may have a complete directory tree underneath it. As with other modules listed here, see the documentation to understand all that it can do. Only the basics are covered here. You can use `autodie` to make error handling a bit safer, but the docs show a slightly different approach.

File::Find::Rule

Object-oriented Perl hasn't been covered yet (that's in Chapter 12), but the `File::Find::Rule` module is so useful that it's explained briefly now. If you don't understand what's going on, bookmark this page to return to after you read Chapter 12.

`File::Find::Rule` is an excellent alternative to the `File::Find` module because it has a cleaner syntax that is easier to follow. The code to find HTML documents becomes this:

```
my @html_docs = File::Find::Rule
  ->file
  ->name(qr/\.html?$/)
  ->in(@directories);
```

The `->` syntax, as you may recall, is the *dereferencing operator*. In this case it's also used when you call methods on an object. Chapter 12 covers objects more, but for now, be aware that `->file`, `->name`, and `->in` are sort of like subroutine calls. With the `File::Find::Rule` examples, just note the syntax, and try these examples on your own. You'll understand this better when objects are covered.

Moving along, here's how to find empty files:

```
my @empty = File::Find::Rule->file->empty->in(@directories);
```

You'll note how naturally that reads. The `file()` method means Find Only Files. The `empty()` method means Find Only Empty Files (or directories, if you asked for directories). The `in()` method means, well, I'm sure you get the idea by now. The `name()` method seen just a bit earlier takes a glob or regex and returns everything matching that.

So say you're converting a project from the Subversion source control system to git, and you want to delete all of Subversion's annoying `.svn` directories; you could do this:

```
use File::Path 'remove_tree';
use File::Find::Fule;
my @svn_dirs = File::Find::Rule->directory->name('.svn')->in($dir);
foreach my $svn_dir (@svn_dirs) {
    remove_tree($svn_dir)
      or die "Cannot rmdir($svn_dir): $!";
}
```

`File::Find::Rule` also provides an `exec()` method. Like `File::Find`, it takes a callback (a subreference passed to it). Unlike `File::Find`, it passes relevant variables to the subref as arguments, so the preceding could be written as this:

```
File::Find::Rule->find->directory->name('.svn')->exec( sub {
    my ( $short_name, $directory, $fullname ) = @_;
    remove_tree($svn_dir)
      or die "Cannot rmdir($svn_dir): $!";
} )->in(@directories);
```

If the `exec()` method is encountered, the `$short_name`, `$directory`, and `$fullname` are passed to the subref. These are analogous to the `$_`, `$File::Find::dir`, and `$File::Find::name` variables used with `File::Find`.

Of course, sometimes you prefer an iterator. This is handy when you work with a large directory structure and you want to process everything as it's encountered rather than waiting for a list to be generated. So instead of this:

```
my @html_docs = File::Find::Rule->file
                            ->name(qr/\.html?$/)
                            ->in(@directories);
```

You could write this:

```
my $find = File::Find::Rule->file
                        ->name(qr/\.html?$/)
                        ->start(@directories);

while ( defined ( my $html_document = $find->match ) ) {
    # do something with $html_document
}
```

Or maybe you want to print all files greater than a half meg?

```
File::Find::Rule
  ->file
  ->size('>.5M')
  ->exec(sub {
      my ( $short_name, $directory, $fullname ) = @_;
      print "$fullname\n";
  })->in(@ARGV);
```

Like `File::Find`, `File::Find::Rule` has many options, so reading the documentation is useful.

TRY IT OUT **Recursively Printing a Directory Structure**

Some systems come with a command-line utility named `tree` that prints out a text representation of a file tree. For example, your author wrote this book using the Vim editor and wrote a filetype plug-in named `wroxbook.vim` and a syntax file with the same name. He stored them in a `vim/` directory in `ftplugin/` and `syntax/` directories. The directory structure looks like this (produced by the afore-mentioned `tree` utility):

```
vim
|-- ftplugin
|   `-- wroxbook.vim
`-- syntax
    `-- wroxbook.vim
```

We'll write a simple Perl version of this that will print the following output for that directory structure:

```
vim/
|   ftplugin/
|   |--wroxbook.vim
|   syntax/
|   |--wroxbook.vim
```

It's not quite as pretty as the tree utility, but it works for files and directories. You may want to keep this program handy (and have it somewhere in your path) as it's used to refer to file and directory layout in later chapters. All the code in this Try It Out can be found in the code file example_9_2_tree.pl.

1. Type in the following program, and save it as example_9_2_tree.pl. Use the autodie module here. You need to install this from the CPAN.

```perl
use strict;
use warnings;
use autodie ':all';
use File::Spec::Functions qw(catdir splitdir);

# The starting directory wil be passed on the command line.
# Otherwise, use the current directory.
my $dir = @ARGV ? $ARGV[0] : '.';

unless ( -d $dir ) {
    die "($dir) is not a directory";
}
print_entries( $dir, 0 );
exit 0;

sub print_entries {
    my ( $dir, $depth ) = @_;
    my @directories = grep { $_ } splitdir($dir);
    my $short_name  = $directories[-1];
    my $prefix      = '|   ' x $depth;

    print "$prefix$short_name/\n";
    opendir( my $dh, $dir );

    # grab everything that does not start with a .
    my @entries = sort grep { !/^\./ } readdir($dh);
    foreach my $entry (@entries) {
        my $path = catdir( $dir, $entry );
        if ( -f $path ) {
            print "$prefix|--$entry\n";
        }
        elsif ( -d _ ) {
            print_entries( $path, $depth + 1 );
        }
        else {
            # skip anything not a file or directory
        }
    }
}
```

2. Run the program with `perl example_9_2_tree.pl dirname`. You should see a text representation of the directory you passed to it as an argument. If you had the same `vim/` directory structure as previously outlined, you should see the following output:

```
vim/
|   ftplugin/
|   |--wroxbook.vim
|   syntax/
|   |--wroxbook.vim
```

How It Works

The `File::Spec::Functions` module is used, and you can import the `catdir()` and `splitdir()` functions. These are used to join directories together and to split them into their component parts. Under the hood, this module recognizes your operating system and, most important, how to recognize directories and files. For example, in Macs prior to OS X, the path separator was the colon, `:`. You don't have to know this because `File::Spec::Functions` can take care of it for you.

When you first call `print_entries()`, you can see the following three lines of code:

```
my @directories = grep { '' ne $_ } splitdir($dir);
my $short_name  = $directories[-1];     # grab the last parth
my $prefix      = '|  ' x $depth;
```

The `grep { '' ne $_ }` looks strange, but `splitdir()` may return empty strings for directory separators because these are significant on some operating systems. If you passed `vim/` as the argument to this program, the first time you called this function, `@directories` would be set to (`'vim'`, `''`) and the name would then be the empty string. You can avoid this by using `grep` to select only directory parts not equal to the empty string. (`grep { $_ }` fails because a `0` (zero) is a perfectly valid directory name but evaluates as false.)

The `$short_name` is the last directory in the path. Otherwise, you could end up with output that keeps repeating irrelevant information that obscures our intent. You would have this:

```
beginning_perl/
|   beginning_perl/vim/
|   |   beginning_perl/vim/ftplugin/
|   |   |-- wroxbook.vim
|   |   beginning_perl/vim/syntax/
|   |   |-- wroxbook.vim
```

Instead of this:

```
beginning_perl/
|   vim/
|   |   ftplugin/
|   |   |-- wroxbook.vim
|   |   syntax/
|   |   |-- wroxbook.vim
```

The $prefix variable is a string like '| | | ', corresponding to the number of directories ($depth) you have. You could have used splitdir() and counted them if you didn't want to pass the $depth variable.

Then you can print the current directory:

```
print "$prefix$short_name/\n";
```

Then open the directory, and for everything in it that does not start with a dot, add it to the @entries array:

```
opendir( my $dh, $dir );
my @entries = sort grep { !/^\./ } readdir($dh);
```

Then go through every entry, using File::Spec::Functions::catdir() to add the original directory name to the entry. Otherwise, -f and -d won't find the file you want.

```
foreach my $entry (@entries) {
    my $path = catdir( $dir, $entry );
    if ( -f $path ) {
        print "$prefix|--$entry\n";
    }
    elsif ( -d _ ) {
        print_entries( $path, $depth + 1 );
    }
    else {
        # skip anything not a file or directory
    }
}
```

You can use _ with -d to avoid calling stat() on the file again and minimizing disk I/O. (This can get expensive if you have a large number of files and directories.)

The trailing else block is not necessary here, but it's good practice to remind programmers that you are deliberately not processing symbolic links, sockets, or anything else that might not be a file or directory. Otherwise, a maintenance programmer might assume this is a bug in your code. Remember: Always double-check if/elsif conditions if they do not have a trailing else block.

And just to remind you of the value of using modules and CPAN, the following is the same code rewritten in an iterative fashion with File::Find::Rule.

```
use strict;
use warnings;
use File::Spec::Functions 'splitdir';
use File::Find::Rule;

my $dir = @ARGV ? $ARGV[0] : '.';
my $rule = File::Find::Rule->any(
    File::Find::Rule->directory,   # only directories
    File::Find::Rule->file,        # or files
)->start($dir);
```

```
while ( defined( my $found = $rule->match ) ) {
    next if $found =~ /^\./;
    my @directories = splitdir($found);
    my $name        = pop @directories;

    if ( -f $found ) {
        print "|    " x ( @directories - 1 );
        print "|-- $name\n";
    }
    else {
        print "|    " x @directories;
        print "$name/\n";
    }
}
}
```

Many times in the rest of this book, we'll find this ability to print out the tree structure of directories useful, so we'll be running this program a lot and will refer to it as `tree.pl` for simplicity.

SUMMARY

This chapter covered the basics of file and directory manipulation in Perl. You learned how to open files and read and write to them. You learned about file test operators to check for interesting properties about your filesystem and how to use `binmode()` to tell Perl how it's supposed to read and write the data in filehandles.

Also, because this is the first chapter to start working with data outside of your program, Unicode was introduced. It's a complicated topic and one that more and more programmers are expected to understand. Due to the Internet, what was previously a problem encountered by only a handful of people is one that many must now deal with and understand. You can save yourself much grief in your future career by coming to grips with it now.

EXERCISES

1. The Unix `cat` utility takes a list of files as arguments and concatenates them, printing the result to STDOUT. Write this utility in Perl as `cat.pl`. (If you know the UNIX `cat` utility, you don't need to provide the rest of the behavior.)

2. Modify `cat.pl` to strip comments and blank lines. Consider a comment to be any line in a file that begins with zero or more spaces followed by a # symbol.

3. Write a program, `codepoints2char.pl`, that can take a list of decimal (not hexadecimal) numbers and print the Unicode character. Assume UTF-8. Try running it with the following:

```
perl codepoint2char.pl 3232 95 3232
```

> **NOTE** This exercise is problematic because it requires the proper fonts installed for the code points you want to display. The 3232 (U+0CA0) code point is from Kannada, one of the Dravidian languages of India. You may need to search for an install of a free Kannada font.

4. Write a program, `chars2codepoints.pl`, which can take a list of words on the command line and print out, in decimal, their code points separated by spaces, having each word's list of code points on a separate line. You can search Wikipedia for interesting lists of words written in other scripts.

5. (Extra Credit) Print out the values from exercise as Unicode code points. In other words, decimal 3232 becomes U+0CA0. (Hint: see `sprintf()` or `printf()` in Chapter 4.)

▶ WHAT YOU LEARNED IN THIS CHAPTER

TOPIC	KEY CONCEPTS
open()	The function for opening files for reading and writing.
File test operators	Used for testing various properties of files and directories.
The diamond operator	A shortcut for opening files from the command line.
Temporary files	Files that are deleted when your program ends.
The DATA section	Storing data in your program as a file.
Binmode	Used to give hints to Perl on how to read/write files.
opendir, readdir	Functions for reading directories.
Globbing	Patterns to match files and directories.
Unicode	A standard for describing all character sets.
UTF-8	The most popular Unicode encoding.
Unicode character properties	Ways to identify interesting features of a character.
File::Find	A module used to make directory traversal easier.
File::Path	A module that makes path manipulation easier.
File::Find::Rule	A clean alternative to File::Find.

10

sort, map, and grep

WHAT YOU WILL LEARN IN THIS CHAPTER:

➤ Sorting lists alphabetically and numerically

➤ Creating custom sorts with sort subroutines

➤ Using map and grep to efficiently transform and filter lists and avoiding their traps

➤ Combing map, sort, and grep to create powerful list manipulations

WROX.COM CODE DOWNLOAD FOR THIS CHAPTER

The wrox.com code downloads for this chapter are found at http://www.wrox.com/remtitle .cgi?isbn=1118013840 on the Download Code tab. The code for this chapter is divided into the following major examples:

➤ example_10_1_soldier.pl

➤ example_10_2_is_prime.pl

➤ example_10_3_celsius.pl

➤ listing_10_1_employee.pl

➤ listing_10_2_collate.pl

➤ listing_10_3_locale_sort.pl

By this time in the book you should have a sufficient understanding of Perl that you're able to use it for small tasks in relation to your day-to-day work. However, there's an odd sort of "litmus test" for Perl developers. For some reason, understanding sort, map, and grep seems to be the difference between beginner and intermediate Perl developers. When you cross this threshold, you're well on your way to being a Perl expert.

Though sort, map, and grep have been mentioned briefly, their usage has deliberately been kept simple. Now you can see a bit more about their full power.

The one thing to remember is that each of these creates a new list from an old list.

BASIC SORTING

The sort builtin sorts a list and returns a new list. It has three forms:

```
sort LIST
sort BLOCK LIST
sort SUBNAME LIST
```

As an example of each:

```
@passengers = sort                          @passengers;
@passengers = sort { $a->{age} <=> $b->{age} } @passengers;
@passengers = women_and_children_first      @passengers;
```

Sorting Alphabetically

The simplest sort in Perl is this:

```
my @list = sort qw(this is a list);
print "@list";
```

That prints out the Yoda-esque phrase: a is list this. By default, sort sorts items with a string comparison. Well, actually, it sorts items via a numeric comparison of the string's code point, from lower to higher values. So the following line:

```
# declare our source code as UTF-8
use utf8;
# and we're printing UTF-8
binmode STDOUT, 'encoding(UTF-8)';
print join ' ', sort qw/b 日 aa 国 1 本 a A/;
```

Prints this:

```
1 A a aa b 国 日 本
```

> **NOTE** *If you're unsure of why Perl sorts in this order, you can convert each character to its UTF-8 code point with this (obviously, the aa is left out for this example):*
>
> ```
> use utf8::all;
> print join ' ', map { as_code_point($_) } sort qw/b 日 国 1 本 a
> A/;
> sub as_code_point {
>     my $char = shift;
>     die "Only characters!" if length($char) > 1;
>     return "U+" . uc sprintf "%04x", ord $char;
> }
> ```
>
> *And that prints out this:*
>
> ```
> U+0031 U+0041 U+0061 U+0062 U+56FD U+65E5 U+672C
> ```
>
> *As you can see, by default Perl's sort will sort characters in ascending order by their numerical* ord() *value. If you don't understand the* map, *don't worry. It is explained carefully in the "map and grep" section later in this chapter.*
>
> *If you want to see the decimal value of the numbers, use this:*
>
> ```
> use utf8::all;
> print join ' ', map ord, sort qw/b 日 国 1 本 a A/;
> ```

Sorting Numerically

Perl's default `sort` (more or less) sorts strings as characters. This means that if you do this:

```
print join "\n", sort qw/1 9 10 99 222/;
```

You get this:

```
1
10
222
9
99
```

You probably meant to sort your numbers numerically. In this case, you can provide a `sort` block:

```
print join "\n", sort { $a <=> $b } qw/1 9 10 99 222/;
```

And now you get the correct sort order:

```
1
9
10
99
222
```

In the form sort BLOCK LIST, Perl iterates over the pairs of items in the list and sets the special package variables $a and $b to each element in the list in turn. The <=> operator (sometimes called the spaceship operator) was covered in Chapter 4. In this case, it tells Perl to compare $a and $b as numbers instead of strings.

> **WARNING** *The $a and $b variables are special package variables. Do not declare them with* my *or else your* sort *blocks are likely to break.*

Reverse Sorting

Many times you want a list reversed. You could do this:

```
my @reversed_names = reverse sort @names;
```

That reads clearly, but for larger lists, this is inefficient. It sorts the list into ascending order and then reverses it into descending order. Why not just sort directly into reverse descending order? In this case, you can use a sort block and swap the $a and $b variables.

```
my @reversed_names = sort { $b cmp $a } @names;
This works when sorting numbers in descending order, too:
my @descending = sort { $b <=> $a } @numbers;
```

Complex Sort Conditions

When sorting on a single value, sorting is straightforward, but if you need to sort on multiple values, you need to use a sort block or sort subroutine. Listing 10-1 (code file listing_10_1_employee. pl) shows an example of complex sorting.

LISTING 10-1: Complex Sorting in Perl

```perl
use strict;
use warnings;
use diagnostics;
my @employees = (
    {
        name     => 'Sally Jones',
        years    => 4,
        payscale => 4,
    },
    {
        name     => 'Abby Hoffman',
        years    => 1,
        payscale => 10,
    },
```

```
        {
            name     => 'Jack Johnson',
            years    => 4,
            payscale => 5,
        },
        {
            name     => 'Mr. Magnate',
            years    => 12,
            payscale => 1,
        },
    );
    @employees =
        sort {
            $b->{years}    <=> $a->{years}
            ||
            $a->{payscale} <=> $b->{payscale}
        }
        @employees;
    printf "Name            Years Payscale\n";
    foreach my $employee (@employees) {
        printf "%-15s %2d        %2d\n" => @{$employee}{qw/name years payscale/};
    }
```

Running `listing_10_1_employee.pl` prints the following:

```
Name           Years Payscale
Mr. Magnate     12        1
Sally Jones      4        4
Jack Johnson     4        5
Abby Hoffman     1       10
```

The idea in this case is that you want to print a list of employees. They should be printed from the highest number of years in the company to the lowest. That's your first sort condition:

```
$b->{years} <=> $a->{years}
```

The $b and the $a are reversed to provide a descending sort.

But Sally Jones and Jack Johnson have the same number of years with the company. The highest payscale is 1 and the lowest is 10, and if a tie occurs, you need to print employees from highest to lowest payscale (in other words, from 1 to 10).

```
$a->{payscale} <=> $b->{payscale}
```

You may remember that the <=> operator returns 0 (zero) if the two terms are equal, so you can use the || operator to sort by payscale if the employees have the same number of years with the company:

```
@employees =
    sort {
        $b->{years}    <=> $a->{years}
        ||
```

```
      $a->{payscale} <=> $b->{payscale}
    }
    @employees;
```

What happens if the employees have the same number of years and the same payscale? Well, just throw in a sort by name:

```
@employees =
  sort {
      $b->{years}    <=> $a->{years}
      ||
      $a->{payscale} <=> $b->{payscale}
      ||
      $a->{name}     cmp $b->{name}
  }
  @employees;
```

This looks like a lot of work, but the || operator short-circuits. That means that because only one of the conditions is required to be true, as soon as one of the conditions evaluates as true, the subsequent conditions are not evaluated. It's actually a fairly efficient sort.

Writing a sort Subroutine

In handling complex sorts, you might find that this is a bit daunting:

```
@employees =
  sort {
      $b->{years}    <=> $a->{years}
      ||
      $a->{payscale} <=> $b->{years}
      ||
      $a->{name}     cmp $b->{name}
  }
  @employees;
```

The fix is simple. Put that sort block into a subroutine, and replace the block with the subroutine name:

```
sub by_seniority_then_pay_then_name {
    $b->{years}    <=> $a->{years}
    ||
    $a->{payscale} <=> $b->{years}
    ||
    $a->{name}     cmp $b->{name}
}
@employees = sort by_seniority_then_pay_then_name @employees;
```

When you have a complex sort condition, giving it a named sort subroutine improves readability quite a bit. As an added bonus, if you need to replicate a complex sort elsewhere, you already have the code handy.

> **NOTE** For those who are curious, Perl's `sort`, by default, is stable. This means that if two values compare the same way, they will be returned in the same order they were originally found. Thus, if you left off the sorting by name condition in your employee sort, all employees with the same years and payscale would be guaranteed to be returned in the order they were in on the original list. This is useful, particularly if you have a list that is already partially sorted. This is far more common than you think.

Some people prefer to not use the $a and $b variables. They are not strictly required in the `sort` subroutine. If you want to use variables with names of your choosing (and not $a or $b) you need to use a $$ prototype to force passing $a and $b to the sort sub for assignment to your variables:

```
sub by_seniority_then_pay_then_name($$) {
    my ( $employee1, $employee2 ) = @_;
    $employee2->{years}    <=> $employee1->{years}
    ||
    $employee1->{payscale} <=> $employee2->{years}
    ||
    $employee1->{name}     cmp $employee2->{name}
}
@employees = sort by_seniority_then_pay_then_name @employees;
```

Be aware that if you do this, the `sort` subroutine will be a bit slower because as an optimization in Perl, the $a and $b variables are automatically aliased by Perl when `sort` is encountered.

Sorting and Unicode Fun!

Why do you sort data? You do so to make it faster for:

➤ Computers to find data

➤ Humans to find data

If all you care about is to make it faster for computers to find data, the default `sort` behavior is often fine. However, humans are an annoyingly troublesome lot. In Swedish, the letter z comes before the letter ö, but in German it's the other way around. If you're sorting data for display to people, they will complain bitterly (and quite rightly) if they have trouble finding what they need because the sort order of the data is not what they expect, so you need to make sure that you're sorting correctly for your target audience.

And here's another fun example. Run the following code:

```
use utf8::all;
use charnames ":full";
print "\N{ANGSTROM SIGN}\n";
print "\N{LATIN CAPITAL LETTER A WITH RING ABOVE}\n";
```

That prints out this:

o

Å

Those are the Unicode code points U+212B and U+00C5, respectively, but for purposes of sorting or comparison, they are supposed to be considered the same character. Further, Unicode has a combining-character to indicate that two symbols should be combined. This gives Unicode great flexibility in representing different characters. Using the two preceding code points along with an uppercase A and a COMBINING RING ABOVE gives this code:

```
use charnames ':short';
binmode STDOUT, ':encoding(UTF-8)';
print "\N{U+212B}\n";
print "\N{U+00C5}\n";
print "\N{U+0041}\N{U+030A}\n";
```

Which prints this:

o

Å

Å

Many computers can actually print those slightly differently, but they should look generally similar, and for purposes of sorting and comparing (cmp), they must, as already stated, be considered the same character despite being different code points. This information is repeated because it's important, and there's a good chance you'll get it wrong. But don't feel bad. Perl's default sort builtin also gets this wrong.

> **WARNING** Although Å (U+212B), Å (U+00C5) and Å (U+0041 U+030A) are considered to be identical characters, the fact that they look the same is an accident. Do not rely on a character's appearance to decide whether two characters are the same.

So how do you get this right? Collation. *Collation*, for our purposes, is defining the correct order for data. Sorting, by contrast, is putting data into that correct order. The Unicode Collation Algorithm, described at http://www.unicode.org/reports/tr10/, tells you how to do properly collate Unicode data. Fortunately, the Unicode::Collate module was first included with Perl in version 5.7.3 and implements the Unicode Collation Algorithm for you.

So as a general rule, sorting is handled correctly with the code shown in Listing 10-2 (code file listing_10_2_collate.pl).

LISTING 10-2: Using Unicode::Collate

```
use strict;
use warnings;
use diagnostics;
use utf8::all;
```

```
use Unicode::Collate;
my @apples = (
    "\N{U+212B}pples",
    "\N{U+00C5}pples",
    "\N{U+0041}\N{U+030A}pples",
    "apples",
    "Apples",
);
my @bad    = sort @apples;
my @sorted = Unicode::Collate->new->sort(@apples);
print "Original: @apples\n";
print "Sorted:   @bad\n";
print "Collated: @sorted\n";
```

Running `listing_10_2_collate.pl` prints out this:

```
Original: Åpples Åpples Åpples apples Apples
Sorted:   Apples Åpples apples Åpples Åpples
Collated: apples Apples Åpples Åpples Åpples
```

The second line, `Sorted:`, starts with `Apples Åpples apples`. Clearly that's not right, but Perl's default sort does not recognize the U+0041 U+0030A as being combined. It merely sorts on the numeric value of the individual octets, leading to incorrect sorting.

`Unicode::Collate` is great, but you often need to sort according to a specific locale. In Perl, you can do this:

```
use locale; # but don't really do this
```

That tells Perl to use the proper sorting for your system's LC_COLLATE environment variable. Unfortunately, many programmers have been bitten by this because not all operating systems support this, nor are the locales guaranteed to be installed, ensuring that this method is not portable. Instead, use `Unicode::Collate::Locale`.

As previously mentioned, in Swedish the letter z comes before the letter ö, but the sort order is reversed in German. Listing 10-3 shows the use of `Unicode::Collate::Locale` to get the correct sort order (code file `listing_10_3_locale_sort.pl`).

LISTING 10-3: Using Unicode::Collate::Locale to Sort According to Locale

```
use strict;
use warnings;
use utf8::all;
use Unicode::Collate::Locale;
my @letters  = qw(z ö);
my @reversed = reverse @letters;
my $german  = Unicode::Collate::Locale->new( locale => 'de_DE' );
my $swedish = Unicode::Collate::Locale->new( locale => 'sv_SE' );
foreach my $letters ( \@letters, \@reversed ) {
    print "Original: @$letters\n";
    my @german  = $german->sort(@$letters);
```

continues

LISTING 10-3 *(continued)*

```
    my @swedish = $swedish->sort(@$letters);
    print "German:   @german\n";
    print "Swedish:  @swedish\n\n";
}
```

When you run `listing_10_3_locale_sort.pl`, you should see the following:

```
Original: z ö
German:   ö z
Swedish:  z ö
Original: ö z
German:   ö z
Swedish:  z ö
```

`Unicode::Collate::Locale` was first released with `Unicode::Collate` version 0.55 in August 2010, so you may need to install a newer version of `Unicode::Collate` from the CPAN.

TRY IT OUT   **Sorting by External Criteria**

Sometimes you need to sort by criteria that is not directly represented in your data. One way to handle this is to define your sort criteria in a separate data structure. Imagine a fictitious military that has Generals, Colonels, Majors, Captains, and Privates. They're a bit top-heavy on officers and they like their personnel reports to have those important officers sorted at the top. All the code in this Try It Out is found in code file `example_10_1_soldier.pl`.

1. Type in the following program, and save it as `example_10_1_soldier.pl`:

```
use strict;
use warnings;
my %sort_order_for = (
    General => 1,
    Colonel => 2,
    Major   => 3,
    Captain => 4,
    Private => 5,
);
my @soldiers = (
    { name => 'Custer',
      rank => 'General' },
    { name => 'Crassus',
      rank => 'General' },
    { name => 'Burnside',
      rank => 'General' },
    { name => 'Potter',
      rank => 'Colonel' },
    { name => 'Bickle',
      rank => 'Private' },
);
@soldiers = sort {
    $sort_order_for{$a->{rank}} <=> $sort_order_for{$b->{rank}}
    ||
    $a->{name} cmp $b->{name}
```

```
    } @soldiers;
    foreach my $soldier (@soldiers) {
        print "$soldier->{rank} $soldier->{name}\n";
    }
```

2. Run the program with `perl example_10 1_soldier.pl`. You should see the following output:

```
General Burnside
General Crassus
General Custer
Colonel Potter
Private Bickle
```

How It Works

None of the soldier records actually contain the value you first need to sort on, so construct a hash named `%sort_order_for` to contain your sort value. The first `sort` criteria evaluates as the numeric value you need to sort on. Had you merely sorted on rank, `Colonel Potter` would have been listed higher than those Generals (not a bad thing given those Generals' records for historic defeats).

However, for each of `Burnside`, `Crassus`, and `Custer`, the first sort condition evaluates to `1 <=> 1`, so you can fall back to your second sort condition, their name, to complete the sorting:

```
    ||
    $a->{name} cmp $b->{name}
```

Had you left off the second sort condition, the list would look like this:

```
General Custer
General Crassus
General Burnside
Colonel Potter
Private Bickle
```

That shows that you have a stable sort, preserving the original order for values considered "equal."

map and grep

Many times you want to filter or transform a list instead of (or in addition to) sorting the list. The `grep` builtin is for filtering lists. Maybe you want to create a new list of all elements of an old list that are greater than zero? The `grep` builtin is the tool you're looking for.

The `map` builtin allows you to take a list and transform in into another list. For example, you might want to multiply all list elements by two, but assign it to a new list rather than altering the original.

Let's start with filtering the list first.

Using grep

You used the grep builtin a few times in this book and the examples are deliberately kept simple to make the basic use clear. However, pretend you've never heard of it just to give you a quick refresher. The grep builtin takes a list and produces another list of all values matching grep's criteria. For example, to use only numbers greater than zero, use this code:

```
my @greater = grep { $_ > 0 } @numbers;
```

The grep builtin takes two forms:

```
NEWLIST = grep BLOCK        LIST;
NEWLIST = grep EXPRESSION, LIST;
```

The first form, used in the preceding code is probably the most popular. You could have written the "greater than zero" filter as any of these three:

```
my @greater = grep { $_ > 0 } @numbers;
my @greater = grep   $_ > 0,   @numbers;
my @greater = grep(  $_ > 0,   @numbers );
```

The grep BLOCK does not take a comma after the block, whereas grep EXPRESSION does.

When using grep, you can iterate over every element in the LIST, setting each element in turn to $_. The grep builtin returns only elements for which the BLOCK or EXPRESSION returns true. You can have arbitrarily complex expressions in the grep. To grab the palindromes from a list, use this code:

```
my @palindromes = grep { uc eq reverse uc } @words;
```

NOTE *Your author debated quite a bit about writing this palindrome checker:*

```
my @palindromes = grep { uc eq reverse uc } @words;
```

Ignoring Unicode issues here (in some encodings, characters are different depending on their location in a word), it might seem "friendlier" to write the code like this:

```
my @palindromes = grep { uc($_) eq scalar reverse uc($_) }
    @words;
```

The reason the first version works is because uc *operates on the* $_ *version by default. The* scalar *builtin is often used with* reverse *to force it to reverse a string, but the* eq *forces scalar context, rendering the* scalar *keyword redundant. Although you should use the longer form to avoid confusion, you need to get used to seeing the shorter forms, so they will be used from time to time.*

Because a bare regex matches against $_, this is often seen in grep. To find words beginning with the vowels a, e, i, o, or u, use this code:

```
my @starts_with_vowels = grep { /^[aeiou]/ } @words;
```

Because grep returns a list, you can combine this with sort. To find all numbers greater than or equal to 10 and return them sorted from lowest to highest, use this code:

```
my @numbers = ( 13, 3, -2, 7, 270, 19, -3.2, 10.1 );
my @result = sort { $a <=> $b } grep { $_ >= 10 } @numbers;
print join ', ', @result;
```

And that prints the following:

```
10.1, 13, 19, 270
```

When chaining list builtins like this, many people prefer to write them on separate lines to make things more clear:

```
my @result = sort { $a <=> $b }
                grep { $_ >= 10  } @numbers;
```

When using list builtins such as grep, they can operate on an entire list. Sometimes you see code like this:

```
my @positive = grep { $_ > 0 } @numbers;
my $first    = $positive[0];
```

That can be inefficient, particularly if you have a lot of @numbers. A for loop with last is better.

```
my $first;
for (@numbers) {
    if ( $_ > 0 ) {
        $first = $_;
        last;
    }
}
```

That for loop terminates the search through @numbers on the first successful match, if any. Of course, if none of the @numbers are greater than zero, it's not more efficient than the grep.

TRY IT OUT   Grepping for Prime Numbers

Often, you might want to create a new list from an old list based on particular criteria, but that criteria can be expensive to compute. The following program returns a list of primes from a list but caches all prime numbers found so that you don't waste time recalculating whether a given number is prime.

Assume that your resulting list of primes should contain all primes from the supplied list of numbers, even if they're duplicates. Also assume that you're printing only unique primes. Otherwise, your list will be rather large and filled with duplicate numbers. All the code for this Try It Out can be found in the code file example_10_2_is_prime.pl.

1. Type in the following program, and save it as `example_10_2_is_prime.pl`:

```perl
use strict;
use warnings;
use diagnostics;
use List::MoreUtils 'uniq';
use Time::HiRes qw(gettimeofday tv_interval);
my $is_slow = 0;
my @numbers = qw( 3 2 39 7919 997 631 200 7919 459 7919 623 997 867 15 );
@numbers = (@numbers) x 200000;
my @primes;
my $start = [gettimeofday];
if ( $is_slow ) {
    @primes = grep { is_prime($_) } @numbers;
}
else {
    my %is_prime;
    @primes = grep {
                ( exists $is_prime{$_} and $is_prime{$_} )
                or
                ( $is_prime{$_} = is_prime($_) )
            } @numbers;
}
my $elapsed = tv_interval($start);
printf "We took %0.1f seconds to find the primes\n", $elapsed;
print join ', ' => sort { $a <=> $b } uniq @primes;
sub is_prime {
    my $number = $_[0];
    return   if $number < 2;
    return 1 if $number == 2;
    for ( 2 .. int sqrt($number) ) {
        return if !($number % $_);
    }
    return 1;
}
```

2. Run the program with `perl example_10_2_is_prime.pl`. You should see output similar to the following:

```
We took 2.7 seconds to find the primes
2, 3, 631, 997, 7919
```

The exact number of seconds depends on how fast your computer is.

3. Now, change `my $is_slow = 0;` to `my $is_slow = 1;` and run it again. You see output similar to the following, again dependent on how fast your computer is:

```
We took 10.1 seconds to find the primes
2, 3, 631, 997, 7919
```

When you use the slow version, finding primes takes almost four times longer than your fast version.

How It Works

Let's revisit the definition of a prime number. A *prime number* is any integer greater than 1 that is evenly divisible (in other words, no remainder) only by 1 and itself. You know 5 is prime because dividing it by 2 leaves a remainder of 1, 3 leaves a remainder of 2, and 4 leaves a remainder of 1. The number 15 is not prime because dividing it by 5 leaves a remainder of 0, so it's evenly divisible by 5.

That leaves you with the following definition of is_prime():

```
sub is_prime {
    my $number = $_[0];
    return    if $number < 2;
    return 1 if $number == 2;
    for ( 2 .. int sqrt($number) ) {
        return if !($number % $_);
    }
    return 1;
}
```

This is not the most efficient primality test, but it's easy to understand. It's also slow, so you can cache its results.

You return false (return with no arguments) if the number is less than 2 ($number < 2) because by definition, it's not prime. You also return true (1) if the number is 2. That's because the test in the for loop would incorrectly return false for 2, which is prime:

```
return if !($number % 2);
```

Now break that down so you can understand this rather common idiom.

The % operator is the modulus operator. (See Chapter 4 if you don't remember this.) If your number is 8, you know that 8 % 2 returns zero, so that line evaluates to this:

```
return if !(0);
```

The ! symbol negates the truth value of its argument, so the line then evaluates to the following:

```
return if 1;
```

And that is equivalent to:

```
return;
```

Because a bare return (a return that doesn't return any arguments) is evaluated as false, you are effectively returning false from this function. However, the return if !($number % 2) line would return false for 2, so check to see if your $number is 2 on the line prior to the for loop.

Then you have the actual loop:

```
    for ( 2 .. int sqrt($number) ) {
        return if !($number % $_);
    }
    return 1;
```

The loop iterates from 2 to the square root of the number passed to it. Remember that the range operator, `. .` , (see Chapter 4) creates a range from the left number to the right number. For every iteration through the loop, if any number you test returns 0 for `$number % $_`, you know that the `$number` is evenly divisible by some number other than 1 and itself, and you thus `return`. When you get to the end of the loop, you return a true value to indicate that you have a prime number. You may want to walk through this function a couple of times to understand it.

Now that you have the prime number check out of the way, take a look at the rest:

```
use List::MoreUtils 'uniq';
use Time::HiRes qw(gettimeofday tv_interval);
```

Import the `uniq` function from `List::MoreUtils`. (You may have to install this module from the CPAN.) That later enables you to have only `uniq` number for printing. The `Time::HiRes` module was included in Perl 5.7.3 and later, so you probably already have it on your system. See the documentation for how it works. You are just going to use it to show elapsed time.

The `$is_slow` variable is merely a boolean indicating whether you're going to use the slow version of your `grep` or the fast version.

Next, you have this curious bit:

```
my @numbers = qw( 3 2 39 7919 997 631 200 7919 459 7919 623 997 867 15 );
@numbers = (@numbers) x 200000;
```

The `@numbers` array contains 14 numbers. The line after this uses the `(VARIABLE) x REPEAT` syntax. As explained in Chapter 4, when you put parentheses around the value to the left of the x operator, it's in list context and replicates that list REPEAT times. Thus, your original 14 numbers expand into a list of 2,800,000 elements (almost 3 million elements!). That's quite a large list to search through.

If `$is_slow` is true, you executes the following normal `grep` statement:

```
@primes = grep { is_prime($_) } @numbers;
```

However, because you must recompute the value of `is_prime()` every time, it can be quite slow, particularly when you have a list of almost 3 million elements to search through.

If `$is_slow` is false, you execute the following code:

```
my %is_prime;
@primes = grep {
            ( exists $is_prime{$_} and $is_prime{$_} )
            or
            ( $is_prime{$_} = is_prime($_) )
        } @numbers;
```

The `%is_prime` hash is your cache. If a number is in that hash, you know you already calculated its primality:

```
( exists $is_prime{$_} and $is_prime{$_} )
```

Otherwise, you calculate its primality and store it in the hash, taking advantage that an assignment also returns the value assigned.

```
( $is_prime{$_} = is_prime($_) )
```

Finally, you have your `print` statement:

```
print join ', ' => sort { $a <=> $b } uniq @primes;
```

You sort *after* you find the unique values because there's no point to sort the entire list only to throw away duplicates.

Because you put the prime number calculation into the function `is_prime()`, if you have a faster prime number calculation function, you can easily replace just this one function and not touch the rest of the program.

If some of this program is unclear, download it from `Wrox.com` and play around with it. (Better yet, type it in yourself.) You'll learn a lot about various issues in programming.

Using map

The `map` builtin, like the `grep` builtin, takes a list and returns a new list. It maps old values to new values. Its syntax is virtually identical to `grep`'s:

```
NEWLIST = map BLOCK        LIST;
NEWLIST = map EXPRESSION, LIST;
```

So to uppercase every word in a list, use this code:

```
my @UPPER = map { uc } @words;
```

Like `grep`, `map` operates on every element in a list, so use it only if you want to transform an entire list. And like `grep`, because it returns a list, you can chain with `grep` and `sort`. Say you have an array of numbers, and you want to take the square roots of those numbers greater than zero:

```
my @roots = map  { sqrt($_) }
                grep { $_ > 0 } @numbers:
```

TRY IT OUT   Printing Celsius Values from Fahrenheit

Often, you need to convert a list to a new set of values. Converting from Fahrenheit to Celsius is an age-old problem. Following is one way to do this, using `map`. All the code in this Try It Out is found in code file `example_10_3_celsius.pl`.

1.   Type in the following program, and save it as `example_10_3_celsius.pl`.

```
use strict;
use warnings;
binmode STDOUT, ':encoding(UTF-8)';
my %fahrenheit = (
    'absolute zero'   => -459.67,
```

```
            'freezing water'   => 32,
            'body temperature' => 98.6,
            'boiling water'    => 212,
   );
   my %celsius =
      map { $_ => 5 / 9 * ( $fahrenheit{$_} - 32 )  }  keys %fahrenheit;
   while ( my ( $name, $temp ) = each %celsius ) {
       print "The temperature for $name is $temp\N{U+00B0} celsius\n";
   }
```

2.   Run the program with `perl example_10_3_celsius.pl`. You should see the following output (because this is a hash, the order on your system may be different):

```
The temperature for freezing water is 0° celsius
The temperature for body temperature is 37° celsius
The temperature for boiling water is 100° celsius
The temperature for absolute zero is -273.15° celsius
```

How It Works

Transforming a hash via a `map` is a bit trickier than transforming a list, but it still uses everything you learned so far. The main magic is right here:

```
my %celsius =
   map { $_ => 5 / 9 * ( $fahrenheit{$_} - 32 )  }
   keys %fahrenheit;
```

You'll note that `keys %fahrenheit` returns a list of the keys. Each one is set to `$_`. That's the "left side" of the hash in the `$_ =>` construct. The right side (the value you need to create), needs the appropriate value for the key, so merely use `$fahrenheit{$_}` to do this, and use the standard Fahrenheit-to-Celsius formula.

In reality, what the `map` does is return an even-sized list like this:

```
"freezing water", 0, "body temperature", 37, "boiling water", 100,
"absolute zero", -273.15
```

The order of each pair is effectively random; however when this list is assigned to `%celsius`, you have the wanted hash.

The `while` loop prints out your `%celsius` hash.

```
while ( my ( $name, $temp ) = each %celsius ) {
    print "The temperature for $name is $temp\N{U+00B0} celsius\n";
}
```

The `U+00B0` Unicode code point is the degree symbol, °, and you can use the `\N{...}` syntax for this. The `binmode` tells STDOUT that it's going to get UTF-8 and avoids the `Wide character in print` warnings.

Aliasing Issues

One significant issue to be aware of with both map and grep is that when individual elements of the list are assigned to $_, they are *aliased* to the original value. This means that if you change the value of $_, you change the value of the original item. The following is a short program to demonstrate just how terribly wrong things can go if you're not aware of this. Use a lesser-known feature of Data::Dumper to name your variables in your output to make it easier to follow.

```
use Data::Dumper;
my @numbers = qw{ 1 2 3 4 5 };
my @incremented = map $_++, @numbers;    # No!
print Data::Dumper->Dump(
    [ \@numbers, \@incremented ],
    [ '*numbers', '*incremented' ]
);
```

And that prints out the following:

```
@numbers = (
            '2',
            '3',
            '4',
            '5',
            '6'
          );
@incremented = (
                '1',
                '2',
                '3',
                '4',
                '5'
              );
```

What's going on here? You haven't incremented the numbers you intended, and you incremented the original list you meant to leave alone!

Because $_ is an alias, the $_++ changes the original numbers, but because the ++ is the postfix version of the autoincrement operator, it changes the value after it's been returned. Thus, your new list gets the old values and your old list gets the new values! Here is one way to write that the way you intended it:

```
my @incremented = map $_ + 1, @numbers;
```

Also, if you use the block form of map, you can localize the value of $_ in the block, but it's beginning to look like an ugly hack.

```
my @incremented = map { local $_ = $_; ++$_ }, @numbers;
```

> **NOTE** *Many Perl developers are not aware of this alternative syntax for* Data::Dumper, *and if they are, they often avoid it because it's rather cumbersome to use. See* perldoc Data::Dumper *to understand it.*
>
> *You author has released* Data::Dumper::Names *and* Data::Dumper::Simple *to the CPAN to make this easier to use. They behave slightly differently, so read their documentation to understand the differences.*

Trying to Do Too Much

At their core, sort, map, and grep all take an existing list and return a new list. There's nothing complicated about this, but the sorting, filtering, or transforming may be complicated. Keep them simple or else they're hard to follow. You've already shown how to do it with sort by taking this:

```
@employees= sort {
    $b->{years}    <=> $a->{years}
    ||
    $a->{payscale} <=> $b->{payscale}
    ||
    $a->{name}     cmp $b->{name}
} @employees;
```

And turning it into this:

```
@employees = sort by_seniority_then_pay_then_name @employees;
```

However, you may remember this rather complicated grep:

```
my %is_prime;
@primes = grep {
            ( exists $is_prime{$_} and $is_prime{$_} )
            or
            ( $is_prime{$_} = is_prime($_) )
        } @numbers;
```

It was deliberately left complicated in the code to show how some people will write a grep statement. Instead, you can push the caching into the is_prime() function:

```
{
    my %is_prime;
    sub is_prime {
        my $number = $_[0];
        return $is_prime{$number} if exists $is_prime{$number};
        $is_prime{$number} = 0 if $number < 2;
        $is_prime{$number} = 1 if $number == 2;
        for ( 2 .. int sqrt($number) ) {
            if ( !($number % $_) ) {
                $is_prime{$number} = 0;
                last;
```

```
            }
        }
        $is_prime{$number} = 1 if !exists $is_prime{$number};
        return $is_prime{$number};
    }
}
```

By doing that, your `grep` then becomes this:

```
@primes = grep { is_prime($_) } @numbers;
```

Not only is that much easier to read, but also any other code that now calls `is_prime()` gets to take advantage of the caching.

Also, the actual `grep()` is faster than it was originally. You can discover easier ways to verify that with the `Benchmark` module covered in Chapter 18.

Trying to Be Clever

The `sort`, `map`, and `grep` functions are the type of functions that developers love to abuse. Sadly, many developers think being clever is more important than writing maintainable code so they write something like this:

```
my %person = (
    id         => 6,
    name       => 'The Prisoner',
    profession => 'Ex-Spy',
    status     => 'Silent',
);
my $result = '';
foreach ( sort { $a ne 'id' } keys %person ) {
    my $value = $person{$_};
    $result .= sprintf "%-10s - $value\n", $_;
}
print $result;
```

And that prints out this:

```
id         - 6
name       - The Prisoner
status     - Silent
profession - Ex-Spy
```

The order of `name`, `status`, and `profession` may be different on your system, but `id` is guaranteed to be first. Why? Because of the strange `sort { $a ne 'id' }` construction. As you may recall, both the `cmp` and `<=>` operators return –1, 0, or 1 depending on whether the left value is less than, equal to, or greater than the right value. The `$a ne 'id'` returns false (the empty string, in this case) that Perl treats as 0 (zero) and `$a ne $anything_else` returns 1, ensuring that the value `'id'` is always sorted first.

This sort of cleverness can be fun if you're just playing around, but for serious code, particularly in a Comp environment in which someone may need to fix something quickly, try to be clear. The following is a better solution:

```
my $format = "%-10s - %s\n";
# always have id as the first line
my $result = sprintf $format, 'id', delete $person{id};
foreach ( keys %person ) {
    my $value = $person{$_};
    $result .= sprintf $format, $_, $value;
}
```

PUTTING IT ALL TOGETHER

Now that you've covered sort, map, and grep, it's time to put all of them together for some more advanced techniques. The techniques presented here can help make your sorting much faster. They combine map and sort to great effect. You can also combine grep with sort and you'll see an example of that in the Exercises for this chapter. You won't see these as often in your code, but when you need them, they can help you out.

Schwartzian Transform (aka decorate, sort, undecorate)

Many sorting operations can be extremely expensive if you need to calculate the value to be sorted on. The Schwartzian Transform enables you to calculate once and only once a sort key, sort on it, and then strip the sort key. In other languages, this technique is sometimes known as decorate, sort, and undecorate.

Assume you have the following data in a file:

```
James|007|Spy
Number 6|6|Ex-spy
Agent 99|99|Spy with unknown name
Napoleon Solo|11|Uncle spy
Unknown|666|Maybe a spy
```

Except it's actually approximately 300,000 lines or so, and you need to sort on the number between the pipes, such as |007|. So you try a straightforward sort like this:

```
my @sorted = sort by_id <>;
sub by_id {
    $a =~ /\|(\d+)/;
    my $a_id = $1;
    $b =~ /\|(\d+)/;
    my $b_id = $1;
    return $a_id <=> $b_id;
}
```

What you've done is use a regular expression to extract the number into a variable, and then you return the variables compared with the spaceship operator. You've also been good, and you've written a sort subroutine to make the `sort` operation easier to follow, but when you run this, you find it takes 7 or 8 seconds to run.

This might be fast enough for you. If this is a one-off script, you may not care about speed. If this is part of a process that runs once a night, again you may not care about speed. However, if you call this a lot, that extra time might be problematic, so switch to the Schwartzian Transform.

```
my @sorted = map  { $_->[0] }                      # undecorate
             sort { $a->[1] <=> $b->[1] }          # sort
             map  { /\|(\d+)/; [ $_, $1 ] } <>;    # decorate
```

Now, instead of 7 or 8 seconds, it takes about 2 seconds to sort 300,000 lines, but how does it work?

> **NOTE** If you don't remember <>, the diamond operator, go to Chapter 9 and reread "The Diamond Operator" section. This operator takes a bit of time to get used to.

Both sorts compare every number to every other number, but the naïve `sort` must use a regular expression to extract the ID every time, even if it's been previously extracted. With the Schwartzian Transform, you can extract the number only once with the first `map`, known as the "decorate" step.

```
map  { /\|(\d+)/; [ $_, $1 ] } <>;  # decorate
```

The `[ $_, $1 ]` is an array reference that has the original value in the first element (remember, that's index 0) and the sort key (the ID, in this case) from `$1` in the second element (index 1).

Then the second step, the `sort`, just sorts on element 1, the sort key:

```
sort { $a->[1] <=> $b->[1] }        # sort
```

Finally, the last `map` (undecorate) returns element 0, the original string.

```
my @sorted = map  { $_->[0] }       # undecorate
```

By not re-extracting the ID for every comparison, you gain a significant speed improvement, which is the beauty of the Schwartzian Transform.

The intermediate container doesn't need to be an array. You can use a hash reference if you prefer.

```
my @sorted = map  { $_->{original} }
             sort { $a->{id} <=> $b->{id} }
             map  { /\|(\d+)/; { original => $_, id => $1 } } <>;
```

Hash lookups are slightly slower than array lookups, but even the preceding code is twice as fast as the naïve `sort`.

> **NOTE** *The Schwartzian Transform is a famous technique named after the well-known Perl hacker Randal Schwartz. He explains this technique in a UNIX Review column at* `http://www.stonehenge.com/merlyn/UnixReview/col64 .html`.

For the micro-optimization fans, you can shave another 5 to 10 percent of the time by using `index` instead of regular expressions.

```
my @sorted = map  { $_->[0] }
             sort { $a->[1] <=> $b->[1] }
             map  { my $i      = 1 + index $_, "|";
                    my $length = index( $_, "|", $i ) - $i;
                    [ $_, substr $_, $i, $length ]
             } <>;
```

How that works is an exercise left for you. You will find people trying to shave tiny amounts of time with code like this, but unless you can prove why you need to save that time, the author strongly urges you not to write code this tricky. It's a beast to maintain and can make your coworkers unhappy with your "cleverness." If you must write that, document it well.

Guttman-Rosler Transform

The *Guttman-Rosler Transform* sort technique is advanced, and you can skip this section if you want, but it's included for completeness.

When using `sort`, if you can eliminate the dereferencing in the `sort` block, you can have a faster sort. The paper "A Fresh Look at Efficient Perl Sorting" (`http://www.sysarch.com/Perl/ sort_paper.html`) by Uri Guttman and Larry Rosler, introduces the Guttman-Rosler Transform. (Although they did not call it that.)

```
my @sorted = map { substr $_, 4 }
    sort
    map { /\|(\d+)/; pack("A4", $1).$_ } <>;
```

This looks strange and you need to read `perldoc perlpacktut` to understand how `pack` works. The `pack` template, `A4`, creates a four-octet ASCII string out of the ID and that is prepended to the beginning of the string. As a result, the `sort` itself can rely on its standard sort behavior, and the final map removes the packed data. On the computer your author used to write this chapter, Table 10-1 shows the typical performance of each sort method on the test file with a 300,000 line file with random integers for IDs.

TABLE 10-1: Sort Time Comparisons

SORT METHOD	APPROXIMATE TIME
Naïve sort	7.5 seconds
Schwartzian Transform	2.5 seconds
Guttman-Rosler Transform	1.5 seconds

As you can see, the Guttman-Rosler transform is fast, but it is rarely used because most Perl developers are not familiar with the `pack` function.

SUMMARY

In this chapter you've learned about `sort`, `map`, and `grep`, three powerful functions that transform a list into a new list. You've learned a variety of sorting techniques and how to use `sort` subroutines. And you now know how to efficiently filter a list of values with `grep` and how to transform an old list of values into a new list of values with `map`. Finally, you've learned ways to combine these functions together to get powerful data manipulation techniques.

EXERCISES

1. Given the following list of hexadecimal numbers, print them in descending numeric order;

```
my @numbers = ( 0x23, 0xAA, 0xaa, 0x01, 0xfB );
```

2. Given a list of numbers, use `grep` to return only the numbers that are perfect squares. Then print them in ascending numeric order.

Assume the following list of numbers:

```
my @numbers = ( 28, 49, 1000, 4, 25, 49, 529 );
```

Write the `grep` in both BLOCK and EXPRESSION form.

```
NEWLIST = grep BLOCK        LIST;
NEWLIST = grep EXPRESSION, LIST;
```

What happens if one of the values in the `@numbers` array is actually the string `Get a job, hippy!`? How would this change your code?

3. Given the following list, write a `grep` statement that creates a new list but without duplicate elements. There are several ways you can solve this.

```
my @list = qw(
    bob
    sally
    Andromalius
    sally
    bob
    ned
    Andromalius
);
```

4. Given the following array:

```
my @employees = (
    {
        first_name => 'Sally',
        last_name  => 'Jones',
        years      => 4,
        payscale   => 4,
    },
    {
        first_name => 'Abby',
        last_name  => 'Hoffman',
        years      => 1,
        payscale   => 10,
    },
    {
        first_name => 'Jack',
        last_name  => 'Johnson',
        years      => 4,
        payscale   => 5,
    },
    {
        first_name => 'Mr.',
        last_name  => 'Magnate',
        years      => 12,
        payscale   => 1,
    },
);
```

Use `map` to create a new array that looks like this:

```
my @names = (
    'Jack Johnson',
    'Sally Jones',
    'Mr. Magnate',
);
```

The names are sorted by last name, ascending, and exclude employees who have been with the company a year or less.

▶ WHAT YOU LEARNED IN THIS CHAPTER

TOPIC	KEY CONCEPTS
`sort`	Used to order a list of data.
Sort subroutines	Making complex sorts easier to understand.
Sorting Unicode	Using the Unicode Collation Algorithm to sort different character sets.
`grep`	Only select elements of a list that pass wanted criteria.
`map`	Transform every element of a list, making a new list.
`map` and `sort` traps	Aliasing, complexity, and "clever" code are not your friends.
Complex sorts	Using `map` and `sort` together for more efficient sorting.

11

Packages and Modules

WHAT YOU WILL LEARN IN THIS CHAPTER:

➤ Understanding packages and namespaces

➤ Defining and exporting subroutines in packages

➤ Using `BEGIN`, `CHECK`, `INIT`, and `END`

➤ Writing POD: Plain Old Documentation

➤ Creating packages with `Module::Build` and `ExtUtils::MakeMaker`

➤ How to create and install modules

WROX.COM CODE DOWNLOAD FOR THIS CHAPTER

The wrox.com code downloads for this chapter are found at `http://www.wrox.com/remtitle` `.cgi?isbn=1118013840` on the Download Code tab. The code for this chapter is divided into the following major examples:

➤ `example_11_1_convert.pl`

➤ `lib/Convert/Distance/Imperial.pm`

➤ `lib/Convert/Distance/Metric.pm`

➤ `lib/My/Number/Utilities.pm`

➤ `listing_11_1_primes.pl`

Up to now, all the code has been in a single file. However, that doesn't work when you build larger systems. You need to understand how to logically break apart your applications into separate, preferably reusable components called packages or modules. These modules generally live in different files. This chapter explains how to create and organize these packages. Some professional Perl programmers never get beyond this step and still have successful careers, and by the end of this chapter, you'll be well on your way to being a professional Perl programmer.

In the real world, mission-critical Perl applications range from a few lines of code to more than a million (your author has worked on the latter).

When you have huge systems, would you actually want all that in one file? Probably not. Creating modules enables you to break your application down into small, manageable chunks. Doing so makes it easier to understand and design different parts of your system and helps to avoid what your author thinks of as "a steaming pile of ones and zeros."

NAMESPACES AND PACKAGES

Namespaces were very briefly discussed in Chapter 3. A namespace is a place to organize logically related code and data. It's given a package name and all subroutines and package variables declared in that namespace cannot be accessed outside of that namespace unless you prepend the package name to them or if the package "exports" the subroutines to other packages. This allows you to reuse names in different namespaces without worrying about collision. Declaring the subroutine `is_stupid()` twice in the same namespace can generate a warning. (And the first subroutine will be overwritten.) Declaring it twice in separate namespaces is just fine.

A package name is one or more identifiers separated by double colons. As you can recall from Chapter 3, an identifier must start with a letter or underscore. You can optionally follow that with one or more letters, numbers, or underscores. The following are all valid package names from modules you can find on the CPAN:

➤ `File::Find::Rule`

➤ `Module::Starter`

➤ `DBIx::Class`

➤ `Moose`

➤ `aliased`

Note the last one, `aliased`. It starts with a lowercase letter. By convention in Perl, a module whose name is all lowercase should be a pragma that affects Perl's compilation (as `aliased` and `autodie` do). Think carefully about using a lowercase name for a module because it's usually a bad idea.

> **NOTE** *Actually, as a legacy from earlier versions of Perl, you can use a single quote mark, `'`, in place of a double colon. So you could refer to the* `My::Preferred::Customer` *package as* `My'Preferred'Customer`. *However, this is highly frowned upon today. I mention this because you might sometimes find a programmer trying to be "clever" and using this older style of package name. Be wary of "clever" programmers.*

Start with a simple package named `My::Number::Utilities`. By convention, this should correspond to a path and filename of `My/Number/Utilities.pm` and it should usually be located in a `lib/` directory (in other words, `lib/My/Number/Utilities.pm`). The `.pm` extension is what Perl uses to identify a given module. A module is simply a file that contains one or more packages; although it's generally recommended to have one package per module. It's also strongly recommended that your module and package names correspond. You can have a file called My/Sekret/Stuff.pm containing a package named I::Am::A::Lousy::Programmer, but this tends to be confusing. That module should contain a package named My::Sekret::Stuff.

Now create the lib/My/Number/ directory and create an empty Utilities.pm file in it. If you saved the tree.pl utility created in Chapter 9, your file structure should look like this:

```
lib/
|  My/
|  |  Number/
|  |  |--Utilities.pm
```

Take the first is_prime() function created in Chapter 10 and use that to make your My::Number::Utilities package. Save the following code in lib/My/Number/Utilities.pm:

```perl
package My::Number::Utilities;

use strict;
use warnings;

our $VERSION = 0.01;

sub is_prime {
    my $number = $_[0];
    return    if $number < 2;
    return 1 if $number == 2;
    for ( 2 .. int sqrt($number) ) {
        return if !($number % $_);
    }
    return 1;
}

1;
```

That's it! You've successfully created your first module. Now see how to use it.

In the directory containing the lib/ directory, create a file named listing_11_1_primes.pl and save the code in Listing 11-1 to it (code file listing_11_1_primes.pl and lib/My/Number/Utilities.pm). It should look familiar.

LISTING 11-1: Using OurSimple Module

```perl
use strict;
use warnings;
use diagnostics;

use lib 'lib'; # tell Perl we'll find modules in lib/

use My::Number::Utilities;

my @numbers = qw(
3 2 39 7919 997 631 200
```

continues

LISTING 11-1 *(continued)*

```
7919 459 7919 623 997 867 15
);

my @primes  = grep { My::Number::Utilities::is_prime($_) }
 @numbers;
print join ', ' => sort { $a <=> $b } @primes;
```

When you run `perl listing_11_1_primes.pl`, you should see the following output and you've successfully used the module:

```
2, 3, 631, 997, 997, 7919, 7919, 7919
```

> **NOTE** *It's possible, however, that you'll get an error similar to the following:*
>
> ```
> Can't locate My/Number/Utilities.pm in @INC
>   (@INC contains: lib t /home/ovid/perl5/perlbrew/...
> BEGIN failed--compilation aborted at primes.pl line 6 (#1)
>     (F) You said to do (or require, or use) a file that
> couldn't be found. Perl looks for the file in all the
> locations mentioned in @INC,unless the file name
> included the full path to the file.  Perhaps youneed
> to set the PERL5LIB or PERL5OPT environment variable
> to say wherethe extra library is, or maybe the script
> needs to add the library nameto @INC.  Or maybe you
> just misspelled the name of the file.  See
>     perlfunc/require and lib.
> ```
>
> *Reading through that carefully should tell you where to look. In this case, you've either misspelled the module name, misspelled a directory or filename when creating the module, or your* `use lib` *line doesn't actually point to the* `lib/` *directory where the module lives. (You can use absolute paths if you need to, but they tend not to be portable.) If you read through the* `@INC` *line, you can see where Perl is looking for your module.*
>
> *And be aware that some file systems are case-sensitive and others are not. For example, on a case-insensitive file system you might be able to load a module named* `My::Module` *with this (note the lowercase letters), but get strange error messages when you try to use the code:*
>
> ```
> use my::module;
> ```
>
> *This is because* `lib/My/Module.pm` *and* `lib/my/module.pm` *are seen as the same thing on case-insensitive file systems.*
>
> *Be aware of this issue and make sure that the* `use` *statement, the module's package name and the filename all have matching case.*
>
> *Reading through error messages seems to almost be a lost art because so many error messages are awful, but learning to pay attention to them can make your programming life much easier.*

Most of your modules have effectively the same core:

```
package Module::Name;

use strict;
use warnings;

our $VERSION = 0.01; # or some other version number

# module code here

1;
```

Now look at the code for My::Number::Utilities again. The package statement is the first line:

```
package My::Number::Utilities;
```

This declares that everything after this declaration belongs to the My::Number::Utilities package. The package statement is either file-scoped or block-scoped. In this case, from the package declaration to the bottom of the file, everything is in the My::Number::Utilities package. If another file-scoped package declaration is found, the subsequent code belongs to the new package:

```
package My::Math;

use strict;
use warnings;

our $VERSION = 0.01;

sub sum {
    my @numbers = @_;
    my $total = 0;
    $total += $_ foreach @numbers;
    return $total;
}

# same file, different package
package My::Math::Strict;

use Scalar::Util 'looks_like_number';

our $VERSION = 0.01;

sub sum {
    my @numbers = @_;
    my $total = 0;
    $total += $_ foreach grep { looks_like_number($_) } @numbers;
    return $total;
}

1;
```

The preceding code has slightly different variants of the `sum()` function, but the first can be called with `My::Math::sum(@numbers)` and the second can be called with `My::Math::Strict::sum()`. Both the `strict` and `warnings` pragmas are in effect until the end of the file, thus affecting `My::Math::Strict`.

Sometimes, though, you may want to limit the scope of a `package` declaration. You do this by enclosing the package declaration in a block:

```
package My::Package;
use strict;
use warnings;
our $VERSION = 0.01;
{
    package My::Package::Debug;
    our $VERSION = 0.01;
    # this belongs to My::Package::Debug
    sub debug {
        # some debug routine
    }
}
# any code here belongs to My::Package;
1;
```

Generally, though, putting each package in its own appropriately named file makes it much easier to track that package down later.

You may also be curious about the bare 1 at the end of the package:

```
1;
```

In Perl, when you use a package, it must return a true value. If it does not, the use fails at compile time. Putting a `1;` at the end of the package solves this.

> **NOTE** *Ordinarily, a bare value generates a warning:*
>
> ```
> use strict;
> use warnings;
>
> 'one';
> ```
>
> *And that warns about:*
>
> ```
> Useless use of a constant (one) in void context at ...
> ```
>
> *This warning is to let you know that you're not assigning the constant to anything (hence, "void context"). However, a bare value of 1 or 0 does not emit a warning. This is a special case in Perl because there are a few times you will find a bare 1 or 0 useful, such as the 1; at the end of the module declaration.*

use Versus require

Generally, when you need to load a module, you use it:

```
use My::Number::Utilities;
```

The use statement has a variety of different uses and these can be a bit confusing:

```
use VERSION
use Module VERSION LIST
use Module VERSION
use Module LIST
use Module
```

The use VERSION form tells Perl that it must use a minimum version of Perl. This being Perl, there are a variety of different formats for the version number. So if you want to declare that your code requires Perl version 5.8.1 or above:

```
use v5.8.1;
use 5.8.1;
use 5.008_001;
```

If you require Perl version 5.9.5 or above, all features available via use feature will be loaded. Thus, instead of saying:

```
use feature "say";
# or
use feature ":5.12";
```

You can say:

```
use v5.12.0;
```

Prefixing the number with a v (as in v5.12.0) requires a 3-part number called a version string, or v-string. They have some issues and not everyone likes them. See "Version Strings" in perldoc perldata.

> **NOTE** If you use Perl version 5.11.0 or better in your code, strict is automatically enabled in your code. In other words, use strict is not required.

```
use Module
use Module LIST
use Module VERSION
use Module VERSION LIST
```

Many times you use a module with:

```
use Test::More;
```

`Test::More` is used in testing your code (see Chapter 14). You may find that you enjoy the `subtest()` feature of `Test::More`, but it's not available until version 0.96, so you can assume that you need at least that version of `Test::More`:

```
use Test::More 0.96;
# or
use Test::More v0.96.0;
```

> **WARNING** *If the version number is less than* `1.0` *and you're not using v-strings, you must have a leading* `0`*:*
>
> ```
> use Some::Module  .32;   # Syntax error, do not use!
> use Some::Module 0.32;   # Properly asserting the version
> ```
>
> *This broken form is a syntax error in Perl and is related to how Perl's* use *statement parses version numbers. Just remember that when using version numbers, you must always have a digit before the decimal point.*

When Perl loads `Test::More`, if its version is less than the supplied version, it will automatically `croak()`.

`Test::More` accepts an import list. When you use a module, Perl automatically looks for a function in that module named `import()` and, if it's found, it calls it for you, passing in any arguments included in the import list when you use the module. So you might use `Test::More` like this:

```
use Test::More tests => 13;
```

Then, the list `tests, =>13` is passed as arguments to `Test::More::import()`.

Finally, you can combine the version check and import list:

```
use Test::More 0.96 tests => 13;
```

That tells Perl that `Test::More` must be version `0.96` or better and passes the arguments `tests` and `13` to the import method.

> **NOTE** *Sometimes you want to load a module and not call its* `import()` *method. Use parentheses for the* LIST *when you use the module:*
>
> ```
> # Don't export Dumper() into our namespace
> use Data::Dumper ();
> ```

You can also `require` a module:

```
require My::Number::Utilities;
```

The use statement happens at compile time, even if it's embedded in a code path that would not normally be executed. The require happens at runtime. Loading a module with use is usually what you want. However, sometimes you want to delay loading a module if you don't need it. For example, if you want to debug output with Data::Dumper, it automatically exports the Dumper() subroutine (unless you use Data::Dumper ()).

```
use Data::Dumper;
print Dumper($some_variable);
```

However, sometimes you don't want to load Data::Dumper unless there's a problem. You might wrap this in a subroutine and use require:

```
sub debug {
    my @args = @_;
    require Data::Dumper;
    warn Data::Dumper::Dumper(\@args);
}
```

With the debug() subroutine, Data::Dumper will never be loaded unless debug() is called. Because it's loaded with require and not use, Data::Dumper's import() method is not called, so you must call Dumper() with its fully qualified subroutine name: Data::Dumper::Dumper().

Package Variables

Up to now you've primarily seen lexically scoped variables declared with the my builtin:

```
my $foo;
my @bar;
my %baz;
```

Those are file or block scoped and not visible elsewhere. However, sometimes you want a variable to be seen by other packages. To enable the visibility you need to use *fully qualified* package variables (variables with a package name prefixed to them) or declare the variables with our. The our builtin is like my, but it's for package variables and not lexically scoped ones.

For example, the Data::Dumper module lets you control much of its behavior with package variables:

```
use Data::Dumper;

# sort hash keys alphabetically
local $Data::Dumper::Sortkeys = 1;

# tighten up indentation
local $Data::Dumper::Indent   = 1;

print Dumper(\%hash);
```

Typing long package names can be frustrating and your author repeatedly types `$Data::Dumper::SortKeys = 1` and then tries to figure out what went wrong. Fortunately, `Data::Dumper` provides an alternative, cleaner interface, so read the documentation.

> **NOTE** Using `local()` to restrict the changes to package variables to the current scope is not strictly required when using package variables, but it's usually good practice. Your author has stumbled on numerous bugs in Perl modules due to authors changing package variables (or not realizing that some other code is doing this).

You would use a package variable when you need a variable that other packages can access using its fully qualified name. Why this is usually a bad idea is explained later, but for now, here's how you might declare them:

```
package My::Number::Utilities;

use strict;
use warnings;

our $VERSION = 0.01;

$My::Number::Utilities::PI  = 3.14159265359;
$My::Number::Utilities::E   = 2.71828182846;
$My::Number::Uitlities::PHI = 1.61803398874; # golden ratio
@My::Number::Utilities::FIRST_PRIMES = qw(
   2  3  5  7 11 13 17 19 23 29
  31 37 41 43 47 53 59 61 67 71
);

sub is_prime {
    #
}

1;
```

As you can see, several package variables are declared, but the sharp-eyed amongst our readers may notice the problem. The `$My::Number::Uitlities::PHI` variable has a misspelled package name. Oops!

Instead, you use the `our` declaration to omit the package name:

```
our $PI  = 3.14159265359;
our $E   = 2.71828182846;
our $PHI = 1.61803398874; # golden ratio
our @FIRST_PRIMES = qw(
   2  3  5  7 11 13 17 19 23 29
  31 37 41 43 47 53 59 61 67 71
);
```

> **NOTE** By convention, variables declared with a package scope have UPPER-CASE identifiers. When you're debugging a subroutine and see an UPPERCASE variable, it not only makes it much easier to know that it's declared outside of this subroutine, but it also makes it harder for you to accidentally override the value of $PHI with a my $phi declaration later.

Versions of Perl prior to version 5.6.1 did not have the our builtin, so they used the vars pragma instead:

```
use vars qw($PI $E $PHI @FIRST_PRIMES);

$PI  = 3.14159265359;
$E   = 2.71828182846;
$PHI = 1.61803398874; # golden ratio
@FIRST_PRIMES = qw(
  2  3  5  7 11 13 17 19 23 29
 31 37 41 43 47 53 59 61 67 71
);
```

Today if you must use package variables, it is recommended that you use the our builtin instead of the vars pragma.

So what's wrong with package variables?

```
package Universe::Roman;
use My::Number::Utilities;
$My::Number::Utilities::PI = 3;
```

And all the other universes fall apart. The proper way to do that is:

```
package Universe::Roman;
use My::Number::Utilities;
local $My::Number::Utilities::PI = 3;
```

However, because you can't force other packages to declare your package variables with local, it's better to just provide a subroutine that encapsulates this value:

```
package My::Number::Utilities;
use strict;
use warnings;

our $VERSION = 0.01;

sub pi { 3.14159265359 }
```

And now the value of PI is read-only.

```
package Universe::Roman;
use My::Number::Utilities;
my $PI = My::Number::Utilities::pi();
```

TRIVIA TIME: A SHORT HISTORY OF MISUNDERSTANDING PI

It's a widely held belief that the ancient Romans thought the value of π (PI) was 3. This is a myth. The Roman mathematician Ptolemy calculated the value of π as approximately 3.14166. Although this value is wrong, it was close enough for Roman construction needs.

The stories of Alabama trying to pass a law legislating the value of π as 3 are also not true, but Indiana did attempt to pass a law altering the value of π in 1897. It was stopped due to a mathematician visiting the Indiana legislature during the debate.

```
http://www.agecon.purdue.edu/crd/Localgov/Second%20Level%20pages/
Indiana_Pi_Story.htm
```

WARNING *You often see code like this at the top of modules:*

```
package Foo;

use strict;
use warnings;

our ( $THIS, $THAT, $OTHER ) = qw( foo bar baz );
```

When a variable should be available throughout the entire package, program-mers often use the our *builtin to declare these variables at the top of the pack-age. Unless you have a good reason for allowing other packages to read (and change) these variables directly, this is a bad idea. Just declare the variables with* my.

```
my ( $THIS, $THAT, $OTHER ) = qw( foo bar baz );
```

This at least protects these variables from other packages changing their value.

Do not package variables unless absolutely necessary. There is one clear exception: declaring version numbers.

Version Numbers

In the `My::Number::Utilities` module, a version number is declared with `our`:

```
our $VERSION = 0.01;
```

Although not strictly needed, it's strongly recommended that you declare a version number for your modules. Thus, if your `Time::Dilation` module version 2.3 has a bug and you release version 2.4, programmers who want to avoid your bug can do this:

```
use Time::Dilation 2.4;
```

When you assert a version of a module in a use statement, Perl checks the package variable $Module::Name::VERSION and throws an exception if the version is lower than the version needed.

If you do not provide a version number for the module, it makes life difficult for other developers trying to use your code. As a general rule, the version declaration previously shown should be sufficient for your needs, but some argue for the following:

```
our $VERSION = '0.001';   # make sure it's in quotes!
$VERSION = eval $VERSION;
```

David Golden has an excellent description of why this is the preferred way to write version numbers:

```
http://www.dagolden.com/index.php/369/version-numbers-should-be-boring/
```

In short, it allows Perl's version number to always be considered the same, regardless of how the module is used, such as when the $VERSION is parsed for a CPAN upload or which version of Perl you use. The full reasons are beyond the scope of this book, but it's worth reading David Golden's writing on this topic.

SUBROUTINES IN OTHER PACKAGES

When building software, you have different parts of the software for different tasks. However, you probably don't want to type my $pi = My::Number::Utilities::pi() all the time. Also, the My::Number::Utilities module likely has "private" subroutines that you should not be able to call. The former is handled by exporting, and the latter is handled by naming conventions.

Exporting

Now look at theMy::Number::Utilities package again:

```
package My::Number::Utilities;

use strict;
use warnings;

our $VERSION = 0.01;

sub  pi() { 3.14166 }   # good enough for 2,000 year
                        # old aqueducts and bridges
sub is_prime {
    my $number = $_[0];
    return    if $number < 2;
    return 1 if $number == 2;
    for ( 2 .. int sqrt($number) ) {
        return if !($number % $_);
    }
    return 1;
}

1;
```

Others using this package will be annoyed at typing `My::Number::Utilities::pi()` and `My::Number::Utilities::is_prime()` every time they want to use those functions, so you can export those functions to the calling code's namespace. The most popular module for doing this is `Exporter`, which has shipped with Perl since version 5. Here's another case in which you need to use package variables because `Exporter`'s interface requires it.

Near the top of module code you review, you'll often see the following:

```
use base 'Exporter';
our @EXPORT_OK = qw(pi is_prime);
our %EXPORT_TAGS = ( all => \@EXPORT_OK );
```

This means that those functions, `pi()` and `is_prime()`, can be exported. Now, when someone wants to use your module, they can import those functions by specifying their names in the import list:

```
use My::Number::Utilities 'pi', 'is_prime';
```

Or if they prefer, they can import only the functions they want:

```
use My::Number::Utilities 'is_prime';
print is_prime($number)
  ? "$number is prime"
  : "$number is not prime";
```

When you `use base 'Exporter'`, you inherit from the Exporter module. (Chapter 12 covers inheritance. For now, just follow along.) When someone uses your module, the `Exporter::import()` function is called. It uses your module name and finds the `@EXPORT`, `@EXPORT_OK`, and `%EXPORT_TAGS` package variables to determine what functions can be exported. Only function names in `@EXPORT_OK` and `@EXPORT` can be exported, but using `@EXPORT` is usually not recommended because `@EXPORT` exports all the functions listed in the array, and the programmer using your module no longer has control over what is imported into their namespace. It's no fun accidentally importing a `build()` function and overwriting the `build()` function you have in your namespace.

> **NOTE** Although Chapter 12 explains inheritance when you cover objects, for modules not object oriented, some people object to inheriting from `Exporter`. `Exporter` enables you to import the `import()` subroutine, if preferred:
>
> ```
> use Exporter 'import';
> ```
>
> This imports the `import()` subroutine directly into your namespace. No other change in your code is required.

With the preceding code, if programmers want all the functions, they can ask for that with `:all`.

```
use My::Number::Utilities ':all';
```

The `%EXPORT_TAGS` package hash has key/value pairs specifying groups of functions that can be exported. When using your module, a developer uses a key name from `%EXPORT_TAGS`, prefixed with a colon, `:`, to say the he wants that group of functions.

> **NOTE** *You can also export package variables with* `Exporter`, *but this is a bad idea for the reasons already discussed in the "Package Variables" section of this chapter.*

If your `My::Number::Utilities` module has subroutines for mathematical constants such as `pi`, `e`, and `phi`, you can allow those to be imported separately from the `:all` tag:

```
our %EXPORT_TAGS = qw(
    all       => \@EXPORT_OK,
    constants => [qw(ph e phi)],
);
```

NULL PROTOTYPES

You may have noticed that the `pi` constant subroutine was declared with a null prototype:

```
sub pi() { 3.14159265359 }
```

When Perl sees such a prototype, if the body of the subroutine is simple, Perl tries at compile time to replace all instances of that subroutine call with the value it returns. This is faster than the subroutine call and is called *inlining*. So if you have a null prototype, this:

```
use My::Number::Utilities 'pi';
print pi;
```

Is equivalent to this:

```
use My::Number::Utilities 'pi';
print 3.14159265359;
```

See "Constant Functions" in `perldoc perlsub`.

And someone who just wants the constants and not the `is_prime()` function can ask for them:

```
use My::Number::Utilities ':constants';
```

You often see the `constant` pragma used to declare constants. These can be exported just like any other subroutine because they're just created as subroutines with null prototypes.

```
our @EXPORT_OK = qw(PI E PHI);
use constant PI  => 3.14159265359;
use constant E   => 2.71828182846;
use constant PHI => 1.61803398874;
```

Though `Exporter` is the most common way of exporting functions into other namespaces, modules such as `Exporter::NoWork`, `Perl6::Export` and others exist for those who do not care for the `Exporter` syntax. See a CPAN near you for the latest and greatest alternatives.

Naming Conventions

You've seen that subroutines representing constants are often UPPERCASE subroutines, but what about other functions?

For a function that other modules are allowed to use, a normal function name is standard:

```
sub unique {
    #
}
```

However, for subroutines you want to remain private, by convention those are prefixed with an underscore:

```
sub _log_errors {
    #
}
```

Although developers may know about those subroutines, they also know that they should not rely on them. This is no guarantee that they won't try to use these subroutines, but good developers knows that they should not. Perl doesn't try to rigorously enforce privacy by default. You're expected to behave yourself.

> **NOTE** *If you insist on truly private subroutines, use an anonymous subroutine assigned to a scalar, for example:*
>
> ```
> package Really::Private;
>
> use strict;
> use warnings;
> use Carp 'croak';
>
> our $VERSION = '0.01';
>
> my $is_arrayref_of_hashrefs = sub {
>     my $arg = shift;
>     # is it an array ref?
>     return unless 'ARRAY' eq ref $arg;
>     # return boolean indicating if all elements are hashrefs.
>     return @$arg == grep { 'HASH' eq ref $_ } @$arg;
> };
> ```

```
sub process_records {
my ( $records ) = @_;
    unless ( $is_arrayref_of_hashrefs->($records) ) {
        croak "process_records() needs an array ref of hashrefs";
    }
    # process records here
}

1;
```
In the `Really::Private` *package described, the* `$is_arrayref_of_hashrefs`
variable contains an anonymous subroutine reference called by `process_`
`records()`. *Because the subroutine reference is bound to a lexical scalar, it is
not available outside of this package.*

For subroutines that should return a boolean value, start them with `is_`.

```
sub is_prime { … }
```

Also, you're strongly urged to `use_underscores_to_separate_names insteadOfUpperCase`
`Letters`. Underscores are much easier to read, particularly if English is not your first language.

TRY IT OUT   Distance Conversion

All the code in this Try It Out comes from code file `lib/Convert/Distance/Imperial.pm`, and
`example_11_1_convert.pl`.

Write a module with six functions:

➤   `miles_to_yards`

➤   `yards_to_miles`

➤   `miles_to_feet`

➤   `feet_to_miles`

➤   `miles_to_inches`

➤   `inches_to_miles`

Each of these functions is exported only if requested or all may be requested at once.

1.   In `lib/Convert/Distance/Imperial.pm`, type the following code:

```
package Convert::Distance::Imperial;

use strict;
use warnings;
use diagnostics;

our $VERSION = '0.001';
```

```
$VERSION = eval $VERSION;

use Exporter 'import';
our @EXPORT_OK = qw(
  miles_to_yards
  yards_to_miles
  miles_to_feet
  feet_to_miles
  miles_to_inches
  inches_to_miles
);
our %EXPORT_TAGS = ( all => \@EXPORT_OK );

use constant FEET_PER_MILE   => 5_280;
use constant FEET_PER_YARD   => 3;
use constant INCHES_PER_FOOT => 12;

sub miles_to_yards {
    my $miles = shift;
    return miles_to_feet($miles) / FEET_PER_YARD;
}

sub yards_to_miles {
    my $yards = shift;
    return feet_to_miles( $yards * FEET_PER_YARD );
}

sub miles_to_feet {    my $miles = shift;
    return $miles * FEET_PER_MILE;
}

sub feet_to_miles {
    my $feet = shift;
    return $feet / FEET_PER_MILE;
}

sub miles_to_inches {
    my $miles = shift;
    return miles_to_feet($miles) * INCHES_PER_FOOT;
}

sub inches_to_miles {
    my $inches = shift;
    return feet_to_miles( $inches / INCHES_PER_FOOT );
}

1;
```

2. Create a program, example_11_1_convert.pl, with the following code:

```
use strict;
use warnings;
use diagnostics;
use lib 'lib';
```

```
use Convert::Distance::Imperial ':all';

printf "there are %d yards in a mile\n"   => miles_to_yards(1);
printf "there are %d feet in a mile\n"    => miles_to_feet(1);
printf "there are %d inches in a mile\n" => miles_to_inches(1);

printf "there are %0.2f miles in a %d yards\n"  => yards_to_miles(5000),  5000;
printf "there are %0.2f miles in a %d feet\n"   => feet_to_miles(5000),   5000;
printf "there are %0.2f miles in a %d inches\n" => inches_to_miles(5000), 5000;
```

If you have created this in the same directory you created the lib/My/Number/Utilities.pm and the listing_11_1_primes.pl program from Listing 11-1, you should have the following directory structure, as output from tree.pl:

```
|--convert.pl
|   lib/
|   |   Convert/
|   |   |   Distance/
|   |   |   |--Imperial.pm
|   |   My/
|   |   |   Number/
|   |   |   |--Utilities.pm
|--primes.pl
```

3. Run the program with `perl example_11_1_convert.pl`. You should see the following output:

```
There are 1760 yards in a mile
There are 5280 feet in a mile
There are 63360 inches in a mile
There are 2.84 miles in a 5000 yards
There are 0.95 miles in a 5000 feet
There are 0.08 miles in a 5000 inches
```

By an astonishing stroke of luck, those numbers turn out to be correct.

How It Works

Start with the standard `strict`, `warnings`, and `diagnostics`. (Although at this point, you could probably do without `diagnostics` and figure out what's going on.) Then you have the use `lib` line:

```
use lib 'lib';
```

This tells Perl that before searching for modules in `@INC`, check the `lib/` directory. If you had several extra places you wanted Perl to look for modules, you could pass them all to `lib`'s import list:

```
use lib 'lib', 'mylib', 'other/lib';
```

Next, set up your subroutine exporting with the following:

```
use Exporter 'import';
our @EXPORT_OK = qw(
  miles_to_yards
```

```
        yards_to_miles
        miles_to_feet
        feet_to_miles
        miles_to_inches
        inches_to_miles
    );
    our %EXPORT_TAGS = ( all => \@EXPORT_OK );
```

This lets you import any of those functions individually upon request, or in the case of your convert.pl program, you imported them via the :all tag.

Next, define several useful constants:

```
    use constant FEET_PER_MILE   => 5_280;
    use constant FEET_PER_YARD   => 3;
    use constant INCHES_PER_FOOT => 12;
```

You could have simply typed these directly into your subroutines, but if you did something silly like mistakenly assume that there are 5,200 feet per mile, you'd need to change this value in several places. Instead, use the constant pragma to create easy-to-read labels for each value, and later if you find one is in error, you have to change it only in one place.

Also, you could have declared the constants all at one time like this:

```
    use constant {
        FEET_PER_MILE   => 5_280,
        FEET_PER_YARD   => 3,
        INCHES_PER_FOOT => 12,
    };
```

Next, you have the functions implementing your actual code. The miles_to_feet() and feet_to_miles() functions are actually your core functions here:

```
    sub miles_to_feet {
        my $miles = shift;
        return $miles * FEET_PER_MILE;
    }

    sub feet_to_miles {
        my $feet = shift;
        return $feet / FEET_PER_MILE;
    }
```

Those should be clear. Each of them depends only on the FEET_PER_MILE constant and the value passed into it. Note that even when these subroutines are exported into your namespace, they can still reference the value in FEET_PER_MILE, despite it being defined in a different package.

Looking at other subroutines, such as miles_to_yards(), you can see that they are defined in terms of miles_to_feet().

```
    sub miles_to_yards {
        my $miles = shift;
```

```
        return miles_to_feet($miles) / FEET_PER_YARD;
    }
```

You do this to make things more clear and to avoid repeating your miles-to-feet calculation.

The miles_to_yards() function relies on FEET_PER_YARD and miles_to_feet(). When exported, miles_to_yards() still knows about those and returns correct answers even if FEET_PER_YARD and miles_to_feet() are not exported. You can verify that by only exporting miles_to_yards() and see that it still works correctly:

```
use lib 'lib';
use Convert::Distance::Imperial 'miles_to_yards';
printf "There are %d yards in a mile\n"  => miles_to_yards(1);
```

BEGIN, UNITCHECK, CHECK, INIT, AND END

There are four special blocks, BEGIN, CHECK, INIT, and END, which are executed at different stages of your program. There is also UNITCHECK, which was introduced in Perl version 5.9.5. These blocks execute code at specific times of the program. They sometimes check that a necessary resources, such as data files, exist, but you can use them any time you feel you must have code execute at a particular time in your program's compilation, rather than explicitly calling it.

These blocks look like subroutines, but they're not. (You can prefix them with the sub keyword, but it's considered bad style.) They automatically execute and cannot be called. Furthermore, you can have multiples of each of these blocks, for example:

```
package Foo;

use strict;
use warnings;

BEGIN {
    print "This is the first BEGIN block\n";
}

BEGIN {
    print "This is the second BEGIN block\n";
}
```

And when you use Foo (or even if you just check its syntax with perl -c Foo.pm), it prints out:

```
This is the first BEGIN block
This is the second BEGIN block
```

> **NOTE** *You can read more about* BEGIN, INIT, CHECK, UNITCHECK, *and* END *in* perldoc perlmod.

To understand these special blocks, think of a Perl program's "lifecycle" in terms of the following steps. (This is an oversimplification.)

1. The program is compiled.

2. The program is executed.

3. The program is finished.

BEGIN blocks

BEGIN blocks fire during program compilation (step 1), as soon as the trailing } is found. BEGIN blocks are useful for a variety of purposes, such as checking whether or not necessary files exist before the program runs or verifying that you are on the correct operating system.

Ordinarily a print statement happens in step 2, when the program is executed, so this:

```
BEGIN {
    print "This is the first BEGIN block\n";
}

print "The program is running\n";

BEGIN {
    print "This is the second BEGIN block\n";
}
```

Prints this:

```
This is the first BEGIN block
This is the second BEGIN block
The program is running
```

If your program contains a syntax error after a BEGIN block, the BEGIN block still executes because it is executed as soon as it is compiled and before the program finishes compiling. So this:

```
BEGIN {
    print "This is the first BEGIN block\n";
}

print "The program is running\n";

BEGIN {
    print "This is the second BEGIN block\n";
}
my $x =;
```

Prints something like this:

```
syntax error at some_program.pl line 8, near "=;"
Execution of some_program.pl aborted due to compilation errors.
This is the first BEGIN block
This is the second BEGIN block
```

Because STDERR and STDOUT are separate filehandles, they are not guaranteed to print in sequence, thus leading to this strange case in which you may get the syntax error printed before you have the BEGIN block output printing. This is an artifact of how operating systems work and is not a flaw in Perl.

BEGIN blocks always execute in the order they are found.

> **NOTE**   Note that this:
>
> ```
>     use Module ();
> ```
>
> Is equivalent to this:
>
> ```
>     BEGIN{ require Module; }
> ```
>
> That's because the parentheses with use Module () tell Perl not to call the import() function and the BEGIN block using require, therefore it does the same thing.

END Blocks

END blocks are like BEGIN blocks, but they happen in step 3, when the program is exiting. They will even be called if you die(), but signals and (the incredibly rare) segfaults can cause them to be skipped. They are useful if you need to clean anything up after your program finishes running.

They are executed in the reverse order that they are defined. Thus, this:

```
END {
    print "This is the first END block\n";
}
END {
    print "This is the second END block\n";
}
```

Prints this:

```
This is the second END block
This is the first END block
```

INIT, CHECK, and UNITCHECK Blocks

When your program finishes compiling but before it executes is when INIT, CHECK, and UNITCHECK blocks fire. Because of this, unlike BEGIN blocks, they do not execute if there is a syntax error. A CHECK blocks runs immediately after step 1 (compilation) is finished, in a *LIFO* (last in, first out) order. INIT blocks run after CHECK blocks and just before step 2, the program execution. They run in the order they are defined (*FIFO*, first in, first out).

```
INIT {
    print "This is the first INIT block\n";
}
CHECK {
    print "This is the first CHECK block\n";
}
INIT {
    print "This is the second INIT block\n";
}
CHECK {
    print "This is the second CHECK block\n";
}
```

That prints out:

```
This is the second CHECK block
This is the first CHECK block
This is the first INIT block
This is the second INIT block
```

As you can see, the CHECK blocks run before the INIT blocks, in reverse order. The INIT blocks are run in the order defined.

UNITCHECK was introduced in Perl 5.9.5. It was designed to solve a problem in which code loaded during program execution (such as with a `require MODULENAME` or a string `eval`) will not execute CHECK and INIT blocks. They would not be executed because those blocks execute only after program compilation and before program execution, not during program execution.

A UNITCHECK runs immediately after the code containing it is compiled, even if you are already in the program execution phase. This allows you to "check" necessary conditions before the containing code is executed.

PLAIN OLD DOCUMENTATION (POD)

> *Documentation is worth it just to be able to answer all your mail with 'RTFM'—Alan Cox*

So you've written a lot of code by now, but what about documenting it? Whenever you read a module's documentation on the CPAN, you're reading POD, short for Plain Old Documentation. POD is a quick-and-easy way to write documentation for your modules, and it's quick to learn.

> **NOTE** *POD is not just for modules. You are encouraged to use it in all your code that has a lifespan greater than a few hours. You will thank yourself.*

When reading module documentation on your computer, you generally do so with the `perldoc` command. When you type something like `perldoc Convert::Distance::Imperial`, it searches through @INC for `Convert/Distance/Imperial.pm` and `Convert/Distance/Imperial.pod`. It attempts to format a .pm file if it contains POD. It automatically assumes that a .pod file is POD. This allows you to write a module and keep the documentation in a separate file, if wanted:

```
|--convert.pl
|  lib/
|  |  Convert/
|  |  |  Distance/
|  |  |  |--Imperial.pm
|  |  |  |--Imperial.pod
```

POD starts with a command paragraph. A command paragraph is any text starting with = and followed by an identifier. Though it's called a *paragraph*, it is usually on a single line. POD ends with the =cut command paragraph (or the end of the file). There must be no whitespace to the left of the =.

> **WARNING** *Though the* =cut *on a line by itself is usually sufficient to indicate the end of the POD section, some POD parsers require a blank line before (and sometimes after) the* =cut.

In general, any text typed as a paragraph in POD is rendered as such. Here's a POD paragraph between two subroutines:

```
sub reciprocal { return 1 / shift }

=pod

This is a paragraph in a POD section. When run through a formatter, the
paragraph text will rewrap as necesseary to fit the needs of your
particular output format.

=cut

sub not_reciprocal { return shift }
```

The following command paragraphs are recognized. You may create custom ones if you create your own POD parser.

```
=pod
=head1 Heading Text
=head2 Heading Text
=head3 Heading Text
=head4 Heading Text
=over indentlevel
=item stuff
=back
=begin format
=end format
=for format text...
=encoding type
=cut
```

Although POD documentation is often interspersed with code, particularly with a documentation section before each subroutine, many programmers prefer to put their documentation at the end of the module, after a __END__ or __DATA__ literal. There are arguments for and against each style. It's up to you.

Documentation Structure

Though the exact format varies, you can notice that most modules on the CPAN follow a documentation layout similar to the following (and generally in this order):

➤ NAME: The module name

➤ SYNOPSIS: A brief code snippet showing usage

➤ DESCRIPTION: A description of what the module is for

➤ EXPORT: An optional list, if any, of what the module exports

➤ FUNCTION/METHODS: Detailed descriptions of every subroutine/method

➤ BUGS: Known bugs and how to report new ones

➤ AUTHOR: Who wrote the module (often more than one author)

➤ LICENSE: The license terms of the module

It is strongly recommended that you follow this format unless you have a strong reason not to. This makes your documentation consistent with other Perl modules and makes it easier to read. See the documentation for DBIx::Class for a good example of why you might want a slightly different format.

Other common sections include VERSION, DIAGNOSTICS, SEE ALSO (related modules) and CONTRIBUTORS (nonauthors who've nonetheless offered useful feedback or patches).

The sections generally begin with a =head1 command paragraph:

```
=head1 NAME

Convert::Distance::Imperial - Convert imperial units to other units

=head1 VERSION

VERSION 0.001

=head1 SYNOPSIS

 use Convert::Distance::Imperial 'miles_to_inches';
 my $miles = miles_to_inches(453285);
```

Headings

POD, by default, supports four levels of headings:

➤ =head1 ALL CAPS TEXT

➤ =head2 Some Text

> ➤ =head3 Some text

> ➤ =head4 Some text

The pod2html formatter, included with Perl, renders these as <h1>, <h2>, <h3>, and <h4>, respectively. Other POD formatters obviously make different choices. The ALL CAPS for the =head1 command is not strictly required for all POD formatters, but some require it, so you should probably stick with it.

Paragraphs

A paragraph in POD, as mentioned, is merely text you type in a POD section. Note that there must be no whitespace at the start of any paragraph line:

```
=pod

This is a POD paragraph.

This is a second POD paragraph.

=cut
```

Lists

A list begins with =over *indentlevel* (typically the number 4), has one or more =item commands, and ends with a =back command.

```
=over 4

=item * This is a list item

=item * This is a second list item.

This is an optional paragraph explaining the second list item.

=back
```

You may have an optional paragraph after an =item command. No =head*n* commands are allowed, and although you might think that a nested list is handy, not all POD formatters respect them.

If you don't want a bulleted list, you can create a numbered list manually. Use 1., 2., 3., and so on after each =item. Many POD parsers are weak in this area, so double-check that your desired POD parser handles this correctly.

```
=over 4

=item 1. This is a list item

=item 2. This is a second list item.
```

```
    This is an optional paragraph explaining the second list item.

    =item 3.

    =back
```

If you don't want a bulleted or numbered list, just use =item followed by your desired list text.

The *indentlevel* is optional as it defaults to 4. Many POD formatters ignore it entirely, whereas others consider that to be the number of *ems* width of indent (An em is the width of the capital letter M in the base font of the document.)

Verbatim

So why can't we have any whitespace at the start of a line of normal POD paragraph? Because any text with leading whitespace is rendered verbatim. This makes it easy to insert code in your documentation.

```
=head1 SUBROUTINES

=head2 C<miles_to_yards>

use Convert::Distance::Imperial 'miles_to_yards';
my $yards = miles_to_yards($miles);
print "$miles miles is $yards yards\n";

The C<miles_to_yards()> subroutines takes a number, in
miles, and returns anumber, in yards.
```

That funky C<> stuff is explained in just a bit.

> **NOTE** *When writing documentation for your functions, try to focus on what they do, not how they do it. This makes it more likely that you will not need to update your documentation later if you change how your function behaves internally, but its use remains the same.*

Miscellaneous

With headings, paragraphs, lists, and verbatim text, you now know most of the POD syntax people use. However, there are a few other commands we'll take the time to explain. These are merely the most popular and you should read perldoc perlpod to understand what else you can do.

Formatting codes

Sometimes you want to have a bit more control over the output. It can be useful to have fixed-width text, **bold**, or *italic* text. All paragraphs and some command paragraphs allow formatting codes, also known as *interior sequences*. Here's how you might format this paragraph in POD:

```
Sometimes you want to have a bit more control over the
output. It can be useful to have C<fixed-width text>,
```

```
B<bold> or I<italic> text. All paragraphs and some
command paragraphs allow formatting codes, also known
as I<interior sequences>. Here's how you might format
this paragraph in POD:
```

Formatting codes begin with a single uppercase letter, followed by a <, followed by the wanted text, and ending with a >. Some POD formatters require all these to be on the same line. Table 11-1 shows common POD formatting codes.

TABLE 11-1 Common Formatting Codes

CODE	MEANING
C<text>	Fixed-width ('C'ode)
C<< text >>	Fixed-width and doesn't let the next > end the interior sequence. (C<< $age >= 18 >>)
B<text>	'B'old
I<text>	'I'talics
E<text>	'E'scape text (generally, you can use HTML escape names such as E<lt> for the < character)
S<text>	All 's'paces are nonbreaking
L<text>	Create a 'l'ink

Linking

Linking is often skipped in Perl modules, but it's good to know, particularly because good linking will show up on CPAN modules and make it easier to cross-reference other documents. Note that names must not contain | or / and if they contain < or >, they must be balanced.

There are three primary linking formats:

➤ L<name>: This links to a Perl manual page, such as L<Scalar::Util> or L<perlunitut>. This form of linking does not allow spaces in the name.

➤ L<name/"sec"> or L<name/sec>: A link to a section of a man page. For example, L<perlpod/"Formatting Codes">.

➤ L</"sec"> or L</sec>: A link to another section of the current POD document.

If you prefer, you can prefix any of these with a *text/* to give them a more readable name:

```
L<Read about formatting codes|perlpod/"Formatting Codes">
```

Or that's the theory, at least. Some POD formatters struggle with this syntax.

Finally, you can link to a URL:

```
L<http://www.overseas-exile.com/>
```

The `perlpod` documentation claims you cannot give a nice "text" name to a URL, meaning that the `text|link` syntax does not work:

```
L<Overseas Exile|http://www.overseas-exile.com/>
```

However, that was apparently fixed in Perl version 5.8.9, though the `Pod::Checker` module would apparently complain about this syntax. If you have problems using this syntax, be sure to update `Pod::Parser` with the latest version from the CPAN.

Encoding

Your POD documents are generally written in ASCII or Latin-1. However, if you need them to be in another encoding, you must specify this with the `=encoding` command:

```
=encoding UTF-8
```

The `Encoding::Supported` module from the CPAN can give you a list of supported encodings.

CREATING AND INSTALLING MODULES

Writing a module is all fine and dandy, but what about installing it? When a module is properly installed, you no longer require a `use lib 'lib';` line to tell Perl where to find it. The module will probably be installed in one of the paths in `@INC` and Perl will find it when you use it. This is also the first step to create a distribution that can be given to other programmers for installation or uploaded to the CPAN. Sharing is good. Installable modules are shareable modules.

Creating a Simple Module

In the old days, people used a program that ships with Perl called `h2xs`, but it's so old and out of date it's mentioned just to say "Don't bother." Today many people use `Dist::Zilla` to create and install modules, and while we recommend it, it's beyond the scope of this book. Instead, we recommend that you start by installing `Module::Starter` from the CPAN. It can provide a module-starter program. Now create an installable version of the `Convert::Distance::Imperial` program:

```
module-starter --module=Convert::Distance::Imperial \
               --author='Curtis "Ovid" Poe'          \
    --email=ovid@cpan.org
```

That creates a directory named `Convert-Distance-Imperial/`. Using your `tree.pl` program, you can see the following directory structure:

```
$ tree.pl Convert-Distance-Imperial/
Convert-Distance-Imperial/
|--Changes
|--MANIFEST
|--Makefile.PL
|--README
|--ignore.txt
|   lib/
```

```
|   |   Convert/
|   |   |   Distance/
|   |   |   |--Imperial.pm
|   t/
|   |--00-load.t
|   |--boilerplate.t
|   |--manifest.t
|   |--pod-coverage.t
|   |--pod.t
```

There's a lot of stuff here, so let's go over each item.

➤   The `Changes` file contains a list of changes for each version of your program.

➤   The `MANIFEST` should list each file that must be included in the actual distribution.

➤   The `Makefile.PL` is a Perl program that creates a `Makefile` that you use with `make` (or sometimes `nmake` or `dmake` in Windows). A `Makefile` is a file that explains how to build your software. If you decide to read the `Makefile`, be careful not to change it unless you're familiar with writing a `Makefile`. It contains embedded tabs and if you accidentally convert them to spaces, you will break the `Makefile`.

➤   The `README` is for the user to understand how to build and install the distribution and often has the distribution documentation embedded in it.

➤   The `ignore.txt` is a template to use with various version control systems, such as git or Subversion, to know which files to ignore. You often want to copy that file (or its contents) to an appropriately named file for your version control system.

➤   The `lib/` directory contains the modules you want to install.

➤   The `t/` directory contains the tests for the module, which Chapter 14 covers.

You can just copy your copy of `Convert/Distance/Imperial.pm` to `Convert-Distance-Imperial/lib/Convert/Distance/Imperial.pm` and you have an installable module.

> **NOTE**   *You may find it annoying to type your name and e-mail every time you run module-starter.* `perldoc Module::Starter` *doesn't (as of this writing) suggest how to avoid that, but* `perldoc module-starter` *tells you that you can create a* `$HOME/.module-starter/config` *file (where* `$HOME` *is your home directory) and add your name and e-mail in that:*
>
> ```
>     author: Curtis "Ovid" Poe
>     email:  ovid@cpan.org
> ```
>
> *Then you can just type:*
>
> ```
>     module-starter --module=My::Module
> ```
>
> *And the author and e-mail information will be filled in for you.*

You're going to do that now in the following Try It Out.

TRY IT OUT   Creating an Installable Distribution

In this Try It Out, you create an installable package for `Convert::Distance::Imperial` and optionally install it. This shows you the basic process.

1. Run `module-starter`, using your name and e-mail address:

```
module-starter --module=Convert::Distance::Imperial \
  --author='Curtis "Ovid" Poe' --email=ovid@cpan.org
```

On Linux and OS X, the \ at the end of the line tells the operating system to continue the command on the next line rather than execute it immediately. You can put all those on the same line if you like.

2. Copy your version of `Convert/Distance/Imperial.pm` to `Convert-Distance-Imperial/lib/Convert/Distance/Imperial.pm`. As an alternative, you can open up the new `Convert-Distance-Imperial/lib/Convert/Distance/Imperial.pm` file and add your code to it directly. This is good because most of the POD boilerplate is filled out for you.

3. Change to the `Convert-Distance-Imperial/` directory.

4. Type the following commands, one at a time. If you use an alternative `make` command such as `dmake` or `nmake`, substitute that command for `make`.

```
perl Makefile.PL
make
make test
```

Many developers just type those on a single line:

```
perl Makefile.PL && make && make test
```

5. If `make test` reports that all tests passed (and it should), then type (if you want to install this module):

```
make install
```

If you use your system Perl (and I generally recommend against this), you may need superuser privileges to install the module. On Linux or OS X, you can type this:

```
sudo make install
```

That prompts you for your password. Windows users often have Administrator privileges and won't need to worry about that. Plus, because Perl is not included by default on Windows, you don't need to worry as much about breaking something your system depends on.

6. If all went well, you should see something similar to this:

```
$ perl Makefile.PL && make && make test
Checking if your kit is complete...
```

```
Looks good
Writing Makefile for Convert::Distance::Imperial
cp lib/Convert/Distance/Imperial.pm
blib/lib/Convert/Distance/Imperial.pm
Manifying blib/man3/Convert::Distance::Imperial.3
t/00-load.t ....... 1/1 # Testing Convert::Distance::Imperial 0.01
t/00-load.t ....... ok
t/manifest.t ...... skipped: Author tests not required
All tests successful.
Files=2, Tests=1,  0 wallclock secs ( 0.03 usr  0.02 sys +
 0.06 cusr  0.01 csys =  0.12 CPU)
Result: PASS
```

These files are not included for download because you can generate them automatically with
module-starter.

How It Works

When you first run module-starter, it creates a shell of a distribution, and you need to fill out the
important bits. If you know in advance that your distribution contains multiple modules, you can list
all of them, separated by commas (but no spaces).

```
module-starter --module=Convert::Distance::Imperial,\
Convert::Distance::Metric
```

When you change into the Convert-Distance-Imperial/ directory, take a look at the Makefile.PL.
It looks something like this:

```
use 5.006;
use strict;
use warnings;

use ExtUtils::MakeMaker;

WriteMakefile(
    NAME          => 'Convert::Distance::Imperial',
    AUTHOR        => q{Curtis "Ovid" Poe <ovid@cpan.org>},
    VERSION_FROM  => 'lib/Convert/Distance/Imperial.pm',
    ABSTRACT_FROM => 'lib/Convert/Distance/Imperial.pm',
    ($ExtUtils::MakeMaker::VERSION >= 6.3002
      ? ('LICENSE'=> 'perl')
      : ()),
    PL_FILES          => {},
    PREREQ_PM => {
        'Test::More' => 0,
    },
    dist => { COMPRESS => 'gzip -9f', SUFFIX => 'gz', },
    clean => { FILES => 'Convert-Distance-Imperial-*' },
);
```

I won't go into details, but the PREREQ_PM should point to a hash reference whose keys are all modules
your code depends on and whose values are the minimum version numbers required. If you install
a module from the CPAN using standard tools, it consults the PREREQ_PM and if you do not have the
modules listed (or their minimum versions), then those modules will be installed before yours.

To choose a mininum version number for a required module, you might want to check the Changes file included in almost every module's distribution (you'll find a link to it on its Web page on the CPAN) and make sure that the features you need are listed in that version.

When you run perl Makefile.PL, the ExtUtils::MakeMaker module's WriteMakefile() function will, unsurprisingly, write the Makefile for you.

Running make can read the Makefile and build your module correctly. The make test runs the tests in the t/ directory. Finally, make install installs your module.

The t/boilerplate.t, t/pod.t, t/pod-coverage.t, and t/manifest.t modules are all likely to pass or be skipped because you won't have the proper modules installed to run them, or you won't have removed the "boilerplate" code that module-starter generates. To see the full list of boilerplate that you should edit and replace, you can do this:

```
$ prove -l -v t/boilerplate.t
```

The prove command comes standard with Perl and is used to run tests. The -l switch tells prove to look for your modules in the lib/ directory and -v says "use verbose output." Finally, you include the name of the test program you want to run. You can bundle the -l and -v switches into a single -lv if you prefer. The output looks similar to this (reformatted slightly to fit):

```
$ prove -lv t/boilerplate.t
t/boilerplate.t ..
1..3
not ok 1 - README # TODO Need to replace the boilerplate text
#   Failed (TODO) test 'README contains boilerplate text'
#   at t/boilerplate.t line 24.
# The README is used... appears on lines 3
# 'version information here' appears on lines 11
not ok 2 - Changes # TODO Need to replace the boilerplate text
#   Failed (TODO) test 'Changes contains boilerplate text'
#   at t/boilerplate.t line 24.
# placeholder date/time appears on lines 3
not ok 3 - Convert/Distance/Imperial.pm # TODO replace boilerplate
#   Failed (TODO) test 'lib/Convert/Distance/Imperial.pm'
#   at t/boilerplate.t line 24.
# stub function definition appears on lines 38 42 45 49
# boilerplate description appears on lines 22
# the great new $MODULENAME appears on lines 9
ok
All tests successful.
Files=1, Tests=3,  0 wallclock secs ( 0.02 usr  0.01 sys +
 0.02 cusr  0.00 csys =  0.05 CPU)
Result: PASS
```

This text is fairly human-readable, and if you're careful, you can figure out what the test output means. However, we'll say no more about this until testing is covered in Chapter 14.

Now that you've created your first "proper" module, turning it into a distribution is a snap. After you've done perl Makefile.PL, make, and maketest, you can type **make dist** and something called a tarball is created for you. In this case it has a name similar to

`Convert-Distance-Imperial-0.01.tar.gz`. That's suitable for uploading to the CPAN. If you want to do that, you need a PAUSE (Perl Authors Upload Server) account. You can apply for one at `https://pause.perl.org/` and start sharing your CPAN modules with everyone else.

After you type **make**, there are many extra files that have been built, such as a `Makefile`, a `blib/` directory and a `pm_to_blib/` directory. They can be useful for debugging build problems, but to make them go away, you can just type **make realclean**. They return the next time you type **make**.

Makefile.PL or Module::Build?

You might think it odd that a language such as Perl uses an external tool like a `Makefile` to control how it builds its modules. After all, Java has `ant` and Ruby has `rakefiles`, why not a pure Perl alternative? This is because when Perl was first introduced, long before either Java or Ruby, it was common on UNIX-like systems, and people who were likely to use Perl already knew about `Makefiles`.

The Perl module that creates the actual `Makefile` is called `ExtUtils::MakeMaker` (often referred to simply as `EUMM`) and it's a beast to maintain. This is because there are many different implementations of the `make` program, not all of which are compatible with one another. Further, different operating systems have different constraints about filenames, paths, how commands get executed, and so on. Because the `Makefile` must respect those constraints, the job gets harder. Imagine all the different types of `make` utilities and the different incompatible operating systems, and you can understand why this system has been hard to maintain.

As a result, the `Module::Build` project was started. It's written entirely in Perl and is much easier to extend than `EUMM`. Unfortunately, `Module::Build` was buggy when it first came out. Further, because `EUMM` had some design flaws when it was implemented, `Module::Build` fixed some of those flaws, and this led to subtle incompatibilities between the two. Michael Schwern, the maintainer of `EUMM`, has tried to convince people to switch to `Module::Build`, but many developers have chosen not to.

If you want to use `Module::Build` with `module-starter`, just pass the `--mb` switch to `module-starter`. You'll also want to read `Module::Build::Authoring`. The build process is then:

```
perl Build.PL
./Build
./Build test
./Build install
```

Finally, there's the `Module::Install` module. This is designed primarily to work with `ExtUtils::MakeMaker` and is easy to learn, particularly for new programmers. If you have Perl version 5.9.4 or better, you already have `Module::Build` installed. You have to install `Module::Install` separately.

SUMMARY

In this chapter, you have learned the basics of writing modules and building distributions. You've learned about the phases of program execution and how to export subroutines to other packages. You've also learned how to document your modules. You should read `perldoc perlmod` for more information.

EXERCISES

1. Write a module, `Convert::Distance::Metric`, which contains the following subroutines:

- ➤ `kilometers_to_meters`
- ➤ `meters_to_kilometers`

Make those subroutines optionally exportable, and let people also import all of them with:

```
use Convert::Distance::Metric ":all";
```

2. Add this module to your `Convert-Distance-Metric` distribution. Don't forget to add it to the `MANIFEST`.

3. Add full POD to the `Convert::Distance::Metric` module. Include the following sections:

- ➤ NAME: The module name.
- ➤ SYNOPSIS: A brief code snippet showing usage.
- ➤ DESCRIPTION: A description of what the module is for.
- ➤ EXPORT: An optional list, if any, of what the module exports.
- ➤ FUNCTION: Detailed description of every subroutine.
- ➤ BUGS: Known bugs and how to report new ones.
- ➤ SEEALSO: A link to `Convert::Distance::Imperial`.
- ➤ AUTHOR: Who wrote the module (often more than one author).
- ➤ LICENSE: The license terms of the module.

Be sure to type **perldoc lib/Convert/Distance/Metric.pm** to verify the POD output. You can also run **podchecker lib/Convert/Distance/Metric.pm** to look for errors in your POD.

4. Write a short program to convert 3.5 kilometers to meters and convert the answer back to kilometers using the `Convert::Distance::Metric` module you created for Exercise 1.

5. (Optional). Although testing hasn't been covered yet, edit the `t/00-load.t` test program in the `Convert-Distance-Imperial` distribution and try to add a test to verify that you can load `Convert::Distance::Metric`. You can check to see if it works with:

```
prove -lv t/00-load.t
```

Or just run:

```
perl makefile.pl
make
make test
```

▶ WHAT YOU LEARNED IN THIS CHAPTER

TOPIC	KEY CONCEPTS
Namespace	A container which groups names.
Package	A namespace for package variables, subroutines, and so on.
Module	A file that contains one or more packages.
Distribution	A single file containing everything need to build and install a module or group of modules.
use and require	Loading modules at compile time and run time.
Exporting	A way to put subroutines in other packages.
BEGIN, et al.	Blocks of code that execute at specific phases of the program run.
POD	How to document your code.

12

Object Oriented Perl

WHAT YOU WILL LEARN IN THIS CHAPTER:

➤ Understanding what an object is

➤ Learning the three rules of Perl's OO system

➤ Creating a class

➤ How to subclass a class

➤ Overloading classes

➤ Learning OO traps for the unwary

WROX.COM CODE DOWNLOAD FOR THIS CHAPTER

The wrox.com code downloads for this chapter are found at `http://www.wrox.com/remtitle` `.cgi?isbn=1118013840` on the Download Code tab. The code for this chapter is divided into the following major examples:

➤ `example_12_1_shopper.pl`

➤ `example_12_2_episode.pl`

➤ `lib/Shopper/Personal.pm`

➤ `lib/TV/Episode.pm`

➤ `lib/TV/Episode/Broadcast.pm`

➤ `lib/TV/Episode/OnDemand.pm`

➤ `lib/TV/Episode/Version.pm`

➤ `listing_12_1_episode.pl`

Chapter 10 mentioned that knowledge of the `sort`, `map`, and `grep` functions is sort of a litmus test that some programmers use to know if a Perl developer is at least at an intermediate level. Knowledge of object-oriented programming (often referred to as OOP, or just OO) is your first step toward being an advanced Perl developer. Many languages support OO programming, and learning about it in Perl will help you in many other languages.

Two chapters discuss OOP. This chapter describes Perl's built-in OO tools. They're minimal, but this minimalism gives you a lot of freedom. You need to understand how Perl's built-in OO works because much of the Perl software in the wild is written with this.

The next chapter, Chapter 13, covers `Moose` which is an incredibly powerful object system built on top of Perl's OO tools. It's so powerful that it's rapidly becoming Perl's de facto OO system for many developers and companies and has had a large influence over the development of Perl.

WHAT ARE OBJECTS? THE ÆVAR THE PERSONAL SHOPPER

Many books have been written about OOP and even among experts, there is often disagreement about what OOP is. Many programmers have tried to explain OOP and leave the programmer confused. A case in point is the classic "An object is a data structure with behaviors attached to it." Although that's correct, that's also an awful description and tells you almost nothing you need to know, so instead of giving you a textbook definition, we're going to tell you a story.

You're an awfully busy person and have little free time but plenty of disposable income, so you've decided to hire a personal shopper. His name is Ævar (any resemblance to reviewers of this book, living or dead, is purely coincidental) and he's friendly, flamboyant, and most of all, cheap.

Because Ævar is new to both your city and the job, you have to tell him carefully how much money he can spend, exactly what quality of products you want, and where to buy them. You may even have to tell him which route to drive to pick up the goods and how to invoice you.

That, in essence, is procedural code and that's what you've been doing up to now. You've been carefully telling the computer every step of the way what to do.

After a few months of explaining every little detail, Ævar gets upset and says, "*þegiðu maður, ég veit alveg hvað ég er að gera*" (Icelandic for "Shut up dude; I know what I'm doing"). And he does. He knows what you like and where to get it. He's become an expert. In OO terms, you might now be doing this:

```
my $aevar = Shopper::Personal->new({
    name   => 'Ævar',
    budget => 100
});
$aevar->buy(@list_of_things_to_buy);
my $invoice = $aevar->get_invoice;
```

You're no longer telling Ævar every little step he needs to take to get your shopping done. He's an expert, and he has all the knowledge needed to do your shopping for you and present you with the bill.

And that's all objects are: experts about a problem you need solved. They have all the knowledge you need to get a task done, and you don't *tell* them how to do something, you merely *ask* them to do something.

THREE RULES OF PERL OO

We've already said that Perl has a minimalist OO system. This is both good and bad. It's bad because if you're familiar with OO from another language, you may be frustrated with the differences in Perl or its lack of native facilities to handle things you take for granted. However, it's good because it's easy to learn and extend.

There are three simple rules to know about Perl's OO system.

- ➤ A class is a package.

- ➤ An object is a reference that knows its class.

- ➤ A method is a subroutine.

When you understand and memorize those three rules, you'll know most of what there is to know about basic OO programming in Perl.

Class Is a Package

In OO programming, we often speak of classes. A *class* is a blueprint for something you want to create. Just as you can use a blueprint of a house to make several houses, each painted in different colors, you can use a Shopper::Personal class to create several personal shoppers, each with different buying habits. The Shopper::Personal class is not the object, but it's the blueprint you can use to create one.

> **NOTE** Given that Perl has been heavily influenced by linguistics, it might also be fair to describe a class as a noun and an instance as a proper noun. It's the difference between the generic idea of a "city" (a noun) and "Paris" (a proper noun).

> **NOTE** Perl's OO is based on classes. However, this is not the only way to do OO programming. For example, JavaScript uses a prototype-based object system. There's actually some disagreement about many aspects of OO programming, but most of the OO world today (outside of JavaScript, ActionScript, and a few other languages) have settled on class-based OO programming.

For the Shopper::Personal snippet, you can have this:

```perl
my $aevar = Shopper::Personal->new({
    name   => 'Ævar',
    budget => 100
});
```

You'll note the `Shopper::Personal->new` bit. `Shopper::Personal` is the class name. It looks like a package name because it is! In Perl a class is a package and it's declared the same way. There is no special syntax for declaring a class. In `Shopper/Personal.pm`, declaring the class might start with this:

```
package Shopper::Personal;
use strict;
use warnings;

sub new {
    # more code here
}
```

Pretty simple, eh? Sure, there's more to the code, but a class is nothing special in Perl.

An Object Is a Reference That Knows Its Class

When you create an object, you create a reference that knows what class it belongs to. You can do that by blessing the reference into the class using the `bless` builtin. The syntax looks like this:

```
OBJECT = bless REFERENCE, CLASSNAME;
```

The `bless` builtin tells a reference that it belongs to a class. When the object is used, it knows where its methods are.

When you created your `Shopper::Personal` object and passed in a hash reference:

```
my $aevar = Shopper::Personal->new( {
    name   => 'Ævar',
    budget => 100
} );
```

The code to create it may have looked like this:

```
package Shopper::Personal;
use strict;
use warnings;
sub new {
    my ( $class, $arg_for ) = @_;
    return bless {
        name   => $arg_for->{name},
        budget => $arg_for->{budget},
    }, $class;
}
```

In this code, the `$arg_for` hashref has now been blessed into the `Shopper::Personal` personal class. When you or anyone else uses the object and call methods on it, the blessed reference knows where it is, in this case the `Shopper::Personal` class.

> **WARNING** *Some OO tutorials show you this:*
>
> ```
> sub new {
>     my ( $class, $arg_for ) = @_;
>     return bless {
>         name   => $arg_for->{name},
>         budget => $arg_for->{budget},
>     }; # assume current package, bad form
> }
> ```
>
> *You blessed the reference but did not say what class to bless it in. When this happens, Perl blesses the object into the current package. This is considered to be bad form because if you later need to inherit from this class (explained later), you may want to reuse the* new() *constructor, but you can't because it blesses the reference into the current class.*
>
> *This is called the* one-argument bless *and its use is heavily discouraged.*

For some other languages that allow OO programming, new is actually a keyword used to construct objects. In Perl this is not the case. The new() method is just another method. You could easily have called the constructor hire() and written Shopper::Personal->hire(). However, unless you have good reason to do so, the best thing to do is name your constructors new() to avoid confusion.

When you see this:

```
my $aevar = Shopper::Personal->new( {
    name   => 'Ævar',
    budget => 100
} );
```

The Shopper::Personal->new bit is important. When you use the dereferencing operator, ->, with a class name on the left and a method name on the right (remember that a method is a subroutine in the class), the method receives the class name as the first argument in @_ with the other arguments added to @_ as normal.

> **NOTE** *The first argument to a method is either a class name or an object. Because it's what is responsible for invoking the method, it's referred to as the* invocant.

So the new() method, in the preceding example, can have the following arguments:

```
@_ = ( 'Shopper::Personal', { name => 'Ævar', budget => 100 } );
```

So look at the constructor again:

```perl
sub new {
    my ( $class, $arg_for ) = @_;
    return bless {
        name   => $arg_for->{name},
        budget => $arg_for->{budget},
    }, $class;
}
```

You can see that `$class` contains `Shopper::Personal` and `$arg_for` contains the hash reference.

You don't actually need to pass a hash reference. You could pass a list:

```perl
my $aevar = Shopper::Personal->new( 'Ævar', 100 );
```

And then the `new()` constructor might look something like this:

```perl
sub new {
    my ( $class, $name, $budget ) = @_;
    return bless {
        name   => $name,
        budget => $budget,
    }, $class;
}
```

> **NOTE** You can use `bless` with any kind of reference. Here, you bless an array reference:
>
> ```perl
> sub new {
>     my ( $class, $name, $budget ) = @_;
>     return bless [ $name, $budget ], $class;
> }
>
> # these methods will make more sense in the next section
> sub name {
>     my $self = shift;
>     return $self->[0];
> }
>
> sub budget {
>     my $self = shift;
>     return $self->[1];
> }
> ```
>
> However, as you get more experience with OO programming, blessing a hash reference is much easier to work with than blessing other types of references, particularly if the class may be subclassed.

A Method Is a Subroutine

Moving along, you see this:

```perl
$aevar->buy(@list_of_things_to_buy);
my $invoice = $aevar->get_invoice;
```

Here you call two methods, `buy()` and `get_invoice()` against the $aevar object. When this happens, $aevar is passed as the first argument in @_ with the other arguments following. Before looking at those methods, look at the name and budget attributes passed to the constructor.

```perl
my $aevar = Shopper::Personal->new( {
    name   => 'Ævar',
    budget => 100
} );

print $aevar->get_name;
print $aevar->get_budget;
```

Now expand the Shopper::Personal class just a bit to provide those methods.

```perl
package Shopper::Personal;

use strict;
use warnings;

sub new {
    my ( $class, $arg_for ) = @_;
    return bless {
        name   => $arg_for->{name},
        budget => $arg_for->{budget},
    }, $class;
}

sub get_name {
    my $self = shift;
    return $self->{name};
}

sub get_budget {
    my $self = shift;
    return $self->{budget};
}

1;
```

> **NOTE** By now, some of you are wondering why the constructor is blessing a hash reference without checking the validity of those arguments:
>
> ```perl
> sub new {
>     my ( $class, $arg_for ) = @_;
>     return bless {
>         name   => $arg_for->{name},
>         budget => $arg_for->{budget},
>     }, $class;
> }
> ```
>
> What if some of the keys are misspelled or the values contain invalid values? The new() constructor here is actually not good practice, but it has the advantage of being simple enough to not get in the way of explaining the basics of OOP in Perl.

When you call a method using a class name:

```
my $shopper = Shopper::Personal->new($args);
```

The class name is passed as the first argument to @_. Naturally, when you call a method using the instance:

```
my $budget = $shopper->get_budget();
```

The $shopper instance gets passed as the first argument to @_. Thus, for the get_budget() method:

```
sub get_budget {
    my $self = shift @_;
    return $self->{budget};
}
```

You can refer to the object as $self (this is by convention, but other popular names are $this and $object) and because it's the first argument to get_budget(), you can shift it off @_. Because $self is a blessed hash reference it "knows" that it wants the get_budget() method from the Shopper::Personal class. Therefore, you can fetch the budget attribute with normal dereferencing syntax:

```
return $self->{budget};
```

> **WARNING** When you read the data in a blessed object by directly accessing the reference, this is called *reaching inside* the object. In general, the only time this should be done is for the getters and setters and even then, only inside the class. Otherwise, use the proper methods to get the data.
>
> ```
> my $budget = $shopper->budget;      # Right.
> my $budget = $shopper->{budget};    # WRONG, WRONG, WRONG!
> ```
>
> *DO NOT REACH INSIDE THE OBJECT IF YOU DO NOT HAVE TO. I cannot emphasize this strongly enough; even though many developers seem to think it's Okay. The reason is simple: When you use a method call to get the value, you do not know or care how the data is "gotten." The maintainer of the object class is free to change the internals of the object at any time so long as they keep the interface the same. By reaching inside the object, you're relying on behavior that is not and should not be guaranteed. Many a programmer (including your author) has learned this the hard way.*
>
> *Let me repeat that: DO NOT REACH INSIDE THE OBJECT IF YOU DO NOT HAVE TO. It's important.*

By now you can see that if you want to change the budget value, it's fairly trivial:

```
sub set_budget {
    my ( $self, $new_budget ) = @_;
    $self->{budget} = $new_budget;
}
```

In fact, many objects in Perl overload the budget() method to be both a setter and a getter (or mutator/accessor, if you prefer big words).

```
sub budget {
    my $self = shift;
    if (@_) { # we have more than one argument
        $self->{budget} = shift;
    }
    return $self->{budget};
}
```

That allows you to do this:

```
my $budget = $aevar->budget;     # get the existing budget
$aevar->budget($new_budget);     # set a new budget
```

Some developers prefer to keep the get_ and set_ behaviors separate, such as:

```
my $budget = $aevar->budget;          # get the existing budget
$aevar->set_budget($new_budget);      # set a new budget
```

Others prefer to have the budget() method used for both the getter and the setter. It's a matter of personal choice, but whichever style you choose, stick with it to avoid confusing later developers.

One strong recommendation in favor of separate getters and setters is the case in which some getters do not have corresponding setters because that data is read-only:

```
my $customer = Customer->find($customer_id);
print $customer->name;

$customer->name($new_name);
print $customer->id;

$customer->id($new_id);    # boom! this is read-only
```

In this example, the id() method of a Customer object is assumed to be read-only, but you can't tell this directly from the API methods. However, if you prefixed all setters with set_ and there was no set_id() method, the run-time error Can't locate object method "set_id" via package "Customer" is a good clue that you cannot set the ID to a new value. What's worse, the minimalist getters that many developers write can obscure the problem:

```
sub id {
    my ($self) = @_;
    return $self->{id};
}
```

As you can see, if you tried to set a new ID with this method, it would fail, but it would do so silently. This could be hard to debug. Failures should be loud, painful, and clear.

Getting back to Shopper::Personal, you have the following code:

```
package Shopper::Personal;

use strict;
```

```
use warnings;

sub new {
    my ( $class, $arg_for ) = @_;
    return bless {
        name   => $arg_for->{name},
        budget => $arg_for->{budget},
    }, $class;
}

sub get_name {
    my $self = shift;
    return $self->{name};
}

sub get_budget {
    my $self = shift;
    return $self->{budget};
}

1;
```

But what does the buy() method look like? Well, it might look something like this:

```
sub buy {
    my ( $self, @list_of_things_to_buy ) = @_;

    my $remaining_budget = $self->get_budget;
    my $name             = $self->get_name;

    foreach my $item (@list_of_things_to_buy) {
        my $cost = $self->_find_cost_of($item);

        if ( not defined $cost ) {
            carp("$name doesn't know how to buy '$item'");
        }
        elsif ( $cost > $remaining_budget ) {
            carp("$name doesn't have enough money buy '$item'");
        }
        else {
            $remaining_budget -= $cost;
            $self->_buy_item($item);
        }
    }
}
```

You can see that this method is calling out to other methods, some of which start with an underscore (_find_cost_of(), and _buy_item()), indicating that they are private methods that should not be used outside of this package.

For each item, you have three possibilities:

➤ Ævar can't find the item.

➤ Ævar can't afford the item.

➤ The item is purchased.

Oh, and you can use the `carp()` subroutine, so don't forget to include the `use Carp 'carp';` line at the top of the code.

When you call a method against a class, such as this:

```
my $aevar = Shopper::Personal->new($hashref);
```

This method is called a class method because it can be safely called with the class name instead of an instance of the class. In this case, the constructor is returning `$aevar`, an instance of the `Shopper::Personal` class. Later, when you call a method against `$aevar`:

```
my $invoice = $aevar->get_invoice;
```

`get_invoice()` is called an instance method because you must have an instance of the object to safely call that method. When you try to call a method and you get an error message like this:

```
Can't use string ("Shopper::Personal") as a HASH ref ...
```

It's probably because you accidentally called an instance method as a class method:

```
Shopper::Personal->buy(@list_of_things_to_buy);
```

When you should have called it on an instance:

```
$aevar->buy(@list_of_things_to_buy);
```

New OO programmers are often confused by this, but think about blueprints again. If you use a blueprint (class) to build several houses (instances), you could see how many bedrooms each house (instance) has by reading the blueprint (class). However, you probably wouldn't know what furniture each house (instance) has.

TRY IT OUT **Your First Class**

Because you wrote a lot of the code for the `Shopper::Personal` class, finish writing the entire class. All the code in this Try It Out is found in the code file `lib/Shopper/Personal.pm` and `example_12_1_shopper.pl`.

1. Make a directory path called `chapter12/lib/Shopper/`. Change to the `chapter12` directory. Type in the following class and save it as `lib/Shopper/Personal.pm`:

```
package Shopper::Personal;

use strict;
use warnings;
```

```perl
use Carp qw(croak carp);
use Scalar::Util 'looks_like_number';

our $VERSION = '0.01';

sub new {
    my ( $class, $arg_for ) = @_;
    my $self = bless {}, $class;
    $self->_initialize($arg_for);
    return $self;
}

sub _initialize {
    my ( $self, $arg_for ) = @_;
    my %arg_for = %$arg_for;        # make a shallow copy
    my $class = ref $self;
    $self->{purchased_items} = [];
    $self->{money_spent}     = 0;
    my $name = delete $arg_for{name};
    unless ( defined $name ) {
        croak("$class requires a name to be set");
    }
    $self->set_budget( delete $arg_for{budget} );
    $self->{attributes}{name} = $name;
    if ( my $remaining = join ', ', keys %arg_for ) {
        croak("Unknown keys to $class\::new: $remaining");
    }
}

sub get_name {
    my $self = shift;
    return $self->{attributes}{name};
}

sub set_budget {
    my ( $self, $budget ) = @_;
    unless ( looks_like_number($budget) && $budget > 0 ) {
        croak("Budget must be a number greater than zero");
    }
    $self->{attributes}{budget} = $budget;
}

sub get_budget {
    my $self = shift;
    return $self->{attributes}{budget};
}

sub buy {
    my ( $self, @list_of_things_to_buy ) = @_;
    my $remaining_budget = $self->get_budget;
    my $name             = $self->get_name;
    foreach my $item (@list_of_things_to_buy) {
        my $cost = $self->_find_cost_of($item);
        if ( not defined $cost ) {
```

```
                carp("$name doesn't know how to buy '$item'");
            }
            elsif ( $cost > $remaining_budget ) {
                carp("$name doesn't have enough money buy '$item'");
            }
            else {
                $remaining_budget -= $cost;
                $self->_buy_item($item);
            }
        }
    }
}

sub get_invoice {
    my $self        = shift;
    my @items       = $self->_purchased_items;
    my $money_spent = $self->_money_spent;
    my $shopper     = $self->get_name;
    my $date        = localtime;
    unless (@items) {
        return "No items purchased";
    }
    my $invoice =<<"END_HEADER";
Date:     $date
Shopper: $shopper
Item        Cost
END_HEADER
    foreach my $item (@items) {
        $invoice .= sprintf "%-10s %0.2f\n", $item,
 $self->_find_cost_of($item);
    }
    $invoice .= "\nTotal + 10%: $money_spent\n";
    return $invoice;
}

sub _purchased_items { @{ shift->{purchased_items} } }

sub _money_spent {
    my $self = shift;
    # we assume personal shoppers add 10% to the price
    # to cover the cost of their services
    return $self->{money_spent} * 1.10;
}

sub _find_cost_of {
    my ( $class, $item ) = @_;
    my %price_of = (
        beer    => 1,
        coffee  => 3.5,
        ravioli => 1.5,
        ferrari => 225_000,
    );
    return $price_of{lc $item};
}
```

```
sub _buy_item {
    my ( $self, $item ) = @_;
    $self->{money_spent} += $self->_find_cost_of($item);
    push @{ $self->{purchased_items} }, $item;
}

1;
```

2. In your `chapter12` directory, save the following program as `example_12_1_shopper.pl`:

```
use strict;
use warnings;

use lib 'lib';
use Shopper::Personal;

my $shopper = Shopper::Personal->new({
    name   => 'aevar',
    budget => 10,
});

$shopper->buy(
    'beer',
    'Ferrari',
    ('coffee')  x 2,
    ('ravioli') x 2,
    'beer',
);
print $shopper->get_invoice;

my $next_shopper = Shopper::Personal->new({
    name  => 'bob',
    limit => 10,
});
```

When you finish, your current directory structure should look like this:

```
./
|  lib/
|  |  Shopper/
|  |  |--Personal.pm
|--example_12_1_shopper.pl
```

3. Run the program with `perl example_12_1_shopper.pl`. You should see output similar to the following (obviously your date will be different):

```
aevar doesn't have enough money buy 'Ferrari' at shopper.pl line 11
aevar doesn't have enough money buy 'ravioli' at shopper.pl line 11
aevar doesn't have enough money buy 'beer' at shopper.pl line 11
Date:    Sun Feb 26 16:15:29 2012
Shopper: aevar
Item      Cost
beer      1.00
```

```
coffee     3.50
coffee     3.50
ravioli    1.50
Total + 10%: 10.45
Budget must be a number greater than zero at shopper.pl line 21
```

How It Works

Obviously this Try It Out is far more involved that much of what you've done before. Nothing new was introduced in the Try It Out, but I've reached into my bag of tricks and put together a lot of interesting things here. First, look at object construction. Start numbering lines of code for longer bits like this.

```
 1:  package Shopper::Personal;
 2:  use strict;
 3:  use warnings;
 4:  use Carp qw(croak carp);
 5:  use Scalar::Util 'looks_like_number';
 6:
 7:  our $VERSION = '0.01';
 8:
 9:  sub new {
10:      my ( $class, $arg_for ) = @_;
11:      my $self = bless {}, $class;
12:      $self->_initialize($arg_for);
13:      return $self;
14:  }
15:
16:  sub _initialize {
17:      my ( $self, $arg_for ) = @_;
18:      my %arg_for = %$arg_for;    # make a shallow copy
19:      my $class = ref $self;
20:
21:      $self->{purchased_items} = [];
22:      $self->{money_spent}     = 0;
23:
24:      my $name = delete $arg_for{name};
25:      unless ( defined $name ) {
26:          croak("$class requires a name to be set");
27:      }
28:
29:      $self->set_budget( delete $arg_for{budget} );
30:
31:      $self->{attributes}{name} = $name;
32:
33:      if ( my $remaining = join ', ', keys %arg_for ) {
34:          croak("Unknown keys to $class\::new: $remaining");
35:      }
36:  }
```

Lines 1 through 7 are standard boilerplate, making your code safer and importing carp, croak, and looks_like_number, three utility subroutines that your methods can find useful.

The constructor, new() (lines 9–14), now blesses only a hash ref and then immediately passes control to the _initialize() method. This allows the constructor to do only one thing. The _initialize()

method handles setting up the actual object state and making sure it's sane. In fact, _initialize() does three things:

1. Create entries in the hashref for storing important data (lines 21–29).

2. Make sure data supplied in the constructor is valid (lines 25–27).

3. Make sure no extra keys are supplied (lines 33–33).

It's important to look closely at lines 12 and 18:

```
12:     $self->_initialize($arg_for);
18:     my %arg_for = %$arg_for;     # make a shallow copy
```

Notice that you pass the hashref, $arg_for and then dereference it in the %arg_for variable. By doing this, you can ensure to provide a shallow copy of the hash to _initialize(). Otherwise, when you do this:

```
24:     my $name = delete $arg_for{name};
```

If it were a reference, you would have deleted $arg_for->{name} and that would have altered the value of the hash reference that's passed to the constructor! You don't want to do that.

So why delete the keys? You don't actually need to, but if you delete all allowed keys, it makes it easy for lines 33–35 to see that there are extra keys left over and croak() with a list of said keys. Note that there are many other ways to verify passing the correct arguments. This is merely one of them.

If this seems like a bit of extra work, that's because it is. Many OO authors assume that people will just read the documentation and use the class correctly. Unfortunately, without tight validation of your arguments, it's easy to get this wrong and have unexpected side effects. In Chapter 13, when discussing Moose, you'll see how much easier classes like this are to write.

Next, you have three methods for your attributes:

```
38:   sub get_name {
39:       my $self = shift;
40:       return $self->{attributes}{name};
41:   }
42:
43:   sub set_budget {
44:       my ( $self, $budget ) = @_;
45:       unless ( looks_like_number($budget) && $budget > 0 ) {
46:           croak("Budget must be a number greater than zero");
47:       }
48:       $self->{attributes}{budget} = $budget;
49:   }
50:
51:   sub get_budget {
52:       my $self = shift;
53:       return $self->{attributes}{budget};
54:   }
```

The get_name() and get_budget() methods are straightforward, but the set_budget() takes a bit more work because line 45 checks to make sure that the budget is actually a number greater than zero.

Note how the _initialize() method takes advantage of the set_budget() method on line 29. That makes it easier to avoid duplicating logic.

Next, you have the buy() method:

```
56:  sub buy {
57:      my ( $self, @list_of_things_to_buy ) = @_;
58:      my $remaining_budget = $self->get_budget;
59:      my $name             = $self->get_name;
60:
61:      foreach my $item (@list_of_things_to_buy) {
62:          my $cost = $self->_find_cost_of($item);
63:
64:          if ( not defined $cost ) {
65:              carp("$name doesn't know how to buy '$item'");
66:          }
67:          elsif ( $cost > $remaining_budget ) {
68:              carp("$name doesn't have enough money buy '$item'");
69:          }
70:          else {
71:              $remaining_budget -= $cost;
72:              $self->_buy_item($item);
73:          }
74:      }
75:  }
```

This method iterates over the list of items to buy and, so long as you have enough money left in your budget, you buy the item (line 72). You carp() if you cannot find the price for the item (line 65) or if you don't have enough money left (line 68).

In particular, pay attention to lines 58 and 59:

```
58:      my $remaining_budget = $self->get_budget;
59:      my $name             = $self->get_name;
```

Because you're inside the Shopper::Personal class, why not just grab the data directly instead of the calling these accessors?

```
58:      my $remaining_budget = $self->{attributes}{budget}
59:      my $name             = $self->{attributes}{name};
```

There are several reasons for this:

➤   Calling the method is often more readable.

➤   You don't need to worry about misspelling the hash keys.

➤   If you change the logic of the methods, you don't have to change this code.

The final point is particularly true when you learn about inheritance in the "Subclassing" section later in this chapter.

Looking at get_invoice():

```
77:  sub get_invoice {
78:      my $self        = shift;
```

```
79:        my @items       = $self->_purchased_items;
80:        my $money_spent = $self->_money_spent;
81:        my $shopper     = $self->get_name;
82:        my $date        = localtime;
83:        unless (@items) {
84:            return "No items purchased";
85:        }
86:        my $invoice =<<"END_HEADER";
87:  Date:      $date
88:  Shopper:  $shopper
89:
90:  Item         Cost
91:  END_HEADER
92:        foreach my $item (@items) {
93:            $invoice .= sprintf "%-10s %0.2f\n", $item, \
$self->_find_cost_of($item);
94:        }
95:        $invoice .= "\nTotal + 10%: $money_spent\n";
96:        return $invoice;
97:    }
```

You may not be familiar with `localtime`, a Perl builtin used in line 82, but `perldoc -f localtime` can reveal that in scalar context it returns a human-readable form of the current date and time, which is exactly what you need for the header of the report that you generate in lines 86–89.

Lines 92–94 add the individual items to the invoice, and line 95 adds the total. Actually, `get_invoice()` is a normal method.

After `get_invoice()`, however, all methods begin with underscores. These are private methods that only the class should use. There are only a couple of them you might find interesting.

First, the `_purchased_items()` method is rather simple:

```
99:  sub _purchased_items { @{ shift->{purchased_items} } }
```

Why wouldn't you just go ahead and make that public so that anyone can use it to get a list of purchased items? A good rule of thumb is to make nothing in a class public unless absolutely necessary. As soon as you make something a public method, you've now committed your class to maintaining that interface because you don't want to break others' code. By making it a private method, you give yourself flexibility. You can always make a private method public later, but making a public method private is much more likely to break someone's code.

The `get_name()` and `get_budget()` methods should have been private and the `set_budget()` budget method should not have existed at all. Why? Because if you look at the sample code, you see that you need only the `new()`, `buy()` and `get_invoice()` methods. Those are the only three methods that need to be made public, but you made a few others public just to show a bit more about how getters/setters typically work in Perl.

Remember: If you don't need to make a method public, don't.

The other potentially interesting method here is the `_buy_item()` method:

```
120:  sub _buy_item {
121:      my ( $self, $item ) = @_;
122:      $self->{money_spent} += $self->_find_cost_of($item);
123:      push @{ $self->{purchased_items} }, $item;
123:  }
```

What do you do when you buy an item at a store: You pay for it and take it with you. That's exactly what the _buy_item() method does and it does nothing else. Just as a class should contain all the logic necessary to be an "expert" on whatever problem domain the class is for — and not do anything else — individual methods should contain all the logic needed to handle their smaller piece of the problem — and not do anything else.

OBJECTS – ANOTHER VIEW

Sometimes objects don't do complicated tasks like buying things. Sometimes they're just there to encapsulate a complex data structure and make sure it has all the needed properties of a class and doesn't allow invalid data to be created.

When your author worked at the BBC, he was one of the developers responsible for handling metadata. *Metadata* is information about information. It seems strange, but it's fairly natural when you get used to it. For example, an episode of a TV show might present a lot of information about animals, but what about the information regarding the episode? For your purposes, TV show episode objects won't model everything you need, but you'll have just enough to show how this works. You can create a small class to model this.

This really isn't different from the "objects as experts" example earlier, but it's a good foundation to show how objects can sometimes be viewed as complex data types.

Using TV::Episode

You'll startout with a basic TV::Episode class, making read-only accessors for all your data. You can find the following code in the code file lib/TV/Episode.pm:

```perl
package TV::Episode;

use strict;
use warnings;

use Carp 'croak';
use Scalar::Util 'looks_like_number';

our $VERSION = '0.01';

my %IS_ALLOWED_GENRE = map { $_ => 1 } qw(
  comedy
  drama
  documentary
```

```perl
    awesome
);

sub new {
    my ( $class, $arg_for ) = @_;
    my $self = bless {} => $class;
    $self->_initialize($arg_for);
    return $self;
}

sub _initialize {
    my ( $self, %arg_for ) = @_;
    my %arg_for = %$arg_for;
    foreach my $property (qw/series director title/) {
        my $value = delete $arg_for{$property};
        # at least one non-space character
        unless ( defined $value && $value =~ /\S/ ) {
            croak("property '$property' must have at a value");
        }
        $self->{$property} = $value;
    }
    my $genre = delete $arg_for{genre};
    unless ( exists $IS_ALLOWED_GENRE{$genre} ) {
        croak("Genre '$genre' is not an allowed genre");
    }
    $self->{genre} = $genre;
    foreach my $property (qw/season episode_number/) {
        my $value = delete $arg_for{$property};
        unless ( looks_like_number($value) && $value > 0 ) {
            croak("$property must have a positive value");
        }
        $self->{$property} = $value;
    }
    if ( my $extra = join ', ' => keys %arg_for ) {
        croak("Unknown keys to new(): $extra");
    }
}

sub series         { shift->{series} }
sub title          { shift->{title} }
sub director       { shift->{director} }
sub genre          { shift->{genre} }
sub season         { shift->{season} }
sub episode_number { shift->{episode_number} }

sub as_string {
    my $self      = shift;
    my @properties = qw(
      series
      title
      director
      genre
      season
      episode_number
```

```
        );
        my $as_string = '';
        foreach my $property (@properties) {
            $as_string .= sprintf "%-14s - %s\n", ucfirst($property),
              $self->$property;
        }
        return $as_string;
    }

    1;
```

There's nothing terribly unusual about it; though there is a huge amount of tedious validation in the _initialize() method. Chapter 13 covers the Moose object system and shows you how to make most of this code go away.

One strange bit you'll notice in the as_string() method is this:

```
    $self->$property;
```

If you have code like this:

```
    my $method = 'genre';
    print $self->$method;
```

That's equivalent to:

```
    $self->genre;
```

Using a variable as a method name is illegal in many other OO languages, but Perl allows this, and it's handy because there are times when you might want to delay the decision about which method to call until runtime. Otherwise, the previous code may have had this:

```
    my $format = "%-14s - %s\n";
    my $episode = sprintf $format, 'Series',   $self->series;
    $episode .=  sprintf $format, 'Title',    $self->title;
    $episode .=  sprintf $format, 'Director', $self->director;
    $episode .=  sprintf $format, 'Genre',    $self->genre;
    $episode .=  sprintf $format, 'Season',   $self->season;
    $episode .=  sprintf $format, 'Episode number',
      $self->episode_number;
    return $episode;
```

That is error prone and the foreach loop makes it simpler.

Moving along, you can use your class like this (code file listing_12_1_episode.pl):

```
    use strict;
    use warnings;

    use lib 'lib';
    use TV::Episode;
```

```perl
my $episode = TV::Episode->new({
    series         => 'Firefly',
    director       => 'Marita Grabiak',
    title          => 'Jaynestown',
    genre          => 'awesome',
    season         => 1,
    episode_number => 7,
});
print $episode->as_string;
```

And that prints out:

```
Series         - Firefly
Title          - Jaynestown
Director       - Marita Grabiak
Genre          - awesome
Season         - 1
Episode_number - 7
```

And that's great! Except for one little problem you probably don't know about. When you create objects, you must model your objects to fit real-world needs, and you've never actually seen an episode. In reality, you've seen a broadcast on television or an *ondemand*, a streaming version that you can watch on demand on a website (and you're ignoring that there are different versions of episodes, DVDs and other issues). A broadcast might have a broadcast date and an ondemand might have an availability date range. What you need is more specific examples of your TV::Episode class. That's where subclassing comes in.

Subclassing

A *subclass* of a class (also known as a *child class*) is a more specific version of that class. For example, a Vehicle class might have Vehicle::Automobile and Vehicle::Airplane subclasses. The Vehicle::Airplane class might in turn have Vehicle::Airplane::Jet and Vehicle::Airplane::Propeller subclasses.

A subclass uses *inheritance* to provide all the *parent* (also known as a *superclass*) behavior. A method provided by a parent class and used by the subclass is called an *inherited method*. For example, if class A provides a foo() method and class B inherits from A, class B will also have the foo() method, even if it does not implement one itself. (If B does have a foo() method, this is called *overriding* the inherited method.)

> **NOTE** From here on out, I'll use parent and superclass, child and subclass interchangeably. This is because they mean the same thing in Perl and the literature on the subject uses both. Thus, I want you to be very familiar with both terms.

For the TV::Episode class, you need a TV::Episode::Broadcast subclass and a TV::Episode::OnDemand subclass.

THE LISKOV SUBSTITUION PRINCIPLE

I mentioned that subclasses should extend the behavior of their parent classes but not alter this behavior. This is due to something known as the *Liskov Substitution Principle*. This principle effectively states the same thing. The purpose of this principle is to ensure that in any place in your program you can use a given class; if you actually use a subclass of that class, your program should still function correctly.

It has a few more subtleties than merely not changing parent behavior. For example, subclasses are allowed to be less restrictive in the data they accept but not in the data they emit. There is some controversy over the Liskov Substitution Principle, but it's a good idea to follow unless you have strong reasons not to.

The principle was created by Barbara Liskov, Ph.D. She won the 2008 Turing Award (the Nobel prize for computer science) for her work in computer science and her work has influenced much of computing today.

See http://en.wikipedia.org/wiki/Liskov_substitution_principle and http://en.wikipedia.org/wiki/Barbara_Jane_Liskov for more information. Just remember that if you cannot use a subclass in the same place where you can use a parent class, you might have a design flaw.

Using TV::Episode::Broadcast

When something like the TV::Episode::Broadcast class uses the TV::Episode class as its parent, you can say that TV::Episode::Broadcast *inherits* from TV::Episode. To represent the broadcast date, use the DateTime module you can download from the CPAN. Here's how TV::Episode::Broadcast class works. You can find the following code in code file lib/TV/Episode/Broadcast.pm.

```perl
package TV::Episode::Broadcast;

use strict;
use warnings;

use Try::Tiny;
use Carp 'croak';
use base 'TV::Episode';   # inherit!

sub _initialize {
    my ( $self, $arg_for ) = @_;
    my %arg_for = %$arg_for;
    my $broadcast_date = delete $arg_for{broadcast_date};
    try {
        $broadcast_date->isa('DateTime') or die;
    }
    catch {
        croak("broadcast_date must be a DateTime object");
    };
```

```
        $self->{broadcast_date} = $broadcast_date;
        $self->SUPER::_initialize( \%arg_for );
    }

    sub broadcast_date { shift->{broadcast_date} }

    sub as_string {
        my $self    = shift;
        my $episode = $self->SUPER::as_string;
        my $date    = $self->broadcast_date;
        $episode .= sprintf "%-14s - %4d-%2d-%2d\n"
    => 'Broadcast date',
    $date->year,
    $date->month,
    $date->day;
        return $episode;
    }

    1;
```

And this looks similar to TV::Episode, but now you supply the broadcast date:

```
    my $broadcast = TV::Episode::Broadcast->new(
        {
            series         => 'Firefly',
            director       => 'Allan Kroeker',
            title          => 'Ariel',
            genre          => 'awesome',
            season         => 1,
            episode_number => 9,
            broadcast_date => DateTime->new(
                year  => 2002,
                month => 11,
                day   => 15,
            ),
        }
    );
    print $broadcast->as_string;
    print $broadcast->series;
```

Running the program prints out:

```
    Series         - Firefly
    Title          - Ariel
    Director       - Allan Kroeker
    Genre          - awesome
    Season         - 1
    Episode_number - 9
    Broadcast date - 2002-11-15
    Firefly
```

Because TV::Episode::Broadcast has inherited from TV::Episode, broadcasts have all the behavior of episodes, so you can still call $broadcast->series, $broadcast->director, and so on.

There's no need to re-implement these behaviors. This is because when you call a method on an object, Perl checks to see if that method is defined in the object's class. If it's not, it searches the parent class, and then the parent's parent class, and so on, until it finds an appropriate method to call, or dies, telling you that the method is not found.

This is why `TV::Episode::Broadcast` does not have a `new()` method. When you try to call `TV::Episode::Broadcast->new(...)`, Perl looks for `TV::Episode::Broadcast::new()` and, not finding it, starts searching the superclasses and calls the first `new()` method it finds (`TV::Episode::new()` in this case). This is one of the reasons why OO is so powerful: It makes it easy to reuse code.

Perl knows that `TV::Episode` is the parent of `TV::Episode::Broadcast` because of this line:

```
use base 'TV::Episode';
```

The `base` module is commonly used to establish inheritance. There's a newer version named `parent` that does the same thing:

```
use parent 'TV::Episode';
```

It's a fork of the `base` module and mostly involves cleaning up some of the internal cruft that `base` has accumulated over the years. It's not entirely compatible with it, but you'll likely not notice the difference.

> **NOTE** The `base` and `parent` modules also take lists allowing you to inherit from multiple modules at once:
>
> ```
> TV::Episode::AllInOne;
> use base qw(
>   TV::Episode::Broadcast
>   TV::Episode::OnDemand
> );
> ```
>
> This is referred to as multiple inheritance. It's usually a bad idea and its use is controversial enough that many programming languages forbid it outright. Chapter 13 talks about multiple inheritance when discussing roles.

For some older Perl modules, you see inheritance established with the `@ISA` array:

```
package TV::Episode::Broadcast;

# with @ISA, you must first 'use' the modules
# you wish to inherit from

use TV::Episode;
use vars '@ISA';
@ISA = 'TV::Episode';
# optionally: our @ISA = 'TV::Episode';
```

When Perl tries to figure out a module's parent or parents, it looks at the module's @ISA package variable and any classes contained therein are considered parents. Although this method to establish inheritance is now discouraged, you can still sometimes see code messing with the @ISA array, so it's important to remember it. The base and parent modules are merely loading the parents and assigning to @ISA for you. They make it harder to forget to use the parent modules and also protect from *circular inheritance*, a problem whereby a class accidentally inherits from itself.

Now look at your new _initialize() method. This overrides the _initialize() method from the parent class. Because it overrides, the TV::Episode::_initialize() method will not be called unless you call it explicitly, as you do in line 13:

```
 1:  sub _initialize {
 2:      my ( $self, $arg_for ) = @_;
 3:      my %arg_for = %$arg_for;
 4:      my $broadcast_date = delete $arg_for{broadcast_date};
 5:
 6:      try {
 7:          $broadcast_date->isa('DateTime') or die;
 8:      }
 9:      catch {
10:          croak("Not a DataTime object: $broadcast_date");
11:      };
12:      $self->{broadcast_date} = $broadcast_date;
13:      $self->SUPER::_initialize(\%arg_for);
14:  }
```

The $self->SUPER::_initialize() syntax is what you use to call the superclass method. If it doesn't exist, you'll get an error like:

```
Can't locate object method "_initialize" via package "main::SUPER"
```

This allows you to override a parent method but still rely on its behavior if you need to. In this case, you supply an extra parameter but remove it from the %arg_for hash to ensure that the parent _initialize() method does croak() when it sees the extra argument. You can test that the parameter is suitable with a try/catch block and an isa() test, but this is explained a bit more when I cover the UNIVERSAL package in the "Using UNIVERSAL" section of this chapter.

> **NOTE** *Although the example code shows an overridden method calling their parent versions with* $self->SUPER::some_method, *there is actually no requirement that you call the parent method. Use this technique here to show how you can supplement parent method behavior, but replace it entirely with an overridden method, which is fine so long as you don't change the semantics of the method. (Well, you could have your* as_string() *method do something radically different from the parent method, such as return an array reference, but that's not a good idea.)*

You can do the same thing on line 3 with the as_string() method:

```
 1:  sub as_string {
 2:      my $self    = shift;
 3:      my $episode = $self->SUPER::as_string;
 4:      my $date    = $self->broadcast_date;
 5:      $episode .= sprintf "%-14s - %4d-%2d-%2d\n" => 'Broadcast date',
 6:          $date->year,
 7:          $date->month,
 8:          $date->day;
 9:      return $episode;
10:  }
```

In this case, you use the parent's `as_string()` method to create the text representation of the object and then add an extra line of data. You probably should have pulled the format out into its own method so that you could override the format if needed. You could have done something like this:

```
sub _as_string_format { return "%-14s - %4d-%2d-%2d\n" }
sub as_string {
    my $self    = shift;
    my $episode = $self->SUPER::as_string;
    my $date    = $self->broadcast_date;
    $episode .= sprintf $self->_as_string_format => 'Broadcast date',
        $date->year,
        $date->month,
        $date->day;
    return $episode;
}
```

But that would have required a change to the base class to support the same `_as_string_format()` and you may have not had access to change the base class. If that's the case and you needed a different format, you would have to override the parent `as_string()` method and duplicated most of its logic and not call `$self->SUPER::as_string`.

Class Versus Instance Data

Sometimes you want to share data across all instances of a class, for example:

```
package Universe;
sub new {
    my ( $class, $name ) = @_;
    return bless { name => $name }, $class;
}
sub name { shift->{name} }
sub pi   { 3.14159265359 }
1;
```

That creates a read-only `pi()` method that you can access via `Universe->pi`. You can also call it on an instance and it behaves the same way:

```
my $universe1 = Universe->new('first universe name');
print $universe1->pi, "\n";

my $universe2 = Universe->new('second universe name');
print $universe2->pi, "\n";
```

Each Universe you create will have a different name, but share the same value of pi().

You can also make it read-write:

```perl
package Universe;

sub new {
    my ( $class, $name ) = @_;
    return bless { name => $name }, $class;
}

sub name { shift->{name} }

{
    my $pi = 3.14159265359;
    sub pi {
        my $class = shift;
        if ( @_ ) {
            $pi = shift;
        }
        return $pi;
    }
}
1;
```

However, be aware that this is little more than a global variable. If you change it for one universe, you will change it for all of them. (And you didn't even have data validation for it!)

There is, as you probably suspect by now, a CPAN module to make this easier: Class::Data::Inheritable. This allows you to easily define class data but override it in a subclass, if needed:

```perl
package Universe;
use parent 'Class::Data::Inheritable';
__PACKAGE__->mk_classdata( pi => 3.14159265359 );
```

With that, you can now call Universe->pi and get the right answer. Of course, you can still change it:

```perl
Universe->pi(3);    # oops
```

A better strategy, instead of allowing this hidden global into your code, is sometimes to provide a default:

```perl
sub new {
    my ( $class, $arg_for ) = @_;
    $arg_for->{pi} ||= $class->_default_pi;
    my $self = bless {}, $arg_for;
    $self->_initialize($arg_for);
    return $self;
}

# You can override this in a subclass, if desired
sub _default_pi { 3.14159265359 }
```

With that, all instances of a class default to a valid value of pi, but if you change it later for one class, it does not impact other instances. Whether this is appropriate depends on your needs. Sometimes it's easier to share data across instances.

A BRIEF RECAP

You've covered the basics of OO, so now, have a brief recap of what you've learned so far.

First, there are three rules to Perl's Object-Oriented programming:

➤   A class is a package.

➤   An object is a reference blessed into a class.

➤   A method is a subroutine.

Classes can inherit from other classes to provide more specific types of a class. A class that inherits from another class is called a subclass or child class, and the class it inherits from is the superclass or parent class.

Methods are inherited from parent classes, but the child class can override the methods to provide more specific behavior, including calling back to the parent class methods if need be. The child class can also provide additional attributes or methods as needed.

And that's it for basic OOP in Perl. There's nothing complicated about it, and you can get most of the basics down in a couple of hours. Now, however, it's time to move along and explain a few more things about classes that you should know about.

Overloading Objects

When you have normal variables such as scalars, it's easy to print them, compare them, add or concatenate them, and so on. You can do this with objects, too, by overloading them. You use the overload pragma to do this. You're going to create a TV::Episode::OnDemand subclass to show how this works. You can skip (some) of the data validation to focus on the actual overloaded behavior. You also take advantage of assuming that your new attributes use DateTime objects. DateTime is also overloaded and you can see how several overloaded objects can work together to make life easier. We're not going to explain in-depth how overloading works (but see perldoc overload) because most objects don't actually use overloading, but you should be familiar with this technique when you come across it and want to use it later.

An ondemand is industry shorthand for *Video On Demand* (*VOD*) and refers to technology allowing you to watch the video when you want (in other words, "on demand"), such as when you watch something on Hulu, YouTube, or the BBC's iPlayer service. Rather than having a broadcast date, an ondemand has availability. In loose terms, this means "when you can watch it." Now you'll create a subclass of TV::Episode named TV::Episode::OnDemand and it will have start_date and end_date attributes along with an available_days method. The following code uses the code file lib/TV/Episode/OnDemand.pm and listing_12_1_episode.pl:

```perl
package TV::Episode::OnDemand;

use strict;
use warnings;
use Carp 'croak';

use overload '""' => 'as_string';

use base 'TV::Episode';

sub _initialize {
    my ( $self, $arg_for ) = @_;
    my %arg_for = %$arg_for;

    # assume these are DateTime objects
    $self->{start_date} = delete $arg_for{start_date};
    $self->{end_date}   = delete $arg_for{end_date};

    # note the > comparison of objects
    if ( $self->start_date >= $self->end_date ) {
        croak("Start date must be before end date");
    }
    $self->SUPER::_initialize( \%arg_for );
}

sub start_date { shift->{start_date} }
sub end_date   { shift->{end_date} }

sub as_string {
    my $self       = shift;
    my $episode    = $self->SUPER::as_string;
    my $start_date = $self->start_date;
    my $end_date   = $self->end_date;

    # overloaded stringification
    $episode .= sprintf "%-14s - $start_date\n" => 'Start date';
    $episode .= sprintf "%-14s - $end_date\n"   => 'End date';
    $episode .= sprintf "%-14s - %d\n"          => 'Available days',
      $self->available_days;
    return $episode;
}

sub available_days {
    my $self       = shift;
    # hey, we can even subtract DateTime objects
    my $duration = $self->end_date - $self->start_date;
    return $duration->delta_days;
}
1;
```

And the script to show how this works:

```perl
use strict;
use warnings;
use DateTime;
```

```perl
use lib 'lib';
use TV::Episode::OnDemand;

my $ondemand = TV::Episode::OnDemand->new(
    {
        series         => 'Firefly',
        director       => 'Allan Kroeker',
        title          => 'Ariel',
        genre          => 'awesome',
        season         => 1,
        episode_number => 9,
        start_date => DateTime->new(
            year  => 2002,
            month => 11,
            day   => 21,
        ),
        end_date => DateTime->new(
            year  => 2002,
            month => 12,
            day   => 12,
        ),
    }
);
print $ondemand;
```

Running the script should produce output similar to the following:

```
Series         - Firefly
Title          - Ariel
Director       - Allan Kroeker
Genre          - awesome
Season         - 1
Episode_number - 9
Start date     - 2002-11-21T00:00:00
End date       - 2002-12-12T00:00:00
Available days - 21
```

Note that this code prints $ondemand and not $ondemand->as_string. What allows you to do that is this line:

```perl
use overload '""' => 'as_string';
```

The '""' argument says "we want to overload this object's behavior when it is used as a string" and the "as_string" is the name of the method you will use to handle this behavior. Without this, the print $ondemand line would produce something useless like this:

```
TV::Episode::OnDemand=HASH(0x7f908282c9a0)
```

The DateTime objects have even more overloading. You can compare dates in your _initialize() method:

```perl
if ( $self->start_date >= $self->end_date ) {
    croak("Start date must be before end date");
}
```

If overloading was not provided, you would either have to do something like this (assuming that `DateTime` offered the appropriate method):

```
if ( $self->start_date->is_greater_than_or_equal_to($self->end_date) ) {
    ...
}
```

Or worse, try to figure out the date math yourself. (And that's harder than it sounds.)

> **NOTE** The `TV::Episode`, `TV::Episode::Broadcast` and `TV::Episode::OnDemand` classes all provide private `_initialize()` methods and public `as_string()` methods. When you call the `as_string()` method on an `$episode`, `$broadcast`, or `$ondemand`, Perl calls the correct `as_string()` method for you. This behavior is known as subtype polymorphism; though most people just call it polymorphism. It allows you to have a uniform interface for related objects of different types.

The `DateTime` objects also have stringification overloaded, allowing you to do this:

```
$episode .= sprintf "%-14s - $start_date\n" => 'Start date';
$episode .= sprintf "%-14s - $end_date\n"   => 'End date';
```

Otherwise, we would have to fall back to this:

```
$episode .= sprintf "%-14s - %4d-%2d-%2d\n" => 'Broadcast date',
    $date->year,
    $date->month,
    $date->day;
```

> **NOTE** The `DateTime` format wasn't pretty when you printed the `DateTime` objects directly. Read "Formatters And Stringification" in `perldoc DateTime` for fine-grained control of the print format.

You can also overload subtraction. When you subtract one `DateTime` object from another, it returns a `DateTime::Duration` object:

```
sub available_days {
    my $self     = shift;
    my $duration = $self->end_date - $self->start_date;
    return $duration->delta_days;
}
```

If you've realized how annoying it can be to figure out if one date is greater than another (think about time zones and daylight savings time, among other things), then you can imagine how painful calculating the actual distance between two dates can be. A well-designed module coupled with intelligently overloaded behavior makes this simple.

Using UNIVERSAL

All objects ultimately inherit from the UNIVERSAL class. The TV::Episode inherits directly from UNIVERSAL and TV::Episode::Broadcast and TV::Episode::OnDemand inherit from TV::Episode, meaning that they both inherit directly UNIVERSAL through TV::Episode. The object graph looks like Figure 12-1.

The UNIVERSAL class provides three extremely useful methods that all classes will inherit: isa(), can(), and VERSION(). As of 5.10.1 and better, there is also a DOES() method provided, but we won't cover that until we explain roles in Chapter 13.

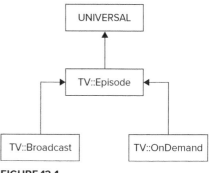

FIGURE 12-1

Understanding the isa() Method

The isa() method tells you whether your object or class inherits from another class. It looks like this:

```
$object_or_class->isa(CLASS);
```

Where $object_or_class is the object (or class) you want to test and CLASS is the class you're comparing against. It returns true if $object_or_class matches CLASS or inherits from it. The following will all return true:

```
$broadcast->isa('TV::Episode::Broadcast');
$broadcast->isa('TV::Episode');
TV::Episode::OnDemand->isa('TV::Episode');
$ondemand->isa('UNIVERSAL');
$episode->isa('UNIVERSAL');
```

In fact, every object will respond true if you test it against UNIVERSAL.

Naturally, all the following return false:

```
$broadcast->isa('TV::Episode::OnDemand');
$episode->isa('TV::Episode::OnDemand');
UNIVERSAL->isa('TV::Episode');
```

You may recall that the TV::Episode::Broadcast::_initialize() method had the following bit of code to check to see if you had a valid broadcast date:

```
try {
    $broadcast_date->isa('DateTime') or die;
}
```

```
catch {
croak("Not a DateTime object: $broadcast_date");
};
```

You could have written it like this:

```
if ( not $broadcast_date->isa('DateTime') ) {
    croak("broadcast_date must be a DateTime");
}
```

However, what if someone passed something strange for the broadcast_date parameter, or passed nothing at all? The $broadcast_date->isa() check would be called against something that might not be an object, and you could get a strange error message. Trapping the error with a try/catch block allows you to ensure the user gets exactly the error message you want them to get.

Please note that sometimes you'll see the following mistake:

```
if ( UNIVERSAL::isa($broadcast_date, 'DateTime') ) {
    # BAD IDEA!
}
```

The idea behind this is simple: Because the first argument to a method call is the invocant, calling a method like a subroutine and passing the invocant manually is the same thing. Plus, you don't have to do that annoying try/catch stuff or check to see if the invocant is actually an object.

It's a bad idea, though. Sometimes classes override isa(), and if you call UNIVERSAL::isa() instead of $object->isa(), you won't get the class's overridden version, thus leading to a possible source of bugs. Most of the time UNIVERSAL::isa() will work just fine, but the one time it doesn't can lead to hard-to-find bugs.

Understanding the can() Method

The can() method tells you whether a given object or class implements or inherits a given method. It looks like this:

```
$object_or_class->can($method_name);
```

Because TV::Episode::Broadcast and TV::Episode::OnDemand both inherit from TV::Episode, they will respond to true the following:

```
$episode->can('episode_number');
$broadcast->can('episode_number');
$broadcast->can('episode_number');
```

However, because TV::Episode does not implement the broadcast_date() method, $episode->can('broadcast_date') will return false.

> **NOTE**   In reality, the `can()` method returns a reference to the method that
> would be invoked. Some programmers use this to avoid having Perl look up the
> method twice:
>
> ```
> if ( my $method = $object->can($method_name) ) {
>     $object->$method;
> }
> ```
>
> Because a subroutine reference can evaluate to true, that's the same as:
>
> ```
> if ( $object->can($method_name) ) {
>     $object->$method_name;
> }
> ```
>
> And yes, objects can call a method that is in a variable name, as shown here.
> Use this with care to make sure you're not calling a method you don't want to
> call. Your author has seen many bugs and security holes in Perl code that allows
> someone to pass in the name of the method to be called.

Just like that, you'll sometimes see:

```
if ( UNIVERSAL::can( $object, $method_name ) ) {
    # BAD IDEA!
}
```

Again, this is a bad idea because if one of your objects provides its own `can()` method (and this is even more common than providing a new `isa()` method), then the above code is broken. Use the proper OO behavior: `$object->can($method)`.

Understanding the VERSION() Method

The UNIVERSAL class also provide a VERSION() method. (Why it's in ALL CAPS when the `is()` and `can()` are not is merely one of life's little mysteries.) This returns the version of the object. You'll notice that your code often has things like:

```
our $VERSION = '3.14';
```

That `$VERSION` is precisely what `$object->VERSION` returns, but in a clean interface. As you defined the version as being `'0.01'` for all of our `TV::` classes, calling `->VERSION` on any of them will return `'0.01'`.

Understanding Private Methods

This chapter already mentioned that private methods traditionally begin with an underscore. This bears a bit of explaining. In Perl, all methods are actually public. There is nothing to stop someone from calling your "private" methods. Most good programmers know better than to call these methods, but sometimes they get sloppy or they need behavior from the class that was not made "public."

This also means that subclasses inherit your "private" methods, effectively making them what some other languages would call a protected method. This is a method that is inherited but should not be called outside the class. Generally this is not a problem, but look at the following code:

```perl
package Customer;

sub new {
    my ( $class, $args ) = @_;
    return bless $args, $class;
}

sub outstanding_balance {
    my $self = shift;
    my @accounts = $self->_accounts;
    my $total = 0;
    $total += $_->total foreach @accounts;
    return $total;
}

sub _accounts {
    my $self = shift;
    # lots of code
    return @accounts;
}

# more code here
```

Now imagine a `Customer::Preferred` class that inherits from `Customer` but implements its own `_accounts()` method that returns an array reference of the customer accounts. If the `outstanding_balance()` method is not overridden, you'll have a run-time error when `outstanding_balance()` expects a list instead of an array reference.

In reality, this problem doesn't happen a lot. Part of the reason is simply because programmers who want to subclass your code often read it and make sure they're not breaking anything, or they write careful tests to verify that they haven't broken anything. However, as your systems get larger, you're more likely to accidentally override methods, and you should consider yourself lucky if it causes a fatal error. It's also possible to cause a subtle run-time error that generates bad data rather than killing your program. When you try to debug a problem in a system with a few hundred thousand lines of code, this type of error can be maddening.

If you are concerned about this, there are a couple of ways to deal with this. One is to simply document your "private" methods and whether they're appropriate to subclass. Another strategy is to declare private methods as subroutine references assigned to scalars:

```perl
package Customer;

sub new {
    my ( $class, $args ) = @_;
    return bless $args, $class;
}

my $_accounts = sub {
```

```
    my $self = shift;
    # lots of code
    return @accounts;
};

sub outstanding_balance {
    my $self = shift;
    my @accounts = $self->$_accounts;
    my $total = 0;
    $total += $_->total foreach @accounts;
    return $total;
}
```

Here, you assign a code reference to the $_accounts variable and later call it with $self->$_accounts. You can even pass arguments as normal:

```
    my @accounts = $self->$_accounts(@arguments);
```

Note that this technique creates truly private methods that cannot be accidentally overridden. (Actually, you can change them from outside the class, but it's an advanced technique that requires advanced knowledge of Perl.) Most Perl programmers do not actually use this technique and expect people who subclass their modules to test that they haven't broken anything.

NOTE *For what it's worth, your author did an informal poll of Perl developers and all of them denied that they have ever worked on code where someone has accidentally overridden a private method. This leaves me in the awkward position of recommending a solution to a problem that no one seems to have experienced.*

TRY IT OUT Creating Episode Versions

Earlier this chapter pointed out that you don't watch episodes; you usually watch a broadcast of an episode or an ondemand of an episode. That was actually a bit of a lie. You watch a broadcast of a version of an episode, or an ondemand of a version of an episode. It might be the original version, edited for adult content (such as naughty words bleeped out), edited for legal reasons (accidentally defaming someone, for example), or any number of reasons. So you're going to create a version subclass of episodes and alter your ondemands and broadcasts to inherit from that instead. All the code in this Try It Out is available in the code file lib/TV/Episode/Version.pm.

1. Type in the following program and save it as lib/TV/Episode/Version.pm:

```
package TV::Episode::Version;

use strict;
use warnings;
use base 'TV::Episode';

our $VERSION = '0.01';
```

```perl
sub new {
    my ( $class, $arg_for ) = @_;
    my $self = bless {} => $class;
    $self->_initialize($arg_for);
    return $self;
}

sub _initialize {
    my ( $self, $arg_for ) = @_;
    my %arg_for = %$arg_for;
    $self->{description} = exists $arg_for{description}
        ? delete $arg_for{description}
        : 'Original';
    $self->SUPER::_initialize( \%arg_for );
}

sub description { shift->{description} }

sub as_string {
    my $self       = shift;
    my $as_string = $self->SUPER::as_string;
    $as_string .= sprintf "%-14s - %s\n" => 'Version',
        $self->description;
    return $as_string;
}

1;
```

2. At this point, you have a decision to make. Many developers prefer to have the class struc-
    ture reflected in the name of the class, meaning the `TV::Episode::Broadcast` and
    `TV::Episode::OnDemand` would become `TV::Episode::Version::Broadcast`
    and `TV::Episode::Version::OnDemand`. Each part of the class name shows how you're getting
    more and more specific. But what if your code is used in other projects that you don't have control
    over? Instead, you'll decide to keep their class names, and for broadcasts and on demands, you'll
    merely change their inheritance line to:

    ```perl
    package TV::Episode::Broadcast;
    # snip
    use base 'TV::Episode::Version';
    ```

    This may not be the best name for the broadcast or ondemand classes, but it's the sort of
    compromises you make in real-world code.

    Another choice (which, for the sake of simplicity, you're not taking) is to create the new classes
    like this:

    ```perl
    package TV::Episode::Version::Broadcast;
    use base 'TV::Episode::Broadcast::_initialize;
    1;
    ```

    That allows people to use either name, but there's one more change to make:

```
package TV::Episode::Broadcast;

use Carp 'cluck';

sub new {
    my ( $class, $arg_for ) = @_;
    if ( $class eq __PACKAGE__ ) {
        cluck(<<"END");
Package TV::Episode::Broadcast is deprecated. Please use
TV::Episode::Version::Broadcast instead.
END
    }
    my $self = bless {} => $class;
    $self->_initialize($arg_for);
    return $self;
}
```

By adding such a deprecation warning (and documenting this in your POD!), you can give other programmers advance warning of the package name change. This allows their code to continue working and gives them time to make the needed updates to their code.

3. After you update TV::Episode::OnDemand to inherit from TV::Episode::Version, write the following and save it as example_12_2_episode.pl:

```
use strict;
use warnings;
use DateTime;

use lib 'lib';
use TV::Episode::OnDemand;

my $ondemand = TV::Episode::OnDemand->new(
    {
        series          => 'Firefly',
        director        => 'Allan Kroeker',
        title           => 'Ariel',
        genre           => 'awesome',
        season          => 1,
        episode_number => 9,
        start_date => DateTime->new(
            year  => 2002,
            month => 11,
            day   => 21,
        ),
        end_date => DateTime->new(
            year  => 2002,
            month => 12,
            day   => 12,
        ),
    }
);
print $ondemand;
```

4. Run the program with `perl example_12_2_episode.pl`. You should see the following output:

```
Series        - Firefly
Title         - Ariel
Director      - Allan Kroeker
Genre         - awesome
Season        - 1
Episode_number - 9
Version       - Original
Start date    - 2002-11-21T00:00:00
End date      - 2002-12-12T00:00:00
Available days - 21
```

How It Works

By this time you should have an idea of how subclassing works, and there is nothing new here, but now look at a couple of interesting bits, starting with the `_initialize()` method:

```
1:  sub _initialize {
2:      my ( $self, $arg_for ) = @_;
3:      my %arg_for = %$arg_for;
4:
5:      $self->{description} = exists  $arg_for{description}
6:          ? delete $arg_for{description}
7:          : 'Original';
8:      $self->SUPER::_initialize( \%arg_for );
9:  }
```

Instead of calling `croak()` when you don't have a `description`, note how lines 5 through 7, assign the value `Original` to it. This allows you to create a new version and, if this value is not present, assume that it's the original version. However, it has a more important benefit. If other developers are already using the `TV::Episode::Broadcast` and `TV::Episode::OnDemand` classes, they are not setting the description property. If you simply called `croak()` here, you'd break everyone's code and they'd probably be upset with you.

Also, note the `as_string()` method:

```
1:  sub as_string {
2:      my $self      = shift;
3:      my $as_string = $self->SUPER::as_string;
4:      $as_string .= sprintf "%-14s - %s\n" => 'Version',
5:          $self->description;
6:      return $as_string;
7:  }
```

You have again duplicated the `"%-14s - %s\n"` format, so it's probably a good time to abstract this out into a method in your `TV::Episode` base class. If you want to change how this behavior formats in the future, it will be easier to do so.

GOTCHAS

When writing object-oriented code, there are a number of problem areas you should be aware of. We'll only cover a few, but these are important issues that can make your code harder to use or more likely to break.

Unnecessary Methods

Often when people write objects, they correctly think of them as "experts." However, they then rationalize that the object must do everything conceivable that someone wants, rather than simply provide an intended behavior. Rule: Don't provide behavior unless you know that people need it. A good example is people making all object attributes read-write. For example, with TV::Episode, say that you want to make the episode number optional and people can set it later if they want to:

```
use Scalar::Util 'looks_like_number';
sub episode_number {
    my $self = shift;
    if (@_) {
        my $number = shift;
        unless ( looks_like_number($number) and $number > 0 ) {
  croak("episode_number is not a positive integer: $number");
        }
        $self->{episode_number} = $number;
    }
    return $self->{episode_number};
}
```

That looks harmless enough, right?

Later on you create a TV::Season object and it looks like this:

```
my $season = TV::Season->new({
    season_number => 3,
    episodes      => \@episodes,
});
```

If you assume that all TV::Episode objects in @episodes must have unique number, you can easily validate this when you construct the TV::Season object. However, if you later do this to one of the objects passed to TV::Season:

```
$episode->episode_number(3);
```

If another one of the episodes already has an episode_number of 3, you may have two episodes in a season with the same episode_number! That's because objects are merely blessed references. Change the data contained in a reference, and the place you store that reference will be pointing to the same data. Errors like this are much harder to avoid if you allow attributes to be set after you've constructed the object. Think carefully if this is a design requirement.

"Reaching Inside"

If you know something is an attribute, it can be tempting to do this:

```
my $name = $shopper->{name};
```

That seems OK because you know that name is in that hash slot, and hey, dereferencing the hash is faster than calling an object method!

And it's stupid, too. The reason that OO developers provide methods to let you get that data is because they must be free to change how the objects work internally, even if you don't see the change on the outside. You want to use $shopper->name because although it may be defined like this:

```
sub name { $_[0]->{name} }
```

The next release of the software might define it like this:

```
sub name {
    my $self = shift;
    return join ' ' => $self->first_name, $self->last_name;
}
```

Even inside the class you should avoid reaching inside of the object. You might say, "But I know that $self->{name}" is okay — until someone subclasses your module and the name() method is completely redefined. Or you are moaning over a nasty bug, not realizing that $self->{naem} is embedded somewhere in your code.

Finally, the object method that sets a value might validate that the value is valid. Reaching inside the object completely skips this validation.

Multiple Inheritance

Tighten up your seat belts. This is going to get a little rough, and it's worth reading through a couple of times to understand what's going on.

Multiple inheritance is inheriting from more than one class at the same time. For example, imagine you're writing a game and you want to create a talking box. Because your Creature class can speak and your Box class is a box, you decide that you want to inherit from both of them rather than rewrite the behaviors:

```
package Creature;
use base 'Physical::Object';
sub speak { ... }
package Box
use base 'Physical::Object';
sub put_inside { ... }
sub take_out { ... }
package Box::Talking;
use base qw(Creature Box);
```

And now your `Box::Talking` can respond to the `speak()`, `put_inside()`, and `take_out()` methods.

On the surface, this looks okay, but multiple inheritance is so problematic that many programming languages ban it outright. What are the constructors going to look like? Do you call both of your parent constructors? What if they do conflicting things?

Imagine what happens if the classes `Box` and `Physical::Object` both have a `weight()` method. When you want to find out its weight you might do this:

```
my $weight = $talking_box->weight;
```

However, Perl, by default, uses a left-most, depth-first inheritance search strategy. Now look at the inheritance hierarchy in Figure 12-2.

In this case, when you call `$talking_box->weight()`, it looks for the weight method in `Box::Talking` and, not finding it, searches `Creature`. And failing to find that, it looks for the `weight()` method in `Physical::Object` and calls that. The `Box::weight()` method will never get called. The `Physical::Object` might simply report its weight even though you wanted the `Box` class's `weight()` method because it responds with its weight plus all the objects inside of it.

You could fix that by reversing the order in which you inherit from those:

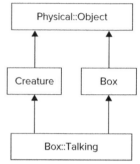

FIGURE 12-2

```
use base qw(Box Creature);
```

Then, when you call `$talking_box->weight()`, you'll get the `weight()` method from `Box`.

You can solve this problem without changing the inheritance order by using something called C3 linearization. (See the `C3` or `mro` modules on the CPAN.) They use a left-most, breadth-first method resolution strategy. Perl would search, in order, `Box::Talking`, `Creature`, `Box`, and then `Physical::Object` methods and would find `Box::weight()` before `Physical::Object::weight()`.

NOTE *If Perl cannot find the method, you usually get an error message similar to:*

```
Can't locate object method "do_stuff" via package "MyPackage"
```

However, sometimes there is an AUTOLOAD method available. If Perl does not find the method, it resumes its search through the inheritance hierarchy looking for a method named AUTOLOAD and calls the first AUTOLOAD method it finds. We generally do not recommend this because it is tricky to write properly, is slow, and can easily hide errors. See the Autoloading section in `perldoc perlsub` *for more information.*

Confused yet? It gets worse.

Now assume that `Box::Talking` has inherited from `Box` first and then Creature?

```
use base ('Box', 'Creature');
```

Now imagine that you have a `move()` method in both `Create` and `Box` and you want to call the `Creature` method instead of the `Box` method? Perl's default method resolution order would be to search `Box::Talking`, `Box`, `Physical::Object`, and then `Creature`. You would never call the `Creature::move()` method.

If you switch to the C3 method resolution order, Perl searches `Box::Talking`, `Box`, `Creature`, and `Physical::Object`. Because it can still find the `Box::move()` method first, you still get the wrong method.

> **NOTE** The order in which Perl searches for the method in classes is called the method resolution order, or MRO for short. There is an `mro` module on the CPAN that enables you to change the method resolution order.
>
> If you don't like Perl's default method order, your author recommends that you do not change it. Simply use the `Moose` OO system as explained in Chapter 13. It uses the left-most, breadth-first C3 MRO by default.
>
> Fortunately, if you never use multiple inheritance, the MRO issues do not apply to your code.

You can solve this in your `Box::Talking` class with the following ugly code:

```
sub move {
    my ( $self, $movement ) = @_;
    return $self->Creature::move($movement);
}
```

Calling fully qualified method names like this is legal, but it's not common, and it's a symptom of bad class design. If you decided to refactor your classes, these hard-coded class names in your code can lead to confusing errors.

If this section of the chapter confused you, don't worry. Many good programmers have been bitten by multiple inheritance, and every year there seems to be a new computer science paper describing why it's bad. Strong advice: Even though Perl lets you use multiple inheritance, don't use it unless you're very, very sure you have no other choice.

Chapter 13 explains how to avoid this problem by using `Moose`. (Have we hyped `Moose` enough yet for you?)

SUMMARY

Object-oriented programming is a way to create "experts" for particular problems your software may need to solve. A class is a package and describes all data and behavior the object needs to deal with. The object is a reference blessed into that class. Methods are subroutines and the class name or object is always the first argument.

Inheritance is where you create a more-specialized version of a class. It inherits from another class and gains all its behavior and data, along with adding its own behavior and possibly data. If you call a method on an object and the objects class does not provide that method, Perl searches the objects inheritance tree to find the correct method to call.

All objects ultimately inherit from the UNIVERSAL class. This class provides isa(), can(), and VERSION() methods to all classes.

So you've taken a long time to get to this incredibly short summary. Objects in Perl are straightforward, but you've taken the time to consider examples of real-world objects to give you a better idea of what they're often like in Comp code.

EXERCISES

1. Representing people in software systems is a common task. Create a simple Person class with a name attribute and a birthdate attribute. The latter should be a DateTime object. Provide a method named age() that returns the person's age in years.

Hint: You can use DateTime->now to get a DateTime object for today's date. Subtracting the person's birthdate from today's date returns a DateTime::Duration object.

2. The following code works, but it will likely break if you try to subclass it. Why?

```perl
package Item;
use strict;
use warnings;
sub new {
    my ( $class, $name, $price ) = @_;
    my $self = bless {};
    $self->_initialize( $name, $price );
    return $self;
}
sub _initialize {
    my ( $self, $name, $price ) = @_;
    $self->{name}  = $name;
    $self->{price} = $price;
}
sub name  { $_[0]->{name} }
sub price { $_[0]->{price} }
1;
```

3. Using the Person class described in exercise 1 of this chapter, create a Customer subclass. Per company policy, you will not accept customers under 18 years of age.

▶ **WHAT YOU LEARNED IN THIS CHAPTER**

TOPIC	KEY CONCEPTS
Class	An abstract "blueprint" for an object.
Method	A subroutine in a class that takes the class name or object as its first argument.
Object	An "expert" about a problem domain.
`bless`	A builtin that binds a reference to a class.
Inheritance	How Perl creates a more specific version of a class.
Subclass	A more specific type of a class. Also called a child class.
Superclass	The parent of a subclass.
`UNIVERSAL`	The ultimate parent of all classes.

13

Moose

WHAT YOU WILL LEARN IN THIS CHAPTER:

➤ Understanding Moose Syntax including attributes, constructors, and inheritance

➤ Using Type constraints, Method modifiers, roles, and popular Moose extensions

➤ Understanding Moose Best Practices

WROX.COM CODE DOWNLOAD FOR THIS CHAPTER

The wrox.com code downloads for this chapter are found at http://www.wrox.com/remtitle .cgi?isbn=1118013840 on the Download Code tab. The code for this chapter is divided into the following major examples:

➤ example_13_1_person.pl

➤ example_13_2_episode.pl

➤ lib/Person.pm

➤ lib/My/Company/Moose/Types.pm

➤ lib/TV/Episode.pm

➤ lib/TV/Episode/Broadcast.pm

➤ listing_13_1_age.pl

In the beginning there was Perl and on the fifth version Larry blessed references and said, "Let there be objects" and all was good.

Well, sort of. Chapter 12 showed how to create objects with Perl's builtin `bless` syntax, but there's a lot of tedium in validating that your data is correct and setting up your classes properly. If you're familiar with object-oriented programming (OOP) in other languages, you may have found Perl's implementation to be a bit crufty. You'd be right.

To work around Perl's rather simple object facilities, many programmers have taken a swing at making it easier to write objects. There is `Class::MakeMethods`, `Class::MethodMaker`, `Class::BuildMethods`, `Class::Accessor`, `Object::Tiny`, and so on. As of this writing, there are approximately 500 different packages in the `Class::` and `Object::` namespaces, many of which aren't actually object builders. How do you figure out which one you want? They offer bewildering sets of features, and you certainly don't have time to evaluate all of them.

Eventually, a rather brilliant programmer named Stevan Little wrote `Moose`, which is probably one of the most advanced object systems available. It draws heavily on theory from a wide variety of sources, but puts it all together in a way that suits Perl. Many companies are now adopting `Moose` as the standard way todo object-oriented programming in Perl and the benefits are huge, not the least of which is that it has a predictable syntax, meaning that it's often much easier to understand a `Moose` class than a regular Perl class.

Though you see quite a bit of `Moose` in this chapter, I'm only going to scratch the surface of its capabilities, so consider this chapter an introduction to the most common features, not an in-depth tutorial.

`Moose` is not shipped with Perl, so you need to install it from the CPAN.

UNDERSTANDING BASIC MOOSE SYNTAX

Writing a `Moose` class is mostly a matter of declaring attributes and methods. For example, say you want to create a drawing program. You might start with a simple x and y coordinate system:

```
package Point;

use Moose;

has 'x' => ( is => 'ro', isa => 'Num', required => 1 );
has 'y' => ( is => 'ro', isa => 'Num', required => 1 );

1;
```

And that's all you need! Here's an example of how to use it:

```
my $point = Point->new( { x => 3.2, y => -7 } );
printf "x: %f y: %f\n" => $point->x, $point->y;
```

And that prints out:

```
x: 3.200000 y: -7.000000
```

What's going on is that the `has` function is exported by `Moose` and it's used to declare attributes. When used correctly, you no longer need a constructor (a `new()` method), nor do you need to create a bunch of helper methods to fetch these values. I'll explain in-depth how to use them in the "Using Attributes" section of this chapter.

Now maybe you want a line. A line is defined by its two endpoints:

```
package Line;

use Moose;

has 'point1' => ( is => 'ro', isa => 'Point', required => 1 );
has 'point2' => ( is => 'ro', isa => 'Point', required => 1 );

sub length {
    my $self = shift;
    return sqrt(
        ($self->point1->x - $self->point2->x)**2
        +
        ($self->point1->y - $self->point2->y)**2
    );
}

1;
```

And to use it:

```
my $line = Line->new({
    point1 => Point->new({ x => 1, y => -1 }),
    point2 => Point->new({ x => 4, y => -5 }),
});
print $line->length;
```

And that prints 5 as the length of that line.

> **NOTE** *Chapter 12 shows constructors as always receiving a hash reference as the argument. This makes it easier to know that you have key/value pairs, and you see the error quickly when the object code tries to dereference something that is not a hash reference.*
>
> Moose *makes this optional. Although hash references to the constructors are in the examples, you don't need them with* Moose. *You may find your code cleaner without them.*
>
> ```
> my $line = Line->new(
>     point1 => Point->new( x => 1, y => -1 ),
>     point2 => Point->new( x => 4, y => -5 ),
> );
> print $line->length;
> ```
>
> *However, if you always stick to a hash references, you'll get a warning if you pass an odd number of elements by accident. (Remember, a hash is a set of key and value pairs.)*

Among other things, you can note that `strict` or `warnings` are not used. Why not? Because when you use `Moose`, it automatically uses `strict` and `warnings` for you.

You also don't have to declare a `new()` constructor. `Moose` provides that for you, enabling you to assign values to the declared attributes. Much easier, right? And if you tried to do this:

```
Point->new({ x => 'Foo', y => 3 });
```

You get a long stack trace starting with the message:

```
Attribute (x) does not pass the type constraint because:
   Validation failed for 'Num' with value Foo at ...
```

Needless to say, this is much easier than working with Perl's standard bare-bones OO. The CPAN page `Moose::Manual::Unsweetened` shows how much easier with a `Moose` versus Perl 5 OO example.

> **NOTE** *A stack trace is a list of every subroutine called, along with their arguments, from the point where the error occurred back to the calling code that generated the error. They're long and messy, but they're invaluable to help you understand how your code committed suicide.*

Using Attributes

An attribute is a piece of data, such as quantity or color, associated with an object. They're described in full in `perldoc Moose::Manual::Attributes`. The simplest attribute looks like this:

```
has 'name' => ( is => 'ro' );
```

The `is => 'ro'` means that the attribute is read-only. You can set it when you create the object, but you cannot change it later. If you want it to be read-write, declare it with `'rw'`.

```
has 'name' => ( is => 'rw' );
```

> **NOTE** *Actually, you don't even need the is => '...' for the attribute, but that creates an attribute with no accessor. There are reasons you might want to do that, but they aren't covered here.*

Usually you want to specify what types the attribute can accept. For example, a name attribute should probably be a string:

```
has 'name' => ( is => 'ro', isa => 'Str' );
```

The isa => 'Str' says "this attribute *isa* string." You can see the full list of built-in types with
perldoc Moose::Util::TypeConstraints:

```
Any
Item
    Bool
    Maybe[`a]
    Undef
    Defined
        Value
            Str
                Num
                    Int
                ClassName
                RoleName
        Ref
            ScalarRef[`a]
            ArrayRef[`a]
            HashRef[`a]
            CodeRef
            RegexpRef
            GlobRef
            FileHandle
        Object
```

Most of those types should be self-explanatory, except for a few items we haven't gone in-depth
about:

➤   Any means "anything." An Item is the same as Any. You could think of it as the difference
   between "something" and "anything." In other words, it will not be of much practical
   difference in your work.

➤   A Str is a string, a Num is any number, an Int is an integer, and so on. A Bool may be
   undef, the empty string, 0 or 1.

➤   A Value is "anything which is defined and not a reference." This can include something
   called a glob (instead of a GlobRef, as listed in the Ref types).

➤   The [`a] is a type parameter. For any types, you can follow them with the type parameter,
   replacing the `a with a given type, for example:

```
has 'temperatures' => (
    is       => 'rw',
    isa      => 'ArrayRef[Num]',
    required => 1,
);
```

And that enables you to create a temperatures attribute that, if present, must be an array reference
containing only numbers. You could use that to create an average_temperature() method. We
used required => 1 to ensure that the temperatures attribute must be supplied.

```
use List::Util 'sum';

sub average_temperature {
    my $self = shift;
    my $temperatures = $self->temperatures;
    my $num_temperatures = @$temperatures
      or return; # an empty temperatures arrayref
    return sum(@$temperatures) / $num_temperatures;
}
```

You can force the $temperatures array reference to have at least one value:

```
use Moose;
use Moose::Util::TypeConstraints; # for subtype, as, where

has 'temperatures' => (
    is       => 'rw',
    isa      => subtype( as 'ArrayRef[Num]', where { @$_ > 0 } ),
    required => 1,
);
```

Then, if you try to pass an empty array reference, Moose throws an exception. That's a bit obscure right now but is covered with type constraints in the "Using Type Constraints" section of this chapter. (And inline subtypes like that are generally not recommended in case other modules will want to use that subtype.)

A Maybe[`a] value enables you to have either undef or a specific value in an attribute. So Maybe[Int] enables either undef or Int.

If you don't like your setter and getter to be a single method, then separate them:

```
has 'name' => (
    is     => 'rw',
    isa    => 'Str',
    writer => 'set_name',
    reader => 'get_name',
);
```

Or you can use the MooseX::FollowPBP, and all attributes will be named get_* and set_* for you. (But you won't get set_* unless you use is => 'rw'.)

```
use Moose;
use MooseX::FollowPBP; # get_name and set_name will now be created
has 'name' => (
    is  => 'rw',
    isa => 'Str',
);
```

You can also use isa to declare that the attribute is a specific type of object:

```
has 'birthdate' => (
    is  => 'ro',
    isa => 'DateTime',
);
```

And now if you pass something that is not a `DateTime` object to `birthdate`, `Moose` throws an exception.

You can also assign defaults to attributes. With the following, if you don't supply a `minimum_age` to the constructor, it defaults to `18`:

```
has 'minimum_age' => (
    is      => 'ro',
    isa     => 'Int',
    default => 18,
);
```

If your default is a reference, you must wrap it in `sub {}` to ensure a new reference is returned every time:

```
has 'minimum_age' => (
    is      => 'ro',
    isa     => 'DateTime::Duration',
    default => sub { DateTime::Duration->new( years => 18 ) },
);
```

`Moose` will throw an exception if your default is a reference without the `sub {}` around it. The `sub{}` ensures that every instance of the class will get a different reference.

> **NOTE** The name `MooseX::FollowPBP` refers to Perl Best Practices, by Damian Conway. It's a few years old, and some module recommendations are out of date, particularly the reference to using `Class::Std` to create your classes, but it's still an excellent book.

There's a lot more power in attributes, so read `Moose::Manual::Attributes` to see what other nifty things you can do.

Using Constructors

As explained, `Moose` provides a `new()` constructor for you. If you need to alter its behavior, do not override `new()`. Instead, use `BUILDARGS` to modify arguments before `new()` is called, with `BUILD` being used after the constructor is called when you need further validation of the state of the object. Consider `BUILDARGS` first, which has an unusual syntax.

BUILDARGS

You saw from the `Point` example that you can create a point like this:

```
my $point = Point->new( x => 3, y => 2 );
```

But you might want to write `Point->new( 3, 2 )`. That's what BUILDARGS is for.

```
package Point;

use Moose;

has 'x' => ( is => 'ro', isa => 'Num', required => 1 );
has 'y' => ( is => 'ro', isa => 'Num', required => 1 );

around 'BUILDARGS' => sub {
    my $orig  = shift;
    my $class = shift;
    if ( @_ == 2 ) {
        my ( $x, $y ) = @_; # Point->new( x, y );
        return $class->$orig( x => $x, y => $y );
    }
    else {
        # Point->new(@list_or_hashref);
        return $class->$orig(@_);
    }
};   # Needs a trailing semicolon

1;
```

That lets you write:

```
my $point = Point->new( 3, 2 );

# or, the same thing
my $point = Point->new( x => 3, y => 2 );
```

The `Point->new( 3, 2 )` version works because the first branch of the `if`/`else` block sees that you have two arguments and rewrites the arguments for you.

When you include the use `Moose` line, your class inherits from `Moose::Object`. There is a BUILDARGS method that checks to see if you've passed a hashref or a list and ensures that the object is called correctly.

The `around()` function takes the name of a method and a subroutine reference. A reference to the original method is passed as the first argument (`$orig`) and the invocant (a class name in this case, but it can also be an instance of an object) is the second argument. Any further arguments are passed as normal in `@_`. You can then test your arguments and call `$class->$orig (@new_arguments)` to build your object.

The `around()` function is called a *method modifier*, which is covered in the "Method Modifiers" section of this chapter.

BUILD

The BUILD method is called after `new()` and can be used to validate your object. Its return value is ignored, and, unlike BUILDARGS, it has a normal method syntax. You should throw an exception if you encounter any errors. For your `Line` example, assume that your two points cannot be the same.

```
    package Line;

    use Moose;
    use Carp 'croak';

    has 'point1' => ( is => 'ro', isa => 'Point', required => 1 );
    has 'point2' => ( is => 'ro', isa => 'Point', required => 1 );

    sub BUILD {
        my $self = shift;
        if (    $self->point1->x == $self->point2->x
             && $self->point1->y == $self->point2->y )
        {
            croak("Line points must not be the same");
        }
    }

    sub length {
        my $self = shift;
        return sqrt(
            ($self->point1->x - $self->point2->x)**2
            +
            ($self->point1->y - $self->point2->y)**2
        );
    }

    1;
```

You can see that this BUILD method lets you have tighter validation of your object than attributes alone can provide. If you pass in the same point twice, or two separate points with the same coordinates, Line->new will croak() with an appropriate error message.

> **NOTE** If you're curious about how BUILD works, internally your code inherits from Moose::Object. It has a BUILDALL method that gets called and checks if you have any BUILD methods defined. If you do, BUILDALL calls these methods for you. If you have inherited from other classes, the BUILD methods for every class are called. However, parent class BUILD methods are called before child class BUILD methods. This guarantees that by the time your class are built, everything in the parent classes is already set up correctly for you.

You could have used BUILDARGS, too, to pass a list of two points. This would have looked similar to the Point::BUILDARGS method.

```
    around 'BUILDARGS' => sub {
        my $orig  = shift;
        my $class = shift;
        if ( @_ == 2 ) {
```

```
        my ( $point1, $point2 ) = @_;
        return $class->$orig(
            point1 => $point1,
            point2 => $point2,
        );
    }
    else {
        return $class->$orig(@_);
    }
};   # Don't forget that trailing semicolon!
```

And now you can write:

```
my $line = Line->new(
    Point->new( 1, -1 ),
    Point->new( 4, -5 ),
);
```

Instead of the more verbose:

```
my $line = Line->new(
    point1 => Point->new( x => 1, y => -1 ),
    point2 => Point->new( x => 4, y => -5 ),
);
```

Understanding Inheritance

Inheritance in `Moose` is easy. With Perl's basic OO behavior, `TV::Episode::Broadcast` would inherit from `TV::Episode` via one of these techniques:

```
use base 'TV::Episode';
# or
use parent 'TV::Episode';
# or
use TV::Episode;
our @ISA = 'TV::Episode';
```

In `Moose`, every `Moose` object inherits from `Moose::Object`. So you can't use those techniques directly or else you lose your inheritance from `Moose::Object`. Instead, you use the `extends` function:

```
package TV::Episode::Broadcast;

use Moose;

extends 'TV::Episode';
```

That does assume your parent class is a `Moose` class. If you're using `Moose`, that's usually the case, but sometimes you need to inherit from a class not built with `Moose`. See `MooseX::NonMoose` for that. If `TV::Episode::Broadcast` is written with `Moose` and `TV::Episode` is not a `Moose` class,

```
package TV::Episode::Broadcast;

use Moose;
use MooseX::NonMoose;

extends 'TV::Episode';
```

That will take care of lots of fiddly bits for you and everything should work fine.

Taking Care of Your Moose

When you use `Moose`, it exports a lot of helper functions into your class, such as:

➤   `after`

➤   `around`

➤   `augment`

➤   `before`

➤   `extends`

➤   `has`

➤   `inner`

➤   `override`

➤   `super`

➤   `with`

You've seen a couple of them, such as `has` and `around`. Later, when someone is using your class, if they write:

```
$moose_object->can('around');
```

That returns a true value because subroutines and methods are treated the same way by Perl. You probably don't want this behavior, and there's no need to leave all those helper functions lying around. To deal with this, use `namespace::autoclean` (available on the CPAN):

```
package TV::Episode::Broadcast;

use Moose;
use namespace::autoclean;

# more code here

1;
```

That automatically removes all those helper functions for you.

Also, just before that trailing 1, you want to make your class immutable. A standard skeleton of a good `Moose` class looks like this:

```
package My::Class::Name;
use Moose;
use namespace::autoclean;

# your code here

__PACKAGE__->meta->make_immutable;

1;
```

The `__PACKAGE__->meta->make_immutable` doesn't change the behavior, but it does a few internal things that make your code run a bit faster. The trade-off is that you can't use metaprogramming (that's what the `__PACKAGE__->meta` is often used for) to change your class later unless you first call the `__PACKAGE__->meta->make_mutable` method. We don't cover this here but if you know what that is, you know when to not make your class immutable.

> **NOTE** *What is meta programming? If you like the* `Moose` *object system but you want to change or extend some of its core behavior, then you're beginning to get an idea of what metaprogramming is. See the full* `Moose` *docs on the CPAN. Every time you use* `has`, `extends`, *and a variety of other functions, you're altering a class definition and, under the hood, it's done with metaprogramming.*
>
> *If you actually want to know, you can start with* `perldoc Moose::Manual::MOP` *(MOP stands for Meta Object Protocol) and then start reading* `Moose::Cookbook::Meta::Recipe1` *through* `Moose::Cookbook::Meta::Recipe7`. *It's advanced stuff, so don't worry if it doesn't make much sense to you.*

When using `Moose`, the Method Resolution Order (`mro`) pragma is in effect. Not only does this use breadth-first C3 method resolution order that was described in Chapter 12, it also substitutes the `SUPER::some_method` call with `next::method`, and `$object->can($some_method)` becomes `$object->next::can($somet_method)`. If you do not use multiple inheritance — and its use is discouraged — you will likely see no difference in behavior aside from the syntax.

For example, you may recall the `as_string()` method from `TV::Episode::Broadcast`:

```
sub as_string {
    my $self    = shift;
    my $episode = $self->SUPER::as_string;
    my $date    = $self->broadcast_date;
    $episode .= sprintf "%-14s - %4d-%2d-%2d\n" => 'Broadcast date',
      $date->year,
      $date->month,
      $date->day;
    return $episode;
}
```

That overrides the `TV::Episode::as_string()` method. When you convert it to `Moose`, you might want to make the following change:

```
# my $episode = $self->SUPER::as_string;
my $episode = $self->next::method;
```

Note that there is no need to embed the method name in the call to the parent method. This can avoid annoying bugs if you try to rename a method. For our example code, there is no functional difference, but there are times, not covered here, when it will make a difference and it's something you'll often see in Moose code.

As a lovely bit of syntactic sugar, you can also override `Moose` methods with the `override` function:

```
package TV::Episode::Broadcast;

use Moose;
extends 'TV::Episode';

# lots of code

override 'as_string' => sub {
    my $self    = shift;
    my $episode = super();
    my $date    = $self->broadcast_date;
    $episode .= sprintf "%-14s - %4d-%2d-%2d\n" => 'Broadcast date',
        $date->year,
        $date->month,
        $date->day;
    return $episode;
}
```

This has two strong advantages. First, it's excellent documentation to a maintenance programmer that this method overrides a parent method. Second, the call to `super()` passes the same arguments to the parent method (if any) that were passed to the child's `as_string()` method, ensuring that you do not accidentally change the interface. Any arguments to `super()` are ignored and you cannot change `@_`.

TRY IT OUT   Write a Person Class

In the first exercise of Chapter 12, you created a `Person` class. It had two attributes, a `name` and a `birthdate`, plus an `age()` method for returning the `Person`'s age in years. Writing this in `Moose` is much simpler. Note that all the code for this Try It Out is found in code file `lib/Person.pm`.

1. Type in the following program and save it as `lib/Person.pm`.

```
package Person;
use Moose;
use namespace::autoclean;
use DateTime;
has 'name' => (
    is       => 'ro',
    isa      => 'Str',
    required => 1,
);
```

```
    has 'birthdate' => (
        is          => 'ro',
        isa         => 'DateTime',
        required => 1,
    );
    sub age {
        my $self = shift;
        my $duration = DateTime->now - $self->birthdate;
        return $duration->years;
    }
    __PACKAGE__->meta->make_immutable;
    1;
```

2. Write the following code and save it as `example_13_1_person.pl`:

```
    use lib 'lib';
    use strict;
    use warnings;
    use DateTime;
    use Person;
    my $person = Person->new({
        name        => 'Bertrand Russell',
        birthdate => DateTime->new(
            year  => 1872,
            month => 5,
            day   => 18,
        ),
    });
    print $person->name, ' is ', $person->age, ' years old';
```

3. Run the program with `perl example_13_1_person.pl`. You should see the following output:

```
    Bertrand Russell is 139 years old
```

How It Works

There's actually not much to say here. `Moose` is so simple to use that the preceding code should be self-explanatory. However, if you did the exercises for Chapter 12, you probably wound up with something like this:

```
package Person;

use strict;
use warnings;

use DateTime;
use Carp 'croak';

sub new {
    my ( $class, $args ) = @_;
    my $self = bless {} => $class;
    $self->_initialize($args);
    return $self;
}
```

```perl
sub _initialize {
    my ( $self, $args ) = @_;
    my %args       = %$args;
    my $name       = delete $args{name};
    my $birthdate = delete $args{birthdate};

    # must have at least one non-whitespace character
    unless ( $name && $name =~ /\S/ ) {
        croak "Person name must be supplied";
    }

    # trap the error if it's not an object
    unless ( eval { $birthdate->isa('DateTime') } ) {
        croak "Person birthdate must be a DateTime object";
    }
    $self->{name}      = $name;
    $self->{birthdate} = $birthdate;
}

sub name      { $_[0]->{name} }
sub birthdate { $_[0]->{birthdate} }

sub age {
    my $self = shift;
    my $duration = DateTime->now - $self->birthdate;
    return $duration->years;
}

1;
```

That's much longer and harder to read. Further, the more attributes you have, the shorter the Moose code tends to be in comparison to the standard OO code. That's why you often see many programmers creating their objects like this:

```perl
sub new {
    my ( $class, $arg_for ) = @_;
    return bless {
        name      => $arg_for->{name},
        birthdate => $arg_for->{birthdate},
    }, $class;
}
```

That works if, and only if, the person using your class never messes up and passes in the wrong data. With Moose, you have a simple, declarative interface, and it's much easier to use.

ADVANCED MOOSE SYNTAX

In a few short pages, you've seen Moose and how easy it is to create objects with it. We've also mentioned several times that there are "advanced" features of Moose. What we've already covered deals primarily with using Moose to easily replicate what you can do with standard Perl classes.

The advanced features will show you how easy it is to have full control over your class behavior with very little code.

Using Type Constraints

When you declare an attribute, you can also declare what type it is:

```
package Hand;

use Moose;

has 'fingers' => (
    is       => 'ro',
    isa      => 'Int',
    required => 1,
);
```

Now presumably, your Hand can't have less than zero fingers. You could write a BUILD method and validate that your object has zero or more fingers, but you really don't want to do that for every class where you need to assert a non-negative integer. So you can use Moose::Util::TypeConstraints to create a custom type:

```
package Hand;

use Moose;
use Moose::Util::TypeConstraints;

use namespace::autoclean;

subtype 'NonNegativeInteger'
    => as       'Int'
    => where    { $_ >= 0 }
    => message { "A Hand must have 0 or more fingers, not $_" };

has 'fingers' => (
    is       => 'ro',
    isa      => 'NonNegativeInteger',
    required => 1,
);

__PACKAGE__->meta->make_immutable;
1;
```

With that subtype, when you try to create an object with fewer than 0 fingers:

```
Hand->new( fingers => -3 );
```

You get a useful error message (with a stack trace that I've omitted):

```
Attribute (fingers) does not pass the type constraint because:
  A Hand must have 0 or more fingers, not -3 at ...
```

To create your own subtypes, you use the `Moose::Util::TypeConstraints` module to add a few new helper functions to your code.

A subtype is a more specific version of an existing type. In this case, it's a more specific version of an `Int` (integer). That's what the `as => 'Int'` is for.

```
subtype 'NonNegativeInteger'
    => as       'Int'
    => where    { $_ >= 0 }
    => message { "You must provide an integrer> 0, not $_" };
```

The `where { ... }` is a code block that is executed with $_set to the supplied value of the attribute. If it returns false, the type check fails and the optional `message { ... }` is displayed. If you don't supply the message, the error can be rather confusing:

```
Attribute (fingers) does not pass the type constraint because:
  Validation failed for '__ANON__' with the value -3 ...
```

However, what you actually want to do is create your own type library so that you can share these types across your various classes. It's recommended that you do two things:

➤ Put all your subtypes in one package that you `use`.

➤ Name yoursubtypes so that they won't conflict with other subtypes.

Say that you work for a company named My Company. Customers must be 18 years old or older, so you must create a subtype to handle that. Here's one way to create the type package (code file `lib/My/Company/Moose/Types.pm`):

```
package My::Company::Moose::Types;

use Moose::Util::TypeConstraints;
use DateTime;

subtype 'MyCompany:NonNegativeInteger'
    => as       'Int'
    => where    { $_ >= 0 }
    => message { "You must provide a non-negative integer, not $_" };

subtype 'MyCompany:18orOlder'
    => as        'DateTime'
    => where    { ( DateTime->now - $_ )->years >= 18 }
    => message {
        my $age = ( DateTime->now - $_ )->years;
        "DateTime supplied must be 18 years old or older, not $age years"
    };

1;
```

> **NOTE** The names of the sample subtypes are `My:CompanyNonNegativeInteger` and `MyCompany:18orOlder`. Neither of those is a valid package name, but that's okay. Just make sure that your names don't conflict with anything else.

Now you create a little test program for it (code file `listing_11_1_age.pl`):

```perl
{
    # remember that the package declaration is lexically scoped,
    # so the brackets around this package keep it separate from
    # the rest of your code
    package Person;

    use Moose;
    use DateTime;
    use My::Company::Moose::Types;

    has 'name' => (
        is       => 'ro',
        isa      => 'Str',
        required => 1,
    );

    has 'age' => (
        is       => 'ro',
        isa      => 'MyCompany:18orOlder',
        required => 1,
    );
}

my $youngster = Person->new(
    name => 'Youngster',
    age  => DateTime->new(
        year  => 2000,
        month => 1,
        day   => 1,
    ),
);
```

When you run that, it generates an error similar to the following (at the time the author wrote this):

```
Attribute (age) does not pass the type constraint because:
    DateTime supplied must be 18 years old or older, not 12 years at ...
```

> **NOTE** *You may have been curious about this construct:*
>
> ```
>     my $age = ( DateTime->now - $_ )->years;
> ```
>
> *Chapter 12 showed how subtracting one* DateTime *object from another returns a* DateTime::Duration *object. The Exercises for Chapter 12 showed how to use the* years() *method with* DateTime::Duration *to determine the number of years the duration represents. When you wrap parentheses around expressions, the code inside of the parentheses is executed, and the return value is substituted for the parentheses, making the code more or less equivalent to the following:*
>
> ```
>     my $duration = DateTime->now - $_;
>     my $age      = $duration->years;
> ```
>
> *This type of code is moderately common with experienced Perl hackers, and you will see it in Comp code, so it seemed appropriate to twist your brain a little more at this time.*

Using Method Modifiers

One interesting feature of Moose is the concept of method modifiers. These are subroutines that you can attach to existing Moose subroutines to add to or alter behavior. You have already seen the around and override modifiers. There are also before, after, augment, and inner modifiers.

The before and after Modifiers

As you might expect, the before modifier runs before the method is called. Sometimes you want additional checks on methods that may not make sense for a type constraint, or a subclass may have different checks from another subclass. A before modifier can make life simpler. The modifier is passed the same arguments as the original method, for example:

```
before 'buy_item' => sub {
    my ( $self, $item ) = @_;
    if (    $item->is_age_restricted
         && $self->age < $self->locale->minimum_age_to_purchase($item) )
    {
        my $name      = $self->name;
        my $item_name = $item->name;
        croak "$name is not old enough to buy $item";
    }
}; # don't forget that trailing semicolon!
```

Note that unlike the example with around and override, you do not need to explicitly call the actual method. The before modifier is called automatically before the modified method is called. Also, any changes made to @_ are ignored, as is any return value from the modifier.

The `after` modifier behaves similarly to the `before` modifier and runs immediately after the execution of the method:

```
after 'buy_item' => sub {
    my ( $self, $item ) = @_;
    if ( $item->is_age_restricted ) {
        $self->log_purchase($item);
    }
};
```

As with the `before` modifier, changes to `@_` are ignored, as is the return value.

The augment/inner Pair

The `augment` and `inner` modifiers work together and are the two modifiers that Perl programmers get the most confused about. Effectively, they let you call the parent method instead of the child method. The parent is responsible for calling the child methods for you. Or to put it another way: It sort of inverts the inheritance tree. Got that?

No, you may not have gotten that, so let's go with an example.

When you have a name attribute, it can be kind of hard to stop someone from setting a name to `dsn334548h21234;&` and, in fact, there's a good chance you don't want to do that. Some people have names that are just numbers, or unpronounceable symbols, or perhaps written in a character set you don't recognize. More important, getting a name wrong is common and tends not to be disastrous.

Calculating the payroll wrong would be disastrous, however, so you might want a bit more protection for the `salary()` method. When you create an `Employee` class and you've designed it to be subclassed, there might be a variety of subclasses that implement the `salary()` method in different ways. Now look at how someone writing payroll code might calculate the payroll:

```
my @employees = $company->get_employees;
my $month     = $company->get_fiscal_month;
my $payroll   = 0;

foreach my $employee (@employees) {
    $payroll += $employee->salary($month);
}
```

The `@employees` array might contain a wide variety of different payroll subclasses, including `Employee::Standard`, `Employee::Manager`, `Employee::Consultant`, and so on. Each of those might have salary methods that behave differently, such as `Employee::Consultant` returning a `Salary::External` object, `Employee::Standard` expecting to receive "hours worked" instead of a fiscal month, and a completely different subclass with a bug returning a negative salary if the month is February.

In short, you don't want the `salary()` method to be wrong. This is how you might implement `salary()` in your Moosified (your author should trademark that term) `Employee` base class, using the `inner()` function.

```
package Employee;

use Moose;

# lots of code omitted

sub salary {
    my ( $self, $fiscal_month ) = @_;
    unless ( $fiscal_month->isa('Fiscal::Month') ) {
        croak "Argument to salary() must be a Fiscal::Month object";
    }
    my $salary = inner(); # this calls the child version of salary()
    if ( ref $salary or $salary < 0 ) {
        croak "Salary must be a non-negative number: $salary";
    }
    return $salary;
}
```

The `inner()` function calls your subclass implementation of `salary()` and that must be declared with `augment()`:

```
package Employee::Manager.

use Moose;
extends 'Employee';

# lots of code omitted

augment 'salary' => sub {
    my $self = shift;
    # lots of code
    return $salary;
};
```

Assuming all subclasses properly declared `salary()` with `augment`, when you call `$employee->salary`, regardless of what subclass you use, you get the superclass `Employee::salary()` method, and it calls `inner()` to call the `augmented` salary method in the child class, passing it the same arguments that you passed to `salary()`. You can have program pre- and post-conditions into your `salary()` method to verify that you are not accepting or returning incorrect values.

> **NOTE** *Those of you with a computer science background may recognize* `augment/inner` *as implementing a technique known as* Design by Contract. *See* `http://en.wikipedia.org/wiki/Design_by_contract` *for more details.*

If you want to use this technique with non-`Moose` classes, you can have this in your `Employee` class:

```
sub salary {
    my ( $self, $fiscal_month ) = @_;
    unless ( $fiscal_month->isa('Fiscal::Month') ) {
        croak "Argument to salary() must be a Fiscal::Month object";
```

```
    }
    my $salary = $self->_salary($fiscal_month); # inner()
    if ( ref $salary or $salary < 0 ) {
        croak "Salary must be a non-negative number: $salary";
    }
    return $salary;
}
```

And in your documentation, explain that all subclasses must implement `salary()` as `_salary()` (note the leading underscore).

Understanding and Using Roles

A role provides additional methods for a class, along with listing methods it requires to implement those methods. Effectively, it's a named set of methods that you can't use independently but a class can include to provide extra behavior. In fact, multiple unrelated classes can use the same role or roles to provide identical behavior. There are several implementations in Perl, but the most common is `Moose::Role`. It's a fairly advanced technique, but it's powerful enough that you should take some time to understand it.

Generally speaking, the set of methods a role provides should be something that the class might provide but is not inherent to the class's expert knowledge. For example, with a `Person` class, she may have a `name`, a `birthdate`, and be able to "talk." But should a person intrinsically know how to serialize herself with an `as_json()` method? Probably not, but you'll notice that the `TV::Episode` classes and subclasses all had the capability to serialize themselves as strings with an `as_string()` method. In fact, many completely unrelated classes might have an `as_json()` method, so it's a perfect candidate to put into a role.

> **NOTE** *Though not covered extensively in this book, JSON, short for JavaScript Object Notation, is a popular method of serializing data, converting it to a format that can be shared or stored. It is formally described at* `http://www.json.org/`, *but the Wikipedia article gives better examples:* `http://en.wikipedia.org/wiki/Json.`

For the examples that require the JSON module, you need to install it from the CPAN.

Basic Roles

A class that uses one or more roles is said to *consume* those roles. As for the roles, they are defined by the methods they require the class to provide and the methods the role provides to the class. Here's how your role providing the `as_json()` method might look:

```
package Role::Serializable::JSON;

use Moose::Role;
use JSON 'encode_json';
```

```
# you can list multiple methods here

requires qw(
  serializable_attributes
);

sub as_json {
    my $self = shift;
    my %object = map { $_ => $self->$_ } $self->serializable_attributes;
    return encode_json( \%object );
}

1;
```

This role requires the consuming class to have a method named `serializable_attributes()`. If the class does not have this method, your class throws an error similar to:

```
'Role::Serializable::JSON' requires the method
'serializable_attributes'to be implemented by
'Some::Class::Name'
```

This error will be thrown at compile time. No more 2:30 A.M. frantic phone calls from work about `Method Not Found` errors!

> **NOTE** A role might have only a `requires` section and provide no methods. When it does, it's what other languages define as an *interface*: It guarantees that any class consuming the role has a well-defined set of methods the class provides.

The `Role::Serializable::JSON` method provides the `as_json()` method to the class. However, the `encode_json()` function, imported into the role namespace, will not be provided.

A class consuming this role may look like this:

```
package Soldier;

use Moose;
use namespace::autoclean;
with "Role::Serializable::JSON";

has 'name' => ( is => 'ro', isa => 'Str', required => 1 );
has 'rank' => ( is => 'ro', isa => 'Str', required => 1 );

sub serializable_attributes {
    return qw( name rank );
}

__PACKAGE__->meta->make_immutable;

1;
```

And here's a sample program:

```
my $soldier = Soldier->new(
    {
        name => "Schultz",
        rank => "Sergeant",
    }
);
print $soldier->as_json;
```

And that prints out the attribute key/value pairs as JSON:

```
{"name":"Schultz","rank":"Sergeant"}
```

You can reuse this role with many other classes, regardless of whether they inherit from one another.

> **NOTE** We've had a few examples of classes that have a hard-coded list of methods. You might find that annoying and so does your author. This is an example of where metaprogramming can make your life easier. Instead of requiring the serializable_attributes() method, you could write something like this:
>
> ```
> sub as_json {
>     my $self       = shift;
>     my @attributes = map { $_->name }
>         $self->meta->get_all_attributes;
>     my %object     = map { $_ => $self->$_ } @attributes;
>     return encode_json( \%object );
> }
> ```
>
> The $self->meta call returns an instance of the metaclass for the object and the get_all_attributes() method returns a set of attribute objects. Of course, you might wonder if some of those should not be serialized into a JSON data structure (such as a password attribute). Metaprogramming enables you to extend your class behavior to say which data can and cannot be exposed like this.
>
> Also, not all attributes will have accessor methods with the same attribute name, so this code will often work, but it's not entirely generic.

If you use a class and want to know if the class has a particular role, you cannot use the `$object->isa($some_class)` method. That's because roles are not inherited. Instead, you use the `does()` method:

```
print $soldier->does('Role::Serializable::JSON') ? 'Yes' : 'No';
```

That snippet prints Yes. Also, note that role methods are added directly into your class definition during role composition (when you use the with() function). This is known as *flattening* the methods into your class.

Advanced Roles

Roles allow you to share behavior among unrelated classes, but if that's all they did, they wouldn't be terribly exciting. After all, other languages have various strategies for accomplishing this, such as mixins in Ruby.

Roles, however, attempt to guarantee compositional safety. This is easier to explain with an example. Say that you are writing a game and you want to create a PracticalJoke class. When someone walks into a room, a fuse() method is called on the PracticalJoke instance, and it will explode() after the fuse() is done. Being a good programmer, you know that your Bomb and Spouse classes each have fuse() and explode() methods. Table 13-1 explains their properties.

TABLE 13-1: Available methods in our parent classes

METHOD	DESCRIPTION
Bomb::fuse()	Burns for a fixed amount of time
Spouse::fuse()	Burns for a random amount time
Bomb::explode()	Lethal
Spouse::explode()	Wish it were lethal

For your practical joke, you want the Bomb::fuse() method because you want to control the time it takes to explode, but you want the Spouse::explode() method because you don't want to actually kill the player. With inheritance, this is tricky and you need to set up delegates for one or the other.

```
package PracticalJoke;

use strict;
use warnings;

use base qw(Bomb Spouse);

sub new {
    ...
}

sub explode {
    my $self = shift;
    $self->Spouse::explode();
}
```

Having to write a delegate to `$self->Spouse::explode()` is because you inherit from `Bomb` first, and if you just relied on inheritance, you would call the `Bomb::explode()` method and kill your hapless player. But hard-coding class names like this is doing work that object-oriented programming is supposed to do for you! And if you later decide to inherit from a different class that provides an `explode()` method, you have to find all the places where you've hard-coded the `Spouse::explode()` method and rewrite them. This is begging for bugs, and it's more work than you should have to do.

Instead, assume that you want to share the `Bomb` and `Spouse` behavior with many different classes and put them into roles:

```
{
    package Bomb;
    use Moose::Role;
    sub fuse    { print "Bomb fuse\n" }
    sub explode { print "Bomb explode\n" }
}
{
    package Spouse;
    use Moose::Role;
    sub fuse    { print "Spouse fuse\n" }
    sub explode { print "Spouse explode\n" }
}
{
    package PracticalJoke;
    use Moose;
    with qw(Bomb Spouse);
}
my $joke = PracticalJoke->new();
$joke->explode();
$joke->fuse();
```

If you try to run this code, you get the following error at compiletime:

```
Due to method name conflicts in roles 'Bomb' and 'Spouse',
the methods 'explode' and 'fuse' must be implemented or
excluded by 'PracticalJoke' at ...
```

> **NOTE** *We've mentioned a couple of times that certain errors with roles will happen at compile time. This is a lie. They actually happen at composition time. This is a Moose-specific term, and it happens after compile time but before your program runs.*

This error happens because Moose sees that `Bomb` and `Spouse` each provide `explore()` and `fuse()` methods, but Moose has no way to know which you want. You can either implement the methods yourself in your class, thus causing the corresponding role methods to be ignored, or you can exclude the methods you don't want, keeping only the methods you do:

```
package PracticalJoke;
use Moose;
with 'Bomb'   => { excludes => 'explode' },
     'Spouse' => { excludes => 'fuse' };
```

If you make that change and rerun the code, it prints out:

```
Spouse explode
Bomb fuse
```

And that's exactly what you were looking for.

Note that the order in which you consume the roles is not relevant (though if you have method modifiers on role methods, this may not be true). Further, because most developers list the roles the class consumes at the top, a well-named set of roles can allow maintenance programmers a quick-and-easy way to glance at a class and understand which behaviors it implements without necessarily digging deep into an inheritance hierarchy. When you understand them, roles can make your OO codebase easier to manage and extend.

> **NOTE** *On a somewhat controversial note, your author has built large OO systems using only roles and no inheritance. By viewing roles as a collection of building blocks to assemble into classes, he's found it easy to add new behavior safely to large systems. Others with whom he has spoken have reported similar results. However, the idea of completely eliminating inheritance in favor of roles is controversial, so just pretend you didn't read this note.*

To better understand roles, we recommend:

➤ `perldoc Moose::Role`

➤ Various role recipes in the `Moose::Cookbook`

➤ `http://www.slideshare.net/Ovid/inheritance-versus-roles-1799996`

Exploring MooseX

When learning `Moose`, you'll sometimes find that you want to do things a bit differently. We've alluded to metaprogramming, but you'll be happy to know that for many of the most common tasks, there are modules on the CPAN that handle them for you. By convention, modules that are "unofficial" extensions to other modules have an X in the name, so the unofficial `Moose` extension modules are in the `MooseX::` namespace. The ones that the core `Moose` team likes are described in `Moose::Manual::MooseX`. We'll cover a few of the `MooseX::` modules here. These modules are not included with `Moose` and must be installed separately.

MooseX::StrictConstructor

Chapter 12 often had the following bit of code at the end of the _initialize() methods to ensure that no unknown arguments were passed to the constructor.

```
if ( my $remaining = join ', ', keys %arg_for ) {
    croak("Unknown keys to $class\::new: $remaining");
}
```

By default, Moose checks only known arguments to the constructor. However, if you have an optional birthdate attribute and you misspell it as birtdhate, Moose assumes you didn't supply the birthdate and ignores the birtdhate argument. With MooseX::StrictConstructor, this becomes a fatal error.

```
package Person;
use Moose;
use MooseX::StrictConstructor;
has 'name'      => ( is => 'ro', isa => 'Str',      required => 1 );
has 'birthdate' => ( is => 'ro', isa => 'DateTime', required => 0 );
```

And later when you do this:

```
Person->new(name=>'foo', birtdhate => 1);
```

You get the following error:

```
Found unknown attribute(s) passed to the constructor: birtdhate
```

If you want a strong OO system, this module is highly recommended.

MooseX::Method::Signatures

The MooseX::Method::Signatures module is lovely. It gives you proper method signatures for your methods. Your author knows of one team who is using this on high-volume BBC code, so it may be an excellent choice if you long for the method signatures found in other languages.

> **NOTE** *A method signature is a common feature of many programming languages. Consider the following function:*
>
> ```
> sub reciprocal {
>     my $number = shift;
>     return 1/$number;
> }
> ```
>
> *For many languages, that would be written like this pseudo-code:*
>
> ```
> float reciprocal(int $number) {
>     return 1/$number;
> }
> ```

> *Method signatures make it easier to see what kind of data your functions accepts and returns. Plus, they can handle some of the data validation for you. For languages with proper method signatures, they'll throw an exception (or fail to compile) if you try to pass a string to a function expecting an integer.*
>
> *The* `MooseX::Method::Signatures` *module does not specify the return type.*

From the documentation (note that this package declares no attributes):

```
package Foo;
use Moose;
use MooseX::Method::Signatures;
method morning (Str $name) {
    $self->say("Good morning ${name}!");
}
method hello (Str :$who, Int :$age where { $_ > 0 }) {
    $self->say("Hello ${who}, I am ${age} years old!");
}
method greet (Str $name, Bool :$excited = 0) {
    if ($excited) {
        $self->say("GREETINGS ${name}!");
    }
    else {
        $self->say("Hi ${name}!");
    }
}
$foo->morning('Resi');                      # This works.
$foo->hello(who => 'world', age => 42);     # This too.
$foo->greet('Resi', excited => 1);          # Yup.
$foo->hello(who => 'world', age => 'fortytwo'); # Nope.
$foo->hello(who => 'world', age => -23);    # Too bad.
$foo->morning;                              # Won't work.
$foo->greet;    # Fail!
```

You don't need to declare the variables with `my` and you don't need to declare `$self`. In your author's opinion, this is one of the most exciting things to happen in Perl for years. Lacking proper subroutine and method signatures is one of the biggest complaints registered about Perl.

MooseX::SemiAffordanceAccessor

The `MooseX::SemiAffordanceAccessor` module automatically names your read-write attributes as `$attribute` and `get_$attribute`. Try running this code:

```
{
    package Soldier;
    use Moose;
    use MooseX::SemiAffordanceAccessor;
    has name => ( is => 'ro', isa => 'Str', required => 1 );
    has rank => ( is => 'rw', isa => 'Str', required => 1 );
}
```

```
my $soldier = Soldier->new(
    name => "Billy",
    rank => "Private",
);
$soldier->set_rank("Corporal");
$soldier->set_name("Barbara");
```

That will fail with:

```
Can't locate object method "set_name" via package "Soldier" at ...
```

As you can see, while a soldier's rank is read-write, the name cannot be changed. We assume the military is happy with this.

There are many more MooseX modules, of course, but these give you a great idea of some of the potential out there.

Rewriting Television::Episode

Now use Moose to rewrite our TV::Episode class from Chapter 12. It looked like this:

```
package TV::Episode;

use strict;
use warnings;

use Carp 'croak';
use Scalar::Util 'looks_like_number';

our $VERSION = '0.01';

my %IS_ALLOWED_GENRE = map { $_ => 1 } qw(
  comedy
  drama
  documentary
  awesome
);

sub new {
    my ( $class, $arg_for ) = @_;
    my $self = bless {} => $class;
    $self->_initialize($arg_for);
    return $self;
}

sub _initialize {
    my ( $self, %arg_for ) = @_;
    my %arg_for = %$arg_for;
    foreach my $property (qw/series director title/) {
        my $value = delete $arg_for{$property};

        # at least one non-space character
        unless ( defined $value && $value =~ /\S/ ) {
```

```
                croak("property '$property' must have at a value");
            }
            $self->{$property} = $value;
        }
        my $genre = delete $arg_for{genre};
        unless ( exists $IS_ALLOWED_GENRE{$genre} ) {
            croak("Genre 'genre' is not an allowed genre");
        }
        $self->{genre} = $genre;
        foreach my $property (qw/season episode_number/) {
            my $value = delete $arg_for{$property};
            unless ( looks_like_number($value) && $value > 0 ) {
                croak("$value must have a positive value");
            }
            $self->{$property} = $value;
        }
        if ( my $extra = join ', ' => keys %arg_for ) {
            croak("Unknown keys to new(): $extra");
        }
    }
}
sub series         { shift->{series} }
sub title          { shift->{title} }
sub director       { shift->{director} }
sub genre          { shift->{genre} }
sub season         { shift->{season} }
sub episode_number { shift->{episode_number} }

sub as_string {
    my $self      = shift;
    my @properties = qw(
      series
      title
      director
      genre
      season
      episode_number
    );
    my $as_string = '';
    foreach my $property (@properties) {
        $as_string .= sprintf "%-14s - %s\n", ucfirst($property),
          $self->$property;
    }
    return $as_string;
}

1;
```

There are many strategies you could reuse to rewrite that. For this example, embed
`Moose::Util::TypeConstraints` directly into your module and use an anonymous `enum` type for
the genre to create an `IntPositive` type for the `episode_number` and `season`, as shown in the
following code (code file `TV/Episode.pm`):

```
package TV::Episode;

use Moose;
use MooseX::StrictConstructor;
use Moose::Util::TypeConstraints;

use namespace::autoclean;

use Carp 'croak';
our $VERSION = '0.01';

subtype 'IntPositive',
        as     'Int',
        where { $_ > 0 };

has 'series'   => ( is => 'ro', isa => 'Str', required => 1 );
has 'director' => ( is => 'ro', isa => 'Str', required => 1 );
has 'title'    => ( is => 'ro', isa => 'Str', required => 1 );
has 'genre'    => ( is => 'ro', isa => 'Genre', required => 1 );
has 'season'   => ( is => 'ro', isa => 'IntPositive', required => 1 );
has 'episode_number' => (is => 'ro', isa => 'IntPositive', required => 1);

sub as_string {
    my $self = shift;
    my @attributes =
      map { $_->name }
      $self->meta->get_all_attributes;
    my $as_string = '';
    foreach my $attribute (@attributes) {
        $as_string .= sprintf "%-14s - %s\n",
          ucfirst($attribute),
          $self->$attribute;
    }
    return $as_string;
}

__PACKAGE__->meta->make_immutable;

1;
```

As you can see, this version is much shorter than the original version. In fact, if you pushed the as_string method into a role, you could reduce the class to this:

```
package TV::Episode;

use Moose;
use MooseX::StrictConstructor;
use My::CustomTypes;       # for Genre and IntPositive

with 'Does::ToString';     # for the as_string method

use namespace::autoclean;

our $VERSION = '0.01';
```

```
has 'series'    => ( is => 'ro', isa => 'Str', required => 1 );
has 'director'  => ( is => 'ro', isa => 'Str', required => 1 );
has 'title'     => ( is => 'ro', isa => 'Str', required => 1 );
has 'genre'     => ( is => 'ro', isa => 'Genre', required => 1 );
has 'season'    => ( is => 'ro', isa => 'IntPositive', required => 1 );
has 'episode_number' => (is => 'ro', isa => 'IntPositive', required => 1);

__PACKAGE__->meta->make_immutable;

1;
```

As you can see, by carefully planning out your code, you can make new classes simple and easy to build and maintain. This is why Moose has become the OO system of choice for many Perl programmers.

Considering that the original version was almost twice as long as our revised version, and almost four times longer than our "ideal" version, which would you rather write?

TRY IT OUT   **Rewrite Television::Episode::Broadcast with Moose**

You might recall the old version of TV::Episode::Broadcast. All the code in this Try It Out is in the code file TV/Episode/Broadcast.pm.

```
package TV::Episode::Broadcast;
use strict;
use warnings;
use Try::Tiny;
use Carp 'croak';
use base 'TV::Episode';
sub _initialize {
    my ( $self, $arg_for ) = @_;
    my %arg_for = %$arg_for;
    my $broadcast_date = delete $arg_for{broadcast_date};
    try {
        $broadcast_date->isa('DateTime') or die;
    }
    catch {
        croak("broadcast_date requires a DateTime object");
    };
    $self->{broadcast_date} = $broadcast_date;
    $self->SUPER::_initialize( \%arg_for );
}
sub broadcast_date { shift->{broadcast_date} }
sub as_string {
    my $self    = shift;
    my $episode = $self->SUPER::as_string;
    my $date    = $self->broadcast_date;
    $episode .= sprintf "%-14s - %4d-%2d-%2d\n"
      => 'Broadcast date',
          $date->year,
          $date->month,
          $date->day;
    return $episode;
}
1;
```

With Moose, that is tremendously simplified. We'll go ahead and extend our Moosified version to TV::Episode.

1. Type in the following class and save it as lib/TV/Episode/Broadcast.pm.

```
package TV::Episode::Broadcast;
use Moose;
use namespace::autoclean;
extends 'TV::Episode';
has 'broadcast_date' => (
  is       => 'ro',
  isa      => 'DateTime',
  required => 1,
);
__PACKAGE__->meta->make_immutable;
1;
```

2. Type in the following program and save it as example_13_2_episode.pl.

```
use strict;
use warnings;
use DateTime;

use lib 'lib';
use TV::Episode;
use TV::Episode::Broadcast;

my $episode = TV::Episode->new(
    {
        series         => 'Firefly',
        director       => 'Marita Grabiak',
        title          => 'Jaynestown',
        genre          => 'awesome',
        season         => 1,
        episode_number => 7,
    }
);
print $episode->as_string;
print "----\n";

my $broadcast = TV::Episode::Broadcast->new(
    {
        series         => 'Firefly',
        director       => 'Allan Kroeker',
        title          => 'Ariel',
        genre          => 'awesome',
        season         => 1,
        episode_number => 9,
        broadcast_date => DateTime->new(
            year  => 2002,
            month => 11,
            day   => 15,
        ),
    }
);
print $broadcast->as_string;
```

3. Run the program with `perlexample_13_2_episode.pl`. You should see output similar to the following:

```
Director        - MaritaGrabiak
Episode_number  - 7
Genre           - awesome
Season          - 1
Series          - Firefly
Title           - Jaynestown
----
Broadcast_date  - 2002-11-15T00:00:00
Director        - Allan Kroeker
Episode_number  - 9
Genre           - awesome
Season          - 1
Series          - Firefly
Title           - Ariel
```

How It Works

This one is awesome. We've gone from a third-one-line version of `TV::Episode::Broadcast` to a seven-line version.

In this case, the magic was adding the `broadcast_date` attribute and taking advantage of the following line in our `TV::Episode::as_string()` method:

```
my @attributes = sort map { $_->name }
$self->meta->get_all_attributes;
```

When you subclass and call an inherited method, the metaclass returned by `$self->meta` is for the subclass, not the parent class. Because the subclass inherits the superclass's behavior, all of its attributes are reported in the `get_all_attributes()` method class. This power is part of what allows you to do things with Moose much more easily than with Perl's built-in OO.

And for those developers who object that they now lack control over how the items in `as_string()` are ordered: they're quite right. However, there are several strategies to get around this, such as providing an `_ordered_attributes()` method and overriding it in a subclass, or delving into more metaprogramming to allow you to attach additional information to attributes to better control their sort order. We'll leave that as an exercise for you.

MOOSE BEST PRACTICES

If you read `perldocMoose::Manual::BestPractices`, you can get a handful of best practices for using `Moose`. Following them can make your code cleaner and easier to maintain. We'll highlight a few of them here and toss in some of our own, but remember, there's an exception for every rule. The key thing to remember here is that you should understand why these are best practices. If you don't, you will likely make bad decisions when you decide to break them.

Note that this is not an exhaustive list.

Use namespace::autoclean and Make Your Class Immutable

A shell of all Moose classes should look like this:

```
package Person;
use Moose;
use namespace::autoclean;
# extends, roles, attributes, etc.
# methods
__PACKAGE__->meta->make_immutable;
1;
```

By using namespace::autoclean, you guarantee that imported functions are not accidentally treated as methods. By making your class immutable, you gain a significant performance improvement in your code.

Never Override new()

BUILDARGS enables you to alter the argument list before calling new(), and BUILD allows you to do validation on your object that may be difficult in the constructor.

Always Call Your Parent BUILDARGS Method

If you inherit from a class providing a BUILDARGS method, use super() to call that parent method. You've seen this from the override() function described earlier.

Provide Defaults if an Attribute is Not Required

This is often bad:

```
has 'budget' => ( is => 'ro', isa => 'Num' );
```

If you are not going to require an attribute to be provided, your code may blow up when you try to use the attribute value. A better strategy is to provide a default and document it:

```
has 'budget' => ( is => 'ro', isa => 'Num', default => 100 );
```

Remember that if the default is a reference, you must wrap it in an anonymous subroutine:

```
has 'birthday' => (
    is      => 'ro',
    isa     => 'DateTime',
    default => sub { DateTime->now } );
```

Default to Read-Only

Generally you want your attributes to be read-only. This makes it much harder for someone to change the state of the object to something invalid later on. Sometimes, though, your class needs to change the attribute value internally, so make a private "writer":

```
has 'budget' => (
    is      => 'ro',
    isa     => 'Num',
    writer  => '_set_budget',
);
```

Put Your Custom Types in One Module and Give Them a Namespace

```
subtype 'My::Company::NonNegativeInteger'
    => as       'Int'
    => where    { $_ >= 0 }
    => message { "A Hand must have 0 or more fingers, not $_" };
```

By doing this, it's easy to find the types and manage them. Also, by adding a custom `My::Company::` prefix to the subtype name, you are less likely to conflict with another subtype of the same name.

Don't Use Multiple Inheritance

Use roles instead.

If you feel that you must use multiple inheritance to solve a problem, pull out the code you want to share, and put it in a role. The extra class (or classes!) you want to inherit from should now use that role, and the new class you are writing can use that role, too. This should make your code much easier to maintain and avoids bugs in inheritance order and accidentally overriding methods you did not mean to override.

Always Consume All Your Roles at Once

It's perfectly legal to do this:

```
package Foo;
use Moose;
with 'RoleA';
with 'RoleB';
```

But what happens if both `RoleA` and `RoleB` provide a `discharge()` method? Well, `RoleA` will provide the `discharge()` method and `RoleB`'s `discharge()` method will be silently ignored. This is because when you consume a role, `Moose` assumes that your class's methods take precedence over role methods. Thus, when `RoleA`'s `discharge()` method is added to your class, by the time you consume `RoleB`, Moose sees that your `Foo` class already has a `discharge()` method and ignores the one from `RoleB`.

Instead, be explicit about what you want:

```
package Foo;
use Moose;
with 'RoleA' => { excludes => "discharge" },
     'RoleB';
```

Even if you actually did want to exclude the RoleB discharge method:

```
package Foo;
use Moose;
with 'RoleA',
     'RoleB' => { excludes => "discharge" };
```

In this case, it might be functionally equivalent to consuming those roles separately; it's cleaner and self-documenting. To understand this, consider our PracticalJoke class from earlier:

```
package PracticalJoke;
use Moose;
with 'Bomb'   => { excludes => 'explode' },
     'Spouse' => { excludes => 'fuse' };
```

If you had written:

```
package PracticalJoke;
use Moose;
with 'Bomb';
with 'Spouse';
```

You may not have spotted the method conflicts and thus had your code fail in ways you did not expect.

Consume all your roles at once, and be explicit about what you are doing.

SUMMARY

In this chapter, you've learned about Moose, the OO programming module that is becoming the de facto standard for OO programming in Perl. Moose allows you to easily declare attributes, their types, whether they are required or read-only, what their default values are, and much more. The type constraints in Perl are easily extended, and you can share behavior between unrelated classes with roles. Classes are easier to write, easier to read, and easier to maintain.

Your author has been known to write non-Moose classes from time to time, but that's the exception rather than the rule. If you want to do OO programming in Perl, you should understand Perl's default OO facilities, but write your classes in Moose if you have the choice.

EXERCISES

1. Passwords are generally supplied in plain text. However, it's a very, very bad idea to ever store them like this. Many developers use an MD5 "digest" to rewrite the password. An MD5 digest takes a string and converts it into a series of characters that are unique to that string. However, the process is one-way. Without using software such as rainbow tables (http://en.wikipedia.org/wiki/Rainbow_table), you cannot get the original string back.

Write a User class that requires a username and password, but has a BUILD method that immediately changes the password to an MD5 digest. The Digest::MD5 module was first released with Perl 5.7.3 and its use looks like this:

```
use Digest::MD5 'md5_hex';
my $digest = md5_hex($string);
```

Make sure to include a password_eq() method to verify that a new password matches the old password.

Note: This example should not be considered cryptographically secure. There are some issues with it, but hey, this isn't a book on software security!

2. Create a role named Does::ToHash that returns a hash reference representation of an object. It should be used only for attributes that do not return a reference. Have your User class from exercise 1 consume this role and print out the resulting object.

Note that Moose automatically provides a dump() method ($user->dump) to do this for you. This exercise is to help you learn how to create roles.

▶ **WHAT YOU LEARNED IN THIS CHAPTER**

TOPIC	KEY CONCEPTS
Moose	A powerful object system available from the CPAN.
Attributes	Basic pieces of data used by your classes.
BUILDARGS	A method to override how arguments are supplied to `new()`.
BUILD	A method to validate your classes after construction.
extends	The keyword to use to inherit from another `Moose` class.
subtype	The keyword to declare new type constraints in `Moose`.
before/after	Method modifiers called before and after methods.
around	A special modifier used to wrap a `Moose` method.
augment/inner	Special modifiers that allow a parent class full control over a method's behavior.
Roles	A new, improved way to share behavior among classes.
MooseX::	The default namespace for modules that extend `Moose`'s capabilities.

14

Testing

WHAT YOU WILL LEARN IN THIS CHAPTER:

➤ Understanding basic tests

➤ Learning the `Test::More` module in depth

➤ Using different testing modules

➤ Understanding xUnit style testing

WROX.COM CODE DOWNLOAD FOR THIS CHAPTER

The wrox.com code downloads for this chapter are found at `http://www.wrox.com/remtitle .cgi?isbn=1118013840` on the Download Code tab. The code for this chapter is divided into the following major examples:

➤ `lib/TestMe.pm`

➤ `t/testit.t.pm`

➤ `lib/TestQuery.pm`

➤ `t/query.t`

➤ `lib/Person.pm`

➤ `t/test_classes.t`

➤ `t/test_classes.t`

➤ `t/lib/TestsFor/Person.pm`

➤ `lib/Customer.pm`

➤ `t/lib/TestsFor/Customer.pm`

➤ `lib/TV/Episode.pm`

The author recently downloaded and built Perl version 5.15.9. All 521,047 tests passed. That's right: Perl ships with more than a half-million tests. Not all of them are perfect, and sometimes they verify that a feature works the way it was written and not the way that was intended, but it's still an incredible number. Few programming languages ship with more than a half-million tests. Testing your software is easy, and the Perl community is keen on testing. A few years ago, some people still argued against testing, but today professional Perl developers test more often than not.

BASIC TESTS

Consider the following line of code:

```
sub reciprocal { return 1 / shift }
```

Because the reciprocal of a number is 1 divided by that number, this looks like the canonical definition of a reciprocal. What could possibly go wrong?

When developers write tests, they often write a test to verify that the code does what it is supposed to do when the input is correct, but they don't think about incorrect input. So what happens if you pass reciprocal() a string? Or a hash reference? Or a zero? There are a variety of subtleties here that you may or may not care about, so let's delve into them.

Using Test::More

The standard testing module for Perl is Test::More, first released in Perl version 5.6.2. Test::More exports many helpful functions into your namespace, enables you to set the test plan (the number of tests), and makes writing tests simple. A basic test script might look like this:

```
use strict;
use warnings;
use Test::More tests => 3;
ok 7, '7 should evaluate to  a true value';
is 5 - 2, 3, '... and 5 - 2 should equal three';
ok 0, 'This test is designed to fail';
```

The tests => 3 arguments to Test::More is called the plan. In this case, it states that you will run three tests. If you run fewer tests or more tests than the number of tests planned, even if all of them pass, the test script reports a failure.

The ok() and is() functions are each considered a single test. Thus, you have three tests in the preceding test script (two ok() and one is()), which are explained in a bit.

If you run this snippet of code, you should see the following output:

```
1..3
ok 1 - 7 should evaluate to  a true value
ok 2 - ... and 5 - 2 should equal three
not ok 3 - This test is designed to fail
#   Failed test 'This test is designed to fail'
#   at some_test_script.t line 7.
# Looks like you failed 1 test of 3.
```

> **NOTE** *The test output format is the* Test Anything Protocol, *also known as TAP. It's designed to be both readable by both humans and machines. If you're curious about this protocol, see* `http://www.testanything.org/`.

The `1..3` bit in the output is from the plan you asserted in the code. It means "we'll be running three tests."

Each line of test output is in this form:

```
ok $test_number - $test_message
```

Or:

```
not ok $test_number - $test_message;
```

Any line beginning with a # is called a diagnostic and should be a human readable message to help you figure out what your tests are doing. It is ignored for purposes of considering whether tests passed or failed.

> **WARNING** *The message for each test is optional. You could have written this:*
>
> ```
> ok 7;
> is 5 - 2, 3;
> ok 0;
> ```
>
> *However, if you do that, your test output looks like this:*
>
> ```
> 1..3
> ok 1
> ok 2
> not ok 3
> #   Failed test  at some_test_script.t line 7.
> # Looks like you failed 1 test of 3.
> ```
>
> *Needless to say, this makes it much harder to read the test output and understand what is going on. Always provide a clear test message for each test.*

As you write tests, it can be annoying to constantly update the test plan every time you add or delete tests, so you can state `no_plan` as the plan. (Note that we're adding parentheses to these test functions just to remind you that you can use them if you prefer them.)

```
use strict;
use warnings;
use Test::More 'no_plan';
```

```
ok( 7, '7 should evaluate to  a true value' );
is( 5 - 2, 3, '... and 5 - 2 should equal three' );
ok( 0, 'This test is designed to fail' );
```

When you run this, you see the following:

```
ok 1 - 7 should evaluate to  a true value
ok 2 - ... and 5 - 2 should equal three
not ok 3 - This test is designed to fail
#   Failed test 'This test is designed to fail'
#   at /var/tmp/eval_3qMq.pl line 7.
1..3
# Looks like you failed 1 test of 3.
```

The plan, `1..3`, now appears at the end of the test output. If you like numeric plans, then you should switch `no_plan` to `tests => $number_of_tests` when you finish writing your test code.

As a recommended alternative, if you use `Test::More` version 0.88 or better, you can do this:

```
use Test::More;
# write a bunch of tests here
done_testing;
```

With `done_testing()` at the end of your test script, if the program exits prior to calling `done_testing()`, you get an error, even if all tests pass. This lets you know whether your tests have completed successfully. If you run the following script with a new enough version of `Test::More`:

```
use strict;
use warnings;
use Test::More;
ok( 7, '7 should evaluate to  a true value' );
is( 5 - 2, 3, '... and 5 - 2 should equal three' );
exit;   # oops!
ok( 0, 'This test is designed to fail' );
done_testing;
```

You should get the following output:

```
ok 1 - 7 should evaluate to  a true value
ok 2 - ... and 5 - 2 should equal three
# Tests were run but no plan was declared and done_testing() was not seen.
```

You are recommended to install the latest version of `Test::More` from the CPAN. It's part of the `Test::Simple` distribution.

Writing Your Tests

As you work your way through this chapter, you start with a simple package named `TestMe`. You test it with a test script named `testit.t`. By convention, test scripts in Perl end with a `.t` extension.

The TestMe package will, of course, be in lib/TestMe.pm. Test scripts, however, usually live in the t/ directory. Your directory structure should look like this:

```
lib/
|--TestMe.pm
t/
|--testit.t
```

Start by creating lib/TestMe.pm like this (code file lib/Test.pm):

```
package TestMe;

use strict;
use warnings;

use Exporter::NoWork;

sub reciprocal { return 1 / shift }

1;
```

The Exporter::NoWork module is similar to Exporter, but it automatically allows exporting of functions in your package that do not start with an underscore. (You need to install it from the CPAN.) You don't always want all functions exportable, but for these testing examples, it's perfect for your needs.

And code file t/testit.t should look like this:

```
use strict;
use warnings;
use Test::More;

use lib 'lib';
# Exporter::NoWork used the :ALL tag to import all functions
use TestMe ':ALL';

ok 1, 'this is a test!';

done_testing;
```

You add to both the TestMe package and the testit.t script as you work through the chapter.

Understanding the prove Utility

The Test::More distribution is used to test your modules. (Actually, it's a convenient wrapper around the Test::Builder module.) Test::More generates TAP output. However, something called the Test::Harness can run the test programs, read the TAP output, and determine if the tests pass or fail. Many large software systems can have tens of thousands of tests spread over hundreds of files. You don't want to run all those by hand, but you can use tools shipped with Test::Harness to do this.

> **NOTE** *Your author, in addition to writing the book, is also the author of the* Test::Harness *module that ships with the Perl language. (It's maintained by his good friend Andy Armstrong.) There might be truth in the rumor that your author is a testing bigot.*

One of the most useful utilities included with Test::Harness is the prove utility. From now on, you use this to run your test scripts:

```
$ prove -l -v t/testit.t
t/testit.t ..
ok 1 - this is a test!
1..1
ok
All tests successful.
Files=1, Tests=1,  0 wallclock secs
Result: PASS
```

The -l switch to prove says "our code is in the lib/ directory" (this is redundant in this case because you have use lib 'lib' in your test script) and the -v tells prove to use verbose output. Note that the bottom line says Result: PASS. If you have many tests, you can just glance at that output at the bottom of the test to see if it passed or failed.

Without the -v switch, you would see this:

```
t/testit.t .. ok
All tests successful.
Files=1, Tests=1,  0 wallclock secs
Result: PASS
```

For a single test script, you probably want to run it verbosely, but for multiple test scripts, leaving the -v switch off of the prove command can make the output easier to read:

```
$ prove -l t
t/01get_tag.t ...... ok
t/01get_token.t .... ok
t/02munge_html.t ... ok
t/03constructor.t .. ok
t/04internals.t .... ok
t/pod-coverage.t ... ok
t/pod.t ........... ok
All tests successful.
Files=7, Tests=188,  0 wallclock secs
Result: PASS
```

UNDERSTANDING TEST::MORE TEST FUNCTIONS

Now that you covered some of the basics of how testing works, it's time to write some tests. There are many testing modules out there, but the section goes through some of the more popular testing functions from the Test::More module.

Using ok

The `ok()` function is the most basic test function in Perl. The `Test::More` module automatically exports `ok()` and its syntax looks like this:

```
ok $true_or_false_expression, $optional_message;
```

The `ok()` function takes a single argument or expression and tests it for "truth." The test passes if the first argument is true:

```
ok 1;
ok "Hi there. I'm true!", "This is a silly test";
```

And it fails if the first argument is false:

```
my $balrog;
ok $balrog, 'You shall not pass!';
```

In your `t/testit.t` script, add the following line, replacing the useless `ok 1` test:

```
ok reciprocal(2), 'The reciprocal of 2 should be true';
```

If you run that script with `prove -lv t/testit.t`, you should see the following output:

```
t/testit.t ..
ok 1 - The reciprocal of 2 should be true
1..1
ok
All tests successful.
Files=1, Tests=1,  0 wallclock secs
Result: PASS
```

Congratulations! You've written your first successful test.

Using is

Obviously, checking that `reciprocal(2)` returns a true value is not useful. You want to ensure that it returns the correct value. You can do this with the `is()` function. Its syntax looks like this:

```
is $have, $want, $message;
```

The `$have` variable contains the value that you have, and `$want` is the value you expect to receive. Instead of replacing your `ok` test, just add another test after it:

```
is reciprocal(2), .5, 'The reciprocal of 2 should be correct';
```

Using the `prove` utility should now generate the following output:

```
t/testit.t ..
ok 1 - The reciprocal of 2 should be true
ok 2 - The reciprocal of 2 should be correct
```

```
1..2
ok
All tests successful.
Files=1, Tests=2,  0 wallclock secs
Result: PASS
```

Now write another test, but this time force it to fail:

```
is reciprocal(3), .5, 'The reciprocal of 3 should be correct';
```

If you add that after your first two tests, your test script should now look like this:

```
use strict;
use warnings;
use Test::More;
use lib 'lib';
use TestMe ':ALL';
ok reciprocal(2), 'The reciprocal of 2 should be true';
is reciprocal(2), .5, 'The reciprocal of 2 should be correct';
is reciprocal(3), .5, 'The reciprocal of 3 should be correct';
done_testing;
```

And running that produces:

```
t/testit.t ..
ok 1 - The reciprocal of 2 should be true
ok 2 - The reciprocal of 2 should be correct
not ok 3 - The reciprocal of 3 should be correct
1..3
#   Failed test 'The reciprocal of 3 should be correct'
#   at t/testit.t line 9.
#          got: '0.333333333333333'
#     expected: '0.5'
# Looks like you failed 1 test of 3.
Dubious, test returned 1 (wstat 256, 0x100)
Failed 1/3 subtests
Test Summary Report
-------------------
t/testit.t (Wstat: 256 Tests: 3 Failed: 1)
  Failed test:  3
  Non-zero exit status: 1
Files=1, Tests=3,  1 wallclock secs
Result: FAIL
shell returned 1
```

> **NOTE** The diagnostics in the failure output may or may not appear immediately after the test failure. This is because the normal test output is sent to the computer's standard out (STDOUT), whereas your diagnostics are sent to standard error (STDERR). Because of how most operating systems work, those are not guaranteed to be in synch.

> If you want those in synch, you can pass the --merge switch to prove:
>
> ```
> prove -v --merge t/testit.t
> ```
>
> That attempts to "merge" the STDOUT and STDERR output streams to make everything come out at the same time. It should be considered an experimental feature, and if something else in your software prints something to STDERR (or STDOUT, for that matter), the test harness may have trouble interpreting the output.

So you focus on the test failure:

```
#   Failed test 'The reciprocal of 3 should be correct'
#   at t/testit.t line 9.
#        got: '0.333333333333333'
#     expected: '0.5'
# Looks like you failed 1 test of 3.
```

The failure output tells you what you $have (the got: line) and what you $want (the expected: line). This makes it easier to diagnose problems.

In this case, you might find it annoying (not to mention error-prone) to type 0.333333333333333 for the $want variable. That's when choosing an appropriate level of rounding and using the sprintf function can help. You can use this to easily make the test pass:

```
use strict;
use warnings;
use Test::More;
use lib 'lib';
use TestMe ':ALL';
ok reciprocal(2), 'The reciprocal of 2 should be true';
is reciprocal(2), .5, 'The reciprocal of 2 should be correct';
is sprintf( "%.4f", reciprocal(3) ), .3333,
   'The reciprocal of 3 should be correct';
done_testing;
```

> **NOTE** The sprintf() trick is also useful when you have floating point issues. For example, the following code, using the printf analogue to sprintf prints 0.41999999999999998446 on my computer. (The answer might be different on yours.)
>
> ```
> printf "%.20f", .42;
> ```
>
> *continues*

> *continued*
>
> *This is due to how computers handle numbers internally. Using* `sprintf()`
> *to guarantee a certain level of precision can make it easier to test when one*
> *floating point number is equal to another.*
>
> ```
> printf "%.5f", .42;
> ```
>
> *And that prints:*
>
> ```
> 0.42000
> ```

Using like

Sometimes you know roughly what your data looks like, but you can't guarantee its exact output.
That's where the `like()` test function comes into play. It looks like this:

```
like $data, qr/$regular_expression/, $message;
```

In your `TestMe` package, add `use DateTime;` to the top of the module, and add the following
function:

```
sub order_date {
    my $today = DateTime->now->subtract( days => rand(30) );
    return join '/' => map { $today->$_ } qw/month day year/;
}
```

Use this to simulate a random order date.

The idea is that you want to output dates like `08/04/2012` for April 4th, 2012. Write a `like()` test
for that, adding it to `testit.t` as usual.

```
# we use the /x modifier on the regex to allow whitespace to be
# ignored. This makes the regex easier to read
like today(), qr{^ \d\d/\d\d/\d\d\d\d $}x,
    'today() should return a DD/MM/YYYY format';
```

Run your `testit.t` script a few times. Because you're using a random value, sometimes it might
pass, but other times it will fail with something like this:

```
not ok 4 - today() should return a DD/MM/YYYY format
1..4
#   Failed test 'today() should return a DD/MM/YYYY format'
#   at t/testit.t line 11.
#                   '3/4/2012'
#     doesn't match '(?x-ism:^ \d\d/\d\d/\d\d\d\d $)'
# Looks like you failed 1 test of 4.
```

The regular expression attempts to match two digits, followed by a slash, two more digits, a slash,
and four digits. The ^ and $ anchors force the regex to match from the start to the end of the string.

At the end it fails because 3/4/2012 clearly does not match the regular expression. You have two choices: If you decide your code is correct, then you fix the test. In this case, you decide that your test is correct and the code is in error. (This is usually the case for failing tests.) So fix the code:

```
sub order_date {
    my $today = DateTime->now->subtract( days => rand(30) );
    return sprintf "%02d/%02d/%04d" =>
        map { $today->$_ } qw/day month year/;
}
```

Now, no matter how many times you run your tests, the tests pass.

The other choice is to decide that your test is wrong and fix the test. The answer is not always this obvious, so pay careful attention to test failures.

Using is_deeply

Sometimes you want to compare data structures. Consider this:

```
is [ 3, 4 ], [ 3, 4 ], 'Identical array refs should match';
```

That may generate an error like this:

```
not ok 1 - Identical array refs should match
#   Failed test 'Identical array refs should match'
#   at some_script.t line 2.
#          got: 'ARRAY(0x7fc9eb0032a0)'
#     expected: 'ARRAY(0x7fc9eb026048)'
```

What happened? The is() functions tests whether two values are equal and, in this case, those values are references, not their contents. That's where the is_deeply() function comes in.

```
use Test::More;
is_deeply [ 3, 4 ], [ 3, 4 ], 'Identical array refs should match';
```

That test passes because the array reference contents are identical. However, if the contents are not identical:

```
is_deeply [ 3, 4 ], [ 3, 4, 1 ], 'Identical array refs should match';
```

You get an array like this:

```
not ok 1 - Identical array refs should match
#   Failed test 'Identical array refs should match'
#   at some_script.t line 2.
#     Structures begin differing at:
#          $got->[2] = Does not exist
#     $expected->[2] = '1'
```

The is_deeply() test function walks through each data structure, in parallel, keeping track of where it is and reports an error at the first item in each structure that is different. If there are multiple differences, it can be annoying to track them all down, but later you look at the `Test::Differences` module that will make this easier.

Using SKIP

Sometimes you need to test code that should not always be run. For example, maybe some features work only if you have a particular module installed. You can use SKIP to skip them. SKIP looks like this:

```
SKIP: {
    skip $why, $how_many if $some_condition;
    # tests
}
```

And if `$some_condition` is true, `skip()` prints out several "successful" test lines (matching `$how_many`) and the rest of the block will be skipped. Here's a concrete example:

```
SKIP: {
    skip "Don't have an internet connection", 2
        unless have_internet_connection();
    my $website;
    ok $website = get_website($some_site),
      'We should be able to get the website';
    is $website->title, 'Some Title',
      '... and the title should be correct';
}
```

And assuming that `have_internet_connection()` returns false, you get output similar to the following:

```
ok 1 # skip Don't have an internet connection
ok 2 # skip Don't have an internet connection
```

Using TODO

Maybe you have a feature that you haven't completed writing, but you still want to write tests for it without necessarily having the test suite fail. You can do this with a SKIP test, but that's not quite what you want. Instead, you want the tests to be run, but not have their failures make the entire test suite fail. Use a TODO test for that. The structure looks like this:

```
TODO: {
    local $TODO = 'These tests do not work yet';
    # some tests
}
```

Let's add the following function to `TestMe`.

```
sub unique {
    my @array = @_;
    my %hash  = map { $_ => 1 } @array;
    return keys %hash;
}
```

And then add this to your `testit.t` program:

```
TODO: {
    local $TODO = 'Figure out how to avoid random order';
    my @have = unique( 2, 3, 5, 4, 3, 5, 7 );
    my @want = ( 2, 3, 5, 4, 7 );
    is_deeply \@have, \@want,
        'unique() should return unique() elements in order';
}
```

When you run your tests, you probably get an error similar to this. (The `not ok` and the `# TODO` lines are broken over two lines here only to fit the formatting of the book. Ordinarily they are on a single line.)

```
not ok 5 - unique() should return unique() elements in order
# TODO Figure out how to avoid random order
#   Failed (TODO) test 'unique() should return unique() elements in order'
#   at t/testit.t line 19.
#     Structures begin differing at:
#          $got->[0] = '0'
#      $expected->[0] = '2'
```

Perl can recognize that everything in the TODO block should not be considered a failure, even if the test fails. When the test does pass, you see output like this:

```
t/testit.t ..
ok 1 - The reciprocal of 2 should be true
ok 2 - The reciprocal of 2 should be correct
ok 3 - The reciprocal of 3 should be correct
ok 4 - today() should return a DD/MM/YYYY format
ok 5 - unique() should return unique() elements in order # TODO ...
1..5
ok
All tests successful.
Test Summary Report
-------------------
t/testit.t (Wstat: 0 Tests: 5 Failed: 0)
  TODO passed:   5
Files=1, Tests=5,  0 wallclock secs
Result: PASS
```

There is a `TODO passed: 5` note in the test output footer. That helps you track down a test that unexpectedly succeeds when it's in a TODO block.

Using eval {}

Sometimes you want to test failures that would ordinarily kill your test program, but you would like to keep your tests running. Consider `reciprocal():`. What happens when you pass a zero? You can use `eval` to trap the error:

```
eval { reciprocal(0) };
my $error = $@;
like $error, qr{Illegal division by zero at t/testit.t},
    'reciprocal(0) should report an error from the caller';
```

> **NOTE** If you don't remember the eval/$@ syntax, see the eval section in Chapter 7.

In this case, you don't want `reciprocal()` to report where the error occurred but to report the calling code that caused the error. The `eval` ensures that your tests can keep running, but your test fails:

```
not ok 6 - reciprocal(0) should report an error from the caller
#   Failed test 'reciprocal(0) should report an error from the caller'
#   at t/testit.t line 25.
#                   'Illegal division by zero at t/testit.t line 23.
# '
#     doesn't match '(?-xism:Illegal division by zero at testit.t)'
```

To make the test pass, make sure that you include `use Carp 'croak'` in `lib/TestMe.pm` and then fix the `reciprocal()` function:

```perl
sub reciprocal {
    my $number = shift;
    unless ($number) {
        croak("Illegal division by zero");
    }
    return 1 / $number;
}
```

Rerun your tests and now they should pass.

Using use_ok and require_ok

Sometimes you want to know if you can use a module you've written. You'll often see people do this:

```perl
use_ok    'My::Module', 'My::Module should load';
require_ok 'My::Module', 'My::Module should load';
```

You shouldn't use either of these; just use `use` *module* or `require` *module* as necessary. If the `use` or `require` fails, your script will die and you'll get a test failure reported. Without going into long, painful technical detail, suffice it to say that both these functions have several problems. People have tried to correct some of the problems with `use_ok` by doing this:

```perl
BEGIN {
    use_ok 'My::Module', 'My::Module should load'
      or die "Cannot load 'My::Module'";
}
```

But at this point, you may as well `use My::Module;` because the above construct doesn't gain you much.

Working with Miscellaneous Test Functions

The `can_ok` function tests whether the first argument (an object or class name) can execute the methods listed in `@list_of_method_names`.

```
can_ok $package_or_class, @list_of_method_names;
```

No description is required because `can_ok()` supplies one for you. It's the same as:

```
ok $package_or_class->can($method), "Package can execute $method";
```

But it works for multiple methods at once.

The `isa_ok` function is similar, but it takes only one class name to test against:

```
isa_ok $object, $class;
```

It's identical to:

```
ok $object->isa($class), "object isa $class";
```

However, you don't have to worry about wrapping it an `eval` and it provides the descriptive test name for you.

The `diag()` function lets you spit out diagnostic messages without worrying about them interfering with test output:

```
diag( "Testing with Perl $], $^X" );
```

If that's in your tests, it might output something like the following when you run your tests:

```
# Testing with Perl 5.012004 ~perl5/perlbrew/perls/perl-5.12.4/bin/perl
```

With well-thought-out `diag()` messages, if someone reports a failure in one of your modules, you can often have them send you the complete test failure output and better understand why your code failed.

> **NOTE** In your sample `diag()` message, you included the `$]` and `$^X` special variables. These represent the Perl version and the path to the currently executing Perl. See `perldoc perlvar` for more information.

TRY IT OUT   Testing a Complex Function

So far you have seen a few trivial examples of testing, but let's look at something a little bit more real world. Generally when you write code, you want to reuse working code from the CPAN (or some other source) rather than write all of it yourself, but in this case, you write a simple query string parser (those extra bits on URLs that you see after a ? sign) and test that it behaves correctly. Though query strings are relatively simple, there are plenty of examples of broken parsers on the web, and you don't want a broken example.

You're not actually going to do the work of decoding the characters from RFC 3986 encoding (http://tools.ietf.org/html/rfc3986). Let URI::Escape do that. Instead, ensure that you can translate a query string into a data structure you can easily test against.

All the code for this Try It Out is in the code file lib/TestQuery.pm and t/query.t.

1. Save the following as lib/TestQuery.pm:

```
package TestQuery;
use strict;
use warnings;
use URI::Escape 'uri_unescape';
use Encode 'decode_utf8';
use Exporter::NoWork;
sub parse_query_string {
    my $query_string = shift;
    my @pairs = split /[&;]/ => $query_string;
    my %values_for;
    foreach my $pair (@pairs) {
        my ( $key, $value ) = split( /=/, $pair );
        $_ = decode_utf8( uri_unescape($_) ) for $key, $value;
        $values_for{$key} ||= [];
        push @{ $values_for{$key} } => $value;
    }
    return \%values_for;
}
1;
```

2. Save the following test script as t/query.t:

```
use strict;
use warnings;
use Test::More;
use lib 'lib';
use TestQuery ':ALL';
my $query = parse_query_string('name=Ovid&color=black');
is_deeply $query, { name => ['Ovid'], color => ['black'] },
  'A basic query string parsing should be correct';
$query = parse_query_string('color=blue&color=white&color=red');
is_deeply $query, { color => [qw/blue white red/] },
  '... and multi-valued params should also parse correctly';
$query = parse_query_string('color=blue;color=white;color=red');
is_deeply $query, { color => [qw/blue white red/] },
  '... even if we are using the alternate ";" delimiter';
$query = parse_query_string('remark=%28parentheses%21%29');
is_deeply $query, { remark => ['(parentheses!)'] },
  '... or URI-encoded characters';
my $omega = "\N{U+2126}";
$query = parse_query_string('alpha=%E2%84%A6');
is_deeply $query, { alpha => [$omega] },
    '... and Unicode should decode correctly';
done_testing;
```

When you finish, your directory structure should look like this, assuming you also wrote the lib/TestMe.pm and t/testit.t programs:

```
lib/
|--TestMe.pm
|--TestQuery.pm
t/
|--query.t
|--testit.t
```

3. Run the test program with `prove -v t/query.t`. You should see the following output, verifying that you have correctly parsed the query strings:

```
t/query.t ..
ok 1 - A basic query string parsing should be correct
ok 2 - ... and multi-valued params should also parse correctly
ok 3 - ... even if we are using the alternate ";" delimiter
ok 4 - ... or URI-encoded characters
ok 5 - ... and Unicode should decode correctly
1..5
ok
All tests successful.
Files=1, Tests=5
Result: PASS
```

How It Works

When you have a query string like `name=value&color=blue`, you want that returned in a hash reference, such as `{ name => 'value', color => 'blue' }`. However, what many people get wrong is that this is a perfectly valid query string:

```
name=value;color=red;color=blue
```

The separator in that query string is a semicolon, `;`, and not an ampersand, `&`. You also have more than one value for `color`. Because you can have multiple values for each parameter, use array references and your resulting data structure should look like this:

```
{
    name  => [ 'value' ],
    color => [ 'red', 'blue' ].
}
```

And that's what your `parse_query_string()` function does:

```perl
sub parse_query_string {
    my $query_string = shift;
    my @pairs = split /[&;]/ => $query_string;
    my %values_for;
    foreach my $pair (@pairs) {
        my ( $key, $value ) = split( /=/, $pair );
        $_ = decode_utf8( uri_unescape($_) ) for $key, $value;
        $values_for{$key} ||= [];
        push @{ $values_for{$key} } => $value;
    }
    return \%values_for;
}
```

This line:

```
my @pairs = split /[&;]/ => $query_string;
```

Splits the query string on ampersands and semicolons into key value pairs.

And the body of the loop

```
my ( $key, $value ) = split( /=/, $pair );
$_ = decode_utf8( uri_unescape($_) ) for $key, $value;
$values_for{$key} ||= [];
push @{ $values_for{$key} } => $value;
```

That splits each key/value pair on the = sign and the following line calls uri_unescape and decode_utf8 on each key and value. Then you create an array reference if you didn't have one, pushing the new value onto that array reference and storing it in the %values_for hash.

The reason you need to decode_utf8 on the unescaped value is because the uri_unescape function can decode the characters into a byte string, but you need decode_utf8 to turn that byte string into a proper UTF-8 string. See the Unicode section in Chapter 9 for more details. You may want to remove the decode_utf8 and run the tests again. You can examine the test failure to see the difference in behavior.

Now look at the first test:

```
my $query = parse_query_string('name=Ovid&color=black');
is_deeply $query, { name => ['Ovid'], color => ['black'] },
    'A basic query string parsing should be correct';
```

In this, you parse a query string and expect two name/value pairs to be returned in a hash reference. The is_deeply() test function does a deep check to verify that the $query returned matches the expected data structure you supply.

Run the test with a variety of different query strings:

- ➤ color=blue&color=white&color=red
- ➤ color=blue;color=white;color=red
- ➤ remark=%28parentheses%21%29
- ➤ alpha=%E2%84%A6

The last one is rather interesting. The Greek letter Omega (Ω) is the Unicode code point U+2126. Its three-byte sequence is \xe2\x84\xa6 and that gets URI encoded as %E2%84%A6. Without the decode_utf8, the uri_unescape function would return that three octets from the URI encoding. The uri_unescape function does not actually know about Unicode, which is why you need to decode it manually. Thus, you want a solid test here to verify that you are properly handling Unicode in query strings.

```
my $omega = "\N{U+2126}";
$query = parse_query_string('alpha=%E2%84%A6');
is_deeply $query, { alpha => [$omega] },
    '... and Unicode should decode correctly';
```

Now that you have a test program, can you think of other use cases you might want to handle in query strings? What do you do if you have no value for a parameter (for example: `name=&color=red`)? If you write another function that validates that your query strings have particular keys and values matching certain parameters, how would you test that? These are the sorts of questions you need to face when writing tests and the answers can vary depending on your needs.

USING OTHER TESTING MODULES

In reality, you could write an entire test suite using only the `ok()` test function. However, that would not provide you with good diagnostic information. Instead, there are a wide variety of other testing functions available from `Test::More` (not all of which are covered in this book). However, `Test::More`, while being great, is often not enough. Instead, you might want to use other testing modules that can make testing your code even easier. Some of the more popular ones are covered next.

Using Test::Differences

Consider the following test:

```
use Test::More;
my %have = (
    numbers => [ 3, 4 ],
    fields  => { this => 'that', big => 'bad' },
    extra   => [ 3, 4 ],
);
my %want = (
    numbers => [ 3, 4 ],
    fields  => { this => 'taht', big => 'bad' },
    extra   => [ 4, 4, ],
);
is_deeply \%have, \%want, 'have and want should be the same';
done_testing;
```

And that prints out:

```
not ok 1 - have and want should be the same
#   Failed test 'have and want should be the same'
#   at /var/tmp/eval_q5aW.pl line 12.
#     Structures begin differing at:
#          $got->{fields}{this} = 'that'
#     $expected->{fields}{this} = 'taht'
1..1
# Looks like you failed 1 test of 1.
```

That tells you the items don't match, but it tells you only the first item that it found that failed to match. And if you data structure is extremely complicated, you might dig through something like:

```
#          $got->{fields}[0][3]{some_value} = 'that'
#     $expected->{fields}[0][3]{some_value} = 'taht'
```

And that's not a lot of fun. Instead, you can use the Test::Differences modules. It exports several test functions, the most common of which is eq_or_diff(). It looks like this:

```
use Test::More;
use Test::Differences;
my %have = (
    numbers => [ 3, 4 ],
    fields  => { this => 'that', big => 'bad' },
    extra   => [ 3, 4 ],
);
my %want = (
    numbers => [ 3, 4 ],
    fields  => { this => 'taht', big => 'bad' },
    extra   => [ 4, 4, ],
);
eq_or_diff \%have, \%want, 'have and want should be the same';
done_testing;
```

When you run that, you get a full diff:

```
not ok 1 - have and want should be the same
#   Failed test 'have and want should be the same'
#   at /var/tmp/eval_1h41.pl line 13.
# +----+-------------------+-------------------+
# | Elt|Got                |Expected           |
# +----+-------------------+-------------------+
# |   0|{                  |{                  |
# |   1|  extra => [       |  extra => [       |
# * |   2|    3,             |    4,             | *
# |   3|    4              |    4              |
# |   4|  ],               |  ],               |
# |   5|  fields => {      |  fields => {      |
# |   6|    big => 'bad',  |    big => 'bad',  |
# * |   7|    this => 'that' |    this => 'taht' | *
# |   8|  },               |  },               |
# |   9|  numbers => [     |  numbers => [     |
# |  10|    3,             |    3,             |
# |  11|    4              |    4              |
# |  12|  ]                |  ]                |
# |  13|}                  |}                  |
# +----+-------------------+-------------------+
1..1
# Looks like you failed 1 test of 1.
```

The Elt column is the line number of the diff. The Got column is what you have, and the Expected column is what you want. Prior to each Elt number matching an incorrect line is an asterisk showing which lines are different.

For extremely large data structures, it show only a range of lines and also has functions to customize the output.

Using Test::Exception

You may remember how you tested a function that might die:

```
eval { reciprocal(0) };
my $error = $@;
like $error, qr{Illegal division by zero at t/testit.t},
    'reciprocal(0) should report an error from the caller';
```

The Test::Exception module makes this a little bit cleaner:

```
use Test::Exception;
throws_ok { reciprocal(0) }
    qr{Illegal division by zero at t/testit.t},
    'reciprocal(0) should report an error from the caller';
```

The first argument to throws_ok is a subroutine reference. Because the prototype to throws_ok is (&$;$) (see the prototypes section in Chapter 7, "Subroutines"), the first argument can be a block, { ... }, without the sub keyword in front of it.

The second argument is a regular expression compiled with the qr// builtin. This is a common mistake:

```
use Test::Exception;
throws_ok { some_code() }
  /some regular expression/,
  'I should get the correct error';
```

When you see a bare regular expression in the form of /.../, that's executed immediately against $_. You must use the qr// compiled form of the regular expression.

NOTE When using Test::Exception::throws_ok function (or any function that has a & prototype), you do not use a trailing comma if you provide a block:

```
throws_ok { some_code() } qr/.../, $message;
```

You do need the trailing comma if you provide the sub keyword:

```
throws_ok sub { some_code() }, qr/.../, $message;
```

Test::Exception exports other test functions, such as dies_ok and lives_ok, so read the documentation for a full understanding of its capabilities.

Using Test::Warn

Sometimes your code throws warnings. There are two types:

➤ Those generated by `perl` (such as the common `Use of uninitialized value`).

➤ Warnings the programmer creates. Warnings issued by `perl` should be dealt with and eliminated because those are warnings to the developer writing some code, but warnings created by the programmer should be tested because those are warnings to the *user* of the code. This is where `Test::Warn` comes in.

Consider the following code snippet:

```
sub read_config {
    my $config = shift;
    unless ( -f $config && -r _ ) {
        carp "Cannot read '$config'. using default config";
        $config = $DEFAULT_CONFIG;
    }
    # read the config
}
```

You can test that with `Test::Warn` with code like the following:

```
use Test::More;
use Test::Warn;
warning_is { read_config($config) }
    "Cannot read '$config'. using default config",
    'Reading a bad config should generate a warning';
```

Code might throw no warnings or multiple warnings, or you may need to test the warnings against a regular expression. `Test::Warn` handles all these cases.

Using Test::Most

Finally, here's your author's favorite `Test::` module (disclaimer: he wrote it), `Test::Most`, a name chosen to gently make fun of the `Test::More` module's name. (The authors are actually good friends, so this isn't mean-spirited.)

When dealing with large test suites, it's common to see something like this at the beginning of each test module:

```
use strict;
use warnings;
use Test::Exception;
use Test::Differences;
use Test::Deep;
use Test::Warn;
use Test::More tests => 42;
```

That's a lot of typing and frankly, it gets annoying re-creating this boilerplate every time. As a result, the `Test::Most` module was created. The above boilerplate (even the `strict` and `warnings`) can be replaced with this:

```
use Test::Most tests => 42;
```

You've now eliminated six lines of code and can just start writing tests without retyping those six lines every time (or forgetting one and going back and adding it). The test modules in question were chosen by running a heuristic analysis over the entire CPAN and seeing which test modules were most commonly used and including the appropriate ones in `Test::Most`.

> **NOTE** If you like this idea but want a different list of modules, you author has also released `Test::Kit`. This allows you to assemble your own list of modules to bundle together.

UNDERSTANDING XUNIT STYLE USING TESTING

If you're familiar with testing in other languages, you may be familiar with *xUnit* style testing. This is a type of testing that is particularly well suited to object-oriented code. Just as you have classes that you want to test, with xUnit style testing, you can create corresponding test classes. These test classes can inherit tests from one another, just as your classes can inherit from other classes.

The most popular xUnit style testing package in Perl is called `Test::Class` and that's what you'll use.

> **WARNING** Sometimes you'll find people using `Test::Unit` for xUnit style testing instead of `Test::Class`. Unfortunately, `Test::Unit` is not compatible with `Test::Builder`, the module that most modern Perl testing tools are built with, so you should not use it. It has not been updated since 2005 and appears to be abandoned.

Using Test::Class

Start by creating a `Person` class. The `Person` has a given name, a family name (analogous to first name and last name), an optional read/write title, such as Dr., and a birth date. The class will look like the following code (code file: `lib/Person.pm`):

```
package Person;
use Moose;
use Moose::Util::TypeConstraints;
use DateTime::Format::Strptime;
use namespace::autoclean;
# Moose doesn't know about non-Moose-based classes.
```

```
class_type 'DateTime';
my $datetime_formatter = DateTime::Format::Strptime->new(
    pattern   => '%Y-%m-%d',
    time_zone => 'GMT',
);
coerce 'DateTime'
  => from 'Str'
  => via { $datetime_formatter->parse_datetime($_) };
use DateTime;
has 'given_name'  => ( is => 'ro', isa => 'Str', required => 1 );
has 'family_name' => ( is => 'ro', isa => 'Str', required => 1 );
has 'title'       => ( is => 'rw', isa => 'Str', required => 0 );
has 'birthdate' =>
  ( is => 'ro', isa => 'DateTime', required => 1, coerce => 1 );
sub name {
    my $self = shift;
    my $name = '';
    if ( my $title = $self->title ) {
        $name = "$title ";
    }
    $name .= join ' ', $self->given_name, $self->family_name;
    return $name;
}
sub age {
    my $self     = shift;
    my $duration = DateTime->now - $self->birthdate;
    return $duration->years;
}
__PACKAGE__->meta->make_immutable;
1;
```

> **NOTE** The `DateTime::Format::Strptime` *module can help you convert date strings like* 1967-06-20 *to a proper* `DateTime` *object. Then use special* `Moose` *code to coerce strings to* `DateTime` *objects for the* `birthdate`. *That lets you do this:*
>
> ```
>         my $person = Person->new(
>             title        => 'President',
>             given_name   => 'Dwight',
>             family_name  => 'Eisenhower',
>             birthdate    => '1890-10-14',
>         );
> ```
>
> *That's much easier than creating the entire* `DateTime` *object every time.*
>
> *Chapter 13 doesn't cover coercions for* `Moose` *because they're a bit more advanced, so you won't see them here, but you can read* `Moose::Cookbook::Basics::Recipe5` *to better understand how to use coercions in your own* `Moose` *classes.*

You could write normal .t scripts for this, but I'll show you how to take advantage of the power of Test::Class to extend these classes.

To start writing your tests, you need a little bit of code to make it easy to run the tests. There are a variety of ways to configure how to run Test::Class tests, but the following method is your author's preferred setup. It is extremely flexible and makes running your classes a breeze.

First, make a "driver" test that can run all your test classes at once. Save the following (code file t/test_classes.t).

```
use strict;
use warnings;
use Test::Class::Load 't/lib';
```

That script can find all Test::Class tests in the t/lib directory and run them. It can also add t/lib to @INC to ensure that Perl can find them, too. (@INC is the special Perl variable telling Perl which paths to look for code in. For more information, see Chapter 11).

Next, create a t/lib directory and add the following code (code file t/lib/TestsFor.pm):

```
package TestsFor;
use Test::Most;
use base 'Test::Class';
INIT { Test::Class->runtests }
sub startup  : Tests(startup)  {}
sub setup    : Tests(setup)    {}
sub teardown : Tests(teardown) {}
sub shutdown : Tests(shutdown) {}
1;
```

Now use the TestsFor:: namespace to ensure that your test classes do not try to use a namespace in use by another package. The INIT block tells Test::Class to run all the tests after they have been compiled. I'll explain the startup, setup, teardown, and shutdown methods in the "Using Test Control Methods" section later in this chapter. The use base 'Test::Class', tells Perl that TestsFor.pm will inherit from the Test::Class module. That's what makes all this work.

A Basic Test Class

The code files t/test_classes.t script and t/lib/TestsFor.pm class are all the code you need for your setup. Now you can begin to write tests for your Person class. You need to create a t/lib/TestsFor/ directory and save the following code as t/lib/TestsFor/Person.pm:

```
package TestsFor::Person;
use Test::Most;
use base 'TestsFor';
use Person;
use DateTime;

sub class_to_test { 'Person' }

sub constructor : Tests(3) {
```

```
    my $test = shift;
    my $class = $test->class_to_test;
    can_ok $class, 'new';
    throws_ok { $class->new }
    qr/Attribute.*required/,
        "Creating a $class without proper attributes should fail";
    my $person = $class->new(
        given_name  => 'Charles',
        family_name => 'Drew',
        birthdate   => '1904-06-03',
    );
    isa_ok $person, $class;
}
1;
```

You can now run `prove -lv t/test_classes.t` to should see the following output:

```
$ prove -lv t/test_classes.t
t/test_classes.t .. #
# TestsFor::Person->constructor
1..3
ok 1 - Person->can('new')
ok 2 - Creating a Person without proper attributes should fail
ok 3 - The object isa Person
ok
All tests successful.
Files=1, Tests=3,  2 wallclock secs
Result: PASS
```

Now break down what's happening here. Here are the opening lines from the `TestsFor::Person` class:

```
package TestsFor::Person;
use Test::Most;
use base 'TestsFor';
use Person;
use DateTime;
```

Use `Test::Most` to avoid repeatedly using many test modules, plus, it turns on `strict` and `warnings`. You inherit from your `TestsFor` module because when you create test classes, it's a good idea to have a common test class that you might have shared methods in, such as methods to connect to a database.

You also have this curious bit:

```
sub class_to_test { 'Person' }
```

Why do you do that? Because you want to ensure that your subclasses can override this method to assert which class they are testing. This becomes more clear when you learn how to inherit from subclasses.

Now take a close look at your test method.

The test method is defined as:

```
sub constructor : Tests(3) {
    ...
}
```

The : `Tests(3)` bit is called a *subroutine attribute*. These are not the same thing as class attributes (data attached to a class). These are special extra bits of information you can attach to a subroutine to provide a bit more information about them. The syntax looks like this:

```
sub NAME : ATTRIBUTES { ... }
```

By themselves they don't do anything, but some authors use the `Attribute::Handlers` module to define custom attributes and describe their meaning. I won't cover them more except to say that `Test::Class` has attributes for test methods to mark them as something that `Test::Class` knows how to deal with. So this:

```
sub customer : Tests(3) { ... }
```

Tells `Test::Class` that you will run three tests in this test method. If you run more, you have a test failure. If you run fewer, `Test::Class` assumes you meant to skip the tests and issues "skipped test" lines in your test output.

> **WARNING** You used the name `constructor()` for the `new()` method because `Test::Class` has its own `new()` method, and overriding that method can cause strange bugs in your test classes. Never override `new()` unless you know exactly what you're doing.

If you're not sure how many tests you will run in a test method, you can omit the number of tests:

```
sub some_test_method : Tests { ... }
```

The next line is this:

```
my $test = shift;
```

Ordinarily the invocant to a method is called `$self` and most developers who use `Test::Class` write my `$self = shift`. Your author prefers to use the `$test` variable to help keep you in the frame of mind of "writing tests." It's silly, but there you go.

The rest of the test method is composed of standard testing code that you already understand.

When you run a test class, the `Test::Class` module can find all methods in all test class with a `:Tests` attribute and execute them sequentially as tests, grouping test results per test class, per test method.

Now add test methods for the `name` and `age` methods. First, because you'll be instantiating the `Person` class several times, pull that out into its own method `default_person()` method:

```perl
sub constructor : Tests(3) {
    my $test = shift;
    my $class = $test->class_to_test;
    can_ok $class, 'new';
    throws_ok { $class->new }
    qr/Attribute.*required/,
        "Creating a $class without proper attributes should fail";
    isa_ok $test->default_person, 'Person';
}
sub default_person {
    my $test = shift;
    return $test->class_to_test->new(
        given_name  => 'Charles',
        family_name => 'Drew',
        birthdate   => '1904-06-03',
    );
}
```

As you can see in the `constructor()` test method, you can write `$test->default_person` to get the `Person` object. If you rerun the tests, you see no change of behavior because `default_person()` does not have a `:Tests` attribute and `Test::Class` will not attempt to run it directly.

Now add the following test methods to the `TestsFor::Person` class:

```perl
sub name : Tests(2) {
    my $test   = shift;
    my $person = $test->default_person;
    is $person->name, 'Charles Drew', 'name() should return the full name';
    $person->title('Dr.');
    is $person->name, 'Dr. Charles Drew',
        '... and it should be correct if we have a title';
}
sub age : Tests(2) {
    my $test = shift;
    my $person = $test->default_person;
    can_ok $person, 'age';
    cmp_ok $person->age, '>', 100,
        'Our default person is more than one hundred years old';
}
```

Notice that in `name()` you take advantage that you made `title()` a read-write object attribute. In both of these, you used your `default_person()` method to avoid rewriting code.

After you've added these methods, you can rerun your tests and get this output:

```
t/test_classes.t .. #
1..8
# TestsFor::Person->age
ok 1 - Person->can('age')
ok 2 - Our default person is more than one hundred years old
```

```
#
# TestsFor::Person->constructor
ok 3 - Person->can('new')
ok 4 - Creating a Person without proper attributes should fail
ok 5 - The object isa Person
#
# TestsFor::Person->name
ok 6 - Person->can('name')
ok 7 - name() should return the full name
ok 8 - ... and it should be correct if we have a title
ok
All tests successful.
Files=1, Tests=8,  0 wallclock secs
Result: PASS
```

You can see diagnostic comments indicating which test methods have run, along with their corresponding tests.

Extending a Test Class

If your classes have subclasses, it's natural that your test classes have subclasses, too. Look at a Customer subclass of Person. It's identical to Person, but it's required to have a minimum age of 18. First, write the Customer class (code file lib/Customer.pm):

```
package Customer;
use Moose;
extends 'Person';
use Carp 'croak';
use namespace::autoclean;
sub BUILD {
    my $self = shift;
    if ( $self->age < 18 ) {
        my $age = $self->age;
        croak("Customers must be 18 years old or older, not $age");
    }
}
__PACKAGE__->meta->make_immutable;
1;
```

As you can see, this is a simple, straightforward subclass with no complications. Now look at its test class (code file t/lib/TestsFor/Customer.pm):

```
package TestsFor::Customer;
use Test::Most;
use base 'TestsFor::Person';
use Customer;
use DateTime;

sub class_to_test { 'Customer' }

sub mininum_age : Tests(2) {
    my $test = shift;
```

```
    my $year = DateTime->now->year;
    $year -= 16;
    throws_ok {
        $test->class_to_test->new(
            given_name  => 'Sally',
            family_name => 'Forth',
            birthdate   => "$year-06-05",
        );
    }
    qr/^Customers must be 18 years old or older, not \d+/,
      'Trying to create a customer younger than 18 should fail';
    $year -= 10;    # take another ten years off
    lives_ok {
        $test->class_to_test->new(
            given_name  => 'Sally',
            family_name => 'Forth',
            birthdate   => "$year-06-05",
        );
    }
    'Trying to create a customer older than 18 should succeed';
}
1;
```

Just as the `Customer` class inherited from the `Person` class, the `TestsFor::Customer` class inherited from `TestsFor::Person` (using slightly different syntax because the classes are written with `Moose` and the test classes are not).

There are two interesting things here:

- ➤ You compute the year rather than hard-code it with something like `my $year = 1999;`. You do that to ensure that these tests don't start to break in the future.

- ➤ You again fetch the name of the class to test from your `class_to_test()` method. You'll see why right now.

So run this test class, but only this test class. Remember this line from in the `t/lib/TestsFor.pm` package?

```
INIT { Test::Class->runtests }
```

Because you have that, loading your tests automatically runs them, but you need to tell the `prove` utility where to find the test classes. You do this by passing `-It/lib` to `prove`.

```
$ prove -lv -It/lib t/lib/TestsFor/Customer.pm
t/lib/TestsFor/Customer.pm .. #
# TestsFor::Person->age
1..18
ok 1 - Person->can('age')
ok 2 - Our default person is more than one hundred years old
#
# TestsFor::Person->constructor
ok 3 - Person->can('new')
ok 4 - Creating a Person without proper attributes should fail
```

```
ok 5 - The object isa Person
#
# TestsFor::Person->name
ok 6 - Person->can('name')
ok 7 - name() should return the full name
ok 8 - ... and it should be correct if we have a title
#
# TestsFor::Customer->age
ok 9 - Customer->can('age')
ok 10 - Our default person is more than one hundred years old
#
# TestsFor::Customer->constructor
ok 11 - Customer->can('new')
ok 12 - Creating a Customer without proper attributes should fail
ok 13 - The object isa Customer
#
# TestsFor::Customer->mininum_age
ok 14 - Trying to create a customer younger than 18 should fail
ok 15 - Trying to create a customer older than 18 should succeed
#
# TestsFor::Customer->name
ok 16 - Customer->can('name')
ok 17 - name() should return the full name
ok 18 - ... and it should be correct if we have a title
ok
All tests successful.
Files=1, Tests=18,  1 wallclock secs
Result: PASS
```

> **WARNING** Sometimes when you run `Test::Class` tests, you get a warning like the following:
>
> ```
> t/lib/TestsFor/Customer.pm .. Invalid CODE attribute:
>   Tests(startup) at
> t/lib/TestsFor/Customer.pm line 12.
> BEGIN failed--compilation aborted at t/lib/TestsFor/Customer.pm
>   line 12.
> t/lib/TestsFor/Customer.pm .. Dubious, test returned 255
> No subtests run
> ```
>
> This usually means that you have forgotten to tell Perl (or `prove`) where to find the test classes. Make sure that you have supplied the appropriate `-It/lib` switch to `prove`. If you run `prove t/test_class.t` and it uses `Test::Class::Load`, this issue will probably not happen.

Whoa! What just happened here? Your `Person` class had only eight tests, and you added only two tests! That means ten tests, right?

Nope.

`Test::Class` knows that `TestsFor::Customer` inherited `TestsFor::Person`. Because of the Liskov Substitution Principle (mentioned in Chapter 12), you know that you should use a subclass in any place you can use a parent class. Thus, when you run the tests for `TestsFor::Customer`, `Test::Class` also runs all the tests you inherit from `TestsFor::Person`, but because of your `INIT` block in the `TestsFor` base class, it also ran the tests for `TestsFor::Person`.

This means that `TestsFor::Person` ran its eight tests, and `TestsFor::Customer` ran its two tests, plus the eight tests it inherited from `TestsFor::Person`. That makes 18 tests in total, even though you've only written 10 tests.

That is why I provided this method:

```
sub class_to_test { 'Person' }
```

Look at the `constructor()` test method again to understand why `TestsFor::Customer` overrode the `TestsFor::Person::class_to_test` method:

```
sub constructor : Tests(3) {
    my $test = shift;
    my $class = $test->class_to_test;
    can_ok $class, 'new';
    throws_ok { $class->new }
    qr/Attribute.*required/,
      "Creating a $class without proper attributes should fail";
    my $person = $class->new(
        given_name  => 'Charles',
        family_name => 'Drew',
        birthdate   => '1904-06-03',
    );
    isa_ok $person, $class;
}
```

Because you now fetch the class to test from a method you can override, that test method outputs the following:

```
# TestsFor::Customer->constructor
ok 11 - Customer->can('new')
ok 12 - Creating a Customer without proper attributes should fail
ok 13 - The object isa Customer
```

If you did not override the class name, you would have had this test out:

```
# TestsFor::Customer->constructor
ok 11 - Person->can('new')
ok 12 - Creating a Person without proper attributes should fail
ok 13 - The object isa Person
```

Clearly that would not be the test you would want. By allowing the code to override the name of the class, you allow your subclasses to use the parent class tests and ensure that your behavior did not change in the subclass.

At this point, you might wonder why your author showed you this:

```
$ prove -lv -It/lib t/lib/TestsFor/Customer.pm
```

Because of the INIT block in your subclass, that causes all tests to run for all loaded classes, not just TestsFor::Customer. However, you can do this with the Person class. (Leave off the -v so that the test output is not so verbose.)

```
$ prove -lv -It/lib t/lib/TestsFor/Person.pm
t/lib/TestsFor/Person.pm .. ok
All tests successful.
Files=1, Tests=8,  1 wallclock secs
Result: PASS
```

This shows that you have run only eight tests, and not the full 18. That's because you loaded TestsFor::Person and not TestsFor::Customer. If you have a large set of test classes, running different test classes like this can make it easier to run subsets of your tests and verify they work. Later, when you finish coding, you can rerun the full test suite with prove -l t/.

Using Test Control Methods

So far you might be getting an inkling of the power of Test::Class, but you're going to start feeding it steroids now and not only see you powerful it can be, but also how powerful object-oriented programming can be (two chapters for the price of one).

Remember the original TestsFor base class:

```
package TestsFor;
use Test::Most;
use base 'Test::Class';
INIT { Test::Class->runtests }
sub startup  : Tests(startup)  {}
sub setup    : Tests(setup)    {}
sub teardown : Tests(teardown) {}
sub shutdown : Tests(shutdown) {}
⊥;
```

You have startup, setup, teardown, and shutdown methods. Each of them has a corresponding :Tests(methodname) attribute. These are test control methods. These are run at the beginning and end of every class, or at the beginning and end of every test method, as shown in Table 14-1.

TABLE 14-1: Test Control Methods

METHOD	WHEN IT'S RUN
startup	Before every test class starts
setup	Before every test method start
teardown	After every test method ends
shutdown	After every test class ends

Now rewrite your `TestsFor` class. Use the `startup` method to load the class you want to test before each test class runs. Also set the class name in `class_to_test()`. Use multiple inheritance to provide class data here, but see `Test::Class::Most` to see a better way to do this:

```
package TestsFor;
use Test::Most;
use base qw(Test::Class Class::Data::Inheritable);
INIT {
    __PACKAGE__->mk_classdata('class_to_test');
    Test::Class->runtests;
}
sub startup : Tests(startup) {
    my $test  = shift;
    my $class = ref $test;
    $class =~ s/^TestsFor:://;
    eval "use $class";
    die $@ if $@;
    $test->class_to_test($class);
}
sub setup    : Tests(setup)    {}
sub teardown : Tests(teardown) {}
sub shutdown : Tests(shutdown) {}
1;
```

You inherited from both `Test::Class` and `Class::Data::Inheritable`. The `INIT` block now creates a class data method before running the tests. Use the `startup` method to do some magic! First, the `$test` invocant passed to the `startup` method is a reference, so use the `ref` function to determine the class name. Then use a substitution to strip off the `TestsFor::` prefix:

```
$class =~ s/^TestsFor:://;
```

That's when it gets interesting. Use `eval` to load the class and, if it succeeds, use `$test->class_to_test($class)` to set the class name on a per class basis!

```
eval "use $class";
die $@ if $@;
$test->class_to_test($class);
```

You can now edit `TestsFor::Person` and `TestsFor::Customer` and delete the use `Person` or use `Customer` lines, along with the `class_to_test()` methods. This is now automatically done for you!

Later, when you write `TestsFor::Order::Item`, the `Order::Item` class automatically loads without asking, and `class_to_test()` returns `Order::Item`, as you would expect. This little trick makes it much easier to build test classes on-the-fly.

You might also remember this method:

```
sub default_person {
    my $test = shift;
    return $test->class_to_test->new(
        given_name  => 'Charles',
```

```
            family_name => 'Drew',
            birthdate   => '1904-06-03',
        );
    }
```

Every time you call that method, the default person is re-created. If you want, you could set this in the setup method prior to every test. Make sure to do this in your TestsFor::Person class and not your TestsFor class because other test classes are likely to inherit from TestsFor and won't necessarily need a default Person object.

By doing this, your TestsFor::Person class now looks like this:

```
package TestsFor::Person;
use Test::Most;
use base 'TestsFor';
sub startup : Tests(startup) {
    my $test = shift;
    $test->SUPER::startup;
    my $class = ref $test;
    $class->mk_classdata('default_person');
}
sub setup : Tests(setup) {
    my $test = shift;
    $test->SUPER::setup;
    $test->default_person(
        $test->class_to_test->new(
            given_name  => 'Charles',
            family_name => 'Drew',
            birthdate   => '1904-06-03',
        )
    );
}
sub constructor : Tests(3) {
    # constructor tests
}
sub name : Tests(3) {
    # name tests
}
sub age : Tests(2) {
    # age tests
}
1;
```

You didn't use Person (because you no longer need to) and the class_to_test() method returns the correct class.

Calling Parent Test Control Methods

Now look at that startup method you created for TestsFor::Person:

```
sub startup : Tests(startup) {
    my $test = shift;
    $test->SUPER::startup;
```

```
    my $class = ref $test;
    $class->mk_classdata('default_person');
}
```

After you shift off the invocant ($test) but before you create the default_person() class data method, call $test->SUPER::startup. Why? Because you want to ensure that your TestsFor::startup method has been called and loaded your test class and set the class_to_test() method. Generally, when you call setup and startup methods, there may be a parent method available, and you should call them first to ensure that your test class has everything it needs to run.

In fact, The setup() method calls $self->SUPER::setup even though you have an empty setup method in your base class. Later, you may find that you need your parent classes to have some code in the setup method and you want to ensure that your subclasses do not mysteriously break by forgetting to call this important code.

The teardown and shutdown test control methods are not called as often, but they're used for things like cleaning up temp files or perhaps closing a database connection. When you use them, make sure to call the SUPER:: method after you have done your cleanup (unless you have a good reason not to). The reason for this is because if you call the parent teardown or shutdown method before you're cleaning up in the subclass method, it's entirely possible that the database handle you needed has been destroyed, or some other critical bit of your test class state is gone. By running your teardown or shutdown code first and then calling the parent method, you can make sure you haven't destroyed anything you need until nothing else needs it.

Given what I've explained, for each test control method you think you need, the methods should look like this:

```
# startup and setup call parent methods before their code
sub startup : Tests(startup) {
    my $test = shift;
    $test->SUPER::startup;
    # startup up code here
}
sub setup : Tests(setup) {
    my $test = shift;
    $test->SUPER::setup;
    # setup up code here
}
# teardown and shutdown call parent methods after their code
sub teardown : Tests(teardown) {
    my $test = shift;
    # teardown up code here
    $test->SUPER::teardown;
}
sub shutdown : Tests(shutdown) {
    # shutdown up code here
    $test->SUPER::shutdown;
}
```

This introduction to Test::Class only skims the surface of what you can do. The author recommends his five-part online tutorial on Test::Class at http://www.modernperlbooks .com/mt/2009/03/organizing-test-suites-with-testclass.html.

TRY IT OUT   Write Tests for the TV::Episode Class

You may recall the `TV::Episode` class from Chapter 13. This Try It Out shows you how to write some
tests for it using `Test::Class` and assumes that you are already using your `TestsFor` class. All the code
for this Try It Out is in code file `lib/TV/Episode.pm`.

1.   Type in the following program and save it as `lib/TV/Episode.pm` (assuming you didn't do that
for Chapter 13):

```perl
package TV::Episode;
use Moose;
use MooseX::StrictConstructor;
use Moose::Util::TypeConstraints;
use namespace::autoclean;
use Carp 'croak';
our $VERSION = '0.01';
subtype 'IntPositive',
        as    'Int',
        where { $_ > 0 };
has 'series'         => ( is => 'ro', isa => 'Str',
  required => 1 );
has 'director'       => ( is => 'ro', isa => 'Str',
  required => 1 );
has 'title'          => ( is => 'ro', isa => 'Str',
  required => 1 );
has 'season'         => ( is => 'ro', isa => 'IntPositive',
  required => 1 );
has 'episode_number' => ( is => 'ro', isa => 'IntPositive',
  required => 1 );
has 'genre'          => (
    is       => 'ro',
    isa      => enum(qw(comedy drama documentary awesome)),
    required => 1
);
sub as_string {
    my $self = shift;
    my @attributes = map { $_->name }
      $self->meta->get_all_attributes;
    my $as_string = '';
    foreach my $attribute (@attributes) {
        $as_string .= sprintf "%-14s - %s\n", ucfirst($attribute),
          $self->$attribute;
    }
    return $as_string;
}
__PACKAGE__->meta->make_immutable;
1;
```

2.   Type in the following program, and save it as `t/lib/TestsFor/TV/Episode.pm`. (Create the
`t/lib/TestsFor/TV` directory first.)

```perl
package TestsFor::TV::Episode;
use Test::Most;
use base 'TestsFor';
sub attributes : Tests(14) {
```

```
    my $test                = shift;
    my %default_attributes = (
        series          => 'Firefly',
        director        => 'Marita Grabiak',
        title           => 'Jaynestown',
        genre           => 'awesome',
        season          => 1,
        episode_number  => 7,
    );
    my $class   = $test->class_to_test;
    my $episode = $class->new(%default_attributes);
    while (my ($attribute, $value) = each %default_attributes) {
        can_ok $episode, $attribute;
        is $episode->$attribute, $value,
          "The value for '$attribute' should be correct";
    }
    my %attributes = %default_attributes;   # copy 'em
    foreach my $attribute (qw/season episode_number/) {
        $attributes{$attribute} = 0;
        throws_ok { $class->new(%attributes) }
        qr/\Q($attribute) does not pass the type constraint/,
          "Setting $attribute to less than zero should fail";
    }
}
1;
```

3. Run the program with `prove -lv t/lib t/lib/TestsFor/TV/Episode.pm`. You should see the following output:

```
$ prove -lv -It/lib t/lib/TestsFor/TV/Episode.pm
t/lib/TestsFor/TV/Episode.pm .. #
# TestsFor::TV::Episode->attributes
1..14
ok 1 - TV::Episode->can('episode_number')
ok 2 - The value for 'episode_number' should be correct
ok 3 - TV::Episode->can('title')
ok 4 - The value for 'title' should be correct
ok 5 - TV::Episode->can('season')
ok 6 - The value for 'season' should be correct
ok 7 - TV::Episode->can('genre')
ok 8 - The value for 'genre' should be correct
ok 9 - TV::Episode->can('director')
ok 10 - The value for 'director' should be correct
ok 11 - TV::Episode->can('series')
ok 12 - The value for 'series' should be correct
ok 13 - Setting the season to a value less than zero should fail
ok 14 - Setting episode_number to less than zero should fail
ok
All tests successful.
Files=1, Tests=14,  1 wallclock secs
Result: PASS
```

4. Run the full test suite in nonverbose mode (leaving off the -v switch to prove) with `prove t/`. If you've worked through all the examples in this chapter, it should run tests for `t/testit.t`, `t/query.t`, and `t/test_classes.t`. The output should resemble the following:

```
$ prove t
t/query.t ........ ok
t/test_classes.t .. ok
t/testit.t ....... ok
All tests successful.
Files=3, Tests=43,  1 wallclock secs
Result: PASS
```

How It Works

At this point you've gone from the point of writing a few individual tests to having a full test suite (admittedly for a grab bag of unrelated modules).

You already know what `TV::Episode` does from Chapter 13, and `t/lib/TestsFor/TV/Episode.pm` are straightforward — there's nothing new there. Because you used the `TestsFor` base class you created earlier in this chapter, you didn't even need to have an explicit use `TV::Episode` line. The base class does that for you and sets the `$test->class_to_test` value.

This command is interesting:

```
$ prove -lv t/lib t/lib/TestsFor/TV/Episode.pm
```

Use the `-It/lib` switch to tell `prove` where the test classes are loaded; the `-l` tells it where the ordinary classes are loaded (`-l` is the same thing is `-Ilib/`); and then you pass `t/lib/TestsFor/TV/Episode.pm` as the argument to `prove`.

When you do that, you run only the 14 tests in that class. You could have run this:

```
$ prove -l t/test_classes.t
t/test_classes.t .. ok
All tests successful.
Files=1, Tests=32,  3 wallclock secs
Rcsult: PASS
```

And that would have run all your test classes without the other `t/*.t` tests. Instead, you ran `prove -l t/` to run the full test suite. Each test program is run, in alphabetical order, until a total of all 43 tests are run. The `prove` utility makes it easy to run and manage tests.

SUMMARY

In this chapter, you learned the basics of writing tests in Perl. You learned about the standard `Test::More` module and how to use other testing modules such as `Test::Differences`, `Test::Exception`, and `Test::Most`. You learned how to catch exceptions in testing with `eval` and `throws_ok` and how to test for warnings with `Test::Warn`.

You also learned quite a bit about advanced usage of Test::Class, an excellent module that is sadly underused in Perl testing. Many of the techniques demonstrated in this chapter are fairly new to many Perl developers (particularly the tricks about auto-loading classes in your startup method) and after you master them, you'll have fairly advanced testing skills.

EXERCISES

1. Earlier you had a unique() function:

```
sub unique {
    my @array = @_;
    my %hash  = map { $_ => 1 } @array;
    return keys %hash;
}
```

Unfortunately, you wrapped the test in a TODO: block because it doesn't do exactly what you want it to do:

```
TODO: {
    local $TODO = 'Figure out how to avoid random order';
    my @have = unique( 2, 3, 5, 4, 3, 5, 7 );
    my @want = ( 2, 3, 5, 4, 7 );
    is_deeply \@have, \@want,
        'unique() should return unique() elements in order';
}
```

Study the test and rewrite the unique() function to make the test pass. Remove the TODO: block around the test.

2. Usually when you have a failing test, the code is wrong and not the test. Take the example from the first exercise and assume that the code is correct and the test is wrong. How might you fix it?

3. The following test fails. Make it pass.

```
use Test::Most;
use Carp 'croak';
sub reciprocal {
    my $number = shift;
    unless ($number) {
        croak("Illegal division by zero");
    }
    return 1 / $number;
}
throws_ok { reciprocal([]) }
  qr/Argument to reciprocal\(\) must be a number/,
  'Passing non-numbers to reciprocal() should fail';
diag reciprocal([]);
done_testing;
```

4. Extra credit: In the second Try It Out for this chapter, you created a test class for the `TV::Episode` class from Chapter 13. Create a test class for `TV::Episode::Broadcast`. Make sure it inherits from `TestsFor::TV::Episode`.

```
package TV::Episode::Broadcast;
    use Moose;
    use namespace::autoclean;
    extends 'TV::Episode';
    has broadcast_date => ( is => 'ro', isa => 'DateTime', required => 1 );
    __PACKAGE__->meta->make_immutable;
    1;
```

You won't actually need to write any tests for this class if you inherit properly. Because your attributes test method will have two extra tests (one for whether `$broadcast->can ('broadcast_date')` and another for whether it returns the correct value), you can use the following special syntax to make that work:

```
sub attributes : Tests(+2) {
    my $test = shift;
    $test->SUPER::attributes;
}
```

That allows you to override the original test method and declare that there are two extra tests (`Tests(+2)`).

Hint: To do this properly, you need to make a small change to `TestsFor::TV::Episode`.

▶ **WHAT YOU LEARNED IN THIS CHAPTER**

TOPIC	DESCRIPTION
Testing	The way you ensure your code does what you want it to do.
`Test::More`	The most popular test module for Perl.
`ok()`	Tests if a value is true.
`is()`	Tests if one scalar matches another scalar.
`like()`	Tests if a scalar matches a regular expression.
`is_deeply()`	Tests if one reference contains the same value as another reference.
`SKIP`	Skips tests that cannot be run.
`TODO`	Marks tests as expected failures.
`Test::Differences`	Produces a diff of data structures that don't match.
`Test::Exception`	Easily tests exceptions.
`Test::Warn`	Tests for warnings in your code.
`Test::Most`	Bundles the most common testing functions into one module.
`Test::Class`	Used to write object-oriented tests.

15

The Interwebs

WHAT YOU WILL LEARN IN THIS CHAPTER:

➤ Understanding the basics of the HTTP, including web servers, web forms, cookies and security issues

➤ Understanding a web client's role

WROX.COM CODE DOWNLOAD FOR THIS CHAPTER

The wrox.com code downloads for this chapter are found at `http://www.wrox.com/remtitle.cgi?isbn=1118013840` on the Download Code tab. The code for this chapter is divided into the following major examples:

➤ `app.psgi` and `anne_frank_stamp.jpg`

➤ `character.psgi`

➤ `example_15_1_google_directions.pl`

➤ `listing_15_1_get_links.pl`

➤ `listing_15_2_get_comments.pl`

➤ `listing_15_3_post_character.pl`

➤ `params.psgi`

➤ `templates/character.tt`

➤ `templates/character_display.tt`

Ah, Perl, the duct tape of the Internet. Duct tape has a reputation for being an amazing, ad hoc supertool for fixing things in a hurry, even as a combat dressing. Perl is the same way. Need something done on the web quickly? Reach for Perl!

This chapter pays particular attention to the *HyperText Transfer Protocol* (*HTTP*). When you view a web page in your browser, it was probably sent to you via HTTP (or HTTPS, the encrypted version of HTTP). HTTP is nothing more than text, and Perl excels at text manipulation. Your author believes you need a foundation of how HTTP flows between systems to effectively program at a higher level.

The first part of this chapter is about responding as a server. It will not be "Here's how to write a web application"; though you create some simple ones, but rather, "Here are some concepts you need to know." Chapter 19 briefly looks at Dancer, (http://perldancer.org/) one of Perl's easiest-to-use frameworks for quickly building web applications.

The next part of the chapter is writing client software: accessing websites, finding links on web pages, using web APIs, and so on. Again, it's not going to be a full "Here's all you wanted to know about web clients," but it can get you off to a great web automation beginning.

> **NOTE** *This chapter assumes that you know a little bit about creating a web page with HTML (the HyperText Markup Language). If you don't, check out* http://www.w3schools.com/html/ *to learn the basics of HTML. However, while they're easy to use, you should also read* http://w3fools.com/ *to understand some of the issues with w3schools.*

A BRIEF INTRODUCTION TO HTTP

HTTP is a client-server protocol. That means that a client, such as a web browser or some software you write, makes a request to a server via HTTP and the server responds with, well, something. It might be a static web page, a page generated on-the-fly, or HTTP responses telling you 404 Page Not Found, the dreaded 500 Server Error, or a 301 Moved Permanently (a redirect).

To understand how the web works, you can use a simple telnet client, a standard tool available on all major operating systems (http://en.wikipedia.org/wiki/Telnet). A simple telnet session might look like this:

```
% telnet example.com 80
Trying 192.0.43.10...
Connected to example.com.
Escape character is '^]'.
HEAD /
HTTP/1.0 302 Found
Location: http://www.iana.org/domains/example/
Server: BigIP
Connection: close
Content-Length: 0
Connection closed by foreign host.
```

> **NOTE** You can use `telnet` to try to connect to any server on the Internet, but it often fails. Historically, there have been a number of security issues surrounding the `telnet` protocol and, as a result, many servers disable `telnet` access.
>
> However, you can use `telnet` and impersonate web, mail, and other clients if you know the rules of the protocol. You can do a bit of that to learn how web clients and servers communicate.

When you `telnet` to a server, you specify the host (`example.com` in this case) and the port (80, the standard HTTP port):

```
% telnet example.com 80
And then you'll see a response similar to:
Trying 192.0.43.10...
Connected to example.com.
Escape character is '^]'.
```

The *escape character*, in this case, is CTRL-] (typing the control and right square bracket at the same time). That causes you to enter a command mode that you can CTRL-C out of.

Then issue a HEAD request against the root of the server:

```
HEAD /
```

When you "surf" to a web page in your browser by clicking a link such as `http://www.example.com/some/page/`, behind the scenes your browser is probably issuing a GET request to that server:

```
GET /some/page
```

That returns a set of headers giving information about the resource you have connected to, separated by two newlines, and the body of the request (also known as the entity-body), often a web page written in HTML.

When you issue a HEAD request, you're saying "I only want the headers for this resource, not the body." In this case, that's great because there is no body available for this request (the Content-Length is 0):

```
HTTP/1.0 302 Found
Location: http://www.iana.org/domains/example/
Server: BigIP
Connection: close
Content-Length: 0
```

The first line is the HTTP protocol version, followed by the HTTP numeric status code, followed by a human readable description.

Next is a list of HTTP header fields. Each consists of a field name, followed by a colon, followed by the value of that field name. In this case, you see that / at www.example.com can actually be found at `http://www.iana.org/domains/example/`. If you go to `www.example.com` in your browser, when it sees the `302 Found`, it redirects you to `http://www.iana.org/domains/example/`.

That's the basics of the HTTP protocol. When you understand it, it's quite simple — plus, because it's plain text, it's easy to view for debugging.

Plack

To start with web development and Perl, you can use Plack (`http://plackperl.org/`). You won't be doing anything too complicated, but you can see the basics of how it works. You can install Plack with your favorite CPAN client:

```
$ cpan PSGI Plack
```

> **NOTE** When installing Plack, you don't actually need to install PSGI because it is only the specification of the PSGI interface. However, `perldoc PSGI` can often help you better understand how Plack works.
>
> Also, if you do serious web development with Plack, it's recommended that you install `Task::Plack`. That installs many modules that are very helpful when developing Plack applications.
>
> The Plack examples given in this chapter are bare-bones without full support of features you find in most applications. For example, the `telnet` and HEAD shown earlier won't work with your Plack app.

Plack and PSGI were created by Tatsuhiko Miyagawa, an extremely talented and prolific programmer. PSGI is a specification of how a web server can talk to a web application. It is modeled after WSGI, a web server/application interface originally developed for the Python language and Ruby's Rack implementation. Plack is an implementation of the PSGI specification.

Prior to PSGI, many companies had to choose between different web servers that accept HTTP requests and web applications that might process those requests. When the server receives a request that should be handled by an application, it needed to know how to talk to that application, and the application needed to know how to respond.

PSGI changes the game tremendously. It sits between the web server and the web application, guaranteeing a standard web interface. As long as both your web server and web application "speak" PSGI (today, most popular options all understand PSGI), you can switch to different servers or applications without needing to reconfigure how they talk to one another. This is one of many examples of why Perl is duct tape in the web world.

Hello, World!

Be aware that Plack is actually a set of building blocks for web applications and is not intended to be used by application developers directly. However, it's easy to use and a great compromise between showing how web applications work and how HTTP operates.

Create a `chapter15/` directory, change into it, and save the following as `app.psgi`:

```
my $app = sub {
    return [
        200,
        [ 'Content-Type' => 'text/plain' ],
        ['Hello World'],
    ];
};
```

A Plack application is a code reference. It's expected to return an array reference with three values:

➤   HTTP status code

➤   Array reference of HTTP headers

➤   "Body" of the HTTP request

After you save the `app.psgi`, run `plackup` (which is installed when you install Plack):

```
$ plackup
HTTP::Server::PSGI: Accepting connections at http://0:5000/
```

> **NOTE** By default, `plackup` looks for an `app.psgi` file. However, you can name this anything you want. To use a file with a name that makes more sense to you, pass that as an argument to `plackup`:
>
> ```
> $ plackup hello.psgi
> ```
>
> See `perldoc plackup` for more information.

Congratulations! You now have a web server running on your computer.

When you run `plackup`, it starts a web server for you. You can configure it to use different web servers, but use the default `HTTP::Server::PSGI` web server installed with Plack.

The `plackup` command appears to hang, but that's because it is waiting for requests. Open your favorite browser and go to `http://localhost:5000/`. You should see the text `Hello World` displayed. After you see the page, look at your terminal window that `plackup` runs in. You see something like this (reformatted for the book, this is all on two lines):

```
HTTP::Server::PSGI: Accepting connections at http://0:5000/
127.0.0.1 - - [11/Apr/2012:11:42:13 +0200] "GET / HTTP/1.1" 200 11 "-"
"Mozilla/5.0 (Macintosh; Intel Mac OS X 10_7_3) AppleWebKit/535.19
(KHTML,like Gecko) Chrome/18.0.1025.151 Safari/535.19"
```

The first line tells you that `HTTP::Server::PSGI` is listening on port 5000.

> **NOTE** *When talking about software, a port is merely a software or process-specific way to wave its little virtual hands and say "Yoo hoo! I'm over here!" Any software or process communicating with that port needs to understand the protocol that port listens on. For the default 5000 port for* plackup, *that protocol is HTTP.*

The second line shows a request from IP address 127.0.0.1 (your browser) came in at a particular time and issued an HTTP GET / request. It also contains information about the response code (200 OK in this case) and the type of client that attempted to connect.

With this simple web application, connecting to any path, such as http://localhost:5000/asdf/ asdf, displays Hello World because that's all you've programmed it to do. Now quickly expand this to take a look at your environment. Stop plackup (CTRL-C) and edit your app.psgi to look like this:

```
use strict;
use warnings;

use Data::Dumper;

$Data::Dumper::Indent   = 1;
$Data::Dumper::Sortkeys = 1;
$Data::Dumper::Terse    = 1;

my $app = sub {
    my $environment = Dumper( \%ENV );
    return [
        200,
        [ 'Content-Type' => 'text/plain' ],
        [ "Hello World\n", $environment ],
    ];
};
```

Restart plackup and refresh your browser page with http://localhost:5000/. You should now see Hello World, followed by a hash listing all your environment variables. Here is an edited version of what your author's browser shows:

```
Hello World
{
    'EDITOR'        => '/usr/bin/vim',
    'GIT_USER'      => 'ovid',
    'HISTFILESIZE'  => '1000000000',
    'HISTSIZE'      => '1000000',
    'LC_CTYPE'      => 'UTF-8',
    'LOGNAME'       => 'ovid',
    'PLACK_ENV'     => 'development',
    'PWD'           => '/Users/ovid/beginning_perl/book/chapter15',
    'SHELL'         => '/bin/bash',
    'TERM'          => 'xterm-256color',
    'TERM_PROGRAM'  => 'iTerm.app',
}
```

Now rewrite your `app.psgi` again to get a little closer to a real-world example using code files `app.psgi`. This time add an image (`anne_frank_stamp.jpg`). Save the following in your `app.psgi` file:

```perl
use strict;
use warnings;

my $app = sub {
    my $env = shift;
    if ( $env->{PATH_INFO} eq '/anne_frank_stamp.jpg' ) {
        open my $fh, "<:raw", "anne_frank_stamp.jpg" or die $!;
        return [ 200, [ 'Content-Type' => 'image/jpeg' ], $fh ];
    }
    elsif ( $env->{PATH_INFO} eq '/' ) {
        return [
          200,
          [ 'Content-Type' => 'text/html' ],
          [ get_index() ]
        ];
    }
    else {
        return [
          404,
          [ 'Content-Type' => 'text/html' ],
          ['404 Not Found']
        ];
    }
};

sub get_index {
    return <<'END';
<html>
  <head><title>Sample page</title></head>
  <body>
    <p>Anne Frank was a young lady living in Amsterdam, hiding
    from the Nazis.</p>
    <p>Everyone should read her diaries.</p>
    <img src="/anne_frank_stamp.jpg"/>
  </body>
</html>
END
}
```

This program loads an image of the German Anne Frank stamp. It is in the public domain and is available at `http://commons.wikimedia.org/wiki/File:Anne_Frank_stamp.jpg`. Download this image, save as `anne_frank_stamp.jpg`, and save it in the same directory as your `app.psgi` file.

> **NOTE** *While you're debugging, be aware that you may see more requests in the* `plackup` *terminal output than you expect. For example, many browsers automatically request something called a* `/favicon.ico`. *If found, it's rendered as the website icon, usually in the URL bar and often on bookmarks.*

Restart `plackup` and go to `http://localhost:5000/`. You should see a web page similar to Figure 15-1.

FIGURE 15-1

This is all normal, but look at the opening lines of the `$app` subroutine reference:

```
my $env = shift;
if ( $env->{PATH_INFO} eq '/anne_frank_stamp.jpg' ) {
    open my $fh, "<:raw", "anne_frank_stamp.jpg" or die $!;
    return [ 200, [ 'Content-Type' => 'image/jpeg' ], $fh ];
}
```

The Plack subroutine reference is passed a single `$env` hashref argument, documented in `perldoc` `PSGI`. The `PATH_INFO` key points to the currently requested path. In this case, because you ask for the Anne Frank image, you use the `open` builtin to create a filehandle, return `image/jpeg` as the content type, and the filehandle is returned as the content of the request. Plack knows how to send that image back to your client.

When you navigate to `http://localhost:5000/` in your browser, the following line of code executes:

```
return [ 200, [ 'Content-Type' => 'text/html' ], [ get_index() ] ];
```

And that returns the HTML from the `get_index()` function:

```
sub get_index {
    return <<'END';
<html>
  <head><title>Sample page</title></head>
  <body>
    <p>Anne Frank was a young lady living in Amsterdam, hiding
    from the Nazis.</p>
    <p>Everyone should read her diaries.</p>
    <img src="/anne_frank_stamp.jpg"/>
  </body>
</html>
END
```

In that HTML is an `img` tag:

```
<img src="/anne_frank_stamp.jpg"/>
```

That tag causes the browser to issue GET `/anne_frank_stamp.jpg` to your Plack server. The `app.psgi` sees that path and returns the image.

In other words, you went to the `http://localhost:5000/` URL in your browser, but your browser actually makes two requests to the server. For most web pages on the Internet, a single page can generate many more requests to get everything the page needs to render properly, including the HTML, JavaScript, CSS, multiple images, Flash, and many other potential requests. It actually can seem quite complicated, as you can see from the previous example — much of this is handled for you and it's not as hard as it seems.

Now rewrite `app.psgi` one more time before moving to the next section:

```
use strict;
use warnings;
use Plack::Builder;
builder {

    mount '/anne_frank_stamp.jpg' => sub {
        open my $fh, "<:raw", "anne_frank_stamp.jpg" or die $!;
        return [ 200, [ 'Content-Type' => 'image/jpeg' ], $fh ];
    };

    mount '/' => sub {
        my $env = shift;
        return $env->{PATH_INFO} eq '/'
          ? [200,['Content-Type' => 'text/html'],[get_index()]]
          : [404,['Content-Type' => 'text/html'],['404 Not Found']];
    };
};
sub get_index {
    return <<'END';
<html>
  <head><title>Sample page</title></head>
  <body>
```

```
        <p>Anne Frank was a young lady living in Amsterdam, hiding
        from the Nazis.</p>
        <p>Everyone should read her diaries.</p>
        <img src="/anne_frank_stamp.jpg"/>
    </body>
</html>
END
}
```

`Plack::Builder` is a module that provides a *domain-specific language* (DSL) to make writing Plack applications a little bit easier. This `app.psgi` does the same thing as your last `app.psgi`, but it does so with the `builder` and `mount` commands. The `builder` function says, "I'm going to take the following code reference and use this to build the app."

The `mount` function allows you to map a particular path to a particular section of code. This is much easier than managing long `if/else/elsif` blocks. You do have a `?:` ternary operator in the `/` path, but that's to show only that you can still use this if needed.

The mount command is implemented with `Plack::App::URLMap` and t does not allow "dynamic" mappings. Thus, there's no way to say "Everything that is not mapped is a `404`." Web frameworks such as Dancer, Catalyst, and Mojolicious give you much more flexibility here, but this is enough to do what you need.

Handling Parameters

Many times you see a URL like this:

```
http://www.example.com/?name=john&color=blue&color=red
```

The question mark in a URL indicates the beginning of a query string. A query string is defined in RFC 3986 (`http://www.ietf.org/rfc/rfc3986.txt`). It's a collection of name/value pairs. Each name and value is separated by an equals (=) sign, and each pair is separated by an ampersand (&) or a semicolon (;).The preceding example has two parameters, `name` and `color`. The `name` has one value, `john`, and `color` has two values, `blue` and `red`. You can use `Plack::Request` to handle query strings.

Save the following code file as `params.psgi`:

```
use strict;
use warnings;

use Plack::Builder;
use Plack::Request;

builder {

    mount '/' => sub {
        my $env     = shift;
        my $request = Plack::Request->new($env);
        my @params  = sort $request->param;
        my $body    = '';
```

```
        foreach my $param (@params) {
            my $values = join ',' => $request->param($param);
            $body .= "$param=$values\n";
        }
        $body ||= "No params found";
        return [ 200, [ 'Content-Type' => 'text/plain' ], [$body] ];
    };

};
```

Open a separate terminal window and run the following command:

```
plackup -r params.psgi
```

> **NOTE** Use -r this time because this can make the web server restart every time you change params.psgi. You'll change it a few times, so this makes it easier to use when developing code. If you get an error similar to Could Not Connect, that probably means you have a syntax error in your code. Go back to your plackup terminal window and look for the error message.

By using -r with plackup, you can have plackup running in one terminal window while you continue to develop in another terminal window.

When you request http://localhost:5000/ in your browser, it should display:

```
No params found
```

However, request http://localhost:5000/?name=john;color=red;color=blue and you should see this in your browser window:

```
color=red,blue
name=john
```

By now, you may be tired of returning a three-element array reference because it can be a bit harder to read:

```
return [ 200, [ 'Content-Type' => 'text/plain' ], [$body] ];
```

You can replace that return statement with a response object, which is much easier to read:

```
my $response = $request->new_response(200);
$response->content_type('text/plain');
$response->content($body);
return $response->finalize;
```

The $response->finalize handles building and returning that final array reference for you.

Templates

Until now, you included your HTML in your code. Although that might be fine for small application, it can be hard to maintain for larger applications, particularly as your code becomes a mess of Perl, HTML, plain text, and SQL (see Chapter 16).

As a general rule, you want the different logical sections of your programs separated. One common way to do this is to use the *Model-View-Controller* pattern, more commonly referred to as MVC. There are a few variants of MVC, but we'll cover a popular one for the web.

A full-blown MVC system isn't shown here, but Table 15-1 describes the basic components.

TABLE 15-1: MVC System Basic Components

COMPONENT	ROLE
Model	Oversees the management of the business logic and data
View	The part the client sees (a web page, in this case)
Controller	Receives data from a view, passes it to the model, and returns the results to a view (possibly the same one)

So if someone visits your web page, the *view*, enters a number on a form, and that data gets sent to a *controller* (the mount points, in your PSGI example). The controller receives the data and passes it to the correct *model* (the subreferences in your examples) and returns the results to a view.

In Plack, there's not a clean separation of these concepts, but you can fake it well enough to get an idea of what's going on, so create small templates with `Template::Tiny`.

`Template::Tiny` is a small templating engine written by Adam Kennedy, which is designed to be minimal, fast, and appropriate for small applications. In short, it's what you need. Later, you'll want to use the Template Toolkit module (the package name of the module is `Template`), `Text::Xslate`, or other, more robust, templating modules than `Template::Tiny`.

First, in the same directory as your `app.psgi` and your `params.psgi` files, create a `templates` directory. In that directory, create a file named `params.tt` that contains the following:

```
<html>
  <head><title>Parameters</title></head>
  <body>
[% IF have_params %]
    <p>Our list of params:</p>
    <table rules="all">
      <tr><th>Name</th><th>Value</th></tr>
  [% FOREACH param IN params %]
      <tr><td>[% param.name %]</td><td>[% param.value %]</td></tr>
  [% END %]
    </table>
[% ELSE %]
```

```
        <p><strong>No params supplied!</strong></p>
    [% END %]
      </body>
    </html>
```

At this point, your directory structure (assuming you've been typing in all the examples), should look like this:

```
./
|--anne_frank_stamp.jpg
|--app.psgi
|--params.psgi
|   templates/
|   |--params.tt
```

This HTML code with the strange syntax is `Template::Tiny` syntax, which actually doesn't know anything about HTML. It does nothing except handle loops, if/else/unless statements, and variable interpolation. All `Template::Tiny` commands are wrapped in [% %] brackets.

Consider the following hash reference:

```
{
    have_params => 1,
    params      => [
        { name => 'name',  value => 'john'     },
        { name => 'color', value => 'red,blue' },
    ],
}
```

If you process this `Template::Tiny` template with this hash reference, this tag:

```
[% IF have_params %]
```

Can evaluate to true, passing control to the block with the `<table>` HTML tag. In that, you can see this:

```
[% FOREACH param IN params %]
    <tr><td>[% param.name %]</td><td>[% param.value %]</td></tr>
[% END %]
```

The [% FOREACH param IN params %] iterates over the `params` array reference, setting `param` to each contained hash reference, in turn. Then when you call [% param.name %] and [% param .value %], it's identical to calling $param->{name} and $param->{value}. In Perl code, the entire template would look like this (omitting the HTML for clarity):

```
my $hashref = { ... };
if ( $hashref->{have_params} ) {
    foreach my $param (@{ $hashref->{params} }) {
        print $param->{name},$param->{value};
    }
}
else {
    print "No params supplied!";
}
```

And that's the entire `Template::Tiny` syntax, and here's how you can use it in your new `params`
`.psgi`. Use `File::Slurp` to make reading the template code a bit easier:

```
use strict;
use warnings;

use Plack::Builder;
use Plack::Request;
use Template::Tiny;
use File::Slurp 'read_file';

builder {
    mount '/' => sub {
        my $env     = shift;
        my $request = Plack::Request->new($env);
        my @params;
        foreach my $param ( sort $request->param ) {
            my $values = join ',' => $request->param($param);
            push @params => { name => $param, value => $values };
        }
        my $content = get_content(
            'templates/params.tt',
            {
                params      => \@params,
                have_params => scalar @params,
            }
        );
        my $response = $request->new_response(200);
        $response->content_type('text/html');
        $response->content($content);
        return $response->finalize;
    };
};

sub get_content {
    my ( $file, $vars ) = @_;
    my $template_code = read_file($file);
    my $output;
    my $template      = Template::Tiny->new;
    $template->process( \$template_code, $vars, \$output );
    return $output;
}
```

You can build up an array reference of parameters and pass that, along with the template name,
to the `get_content` subroutine. Use `read_file` from `File::Slurp` to read the contents of
the template. Then pass the contents of the file as a scalar reference as the first argument to the
instantiated `Template::Tiny` object. The hash referee of variables is passed as the second argument,
and a reference to the scalar containing your output is the third argument. (The syntax is a bit odd to
maintain forward compatibility with the Template Toolkit module.)

```
my $output;
my $template      = Template::Tiny->new;
$template->process( \$template_code, $vars, \$output );
return $output;
```

After the template is processed, return the output variable and set that as your `$response->content`.

Now, when you visit `http://localhost:5000/`, you should see this on your web page:

```
No params supplied!
```

When you visit `http://localhost:5000/?name=john;color=red;color=blue;job=janitor`, you should see a page that looks vaguely like this:

```
Our list of params:
Name    Value
color   red,blue
job     janitor
name    john
```

It's not a pretty web page, but now you can see how to separate the view (sometimes called the presentation layer) from the main logic of your code.

At this point you could even take some code from your anonymous subroutine and put that into a module in `lib/` to start making the `params.cgi` a tiny controller, with your model in `lib/` and your view in `templates/`. As mentioned previously, though, if you try to do too much in Plack, it's time to look at a real web framework.

One last caveat: What do you think happens if you visit this URL?

```
http://localhost/?job=%3Chr/%3E%3Cstrong%3Ehi%20there!%3C/strong%3E
```

That's the URL encoded form of this:

```
http://localhost/?job=<hr/><strong>hi there!</strong>
```

The exact appearance depends on your browser, but basically, in the `Value` column, you should see **hi there!** in bold print with a line above it. Why? Because this is the line in the template after the value is added:

```
<tr><td>job</td><td><hr/><strong>hi there!</strong></td></tr>
```

This is sadly a common problem on the web. People write web applications and forget to encode user-supplied data before sending it to a web page. To fix this, add the following line to your code:

```
use HTML::Entities 'encode_entities';
```

And when you push the parameters onto the array:

```
push @params => { name => $param, value => $values };
```

Change it to this:

```
push @params => {
    name  => encode_entities($param),
    value => encode_entities($values)
};
```

Now when you visit that URL, you should see something like this:

```
Name     Value
job      <hr/><strong>hi there!</strong>
```

> **WARNING** *A common mistake when working with user data submitted from the web is to encode HTML data as soon as you receive it. That ensures that no one can forget to encode the data before it is sent out to a web page. Unfortunately, someone invariably forgets and re-encodes the data, causing strange things like* &amp; *and other weirdness to show up on the web page.*
>
> *A stronger reason, however, is that you might want to use the data for something else that is not web-related. If you export the data to a spreadsheet, your users may not be impressed to see HTML entities there.*
>
> *As a general rule, encode the HTML data right before it's to be rendered in HTML and not before.*

And if you look at the source code, you can see this (formatted to fit the page):

```
<tr>
  <td>job</td>
  <td>&lt;hr/&gt;&lt;strong&gt;hi there!&lt;/strong&gt;</td>
</tr>
```

The `encode_entities` function from `HTML::Entities` encodes strings into their corresponding HTML entities. For example, < becomes `&lt;` and > becomes `&gt;`.

There are hundreds of predefined character entities for HTML that are beyond the scope of what you're doing here, but see `http://en.wikipedia.org/wiki/List_of_XML_and_HTML_character_entity_references` for a complete list. For the brave, you can also read the W3C specification at `http://www.w3.org/TR/REC-html40/sgml/entities.html`. Be warned, though: W3C specifications are not designed to be easy to read. They're designed to be complete.

Handling POST Requests

So far, you've been handling GET requests. If you want to pass extra data to the page, you do so via the query string in the URL. However, if you have data that should not be in a URL, such as a username and password, people will be upset when they share that URL with someone before noticing that they're sharing their private data. This is not to recommend POST as a security tool because clever hackers can still get at POST data if they know what they're doing, but at least sharing a link won't expose the contents of your e-mail.

This is where POST comes in. In HTTP, your client would send a POST request that looks similar to this:

```
POST /login HTTP/1.1
Content-Length: 31
Content-Type: application/x-www-form-urlencoded
```

```
Host: localhost:5000
Origin: http://localhost:5000
Referer: http://localhost:5000/login

username=ovid&password=youwish
```

In this example, the POST tells the server that the data is in the entity body. The entity body begins after two consecutive newlines (after the Referer: header in this example). Because the POST content is sent in the entity body, it does not show up in the URL.

> **WARNING** *Many developers believe that because a* POST *puts the data in the entity body, it's more secure than a* GET. *Aside from people copying and pasting sensitive data in a URL, it is not more secure. If you want more security, there are many things you can do, including switching to HTTPS.*

> **NOTE** *A couple of things about your HTTP* POST *example: First, your author knows that* Referer: *is misspelled. Sadly, this happened a long time ago and became formalized in RFC 1945, released in 1996. Pedants lament; the rest of us deal with it.*
>
> *Also, your* Content-Type: *is* application/x-www-form-urlencoded. *There are plenty of others available but aren't covered here.*

Now create a login page. This page doesn't actually "work" in the sense to allow you to log in (hey, this is an intro!), but it shows how a POST request works and also lets you see a bit more refactoring of the params.psgi application.

First, create templates/login.tt with the following:

```
<html>
  <head><title>Login</title></head>
  <body>
    <fieldset>
      <legend>Pretend to Login, please</legend>
      <form action="/login" method="POST">
        <table>
          <tr><td>Username</td><td><input type="text"
            name="username" /></td></tr>
          <tr><td>Password</td><td><input type="password"
            name="password" /></td></tr>
        </table>
        <div align="center"><input type="submit" value="Submit" /></div>
      </form>
  </body>
</html>
```

This doesn't actually have any template parameters in it, and there are better ways to handle it than putting it in templates/, but this is fine for your purposes. Note that the form's action sends you back to /login because that path is what handles the "login" request.

When you render that HTML, it should resemble Figure 15-2.

Now to see how to render it, modify your `params.psgi` to contain the following code:

FIGURE 15-2

```
use strict;
use warnings;

use Plack::Builder;
use Plack::Request;
use Template::Tiny;
use File::Slurp 'read_file';
use HTML::Entities 'encode_entities';

builder {

    mount '/' => sub {
        my $env     = shift;
        my $request = Plack::Request->new($env);
        my @params  = get_params_array($request);
        my $content = get_content(
            'templates/params.tt',
            {
                params      => \@params,
                have_params => scalar @params,
            }
        );
        return response( $request, $content );
    };

    mount '/login' => sub {
        my $request = Plack::Request->new(shift);
        my $content;
        if ( $request->param('username') && $request->param('password') ) {
            my @params = get_params_array($request);
            $content = get_content(
                'templates/params.tt',
                {
                    params      => \@params,
                    have_params => scalar @params,
                }
            );
        }
        else {
            $content = get_content('templates/login.tt');
        }
        return response( $request, $content );
    };
};

sub get_params_array {
    my $request = shift;
    my @params;
```

```
        foreach my $param ( sort $request->param ) {
            my $values = join ',' => $request->param($param);
            push @params => {
                name  => encode_entities($param),
                value => encode_entities($values)
            };
        }
        return @params;
    }

sub response {
    my ( $request, $content ) = @_;
    my $response = $request->new_response(200);
    $response->content_type('text/html');
    $response->content($content);
    return $response->finalize;
}

sub get_content {
    my ( $file, $vars ) = @_;
    $vars ||= {};
    my $template_code = read_file($file);
    my $template      = Template::Tiny->new;
    my $output;
    $template->process( \$template_code, $vars, \$output );
    return $output;
}
```

You factored out your `response()` generation into its own subroutine. The code to get the content for the parameters has also been factored into `get_params_array()`. It takes the request as an argument and returns the array of parameter key/value pairs. That leaves you with your `builder` section,

You can still recognize the / path when you understand the `get_params_array()` and `response()` code. It does the same thing it did before. The "login" code merely checks to see that you have POSTed both a username and a password (any will do). If you haven't, it renders the login form. If you have, it renders the `templates/params.tt` page that you saw from your previous example.

Try it now by going to `http://localhost:5000/login`. Any username and password combination should return the template that shows the values you entered. For example, if you entered `ovid` and `youwish` for your username and password, you should see this:

```
Our list of params:
Name      Value
password  youwish
username  ovid
```

The URL, however, remains `http://localhost:5000/login`. As far as `Plack::Request` (and many other request handlers) is concerned, it makes no difference if it reads your params from a POST or a GET. Thus, even if you switch this to a GET request, you'll still see the table listing params:

```
http://localhost:5000/login?username=ovid;password=youwish
```

You can protect against this, if you want, by allowing only processing of the username and password with a POST request method:

```
if (   'post' eq lc $request->method
    && $request->param('username')
    && $request->param('password') )
{
    return response( $request, get_params_content($request) );
}
```

> **WARNING** *I can't issue enough warnings in this chapter that say the code presented here is not secure. Internet security is a serious problem and we are presenting this information as examples only. The management regrets harping on this, but it's important.*

Sessions

Your author would ask, at this point, for all serious web professionals to turn to the next section and ignore the horrible, horrible abuse of sessions that happen here.

HTTP is, by design, a stateless protocol. This means that each request is independent of every other request. In the early days of the web, every time you visited a web page, the server had no idea you had been there before. Then a Netscape employee named Lou Montulli had the brilliant idea to take "magic cookies" (no, not the type you buy in Amsterdam), which were already in use in other software, and implement them in Netscape Navigator, a browser popular back in the mid-to-late 1990s. This was one of the most important events in the history of the web. Now, if a browser returns a cookie to a host, the host can know that the user had previously visited.

In the code that follows, Plack::Session uses cookies to pass a session key back and forth between the Plack software and the client. The Plack software uses the value of the cookie to look up its in-memory session data. Because this data is not persistent, it cannot survive between server restarts. In serious Comp applications, session data is generally saved in a persistent state, such as in a database or memcached.

TRY IT OUT   Using Cookies to Pass a Session Key

Now let the abuse begin!

1. Install Plack::Middleware::Session from the CPAN.

2. At the top of your params.psgi, after the modules you use, add the following two lines:

```
use Plack::Session;
use constant SESSION_TIME => 30;
```

The session time is in seconds. You only use 30-second sessions because your author is sadistic. Feel free to adjust that to taste.

3. Add the following two subroutines:

```
sub time_remaining {
    my $session = shift;
    my $remaining = SESSION_TIME - ( time - $session->get('time') );
    $remaining = 0 if $remaining < 0;
    return $remaining;
}

sub session_expired {
    my ( $request, $session ) = @_;
    return if time_remaining($session);
    $session->expire;
    my $response = $request->new_response;
    $response->redirect('/login');
    return $response->finalize;
}
```

➤ The `time_remaining()` subroutine returns the number of seconds left in your session.

➤ The `session_expired()` subroutine returns false if you have time remaining in your session.

4. Change your `templates/params.tt` file to this:

```
<html>
  <head><title>Parameters</title></head>
  <body>
    <p>Hello [% username %]. You have [% time %] seconds left.</p>
[% IF have_params %]
    <p>Our list of params:</p>
    <table rules="all">
      <tr><th>Name</th><th>Value</th></tr>
  [% FOREACH param IN params %]
      <tr><td>[% param.name %]</td><td>[% param.value %]</td></tr>
  [% END %]
    </table>
[% ELSE %]
    <p><strong>No params supplied!</strong></p>
[% END %]
  </body>
</html>
```

The only change is immediately after the body tag where you display the session username and the time remaining.

5. Rewrite your builder, again, to match the following:

```
builder {
    enable 'Session';

    mount '/' => sub {
        my $env     = shift;
        my $request = Plack::Request->new($env);
```

```perl
    my $session = Plack::Session->new($env);
    if ( my $redirect = session_expired( $request, $session ) ) {
        return $redirect;
    }
    my @params = get_params_array($request);
    if ( $session->get('from_login') ) {
        push @params => {
            name  => 'username',
            value => $session->get('username'),
        };
        $session->remove('from_login');
    }
    my %template_vars = (
        params       => \@params,
        have_params  => scalar( @params ),
        username     => $session->get('username'),
        time         => remaining_time($session),
    );
    my $content = get_content( 'templates/params.tt', \%template_vars, );
    return response( $request, $content );
};

mount '/login' => sub {
    my $env     = shift;
    my $request = Plack::Request->new($env);
    my $session = Plack::Session->new($env);
    my $content;
    if ( $request->param('username') && $request->param('password') ) {
        $session->set( 'username', $request->param('username') );
        $session->set( 'time', time );
        $session->set( 'from_login', 1 );
        my $response = $request->new_response;
        $response->redirect('/');
        return $response->finalize;
    }
    else {
        $content = get_content('templates/login.tt');
    }
    return response( $request, $content );
};
};
```

When you first restart the app, you're presented with the login screen. If you log in with a username of Bob and a password of Dobbs. You'll see a screen like this:

```
Hello Bob. You have 30 seconds left.
Our list of params:
Name      Value
username  Bob
```

You can refresh this screen as often as you like, and as soon as you have zero seconds left, you're redirected to the /login screen. Your "username" and the time left on your session are stored in the session.

How It Works

When you create a new session:

```
my $session = Plack::Session->new($env);
```

How does it know that it's the session that belongs to you? More important, when you come back to the site, why is the session still there? How does that extra data (such as the time) magically persist?

There are two components:

➤   The session store

➤   The key to open your bit of the store. That key is stored in a cookie in your browser.

When you first create a session object, the session key is stored in Plack's internal $env hash, and the value is the session data. You don't need to set this manually (though you can) because in the examples used in this chapter, it happens automatically.

When you fill in a username and password with your example code, the server responds with something like the following:

```
HTTP/1.1 302 Found
Content-Length: 0
Date: Thu, 12 Apr 2012 08:58:04 GMT
Location: /
Server: HTTP::Server::PSGI
Set-Cookie: plack_session=9f7539872c9b15d1ac30b8557742f3; path=/
```

The 302 Found, combined with the Location: / header tells the browser to redirect to /. In this case, you'll likely be redirecting to http://localhost:5000/. However, the Set-Cookie line says, "Set a Cookie with the Name plack_session and the Value 9f7539872c ..." Every browser generally receives a different cookie value.

When your browser requests the new location, it returns the following Cookie: header:

```
Cookie: plack_session=9f7539872c9b15d1ac30b8557742f3
```

The software sees the session key and now knows the key to "unlock" your session data.

This has been only a brief discussion of this topic and glosses over many technical issues.

When you have entered a username and password, the following code executes:

```
if ( $request->param('username') && $request->param('password') ) {
    $session->set( 'username', $request->param('username') );
    $session->set( 'time', time );
    $session->set( 'from_login', 1 );
    my $response = $request->new_response;
    $response->redirect('/');
    return $response->finalize;
}
```

This sets the username, time, and from_login values in your session. In your toy example, this session is held in memory.

When the browser is redirected to /, the following is the relevant bit of code related to the session:

```
if ( my $redirect = session_expired( $request, $session ) ) {
    return $redirect;
}
my @params = get_params_array($request);
if ( $session->get('from_login') ) {
    push @params => {
        name  => 'username',
        value => $session->get('username'),
    };
    $session->remove('from_login');
}
```

The session_expired() function returns a redirect to /login if the session is greater than SESSION_TIME seconds ago or if there is no username in the session.

> **NOTE** *You could have accessed the session cookie directly and set the expiration time on that. However, savvy end users can edit their cookies and change the time manually, artificially extending their session life. That's why it's a good idea to not rely on the cookie expiration time for session length.*

The $session->get('from_login') checks to see if the from_login value was set in the session (you can't rely on the Referer: value because the end user can change that, too) and, if it were, the from_login value is cleared, and the username is added to the list of params for rendering.

TRY IT OUT Create a Simple Character Generator for Role-playing Games

Now that you have some of the basics of web application under your belt, put it all together to create a character generator for a game. You can choose your name, place of birth, and profession. You can have statistics for strength, intelligence, and health randomly generated, but they adjust for your profession and birthplace. This example is longer than your author would like because there is a lot of data that should be stored in a configuration file or database, which hasn't been covered yet.

This Try It Out also requires one .psgi file and two templates. All the code for this Try It Out is code file character.psgi, templates/character.tt, and templates/character_display.tt.

1. Type in the following program, and save it as character.psgi:

```
use strict;
use warnings;

use Plack::Builder;
use Plack::Request;
use Template::Tiny;
use File::Slurp 'read_file';
```

```perl
use HTML::Entities 'encode_entities';

builder {

    mount '/' => sub {
        my $env      = shift;
        my $request = Plack::Request->new($env);
        my $template = 'templates/character_display.tt';
        my $content;
        if ( $request->param ) {
            my ( $character, $errors )
              = generate_character($request);
            $template = 'templates/character.tt' if @$errors;
            $content = get_content(
                $template,
                {
                    character => $character,
                    errors    => $errors,
                }
            );
        }
        else {
            $content = get_content(
              $template,
              { no_character_found => 1 }
            );
        }
        return response( $request, $content );
    };

    mount '/character' => sub {
        my $env      = shift;
        my $request = Plack::Request->new($env);
        my $content = get_content('templates/character.tt');
        return response( $request, $content );
    };
};

sub generate_character {
    my $request        = shift;
    my %adjustments_for = (
        profession => {
            programmer => {
                strength     => -3,
                intelligence => 8,
                health       => -2,
            },
            pilot    => { intelligence => 3 },
            redshirt => { strength      => 5 }
        },
        birthplace => {
            earth => {
                strength     => 2,
                intelligence => 0,
                health       => -2,
            },
            mars => { strength      => -5, health => 2 },
```

```perl
                vat  => { intelligence => 2,  health => -2 }
            },
    );

    my @errors;
    my %label_for = (
        profession => {
            pilot      => "Starship Pilot",
            programmer => "Programmer",
            redshirt   => "Doomed",
        },
        birthplace => {
            earth => "Earth",
            mars  => "Mars",
            vat   => "Vat 3-5LX",
        },
    );
    my %value_for = map { $_ => roll_dice() }
      qw/strength intelligence health/;

    foreach my $attribute (qw/name profession birthplace/) {
        if ( my $value = $request->param($attribute) ) {
            if (my $adj=$adjustments_for{$attribute}{$value} ) {
                while (my ($stat, $adjustment) = each %$adj) {
                    $value_for{$stat} += $adjustment;
                }
            }
            $value_for{$attribute} =
              encode_entities(
                $label_for{$attribute}{$value} || $value
              );
        }
        else {
            push @errors => "\U$attribute is required";
        }
    }
    if ( 'redshirt' eq $request->param('profession') ) {
        $value_for{health} = 1;
    }
    return \%value_for, \@errors;
}

sub roll_dice {
    my $total = 0;
    for ( 1 .. 3 ) {
        $total += 1 + int(rand(10));
    }
    return $total;
}

sub response {
    my ( $request, $content ) = @_;
    my $response = $request->new_response(200);
    $response->content_type('text/html');
    $response->content($content);
    return $response->finalize;
```

```
    }

    sub get_content {
        my ( $file, $vars ) = @_;
        $vars ||= {};
        my $template_code = read_file($file);
        my $template      = Template::Tiny->new;
        my $output;
        $template->process( \$template_code, $vars, \$output );
        return $output;
    }
```

2. You need a form to let the users make choices about their character. Save the following as templates/character.tt.

```html
<html>
  <head><title>Character Generation</title></head>
  <body>
    <fieldset>
      <legend>Create your character</legend>
[% FOREACH error IN errors %]
      <p style="color:red; font-weight:bold">[% error %]</p>
[% END %]
      <form action="/" method="POST" name="awesome">
        <table>
          <tr><td>Name</td>
            <td>
              <input type="text" name="name"
                value="[% character.name %]" />
            </td>
          </tr>
          <tr>
            <td>Profession</td>
            <td>
              <select name="profession">
                <option value="programmer">Programmer</option>
                <option value="pilot">Starship Pilot</option>
                <option value="redshirt">Security Officer
                  </option>
              </select>
            </td>
          </tr>
          <tr>
            <td>Birth place</td>
            <td>
              Earth <input type="radio" name="birthplace"
                value="earth" /> |
              Mars <input type="radio" name="birthplace"
                value="mars" /> |
              Vat 3-5LX <input type="radio" name="birthplace"
                value="vat" />
            </td>
          </tr>
        </table>
        <div align="center">
```

```
                <input type="submit" value="Submit" />
              </div>
            </form>
          </fieldset>
        </body>
      </html>
```

3. Next, you need a form to display the generated character. Save the following as `templates/character_display.tt`.

```
<html>
  <head>
    <title>The Awesome "This does nothing!" Game</title>
  </head>
  <body>
    <fieldset>
[% IF no_character_found %]
      <legend>Create your character</legend>
      <p>
        <a href="/character">Click here to create a character</a>
      </p>
[% ELSE %]
      <legend>Character Stats</legend>
      <table style="border-spacing:5px;">
        <tr><td>Name</td>
            <td>[% character.name %]</td></tr>
        <tr><td>Profession</td>
            <td>[% character.profession %]</td></tr>
        <tr><td>Birth place</td>
            <td>[% character.birthplace %]</td></tr>
        <tr><td>Strength</td>
            <td>[% character.strength %]</td></tr>
        <tr><td>Intelligence</td>
            <td>[% character.intelligence %]</td></tr>
        <tr><td>Health</td>
            <td>[% character.health %]</td></tr>
      </table>
      <p>
        <a href="/character">
          Click here to generate another character.
        </a>
      </p>
[% END %]
    </fieldset>
      </body>
      </html>
```

4. Run the program with `plackup character.psgi`. In your favorite web browser, go to `http://localhost:5000/`. You should see a link reading `Click here to create a character`.

When you click that link, you're taken to a form with a field for entering the character name, a drop-down for selecting the character profession, and three radio buttons for choosing `Earth`, `Mars`, or `Vat 3-5LX` as your birthplace. If you fill out the form completely and click Submit, a character is randomly generated for you and displayed. If you forget to fill out one of the options, you'll return to the form to see a list of errors. (Due to limitations in how `Template::Tiny` works, when errors occur, only your name will be filled in.)

How It Works

Each of the templates is simple, and just glancing at them should explain what they do. However, the .psgi file is a little more complex.

The get_content() and response() subroutines were used and explained earlier in the chapter. The roll_dice() subroutine simulates the rolling of three ten-sided dice and sums them for a character stat. Thus, each stat of Strength, Intelligence, and Health can have a base score of 3 to 30 (rolling three ones and rolling three tens, respectively).

The generate_character() code is the same procedural code you've been writing throughout the entire book. It has too much data hard-coded into it, but for illustration purposes, it's fine. It's worth reading to see how well-chosen variable names can make the code clear, so take a moment and do that.

```
 1: my %value_for = map { $_ => roll_dice() }
        qw/strength intelligence health/;
 2: foreach my $attribute (qw/name profession birthplace/) {
 3:     if ( my $value = $request->param($attribute) ) {
 4:         if (my $adj = $adjustments_for{$attribute}{$value}) {
 5:             while ( my ($stat, $adjustment) = each %$adj ) {
 6:                 $value_for{$stat} += $adjustment;
 7:             }
 8:         }
 9:         $value_for{$attribute} =
10:           encode_entities(
                   $label_for{$attribute}{$value} || $value );
11:     }
12:     else {
13:         push @errors => "\U$attribute is required";
14:     }
15: }
```

For this code, consider the following:

➤ Line 1 sets random, default values for strength, intelligence, and health. Starting with line 2, you iterate over the values the user entered, and that's when things are interesting.

➤ On line 3, if you don't have a value for an attribute (actually, because you're testing for truth, this means that the number 0 cannot be a character name), control jumps to line 13 where you push an error onto your errors array.

➤ On line 4, you see if you have $adjustments_for{$attribute}{$value}. That's easy to read, and when you substitute the values for the variables, if someone chose Mars for their birthplace, that line evaluates to $adjustments_for{birthplace}{mars}. That points to the following hash reference:

```
{ strength => -5, health => 2 }
```

You then iterate over the keys and values and adjust the character's base strength and health accordingly.

➤ Lines 9 and 10 assign the label for the attribute. This is the value you display on the resulting templates/character_display.tt page. The || $value is there because you don't have default display values for the character name.

It's the `builder` that you want to focus on because this contains the web application control flow logic you're concerned with. You have two paths mounted, `/` and `/character`. The latter is used to generate the form and you look at that first.

```
mount '/character' => sub {
    my $env     = shift;
    my $request = Plack::Request->new($env);
    my $content = get_content('templates/character.tt');
    return response( $request, $content );
};
```

As you can see, all you do here is get the contents of their form submission and display the `templates/character.tt` page, which displays the form the users will use to fill out their character information. When you work through the logic of the program, you can see that for `/character`, you never have any parameters submitted here.

The `/` path is where the interesting bit is:

```
 1:  mount '/' => sub {
 2:      my $env     = shift;
 3:      my $request = Plack::Request->new($env);
 4:
 5:      my $template = 'templates/character_display.tt';
 6:      my $content;
 7:      if ( $request->param ) {
 8:          my ( $character, $errors )
                = generate_character($request);
 9:          $template = 'templates/character.tt' if @$errors;
10:          $content = get_content(
11:              $template,
12:              {
13:                  character => $character,
14:                  errors    => $errors,
15:              }
16:          );
17:      }
18:      else {
19:          $content = get_content(
                $template,
                {no_character_found=>1}
            );
20:      }
21:      return response( $request, $content );
22:  };
```

The first time you visit `http://localhost:5000/`, the `$template` name is set to `templates/character_display.tt` on line 5. However, line 7 shows that you have not submitted parameters and thus control will fall to line 19, where you get the content of the template and pass it a hashref with `no_character_found` having a true value. In the template, that causes this path to be executed:

```
[% IF no_character_found %]
    <legend>Create your character</legend>
    <p>
```

```
        <a href="/character">Click here to create a character</a>
    </p>
[% ELSE %]
```

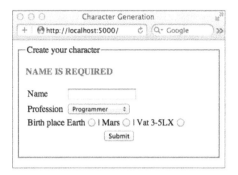

So click the link to create your character, fill out the form, and click Submit. That will POST your data to /. At this point, the test in line 7 shows that you did have parameters submitted and you attempted to generate the character. If there are errors, such as no name found, the template is set back to `templates/character.tt` and the list of errors displays. Figure 15-3 shows an example of what the web page might look like if you have not filled it in correctly.

If you did complete the form, the generated character information is sent to `templates/character_display.tt` and you see your new character in all its glory.

FIGURE 15-3

WEB CLIENTS

Whew! You covered a huge amount about the concepts behind writing web applications, but what about writing web clients? The client most people are familiar with is the web browser, but that's for, well, browsing the web.

Many times you have specific tasks you want a client to accomplish, but a web browser might be a poor choice. So instead, you write your own client to do the task for you. For example, you might want to get all the images from a particular web page. If there are hundreds of images, it might be easier to write a client to get those images for you.

> **WARNING** *Before going any further, you must remember this: Web clients are fun and web clients are easy to write. They can save you a lot of trouble but can also get you in a lot of trouble. Many websites have extremely clear terms of service (TOS) that state that you may not use software to "spider" or "automate" their website. Others require you to go through official channels to get an API key before you write a client.*
>
> *They're not doing this to be mean. They're doing this for a variety of reasons. They might have limited resources and your web client might spider them so fast that they have trouble responding to requests. Or they might have time-sensitive content that should not be stored, or it might be copyrighted, and so on. Before you write a client to automate some work with a website, be sure to read their TOS to understand what your rights and responsibilities are.*
>
> *There are ways to work around websites blocking your clients, but we're not going to discuss them here, and I encourage you to think carefully before you do. If you must run a client you wrote against the website of someone trying to block you, ask permission, and if you don't get it, don't do it.*

As a general pattern for writing a web client, you go through three steps:

1. Navigate to where you're trying to go.

2. Fetch the content.

3. Parse the content.

Now check out some examples.

> **NOTE** *When you write a web client, you need to understand the various HTTP response codes that you may receive. For example, a 200 means the request succeeded, and a 404 is a* `File Not Found`*. There are many possible response codes that can be hard to remember. Check out* `http://www.w3` `.org/Protocols/rfc2616/rfc2616-sec10.html` *to understand a bit more about them.*

Extracting Links from Web Pages

Sometimes you want to fetch the links on a web page. You can use `LWP::Simple` from the `libwww-perl` distribution to get the HTML for a web page and `HTML::SimpleLinkExtor` to extract the links.

You need to download both of these modules from the CPAN:

```
$ cpan libwww-perl HTML::SimpleLinkExtor
```

> **NOTE** *The* `libwww-perl` *module includes many modules that make life easier while writing web clients. However, they do not support HTTPS (encrypted) URLs. You need to install* `LWP::Protocol::https` *separately. Otherwise, you may get strange errors when writing clients.*

So the following (code file `listing_15_1_get_links.pl`) is a little script to get you started:

```
use strict;
use warnings;

use HTML::SimpleLinkExtor;
use LWP::Simple 'get';

my $url       = shift @ARGV or die "Hey, gimme a URL!";
my $html      = get($url) or die "Could not get '$url'";
my $extractor = HTML::SimpleLinkExtor->new;
```

```
    $extractor->parse($html);

    my @links = $extractor->links;

    unless (@links) {
        print "No links founds for $url\n";
        exit;
    }

    for my $link (sort @links) {
        print "$link\n";
    }
```

You can run this against, say, a popular search engine like this:

```
http://searchenginename/
```

It prints out a sorted list of all links found on that page. The get() function exported from LWP::Simple accepts a URL and returns the contents. The HTML::SimpleLinkExtor is used for extracting the links. You can play with this for a few web pages and you'll be amazed at how many links they have. But after a while, you may get tired of the No links found error, particularly if you visit the web page and you know that there are links there. So you can update the program using LWP::UserAgent instead of LWP::Simple:

```
    use strict;
    use warnings;

    use HTML::SimpleLinkExtor;
    use LWP::UserAgent;

    my $url = shift @ARGV or die "Hey, gimme a URL!";
    my $ua = LWP::UserAgent->new;
    $ua->timeout(10);

    my $response = $ua->get($url) or die "Could not get '$url'";

    unless ( $response->is_success ) {
        die $response->status_line;
    }

    my $html = $response->decoded_content;
    my $extractor = HTML::SimpleLinkExtor->new;
    $extractor->parse($html);

    my @links = $extractor->links;

    unless (@links) {
        print "No links founds for $url\n";
        exit;
    }

    for my $link ( sort @links ) {
        print "$link\n";
    }
```

Now try running this with `perl listing_15_1_get_links.pl whitehouse.gov`. (Note the lack of `http://`.) You should get an error similar to the following:

```
400 URL must be absolute at listing_15_1_get_links.pl line 14.
```

Ah! That's better. Now at least you have some idea of what your errors are.

Extracting Comments from Web Pages

Your author has a friend, whom we shall presume wishes to be nameless, who has a habit of responding in online forums in a friendly, informative manner. One of the forums she participates in allows a subset of HTML to be used, including HTML comments. So she embeds HTML comments in her replies. In HTML, they look like this:

```
<!-- this is a comment -->
```

The comments can span multiple lines. Her HTML comments span multiple jurisdictions of vitriol spewed at the person she is responding to. So let's write a small program that prints the HTML comments in a web page (code file `listing_15_2_get_comments.pl`). Sadly, I cannot point you to her comments as this is a family-friendly book, but you'll enjoy the end result nonetheless.

```perl
use strict;
use warnings;

use HTML::SimpleLinkExtor;
use HTML::TokeParser::Simple;

my $url = shift @ARGV or die "Hey, gimme a URL!";
my $ua = LWP::UserAgent->new;
$ua->timeout(10);

my $response = $ua->get($url) or die "Could not get '$url'";

unless ( $response->is_success ) {
    die $response->status_line;
}

my $html   = $response->decoded_content;
my $parser = HTML::TokeParser::Simple->new( \$html );

while ( my $token = $parser->get_token ) {
    print $token->as_is, "\n" if $token->is_comment;
}
```

This program uses `HTML::TokeParser::Simple` to parse the HTML returned by `LWP::UserAgent`. There are a wide variety of parsers available, some more suited to extracting information than others, but this is an easy one to start with. (Disclaimer: Your author wrote it.)

The key portion of this code is here:

```
1:  my $parser = HTML::TokeParser::Simple->new( \$html );
2:  while ( my $token = $parser->get_token ) {
```

```
3:      print $token->as_is, "\n" if $token->is_comment;
4:  }
```

If you have the text of a web page, you must pass it as a reference to the constructor. Then, you can keep calling $parser->get_token to get the next "bit" of the web page. Tokens are things such as HTML tags, HTML comments, text, and so on. I'll walk through all the tokens and only print the ones that are comments. Easy, eh?

One major web comic has an ASCII pterodactyl embedded in his comments. Another site has <!--IE6sux--> 54 times. You can have a lot of fun finding unexpected comments on websites. (Remember to obey their terms of service.)

Filling Out Forms Programmatically

OK, so you wrote two simple examples so far. Boooooring. Now do something a little more involved; write some software to fill out a form on a website to see what happens when you submit it!

Er, except that's hard to do in a book for a couple of reasons: Websites often change their content or TOS and your author would not like to be sued down to his skivvies for encouraging people to do this. Fortunately, you have a workaround.

The last Try It Out section had a web form that you can fill in and submit. Perfect! So go back and run plackup characters.psgi for this example, and leave that running in another terminal window. That's going to be the web server you'll run this example against. You need to install WWW::Mechanize and HTML::TableExtract to make this work.

Type in the following example, and save it as listing_15_3_post_character.pl (a code file is available for this on the website):

```perl
use strict;
use warnings;

use WWW::Mechanize;
use HTML::TableExtract;

my $url  = 'http://localhost:5000/';
my $mech = WWW::Mechanize->new;
$mech->get($url);
$mech->follow_link( text_regex => qr/click here/i );
$mech->submit_form(
    form_number => 1,
    fields      => {
        name       => 'Bob',
        profession => 'redshirt',
        birthplace => 'mars',
    },
);

my $extractor = HTML::TableExtract->new;
$extractor->parse($mech->content);

foreach my $table ( $extractor->tables ) {
```

```
    foreach my $row ( $table->rows ) {
        printf "%-20s - %s\n" => @$row;
    }
}
```

Assuming that you didn't do something silly like change the HTML in the `character.psgi` example, you should get output similar to the following (obviously the numeric values will be different):

```
Name                 - Bob
Profession           - Doomed
Birth place          - Mars
Strength             - 24
Intelligence         - 22
Health               - 1
```

It looks like your poor red shirt is going to die. On the plus side, at least he's smart enough to know it.

`WWW::Mechanize` has a lovely interface. The code looks remarkably similar to what you might do as a human:

```
my $mech = WWW::Mechanize->new;
$mech->get($url);
$mech->follow_link( text_regex => qr/click here/i );
```

As you will recall, when you go the main page, it has a link telling you to `Please click here to create a new character`.

There is only one form on the page, so submit your values to form number 1.

```
$mech->submit_form(
    form_number => 1,
    fields      => {
        name       => 'Bob',
        profession => 'redshirt',
        birthplace => 'mars',
    },
);
```

> **NOTE** HTML forms can also have a `name` attribute. This can make maintaining them much easier if you use `WWW::Mechanize` and don't want to renumber forms if you add a new one to a page.
>
> ```
> $mech->submit_form(
>     form_name   => 'character',
>     fields      => {
>         name       => 'Bob',
>         profession => 'redshirt',
>         birthplace => 'mars',
>     },
> );
> ```

Obviously, you'd have to read the HTML of the page to know the names and appropriate values for a given form, but it's pretty darned easy to do. Just make sure your field refer to the `value="…"` data and not the human-visible names.

Then use `HTML::TableExtract` to get the values from the table printed on the next page:

```
my $extractor = HTML::TableExtract->new;
$extractor->parse($mech->content);
foreach my $table ( $extractor->tables ) {
    foreach my $row ( $table->rows ) {
        printf "%-20s - %s\n" => @$row;
    }
}
```

To be fair, this was a simple example. If you need to do this with more complicated websites, you need to read the documentation carefully.

> **NOTE** *If you had submitted a web form to generate a character's stats, imagine if you hadn't had access to the back-end code. By repeatedly submitting the form and collecting the data, you could eventually get an idea of what's going on behind the scenes, such as calculating the average value and standard deviation of stats based on profession and birth place.*
>
> *This is one of the many reasons why websites have annoying CAPTCHAs: It's hard to stop people from automating things that you don't want automated.*

Be aware that many web developers put all their form validation in JavaScript and not on the back end. Thus, if you use these techniques, you may submit data and generate errors that are hard to reproduce using a browser (sometimes even if you have JavaScript disabled). Be careful with them and don't use them irresponsibly.

TRY IT OUT   Using Google's JSON API to Get Directions

So far, you've been writing a few simple clients that read data from HTML. This is often called *scraping* websites, and it's an unfortunate practice because HTML is not designed to be machine-readable in the sense of "extracting useful information." However, many websites offer APIs for precisely that purpose. You can use the Google Directions API to find driving directions between two points. I won't cover the API in detail, but Google offers excellent documentation at:

`https://developers.google.com/maps/documentation/directions/`

You can use its JSON API because JSON is easy to parse. Essentially, the `JSON::Any` class enables you to convert Google Maps API into a hash reference that you can read directly. Use this API to find the driving directions between the lovely Portland, Oregon, and the somewhat less lovely Boring, Oregon (code file `example_15_1_google_directions.pl`).

1. Type in the following program, and save it as example_15_1_google_directions.pl:

```perl
use strict;
use warnings;

use WWW::Mechanize;
use HTML::Strip;
use JSON::Any;
use URI::Encode 'uri_encode';
use utf8::all;

my $origin      = uri_encode('Boring, OR');
my $destination = uri_encode('Portland, OR');

my $url="http://maps.googleapis.com/maps/api/directions/json";
my $query="origin=$origin&destination=$destination&sensor=false";
my $mech = WWW::Mechanize->new;
$mech->get("$url?$query");

my $object = JSON::Any->new->decode( $mech->content );

unless ( 'OK' eq $object->{status} ) {
    die $object->{status};
}

my $route      = $object->{routes}[0];
my $copyrights = $route->{copyrights};
my $warnings   = $route->{warnings};
my $legs       = $route->{legs}[0];          # only take the first
my $distance   = $legs->{distance}{text};
my $duration   = $legs->{duration}{text};

print
"$copyrights\nThe trip is $distance long and lasts $duration\n";
print join "\n" => @$warnings;
print "\n";

my $strip = HTML::Strip->new;

foreach my $step ( @{ $legs->{steps} } ) {
    my $distance     = $step->{distance}{text};
    my $duration     = $step->{duration}{text};
    my $instructions = $strip->parse($step->{html_instructions});
    $strip->eof;
    print "$instructions for $distance ($duration)\n";
}
```

2. Run the program with perl example_15_1_google_directions.pl. You should see output similar to the following (formatted to fit the page):

```
Map data ©2012 Google, Sanborn
The trip is 23.3 mi long and lasts 37 mins
Head east on OR-212 E/Clackamas-Boring Hwy No 174 toward
  Meadow Creek Ln for 0.6 mi (2 mins)
```

```
Turn left to merge onto US-26 W toward Gresham/Portland
    for 13.6 mi (23 mins)
Turn right onto the I-205 N ramp for 0.1 mi (1 min)
Keep left at the fork and merge onto I-205 N for 1.7 mi
    (2 mins)
Take exit 21B to merge onto I-84 W/U.S. 30 W toward Portland
    for 5.7 mi (6 mins)
Take the I-5 S exit on the left toward
    City Center/Beaverton/Salem for 0.4 mi (1 min)
Keep right at the fork, follow signs for City Center and merge
    onto SE Morrison Bridge for 0.7 mi (1 min)
Continue onto SW Washington St for 0.2 mi (1 min)
Turn right onto SW 6th Ave Destination will be on the right
    for 0.2 mi (1 min)
```

How It Works

In a nutshell, you:

➤ Construct an appropriate URL.

➤ GET the URL from Google.

➤ Parse the JSON response.

➤ Profit!

OK; that last bullet point should have read print.

First, load a bunch of modules you're mostly familiar with:

```
use WWW::Mechanize;
use HTML::Strip;
use JSON::Any;
use URI::Encode 'uri_encode';
use utf8::all;
```

The JSON::Any module is a front end to other JSON modules that you may have installed. You probably want to install the JSON module, but it requires a C compiler. If you can't install that, the JSON::PP (Pure Perl) module is a decent, but slow, substitute. The JSON::Any module tries to load whatever JSON back end it can find.

The HTML::Strip module is used to strip some HTML data from your results. The rest of the modules you should already be familiar with.

Then construct the URL:

```
my $origin      = uri_encode('Boring, OR');
my $destination = uri_encode('Portland, OR');
my $url="http://maps.googleapis.com/maps/api/directions/json";
my $query="origin=$origin&destination=$destination&sensor=false";
```

Naturally, you uri_encode() your $origin and $destination because you don't want them breaking your URL if you use data that must be encoded.

And you fetch the JSON and convert it into a hash reference (called `$object` because that's what JSON calls hashes):

```
my $mech = WWW::Mechanize->new;
$mech->get("$url?$query");
my $object = JSON::Any->new->decode( $mech->content );
```

At this point, you could use `Data:Dumper` and print the hash reference:

```
use Data::Dumper;
print Dumper($object);
```

But you want something a bit easier to read. By reading the Google Maps API documentation, you can figure out how to extract the correct data and print out each part of your route from `Boring, Oregon` to the lovely `Portland, Oregon`.

This example shows you how APIs work, but there is a `Google::Directions` module on the CPAN, along with many other `Google::` modules. Google is awesome and using its APIs can help you solve problems that would otherwise be difficult to solve. Thanks, Google!

SUMMARY

In this chapter, you learned some of the basics to write web applications. You used Plack extensively to learn a bit about HTTP and how to read query parameters sent to your application via GET and POST requests. You created simple templates to keep your HTML or other presentation code separated from your application's main logic. You also learned about how sessions and cookies work.

You have finally started learning to use your powers for evil (that's the web clients), but we'd appreciate it if you didn't do that. You learned how to write software to read the HTML on a website and print out interesting information about it. You also used `WWW::Mechanize` to automate the process to fill out forms on web pages. Finally, you learned a bit about using Web APIs to get access web services.

EXERCISES

1. Update the `character.psgi` and related templates to include `Education`. A character can study `Combat`, `Medicine`, or `Engineering`. These should give +2 to `strength`, `health`, and `intelligence`, respectively.

2. Using the updated `characters.psgi` from Exercise 1, update the `WWW::Mechanize` example to generate 100 `Programmer` characters, born on `Earth`, with an `Engineering` education. Print out the average stats for `Strength`, `Intelligence`, and `Health`, with the high and low values. (Actually, the standard deviation would be better, but this is not a statistics book.)

▶ **WHAT YOU LEARNED IN THIS CHAPTER**

TOPIC	KEY CONCEPT
HTTP	A plain-text protocol to communicate between clients and servers.
PSGI	A specification of how web servers and applications can communicate.
Plack	A Perl implementation of PSGI.
Query string	An encoded way of passing additional information to a web application.
GET	A way to fetch HTTP resources, with an embedded query string.
POST	A way to modify HTTP resources.
Cookies	Small bits of text data stored by your browser and returned to a server.
Sessions	A way to maintain information about a particular web client.
`HTML::SimpleLinkExtor`	Extract links from HTML documents.
`HTML::TokeParser::Simple`	Parse HTML documents.
`WWW::Mechanize`	Automate the navigation of web pages.

16

Databases

WHAT YOU WILL LEARN IN THIS CHAPTER:

➤ Understanding Perl's DBI module

➤ Connecting to databases

➤ Selecting data from databases

➤ Using binding parameters

➤ Changing your data

➤ Using transactions

WROX.COM CODE DOWNLOAD FOR THIS CHAPTER

The wrox.com code downloads for this chapter are found at `http://www.wrox.com/remtitle .cgi?isbn=1118013840` on the Download Code tab. The code for this chapter is divided into the following major examples:

➤ `example_16_1_fetch.pl`

➤ `lib/MyDatabase.pm`

➤ `listing_16_1_make_database.pl`

➤ `listing_16_2_populate_database.pl`

➤ `listing_16_3_select.pl`

A database is a place to store your data. It can be a regular file, a sheet of paper, or a hierarchical database such as IMS (no longer widely used). Today, when most people say "database," they're referring to what most people call *relational databases*. If you have a background in programming, you've probably heard of several of them, such as MySQL, PostgreSQL, Oracle, Sybase, and many others. Each of these offers a variety of different features, some favoring data integrity, others focused on performance, and some striving for both.

In this chapter you acquire a minimum knowledge of using databases in Perl. You will use the SQLite database and Perl's DBI module. I chose SQLite because it's easy to install and Perl's DBI module because it is the standard for connecting to databases. There are other tools, such as object-relational mappers (ORMs) that try to hide some of the complexity of databases, but under the hood, most of them use Perl's DBI module.

Understanding how to use databases generally involves understanding Structured Query Language (SQL). If you're not familiar with it, many short tutorials on the web are available. This chapter does not use complicated SQL, so a beginner's knowledge is enough.

As with most of the chapters, this is an introduction to the topic, not a complete tutorial.

USING THE DBI

The DBI module's name stands for *DataBase Interface*. It was invented by Tim Bunce and solved a thorny problem; at one time, special code was available to connect with a handful of databases. You had Oraperl, a version of Perl compiled with code that let you talk directly to the Oracle database. You could also use Sybperl, a set of modules that let you talk to Sybase, but of course, the syntax was different from Oraperl. This was fine if you wanted to talk to only one database and knew that was never going to change. However, this approach had a couple problems:

➤   Switching databases, if needed, was hard.

➤   New developers had to learn a new interface.

Tim Bunce's DBI module provided a standard interface to a wide variety of databases. All you had to do was implement a DBI compatible database driver (called a DBD), and everyone could use DBI with your database.

Connecting to a Database

To use the code in this chapter, you need to install both DBI and DBD::SQLite. If you prefer another database, you can search the CPAN for a driver for your database. Only DBD::SQLite is covered in this section because it requires no configuration, but if you're savvy enough to configure your own, Table 16-1 lists a few of the more popular database drivers. Most of them require that you can compile C code, but your CPAN client will try to handle this for you. Consult the README for each of these modules on the CPAN.

TABLE 16-1: Popular Database Drivers

DATABASE DRIVER	DATABASE
DBD::DB2	IBM's DB2 Universal Database
DBD::mysql	MySQL driver
DBD::ODBC	ODBC driver
DBD::Oracle	Oracle driver
DBD::Pg	PostgreSQL driver
DBD::PgPP	PostgreSQL driver written in pure Perl (slow)
DBD::Sybase	Sybase driver

You generally connect to a database with DBI's connect method. It returns a database handle, traditionally named $dbh. The syntax looks like this:

```
my $dbh = DBI->connect($data_source, $username, $password, \%attributes);
```

The $username and $password are straightforward, but the $data_source and %attributes require some explaining. The $datasource is a colon-delimited string with three values: the string dbi, the driver you want to connect with and the name of the database you want to connect to.

```
my $data_source = "dbi:mysql:database=customers";
my $data_source = "dbi:SQLite:dbname=wrox.db";
```

The %attributes hash is passed as an optional reference as the fourth parameters to the connect() method. It contains key/value pairs to alter the default settings of various parameters. For example, if you want errors to automatically be fatal (a good idea), you could pass { RaiseError => 1 } as the fourth argument. Table 16-2 shows a few of the common attributes passed to database handles.

TABLE 16-2: Common Attributes Passed to the Database Handles

ATTRIBUTE	MEANING	DEFAULT
AutoCommit	Enables transactions	True
PrintError	Makes errors generate warnings	True
RaiseError	Makes all errors fatal	False
ReadOnly	Makes database read-only	False

> **NOTE** *Not all databases drivers support all attributes. Some, such as* DBD::mysql, *have custom attributes available. In particular, the* AutoCommit *attribute is problematic. Some databases do not support transactions. Others do not support disabling transactions. It is strongly recommended that you always provide an explicit* AutoCommit *value in your* %attributes *hash. Failure to do so may become fatal in future versions of DBI.*
>
> *See the "Creating Transactions" section later in this chapter.*

For example, for MySQL, to connect to the orders database and make errors automatically fatal and disable AutoCommit, you could connect like this:

```
use DBI;
my $dbh = DBI->connect(
    'dbi:mysql:database=orders',
    $username,
    $password,
    { RaiseError => 1, PrintError => 0, AutoCommit => 0 },
);
```

That returns a database handle to the orders database, or croaks if it fails to connect. You set PrintError to false because there's generally no need to print the error and then croak(). If you do not have RaiseError set to a true value, the connect() method returns false if it fails to connect, and you need to check this manually:

```
use DBI;
my $dbh = DBI->connect(
    'dbi:mysql:orders',
    $username,
    $password,
    { RaiseError => 0, AutoCommit => 0 },
) or die $DBI::errstr;
```

Because you use DBD::SQLite, the syntax is:

```
use DBI;
my $dbh = DBI->connect(
    "dbi:SQLite:dbname=$dbfile",
    "",
    "",
    { RaiseError => 1, PrintError => 0, AutoCommit => 1 },
);
```

You do not need to load the DBD:: module. DBI attempts to do this for you. (It's a fatal error if it can't.)

When you no longer need to connect to the database, you can call $dbh->disconnect, but because this generally happens when you exit the program, many programmers don't bother. When the database handle goes out of scope (such as at program exit), the handle disconnects for you.

Also be aware that if `RaiseError` is set to a true value and your code throws an exception, any uncommitted changes to your database will be rolled back.

Using SQLite

The SQLite database is a powerful standalone database used in many applications. If you have a smartphone, such as an Android or an iPhone, many of the applications on it use SQLite to store their data. The SQLite home page (`http://www.sqlite.org/`) has this to say about the software:

> *SQLite is a software library that implements a self-contained, serverless, zero-configuration, transactional SQL database engine. SQLite is the most widely deployed SQL database engine in the world. The source code for SQLite is in the public domain.*

SQLite allows multiple users to read from it at the same time, but only one user can write to it at a time. This is a limitation that is fine for many applications, but if you need to frequently write to the database, a proper client/server database, such as PostgreSQL, MySQL, or Oracle is recommended. For your purposes, though, SQLite is perfect.

If you prefer, you can download a precompiled binary for SQLite from `http://www.sqlite.org/download.html`, or you can download the source code from the same link and try to compile it yourself (not recommended unless you have experience compiling software). After you install SQLite, you can use it via a command line with:

```
sqlite3 databasename
```

Where `databasename` is the name of the database file you want to access.

Using DBD::SQLite

The `DBD::SQLite` module is the database driver for SQLite. Because SQLite does not require configuration, it is embedded directly in the `DBD::SQLite` distribution, allowing you, the user, to install the driver, and you can start working with databases.

For these examples in this chapter, assume that you're a multimedia artist and you want to incorporate video, audio, and images from other sources into your work. To protect against DMCA takedown notices, you create a database tracking the media files you use, their media types, and license, plus the source of your media.

Under the hood, SQLite actually has a fairly primitive set of data types. In contrast to other database implementations, you can generally stick any type of data into any column, regardless of how the type is defined. You can stick the string "round peg" into a column defined as an `INTEGER` (unless the column is a primary key). The data types SQLite supports are listed in Table 16-3 and are described at `http://www.sqlite.org/datatype3.html`. Those types, however, are how SQLite manages the types internally and have little bearing on how you declare types.

Throughout this chapter, you see columns defined as `VARCHAR(255)`. SQLite parses that but does not enforce it. However, it makes it easier to migrate to a different database at a later time.

TABLE 16-3: Data Types that SQLite Supports

TYPE	DESCRIPTION
NULL	The value is a NULL value.
INTEGER	The value is a signed integer.
REAL	The value is a floating point value.
TEXT	The value is a text string.
BLOB	The value is a blob of data, stored exactly as it was input.

> **NOTE** *SQLite can actually parse the type information that other data types provide. For example, you can define a* license_name *column as this:*
>
> ```
> license_name VARCHAR(255) NOT NULL
> ```
>
> *However, SQLite uses its own internal types, and you can actually store any kind of data you want in the* license_name *column.*
>
> *For more information about SQLite data types, see* http://www.sqlite.org/datatype3.html.

To get started, let's create a tiny module named MyDatabase (code file lib/MyDatabase.pm). This can export a single function, db_handle(), which you can use to get a database handle to your SQLite database. This saves you the hassle of retyping the database connection code over and over.

```
package MyDatabase;

use strict;
use warnings;

use DBI;
use Carp 'croak';
use Exporter::NoWork;

sub db_handle {
    my $db_file = shift
      or croak "db_handle() requires a database name";
    no warnings 'once';
    return DBI->connect(
        "dbi:SQLite:dbname=$db_file",
        "",      # no username required
        "",      # no password required
        { RaiseError => 1, PrintError => 0, AutoCommit => 1 },
    ) or die $DBH::errstr;
}

1;
```

All the db_handle function does is return a handle to whatever database you like. It should probably be more configurable, but use the following code (code file listing_16_1_make_database.pl) to write the code that creates the actual database:

```
use strict;
use warnings;

use lib 'lib';
use MyDatabase 'db_handle';

my $dbh = db_handle('rights.db');
my $sql_media_type = <<"SQL";
CREATE TABLE IF NOT EXISTS media_types (
    id         INTEGER PRIMARY KEY,
    media_type VARCHAR(10) NOT NULL
);
SQL

$dbh->do($sql_media_type);

my $sql_license = <<"SQL";
CREATE TABLE IF NOT EXISTS licenses (
    id                INTEGER       PRIMARY KEY,
    name              VARCHAR(255) NOT NULL,
    allows_commercial BOOLEAN       NOT NULL
);
SQL
$dbh->do($sql_license);

my $sql_media = <<"SQL";
CREATE TABLE IF NOT EXISTS media (
    id            INTEGER PRIMARY KEY,
    name          VARCHAR(255) NOT NULL,
    location      VARCHAR(255) NOT NULL,
    source        VARCHAR(511) NOT NULL,
    attribution   VARCHAR(255) NOT NULL,
    media_type_id INTEGER      NOT NULL,
    license_id    INTEGER      NOT NULL,
    FOREIGN KEY (media_type_id) REFERENCES media_types(id),
    FOREIGN KEY (license_id)    REFERENCES licenses(id)
);
SQL
$dbh->do($sql_media);
```

> **NOTE** *If you type in the* listing_16_1_make_database.pl *code directly rather than downloading it from* http://www.wrox.com, *it's normal to make mistakes. That's OK. You can just delete the* rights.db *file and run the* listing_16_1_make_database.pl *program as many times as you need until you get it right —*
> *a SQLite benefit!*

In the `listing_16_1_make_database.pl` program, you have three tables:

➤ One defines your three media types, `video`, `audio`, and `image`.

➤ One defines your licenses, such as public domain or the various Creative Commons licenses (http://creativecommons.org/licenses/). You define only a subset of them needed for your examples.

➤ One defines our media, or the data that you, as the artist formerly known as a Perl programmer, will be creating.

   Unlike other databases, SQLite creates the database for you when you first reference it. Thus, even if you didn't have a file named `rights.db` when you started, you will after you run this code.

After you have your database handle, `$dbh`, you define our three tables and call the `do()` method on `$dbh`. Use the `do()` method if you want to execute a command but don't care about the return values. In the previous examples, because your database handle is defined with `RaiseError => 1`, you don't have to check the return value of `do()` because it automatically dies if the SQL fails to execute. If you did not set `RaiseError` to true, you'd need to wrap every method in something like this:

```
if ( ! $dbh->do($some_sql) ) {
    die $dbh->errstr;
}
```

That gets tedious and it's easy to forget, so `RaiseError => 1` is safer.

> **NOTE** Use the `$DBH::errstr` package variable when you test for a failure with `connect()` because if it fails, you don't have a `$dbh` to call the `errstr()` method with.

Now that you created the database, if you installed an `sqlite3` client, you can check from the command line that it worked:

```
$ sqlite3 rights.db
SQLite version 3.7.7 2011-06-25 16:35:41
Enter ".help" for instructions
Enter SQL statements terminated with a ";"
sqlite> .schema
CREATE TABLE licenses (
    id                 INTEGER      PRIMARY KEY,
    name               VARCHAR(255) NOT NULL,
    allows_commercial  BOOLEAN      NOT NULL
);
CREATE TABLE media (
    id                 INTEGER PRIMARY KEY,
    name               VARCHAR(255) NOT NULL,
    location           VARCHAR(255) NOT NULL,
```

```
    source        VARCHAR(511) NOT NULL,
    attribution   VARCHAR(255) NOT NULL,
    media_type_id INTEGER      NOT NULL,
    license_id    INTEGER      NOT NULL,
    FOREIGN KEY (media_type_id) REFERENCES media_types(id),
    FOREIGN KEY (license_id)    REFERENCES licenses(id)
);
CREATE TABLE media_types (
    id         INTEGER PRIMARY KEY,
    media_type VARCHAR(10) NOT NULL
);
sqlite> .quit
```

Now that you have your database, it's time to add some data (code file listing_16_2_populate_database.pl).

> **WARNING** *You declared foreign key constraints in your media table. This should guarantee that you cannot insert an unknown value into the columns with foreign key constraints. Depending on the version of SQLite you have installed, it may or may not enforce foreign key constraints.*

```perl
use strict;
use warnings;

use lib 'lib';
use MyDatabase 'db_handle';

my $dbh = db_handle('rights.db');
my $sql_media_type = "INSERT INTO media_types (media_type) VALUES (?)";
my $sth            = $dbh->prepare($sql_media_type);
my %media_type_id_for;

foreach my $type (qw/video audio image/) {
    $sth->execute($type);
    $media_type_id_for{$type} = $dbh->last_insert_id("","","","");
}

my $sql_license = <<"SQL";
INSERT INTO licenses (name, allows_commercial)
VALUES               ( ?, ? )
SQL
$sth = $dbh->prepare($sql_license);

my @licenses = (
    [ 'Public Domain',                      1 ],
    [ 'Attribution CC BY',                  1 ],
    [ 'Attribution CC BY-SA',               1 ],
    [ 'Attribution-NonCommercial CC BY-NC', 0 ],
);
```

```perl
my %license_id_for;
foreach my $license (@licenses) {
    my ( $name, $allows_commercial ) = @$license;
    $sth->execute( $name, $allows_commercial );
    $license_id_for{$name} = $dbh->last_insert_id("","","","");
}

my @media = (
    [
        'Anne Frank Stamp',
        '/data/images/anne_fronk_stamp.jpg',
        'http://commons.wikimedia.org/wiki/File:Anne_Frank_stamp.jpg',
        'Deutsche Post',
        $media_type_id_for{'image'},
        $license_id_for{'Public Domain'},
    ],
    [
        'Clair de Lune',
        '/data/audio/claire_de_lune.ogg',
        'http://commons.wikimedia.org/wiki/File:Sonate_Clair_de_lune.ogg',
        'Schwarzer Stern',
        $media_type_id_for{'audio'},
        $license_id_for{'Public Domain'},
    ],
);

my $sql_media = <<'SQL';
INSERT INTO media (
    name, location, source, attribution,
    media_type_id, license_id
)
VALUES ( ?, ?, ?, ?, ?, ? )
SQL

$sth = $dbh->prepare($sql_media);
foreach my $media (@media) {
    $sth->execute(@$media);
}
```

The previous code is conceptually similar to your listing_16_1_make_database.pl program, but instead of calling do(), you call the prepare() and execute() methods. For now, you can run this program to populate your database. You take a closer look at how these work when you get to the "Inserting and Updating Data" section.

After you write and run the code, you can use the command-line client to make sure that you populated your database correctly:

```
$ sqlite3 rights.db
SQLite version 3.7.7 2011-06-25 16:35:41
Enter ".help" for instructions
Enter SQL statements terminated with a ";"
sqlite> select * from media_types;
1|video
```

```
2|audio
3|image
sqlite> select * from licenses;
1|Public Domain|1
2|Attribution CC BY|1
3|Attribution CC BY-SA|1
4|Attribution-NonCommercial CC BY-NC|0
sqlite> select * from media;
sqlite> .quit
```

After you create your database and insert some data, it's time to get it back out.

SELECTING BASIC DATA

The great thing about databases is that the data is persistent. If you stop your application and later restart it, the data is still there. But it's useless until you know how to select that data. This section shows you various ways to do that. You can select data in many ways and need to find one that suits your needs.

Using SELECT Statements

You've seen that if you want to execute an SQL statement once and don't care about the return value, you can do the following:

```
$dbh->do($sql);
```

If you want to execute an SQL statement many times and don't care about the return value, you can do this:

```
my $sth = $dbh->prepare($insert_sql);
foreach my $value (@values) {
    $sth->execute($value);
}
```

For retrieving data, however, you have several options. One of the most common is to prepare the SQL, execute it, and then repeatedly fetch the results. There are many ways to fetch the results, depending on your needs. The following code (code file `listing_16_3_select.pl`) is one way to fetch your media types:

```
use strict;
use warnings;

use lib 'lib';
use MyDatabase 'db_handle';

my $dbh = db_handle('rights.db');
my $sth = $dbh->prepare(<<"SQL");
  SELECT id, media_type
    FROM media_types
```

```
ORDER BY id ASC
SQL
$sth->execute;

while ( my @row = $sth->fetchrow_array ) {
    print "$row[0] - $row[1]\n";
}
```

Running the program should print:

```
1 - video
2 - audio
3 - image
```

A WORD ABOUT ROW ORDER

If you do not specify an ORDER BY clause in your SQL, the order in which the rows
are retrieved are not guaranteed. You should not rely on the default order in which
the database returns the rows, which is why your author put an ORDER BY in his
first SELECT statement in this chapter. If you need something to be in a specific
order, be explicit. Do not assume that a given database will cooperate.

On a related note, if you specify SELECT *, you should not rely on the order in
which your columns are presented, or if they even exist! Your DBA (database
administrator), another developer, and even you, may have altered the database.
This means that the code makes a fragile assumption — that the desired columns
are present and in the correct order. The order of rows, the order or existence of
columns should not be assumed. Developers must be explicit in their intent.

Now break down what's happening here.

1. You prepare a SQL statement, taking care to be explicit about the columns you want and
the order in which the rows should appear. A statement handle, $sth, is returned:

```
my $sth = $dbh->prepare(<<"SQL");
  SELECT id, media_type
    FROM media_types
ORDER BY id ASC
SQL
```

2. You execute the statement handle. No arguments to execute() are required because you
did not have any bind parameters in your SQL. (Bind parameters are explained in the next
section.)

```
$sth->execute;
```

3. You iterate over the results:

```
while ( my @row = $sth->fetchrow_array ) {
    print "$row[0] - $row[1]\n";
}
```

The `fetchrow_array()` method returns an array of the next row's values each time it is called. When there are no more rows, it returns nothing, terminating the loop.

If you consult the DBI documentation (`perldoc DBI`), you can find that there are many such iterators, each custom tailored to a slightly different need. For example, some people prefer hash references to be returned. You can add these lines to your program:

```
$sth->execute;
while ( my $row = $sth->fetchrow_hashref ) {
    print "$row->{id} - $row->{media_type}\n";
}
```

Calling `execute()` on the statement handle executes the SQL again, allowing you to iterate over the rows again. The result is fairly straightforward. The keys in the hash are the column names and the values are, well, the values of each column.

WARNING *One problem you sometimes find with SQL is that it allows duplicate column names. This means that the following is quite legal:*

```
my $sql = <<'SQL';
SELECT first_name as 'name', last_name as 'name'
  FROM customers
SQL

my $sth = $dbh->prepare($sql);
$sth->execute;

while ( my $row = $dbh->fetchrow_hashref ) {
    print $row->{name};    # ???
}
```

You can't tell which name is which! If you use table aliases:

```
my $sql = <<'SQL';
SELECT c.name, p.name
  FROM people c
  JOIN projects  p ON p.manager_id = c.id
SQL
```

The names now look different, but after you call `fetchrow_hashref()`, *the table alias is stripped, and you still have two columns named* name! *Of course, because you put them into a hash reference, there can be only one key named* name, *and you'll lose one of the values. If you can't avoid this SQL, consider returning results as arrays or array references instead of hash references. The two columns with identical names will be fine.*

> **NOTE** When you finish using the statement handle, you can call $sth->finish,
> but there is generally no reason to call it. After you fetch all of your data, or after
> the statement handle has fallen out of scope, finish() is called for you. See the
> DBI documentation for more information.

Many people prefer to return an array reference instead of an array, so you can do that, too:

```
$sth->execute;
while ( my $row = $sth->fetchrow_arrayref ) {
    print "$row->[0] - $row->[1]\n";
}
```

Methods are available that allow you to skip the iterator and return all your data at one time. These methods are generally called directly against the database handle and prepare, execute, and fetch your data all in one go:

```
use Data::Dumper;
my $media_types = $dbh->selectall_arrayref($sql);
print Dumper($media_types);
```

selectall_* methods are good for selecting small amounts of data. If your SQL statement returns a huge amount of data, it may not be a good idea to use them if you're worried about how much memory your program is using. They are, however, convenient for datasets you know will be small.

There are many other ways to select data from your database handle. Browse perldoc DBI to become acquainted with them.

Using Bind Parameters

Selecting all the data from a table is useful, but usually you want to select some data that matches a particular condition. However, a common beginner mistake is to do something like this:

```
my $sql_city_ids = "SELECT id FROM cities WHERE name = '$city_name'";
my $city_ids = $dbh->selectcol_arrayref($sql_city_ids);
```

If the $city_name is R'lyeh, you have a serious nightmare on your hands. After the variable $city_name is interpolated, your resulting SQL will look like this:

```
"SELECT id FROM cities WHERE name = 'R'lyeh'";
```

That's not valid SQL. If you're lucky, it will die. If you're unlucky, you may fall victim to something known as a *SQL injection attack*. This is one of the most common ways to attack software.

Thus, you should always use placeholders. Instead of embedding the variable in the SQL, embed a question mark:

```
my $sql = "SELECT id FROM media_types WHERE media_type = ?";
my $sth = $dbh->prepare($sql);
```

Then supply your variable (or variables, if you have multiple bind parameters) as the argument(s) to
`execute()`:

```
$sth->execute($media_of_interest);
while ( my @row = $sth->fetchrow_array ) {
    print "Id is '$row[0]\n";
}
```

When you do this, you supply the values of the bind parameters as arguments to the `execute()`
method. Internally, the database takes the prepared SQL and replaces the bind parameters with the
variable or variables you supplied to `execute()`. Even if the variable has quotes or other characters
that may be otherwise dangerous in SQL, the database should properly quote the values for you,
and you can safely run the SQL. As an added bonus, this is often much faster than repeatedly
preparing SQL statements with different variables.

> **WARNING** Sometimes it's hard to avoid embedding variables in your SQL
> because placeholders are allowed only for column data, for example:
>
> ```
> SELECT name, percentage FROM $table WHERE $column = ...
> ```
>
> You can't use placeholders to replace table or column names, only column val-
> ues. Thus, you must take extra care if build your SQL dynamically because SQL
> injection attacks have destroyed more than one company. If you must use a
> variable for an identifier such as the table name or column name, you can use
> the `quote_identifier()` method:
>
> ```
> # Make sure a table name we want to use is safe:
> $table_name = $dbh->quote_identifier($table_name);
>
> # Assume @cols contains a list of column names you need to fetch:
> my $cols = join ',', map { $dbh->quote_identifier($_) } @cols;
> my $sth = $dbh->prepare("SELECT $cols FROM $table_name ...");
> ```
>
> For more information about SQL Injection attacks, see http://www.bobby-tables
> .com/, a website created by Andy Lester. It's a gentle introduction to the prob-
> lem, along with examples of how to avoid the problem in many programming
> languages.

You can use more than one placeholder in a SQL statement. Just be sure to pass the same number
arguments to `execute()` as you have placeholders.

Also, many DBI methods have the following form:

```
$dbh->$method($sql, \%attributes, @bind_params);
```

The `%attributes` hashref in the middle is optional (in the sense that you can pass `undef`
for that argument) and rarely used (see the DBI docs for more information). What the rest

of that statement does is allow you execute a method, passing the SQL and bind parameters at the same time:

```
foreach my $id (@ids) {
    my $name = $new_name_for{$id};
    $dbh->do(
        'UPDATE customers SET name = ? WHERE id = ?',
        undef,
        $name, $id
    );
}
```

The methods that allow this syntax are documented in the SYNOPSIS of the DBI documentation.

TRY IT OUT Fetching Records from a Table

You've collected vast amounts of media that you want to sift through for your multimedia project, and you are looking for images in the public domain that you can include. You can write a small program to do this. All the code in this Try It Out is in the code file example_16_1_fetch.pl.

1. Type in the following program, and save it as example_16_1_fetch.pl:

```
use strict;
use warnings;

use lib 'lib';
use Data::Dumper;
use MyDatabase 'db_handle';

my $dbh = db_handle('rights.db');
my $sql = <<'SQL';
  SELECT m.name, location, attribution
    FROM media m
    JOIN media_types mt ON m.media_type_id = mt.id
    JOIN licenses    l  ON m.license_id    = l.id
   WHERE mt.media_type = ?
     AND l.name        = ?
ORDER BY m.name ASC
SQL

my $sth = $dbh->prepare($sql);
$sth->execute('image','Public Domain');

while ( my $media = $sth->fetchrow_hashref ) {
    print <<"END_MEDIA";
Name:        $media->{name}
Location:    $media->{location}
Attribution: $media->{attribution}
END_MEDIA
}
```

2. Run the program with `perl example_16_1_fetch.pl`. You should see the following output:

```
Name:        Anne Frank Stamp
Location:    /data/anne_fronk_stamp.jpg
Attribution: Deutsche Post
```

How It Works

In this example, you have only one record that satisfies your criteria (the Anne Frank Stamp), so only one record is printed out. The bulk of the logic is in the SQL:

```
SELECT m.name, location, attribution
  FROM media m
  JOIN media_types mt ON m.media_type_id = mt.id
  JOIN licenses    l  ON m.license_id    = l.id
 WHERE mt.media_type = ?
   AND l.name        = ?
ORDER BY m.name ASC
```

This SQL selects the media name, location, and attribution from the media table, but the WHERE clause limits you to a given media type and license name. The JOIN conditions tell the SQL how to match the media type and license to the media record. You have two bind parameters in the SQL.

Next, you prepare the SQL and execute the resulting statement handle, passing in the wanted media type and license name:

```
my $sth = $dbh->prepare($sql);
$sth->execute('image','Public Domain');
```

Then it's printing out each record:

```
while ( my $media = $sth->fetchrow_hashref ) {
    print <<"END_MEDIA";
Name:        $media->{name}
Location:    $media->{location}
Attribution: $media->{attribution}
END_MEDIA
}
```

The m.name column in the SQL is accessed as $media->{name} in the hash reference. That's because the column alias is stripped from the key name when it is put into the hash. However, you had to use m.name in the SQL, or SQLite would not know if you need the media name or the license name.

Inserting and Updating Data

Naturally, you need to add and update data to your database. In this case, you'll be happy to know that your Perl code is almost identical.

Here's the code that inserted your media types:

```
my $sql_media_type = "INSERT INTO media_types (media_type) VALUES (?)";
my $sth            = $dbh->prepare($sql_media_type);
```

```
foreach my $type (qw/video audio image/) {
    $sth->execute($type);
}
```

If you know SQL, this is fairly straightforward. Updating, however, might be tricky, depending on your needs. The execute method actually has a return value you've been ignoring. Specifically, it returns the number of rows you inserted or updated. So if you want to change the name of the Anne Frank Stamp to The Anne Frank Stamp, run the following code:

```
my $sql = 'UPDATE media SET name = ? WHERE name = ?';
my $sth = $dbh->prepare($sql);
my $rows_updated = $sth->execute('The Anne Frank Stamp','Anne Frank Stmap');
print $rows_updated;
```

This code prints (the exact result may vary depending on the database):

```
0E0
```

Which means you've not updated any rows. In this case, it's because you misspelled Stamp as Stmap. When you correct this error in the previous code:

```
my $sql = 'UPDATE media SET name = ? WHERE name = ?';
my $sth = $dbh->prepare($sql);
my $rows_updated = $sth->execute('The Anne Frank Stamp','Anne Frank Stamp');
print $rows_updated;
```

you now get 1 printed because you updated 1 row. Naturally, it's easy to update more than one row at a time (for example, if you were to delete several records at one time). Whenever you change your data, you should consider checking the number of rows that you've affected and make sure that you have a reasonable response.

Creating Transactions

One of the most powerful features of databases, if used correctly, is the capability to minimize data corruption. One way to manage this is with the correct use of transactions. Sometimes you need to execute several SQL statements, and if one of them fails, all of them should fail, and the system should be left in the state it started in. The classic example follows:

```
sub transfer_money {
    my ( $self, $from, $to, $amount ) = @_;
    $self->adjust_account( $from, -$amount );
    $self->adjust_account( $to,    $amount );
}
```

What would happen if the first adjust_account() succeeded but the second failed? In the preceding code, presumably the first account would have the amount deducted, and the second account would have no money added, resulting in money being misplaced. This tends to make people unhappy.

In a database, this is handled with transactions. A *transaction* is a group of SQL statements that must all succeed or fail. After you start the transaction, if all SQL statements succeed, you commit the transaction and the changes take effect. If any of the statements fail, you roll back the results and none of the changes take effect, even for those statements that succeeded after the transaction started.

In your `transfer_money()` example, a transaction would look like the following code (using `Try::Tiny` to catch any exceptions):

```
sub transfer_money {
    my ( $self, $from, $to, $amount ) = @_;

    try {
        $self->begin_work;      # start transaction
        $self->adjust_account( $from, -$amount );
        $self->adjust_account( $to,    $amount );
        $self->dbh->commit;     # commit the changes
    }
    catch {
        my $error = $_;
        $self->dbh->rollback;
        croak "Could not transfer $amount from $from to $to";
    };
}
```

In this simple example, you have an object where the database handle is available as an accessor. You can call `$dbh->begin_work()` to start the transaction and `$dbh->commit()` at the end of the work. However, if an exception is thrown before you call `commit`, the control passes to the catch block and `$dbh->rollback` is called.

The previous code had `AutoCommit => 1` passed as database options to `connect()`. This means that every SQL statement's changes affect the database the moment they are executed. For many simple statements, this is fine, but if you have multiple statements related to one another, you probably want a transaction. You need to read your databases documentation to understand how transactions are handled. You can group databases in roughly three categories:

➤   Databases that do not support transactions

➤   Databases that do not support disabling transactions

➤   Databases where transactions must be explicitly started with `begin_work()`

If your database does not support transactions, setting `AutoCommit` to 0 is a fatal error. If your database requires transactions and you set `AutoCommit` to 1, `commit()` is called for you after every statement either by the database or, if the database does not support this, by `DBI`.

Handling Errors

It is recommended that you set `RaiseError => 1` in your `connect()` options (and `PrintError` to 0 unless you want the error printed twice). However, if you're a glutton for punishment, you can check for errors.

Generally, the connect() method dies only if it cannot load the requested database driver. Otherwise, if it cannot connect to the database, it returns undef. You can then use $DBH::errstr to check for the error:

```
my $dbh = DBI->connect($dsn, $user, $pass, $options)
    or die $DBH::errstr;
```

Many other statements also return false upon failure, such as begin_work(), commit(), rollback(), bind_col(), and other methods not covered here. If you do not set RaiseError to a true value, you must manually check the return value of these methods:

```
$dbh->begin_work or die $dbh->errstr;
```

Some methods, such as execute(), return a value that may be false but doesn't indicate an error. Either spend time memorizing the differences of all these or just set RaiseError => 1 to save yourself the trouble (not to mention the inevitable bugs when you forget to check success or failure of that critical method call).

Of course, you can always trap the error with eval or Try::Tiny. Typically, you use RaiseError with eval { ... } to catch the exception that's been thrown and you follow this with an if ($@) { ... } block to handle the caught exception, for example:

```
eval {
  ...
  $sth->execute();
  ...
};
if (my $error = $@) {
  # $sth->err and $DBI::err will be true if error was from DBI
  warn $error; # print the error
  ... # do whatever you need to deal with the error
}
```

If you do this, make sure you can handle the error properly. Otherwise, it may be better to let the program die rather than risk hiding important errors.

SUMMARY

In this chapter you learned the basics to work with databases. You learned a little about SQLite and how to select data from the database, how to safely insert and update data, and how to manage transactions. You also learned about error handling (and why you should let DBI do it for you).

1. The following code is broken. Explain how to fix it.

```
use strict;
use warnings;

use DBI;

my $dbh = DBI->connect(
    'dbi:SQLite:dbname=customers',
    '',
    '',
    { RaiseError => 1, AutoCommit => 1 },
);

my $sth = $dbh->prepare("SELECT id, name FROM customers");

while ( my @row = $sth->fetchrow_array ) {
    print "ID: $row[0] Name: $row[1]\n";
}
```

2. You realize that all media you put under the `Public Domain` license should be under the `Attribution CC BY` license and everything under the `Attribution CC BY` license should be under the `Public Domain` license. Because other code uses the `Public Domain` and `Attribution CC BY` licenses, you can't switch the license names. Switch the media to their correct licenses, but do so in such a way that if you make an error in one step, you don't wind up with bad data.

▶ **WHAT YOU LEARNED IN THIS CHAPTER**

TOPIC	DESCRIPTION
Databases	A persistent data storage solution.
DBI	The standard database interface for Perl.
DBD	A database driver for connecting to your particular database.
SQLite	A free, public domain database; great for standalone applications.
DBD::SQLite	The database driver for SQLite.
Bind parameters	A safe way to use variable data in SQL queries.
Transactions	Used when you have multiple, related SQL statements that must succeed or fail as a group.
Error handling	Various ways to deal with real and potential database errors.

17

Plays Well with Others

WHAT YOU WILL LEARN IN THIS CHAPTER:

➤ Reading user input from `STDIN` and handling command-line arguments

➤ Reading and writing from/to other programs and understanding `STDOUT` and `STDERR`

WROX.COM CODE DOWNLOAD FOR THIS CHAPTER

You can find the wrox.com code downloads for this chapter at `http://www.wrox.com/remtitle.cgi?isbn=1118013840` on the Download Code tab. The code for this chapter is divided into the following major examples:

➤ `listing_17_1_directions.pl`

➤ `example_17_1_poets.pl`

➤ `example_17_2_capture.pl`

➤ `listing_17_2_wc.pl`

Up to this point, you've learned quite a bit about how Perl programs work, but they've largely been standalone programs. You haven't done much work reading information from the command line or reading from or writing to other programs and you haven't deeply investigated how output is handled. This chapter, although not the last, "wraps up" your beginning Perl knowledge and puts you on the path to becoming a well-rounded Perl developer.

THE COMMAND LINE

If your previous experience with computers has been limited to graphical user interfaces (GUIs), you may have trouble understanding the full power of the command line. Although a pretty graphic interface can make it easy to see how things are organized, it can make some things harder. For example, moving a file to a different directory and renaming it are two steps requiring a few clicks. From the command line, to move `foo.txt` to `backups/mydata.txt`, you can do this in with command:

```
mv foo.txt backups/mydata.txt
```

Or in Microsoft Windows, use `cmd` shell:

```
move foo.txt backups\mydata.txt
```

Or imagine that you have a file named events containing many lines of data like this:

```
ovid:2009-03-12:created:admin
bob:2012-03-12:updated:user
```

That's a colon-delimited list of data. Say that you want to extract all the dates from that file and count the number of times each date occurred, and write that out to a file. You might think that you should write a program to do this, but you can do this from a standard UNIX-style command line:

```
cut -d: -f2 < events | sort | uniq -c > events.txt
```

I'm not going to explain what all that means, but suffice it to say, working with the command line, although not as "pretty" as working with graphic interfaces, can put a huge amount of power at your fingertips. Most of this book is geared toward giving you the basic skills required to write programs, but you may need to run many of those programs from the command line, so I'll start showing you some of the basic techniques you need to understand.

Reading User Input

Perhaps the most basic thing you might want to do from a program is to read what a user types in:

```
use strict;
use warnings;

print "Enter your name: ";
my $name = <STDIN>;
chomp($name);

print "Hello, $name!\n";
```

If you run this program, it prints `Enter your name:` and waits for you to enter something and press Enter. Then it prints that "something." So if you enter `Ovid` for your name, you would see this:

```
Enter your name: Ovid
Hello, Ovid!
```

The <STDIN> syntax looks a bit odd. You already know the angle brackets are generally wrapped around a filehandle to read from that filehandle, but what's STDIN? I'll need to give a bit of a long explanation for you to understand how this work.

For Perl, and for many modern programming languages, you have one input stream of data (STDIN) and two output streams of data, one for normal output (STDOUT) and one for error output (STDERR). STDIN, STDOUT, and STDERR are all special filehandles, and a stream is the sequence of data made available over time. So when you type your name in the previous program, you can take your time typing each character until you finally press Enter. When you press Enter, Perl reads the data from the STDIN and returns it, in this case by assigning it to the $name variable. The STDIN filehandle returns exactly what you typed, the string plus the newline, so you call chomp() to remove that newline.

When you print something in Perl, by default it prints to STDOUT. You may recall that you can print something to a filehandle like this:

```
open my $fh, '>', $filename
or die "Cannot open $filename for writing: $!";
print $fh "Here is a line of text\n";
```

What happens when you omit the filehandle? By default, Perl uses STDOUT. Thus, the following two lines mean the same thing:

```
print "Hello, $name!'n";
print STDOUT "Hello, $name!'n";
```

When you warn or die, the message is instead printed to STDERR. The following two lines are almost the same thing:

```
print STDERR "This is a warning!\n";
warn "This is a warning!\n";
```

> **NOTE** *I've said that the following two are almost the same thing:*
>
> ```
> print STDERR "This is a warning!\n";
> warn "This is a warning!\n";
> ```
>
> *They're not quite the same because you can trap warnings with signal handlers, but you cannot use a signal handler to trap data printing directly to STDERR. Signal handlers are tricky (and a frequent source of obscure bugs), but you can read* perldoc perlipc *to learn more about them.*

When data sent to STDOUT and STDERR shows up on your terminal, it looks the same, but because it is sent to different streams, it doesn't show up in the same order your program output them. Normally this is not a problem, but it's something you should be aware of.

The reason STDOUT and STDERR are sent to separate streams is because you can get more control over them. From the command line, you could redirect STDERR to a log file and have STDOUT show up in the terminal, and vice versa. I won't cover much more of that, but it's part of what's tricky about understanding data streams when you program. Just remember that when you print something, it usually does what you want it to do.

Because STDIN is a stream, you can read from it multiple times:

```
use strict;
use warnings;

print "Enter your name: ";

my $name = <STDIN>;
chomp($name);
print "Hello, $name!\n";
print "Anything else you want to bore me with? ";

my $inane_reply = <STDIN>;
chomp($inane_reply);
print "You bored me with: $inane_reply\n";
```

Any time you want to read from STDIN, it's there, waiting for you patiently, like some creepy little stalker.

Handling Command-Line Arguments

You've seen several examples in this book of reading from @ARGV, which, as you know, contains arguments supplied on the command line. So you could save this as dump_args.pl:

```
use strict;
use warnings;
use Data::Dumper;
print Dumper(\@ARGV);
```

And then run it with:

```
perl dump_args.pl this is a list of arguments
```

And you should get the following output:

```
$VAR1 = [
          'this',
          'is',
          'a',
          'list',
          'of',
          'arguments'
        ];
```

Many times, however, you want to pass arguments to your program and give them specific names to make it easier for your program to understand them. For example, you may recall that in

Chapter 7, "Subroutines," you had a program called `maze.pl`. In that program, you needed to specify the height and width of the maze. A common way to do this follows:

```
perl maze.pl --height 20 --width 40
```

You could handle that in many ways, including writing your own parser, but you have plenty of modules on the CPAN to do this for you. Most of these are in the `Getopt::` namespace. For this example, I'll use `Getopt::Long`, by Johan Vromansbecause this is one of the most popular choices:

```
use strict;
use warnings;

useGetopt::Long;
my ( $height, $width );

GetOptions(
    'height=i' => \$height,
    'width=i'  => \$width,
) or die "Could not parse options";

# the rest of your program here
```

When you use `Getopt::Long`, it exports a `GetOptions` function. This function expects an even size list of name/variable pairs. The "name" of each option is actually a specification of how to read that option from the command line. In this example, the `=i` in `height=i` says "the `--height` option must have an integer value." Of course, that integer value could be negative, so you may need to do some validation after.

The variable `$height` gets passed as a reference. Because you pass by reference instead of value, the `Getopt::Long` module can modify the variable's value directly. Thus, with the previous code, passing either of the following command lines sets `$height` and `$width` to 20 and 30, respectively (because the = sign is optional):

```
perl maze.pl --height 20 --width 30
perl maze.pl --height=20 --width=30
```

What's going on is that when you run the program, `@ARGV` contains all the values passed in the command line. For the two preceding examples, `@ARGV` contains this:

```
# perl maze.pl --height 20 --width 30
@ARGV = ('--height', '20', '--width', '30');
# perl maze.pl --height=20 --width=30
@ARGV = ('--height=20', '--width=30');
```

`Getopt::Long` removes all arguments from `@ARGV` that it can parse, leaving the remaining arguments in `@ARGV`, for example, if you have a program named `print_it.pl`:

```
use strict;
use warnings;
```

```
useGetopt::Long;

my $times = 1;

GetOptions(
    'times=i' => \$times,
) or die "Could not parse options";

if ( $times < 1 ) {
die "The --times argument must be greater than zero";
}
my $args = join '-', @ARGV;

for ( 1 .. $times ) {
print "$args\n";
}
```

And you run it with:

```
perl print_it.pl --times 3 bob dobbs
```

It prints out the following:

```
bob-dobbs
bob-dobbs
bob-dobbs
```

Getopt::Long also takes the minimum unique string for each option. (The single dash is optional.)

```
perl maze.pl -h 20 -w 30
```

Sometimes you don't want to assign a value to an option, you just want to know if it's present. For example, you program might print out additional information such as the directories it's creating, the data it has read from a configuration file, and so on. But you might want this information displayed only if you request it with a --verbose switch:

```
perl some_program.pl --verbose
```

And in your program:

```
useGetopt::Long;

my $is_verbose;

GetOptions(
    'verbose' => \$is_verbose,
) or die "Could not parse options";
```

With this, $is_verbose has a true value if you included --verbose (or -v) on the command line, or a false value if you omitted it.

If you include =s with the option name, it expects a string:

```
useGetopt::Long;

my $name = "Ovid";

GetOptions(
    'name=s' => \$name,
) or die "Could not parse options";

print "Hello, $name\n";
```

And run that with:

```
perl get_name.pl --name Bob
```

That prints `Hello, Bob`. If you do not supply an argument, the `$name` value defaults to `Ovid` because `GetOptions` does not overwrite a value if there is no corresponding value on the command line.

If your string has whitespace in it, you need to quote it (Windows requires double quotes: `"Bob Dobbs"`):

```
perl get_name.pl --name 'Bob Dobbs'
```

That's because when you run your program with the preceding arguments, `@ARGV` is as follows without the quoting:

```
@ARGV = ('--name', 'Bob', 'Dobbs');
```

And this with the quoting:

```
@ARGV = ('--name', 'Bob Dobbs');
```

When using `Getopt::Long`, you find that standalone arguments (like the `--verbose` example), string arguments (`--name='Bob'`), and integer arguments (`--height` and `--width`) are the most common types of command-line arguments, but there are many more ways to handle your parsing. See `perldoc Getopt::Long` for more details.

perlrun

Because I'm going in-depth about how to run Perl programs from the command line, it would be a bad thing to forget to mention the oft-overlooked `perlrun` documentation. By reading `perldoc perlrun`, you can learn many things about how to create useful Perl one-liners to solve thorny problems, or perhaps how to use interesting switches that can make your life easier.

The following sections give some examples.

Using the−I Switch

The `-I` switch tells Perl which paths to include when searching for modules to use or require. For example, I often included this line in sample programs:

```
use lib 'lib/';
```

That line tells Perl to also search for Perl modules in the `lib/` directory. However, you can use the `-I` switch to do this from the command line:

```
perl -Ilib/ some_program.pl
```

You can specify this more than once:

```
perl -Ilib/ -I../mylib/ some_program.pl
```

Using the –e and –l Switches

The `-e` switch is for executing the text that follows, instead of assuming it's a program. That's sometimes used with the `-l` switch that automatically adds a newline after every print statement. Here's one way to find out which version of `Moose` you have installed:

```
perl -l -e 'use Moose; print Moose->VERSION'
```

At the present time on my system, that prints something like:

```
$ perl -l -e 'use Moose; print Moose->VERSION'
2.0402
$
```

Note that the `$` prompt is on a line by itself. Without the `-l` switch, you get the following output:

```
$ perl -l -e 'use Moose; print Moose->VERSION'
2.0402$
```

That may be annoying to you, so the `-l` switch makes it nicer to read.

If the switches don't take arguments, you can "bundle" them together. For example, instead of `perl -l -e`, you can use `perl -le`:

```
perl -le 'use Moose; print Moose->VERSION'
```

Using the –n Switch

The `-n` switch wraps a `while (<>) { ... }` loop around your program. As you might recall, the `while(<>) { ... }` syntax reads each successive line from filenames found in `@ARGV` and assigns the line values to `$_`. Thus, to print out all the comments in a few programs:

```
perl -ne 'print if /^\s*#/' program1.pl program2.pl program3.pl
```

That's more or less equivalent to this:

```
use strict;
use warnings;

PROGRAM: foreach my $program (@ARGV) {
    if (open my $fh, '<', $program) {
        while (<$fh>) {
```

```
            print $_ if /^\s*#/;
        }
    }
    else {
        warn "Could not open $program for reading: $!";
        next PROGRAM;
    }
}
```

As you can see, the command-line switches documented in `perlrun` give you a lot of power from the command line, but they can be daunting to learn. Hit your favorite search engine and search for **perl one-liners** to see many more examples. They're popular.

And don't forget to dive into `perldoc perlrun`.

TRY IT OUT Query the Google API from the Command Line

In Chapter 15, "The Interwebs,"you had a sample program that enabled you to query Google directions from the command line. However, you hard-coded the start and end locations into the program. That's not useful. Now you're going to rewrite this to allow you to change your start and end locations from the command line. All the code for this Try It Out is in the code file `listing_17_1_directions.pl`.

1. Type in the following program and save it as `listing_17_1_directions.pl`:

```
use strict;
use warnings;

use WWW::Mechanize;
use HTML::Strip;
use JSON::Any;
use URI::Encode 'uri_encode';
use utf8::all;
use Getopt::Long;

my ( $start, $end );
GetOptions(
    'start=s' => \$start,
    'end=s'   => \$end,
) or die "Could not parse options";

unless ( $start and $end ) {
    die "Both --start and --end arguments must be supplied";
}

if ( @ARGV ) {
    my $args = join ', ', @ARGV;
    die <<"END";
Your \@ARGV contained '$args'. Did you forget to quote something?
--start=$start
--end=$end
END
}

print "Searching for directions from '$start' to '$end'\n";
```

```
$start = uri_encode($start);
$end   = uri_encode($end);

my $url   = "http://maps.googleapis.com/maps/api/directions/json";
my $query = "origin=$start&destination=$end&sensor=false";
my $mech  = WWW::Mechanize->new;

$mech->get("$url?$query");

my $object = JSON::Any->new->decode( $mech->content );

unless ( 'OK' eq $object->{status} ) {
    die $object->{status};
}
my $route      = $object->{routes}[0];
my $copyrights = $route->{copyrights};
my $warnings   = $route->{warnings};
my $legs       = $route->{legs}[0];          # only take the first
my $distance   = $legs->{distance}{text};
my $duration   = $legs->{duration}{text};

print "$copyrights\nThe trip is $distance long and "
    . "lasts $duration\n\n";
print join "\n" => @$warnings;
print "\n";

my $strip = HTML::Strip->new;

foreach my $step ( @{ $legs->{steps} } ) {
    my $distance     = $step->{distance}{text};
    my $duration     = $step->{duration}{text};
    my $instructions = $strip->parse($step->{html_instructions});
    $strip->eof;
    print "$instructions for $distance ($duration)\n";
}
```

2. Run the program with the following command line (remember to use double quotes on a Windows system):

```
perl listing_17_1_directions.pl \
--start='Paris, France' --end='London, UK'
```

You should see output similar to the following (truncated for length):

```
Continue onto Bd Ornano for 0.8 km (1 min)
Right onto Av. de la Porte de Clignancourt for 0.4 km (1 min)
Continue onto Av. Michelet/D14 Follow D14 for 1.9 km (3 mins)
Turn right onto Rue Francisque Poulbot/D410 for 0.5 km (1 min)
# many lines truncated
Slight left to stay on Westminster Bridge Rd/A302
  Continue to follow A302 Toll road for 0.5 km (1 min)
Right onto Victoria Embankment/A3211 Toll road for 0.6 km (1 min)
Left onto Northumberland Ave/A400 Toll road for 0.4 km (1 min)
At the roundabout, take the 4th exit onto Trafalgar Square/A4/A400
  Continue to follow Trafalgar Square/A400 Toll road
  Destination will be on the left for 0.2 km (1 min)
```

How It Works

Most of this program has already been explained in a Try it Out in Chapter 15, but here's the entire new section:

```
1:  use Getopt::Long;
2:  my ( $start, $end );
3:  GetOptions(
4:      'start=s' => \$start,
5:      'end=s'   => \$end,
6:  ) or die "Could not parse options";
7:
8:  unless ( $start and $end ) {
9:      die "Both --start and --end arguments must be supplied";
10: }
11: if ( @ARGV ) {
12:     my $args = join ', ', @ARGV;
13:     die <<"END";
14: \@ARGV contained '$args'. Did you forget to quote something?
15: --start=$start
16: --end=$end
17: END
18: }
19:
20: print "Searching for directions from '$start' to '$end'\n";
21:
22: $start = uri_encode($start);
23: $end   = uri_encode($end);
```

For the previous code block:

➤ You use Getopt::Long to capture your command-line arguments to the $start and $end variables. That's lines 3 through 6.

➤ Lines 8 through 10 verify that you've received values for both $start and $end. Note how you called this in the example:

```
perl directions.pl --start='Paris, France' --end='London, UK'
```

➤ You had to quote the arguments to make sure that the shell knows to pass these arguments as one "chunk" to Perl, rather than as separate bits. If you had done this:

```
perl directions.pl --start=Paris, France --end=London, UK
```

You would have set $start to Paris, (with the comma) and $end to London, (again, with the comma) and you would have had the strings France and UK left in @ARGV. You trap this error and display this in lines 11 through 18. If you had used the preceding command line, you would have received this error:

```
@ARGV contained 'France, UK'. Did you forget to quote something?
--start=Paris,
--end=London,
```

➤ Finally, line 20 prints out the expected start and end destinations and lines 22 and 23 do the expected URI encoding, and everything else is exactly as you saw in Chapter 15.

OTHER PROGRAMS

Most of this book has covered Perl development geared toward writing usable, standalone software. It's also covered quite a few CPAN modules along the way. However, sometimes you find software that does exactly what you want, but it's not written in Perl. You have many techniques to handling this, but here you see a couple easier ones involving reading another program's output and writing output for another program to use.

Running an External Program

Perl offers a variety of ways to run an external program. This section shows you how to handle the most common ways to do this. Table 17-1 shows the tools that this section covers. Some, such as exec and backticks, are not covered here, but are included for completeness.

TABLE 17-1: Useful Tools For Working With External Programs

COMMAND	USAGE
system	Executes a command when you care only about its success or failure
exec	Ends the Perl program and passes control to another program
backticks and qx	Runs an external program and captures its output
open	Writes to or reads from another program
Capture::Tiny	Captures STDOUT and STDERR from external programs

Some of the commands listed in Table 17-1 overlap and the choice of each depends on your needs.

The most basic way to run another program is the system() command. This builtin is useful when you want to run an external program and care only about its success or failure, not its output. For example, if you run a Perl program that has written several megabytes of output in separate files in a directory, you might want to compress those files into a single file and remove the directory afterwards.

Without going into too much detail, one way to compress a directory of files is to use the tar command:

```
tar zcjf archive.tgz mydir/
```

This creates a file named archive.tgz containing the contents of the mydir/ directory. You can later extract (similar to unzip) this archive with the following command:

```
tar xjf archive.tgz
```

> **NOTE** *This chapter was frustrating to write because many of the command-line tools that I care about are written for UNIX/Linux or Mac OS X, but not for the Windows operating systems. Fortunately, Many UNIX/Linux commands run unchanged on an OS X system. You can run many of them on Windows using the GnuWin project freely downloadable from* `http://gnuwin32.sourceforge.net/`.
>
> *Another option is to use the Cygwin program mentioned in Chapter 1, "What's Perl."*

To compress a directory's contents into a single file and then delete that directory, you can do the following:

```
use strict;
use warnings;

use DateTime;

# concatenating a string to the end of the DateTime object triggers
# its string overloading. This example will create a string
# representation of the current date and time

my $dir = DateTime->now . "";

# lots of code to write data to the $dir directory
my @command = ('tar', 'cjf', "$dir.tgz", $dir);
system(@command) == 0
  or die "Could not '@command': $?";

@command = ('rm', '-fr', $dir);
system(@command) == 0
  or die "Could not '@command': $?";
```

This looks a bit strange (and to be fair, system programming often does when you're not used to it), but look at the first system command to see what's going on.

```
my @command = ('tar', 'cjf', "$dir.tgz", $dir);
system(@command) == 0
  or die "Could not '@command': $?";
```

For this, the `@command` array has the command as the first element, followed by the arguments to the command as successive elements. For this example, you place only the external `tar` command into a separate variable to make it easier to report the command failure in the `die` statement.

The `system()` command takes a string or a list of strings and executes them. You could pack everything into a single string:

```
my $command = "tar cjf $dir.tgz $dir";
system($command) == 0
or die "Could not '$command': $?";
```

However, putting the command and its arguments into a single string is not recommended, because that calls your operating system's shell to execute the command instead of executing the command directly. I won't go into detail, but if you call your operating system's shell to execute the command, not only is it slower, but it also can open up serious security holes. Passing a list to a system is faster, and although it can still be dangerous if you don't know what you're doing, it's a touch safer than using a string.

So why do you test that it returns 0? Because on most operating systems, programs have return values. If that value is 0 (zero), this means the program completed successfully. Thus, what Perl considers a false value is returned upon success! If you hadn't tested for system(@command) == 0, you'd have to write this:

```
system(@command)
and die "Could not '@command': $?";
```

Although that shows up in many programs that use the system command, it's confusing to read.

WHY YOU FOCUS ON SUCCESS OR FAILURE

Programs generally exit with 0 if the program completed successfully. If your program dies because of a failure, it exits with some value other than zero. If you trap an error and want to handle it and then exit with a nonzero value, just pass that value as the argument to exit:

```
eval { some_func() };
if ( my $error = $@ ) {
    warn $error;
    # do cleanup
    exit 1;
}
```

When you call an external command and it dies, the $? variable contains the status that the system() command returns. Usually you hope that the status is zero. If not, you know the command failed. You can get a fair amount of data out of this by applying various bitwise operators, as described in the entry for $? in perldoc perlvar:

```
The status returned by the last pipe close, backtick (``) command,
successful call to wait() or waitpid(), or from the system()
operator. This is just the 16-bit status word returned by the
traditional Unix wait() system call (or else is made up to look
like it). Thus, the exit value of the subprocess is really
("$? >> 8"), and "$? & 127" gives which signal, if any, the
process died from, and "$? & 128" reports whether there was a core
dump.
```

However, I'll just focus on success or failure rather than trying to parse the exit codes because different programs have different exit codes. Unfortunately, they tend to be poorly documented, and given that programs are often not portable between Windows and other operating systems, it's difficult to cover them here.

Reading Another Program's Output

Sometimes you run another program and need to read its output. Both backticks (` `` `) and the qx//
operator help with this (they're the same thing but with different syntax) and they're documented in
perldoc perlop. So in a UNIX system, the uptime command tells you how long the computer has
been running since its last reboot or powerup:

```
print `uptime`;
print qx(uptime);
```

On my system, that currently prints:

```
21:42  up 21 days,   4:41, 3 users, load averages: 0.96 0.92 0.91
21:42  up 21 days,   4:41, 3 users, load averages: 0.96 0.92 0.91
```

UNDERSTANDING THE QX OPERATOR'S QUOTES

The qx operator is a standard "quote like" operator, meaning that you can use
many punctuation characters as delimiters:

```
print qx(uptime);
print qx/uptime/;
print qx'uptime';
print qx"uptime";
print qx<uptime>;
```

This means you can use standard variable interpolation:

```
my $program = 'uptime';
print qx<$program>;
```

If you do not want variable interpolation, be sure to use single quotes or escape the
variable sigils:

```
print qx'$uptime';
print qx<\$uptime>;
```

Be careful when interpolating variables in code that executes other programs. It's
easy to get something wrong. For example, if you read commands to execute from
a file and you want to do a quick qx($command), you'll be disappointed if the
command is rm -fr *.

If you prefer, you can also use what is known as a *piped open* to read program output. Just place the
pipe, |, after the program name:

```
open my $read_fh, "$program |"
  or die "Cannot execute '$program |': $!";
while ( my $output = <$read_fh> ) {
    print $output;
}
```

This is useful if you want to pass a function a filehandle and do not care if the output comes from a file or another program.

If you don't want shell metacharacters to expand when you use a piped open, you should use –| instead of a bare |:

```
open my $read_fh, "$program -|"
or die "Cannot execute '$program -|': $!";
```

These methods capture only a program's STDOUT. To capture its STDERR, you need to redirect it:

```
my $stderr = qx/program 2>&1/;
```

Unfortunately, the 2>&1 is a bit cryptic and not portable. You'll see Capture::Tiny in the STDERR section of this chapter. This module provides an easy, portable solution.

> **NOTE** *The various solutions presented for reading output for a program are blocking solutions. That means that they wait until the program called exits before the output is returned to you. See* `perldoc perlopentut` *for more information. The* `sysread` *and* `sysopen` *functions can help here.*

Writing to Another Program's Input

Sometimes instead of reading from another program, you need to write to it. You can do this by placing the pipe in front of the command:

```
open my $fh, "| $command"
or die "Could not open a pipe to $command: $!";
```

Better still is to use the three-argument form of open, with |- to prevent shell expansion:

```
open my $fh, "|-", $command
or die "Could not open a pipe to $command: $!";
```

For example, say you have a block of text and you want to know how many lines, words, and characters it has. You can use the UNIX wc utility:

```
use strict;
use warnings;

my $text = <<'END';
```

```
I will not be pushed, filed, stamped, indexed,
briefed, debriefed, or numbered.
END

open my $fh, '|-', 'wc' or die $!;
print $fh $text;
```

And that prints out:

```
2       12      79
```

That output says you have 2 lines, 12 words, and 79 characters. The reason this text is printed out is because wc's default output goes to STDOUT. You effectively use wc to filter your output.

> **NOTE** Use the wc *utility to count words, lines, and characters in a block of text.*
> *It is not native to Windows, but you can download a set of core UNIX utilities*
> *for Windows from* http://sourceforge.net/projects/gnuwin32/files/
> coreutils/5.3.0/coreutils-5.3.0.exe/download.

This can also be useful if you want to change how your own STDOUT behaves. For example, if you want your program's output to go through a pager such as less, you could do this (I use |- to avoid calling the shell):

```
my $pager = $ENV{PAGER} || '/usr/bin/less';
open STDOUT, "|-", $pager
  or die "Could not open STDOUT to $pager: $!";
```

Now your program's STDOUT output uses the pager instead of spewing lots of information that might scroll past their terminal window.

If you need to read and write at the same time, see IPC::Open2 and IPC::Open3, both of which are core modules. Or you can install IPC::Run from the CPAN. It's more flexible.

> **NOTE** For more information about using pipes with open, see "Pipe Opens" in
> perldoc perlopentut *and also read* perldoc perlipc.

The topic has generated many questions over the years and perldoc perlfaq8 has more relevant information. Unfortunately, as of this writing, the perlipc information is a touch out of date.

STDERR

Earlier you saw how to capture an external program's STDERR instead of its STDOUT.

```
my $stderr = qx/program 2>&1/;
```

Even if you know you're going to run your program only on Linux, perhaps you want to capture both STDOUT and STDERR? That's where Capture::Tiny comes in.

```
use Capture::Tiny 'capture';
my ($stdout, $stderr, @result) = capture {
    print "This goes to STDOUT\n";
    warn "This goes to STDERR\n";
    returnqw(These are the results);
};

print "STDOUT: $stdout";
print "STDERR: $stderr";
print "Results: @result";
```

Running the code snippet outputs:

```
STDOUT: This goes to STDOUT
STDERR: This goes to STDERR
Results: These are the results
```

You can use Capture::Tiny with capturing STDOUT, STDERR and return values from a regular chunk of code. In the case of an external program, it works just the same. Save the following program as example_17_1_poets.pl.

> **NOTE** *If you use* Capture::Tiny, *be aware that sometimes you'll be producing huge amounts of data and* Capture::Tiny *might consume lots of your computer's memory memory.*

```
use strict;
use warnings;

my @favorite_poets = (
    'PubliusOvidiusNaso',
    'John Davidson',
    'Alfred, Lord Tennyson',
    'Christina Rossetti',
);

foreach my $poet (@favorite_poets) {
    print "$poet\n";
}

warn "We're done here";
```

It should be clear what happens if you run that, but you can capture the output in a different program named example_17_2_capture.pl:

```
use strict;
use warnings;

use Data::Dumper;
use Capture::Tiny 'capture';

my $program = "$^X example_17_1_poets.pl";
my ( $stdout, $stderr, @result ) = capture { qx"$program" };

print Dumper $stdout, $stderr, \@result;
```

> **NOTE** $^X is the name of the current Perl executable.

Running that should produce the following output:

```
$VAR1 = '';
$VAR2 = 'We\'re done here at example_17_1_poets.pl line 14.
';
$VAR3 = [
          'PubliusOvidiusNaso
',
          'John Davidson
',
          'Alfred, Lord Tennyson
',
          'Christina Rossetti
'
        ];
```

In this case, $VAR1 is $stdout, $VAR2 is $stderr, and $VAR3 is the @output. You actually didn't have any STDOUT to capture because the qx operator captured that for you and returned it as the @output of the qx command. The warning from example_17_1_poets.pl was captured and returned as the $stderr.

Capture::Tiny tries hard to be cross platform–friendly and generally works on Windows, OS X, and UNIX/Linux systems. However, the author, David Golden, states that portability is a goal, not a guarantee.

> **NOTE** To know if a given module can work on your system, a good place to start is the CPAN testers' matrix, http://matrix.cpantesters.org/, provided by the Perl testing community. To see Capture::Tiny's results go to http://matrix.cpantesters.org/?dist=Capture-Tiny.

Parsing wc Output

Earlier you learned how to write data to an external utility, but that generally doesn't give you much control because the data is dumped directly to STDOUT. With a piped open, your program and the program to which you're piping data share the same STDIN, STDOUT, and STDERR. Thus, when you print $fh $text and use a piped open, it's the same thing as directly printing the output. Instead, you might want to capture the output in case you want to do something different with it.

All the code in this Try It Out is in code file listing_17_2_wc.pl.

1. Type in the following program and save it as listing_17_2_wc.pl:

```
use strict;
use warnings;
my $text = <<'END';
I will not be pushed, filed, stamped, indexed,
briefed, debriefed, or numbered.
END
use Capture::Tiny 'capture';
my ( $stdout, $stderr, @output ) = capture {
    open my $fh, '|-', 'wc' or die $!;
    print $fh $text;
    close $fh or die "Cannot close piped open to wc: $!";
};
my ( $lines, $words, $characters )
   = ( $stdout =~ /(\d+)\s+(\d+)\s+(\d+)/ );
print "Lines: $lines Words: $words Characters: $characters\n";
```

2. Run the program with perl listing_17_2_wc.pl. You should see the following output:

```
Lines: 2 Words: 12 Characters: 79
```

How It Works

Again, if you've been following along, this one is straightforward:

```
my ( $stdout, $stderr, @output ) = capture {
open my $fh, '|-', 'wc' or die $!;
print $fh $text;
close $fh or die "Cannot close piped open to wc: $!";
};
```

In the capture() subroutine, you have a piped open to the wc executable and then you print out text to its filehandle. Because a piped open shares the same STDOUT as the parent process (the program that prints the filehandle), the standard output from wc goes to your own STDOUT, thus ensuring that capture() returns this to the $stdout variable. You then use a regular expression to extract the line, word, and character count and print them out:

```
my ( $lines, $words, $characters )
   = ( $stdout =~ /(\d+)\s+(\d+)\s+(\d+)/ );
print "Lines: $lines Words: $words Characters: $characters\n";
```

SUMMARY

In this chapter, you learned some of the basics to work with programs on the command line, reading user input and handling command-line arguments. You also learned about perlrun, the documentation that explains many of the switches that are available to control the behavior of the Perl interpreter.

Finally, you learned about running other programs from inside your program. You can read their STDOUT and STDERR, and you can send information to them, as needed.

EXERCISES

1. Write a program called age.pl that prompts a user for her birth date in YYYY-MM-DD format and prints her age in years. You can use the following to parse a string in that format into a DateTime object. What happens if someone enters an invalid date?

```
use DateTime::Format::Strptime;

my $datetime_formatter = DateTime::Format::Strptime->new(
    pattern   => '%Y-%m-%d',
    time_zone => 'GMT',
);

my $string = '1967-33-33';
my $birthdate = $datetime_formatter->parse_datetime($string);
```

2. Modify your program from Exercise 1 to not prompt the user if the birth date has been supplied from the command line. Instead, use the birth date supplied on the command line. If the user supplied any extra arguments, assume that she's the person's name:

```
perl age.pl --birthdate=1955-04-08 Barbara Kingsolver
```

Allow an --age_at parameter to allow a person to specify what day you want to calculate his age at.

```
perl age.pl --birthdate 1964-10-18 --age_at 2007-10-02 Charles Stross
```

3. In Chapter 14, you learned about writing tests. Use qx and Capture::Tiny to write some tests for age.pl from Exercise 2. Use the following to verify your program:

```
perl age.pl --birthdate 1964-10-18 --age_at 2007-10-02 Charles Stross
perl age.pl --birthday 1967-06-20

perl age.pl Ovid
```

▶ **WHAT YOU LEARNED IN THIS CHAPTER**

TOPIC	DESCRIPTION
STDIN	The filehandle that user input is read from.
@ARGV	The built-in array containing command-line arguments.
Getopt::Long	A standard module that parses command-line options.
Perlrun	The documentation explaining standard Perl command-line switches.
exec	Terminates the current program and passes control to a new one.
system	Executes another program when you don't care about its output.
Backticks and qx	Executes another program and captures its STDOUT.
Piped opens	Reads and writes to external programs.
Capture::Tiny	Captures the STDOUT, STDERR, and outputs from a subroutine.

18

Common Tasks

WHAT YOU WILL LEARN IN THIS CHAPTER:

➤ Working with CSV Data

➤ Reading and writing XML

➤ Parsing and manipulating dates

➤ Using the built-in debugger

➤ Profiling your program

WROX.COM CODE DOWNLOAD FOR THIS CHAPTER

The wrox.com code downloads for this chapter are found at `http://www.wrox.com/remtitle`
`.cgi?isbn=1118013840` on the Download Code tab. The code for this chapter is divided into
the following major examples:

➤ `example_18_1_jobs.csv`

➤ `example_18_2_parse_csv.pl`

➤ `example_18_3_write_csv.pl`

➤ `example_18_4_library.xml`

➤ `example_18_5_xml_simple.pl`

➤ `example_18_6_xml_twig.pl`

➤ `example_18_7_xml_writer.pl`

➤ `example_18_8_palindrome.pl`

➤ `example_18_9_factorial.pl`

➤ `listing_18_1_cal.pl`

By now you have a good idea of what Perl programming is about, and you should have a solid grasp of the fundamentals. If you've followed along carefully and worked through the exercises, you could possibly even qualify for some entry-level developer positions. However, developers constantly get strange tasks thrown at them all the time and must handle them. These last two chapters cover some of those tasks. This chapter handles common tasks that you'll likely need to perform and the next chapter touches on some advanced topics that mastering can take you to the next level of Perl.

By now, you should know that the CPAN is the first place you look to see if someone else has already handled your task, and you'll explore a few of the popular CPAN modules to handle various tricky data tasks and also how to analyze your programs when things go awry.

USING CSV DATA

One common file format is CSV, which stands for *comma-separated values* and a quick example makes it easy to understand a CSV file:

```
Name,Age,Occupation
John Public,28,Waiter
Curtis Poe,44,Software Engineer
Leïla Contraire,36,Political Advisor
```

Basically, for CSV data, records are separated by newlines and fields are separated by commas. If a field contains a newline, comma, or double quotes, it's generally enclosed in double quotes. Except that there is no formal specification for CSV data, which can make things a bit more difficult. Sometimes people use single quotes instead of double quotes, or they'll enclose everything in quotes that is not a number.

All these factors can make parsing CSV data a challenge. Here's a common (and broken) method of CSV parsing:

```
use strict;
use warnings;
open my $fh, '<', $file or die "Cannot open $file for reading: $!";
while ( my $line = <$fh> ) {
    chomp($line);
    my @fields = split /,/, $line;
    s/^"|"$//g foreach @fields;
    printf "Name: %20s Age: %3d Occupation: %10s\n", @fields;
}
```

As you can see in the next example, double quotes within double quotes are often escaped with more double quotes, but some files escape double quotes with backslashes. The following code (code file example_18_1_jobs.csv) is a typical bit of CSV data (note the embedded newline in the Alice Baker's occupation):

```
Name,Age,Occupation
John Public,28,Bum
"Curtis ""Ovid"" Poe",44,Software Engineer
"Contraire, Leïla",36,Political Advisor
Alice Baker,44,"CEO,
MegaCorp"
```

Running that with your sample program generates complete garbage:

```
Name:          John Public Age:  28 Occupation:        Bum
Name:  Curtis ""Ovid"" Poe Age:  44 Occupation: Software Engineer
Argument "Leïla" isn't numeric in printf at parse_csv.pl line 13,
  <$fh> line 4.
Name:          Contraire Age:   0 Occupation:         36
Name:          Alice Baker Age:  44 Occupation:        CEO
Missing argument in printf at parse_csv.pl line 13, <$fh> line 6.
Missing argument in printf at parse_csv.pl line 13, <$fh> line 6.
Name:          MegaCorp Age:   0 Occupation:
```

Reading CSV Data

Rather than writing lots of code to handle these special cases, you can install the Text::CSV_XS program from the CPAN. As the author, H. Merijn Brand, points out, the module should probably be referred to as parsing ASV (anything separated values) because of its extreme flexibility. Here's how to parse that file (code file example_18_1_parse_csv.pl):

```perl
use strict;
use warnings;

use Text::CSV_XS;
my $file = 'example_18_1_jobs.csv';

open my $fh, '<', $file or die "Cannot open $file for reading: $!";

my $headers = <$fh>;    # discard headers
my $csv     = Text::CSV_XS->new( { binary => 1, eol => $/ } );

while ( my $row = $csv->getline($fh) ) {
    printf "Name: %20s Age: %3d Occupation: %10s\n", @$row;
}
```

And the output:

```
Name: John Public        Age:  28 Occupation: Bum
Name: Curtis "Ovid" Poe   Age:  44 Occupation: Software Engineer
Name: Contraire, Leïla   Age:  36 Occupation: Political Advisor
Name: Alice Baker        Age:  44 Occupation: CEO,
MegaCorp
```

Notice that Alice Baker has her profession printed over two lines, but that's because that was how it was represented in the original data file.

> **NOTE** If you have trouble compiling Text::CSV_XS, you may consider installing the Text::CSV module from the CPAN. It offers a pure Perl alternative. It's not as fast, but it works.

Note the arguments to the constructor:

```
my $csv = Text::CSV_XS->new( { binary => 1, eol => $/ } );
```

By default, `Text::CSV_XS` assumes all data is ASCII. If you have newlines embedded in your fields or if any of your characters have numeric values above `0x7E` (the tilde), then you must pass `binary => 1` to the constructor to ensure it parses correctly. The `eol` argument is documented as taking `$/`, though you can change this, if needed.

> **NOTE** While I mentioned using `binary => 1` in the constructor if you have non-ASCII data, a better choice for many needs is to use `Text::CSV::Encoded`. The `Text::CSV_XS` module is used in this chapter to keep things simple.

You may recall that Chapter 9 describes `$/`. The `$/` variable is the Perl built-in variable for the input record separator. For example, when you read from a file handle in scalar context, Perl returns data up to the input record separator (and `chomp()` removes that separator). `Text::CSV_XS` uses the `$/` to handle reading lines for you. You use `$csv->getline($fh)` instead of the normal `<$fh>` to read the filehandle because newlines embedded in fields are not actually input record separators.

Writing CSV Data

Obviously, if you can read CSV, you want to write it, too. In this case, just print it to the console so that you can see what's going on (code file `example_18_3_write_csv.pl`).

```
use Text::CSV_XS;

my $csv = Text::CSV_XS->new({ binary => 1, eol => $/ });
my @input = (
    [ 'Name',              'Age', 'Occupation'         ],
    [ 'John Public',        28,   'Bum'                ],
    [ 'Curtis "Ovid" Poe',  44,   'Software Engineer'  ],
    [ 'Contraire, Leïla',   36,   'Political Advisor'  ],
    [ 'Alice Baker',        44,   "CEO,\nMegaCorp"     ],
);

foreach my $input (@input) {
    if ( $csv->combine(@$input) ) {
        print $csv->string;
    }
    else {
        printf "combine() failed on argument: %s\n", $csv->error_input;
    }
}
```

And that prints out:

```
Name,Age,Occupation
"John Public",28,Bum
"Curtis ""Ovid"" Poe",44,"Software Engineer"
"Contraire, Leïla",36,"Political Advisor"
"Alice Baker",44,"CEO,
MegaCorp"
```

You handled escaping quotes correctly without worrying about it. As you can see, the `Text::CSV_XS` constructor takes the same arguments used for reading. Later, you use the `$csv->combine(LIST)` to combine a list of arguments into a single CSV string and then the `$csv->string` method for printing it. If the `$csv->combine` method returns false, you call `$csv->error_input` to understand what input caused the actual error.

The `Text::CSV_XS` module is flexible. If you want to write out the data in a tab-separated format, you could pass `sep_char => "\t"` to the constructor (and use this to read tab-separated format, too). You can change the quote character and many other behaviors within the module to get exactly the data you need.

UNDERSTANDING BASIC XML

The Extensible Markup Language (XML) is a format for encoding documents designed to be readable by both humans and computers. When handled correctly, it is both powerful and flexible. The following code (code file `example_18_4_library.xml`) is a simple example of an XML document that might be used to represent a library of books:

```xml
<?xml version="1.0" encoding="UTF-8" ?>
<library>
  <book isbn="1118013840">
    <title>Beginning Perl</title>
    <authors>
      <author>Curtis "Ovid" Poe</author>
    </authors>
    <publisher>Wrox</publisher>
  </book>
  <book isbn="0596526741">
    <title>Perl Hacks</title>
    <authors>
      <author>chromatic</author>
      <author>Damian Conway</author>
      <author>Curtis "Ovid" Poe</author>
    </authors>
    <publisher>O'Reilly Media</publisher>
  </book>
</library>
```

Obviously, you could fit a lot more information in that document, including synopses, genres, and many other things that are useful. The power of XML is that it is both flexible and moderately easy to read. You'll cover some of the more popular choices for XML reading and writing and use your `example_18_4_library.xml` example for your sample XML document.

> **NOTE** *The problem with XML is that the XML specification (`http://www.w3`* *`.org/XML/Core/#Publications`) is large and complex enough that many authors, thinking XML is just angle brackets for grouping data, write XML parsers and generators that are broken in many ways.*
>
> *The problem is serious enough that your author reluctantly (and with a bit of criticism) released `Data::XML::Variant` to enable authors to systematically write "bad" XML. Generally, you don't want to do this, but when working with other parties, they often have an XML "specification" that requires attributes in a specific order, does not allow quoting of attributes, and allows unclosed tags, illegal characters, and other problems.*
>
> *It's strongly recommended that you do not use `Data::XML::Variant` unless you have no other choice.*

Reading CSV Data

There are many Perl modules for reading and writing XML, and `XML::Simple` is one of the more popular choices, but it has a variety of limitations. Still, it's so easy to use that many people prefer it to more robust solutions.

To show you its ease of use, parse your example XML snippet with (code file `example_18_5_xml_simple.pl`):

```
use strict;
use warnings;
use XML::Simple;
use Data::Dumper;
$Data::Dumper::Indent   = 1;
$Data::Dumper::Sortkeys = 1;

my $document = XMLin( 'library.xml', forcearray => ['author'] );

print Dumper($document);
```

And that prints out:

```
$VAR1 = {
  'book' => [
    {
      'authors' => {
        'author' => [
          'Curtis "Ovid" Poe'
        ]
      },
      'isbn' => '1118013840',
      'publisher' => 'Wrox',
      'title' => 'Beginning Perl'
```

```
        },
        {
          'authors' => {
            'author' => [
              'chromatic',
              'Damian Conway',
              'Curtis "Ovid" Poe'
            ]
          },
          'isbn' => '0596526741',
          'publisher' => 'O\'Reilly Media',
          'title' => 'Perl Hacks'
        }
      ]
    };
```

You can also use XML::Simple to output your XML. With the previous $document variable, you can do this:

```
print XMLout(
    $document,
    ValueAttr => { book => 'isbn' },
    RootName  => 'library',
);
```

And that outputs:

```
<library>
  <book isbn="1118013840" publisher="Wrox" title="Beginning Perl">
    <authors>
      <author>Curtis &quot;Ovid&quot; Poe</author>
    </authors>
  </book>
  <book isbn="0596526741" publisher="O'Reilly Media" title="Perl Hacks">
    <authors>
      <author>chromatic</author>
      <author>Damian Conway</author>
      <author>Curtis &quot;Ovid&quot; Poe</author>
    </authors>
  </book>
</library>
```

The XML is not the same, and the XML::Simple documentation offers suggestions but makes it clear that XML::Simple should be used only when the following is true:

➤   You're not interested in text content consisting only of whitespace.

➤   You don't mind that when things get slurped into a hash the order is lost.

➤   You don't want fine-grained control of the formatting of generated XML.

➤   You would never use a hash key that was not a legal XML element name.

➤   You don't need help converting between different encodings.

In other words, XML::Simple is handy, but it's limited enough that you will likely outgrow it quickly.

Other programmers prefer finer control with the XML::Twig module. This module enables you to treat XML documents as trees. A *tree* is a data structure that enables you to represent complex data as a "tree" with "branches" representing the different elements. For example, in the sample XML, the library element is the root of the tree with two book branches.

By using a tree-based XML parser, you can select any or all the branches of the tree and do something with them. For example, here's one way to fetch just the titles:

```
use XML::Twig;
my @titles;
my $twig = XML::Twig->new(
    twig_handlers => {
        '//library/book/title' => sub { push @titles => $_->text },
    },
);
$twig->parsefile('library.xml');
printf "%s\n" => join ' | ', @titles;
```

And that should print out:

```
Beginning Perl | Perl Hacks
```

There are several ways to use XML::Twig and this method is one of the most memory efficient (which is one of the reasons many people use XML::Twig for XML processing). The keys of the twig_handlers hash references are a subset of XPath, a tool used to select elements and attributes in XML documents. The values are subroutines that enable you to manipulate the XML or fetch data from it. The $_ variable is set to the current node of the tree.

> **NOTE** A handy tutorial for understanding XPath is available at http://
> www.w3schools.com/xpath/.

Or maybe you want to create a hash with the keys being the unique ISBN numbers and the values being the titles:

```
use XML::Twig;
use Data::Dumper;

my %books;
my $twig = XML::Twig->new(
  twig_handlers => {
    '//library/book' =>
      sub {
        $books{ $_->{att}{isbn} } = $_->first_child('title')->text;
```

```
        }
     },
   );
   $twig->parsefile('library.xml');
   print Dumper( \%books );
```

And that prints out:

```
   $VAR1 = {
            '0596526741' => 'Perl Hacks',
            '1118013840' => 'Beginning Perl'
   };
```

If you want to be elaborate, you could rewrite the entire XML document in a manner similar to Extensible Stylesheet Language Transformations (XSLT). Here's how to rewrite the XML as HTML lists (code file example_18_6_xml_twig.pl):

```
   use strict;
   use warnings;
   use XML::Twig;

   my $twig = XML::Twig->new(
       twig_handlers => {
           '//library'              => sub { $_->set_tag('ol') },
           '//library/book'         => sub {
               $_->set_tag('li'); $_->set_atts( {} )
           },
           '//library/book/title' => sub { $_->set_tag('strong') },
           '//library/book/publisher' => sub { $_->delete },
           '//library/book/authors'   => \&rewrite_authors,
       },
       pretty_print => 'indented',
       no_prolog    => 1,
       comments     => 'drop',
   );

   $twig->parsefile('example_18_4_library.xml');
   print $twig->toString;

   sub rewrite_authors {
       my $authors = $_;
       my @authors = map { $_->text } $authors->children('author');
       $authors->set_tag('p');
       $authors->set_text( join ' - ', @authors );
   }
```

Running that with your sample XML should print out the following:

```
   <ol>
     <li>
       <strong>Beginning Perl</strong>
       <p>Curtis "Ovid" Poe</p>
     </li>
```

```
      <li>
        <strong>Perl Hacks</strong>
        <p>chromatic - Damian Conway - Curtis "Ovid" Poe"</p>
      </li>
    </ol>
```

There are, of course, many other powerful modules for parsing XML. XML::LibXML, XML::Parser, XML::Sax, and XML::Compile are today among a few of the many useful (and sometimes incomprehensible) XML parsers available. Just because XML::Simple and XML::Twig were shown does not mean that they are the best. Your choice of module should reflect your needs.

Writing CSV Data

Naturally, if you read XML, you must write it, too. XML::Simple's XMLout() function enables you to do that, but it's not flexible. Instead, turn to XML::Writer to handle this task, which makes writing XML a breeze. It generally needs to write its output to an IO::File object, but for simplicity's sake, use XML::Writer::String to print your XML directly.

You start by designing a good data structure to represent your XML data. XML is a set of tags, each of which may be self-closed (<tag/>) or closed later (<tag>...</tag>). Each tag may have zero or more attributes and either contain a string value or a zero or more tags. You can represent each tag as an array reference. The first item is the tag name, so an empty tag looks like this:

```
# <name/>
[ 'name' ]
```

The tag might have attributes, so the second element is a hash reference. With no values, it means the tag has no attributes. Otherwise, the name/value pairs can represent attributes:

```
# <name version="1.0"/>
[ name => { version => '1.0' } ]
```

Any array elements after the hashref should either be a single string, representing the text value, or more array references for nested tags:

```
# <name version="1.0">Bob</name>
[ name => { version => '1.0' }, 'Bob' ]
# <name version="1.0">
#   <first>Bob</first>
#   <last>Dobbs</last>
# </name>
[ name => { version => '1.0' },
  [ first => {}, 'Bob' ],
  [ last  => {}, 'Dobbs' ],
]
```

If you squint, you can even see that it looks a little bit like XML.

To make it cleaner to read, make empty attribute hash references optional:

```
[ name => { version => '1.0' },
  [ first => 'Bob' ],
  [ last  => 'Dobbs' ],
]
```

Now that you have clean data structure for your XML generation, use XML::Writer and XML::Writer::String to create the sample XML you've been using for this chapter (code file example_18_7_xml_writer.pl):

```perl
use strict;
use warnings;
use XML::Writer;
use XML::Writer::String;

my @to_xml = (
    library =>
        [ book  => { isbn => '1118013840' } =>
            [ title => 'Beginning Perl' ],
            [ authors =>
                [ author => 'Curtis "Ovid" Poe' ],
            ],
            [ publisher => 'Wrox' ],
        ],
        [ book => { isbn => '0596526741' } =>
            [ title => 'Perl Hacks' ],
            [ authors =>
                [ author => 'chromatic' ],
                [ author => 'Damian Conway' ],
                [ author => 'Curtis "Ovid" Poe' ],
            ],
            [ publisher => "O'Reilly Media" ],
        ],
);

my $output = XML::Writer::String->new;
my $writer = XML::Writer->new(
    OUTPUT      => $output,
    DATA_MODE   => 1,
    DATA_INDENT => 2,
);

$writer->xmlDecl;
write_element($writer, @to_xml);
$writer->end;

print $output->value;

sub write_element {
    my ( $writer, $element, @next ) = @_;
    # This allows the attributes hashref to be optional
    my ( $attributes, @elements ) = 'HASH' eq ref $next[0]
```

```
        ? @next           # we had attributes
        : ( {}, @next );  # we did not have attributes
$writer->startTag($element, %$attributes);
foreach my $next_element (@elements) {
    ref $next_element
        ? write_element($writer, @$next_element)
        : $writer->characters($next_element);
}
$writer->endTag;
}
```

Running this code prints the wanted XML:

```
<?xml version="1.0"?>

<library>
  <book isbn="1118013840">
    <title>Beginning Perl</title>
    <authors>
      <author>Curtis "Ovid" Poe</author>
    </authors>
    <publisher>Wrox</publisher>
  </book>
  <book isbn="0596526741">
    <title>Perl Hacks</title>
    <authors>
      <author>chromatic</author>
      <author>Damian Conway</author>
      <author>Curtis "Ovid" Poe</author>
    </authors>
    <publisher>O'Reilly Media</publisher>
  </book>
</library>
```

Note the following about this code:

➤ At the top of the `xml_writer.pl` code, you use `XML::Writer` and `XML::Writer::String`. Ordinarily, `XML::Writer` expects to write the data to an `IO::File` object, but use `XML::Writer::String` to make it easier to directly see the output as you work.

➤ Next, the data structure mirrors the example XML perfectly.

➤ Next, the you have code for writing the XML declaration (that's the `<?xml version="1.0"?>` bit), the actual XML, and finally printing out the result:

```
$writer->xmlDecl;
write_element($writer, @to_xml);
$writer->end;
print $output->value;
```

➤ Finally, you have a recursive subroutine that walks the data structure to print the XML:

```
sub write_element {
    my ( $writer, $element, @next ) = @_;
    # This allows the attributes hashref to be optional
```

```
                my ( $attributes, @elements ) = 'HASH' eq ref $next[0]
                    ? @next          # we had attributes
                    : ( {}, @next ); # we did not have attributes
                $writer->startTag($element, %$attributes);
                foreach my $next_element (@elements) {
                    ref $next_element
                        ? write_element($writer, @$next_element)
                        : $writer->characters($next_element);
                }
                $writer->endTag;
            }
```

Because objects in Perl are references, any changes made to the object will persist, and you don't need to return it. (this simplifies Your code somewhat.) You can write out an XML start tag with this:

```
    $writer->startTag($element, %$attributes);
```

Then you recurse throughout the elements, and if you have an array reference, you recursively call write_element() again with the next elements. If you have a string, such as Wrox, write it directly after the tag:

```
    $writer->characters($next_element);
```

Finally, call $writer->endTag, which automatically prints the closing tag for whichever $writer->startTag you last called.

> **NOTE** *The data structure for writing XML might look a bit strange, but it's a real-world example. Your author had to work from home for a couple of weeks due to a back injury and rewrote the XML generation for the Programme Information Platform (PIPs) for the BBC. The data structure is therefore identical to the data structure used to provide XML data for the world's largest broadcaster's data feeds for meta data. It also has a side effect of being unambiguously serializable in both JSON and YAML formats.*
>
> *If you're curious about a tiny behind-the-scenes look at a powerful application powered by Perl, you can read more about PIPs at* http://www.bbc.co.uk/blogs/bbcinternet/2009/02/what_is_pips.html.

The sample code for this chapter skips much of the data validation and error reporting that was necessary and also doesn't include the work needed to deserialize XML, YAML, and JSON back into the same Perl data structure. (XML is a bit tricky, but the YAML and JSON deserialization is straightforward.)

HANDLING DATES

In 1999, you author was working as a mainframe programmer and some of his job was dealing with the infamous Y2K issue. Many systems had years stored as 2 bytes, thus meaning, for example, that the year 00 would often be interpreted as 1900 rather than 2000. There was a rather strange conspiracy theory running around that programmers across the planet had somehow managed to work together to create a nonexistent problem to guarantee job security. In response, your author penned the following haiku:

```
Is Y2K real?
The problem's being solved by
Those who can't find dates.
```

(For the pedants: yes, it's a senryu).

Today, handling dates is as tricky as ever, and programmers invariably underestimate the subtleties involved. Fortunately, Perl offers a variety of excellent tools to make your life easier. In your programming career, you will eventually be confronted with your first date. Don't blow it; listen to the experts.

Using the DateTime Module

The DateTime module, written by Dave Rolsky, is your first choice when learning to navigate this tricky area. If you need to work with dates and times regularly, you must read the documentation thoroughly, and also read the http://datetime.perl.org/ website.

You've already seen a fair amount of use of this module in the book, but now you'll review a couple features that are easy to forget.

Say that you're passed a DateTime object and you want to know if it's after now:

```perl
if ( $datetime > DateTime->now ) {
    # $datetime is in the future
}
```

Sometimes you get a string containing a date, and you want to parse that into a DateTime object. DateTime::Format::Strptime is a good choice. (You can also use DateTime::Format::Builder for hard-to-parse cases).

```perl
use DateTime::Format::Strptime;
my $parser   = DateTime::Format::Strptime->new( pattern => '%Y-%m-%d' );
my $datetime = $parser->parse_datetime('1967-06-20');
```

And you can even represent time down to the nanosecond level:

```perl
my $dt_ns = DateTime->new(
    year       => 2012,
    month      => 5,
    day        => 23,
    hour       => 22,
```

```
    minute    => 35,
    second    => 16,
    nanosecond => 130,
);
```

Using Date::Tiny and DateTime::Tiny

One problem with using DateTime is that dates are so much harder than people think. The module is slow to load and takes about 3 or 4 megabytes of memory. If all you need to do is represent a date and don't care about durations, comparisons, or other aspects of date math, you might find the Date::Tiny and DateTime::Tiny modules by Adam Kennedy interesting. Not only are they much smaller (approximately 100 kilobytes of memory), but they're much faster. However, they achieve this by deliberately excluding many features that DateTime provides. Their basic usage is similar:

```
my $date = Date::Tiny->new(
    year  => 1967,
    month => 6,
    day   => 20,
);
my $date = DateTime::Tiny->new(
    year   => 2006,
    month  => 12,
    day    => 31,
    hour   => 10,
    minute => 45,
    second => 32,
);
```

The Date::Tiny module is useful when you need only a date, and the DateTime::Tiny module is useful when you need both a date and time. Your author has found these handy on performance sensitive systems when he quickly needs to generate a datetime string for now:

```
my $today = Date::Tiny->now;
my $now   = DateTime::Tiny->now;
```

Unlike DateTime, each of these has a simple, built-in date string parser. The date or datetime strings are expected to be in ISO 8601 format:

```
my $birthday     =Date::Tiny->from_string('1967-06-20');
my $party_like_its=DateTime::Tiny->from_string('1998-12-31T23:59:59');
```

> **NOTE** In case you wonder why the date 1967-06-20 shows up so often in the text, it's because this is your author's birthday. Now you have no excuse for forgetting.

Both the `Date::Tiny` and `DateTime::Tiny` modules provide a `DateTime` method for returning the object as its corresponding `DateTime` object. This is useful if you discover that you need to manipulate the `DateTime` in ways that the `Date::Tiny` and `DateTime::Tiny` modules do not allow.

```
my $dt1   = $birthday->DateTime;
my $party = $party_like_its->DateTime->add( seconds => 1 );
```

TRY IT OUT   **Writing a Calendar Display**

On most Linux systems, there is a standard utility named `cal`. This utility prints out a calendar of a given month and year, defaulting to the current month and year. You can rewrite this in Perl, but instead of the positional arguments used with `cal`, you can use named arguments:

```
perl listing_18_1_cal.pl --month 6 --year 1967
perl listing_18_1_cal.pl -m 6 -y 1967
```

And that should print out:

```
     June 1967
Su Mo Tu We Th Fr Sa
             1  2  3
 4  5  6  7  8  9 10
11 12 13 14 15 16 17
18 19 20 21 22 23 24
25 26 27 28 29 3
```

You're going to use many methods on the `DateTime` object that you probably haven't seen before, but you would learn if you read the documentation (something your author has tried to drill into you quite a bit). Further, you can use a few Perl constructs that are less common, but that you've already seen in this book. If you really know Perl well, you can get a lot of power out of little code.

Further, you can see the POD for this script to get an idea of what a full, proper Perl program looks like in the real world.

All the code in this Try It Out is in the code file `listing_18_1_cal.pl`.

1.   Type in the following program and save it as `listing_18_1_cal.pl`:

```
use strict;
use warnings;

use DateTime;
use Getopt::Long;

my $SPACES_PER_DAY = 3;

my $now   = DateTime->now;
my $year  = $now->year;
my $month = $now->month;

GetOptions(
    'month=i' => \$month,
    'year=i'  => \$year,
```

```perl
) or die "Bad options";

my @header = qw( S M T W T F S );
my %date    = (
    month => $month,
    year  => $year,
    day   => 1,
);

my $date        = DateTime->new(%date);
my $last_day    = DateTime->last_day_of_month(%date)->day;
my $day_of_week = $date->day_of_week;
my $month_name  = $date->month_name;

my ( $start, $end ) = ( 1, $last_day );

my @null_days = $day_of_week == 7 ? () : ("") x $day_of_week;

my @calendar = ( undef, @header, @null_days, 1 .. $last_day );

print centered_title( $month_name, $year );
for my $i ( 1 .. $#calendar ) {
    printf "%${SPACES_PER_DAY}s" => $calendar[$i];
    print "\n" if !( $i % 7 );
}

sub centered_title {
    my ( $month_name, $year ) = @_;
    my $title = "$month_name, $year";
    my $padding = " " x (($SPACES_PER_DAY*7-length($title))/2);
    return " $padding$title\n";
}

__END__

=head1 NAME

listing_18_1_cal.pl - print a calendar for a given month and year

=head1 DESCRIPTION

Often we need to quickly display a calendar for a given month
and year. This program will do this for you:

 perl listing_18_1_cal.pl --month 6 --year 2012
 perl listing_18_1_cal.pl -m 6 -y 2012

      June, 2012
  S  M  T  W  T  F  S
                 1  2
  3  4  5  6  7  8  9
 10 11 12 13 14 15 16
 17 18 19 20 21 22 23
 24 25 26 27 28 29 30

=head1 OPTIONS
```

```
--month,-m  The number of the month (defaults to current month)
--year,-y   The number of the year (defaults to current year)

=head1 EXAMPLES

Current month and year:

 perl listing_18_1_cal.pl

Current month, different year:

 perl listing_18_1_cal.pl --year 1999
 perl listing_18_1_cal.pl -y 1999

Current year, different month:

 perl listing_18_1_cal.pl --month 1
 perl listing_18_1_cal.pl -m 1

Exact month and year:

 perl listing_18_1_cal.pl --month 12 --year 1999
 perl listing_18_1_cal.pl -m 12 -y 1999
```

2. Run the program with `perl listing_18_1_cal.pl -m 8 -y 1957`. You should see the following output:

```
      August 1957
  Su Mo Tu We Th Fr Sa
               1  2  3
   4  5  6  7  8  9 10
  11 12 13 14 15 16 17
  18 19 20 21 22 23 24
  25 26 27 28 29 30 31
```

How It Works

The idea behind this program is to figure out the number of days in a given month for a given year. Then you construct an array with the header, each element of which is the first letter of the day of the week, a number of "empty strings" equivalent to the first days of the week that don't correspond to days of the current month, and then the days of the month.

With that properly constructed array, printing the calendar is merely printing off every seven elements (separated by spaces), followed by newlines.

Lines 1 through 16 set up the initial data, including reading the optional month and year from the command line. The $SPACES_PER_DAY variable defines the padding you'll use for each day when you print the calendar. The @header variable contains the first letter of each day of the week.

```
1:  use strict;
2:  use warnings;
3:  use DateTime;
4:  use Getopt::Long;
```

```
 5:
 6:   my $SPACES_PER_DAY = 3;
 7:
 8:   my $now   = DateTime->now;
 9:   my $year  = $now->year;
10:   my $month = $now->month;
11:   GetOptions(
12:       'month=i' => \$month,
13:       'year=i'  => \$year,
14:   ) or die "Bad options";
15:
16:   my @header = qw( S M T W T F S );
```

Lines 17 through 27 calculate various values you'll need to print your calendar. You've not used the `last_day_of_month` constructor for the `DateTime` object before, but you will know about it if you've read the `DateTime` documentation.

```
17:   my %date   = (
18:       month => $month,
19:       year  => $year,
20:       day   => 1,
21:   );
22:   my $date        = DateTime->new(%date);
23:   my $last_day    = DateTime->last_day_of_month(%date)->day;
24:   my $day_of_week = $date->day_of_week;
25:   my $month_name  = $date->month_name;
26:
27:   my ( $start, $end ) = ( 1, $last_day );
```

Line 29 is interesting. This enables you to insert "empty string" elements into your `@calendar` array. These are used to pad the beginning of the week when you print out your calendar. Use the x infix operator with parentheses around the left argument (`("") x $day_of_week`) to enforce list context. If the day of the week is 4, it returns four empty strings elements.

```
29:   my @null_days = $day_of_week == 7 ? () : ("")x$day_of_week;
```

So if the day of the week for the first day of the month is 5, you see the following:

```
S  M  T  W  T  F  S
            1  2  3
```

The `@null_days` variable is empty if `$day_of_week` is 7. Otherwise, you'd wind up with an empty row in the calendar if you're not careful.

Then construct the actual calendar array. It contains the header (the first letter of every day of the week), the `@null_days`, and the number 1 to the number of the last day of the month:

```
31:   my @calendar = (undef, @header, @null_days, 1..$last_day);
```

Use `undef` for the first element because it makes the later math simpler. You'll see that in a bit.

Line 33 prints the title (the month and year) centered. Lines 39 through 44 contain the subroutine that calculates the centered title.

```
33:   print centered_title( $month_name, $year );
39:   sub centered_title {
40:       my ( $month_name, $year ) = @_;
41:       my $title = "$month_name, $year";
42:       my $padding=" "x(($SPACES_PER_DAY*7-length($title))/2);
43:       return " $padding$title\n";
44:   }
```

Line 43 returns " `$padding$title\n"`. The extra space at the beginning of the string you returned is a tiny hack to improve centering. You'll often see tiny hacks like this in Perl code.

Finally, print the actual calendar:

```
34:   for my $i ( 1 .. $#calendar ) {
35:       printf "%${SPACES_PER_DAY}s" => $calendar[$i];
36:       print "\n" if !( $i % 7 );
37:   }
38:
```

The `@calendar` array included an `undef` as the first element because you wanted to skip it. If you started the elements you wanted print at index 0, line 36 would have looked like this and have been more confusing:

```
print "\n" if !( ( $i - 1 ) % 7 );
```

Also note line 35 carefully:

```
printf "%${SPACES_PER_DAY}s" => $calendar[$i];
```

You interpolate the `$SPACES_PER_DAY` variable in the string to dynamically build the format for the `printf` builtin. The format string becomes `%3s`. The identifier of the scalar is wrapped in curly braces: `${SPACES_PER_DAY}` because that tells Perl where the start and end of the variable name is. Otherwise, the format string would be `%$SPACES_PER_DAYs` and Perl would complain that the `$SPACES_PER_DAYs` (note the trailing "s") variable doesn't exist.

> **NOTE** *The trick to wrap the variable identifier in curly braces in a string also works outside of strings:*
>
> ```
> my ${foo} = 3;
> print $foo;    # prints 3
> ```
>
> *However, do not do this. It doesn't add any value here and is good only for obfuscating code and showing off (usually a bad idea). It is mentioned here for completeness.*
>
> *This program shows off a lot of idiomatic Perl and shows you what a real-world program actually looks like. It's worth going over a few times to make sure you understand what it's doing.*

UNDERSTANDING YOUR PROGRAM

Writing programs is great, but you often might be in a situation in which something has gone wrong and you need to understand what it is. Perl offers a rich variety of tools to help you understand these issues, so you'll look at some of them now.

Using the Debugger

The debugger for Perl is probably one of the most useful tools you can use, but many Perl programmers find it quite intimidating. Basic usage of the Perl debugger is quite simple, but the Fear of the command line seems to intimidate many Perl developers and they avoid the debugger. This is actually rather understandable because the debugger is cryptic. You will find, though, that learning the debugger pays off handsomely when you take the time to learn it. Now look at some of the basics.

There are several ways to use the Perl debugger, the most common of which is this:

```
perl -d some_program.pl
```

That command runs `some_program.pl` in the debugger. Rather than try to explain everything, your author shows you a sample program. Imagine that, for some strange reason, you have a list of strings and you want to return the number of letters in a string if it's a palindrome (hey, you try coming up with interesting examples for a book this long!), but zero if it's not a palindrome. For example, the sentence "Murder for a jar of red rum" should have a length of 21, but "Hey, dude." should return 0. So look at the sample program (code file `example_18_8_palindrome.pl`):

```perl
use strict;
use warnings;
use Data::Dumper;

my @strings = (
    'Dogma? I am God.',
    'I did, did I?',
    'Lager, sir, is regal.',
    'This is not a palindrome',
    'Murder for a jar of red rum.',
    'Reviled did I live, said I, as evil I did deliver.',
);

my %lengths = map { $_ => plength($_) } @strings;

print Dumper \%lengths;

sub plength {
    my $word = @_;
    $word =~ s/\W//g;
    return 0 unless $word eq reverse $word;
    return length $word;
}
```

That's straightforward, but it prints out:

```
$VAR1 = {
        'Reviled did I live, said I, as evil I did deliver.' => 1,
        'This is not a palindrome' => 1,
        'Lager, sir, is regal.' => 1,
        'Dogma? I am God.' => 1,
        'I did, did I?' => 1,
        'Murder for a jar of red rum.' => 1
      };
```

Obviously, it's not true that all of those strings have a length of 1 and clearly, one of them is not a palindrome (which one is an exercise for the reader). So fire up your debugger and figure out what's going on.

```
$ perl -d palindrome.pl
Loading DB routines from perl5db.pl version 1.33
Editor support available.
Enter h or `h h' for help, or `man perldebug' for more help.
main::(palindrome.pl:5):    my @palindromes = (
main::(palindrome.pl:6):        'Dogma? I am God.',
main::(palindrome.pl:7):        'I did, did I?',
main::(palindrome.pl:8):        'Lager, sir, is regal.',
main::(palindrome.pl:9):        'This is not a palindrome',
main::(palindrome.pl:10):       'Murder for a jar of red rum.',
main::(palindrome.pl:11):       'Reviled did I live, said I, as …
main::(palindrome.pl:12):    );
  DB<1>
```

When you first file up the debugger, it shows the first line or lines of code that it's about to run and displays them. Whenever a new line of code shows up in the debugger, it's a line of code that is about to be executed, not one that has already been executed.

So you can see that Perl is about to evaluate the contents of the @palindromes array. The code started with three use statements, but those aren't shown because they happen at compile time, and the debugger (usually) starts at the first run-time statement.

So what do you do? Type n. That advances to the 'n'ext line of code.

```
DB<1> n
main::(palindrome.pl:14)::my %lengths = map { $_ => plength($_) } @palindromes;
```

Now you see that the next line of code to execute is the map statements. Because there are six elements in @palindromes, you could hit n six times to execute this six times:

```
  DB<1> n
main::(palindrome.pl:14): my %lengths=map{$_=>plength($_)}@strings;
  DB<1> n
main::(palindrome.pl:14): my %lengths=map{$_=>plength($_)}@strings;
  DB<1> n
main::(palindrome.pl:14): my %lengths=map{$_=>plength($_)}@strings;
```

```
    DB<1> n
main::(palindrome.pl:14):   my %lengths=map{$_=>plength($_)}@strings;
    DB<1> n
main::(palindrome.pl:14):   my %lengths=map{$_=>plength($_)}@strings;
    DB<1> n
main::(palindrome.pl:14):   my %lengths=map{$_=>plength($_)}@strings;
    DB<1> n
main::(palindrome.pl:15):   print Dumper \%lengths;
```

However, that doesn't let you see what's happening in the `plength` subroutine, so after the first n command, type s to step into the subroutine.

```
    DB<1> s
main::(palindrome.pl:14):   my %lengths=map{$_=>plength($_)}@strings;
    DB<1> s
  main::plength(palindrome.pl:18)::    my $word = @_;
```

The first s steps into the `map` command, and the second s steps into `plength` to shows that you're about to execute the first line of the subroutine. Type n again to go to the next line:

```
    DB<1> n
  main::plength(palindrome.pl:19)::    $word =~ s/\W//g;
```

Now that you've executed the `my $word = @_;` line, `$word` has a value, so look at that by using the p command. The p command is shorthand for print:

```
    DB<2> p $word
  1
```

Ah hah! As you can see, `$word` has a value of 1. So what's in `@_`? You use the x command for this. It's like the debugger version of `Data::Dumper`, but with a slightly different output:

```
    DB<5> x \@_
0   ARRAY(0x7ff0398ac3a8)
    0   'Dogma? I am God.'
```

The x command dumps out the variables. If it's a reference, it displays the reference type and address (something like `ARRAY(0x7ff0398ac3a8)`) and then shows the contents of the variable. In this case, you have a one-element array containing the string `Dogma? I am God.`. Obviously, you're passing in the correct value, but now you should understand what happened. You tried to assign a list to a scalar, and that's why `$word` contained the value of 1. So quit the debugger with the q command, and fix the first line of the subroutine by forcing the list context:

```
my ($word) = @_;
```

Now when you run the program again, you get the following output:

```
$VAR1 = {
        'Reviled did I live, said I, as evil I did deliver.' => 0,
        'This is not a palindrome' => 0,
```

```
            'Lager, sir, is regal.' => 0,
            'Dogma? I am God.' => 0,
            'I did, did I?' => 8,
            'Murder for a jar of red rum.' => 0
        };
```

Hmm, the I did, did I? line worked, but not the rest. Because you have a line that returns 0, it looks suspicious. Now run the debugger again. As you probably noticed, the preceding output was rather limited. You usually saw only one line at a time and that can make it hard to see what's going on. So now fix that.

When you are in the debugger, you can type v to see a "view" of the lines surrounding your current line. The current line is designated with a ==> marker, for example:

```
    DB<1> v
15: print Dumper \%lengths;
16
17  sub plength {
18==>        my $word = @_;
19:        $word =~ s/\W//g;
20:        return 0 unless $word eq reverse $word;
21:        return length $word;
22  }
    DB<1>
```

As you can see, you're on the first line of the plength() subroutine, but with the extra lines before and after, it's much easier to see where you are and to understand what's going on.

Obviously, you don't want to type v after every time you enter a command, so when you enter the debugger, before you type anything else, type {{v. The {{ *command* construct, followed by any debugger command, tells the debugger to execute the debugger command before every debugger prompt, (Hey, we already said the debugger was cryptic!) So do that now, followed by the n command to move to the next line of code.

```
$ perl -d palindrome.pl
Loading DB routines from perl5db.pl version 1.33
Editor support available.
Enter h or `h h' for help, or `man perldebug' for more help.
main::(palindrome.pl:5):    my @strings = (
main::(palindrome.pl:6):        'Dogma? I am God.',
main::(palindrome.pl:7):        'I did, did I?',
main::(palindrome.pl:8):        'Lager, sir, is regal.',
main::(palindrome.pl:9):        'This is not a palindrome',
main::(palindrome.pl:10):       'Murder for a jar of red rum.',
main::(palindrome.pl:11):       'Reviled did I live, said I, as …
main::(palindrome.pl:12):    );
    DB<1> {{v
    DB<2> n
main::(palindrome.pl:14): my %lengths=map {$_=>plength($_)}@strings;
```

```
auto(-1)  DB<2> v
11       'Reviled did I live, said I, as evil I did deliver.',
12  );
13
14==>   my %lengths = map { $_ => plength($_) } @strings;
15: print Dumper \%lengths;
16
17  sub plength {
18:     my ($word) = @_;
19:     $word =~ s/\W//g;
20:     return 0 unless $word eq reverse $word;
   DB<2>
```

The debugger looks better already. Now step into the `plength` subroutine by setting a breakpoint with `b plength` (you can set breakpoints with either line numbers or subroutine names) and then pressing `c` to continue to the breakpoint. Then use `n` a couple of times to get to the desired line of code.

```
   DB<2> b plength
   DB<3> c
main::plength(palindrome.pl:18):         my ($word) = @_;
auto(-1)  DB<3> v
15: print Dumper \%lengths;
16
17  sub plength {
18==>b      my ($word) = @_;
19:     $word =~ s/\W//g;
20:     return 0 unless $word eq reverse $word;
21:     return length $word;
22  }
   DB<3> n
main::plength(palindrome.pl:19):         $word =~ s/\W//g;
auto(-1)  DB<3> v
16
17  sub plength {
18:b      my ($word) = @_;
19==>       $word =~ s/\W//g;
20:     return 0 unless $word eq reverse $word;
21:     return length $word;
22  }
   DB<3> n
::plength(palindrome.pl:20): return 0 unless $word eq reverse $word;
auto(-1)  DB<3> v
17  sub plength {
18:b      my ($word) = @_;
19:     $word =~ s/\W//g;
20==>       return 0 unless $word eq reverse $word;
21:     return length $word;
22  }
   DB<3>
```

> **NOTE** *If you, like your author, prefer to always have several lines of context in your debugger output, create a file in your home directory named* `.perldb`. *Add the following text:*
>
>   @DB::typeahead = ('{{v');
>
> *When you launch the debugger, Perl can find that file and execute those Perl commands. In this case, before you type anything, the debugger "types" the commands present in the array. This gives you the lines of context that you are looking for.*
>
> *See* `perldoc perldebug` *for a full explanation of the debugger and* `perldoc perldebtut` *for a tutorial on using it.*

At this point, remember your output:

```
$VAR1 = {
        'Reviled did I live, said I, as evil I did deliver.' => 0,
        'This is not a palindrome' => 0,
        'Lager, sir, is regal.' => 0,
        'Dogma? I am God.' => 0,
        'I did, did I?' => 8,
        'Murder for a jar of red rum.' => 0
      };
```

Clearly you have a problem where you're returning 0 from `plength()` and you're on the line of code that is responsible for this:

```
return 0 unless $word eq reverse $word;
```

So use the `p` command to print out some values. For `DB<4>` you can even print out the value of an expression (in this case the `eq` check in the line of code that's the problem):

```
  DB<3> p $word
DogmaIamGod
  DB<4> $t = reverse $word
  DB<5> p $t
doGmaIamgoD
  DB<6> p ( $word eq reverse $word ) ? 'Yes' : 'No'
No
```

This makes is clear that you want a case-insensitive check, so change the value of $word:

```
  DB<7> $word = lc $word
  DB<8> p ( $word eq reverse $word ) ? 'Yes' : 'No'
Yes
  DB<9> n
```

```
main::plength(palindrome.pl:21):         return length $word;
auto(-1)  DB<13> v
18:b        my ($word) = @_;
19:       $word =~ s/\W//g;
20:     return 0 unless $word eq reverse $word;
21==>       return length $word;
22  }
  DB<10>
```

As you can see, changing the value of $word to lc $word allows the code to continue correctly. Now it's obvious how to fix it.

Table 18-1 has a list of common debugger commands for a handy reference. This section doesn't cover everything and there's a lot more to learn.

TABLE 18-1: Common Debugger Commands

COMMAND	MEANING
n	Go to the next line of code. Do not enter a subroutine call.
s	Step into a subroutine call.
b subname	Set a breakpoint at a subroutine name.
b line	Set a breakpoint at the specified line number.
c	Continue executing code until the next breakpoint.
p EXPR	Print the value of a variable or expression.
x EXPR	Like the p command, but will "dump" references.
v	View a range of lines around the current line.
T	Show a stacktrace.
q	Quit the debugger.
{{ command	Execute the command before every debugger prompt.
w EXPR	Set a global watch expression.
W EXPR	Delete a global watch expression.
h	Display debugger help.
r	Return from a subroutine.
S pattern	Display all subroutines matching patterns.

Profiling

So you have a large, working piece of software. It's composed of several modules, but it's slow and buggy. You're not sure why, so how do you fix it? That's where various profiling tools come in handy.

Using Devel::Cover

A few years ago in London, your author was at a gathering of London Perl Mongers when one of the attendees sheepishly admitted to them that he had just started testing and only one percent of his code was covered by tests. However, he had started writing tests by focusing on real bugs that were reported in his system, and his phone support people reported a significant drop in help desk calls. Some experienced developers are aware of this, and instead of writing tests for all their code, they focus their tests on the most critical parts of their code and hope to come back later and write tests for the rest.

But what does code coverage mean? Imagine the following subroutine:

```
sub is_temperature_out_of_bounds {
    my $celsius = shift;
    if ( $celsius > 40 ) {
        return 1;
    }
    elsif ( $celsius < 10 ) {
        return 1;
    }
    else {
        return;
    }
}
```

The `is_temperature_out_of_bounds()` subroutine should return a false value if the temperature is greater than 40 degrees Celsius or less than 10 degrees Celsius. Some tests might look like this:

```
ok is_temperature_out_of_bounds(50), '50 degrees is too high';
ok !is_temperature_out_of_bounds(30), '30 degrees is ok';
```

In this case, the tests clearly miss the condition of where the temperature is less than 10 degrees. The subroutine is simple enough that you may think it's not important, but if someone changes this subroutine in the future, it would be unfortunate to not have full tests covering all possible conditions and lines of code.

So how do you know which code is actually covered by your test suite? That's where Paul Johnson's excellent `Devel::Cover` module comes in. This module can give you excellent reports on exactly what is covered in your test suites. Take a look at the code coverage for `AI::Prolog`, a module your author wrote to do logic programming in Perl.

> **NOTE** AI::Prolog *implements an interpreter for a language called Prolog. In most programming languages, you tell the computer how to solve problems step by step. In Prolog and other logic programming languages, you give them all the data you know about a problem and the rules of how the data is related. Then when you present it with a problem, the language figures out how to solve the problem for you! Logic programming languages are fascinating. Your author recommends that anyone who wants to be a top-notch developer learn multiple programming paradigms including logic programming.*

For AI::Prolog, instead of installing it via the CPAN, you download it from the CPAN and untar the distribution. (tar zxvf AI-Prolog-0.741.tar.gz, or Windows users can double-click the icon.) Type perl Makefile.PL, accept the default prompt for installing the aiprolog shell, and then type make.

Now that you've built the distribution, you can test it with Devel::Cover.

```
cover -delete
HARNESS_PERL_SWITCHES=-MDevel::Cover make test
cover
```

The cover -delete command tells Devel::Cover to delete any previous code coverage runs.

The HARNESS_PERL_SWITCHES environment variable tells Perl to load Devel::Cover for every test that it runs. You should see output similar to the following (with some warnings deleted for clarity — your output will not be identical):

```
$ HARNESS_PERL_SWITCHES=-MDevel::Cover make test
t/01pod.t ................ ok
t/05examples.t ........... ok
t/10choicepoint.t ........ ok
t/20term.t ............... ok
t/25cut.t ................ ok
t/25number.t ............. ok
t/30termlist.t ........... ok
t/35clause.t ............. ok
t/35primitive.t .......... ok
t/35step.t ............... ok
t/50engine.t ............. ok
t/60aiprolog.t ........... ok
t/80math.t ............... ok
t/80preprocessor.t ....... ok
t/80preprocessor_math.t .. ok
t/90results.t ............ ok
All tests successful.
Files=19, Tests=461, 16 wallclock secs
Result: PASS
```

Then you issue the `cover` command:

```
$ cover
Reading database from /tmp/AI-Prolog-0.741/cover_db
-------------------------------- ------ ------ ------ ------ ------ ------
File                              stmt   bran   cond   sub    pod    time   total
-------------------------------- ------ ------ ------ ------ ------ ------
lib/AI/Prolog.pm                  69.7   37.5   n/a    72.2   88.9   22.6   67.0
lib/AI/Prolog/ChoicePoint.pm     100.0   n/a    n/a   100.0    0.0    2.2   85.7
lib/AI/Prolog/Engine.pm           83.3   70.3   75.0   77.1   60.0    4.5   78.5
...olog/Engine/Primitives.pm      59.5   12.5    0.0   90.9    0.0    1.0   55.7
...I/Prolog/KnowledgeBase.pm      30.4   16.7    0.0   46.2    0.0    0.4   27.2
lib/AI/Prolog/Parser.pm           82.7   75.0   58.8   75.0    0.0   44.8   76.7
...og/Parser/PreProcessor.pm     100.0   n/a    n/a   100.0    0.0    2.8   94.1
...rser/PreProcessor/Math.pm      96.8   85.7  100.0   95.5    0.0    3.3   93.5
lib/AI/Prolog/Term.pm             77.7   66.7   58.9   82.6    0.0   12.2   68.8
lib/AI/Prolog/Term/Cut.pm        100.0   n/a    n/a   100.0    0.0    0.1   88.5
lib/AI/Prolog/Term/Number.pm     100.0  100.0   66.7  100.0    0.0    0.2   88.2
lib/AI/Prolog/TermList.pm         97.2   83.3   66.7  100.0    0.0    2.1   89.5
...Prolog/TermList/Clause.pm      95.2   75.0   n/a   100.0    0.0    0.7   85.3
...log/TermList/Primitive.pm     100.0   50.0   n/a   100.0    0.0    2.7   84.6
...I/Prolog/TermList/Step.pm     100.0   n/a    n/a   100.0    0.0    0.5   95.0
Total                             76.2   61.8   58.7   81.9   12.7  100.0   70.4
-------------------------------- ------ ------ ------ ------ ------ ------
HTML output written to /tmp/AI-Prolog-0.741/cover_db/coverage.html
done.
```

> **NOTE** If you do not have a `Makefile.PL` or `Build.PL` file for your code, you can run coverage with `prove`:
>
> ```
> HARNESS_PERL_SWITCHES=-MDevel::Cover prove -l t
> ```

For every module in the distribution, you have a percentage of coverage for all statements (`stmt`), branches (`bran`), conditionals (`cond`), subroutines (`sub`), and documentation (`pod`). The `time` column merely represents the percent of time the tests spent in each module. An `n/a` result means that the particular type of code to cover was not found. The totals across the bottom and down the right side are averages for the amounts (except for the time column). The number `70.4` in the bottom right portion of the result shows the overall code coverage percent. `70.4%` is not bad, but it's not particularly great, either.

> **WARNING** Many programmers new to testing make the mistake of thinking they should shoot for 100 percent code coverage with their tests. Many types of code, such as GUIs or threaded code, are intrinsically hard to test, and the amount of stress you find in attempting to test virtually untestable code sometimes means that manual testing is fine. Remember, you have deadlines and code to deliver, and if you have hard to test code, focus your tests on those areas of your code that are the most critical.

Statements represent individual lines of code (as separated by semicolons). Branches represent things like if/else conditions. Conditional coverage examines boolean operators such as if (($x && y) || !$z) { ... }. POD coverage uses a heuristic to determine if subroutines not beginning with underscores have POD documentation for them.

> **NOTE** *Having 100 percent coverage for your code does not mean that it is bug-free because for larger systems, it's generally impossible to test all possible combinations of inputs and all the different paths through the code. Thorough code coverage is good, but it's no "silver bullet" to ensure that your code works as expected.*

Knowing that you have code not covered by your tests isn't helpful unless you know which code is not covered. The second to last line of your output was this:

```
HTML output written to /tmp/AI-Prolog-0.741/cover_db/coverage.html
```

Open that up in a browser and you should see output similar to Figure 18-1.

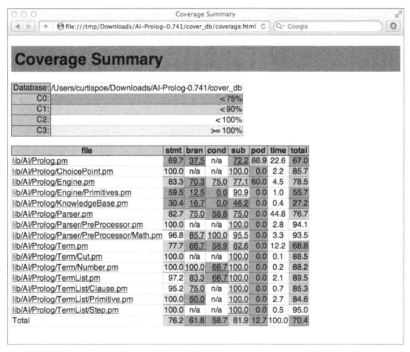

FIGURE 18-1

Many of the items in that report are underlined. These items have hyperlinks that let you drill down to individual modules to see what lines of code your tests have missed. If you have some code with no code coverage, it might actually be dead code you can delete!

Devel::NYTProf

Knowing what code your tests cover is great, but what if your code runs about as fast as a paraplegic cheetah? Not so great. Often in working with large-scale systems, you find that network latency, database access, or simple disk operations are responsible for slow code, but not always. When looking for slow code, the first problem to solve is to identify which code is actually slow. When you work on a system with a few hundred thousand lines of code, this is not a trivial problem. That's where `Devel::NYTProf` comes in. Written by Tim Bunce (the author of the DBI module covered in Chapter 16) and Adam Kaplan, the `Devel::NYTProf` module is often used with test suites to determine where your slow code is.

> **NOTE** *For a better introduction to* `Devel::NYTProf`, *see Tim Bunce's screencast on the topic* at `http://blip.tv/timbunce/devel-nytprof-v4-oscon-201007-3932242`.
>
> *It contains many excellent tips and tricks that you should know when trying to find performance problems in your code.*

`Devel::NYTProf` recommends Perl version 5.8.9 or better, with 5.10.1 or better being preferred.

The basic way to use `Devel::NYTProf` is to execute perl with the -d flag:

```
perl -d:NYTProf some_perl.pl
```

The -d flag, as explained earlier in this chapter, starts Perl with the debugger. However, followed by a colon and an `$identifier`, Perl attempts to load `Devel::$identifier` and runs the `some_perl.pl` program listed on the command line. With the -d:NYTProf argument, Perl loads `Devel::NYTProf` and then runs `some_perl.pl`.

In this case, you'll run in on the `example_7_4_maze.pl` program that you wrote in Chapter 7. Use the downloadable version because that has more interesting timing information.

```
perl -d:NYTProf example_7_4_maze.pl
```

When using `Devel::NYTProf`, the program generally takes 3 to 4 times longer to run, but this is far faster than earlier (and broken) profilers were. Then you can open the `Devel::NYTProf` output in your favorite browser:

```
nytprofhtml --open
```

> **NOTE** The command `nytprofhtml --open` may not work on your system. Instead, you can use this:
>
> `nytprofhtml nytprof.out`
>
> And that creates a directory full of HTML files you can browse. It's the same thing as `nytprofhtml --open` but without the magical opening of a browser window for you.

The output should resemble Figure 18-2.

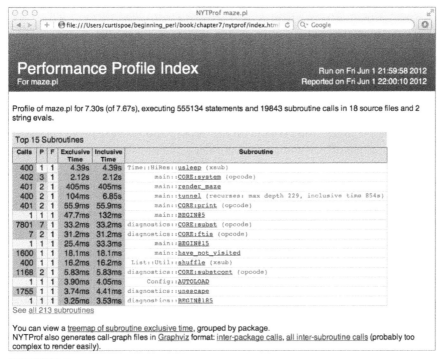

FIGURE 18-2

The first page of this output contains the 15 slowest subroutines (though you can see all the subroutines if you like), but to understand them, you need to know what the columns mean:

➤ **The header information:** This gives you a good idea of what issues to look for.

➤ **The Calls column:** Represents the number of times the subroutine was called. You can see that the relatively fast `diagnostics::CORE::subst` was called a whopping 7,801 times! That makes it slow even if the subroutine is fast.

➤ **The P column:** This represents the number of places the subroutine was called from. For `diagnostics::CORE::subst`, you can see that it was called from seven places.

➤ **The F column:** This represents the number of files the line of the subroutine was called from.

➤ **Exclusive and Inclusive time columns:** These confuse a few people at first. The Inclusive Time represents how much time the subroutine took to run, including the time of any subroutine calls it made. The Exclusive Time column represents the time the subroutine took to run, excluding the timing of any of its subroutine calls. That's why Exclusive Time should always be equal to or less than Inclusive Time.

➤ **The Subroutine column:** This names the offending subroutine.

So how do you use the profiling information? Well, you can guess that `diagnostics::CORE::subst` was probably called from the `diagnostics` pragma, so merely removing that pragma should speed things up a bit.

The top two lines, though, are interesting:

```
Calls  P F Exclusive Inclusive Subroutine
400    1 1 4.39s     4.39s     Time::HiRes::usleep (xsub)
402    3 1 2.12s     2.12s     main::CORE:system (opcode)
```

For the downloadable version of this program, you repeatedly redraw the maze, in slow motion, to see the recursive rendering of the maze. You take out all the `usleep` and system calls to ensure that your code renders as quickly as possible. Running your profiler again gives new results, as shown in Figure 18-3.

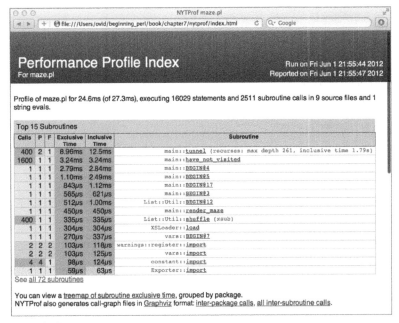

FIGURE 18-3

You've gone from more than 7 seconds to approximately one-half a second. That's great, but clearly this is not a real-world example, and in this case, you dramatically changed the behavior of the code.

Subroutines with names like BEGIN@... represent compile time code, such as loading use warnings. Others, such as the top two tunnel() and have not_visited() subroutines are clearly examples of code you can look at for further optimization. To figure out how to make them run faster, don't guess. Benchmark them! That's covered in the next section.

Benchmark

The Benchmark module is one of the core modules released with Perl version 5. You use it to benchmark some code to see how long it takes to run, and compare it with alternative versions of code that do the same thing.

> **WARNING** *It is very common among developers (sometimes even experienced ones!) to worry about the performance of their programs when they should not. Though there are times this makes sense, programmers tend to be incredibly bad at judging which parts of their software they should optimize. Just because you know that a routine is slow, if it takes only .2% of your program's running time, it's probably not worth speeding up. That's why* Devel::NYTProf *is an excellent tool to find out what parts of your program are the real trouble spots.*
>
> *Just remember one rule: When your program runs fast enough for your needs, stop optimizing.*

Take a look at a concrete example using the example of a factorial. You can define the factorial of a function as that number times the factorial of that number minus one, with the factorial of zero being defined as one. In other words, the factorial of 4 is 24 (4 * 3 * 2 * 1). You could write this with a recursive function that clearly defines your intent:

```
sub fac {
    my $number = shift;
    return 1 if 0 == $number;
    return $number * fac( $number - 1 );
}
```

> **NOTE** *A common error in factorial functions is to return* 0 *for the factorial of* 0 *because programmers forget (or don't know) that the proper result is* 1*. That's why your factorial program has return* 1 *if* 0 == $number *rather than when* 1 == $number.

This seems fine, but what if profiling the code shows that this function is called thousands of times? Would it be worthwhile to eliminate the overhead of the recursive function call? Find out by using the `timethese()` function from `Benchmark`. One way to use this function looks like this. (See the documentation for full details.)

```
timethese(
    $number_of_times_to_run_the_code,
    {
        name1 => \&subref1,
        name2 => \&subref2,
    }
);
```

This is how it works (code file `example_18_9_factorial.pl`):

```
use strict;
use warnings;

use Benchmark 'timethese';

sub recursive_factorial {
    my $number = shift;
    return 1 if 0 == $number;
    return $number * recursive_factorial( $number - 1 );
}

sub loop_factorial {
    my $number = shift;
    return 1 if 0 == $number or 1 == $number;
    my $factorial = 1;
    for ( 2 .. $number ) {
        $factorial *= $_;
    }
    return $factorial;
}

timethese(
    1_000_000,
    {
        'recursive' => sub { recursive_factorial(15) },
        'loop'      => sub { loop_factorial(15) },
    }
);
```

So the `timethese()` function runs your recursive and loop versions of factorial one million times each, computing the factorial of 15. Here's the output from this on the author's computer (reformatted slightly to fit the book):

```
Benchmark: timing 1000000 iterations of loop, recursive...
      loop:  2 wallclock secs (1.92 CPU) @ 520833.33/s (n=1000000)
 recursive:  7 wallclock secs (6.66 CPU) @ 150150.15/s (n=1000000)
```

As you can see, the loop version of the factorial function is more than three times as fast as the recursive version. You might be happy with that, but can you do faster? Sure you can.

The factorial function is a *pure function*. That means the function has no side effects (such as deleting files or altering global variables) and always returns the same output for the same input. Pure functions are great candidates for caching, so cache the factorial and return the cached value if it's found. This can take a bit more code, but for "hot" pieces of code (code that gets run a lot), it can be worth the effort:

```perl
{
    my %factorial_for;

    sub cached_factorial {
        my $number = shift;

        unless (exists $factorial_for{$number}) {
            if ( 0 == $number or 1 == $number ) {
                $factorial_for{$number} = 1;
            }
            else {
                my $factorial = 1;
                for ( 2 .. $number ) {
                    $factorial *= $_;
                }
                $factorial_for{$number} = $factorial;
            }
        }

        return $factorial_for{$number};
    }
}
```

Or if you use Perl version 5.10.0 or better:

```perl
use 5.10.0;
sub cached_factorial {
    state %factorial_for;

    my $number = shift;

    unless (exists $factorial_for{$number}) {
        if ( 0 == $number or 1 == $number ) {
            $factorial_for{$number} = 1;
        }
        else {
            my $factorial = 1;
            for ( 2 .. $number ) {
                $factorial *= $_;
            }
            $factorial_for{$number} = $factorial;
        }
    }

    return $factorial_for{$number};
}
```

And you can add this to your `timethese` function:

```
timethese(
    1_000_000,
    {
        'recursive' => sub { recursive_factorial(15) },
        'loop'      => sub { loop_factorial(15) },
        'cached'    => sub { cached_factorial(15) },
    }
);
```

With these results:

```
Benchmark: timing 1000000 iterations of cached, loop, recursive...
    cached:  0 wallclock secs (0.47 CPU) @ 2127659.57/s (n=1000000)
      loop:  3 wallclock secs (1.96 CPU) @ 510204.08/s (n=1000000)
 recursive:  7 wallclock secs (6.60 CPU) @ 151515.15/s (n=1000000)
```

The `wallclock` time (the amount of time it took from the user's perspective) is rounded off, but when you look at the number after the @ sign, you see that the cached version executed more than two million times per second, whereas the loop version ran only about half a million times per second, so the cached version is roughly 4 times faster than the loop and 14 times faster than the recursive function. Sometimes more lines of code run faster than fewer!

When benchmarking code, you must remember a few things:

➤   There's usually no point in benchmarking code before you've profiled your program.

➤   Always make sure that every version you're benchmarking behaves identically.

➤   Run your benchmark several times. Other processes running on your system can interfere with benchmarks.

➤   If your faster code is too complicated to understand, is it worth it?

➤   When it's fast enough, stop benchmarking!

Perl::Critic

Understanding how much of your code is covered by tests and how well your code performs is great, but how do you know you've written good code? `Perl::Critic` is a highly configurable static analysis tool that can "read" your Perl code, and although it won't tell you if the code is any good, it can identify problem spots your code.

`Perl::Critic` applies policies to your code and analyzes each file to determine if it violates the policies. These policies can have one of five levels of severity, from gentle (level 5) to brutal (level 1). The default policies that ship with `Perl::Critic` are mostly derived from the book *Perl Best Practices*, written by Damian Conway. Some of the policy violations seem a bit out of date (such as RCS keywords `$Id$ not found`, a reference to older version control systems), whereas others catch potentially serious issues with your code (`"return" statement followed by "sort" at line 6, column 5.  Behavior is undefined if called in scalar context.`). `Perl::Critic` is not limited to the Perl best practices. You can write your own policies, and many other policies are on the

CPAN for you to download and apply. You can even create a `.perlcriticrc` file, explained in `perldoc Perl::Critic` (the module) and `perldoc perlcriticrc` (the command-line tool).

Two common ways to use the `perlcritic` tool is to pass it a filename or directory:

```
perlcritic some_program.pl
perlcritic lib/
```

By default, `Perl::Critic` runs in "gentle" mode and reports only on the most severe violations, or ones that are likely to cause your program issues. So run this on the `example_18_9_factorial.pl` benchmarking program you wrote earlier in this chapter:

```
$ perlcritic example_18_9_factorial.pl
example_18_9_factorial.plsource OK
```

That's great. You have no serious violations here. That's equivalent to:

```
$ perlcritic --gentle example_18_9_factorial.pl
$ perlcritic -5 example_18_9_factorial.pl
```

Now kick to the `--stern` level (reformatted slightly):

```
$ perlcritic -4 example_18_9_factorial.pl
Code not contained in explicit package at line 1, column 1.
  Violates encapsulation.  (Severity: 4)
Module does not end with "1;" at line 46, column 1.
  Must end with a recognizable true value.  (Severity: 4)
```

In this case you haven't started your code with a package name, and it doesn't end with a 1 on the last line as you would expect a module to end. The policy violation is described, the line and column where the policy is found is presented, a brief description of why the policy matters is presented, and the severity level is included.

However, those policies are for modules, and this is just a simple script and you don't care about those, so exclude them. The `--exclude` parameter takes a regular expression as its argument and any violations matching that pattern are excluded:

```
$ perlcritic -4 --exclude 'package|module' example_18_9_factorial.pl
example_18_9_factorial.pl source OK
```

Next is the `--harsh` level, or level -3.

```
$ perlcritic -3 --exclude 'package|module' example_18_9_factorial.pl
example_18_9_factorial.pl source OK
```

So far so good.

```
$ perlcritic -2 --exclude 'package|module' example_18_9_factorial.pl
RCS keywords $Id$ not found at line 1, column 1.
  See page 441 of PBP.  (Severity: 2)
RCS keywords $Revision$, $HeadURL$, $Date$ not found at line 1, column 1.
```

```
    See page 441 of PBP.  (Severity: 2)
RCS keywords $Revision$, $Source$, $Date$ not found at line 1, column 1.
    See page 441 of PBP.  (Severity: 2)
"unless" block used at line 28, column 9.  See page 97 of PBP.
    (Severity: 2)
1_000_000 is not one of the allowed literal values (0, 1, 2).
    Use the Readonly or Const::Fast module or the "constant"
    pragma instead at line 45, column 5.  Unnamed numeric
literals make code less maintainable. (Severity: 2)
```

(Note that we've omitted a couple of violations for the sake of brevity).

The RCS keywords violations are references to older source control management systems (used to keep track of changes in your source code) such as CVS or Subversion that we won't cover here. Your author uses a program called git to handle this, so these aren't relevant to him. However, when you run perlcritic you will read See page 441 of PBP if perlcritic detects this issue. In lieu of an explanation of the importance of RCS keywords, you are referred to page 441 of the *Perl Best Practices* book.

The "unless" block used violation is actually a valid concern. Many developers get confused by unless blocks because they can make straightforward logic a bit of a nightmare:

```
unless ( $foo || $bar ) ) {
    ...
}
```

Even the most experienced might be tripped up by this code. It runs only if both $foo and $bar are false, so maybe the perlcritic violation has pointed out something about the code that might make it harder to maintain.

Usually you want to be warned about this, but you don't think it's a problem in this code, so you'll annotate the source code to tell Perl::Critic not to worry about this. You need to read perldoc Perl::Critic::PolicySummary to understand what policy you've violated:

```
unless (exists $factorial_for{$number}) { ## no critic 'ProhibitUnlessBlocks'
```

Or you can add the --statistics switch to get a summary at the end, including the formal names of the policies you've violated:

```
 1 files.
 3 subroutines/methods.
41 statements.
51 lines, consisting of:
      7 blank lines.
      0 comment lines.
      0 data lines.
     44 lines of Perl code.
      0 lines of POD.
Average McCabe score of subroutines was 4.00.
13 violations.
Violations per file was 13.000.
Violations per statement was 0.317.
```

```
Violations per line of code was 0.255.
2 severity 4 violations.
9 severity 2 violations.
2 severity 1 violations.
1 violations of CodeLayout::ProhibitTrailingWhitespace.
1 violations of CodeLayout::RequireTidyCode.
1 violations of ControlStructures::ProhibitUnlessBlocks.
3 violations of Miscellanea::RequireRcsKeywords.
1 violations of Modules::RequireEndWithOne.
1 violations of Modules::RequireExplicitPackage.
1 violations of Modules::RequireVersionVar.
4 violations of ValuesAndExpressions::ProhibitMagicNumbers.
```

In this case, you can see that it was `ControlStructures::ProhibitUnlessBlocks` that you have violated, but just the last part of the name is required when you add an annotation to your code telling Perl critic to ignore the issue.

Now look at the next violation:

```
1_000_000 is not one of the allowed literal values (0, 1, 2).
   Use the Readonly or Const::Fast module or the "constant" pragma
   instead at line 45, column 5.  Unnamed numeric literals make
   code less maintainable. (Severity: 2)
```

This one is certainly a problem. If you're going to hard-code literal values in your code, it's better to declare them at the top of your code and use a descriptive name:

```
use constant NUMBER_OF_TIMES_TO_RUN => 1_000_000;
```

Not only does this help to document your code, but also it makes it easier to find all the values in your code that are more likely to need to change at a later date.

Right now, you've seen a few cases in which there are policies you don't like. Perhaps you want to disable them globally. You can create a `.perlcriticrc` file in your home directory (or a custom one in your code directory) with the following contents:

```
exclude = RequireRCSKeywords RequireTidyCode RequireFinalReturn
[TestingAndDebugging::RequireUseStrict]
equivalent_modules = Dancer
[TestingAndDebugging::RequireUseWarnings]
equivalent_modules = Dancer
```

The `exclude` = line turns off several policies that you don't want (obviously, this is subjective). The `TestingAndDebugging::RequireUseStrict` and `TestingAndDebugging::RequireUseWarnings` sections tell `Perl::Critic` that you don't require `strict` and `warnings` when using the `Dancer` module. (`Dancer` is a lovely web framework and using it turns on strictures and warnings for you.)

You can use your `.perlcriticrc` to include new policies you have created, change the default warning level, and do many other things. `Perl::Critic` can be an excellent tool to ensure your coding standards are met.

SUMMARY

In this chapter you learned about numerous small problems that, although not core Perl, are nonetheless common enough, yet tricky, tasks it's having a basic exposure to. You've learned about reading and writing CSV files, different ways to handle XML, and a bit more about the dates and times.

You also learned about a variety of useful tools, such as the debugger that help you better understand how your programs behave. You learned a bit about `Devel::Cover`, code that can tell you how well your test suites cover your code base. You learned to use `Devel::NYTProf` to uncover performance problems in your code and use the `Benchmark` module to test whether alternative implementations are actually faster.

Finally, you've been exposed to `Perl::Critic`, a tool that enables you uncover potential problems in your code.

EXERCISES

1. Describe at least three potential problems with the following code to read a CSV file:

```
open my $fh, '<', $file
    or die "Cannot open $file for reading: $!";

while ( my $line = <$fh> ) {
    my ( $name, $rank, $notes ) = split /,/ => $line;
    print <<"END";
Name:   $name
Rank:   $rank
Notes:  $notes
}
```

2. Why might you use `DateTime::Tiny` instead of the `DateTime` module? List some strengths and weaknesses of each.

3. Why should you use `Devel::NYTProf`? When should you not use it? What are some of the problems with aggressively optimizing your code for performance?

4. Type in the following program:

```
use Getopt::Long;
my $name  = Nobody;

my $times = 3;

GetOptions(
    'name=s'  => \$name,
    'times=i' => \$times,
) or die;
```

```
hello( $name, $times );

sub hello {
    for ( 1 .. $_[1] ) {
        print "$_[0]\n";
    }
}
```

The program is correct and does what it intended. Try running the program both with and without arguments if you're unsure of what it's doing. Then run this command for the "gentle" warnings from `perlcritic`.

```
perlcritic -5 program.pl
```

Now run `perlcritic -1 program.pl` and read the violations. How do they differ? Do you agree or disagree with what `Perl::Critic` reports?

5. Make the `Perl::Critic` violations reported in Exercise 4 go away. You may want to read the `Perl::Critic` documentation to fix some of these issues. See `--profile` in `perldoc perlcritic` for a useful start. You may want to run `perlcritic` with `--statistics` to see the full names of the policy violations.

▶ WHAT YOU LEARNED IN THIS CHAPTER

TOPIC	DESCRIPTION
`Text::CSV_XS`	A Perl module to handle correctly reading and writing CSV data.
`XML::Simple`	A simple but inflexible method to read and write XML data.
`XML::Twig`	An excellent XML parsing module.
`XML::Writer`	A useful module for writing correct XML.
`DateTime`	A full-featured date and time manipulation/presentation module.
`Date::Tiny`	A minimalistic date object. Good when you don't need date math.
`DateTime::Tiny`	Like `Date::Tiny`, but for dates and times.
Perl Debugger	Used to run Perl programs in debug mode and understand their behavior.
`Devel::Cover`	A module that tells you what code is covered by your test suite.
`Devel::NYTProf`	A module that profiles your program and identify slow code.
`Benchmark`	A module that compares the performance characteristics of different versions of code.
`Perl::Critic`	A code analysis module that enables you to find possible problems in your code.
`perlcritic`	The command-line interface to the `Perl::Critic` module.

19

The Next Steps

WHAT YOU WILL LEARN IN THIS CHAPTER:

➤ What this book covers… and what it leaves out

➤ Using an `DBIx::Class` and other mappers to map relations

➤ How to use the Template Toolkit

➤ Building web applications with `Catalyst`

WROX.COM CODE DOWNLOAD FOR THIS CHAPTER

The wrox.com code downloads for this chapter are found at `http://www.wrox.com/remtitle.cgi?isbn=1118013840` on the Download Code tab. The code for this chapter is divided into the following major examples:

➤ `lib/My/Schema.pm`

➤ `lib/My/Schema/Result/License.pm`

➤ `lib/My/Schema/Result/Media.pm`

➤ `lib/My/Schema/Result/MediaType.pm`

➤ `listing_19_1_dbic.pl`

➤ `listing_19_2_letter.pl`

➤ `templates/en/letter.tt2`

➤ `templates/fr/letter.tt2`

You've finally made it to the last chapter! (Be honest, you've skipped ahead and started reading this.) Chapters 1 through 11 gave you the skills you need to be an entry level Perl programmer (Chapter 17 helps there, too). Chapters 12 through 16 gave you the skills to take the next step in your Perl programming career. Chapter 18 covers a few skills that explain some common tasks you'll encounter, and strong skills for understanding your code. This chapter introduces you to the skills that can take you to the next level.

WHAT NEXT?

It's difficult to say that you truly understand a programming language until you understand the libraries for that language. Your author, for example, "knows" Java and has programmed in it from time to time, but he doesn't actually know the common libraries for the language. Thus, although he may be a strong programmer, many companies would think twice about hiring him as a Java programmer. (Or he'd take such a serious pay cut that it wouldn't be worth it.) This chapter introduces you to the unholy trinity of Perl: `DBIx::Class`, Template Toolkit, and `Catalyst`. These three modules are probably the most common modules used to build large-scale websites. They give you incredible power, but they take quite a while to learn.

A full book could be used to cover each of `Catalyst`, Template Toolkit, and `DBIx::Class`. The first two modules have published books and `DBIx::Class` has a book in progress (https://github.com/castaway/dbix-class-book). These are large modules that take quite a bit of time to exercise their full power. `DBIx::Class` was written by Matt Trout, and he's also one of the major figures behind the `Catalyst` framework. Template Toolkit (just `Template` on the CPAN), was written by Andy Wardley. All three of these modules are well maintained and updated regularly. This chapter doesn't have the room to cover them in-depth, but you get a quick introduction to each.

First, quickly recap what has and hasn't been covered.

What This Book Covers

So far, you've learned about or received:

➤   The core syntax of the Perl language.

➤   Quite a bit about where to go for help.

➤   Where to download new modules.

➤   (Constantly reinforced) where to look for documentation (and to actually read it). This alone can put you a step ahead of many programmers.

➤   How packages and modules work.

➤   Different strategies for writing object-oriented code.

➤   A good introduction to writing tests for your code.

These are skills that can separate the complete beginners from those who are ready for the workforce.

What This Book Leaves Out

You're going to be surprised, but you've not learned how to be a programmer. There is a huge difference between understanding the syntax of a programming language and understanding how to be a programmer. That's why, if you've never programmed before but you've mastered the techniques in this book, you are still probably an entry-level programmer. There is much, much more to it. That being said, you must start somewhere, and learning how to program by learning a programming language is, well, probably not a bad idea.

> **NOTE** *If you want to learn the skills needed to be a good programmer and not just be someone who knows a programming language, your author recommends* Code Complete, *2nd edition, written by Steve McConnell for Microsoft Press. It's an excellent, well-researched book.*

A huge amount of information about solving math issues, manipulating dates and times, and various clever algorithms for complex data-structures has not been covered. Symbol table manipulation (it's not too hard, but you really need to know Perl well first), tying variables, and GUI programming has not been covered. There's also plenty of stuff with process management, sockets, and networking tools that are useful when you want to do system programming, but that requires plenty of other skills that are far beyond what this book is designed to cover.

In fact, your author expects plenty of e-mail mentioning things that he should have covered and didn't, but in a book this size, the web-centric text worked well to keep things focused.

Perl is, at the end of the day, a huge language. There aren't many popular languages that rival it in sheer size and complexity (C++ is one, but it's a bit easier to use), but that's OK. In Perl, it's perfectly OK to specialize in those areas that you actually need to know and just look up the others.

Now move on to the final bits.

UNDERSTANDING OBJECT-RELATIONAL MAPPERS

An *object-relational mapper* (commonly known as an ORM) is a common tool that's used to provide an OO layer over database access. When they're well written, they make it easier to swap between different databases without changing much of your code other than your database connection. In this sense, they're even more powerful than the DBI module enabling you to change databases: DBI sometimes requires that you write SQL that is specific to a particular database, but a good ORM writes that code for you, taking into account the dialect of SQL that you use.

Using an ORM is easy. Say you have a `customers` table and want to get the first and last name of a customer with a given ID. Basic usage of an ORM often looks like this:

```
my $customer = My::Customer->find($id);
print join ' ', $customer->first_name, $customer->last_name;
```

For DBI, it might look like this:

```
my @customer = $dbh->selectrow_array(
    "SELECT first_name, last_name FROM customer"
    {}, $id
);
print join ' ', @customer;
```

That doesn't seem like much of an advantage, but aside from being easier to read, it also makes your life more flexible. Because you have an object instead of a class, you could write a full_name() method and do this:

```
print $customer->full_name;
```

With that, you don't need to write that join code every time you want to print the customer's full name.

Or if you want to fetch all the orders associated with a customer, you might do this:

```
my $orders = $customer->orders;
```

But for DBI, you usually must prepare, execute, and fetch another SQL statement. That's extra code that distracts from what you actually want to do: fetch the customer's orders.

Understanding DBIx::Class

Like most major programming languages, there are a number of ORMs available for Perl. Another popular ORM is Rose::DB::Object. It's ridiculously fast and unlike other ORMs does not try too hard to hide the abstraction between the database and the objects. (Whether this is a benefit is left as an exercise for you.) However, DBIx::Class is by far the most popular ORM for Perl, and if called upon to use one in your job, this is the one you might choose.

DBIx::Class was created a number of years ago by Matt Trout. He was tired of answering questions about how to work around problems in the older Class::DBI ORM, so he wrote his own.

One of the lovely features of DBIx::Class is that it makes a clear distinction between objects (a result), sets of objects (a resultset), and the schema that contains them. By enforcing this distinction, a number of powerful techniques become available.

They are powerful enough and aren't covered in this chapter because this is only an introduction. Deal with it, and hope your author isn't simply hand-waving.

Understanding Basic DBIx::Class Usage

Assume you already have a small database with two tables named customers and orders and a customer can have many orders. You're tired of writing SQL by hand, so you decide to use an ORM.

To use DBIx::Class you must define your schema. For example, if your top-level namespace is Loki::, you might define your schema like this, in lib/Loki/Schema.pm:

```
package Loki::Schema;
use base qw/DBIx::Class::Schema/;

__PACKAGE__->load_namespaces();

1;
```

The load_namespaces() method tells DBIx::Class to look for the actual result classes in Loki::Schema::Result. (This is configurable.) In your code, rather than loading separate classes for every table, you just need to load your schema class, and it takes care of loading the other classes for you.

The connection information isn't embedded in the schema class. This makes it easier for you have to multiple instances of the same schema (for example, a production schema and a test schema) and for the code using the schema to tell it where the database is.

Assuming your customers table has customer_id, first_name, and last_name, fields, your customers table Result class might look like this:

```
Loki::Schema::Result::Customer;

use base qw/DBIx::Class::Core/;

__PACKAGE__->table('customers');
__PACKAGE__->add_columns(qw/ customer_id first_name last_name /);
__PACKAGE__->set_primary_key('customer_id');

__PACKAGE__->has_many(
    orders => 'Loki::Schema::Result::Order',
    'customer_id'
);

sub full_name {
    my $self = shift;
    return join ' ', $self->first_name, $self->last_name;
}

1;
```

Regarding the previous code, you:

1. Inherit from DBIx::Class::Core. That provides the magic that makes everything work.

2. Define the table name, the columns, and the primary key of the table using class methods. Those are the three things you want for every Result:: class.

3. Define your relationships. In this case, you state that each customer *has many* orders. Note that has_many() doesn't necessarily mean that a customer will have orders. It means that they can have zero, one, or many orders.

The has_many() class method takes the accessor name you'll be using ($customer->orders), the name of the class that you are pointing to, and the foreign key in that class that refers to your own primary key. (Thus, the `customer_id` argument in `has_many()` refers to the `orders.customer_id` and not the `customers.customer_id`.)

A `full_name()` method is provided. This shows that this is just an ordinary class, and you can provide additional methods just as you would with any other class.

> **NOTE** To understand how `has_many()` and other relationship columns work, study `perldoc DBIx::Class::Relationship`. Many developers apparently don't read that documentation and, as a result, get confused when trying to describe relationships between tables.

Now see how the class for `orders` is defined:

```
Loki::Schema::Result::Order;

use base qw/DBIx::Class::Core/;

__PACKAGE__->table('orders');
__PACKAGE__->add_columns(qw/order_id number delivered total customer_id/);
__PACKAGE__->set_primary_key('order_id');

__PACKAGE__->belongs_to(
    customer => 'Loki::Schema::Result::Customer',
    'customer_id'
);

1;
```

It's almost the same, but the `belongs_to()` relationship is from the reverse of the `has_many()` relationship. A customer *has many* orders while an order *belongs to* a customer. The first two arguments are still the accessor name (`$order->customer`) and the related class name, but now the third argument is the `orders` foreign key ID (`customer_id`) and not the `id` in the foreign table.

Also, you can actually attach a lot of meta data to a column:

```
__PACKAGE__->add_columns(
    customer_id  => {
        data_type        => 'integer',
        size             => 16,
        is_nullable      => 0,
        is_auto_increment => 1,
    },
    first_name => {
        data_type        => 'varchar',
        size             => 256,
        is_nullable      => 0,
    },
    last_name => {
```

```
            data_type          => 'varchar',
            size               => 256,
            is_nullable        => 0,
        },
    );
```

This meta data is entirely optional and is generally not used by DBIx::Class, but there are plenty of other modules (such as DBIx::Class::WebForm) that do use this meta data to help you create rich meta data.

> **NOTE** *Your author might have avoided some confusion over relationships by naming the ID column of the* customers *table* id *instead of* customer_id. *By having distinct names, it would have been more clear that the* customer_id *in the* belongs_to() *argument list refers to* orders.customer_id *and not* customers.customer_id.*
>
> *However, it's generally good database practice to ensure that columns in different tables that refer to the same thing have the same name. Thus, you never get into a situation in which you're writing* id = customer_id *and wonder if* id *is the identifier for the correct object. By keeping naming consistent, you can write* table1.customer_id = table2.customer_id, *and it's clear that you're really comparing the same thing. This generally isn't done in this book to keep to a convention that many newer developers are familiar with (having the ID simply named* id). *This may have been a mistake.*

Now use your schema:

```
use Loki::Schema;

my $schema = Loki::Schema->connect(
    $dsn,
    $user,
    $pass,
    \%optional_attributes
);

my $customer_rs
  = Loki::Schema::Result::Customer->resultset('Customer');

while ( my $customer = $customer_rs->next ) {
    my $orders_rs = $customer->orders;
    my $total = 0;
    while ( my $order = $orders_rs->next ) {
        $total += $order->total;
    }
    printf "Customer: %40s Total: %0.2f\n",
        $customer->full_name, $total;
}
```

The `connect()` method takes the same arguments as `DBI->connect()`. This is not a coincidence and it makes your life much easier.

The `resultset()` class method returns a `DBIx::Class::ResultSet` object, and you can call `next()` on it repeatedly to iterate over all the objects returned. (The call to the database is not made until you need results returned.) There are many ways you can use it:

```
# find customer Result with given id (must refer to primary key)
my $customer = $customer_rs->find($id);

# Find a customer ResultSet with the last name of 'Smith'
$customer_rs = $customer_rs->search({ last_name => 'Smith' });

# Find a customer ResultSet whose last name begins with 'S',
# ordered by last_name, and then first name
my $customer_rs = Loki::Schema->resultset('Customer')->search(
    { last_name => { like => 'S%' } },
    { order_by  => { -asc => [qw/last_name first_name/] },
);
```

Remember: in `DBIx::Class`, the `ResultSet` returns a set of results that you can search on. Individual `Result` objects correspond to rows in a database, and you can't search on them, but you can call methods on them to get and set data:

```
my $customer = $customer_rs->find($id);
$customer->first_name('Bob');
$customer->update; # save the changed data to the database
```

There's a lot more to `DBIx::Class` than described, but this gives you some idea of the basics. One of the lovely things about this module is that it tends to defer calls to the database unless they are actually needed. For example, if you call the `update()` method on a result that has not been changed, there's no need to update the record in the database, so no UPDATE SQL call is made to the database.

There's a lot more to learn about `DBIx::Class`, so read `DBIx::Class::Manual` for a good start.

Understanding the Pros and Cons of an ORM

Before you reach for an ORM, it's worth being aware of some of the benefits and drawbacks. Further, be aware that many of the benefits and drawbacks are highly dependent on the particular ORM that you use. For example, ORMs are often slower than direct database access, but that's generally not true of `Rose::DB::Object`, but tends to be true of many alternatives. Your specific needs should dictate which ORM, if any, you choose.

ORMs are great for reducing code complexity and, if designed well, often make changing databases easy, such as changing from Oracle to PostgreSQL as your author did at one company. (Although it's your author's experience that changing databases happens rarely, so this benefit is often overstated.) ORMs also tend to remove the SQL from your actual code, so if you need to change your schema (such as a table name), you often have only one spot to do this in. There are other ways to do this, but when people avoid ORMs, they often spread their database knowledge throughout the code and have multiple places in their code that they need to change the data.

On the flip side, you often hear about the *Object-Relational Impedance Mismatch*. In short, it means that the hierarchical nature of objects and the relational nature of databases (for those with a computer science background, think trees versus graphs) often don't map well together. Classes, for example, enable subclassing, but most databases do not support this for tables. So you can map a class to a table, or to a set of related tables, and things can get hairy. Or you find that the data you want to select doesn't map to a single object. Or you have subtle issues when you discover that SQL's NULL is not the same thing as Perl's undef.

For most simple applications, ORMs are helpful, but as your applications grow, it's worth understanding the trade-offs you make when you use an ORM. Your author recommends hitting your favorite search engine and searching for **The Vietnam of Computer Science.** It's a long and fairly technical read, but it's worth digging into and understanding what the author is trying to say.

TRY IT OUT Convert Your DBI Code to DBIx::Class

In Chapter 16 you created a small SQLite database to manage rights data. For your small example, using DBI directly and writing SQL was fine, but as systems grow, it might be harder to maintain, so you can convert them to DBIx::Class. The three tables looked like this:

```
CREATE TABLE media (
    id            INTEGER PRIMARY KEY,
    name          VARCHAR(255) NOT NULL,
    location      VARCHAR(255) NOT NULL,
    source        VARCHAR(511) NOT NULL,
    attribution   VARCHAR(255) NOT NULL,
    media_type_id INTEGER      NOT NULL,
    license_id    INTEGER      NOT NULL,
    FOREIGN KEY (media_type_id) REFERENCES media_types(id),
    FOREIGN KEY (license_id)    REFERENCES licenses(id)
);

CREATE TABLE licenses (
    id                INTEGER      PRIMARY KEY,
    name              VARCHAR(255) NOT NULL,
    allows_commercial BOOLEAN      NOT NULL
);

CREATE TABLE media_types (
    id         INTEGER PRIMARY KEY,
    media_type VARCHAR(10) NOT NULL
);
```

Create three result classes, My::Schema::Result::Media, My::Schema::Result::License, and My::Schema::Result::MediaType.

All the code for this Try It Out is in the code folder lib/My/Schema.pm.

1. Create your schema class and three result classes:

```
package My::Schema;
use strict;
use warnings;

use base 'DBIx::Class::Schema';

__PACKAGE__->load_namespaces;

1;
```

2. Create your media class (code file `lib/My/Schema/Result/Media.pm`):

```
package My::Schema::Result::Media;
use strict;
use warnings;

use base 'DBIx::Class::Core';

__PACKAGE__->table("media");
__PACKAGE__->add_columns(qw{
    id name location source attribution media_type_id license_id
});
__PACKAGE__->set_primary_key("id");

__PACKAGE__->belongs_to(
    license => "My::Schema::Result::License",
    "license_id",
);

__PACKAGE__->belongs_to(
    media_type => "My::Schema::Result::MediaType",
    "media_type_id",
);

1;
```

3. Create your media type class (code file `lib/My/Schema/Result/MediaType.pm`):

```
package My::Schema::Result::MediaType;
use strict;
use warnings;

use base 'DBIx::Class::Core';

__PACKAGE__->table("media_types");
__PACKAGE__->add_columns(qw{id media_type});
__PACKAGE__->set_primary_key("id");

__PACKAGE__->has_many(
    media => "My::Schema::Result::Media",
```

```
        "media_type_id"
    );

    1;
```

3. Create your license class (code file `lib/My/Schema/Result/License.pm`):

```perl
package My::Schema::Result::License;
use strict;
use warnings;

use base 'DBIx::Class::Core';

__PACKAGE__->table("licenses");__PACKAGE__->add_columns(qw{ id name allows_
commercial });
__PACKAGE__->set_primary_key("id");

__PACKAGE__->has_many(
    media => "My::Schema::Result::Media",
    "media_type_id"
);

1;
```

4. Run the scripts from Chapter 16 to create and populate the database schema.

5. Now create a program named `listing_19_1_dbic.pl` (final code is found in code file `listing_19_1_dbic.pl`):

```perl
use strict;
use warnings;

use My::Schema;
my $schema = My::Schema->connect(
    "dbi:SQLite:dbname=rights.db",
    "",
    "",
    { RaiseError => 1, PrintError => 0 },
);

# find anything named 'Anne Frank Stamp'
my $media_rs
  = $schema->resultset('Media')->search(
    { name => 'Anne Frank Stamp' } );
my $count = $media_rs->count;
print "We found $count record(s)\n";

print "\nNow finding all media\n\n";
# find all media, in reverse alphabetical order
$media_rs = $schema->resultset('Media')->search(
    {},    # we want all of them
    { order_by => { -desc => 'name' } },
);
```

```
while ( my $media = $media_rs->next ) {
    my $name      = $media->name;
    my $location  = $media->location;
    my $license   = $media->license->name;
    my $media_type = $media->media_type->media_type;

    print <<"END";
Name:     $name
Location: $location
License:  $license
Media:    $media_type

END
}
```

6.   Run the program with `perl listing_19_1_dbic.pl`. You should see the following output:

```
We found 1 record(s)
Now finding all media
Name:     Clair de Lune
Location: /data/claire_de_lune.ogg
License:  Public Domain
Media:    audio
Name:     Anne Frank Stamp
Location: /data/anne_fronk_stamp.jpg
License:  Public Domain
Media:    image
```

How It Works

Your author had to do a fair amount of setup to get this example working, but after that setup is done, you don't need to do it again. That means that code you write later can rely on your DBIx::Class classes and you don't need to worry about duplicating the code over and over again.

The My::Schema class called this class method:

```
__PACKAGE__->load_namespaces()
```

The load_namespaces() method, inherited from DBIx::Class::Schema, is responsible to find the Result:: and ResultSet:: classes (if any) and load them for you. For example, in your code, you should not need to use My::Schema::Result::Media.

Each of the My::Schema::Result::Media, My::Schema::Result::License, and My::Schema::Result::MediaType classes inherit from DBIx::Class::Core and follow a standard pattern in that they:

➤   Declare the table

➤   Declare the columns

➤   Declare the primary key

➤   Declare the relationships (if any)

And finally, you have `listing_19_1_dbic.pl` to put it all together. Lines 1 through 10 declare `strict`, `warnings`, use the schema, and connect to it:

```
 1:  use strict;
 2:  use warnings;
 3:
 4:  use My::Schema;
 5:  my $schema = My::Schema->connect(
 6:      "dbi:SQLite:dbname=rights.db",
 7:      "",
 8:      "",
 9:      { RaiseError => 1, PrintError => 0 },
10:  );
```

Lines 12 through 16 search for any media named `Anne Frank Stamp` and return a resultset matching your search. In this case, you have only one item found.

```
12:  # find anything named 'Anne Frank Stamp'
13:  my $media_rs
14:    = $schema->resultset('Media')->search(
15:        { name => 'Anne Frank Stamp' } );
16:  my $count = $media_rs->count;
17:  print "We found $count record(s)\n";
```

Lines 18 through 23 search for all media (the empty hash reference in line 21 says "you have no search criteria, so all records will be returned") and line 22 says that you want your records in reverse alphabetical order by name.

```
18:  print "\nNow finding all media\n\n";
19:  # find all media, in reverse alphabetical order
20:  $media_rs = $schema->resultset('Media')->search(
21:      {},     # we want all of them
22:      { order_by => { -desc => 'name' } },
23:  );
```

Finally, you have lines 25 through 38 iterating over your `$media_rs` result set and printing your various bits and pieces of information.

Lines 28 and 29 each take advantage of relationships you declared in `My::Schema::Result::Media` to fetch your related `My::Schema::Result::License` and `My::Schema::Result::MediaType` objects.

```
25:  while ( my $media = $media_rs->next ) {
26:      my $name       = $media->name;
27:      my $location   = $media->location;
28:      my $license    = $media->license->name;
29:      my $media_type = $media->media_type->media_type;
30:
31:      print <<"END";
32:  Name:     $name
33:  Location: $location
34:  License:  $license
```

```
35:   Media:      $media_type
36:
37:   END
38:   }
```

When you have your $media->license and $media->media_type methods, under the hood DBIx::Class makes separate SQL statements for each and (sort of) resemble this:

```
SELECT * FROM licenses me WHERE ( me.id = ? )
SELECT * FROM media_types me WHERE ( me.id = ? )
```

Thus, although you have one call to the database to select your media, for every record, you have two extra calls to the database. This can be expensive if you have lots of records. You can get around this by prefetching the licenses and media types:

```
$media_rs = $schema->resultset('Media')->search(
    {},     # we want all of them
    {   order_by => { -desc => 'me.name' },
        prefetch => [qw/license media_type/],
    },
);
```

The order_by parameter now refers to me.name instead of name. This is because each license record also has a name parameter, and the SQL wouldn't know which name to order by. However, the primary table is always aliased to me, allowing the SQL to know which name to order by. Under the hood, the resulting SQL looks similar to this:

```
 SELECT me.*, license.*, media_type.*
    FROM media me
    JOIN licenses license       ON license.id = me.license_id
    JOIN media_types media_type ON media_type.id=me.media_type_id
ORDER BY me.name DESC
```

By prefetching your related tables, you make a single call to the database and often have a much faster program. This can use a lot more memory, so you have the familiar trade-off between speed and memory usage.

Using DBIx::Class::Schema::Loader

You might find writing DBIx::Class schema classes a bit tedious. That's where DBIx::Class::Schema::Loader comes in handy. It provides the dbicdump utility. You can autogenerate the previous classes with this:

```
dbicdump -o dump_directory=lib My::Schema $dsn $user $pass
```

The dbicdump program uses DBIx::Class::Schema::Loader to read an existing database and automatically create a set of schema classes for it. For SQLite, because you don't require a username and password, you could do this:

```
dbicdump -o dump_directory=lib My::Schema "dbi:SQLite:dbname=rights.db"
```

The output won't be exactly the same as the examples you have, but it can provide documentation on the various columns and richer information about the columns:

```
PACKAGE  ->add_columns(
"id",
{ data_type => "integer", is_auto_increment => 1, is_nullable => 0 },
"name",
{ data_type => "varchar", is_nullable => 0, size => 255 },
"location",
{ data_type => "varchar", is_nullable => 0, size => 255 },
"source",
{ data_type => "varchar", is_nullable => 0, size => 511 },
"attribution",
{ data_type => "varchar", is_nullable => 0, size => 255 },
"media_type_id",
{ data_type => "integer", is_foreign_key => 1, is_nullable => 0 },
"license_id",
{ data_type => "integer", is_foreign_key => 1, is_nullable => 0 },
);
```

Your author strongly recommends that you check this module out. If you have an existing database, it can make your life much easier.

USING THE TEMPLATE TOOLKIT

Chapter 15, introduced you to `Template::Tiny`, a small templating module that makes it easy to create quick-and-dirty templates. However, although fast, it's not powerful. Although there are many alternative templating modules on the CPAN, consider Template Toolkit, one of the most popular. You can read about it at `http://tt2.org/`.

Why Use Templates?

A template is a pattern for data that you want to present to your user. It has variables that can be filled in dynamically to allow you to present the same form of data, but with different values. At its simplest, you can think of string interpolation as a template:

```
foreach my $name (@names) {
    print "Hello, $name\n";
}
```

However, templates go beyond this. They generally mean you can embed simple logic directly in the template. In Chapter 15, one of the example templates had this snippet:

```
[% IF have_params %]
    <p>Our list of params:</p>
    <table rules="all">
      <tr><th>Name</th><th>Value</th></tr>
```

```
   [% FOREACH param IN params %]
      <tr><td>[% param.name %]</td><td>[% param.value %]</td></tr>
   [% END %]
     </table>
[% ELSE %]
     <p><strong>No params supplied!</strong></p>
[% END %]
```

If you wanted to do this in Perl, you must write something like this:

```perl
my $output = '';
if ( $have_params ) {
    $output .= <<'END';
    <p>Our list of params:</p>
    <table rules="all">
      <tr><th>Name</th><th>Value</th></tr>
END
    foreach my $param (@params) {
        $output .=
          "<tr><td>$param->{name}</td><td>$param->{value}</td></tr>";
    }
    $output .= "</table>\n";
}
else {
    $output .= "<p><strong>No params supplied!</strong></p>";
}
```

This tiny example isn't too bad, but as the amount of information (and logic) that you must handle in your output grows, it starts to get unwieldy and may even get in the way to understand your main program logic.

Instead, you often want to separate gathering your data and presenting your data. This could, for example, allow a Perl programmer to focus on writing the code to fetch the data while allowing a web designer to create a lovely template for presenting the data. This can be extremely useful if the data doesn't change but its presentation does. Rather than having to rewrite your code, the designer can create a new set of templates.

Or perhaps you have a set of data that you want to present as HTML, XML, or text? Don't change your program. Just use the same data with different templates.

An Introduction to Template Toolkit

The Template Toolkit module, on the CPAN, is known as Template. For our examples, assume you have a directory named `templates` that contains your templates.

```perl
use Template;

my $template = Template->new(
    INCLUDE_PATH => 'templates',
);
```

```
my %template_data = (
    name     => 'Ovid',
    amount_of => {
        plums => 2,
        books => 8,
        coins => 7,
        sword => 1,
    },
    skills => [qw/cowering hiding running/],
);

$template->process( 'character.tt2', \%template_data )
  or die $template->error;
```

The preceding code looks for a file named `templates/character.tt2` and uses the `%template_data` to fill out the template. Assume that `templates/character.tt2` contained the following template:

```
Hello, [% name %],
Your primary skills are:
[% FOREACH skill IN skills -%]
    [% skill %]
[% END %]
[% IF amount_of -%]
You own:
  [% FOREACH item IN amount_of.keys -%]
    [% amount_of.$item %] [% item %]
  [% END %]
[% ELSE %]
You are empty-handed.
[% END %]
```

When you run the sample program, it prints the following:

```
Hello, Ovid,
Your primary skills are:
    cowering
    hiding
    running
You own:
    1 sword
    2 plums
    8 books
    7 coins
```

The first argument to the `process()` method is the name of the template file you want to process. `Template` looks for this file in the `INCLUDE_PATH` directory. The second argument should be a reference to a hash. The keys of the hash are the names of the variables interpolated in the template.

> **NOTE** *You may find that you don't always want to have Template Toolkit print the data directly to* STDOUT. *You might want to capture it to a variable. In that case, pass a reference to a scalar as the third argument to* process()*:*
>
> ```
>     my $output;
>     $template->process( 'character.tt2', \%template_data, \$output )
>         or die $template->error;
>     print $output;
> ```
>
> *Instead of* $output, *you can also give it a filename (not as a reference!) or file-handle to write the output to.*

When processing the template, you see that the variable can be interpolated directly:

```
Hello, [% name %],
```

And you can iterate over arrays:

```
[% FOREACH skill IN skills -%]
    [% skill %]
[% END %]
```

You can also test if a variable exists and take action upon it:

```
[% IF amount_of -%]
    We have inventory.
[% ELSE %]
    We are the 99%
 [% END %]
```

Note how you iterate over hashes:

```
[% FOREACH item IN amount_of.keys -%]
  [% amount_of.$item %] [% item %]
[% END %]
```

The .keys method is a *vmethod* (virtual method) that's available for hash references. There are vmethods available for scalars, hashes, and lists. See Template::Manual::VMethods for a full list of vmethods available.

That's interesting because you refer to amount_of.$item. The $item tells Template Toolkit that you have a variable named $item and you want to reevaluate it before fetching that item from the amount_of hash reference. Otherwise, amount_of.item would keep trying to fetch a key named item from the %amount_of hash and would return undef every time.

You can also gain some fine-grained control over the output. For example, you could switch your character template to this:

```
Hello, [% name %],
Your primary
[%- IF skills.size == 1 -%] skill is [% skills.0 %]
[% ELSE %] skills are
    [%- FOREACH skill IN skills -%]
        [%- IF skill == skills.last -%]and [%- skill -%]
        [%- ELSE -%] [%- skill -%],
        [%- END -%]
    [%- END -%]
[% END %]
[% IF inventory %]
You own:
[% FOREACH item IN inventory.keys -%]
    [% inventory.$item %] [% item %]
[% END %]
[% ELSE %]
You are empty-handed.
[% END %]
```

And running your program again prints this:

```
Hello, Ovid,
Your primary skills are cowering, hiding, and running
You own:
    1 sword
    2 plums
    8 books
    7 coins
```

But if you only had the hiding skill, the skills line prints:

```
Your primary skill is hiding
```

This makes it easy to change your output on-the-fly without having to change your code.

If you look closely at the template, you can notice that the many of the start and end tags for template commands have a hyphen (-):

```
[%- IF skills.size == 1 -%] skill is [% skills.0 %]
[% ELSE %] skills are
    [%- FOREACH skill IN skills -%]
        [%- IF skill == skills.last -%]and [%- skill -%]
        [%- ELSE -%] [%- skill -%],
        [%- END -%]
    [%- END -%]
[% END %]
```

> **NOTE** *If you don't like the* IN *in the* FOREACH x IN Y *syntax, replace it with =:*
>
> ```
> [% FOREACH item = items %]
>     You have [% item %]
> [% END %]
> ```

If you start the template tag with a pre-chomp tag, `[%-`, you can remove whitespace and newlines before the output. Naturally, a `-%]` removes whitespace and newlines after the output. By understanding where to use these pre- and post-chomp tags, you can make your template output match what you're looking for but still have properly indented template commands to make things much easier to read.

Template Toolkit also supports filtering the data, such as converting characters that have special meaning in HTML:

```
[% name | html %]
```

In the preceding example, you pass a name value to a template, but if you render as HTML you'll be disappointed if someone has supplied a name of `My</html>name` and breaks your web page. The `| html` filter after the name would convert that to `My&lt;/html&gt;name`.

Template Toolkit also allows including headers and footers, sharing common sections between different templates and many other features, but this isn't covered in this introduction.

TRY IT OUT   **Letters in French and English**

The life of a loan shark is a hard one. By definition your customers are not the type of people who find it easy to pay their debts. What's worse, some of your customers speak English and some of them speak French. From time to time, you need to send them a friendly reminder that they owe you money. You can find all the code in this Try It Out in the code files `listing_19_2_letter.pl`, `templates/en/letter.tt2`, and `templates/fr/letter.tt2`.

1.   Type in the following program, and save it as `listing_19_2_letter.pl`:

```perl
use strict;
use warnings;
use Getopt::Long;
use Template;
use DateTime;
use File::Spec::Functions 'catfile';

my ( $name, $amount, $lang );

my %body_parts = (
    en => [qw/arms legs/],
    fr => [qw/bras jambes/],
);
my %supported_lang = map { $_ => 1 } keys %body_parts;

my $template = Template->new(
    INCLUDE_PATH => 'templates',
);

GetOptions(
    'name=s'   => \$name,
    'amount=f' => \$amount,
    'lang=s'   => \$lang,
```

```
    ) or die "Bad options";

$lang ||= 'en';

unless ( $name and $amount ) {
    die "You must provide both name and amount";
}

if ( not exists $supported_lang{$lang} ) {
    die "'$lang' is not a supported lang";
}

my $now             = DateTime->now( locale => $lang );
my @things_to_break = @{ $body_parts{$lang} };
my %template_data   = (
    month     => ucfirst( $now->month_name ),
    day       => $now->day,
    year      => $now->year,
    name      => $name,
    body_part => $things_to_break[rand scalar @things_to_break],
    amount    => $amount,
);

my $file = catfile( $lang, 'letter.tt2' );
$template->process(
    $file,
    \%template_data,
    undef,
    binmode => ':encoding(UTF8)'
) or die $template->error;
```

2. Make a `templates/en` directory and a `templates/fr` directory. In `templates/en`, save the following as `letter.tt2`:

```
[% month %] [% day %], [% year %]

Dear [% name %],

Our records show that you owe us $[% amount %]. If you do not pay
immediately, we will be forced to break your [% body_part %].

Have a nice day :)
Me
```

In the `templates/fr` directory, save the following as `letter.tt2`. (Note that the final filename is identical!) Don't stress too much if you can't figure out how to type the accented characters. Loan sharks aren't always the sharpest.

```
[% month %] [% day %], [% year %]

Cher [% name %],

Nos dossiers indiquent que tu nous dois $[% amount %]. Si tu ne
```

```
payes pas immédiatement, nous seront obligés de te casser les
[% body_part %].

Bonne journée :)
Moi
```

3. Run the program with the following output:

```
perl listing_19_2_letter.pl --lang en --amount 1000.15 --name Bob
```

You should see output similar to the following:

```
June 9, 2012

Dear Bob,

Our records show that you owe us $1000.15. If you do not pay
immediately, we will be forced to break your arms.

Have a nice day :)
Me
```

Run the program again, but change the `--lang` parameter to `fr` (Use the short option form, `-l fr`, to remind you that you can do this):

```
perl listing_19_2_letter.pl -l fr -a 1000.15 -n Robert
```

You should see output similar to this:

```
Juin 9, 2012

Cher Robert,

Nos dossiers indiquent que tu nous dois $1000.15. Si tu ne
payes pas immédiatement, nous seront obligés de te casser les
jambes.

Bonne journée :)
Moi
```

How It Works

Lines 1 through 6 use the various modules you need to make this program work:

```
1:  use strict;
2:  use warnings;
3:  use Getopt::Long;
4:  use Template;
5:  use DateTime;
6:  use File::Spec::Functions 'catfile';
```

Lines 8 through 18 declare and sometimes initialize the variables you need. You can see that line 14 uses the keys from the `%body_parts` hash to avoid duplicating data.

```
 8:  my ( $name, $amount, $lang );
 9:
10:  my %body_parts = (
11:      en => [qw/arms legs/],
12:      fr => [qw/bras jambes/],
13:  );
14:  my %supported_lang = map { $_ => 1 } keys %body_parts;
15:
16:  my $template = Template->new(
17:      INCLUDE_PATH => 'templates',
18:  );
```

Lines 20 through 34 get your command line options and validate them. You die if a required command line option is missing and $lang defaults to en (English) if not supplied.

```
20:  GetOptions(
21:      'name=s'   => \$name,
22:      'amount=f' => \$amount,
23:      'lang=s'   => \$lang,
24:  ) or die "Bad options";
25:
26:  $lang ||= 'en';
27:
28:  unless ( $name and $amount ) {
29:      die "You must provide both name and amount";
30:  }
31:
32:  if ( not exists $supported_lang{$lang} ) {
33:      die "'$lang' is not a supported lang";
34:  }
```

Line 34 creates your DateTime object and sets its locale to $lang. This allows you to fetch the correct month name for your requested language.

```
36:  my $now                = DateTime->now( locale => $lang );
```

Lines 37 through 45 set up the actual template data.

```
37:  my @things_to_break = @{ $body_parts{$lang} };
38:  my %template_data   = (
39:      month     => ucfirst( $now->month_name ),
40:      day       => $now->day,
41:      year      => $now->year,
42:      name      => $name,
43:      body_part =>$things_to_break[rand scalar @things_to_break],
44:      amount    => $amount,
45:  );
```

This bit is a handy trick for randomly selecting one element of an array:

```
$things_to_break[ rand scalar @things_to_break ],
```

Line 47 builds the path to the file in a way that works regardless of which operating system you are on:

```
47:   my $file = catfile( $lang, 'letter.tt2' );
```

And finally you process your template:

```
48:   $template->process(
49:       $file,
50:       \%template_data,
51:       undef,
52:       binmode => ':encoding(UTF8)'
53:   ) or die $template->error;
```

The `undef` as the third parameter tells Template Toolkit to print the results to STDOUT. The optional fourth argument:

```
binmode => ':encoding(UTF8)'
```

Tells Template Toolkit that you want your output filehandle to be encoded as UTF-8. This will be useful if you find that you have Russian or Chinese customers and need to send them friendly reminder letters, too. Customer service is important!

You've noticed that the French and English version of the templates had the same first line:

```
[% month %] [% day %], [% year %]
```

You could extract this into a `header.tt2` file and replace the opening of the letters with:

```
[% INCLUDE header.tt2 %]
```

This can allow you to reuse this data in several files and easily change it in all files at once, if wanted. See the `INCLUDE_PATH` argument to the `Template` constructor to understand this better.

USING CATALYST TO BUILD APPS

Much of this book focuses on teaching you Perl with an emphasis on techniques you need for building web-based applications. The web and web-based applications are one of the driving forces behind many enterprises today, and this is not going to change any time soon. Thus, it's time to finish the book by taking a look at the most popular web framework for Perl.

> **NOTE** *Many other web frameworks for Perl are worth your time to investigate. Your author is rather fond of* `Dancer`, *but* `Mojolicious` *is becoming popular, and* `CGI::Application` *has been around for years. Of course, others are around and still more will appear. Just because* `Catalyst` *is demonstrated doesn't mean you shouldn't consider others. Remember: Different applications have different needs, so investigate your choice of web framework appropriately.*

Catalyst describes itself like this (http://www.catalystframework.org/):

> Catalyst is an open-source Perl MVC web framework that encourages
> rapid development and clean design without getting in your way by
> forcing rules.

What this means is that out-of-the-box, Catalyst provides most of what you need to write web applications, but you can change just about any component to suit your needs.

The Beauty of MVC

Chapter 15 briefly touched on the Model-View-Controller (MVC) pattern. Although originally not created for web applications, this method to organize your code is a useful way to organize a web application to make it easy to maintain and extend.

In MVC for the web, the users (typically people surfing the web), generally see web pages. This is the view. When they click a link or submit a form on your site, the information from the view is sent to a controller that controls what to do with that data.

> **NOTE** *Views do not have to be web pages. They can be RSS feeds, e-mail, JSON, YAML, or any other form of output. A view can also be used to represent the same data in multiple ways. You might request some data in JSON format, whereas another application might request the same data as a spreadsheet. For a web view it may be for a standard browser or a mobile phone. It's common to have the same controller and model be invoked for each of these, but instead have the data sent to different views. This makes for great code reuse.*

The controller generally consults the model (the part of the application that manages the data and business rules) and returns the model's answers to a new view, which is then rendered for the consumer.

To a certain extent, this design pattern should have been named View-Controller-Model because that's the path of behavior from the user's standpoint. (Or perhaps, VCMCV, but that's starting to get cumbersome.)

Catalyst does not require you to follow the MVC pattern, but it defaults to this pattern and it's strongly encouraged.

Setting Up a Catalyst Application

To get up and running with Catalyst, you need to install Catalyst from the CPAN. You should install Task::Catalyst. This contains most of the major modules needed to build your Catalyst applications. It also contains all the new modules you need for this section. If you already have Catalyst installed, you need at least Catalyst version 5.8 for this section because this is the version of Catalyst that was first ported to Moose. Use at least version 5.90012 because this is the version used for these examples.

Autogenerating the Shell of a Catalyst Application

In this section, you start by making a small web application to view the rights data tracked in Chapter 16 (and mentioned previously in the current chapter). In your `chapter19` directory, type the following:

```
catalyst.pl Rights
```

You can see a lot of output about various things being created, including a `Rights/` directory. Now change into that directory to start your new Rights application.

> **NOTE** *All the code for the Rights application is downloadable from* `http://www` `.wrox.com/`. *The usual download message isn't included here because much of this code is autogenerated by* `Catalyst`. *Rest assured the download area will have a* `chapter19/Rights` *directory available for you.*

```
$ perl script/rights_server.pl
[debug] Debug messages enabled
[debug] Statistics enabled
[debug] Loaded plugins:
.------------------------------------------------------------------.
| Catalyst::Plugin::ConfigLoader  0.30                             |
'------------------------------------------------------------------'
[debug] Loaded dispatcher "Catalyst::Dispatcher"
[debug] Loaded engine "Catalyst::Engine"
[debug] Found home "./Rights"
[debug] Loaded Config "./Rights/rights.conf"
[debug] Loaded components:
.-----------------------------------------------------+----------.
| Class                                               | Type     |
+-----------------------------------------------------+----------+
| Rights::Controller::Root                            | instance |
'-----------------------------------------------------+----------'
[debug] Loaded Private actions:
.----------------------+--------------------------+--------------.
| Private              | Class                    | Method       |
+----------------------+--------------------------+--------------+
| /default             | Rights::Controller::Root | default      |
| /end                 | Rights::Controller::Root | end          |
| /index               | Rights::Controller::Root | index        |
'----------------------+--------------------------+--------------'
[debug] Loaded Path actions:
.--------------------------------+---------------------------------.
| Path                           | Private                         |
+--------------------------------+---------------------------------+
| /                              | /index                          |
| /...                           | /default                        |
'--------------------------------+---------------------------------'
[info] Rights powered by Catalyst 5.90012
HTTP::Server::PSGI: Accepting connections at http://localhost:3000/
```

Immediately you can see plenty of useful information about the state of your application and also that it's accepting connections on `http://localhost:3000/`. Go to your favorite web browser and visit that URL. You should see something similar to Figure 19-1.

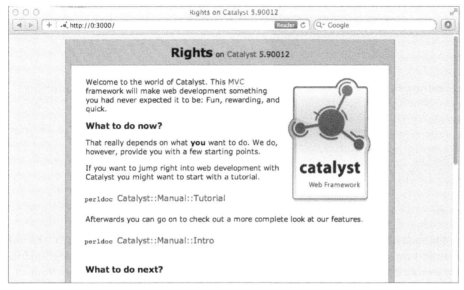

FIGURE 19-1

The default welcome screen in `Catalyst` points to a tutorial, then the manual, and then gives you information on what to do next to build your application. Meanwhile, something similar to the following is printed in your terminal window:

```
[info] *** Request 1 (0.004/s) [46773] [Sun Jun 10 11:08:30 2012] ***
[debug] Path is "/"
[debug] "GET" request for "/" from "127.0.0.1"
[debug] Response Code: 200; Content-Type: text/html; charset=utf-8;
  Content-Length: 5469
[info] Request took 0.002885s (346.620/s)
.------------------------------------------------------------+----------.
| Action                                                     | Time     |
+------------------------------------------------------------+----------+
| /index                                                     | 0.000197s |
| /end                                                       | 0.000189s |
'------------------------------------------------------------+----------'
```

You can see information presented for most requests to help you debug your application. It won't make much sense now, but in reading through it carefully and learning more about `Catalyst`, it's an invaluable resource.

So how does this work? The `scripts/rights_server.pl` program looks like this:

```
BEGIN {
    $ENV{CATALYST_SCRIPT_GEN} = 40;
}

use Catalyst::ScriptRunner;
Catalyst::ScriptRunner->run('Rights', 'Server');


1;
```

Now look at the outline of your code by running your `tree.pl` program on the `lib/` directory:

```
$ tree.pl lib
lib/
|   Rights/
|   |   Controller/
|   |   |-- Root.pm
|   |   Model/
|   |   View/
|-- Rights.pm
```

As you can see, the shell of an MVC application has already been built for you. Currently, the only code is `Rights` and `Rights::Controller::Root`. The `scripts/rights_server.pl` program loads your `Rights.pm` module (which in turn can load everything else for you) and runs it in a built-in web server.

The `Rights.pm` package sets up everything you need to run your application. It looks like this; the actual class has a bunch of POD documentation:

```
package Rights;
use Moose;
use namespace::autoclean;

use Catalyst::Runtime 5.80;
use Catalyst qw/
    -Debug
    ConfigLoader
    Static::Simple
/;
extends 'Catalyst';

our $VERSION = '0.01';

__PACKAGE__->config(
    name => 'Rights',
    # Disable deprecated behavior needed by old applications
    disable_component_resolution_regex_fallback => 1,
    enable_catalyst_header => 1, # Send X-Catalyst header
);

__PACKAGE__->setup();

1;
```

When you use `Catalyst`:

```
use Catalyst qw/
    -Debug
    ConfigLoader
    Static::Simple
/;
```

By default you include the `-Debug` flag (which you should disable for production because there's no need to spam your logs with debugging information) that prints the useful information to the console while running your application. The `ConfigLoader` and `Static::Simple` lines are plug-ins that are used to load a config file (using `Config::General` format) and `Static::Simple` is a plug-in that enables you to serve static files, such as images, CSS, and the like.

Next, you inherit from `Catalyst` (remember that `Moose` uses `extends` to set up inheritance) and configure your application:

```
extends 'Catalyst';

our $VERSION = '0.01';

__PACKAGE__->config(
    name => 'Rights',
    # Disable deprecated behavior needed by old applications
    disable_component_resolution_regex_fallback => 1,
    enable_catalyst_header => 1, # Send X-Catalyst header
);
```

Finally, the `setup()` method loads the other modules and starts the `Rights` application:

```
__PACKAGE__->setup();
```

Next, you have `Rights::Controller::Root`:

```
package Rights::Controller::Root;
use Moose;
use namespace::autoclean;

BEGIN { extends 'Catalyst::Controller' }

__PACKAGE__->config(namespace => '');

sub index :Path :Args(0) {
    my ( $self, $c ) = @_;
    # Hello World
    $c->response->body( $c->welcome_message );
}

sub default :Path {
    my ( $self, $c ) = @_;
    $c->response->body( 'Page not found' );
    $c->response->status(404);
}
```

```
sub end : ActionClass('RenderView') {}

__PACKAGE__->meta->make_immutable;

1;
```

The important parts of `Rights::Controller::Root` are explained next.

➤ The index page (the one you saw in Figure 19-1), is created with the `index` method:

```
sub index :Path :Args(0) {
    my ( $self, $c ) = @_;
    # Hello World
    $c->response->body( $c->welcome_message );
}
```

> **NOTE** The `:Path` `:Args(0)` are called subroutine attributes, which aren't cov-
> ered in this book, but you can read a bit more about them in the `Subroutine`
> `Attributes` section of `perldoc perlsub`. Attributes are a way to provide a bit
> of extra information about a subroutine or method (and other things not covered
> in this book).

➤ In `Catalyst`, URLs are mapped to controllers. For your application, actions (methods) in the `Rights::Controller::Root` namespace are relative to `/`; the `index` method is called when you visit `http://localhost:3000/`. If you change `:Path` to `:Path('hello')`, your `index` method is called when you visit `http://localhost:3000/hello`. This is useful when you don't want your URL names to map directly to your method names.

➤ The `:Args(0)` attribute means that no other path segments are passed to this method. If you had `:Path('hello')` `:Args(1)`, if you visited `http://localhost:3000/hello/2`, then `2` would be the argument passed to the `index` method.

➤ The `$self` argument is the `Catalyst` application instance, but it's `$c` that you're interested in. It's the *context object* for the application. The context object is an instance representing the context in which the current method was called. You'll see more of this later, too.

In this case, this:

```
$c->response->body( $c->welcome_message );
```

Sets the body of the response to the `$c->welcome_message` output. That's the HTML page you saw in Figure 19-1.

Writing Your Catalyst Application

You've seen the shell of your `Rights` application and now it's time to start customizing it to fit your needs.

1. Kill your web server with CTRL-C. (Control-C).

2. Restart it with:

```
perl scripts/rights_server.pl -r
```

The -r switch tells Catalyst to restart the application whenever you change your source code. This makes testing an application while writing it easy.

3. Change your index method to this:

```
sub index :Path  :Args(1) {
    my ( $self, $c, $name ) = @_;
    # Hello World
    $c->response->body( "Hello, $name" );
}
```

If you visit http://localhost:3000/Ovid, the web page says Hello, Ovid. Of course, you want to use HTML::Entities to escape entities put into this output. A clever hacker could use this to inject arbitrary HTML or JavaScript directly into your web page, so don't do that.

In Catalyst, the default() method can be used as a catch-all for other paths that don't match. So if you visit http://localhost:3000/asdf, you receive a 404 NOT FOUND because the default handler matches it:

```
sub default :Path {
    my ( $self, $c ) = @_;
    $c->response->body( 'Page not found' );
    $c->response->status(404);
}
```

The end method is interesting:

```
sub end : ActionClass('RenderView') {}
```

The end of a request usually involves rendering a request, and the :ActionClass action can handle this automatically. Otherwise, you might want something like this:

```
sub end : Private {
    my ( $self, $c ) = @_;
    $c->forward( $c->view('TT') );
}
```

That would forward your action to a TT (Template Toolkit) view and render it for you. However, you don't have a view set up yet, so now do that.

Using Catalyst Views

To use views in Catalyst, you have a useful helper script named rights_create.pl. Create a view using Template Toolkit:

```
$ perl script/rights_create.pl view TT TT
exists "./Rights/script/../lib/Rights/View"
```

```
exists "./Rights/script/../t"
created "./Rights/script/../lib/Rights/View/TT.pm"
created "./Rights/script/../t/view_TT.t"
```

> **NOTE** The output for `Catalyst` commands generally has path information
> like `./Rights/`. However, `Catalyst` actually prints the absolute path. On your
> author's computer, the path actually looks like:
>
> `/Users/ovid/beginning_perl/book/chapter19/Rights/`
>
> The path is deliberately shortened in the examples to make them easier to read
> and fit the format of the book.

When you run `scripts/rights_create.pl`, the first argument is what you're creating. This is usually one of `model`, `view`, or `controller`. For a view, the first `TT` argument is the name you are giving the view. The second argument is the view subclass you're going to use. Because you subclass `Catalyst::View::TT`, the standard `Catalyst` view for Template Toolkit, you must use `TT` for the third argument. If you want your view to be named `Rights::View::Template` and subclass from `Catalyst::View::TT`, you would use this command:

```
perl script/rights_create.pl view Template TT
```

By running this command, you get a module named `Rights::View::TT` and a test named `t/view_TT.t`. (Using the default scripts to create modules, views, and controllers generates default test scripts for them.)

The `Rights::View::TT` module looks like this:

```
package Rights::View::TT;
use Moose;
use namespace::autoclean;

extends 'Catalyst::View::TT';

__PACKAGE__->config(
    TEMPLATE_EXTENSION => '.tt',
    render_die => 1, # die if we encounter rendering errors
);

1;
```

That's all you need to do to make sure you can correctly render Template Toolkit views.

Calling the View from a Controller

In your `Rights::Controller::Root` module, add the following method:

```
sub hello : Path('hello') : Args(1) {
    my ( $self, $c, $my_name ) = @_;
```

```
        $c->stash->{template} = 'hello.tt';
        $c->stash->{my_name}  = $my_name;
}
```

And in the `root/` directory (which should already be created for you), save the following as `hello.tt`:

```
<p>Hello, [% my_name | html %]!</p>
```

Because the path is `hello` and it's relative to the root directory and because it takes one argument, you can visit `http://localhost:3000/hello/World` and the web page would contain the HTML `<p>Hello, World!</p>`. The `| html` filter after the `my_name` variable tells Template Toolkit to encode HTML entities. This is generally a recommended practice to make it harder for someone to send naughty code to your output.

Use the `$c->stash` hash reference to pass data to your templates. The template key is the name of the template you want to render. The `my_name` key, in the example, is a variable you're passing to Template Toolkit and is rendered by `[% my_name %]`.

The method `hello()` is for `Catalyst` to know which method to call, but the `:Path`, although often the same as the method name, is not required to be the same. If you had `:Path('bonjour')` `:Args(1)` for the `hello()` method, you could have visited `http://localhost:3000/bonjour/Monde` and the resulting HTML in your browser would have been `<p>Hello, Monde!</p>`.

> **NOTE** *When building larger applications, it can be difficult to remember what all your paths are. When running* `Catalyst` *under* `-Debug` *mode, you can read the* `Loaded Path Actions` *output to understand what paths are available:*
>
> ```
> [debug] Loaded Path actions:
> .---------------------------------+----------------------------------.
> | Path                            | Private                          |
> +---------------------------------+----------------------------------+
> | /                               | /index                           |
> | /...                            | /default                         |
> | /hello/*                        | /hello                           |
> '---------------------------------+----------------------------------'
> ```
>
> *That output tells you that you can visit* / *and* /hello/$something. *Everything else (*/ . . .*) will be handled by the* default() *method.*

Using Catalyst Models

As explained, a model contains your data and all the business rules for that data. You can quickly create a model for `Catalyst` using the rights database you created in Chapter 16 and reused in the first Try It Out section in this chapter. If you run the scripts to create and populate the database, you should have an SQLite database named `rights.db`. As of this writing, to create the model you need to install `DBIx::Class::Schema::Loader`, `MooseX::NonMoose`, and `MooseX::MarkAsMethods`. Then, run the following, broken up over two lines, but you can run it on one line by omitting the \:

```
perl script/rights_create.pl model Media DBIC::Schema Rights::Schema \
  create=static 'dbi:SQLite:./rights.db'
```

In this example:

➤ The first argument to `rights_create.pl` says you're going to create a model.

➤ The second argument, `Media`, names the model (`Rights::Model::Media`).

➤ The `DBIC::Schema` argument is used to inherit from the `Catalyst::Model::DBIC::Schema` class (you should notice the pattern by now).

➤ The fourth argument specifies the top-level namespace (usually the name of your app, hence `Rights`).

➤ You specify `create=static` to tell `Catalyst::Model::DBIC::Schema` that you're going to read the database to create the schema classes for the model.

➤ Finally, you have the data source name (DSN), just like you'd pass as the first argument to `DBI->connect()`.

If this were a database like MySQL or PostgreSQL that required a username and password, you'd provide those after the DSN.

Now if you run `tree.pl` on your `lib` directory, you should see the following:

```
$ tree.pl lib/
lib/
|   Rights/
|   |   Controller/
|   |   |-- Root.pm
|   |   Model/
|   |   |-- Media.pm
|   |   Schema/
|   |   |   Result/
|   |   |   |-- License.pm
|   |   |   |-- Media.pm
|   |   |   |-- MediaType.pm
|   |-- Schema.pm
|   |   View/
|   |   |-- TT.pm
|-- Rights.pm
```

In your `Rights::Model::Media` file, you have the following:

```
package Rights::Model::Media;
use strict;

use base 'Catalyst::Model::DBIC::Schema';

__PACKAGE__->config(
```

```
        schema_class => 'Rights::Schema',
        connect_info => {
            dsn => 'dbi:SQLite:./rights.db',
            user => '',
            password => '',
        }
    );

    1;
```

And this gives you everything you need to connect to your model. You'll use this, but in the real world, you'd probably want your dsn, user, and password data to be supplied by a config file. This would enable you, for example, to connect to different databases when testing in development and in production.

Creating Schema Classes for the Model

You don't need to see all the result classes because you already have a good idea of what they look like from earlier in this chapter, but here's the Rights::Result::MediaType module:

```
use utf8;
package Rights::Schema::Result::MediaType;

use strict;
use warnings;
use Moose;
use MooseX::NonMoose;
use MooseX::MarkAsMethods autoclean => 1;

extends 'DBIx::Class::Core';

__PACKAGE__->load_components("InflateColumn::DateTime");
__PACKAGE__->table("media_types");
__PACKAGE__->add_columns(
  "id",
  { data_type => "integer",is_auto_increment => 1,is_nullable => 0 },
  "media_type",
  { data_type => "varchar",is_nullable => 0,size => 10 },
);
__PACKAGE__->set_primary_key("id");

__PACKAGE__->has_many(
  "medias",
  "Rights::Schema::Result::Media",
  { "foreign.media_type_id" => "self.id" },
  { cascade_copy => 0, cascade_delete => 0 },
);

__PACKAGE__->meta->make_immutable;

1;
```

Without going over everything this means, suffice it to say that this contains everything you need to access this data via DBIx::Class.

In your `Rights::Controller::Root` class, add the following method:

```
sub media : Path('all_media') : Args(0) {
    my ( $self, $c ) = @_;

    my $media_rs = $c->model('Media::Media')->search(
        {},      # we want all of them
        { order_by => { -desc => 'name' } },
    );

    $c->stash->{template} = 'all_media.tt';
    $c->stash->{media_rs} = $media_rs;
}
```

> **NOTE** *The model is named* `Media` *and you can fetch it via* `$c->model('Media')`. *However, the resultset you're fetching is also named* `Media`. *If you want to fetch all license types, do this:*
>
> ```
> my $licenses = $c->model('Media::LicenseType');
> ```
>
> *Don't be confused by having a model with the same name as one of the result-sets you are fetching.*

And in the root directory, add the following template as `all_media.tt`:

```
<table rules="all">
[% WHILE ( media = media_rs.next ) %]
  <tr>
    <td>[% media.name         |html %]</td>
    <td>[% media.license.name |html %]</td>
  </tr>
[% END %]
</table>
```

Now when you visit your browser and enter `http://localhost:3000/all_media`, you see a table of your media records and the names of their licenses.

This shows a couple of features of Template Toolkit that you haven't seen yet. In Template Toolkit, the condition for a WHILE loop often needs to be wrapped in parentheses to ensure that it parses correctly. You also show that you can call methods on your template objects. (Template Toolkit checks if it's a method and, if not, checks if the variable is a hash reference and then tries to find a key matching the same name.)

Using Catalyst Controllers

You could keep putting new actions in `Rights::Controller::Root`, but that would be hard to maintain. Instead, the following steps show you how to create a new controller, specifically for media.

```
perl script/rights_create.pl controller Media
```

1. The new `Rights::Controller::Media` module is basic:

```perl
package Rights::Controller::Media;
use Moose;
use namespace::autoclean;

BEGIN { extends 'Catalyst::Controller'; }

sub index :Path :Args(0) {
    my ( $self, $c ) = @_;
    $c->response->body('Matched Rights::Controller::Media in Media.');
}

__PACKAGE__->meta->make_immutable;

1;
```

2. Delete the `media()` method from `Rights::Controller::Root` and make that the `index()` method in `Rights::Model::Media`:

```perl
sub index :Path :Args(0) {
    my ( $self, $c ) = @_;

    my $media_rs = $c->model('Video::Media')->search(
        {},     # we want all of them
        { order_by => { -desc => 'name' } },
    );
    $c->stash->{template} = 'media/all.tt';
    $c->stash->{media_rs}  = $media_rs;
}
```

3. You now need to rename the template from `all_media.tt` to `media/all.tt`, so create the `root/media` directory and move `root/all_media.tt` to `root/media/all.tt`. Now you can see your table of all media when you visit `http://localhost:3000/media`. Awesome! You're starting to get some intelligent structure in your application.

4. What about seeing more intelligent information? You want to see a full record, so change `root/media/all.tt` to be the following:

```html
<table rules="all">
[% WHILE ( media = media_rs.next ) %]
  <tr>
    <td><a href="/media/[%media.id%]">[%media.name|html%]</a></td>
    <td>[% media.license.name |html %]</td>
  </tr>
[% END %]
</table>
```

5. You now have hyperlinks to URLs like `/media/1`, `/media/2`, and so on. They currently go to a 404, so add the appropriate action in `Rights::Controller::Media`.

```
sub media : Path : Args(1) {
    my ( $self, $c, $id ) = @_;

    my $media_rs = $c->model('Media::Media')->search(
    $c->stash->{template} = 'media/display.tt';
    $c->stash->{media}    = $media;
}
```

6. By naming this media and specifying 1 argument with `:Args(1)`, you can navigate to `http://localhost:3000/media/1` and try to fetch the media matching ID of 1. Now create `root/media/display.tt`:

```
[% IF media %]
<table>
  <tr>
    <td>Name:</td>
    <td>[% media.name |html %]</a></td>
  </tr>
  <tr>
    <td>Location:</td>
    <td>[% media.location |html %]</a></td>
  </tr>
  <tr>
    <td>Name:</td>
    <td>[% media.source |html %]</a></td>
  </tr>
  <tr>
    <td>License:</td>
    <td>[% media.license.name |html %]</a></td>
  </tr>
</table>
[% ELSE %]
<strong>Media not found</strong>
[% END %]
```

In this example, if you didn't have a matching ID, you'd see `Media not found`. If you do have a matching ID, you see a table similar to:

```
Name:      Anne Frank Stamp
Location:  /data/anne_frank_stamp.jpg
Name:      http://commons.wikimedia.org/wiki/File:Anne_Frank_stamp.jpg
License:   Public Domain
```

Also, in Step 5 above, the code `$c->model('Media::Media')` returns the resultset class. The argument is the model name, `Media`, followed by two colons and then the schema name, also `Media`. For the `Video` schema, you'd have `$c->model('Media::Video')`.

CRUD: Create, Read, Update, and Delete

Viewing your records is great, but as time goes on, you probably get tired of using SQL to directly create, read, update, and delete database records. That's when you want a *CRUD* (Create, Read, Update, and Delete) web interface. When done properly, a CRUD interface makes it easy to manage your data via the web. The author could show you how to do all this directly, but you can cheat because this is only an introduction to Catalyst.

Follow these steps to create an easy-to-use web interface for managing your database data.

1. Enter Catalyst::Plugin::AutoCRUD. This useful module, by Oliver Gorwits, automatically creates a CRUD interface for you. It's configurable, but here's only the basic usage. It assumes that your database has a DBIx::Class schema or such a schema can be loaded with DBIx::Class::Schema::Loader. (This increases your startup time, however.)

2. In your Rights.pm module, change the use Catalyst import list to have AutoCRUD at the end:

```
use Catalyst qw/
    -Debug
    ConfigLoader
    Static::Simple
    AutoCRUD
/;
```

3. Add a display_name() method to each of your Rights::Schema::Result::Media, Rights::Schema::Result::MediaType, and Rights::Schema::Result::License classes. For each of these classes you can notice text near the bottom resembling the following:

```
Created by DBIx::Class::Schema::Loader v0.07024 @ 2012-06-10 17:22:36
# DO NOT MODIFY THIS OR ANYTHING ABOVE! md5sum:OwY2SAMQanKKPXMMfMMpNg
```

> **NOTE** *The reason* DBIx::Class::Schema::Loader *adds this is because you often want to create a* DBIx::Class *schema for your code, but then you want to extend it with extra methods. However, if you add or remove tables, or change existing ones, you might want to run* DBIx::Class::Schema::Loader *again, but you don't want to destroy the extra methods you've added. If you add your methods below the* DO NOT MODIFY THIS OR ANYTHING ABOVE *line, when you run* DBIx::Class::Schema::Loader *again, it changes only the schema code above that line and your added code remains intact.*
>
> *So for your* display_name *methods, add them after the* DO NOT *line.*

4. For Rights::Schema::Result::Media, add this:

```
sub display_name {
    my $self = shift;
    return $self->name;
}
```

5. For `Rights::Schema::Result::License`, add this:

```
sub display_name {
    my $self = shift;
    return $self->name;
}
```

6. For `Rights::Schema::Result::MediaType`, add this:

```
sub display_name {
    my $self = shift;
    return $self->media_type;
}
```

> **NOTE** The `display_name()` methods will be used by `Catalyst::Plugin::AutoCRUD` when it creates drop-down (`<select/>`) menus for tables that link to one another.

7. Restart your `Catalyst` server (or let it restart automatically if you started it with the `-r` switch) and navigate to `http:://localhost:3000/autocrud`. You should see a page similar to Figure 19-2.

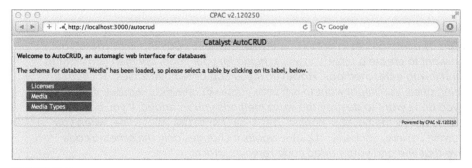

FIGURE 19-2

You should see links for each of the three tables, Licenses, Media, and Media Types. Click the `License` link, and you should be taken to `http://localhost:3000/autocrud/media/licenses` where you'll see a page similar to Figure 19-3. From here you can add new licenses, delete them, modify the data, or filter them by value. (This is useful when you search through a lot of data.)

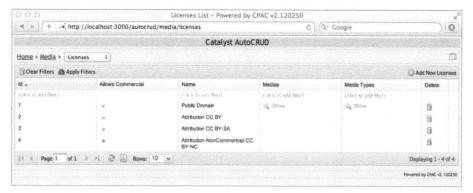

FIGURE 19-3

> **WARNING** `Catalyst::Plugin::AutoCRUD` *is powerful, but it's easy to misconfigure a server and possibly expose to the outside world an interface to destroy your data! Your author recommends (and the author of* `Catalyst::Plugin::AutoCRUD` *has stated his agreement) that if you use this module, that you consider doing so on a separate web server (or a separate application within a web server) with much tighter security than your normal application interface. This isn't strictly necessary, but it makes it much easier to ensure that an accidental server misconfiguration doesn't expose this interface to the outside world.*

`Catalyst::Plugin::AutoCRUD` does have a few limitations as described in the documentation. However, it's harder to imagine a faster and easier editing tool for your web-facing database than this one.

SUMMARY

To give you an idea of where to go from here, this chapter explained what the entire book covers and, more important, some of the things it doesn't cover. Then you got a taste of a few advanced concepts for Perl that, after you learn them, can give you a good start on a solid programming career.

The `DBIx::Class` object-relational mapper, along with some of the strengths and weaknesses of ORMs was covered. You saw how to use `DBIx::Class::Schema::Loader` to make generating your classes easy. See also the `DBIx::Class` tutorial at `http://search.cpan.org/dist/DBIx-Class-Tutorial/`.

A bit of the (very) basic usage of Template Toolkit was also explained and you saw how to separate the data you gather from its presentation. Be sure to read the Template Toolkit tutorial at `http://template-toolkit.org/docs/tutorial/`.

Finally, you took a nice tour of `Catalyst`, the most popular web framework for Perl. The Model-View-Controller pattern was explained and you saw examples of implementing each component in `Catalyst`. The section finished by showing you a quick method for generating an interface for managing your database data via the web. Read the `Catalyst Manual` (http://search.cpan.org/dist/Catalyst-Manual/) for more information.

By now you should have a solid grasp of Perl and be ready to go out there and get a great job!

EXERCISES

1. Briefly describe an object-relational mapper and why you might want to use one.

2. Using Google Translate (http://translate.google.com/) or your own knowledge of a foreign language, modify `listing_19_2_letter.pl` to include a new language. You might want to check `DateTime::Locale` to see if it supports the language you want to translate to.

3. This exercise requires a moderate amount of work. You can think of it as the "final exam" for this book. You can probably do everything in this exercise merely by having followed this book, but there are a couple of places where reading the documentation may be helpful. This exercise brings together your knowledge of Perl, `Catalyst`, `DBIx::Class`, Templates, HTML, and SQL. Despite that, it's actually a straightforward task. Be sure to read your resulting `Rights::Schema::Result::` classes to know what methods are available.

You now have a small website for managing rights data, but maybe you want to do something with it? Like fighting DMCA notices when someone tries to take your videos off Vimeo or YouTube? For this final exercise of the book, you need to add the following table to your rights database:

```
CREATE TABLE IF NOT EXISTS videos (
    id        INTEGER PRIMARY KEY,
    name      VARCHAR(255)  NOT NULL,
    url       VARCHAR(1000) NOT NULL,
    released  DATETIME            NULL
);
```

Because one video might have many media items and one media item might be in several videos, you need to create a `video_to_media` lookup table. It looks like this:

```
CREATE TABLE IF NOT EXISTS video_to_media (
    id        INTEGER PRIMARY KEY,
    video_id  INTEGER NOT NULL,
    media_id  INTEGER NOT NULL,
    FOREIGN KEY (video_id) REFERENCES videos(id)
    FOREIGN KEY (media_id) REFERENCES media(id)
);
```

Add a `Rights::Schema::Result::Video` class and a `Rights::Schema::Result::MediaToVideo` class to your `Rights Catalyst` application. You also need to update your

`Rights::Schema::Result::Media` class because each media can refer to the `video_to_media` table. Finally, create new controllers and templates to display all videos and individual videos.

As a tip to help you get around an issue with how Template Toolkit works, if you want to list all the media associated with a video, you might write the following code:

```
[% video_to_medias_rs = video.video_to_medias %]
  <td>Media</td>
[% IF video_to_medias_rs.count %]
  <td>
    <ul>
  [% WHILE ( v2m = video_to_medias_rs.next ) %]
      <li>
        <a href="/media/[%v2m.media.id%]">[%v2m.media.name%]</a>
      </li>
  [% END %]
    </ul>
  </td>
[% ELSE %]
  <td><strong>No media found</strong></td>
[% END %]
```

This looks perfectly reasonable, but no matter how many `video_to_medias` (the name is awkward, but that's how `DBIx::Class::Schema::Loader` creates it) results are found, you always get the `No media found` message displayed. This is because Template Toolkit always calls methods in list context, and for the `video_to_medias` resultset method, this returns a list of results to the `video_to_medias_rs` variable instead of a single resultset object. The `DBIx::Class::Manual::FAQ` explains the workaround. Every resultset method created for a result relationship can also be called by appending an `_rs` to the end of it. If you do that, it ignores context and always returns a single resultset. Thus, the first line of the preceding template code should be changed to:

```
[% video_to_medias_rs = video.video_to_medias_rs %]
```

By making this change, your template code can work correctly.

► **WHAT YOU LEARNED IN THIS CHAPTER**

TOPIC	DESCRIPTION
`ORM`	An object-relational mapper. An easy way to use database records as objects.
`DBIx::Class`	One of the most popular ORMs for Perl.
`DBIx::Class::Schema::Loader`	An easy way to create a `DBIx::Class` schema.
`Template Toolkit`	A powerful, complete templating system for Perl.
`Catalyst`	A web framework for Perl, designed to make building websites easy.
`MVC`	The Model, View, Controller pattern for organizing websites.
`Model`	Where your data and business rules are managed.
`View`	The external interface to your application. Often an HTML page.
`Controller`	The code that connects your model and view together.
`Catalyst::Plugin::AutoCRUD`	An easy way to create a web interface to your database.

APPENDIX

Answers to Exercises

CHAPTER 3 ANSWERS TO EXERCISES

Exercise 1 Solution

The major difference between strict and warnings is that strict prevents your program from running when it encounters some unsafe code, such as using an undeclared variable.

In contrast, warnings do not prevent your program from running but instead emit "warnings" when your code exhibits behavior that may be problematic, such as when you attempt to use an uninitialized variable or try to add a number to a string.

Exercise 2 Solution

The following is an example (code file exercise_3_2a_array.pl) to create an array with the values Andrew, Andy, and Kaufman and writing a program that prints Andrew "Andy" Kaufman:

```
use strict;
use warnings;
use diagnostics;

my @name = qw(Andrew Andy Kaufman);
print qq{$name[0] "$name[1]" $name[2]\n};
```

Another way to accomplish this is as follows (code file exercise_3_2b_array.pl):

```
use strict;
use warnings;
use diagnostics;

my @name = ('Andrew', 'Andy', 'Kaufman');
my ( $first, $nick, $last ) = @name;
print qq{$first "$nick" $last\n};
```

Exercise 3 Solution

The following code (code file `exercise_3_3_fruit.pl`) is an example of how to create a hash with the keys being names of fruits and the values being their normal color, and then printing every key/value pair as a separate line similar to `bananas are yellow`:

```
use strict;
use warnings;
use diagnostics;

my %color_for = (
    bananas => 'yellow',
    apples  => 'red',
    oranges => 'orange',
);
for my $fruit (keys %color_for) {
    my $color = $color_for{$fruit};
    print "$fruit are $color\n";
}
```

CHAPTER 4 ANSWERS TO EXERCISES

Exercise 1 Solution

`$second`, `$fourth`, and `$sixth` all evaluate to true. The `$fourth` variable is a bit of a trick. Even though it looks like `0.0` because it's a string, it evaluates as true because all nonempty strings evaluate as true. To make it evaluate as false, add zero to it:

```
0+$fourth;
```

That forces Perl to consider it a number.

Exercise 2 Solution

One way to create the `@celsius` array is as follows:

```
my @fahrenheit = ( 0, 32, 65, 80, 212 );
my @celsius    = map { ($_ - 32) * 5/9 } @fahrenheit;
```

Exercise 3 Solution

The `@upper` array can be created with:

```
my @ids   = qw(AAA bbb Ccc ddD EEE);
my @upper = grep { $_ eq uc($_) } @ids;
```

Exercise 4 Solution

$answer1 contains 28 because the multiplication operator has a higher precedence than addition.

$answer2 initially contains 6 because subtraction is left associative, but after the autoincrement in the third line, it contains 7.

$answer3 contains 4 because $answer2 will be subtracted from 10 before it is incremented. If the ++ autoincrement operator were before the $answer2 (10 - ++$answer2), it would have contained 3.

If the autoincrement operator confused you, that's okay. That's why your author often recommends that those lines be rewritten as follows:

```
my $answer2 = 9 - 2 - 1;
my $answer3 = 10 - $answer2;
$answer2++;
```

By having autoincrement and autodecrement operators in their own statements, the code is often easier to understand.

CHAPTER 5 ANSWERS TO EXERCISES

Exercise 1 Solution

The code prints 12345678910. If you want those numbers on separate lines, you can do this:

```
print "$_\n" for 1..10;
```

Exercise 2 Solution

Remember that the ternary operator requires both the "if true" and "if false" conditions, but you're missing that for the second ternary operator.

```
my $temperature = 22;
print $temperature < 15? "Too cold!\n"
    : $temperature > 35? "Too hot!\n"
    :                    "Just right!\n";
```

Exercise 3 Solution

As usual, there are many ways to do this. If you get the correct answer, your code still probably looks different from this answer. Here's one way.

```
my @numbers = qw< 3 9 0 7 8 >;

my $total = 0;
$total += $_ foreach @numbers;
```

```
my $average = $total / @numbers;

print "The numbers are: @numbers\n";
print "The average is $average\n";
```

Remember that an array in scalar context returns the number of elements in the array, so `$total / @numbers` evaluates to `27 / 5`.

Exercise 4 Solution

The logic error is in the loop terminating condition of `$i <= $num_elements`. This is called an *off by one* error because the final value of `$i` is one greater than the final index in `@array`. This is a common problem with C-style for loops. Changing the loop to `$i < $num_elements` fixes the problem.

The programmers see the error at run time by adding a use warnings statement at the beginning of their program. You get a warning similar to the following:

```
Use of uninitialized value within @array in concatenation (.) or string
```

However, the previous code is much simpler if you use a Perl-style `for`/`foreach` loop. (Remember that they're exactly the same thing,)

```
my @array = qw( fee fie foe fum );
for my $word (@array) {
    print "$word\n";
}
```

The Perl-style loop not only avoids off-by-one errors, but the code executes faster, too.

Exercise 5 Solution

For the `add your code here` bit, you might write something like the following:

```
foreach my $stat (keys %stat_for) {
    my $random = 2 + int(rand(6)) + int(rand(6));
    $stat_for{$stat} = $random;
}
```

Exercise 6 Solution

The full code is:

```
my %stat_for = (
    strength     => undef,
    intelligence => undef,
    dexterity    => undef,
);

foreach my $stat (keys %stat_for) {
```

```
    my $random = 2 + int(rand(6)) + int(rand(6));
    redo if $random < 6;
    $stat_for{$stat} = $random;
}

print <<"END_CHARACTER";
Strength:       $stat_for{strength}
Intelligence:   $stat_for{intelligence}
Dexterity:      $stat_for{dexterity}
END_CHARACTER
```

CHAPTER 6 ANSWERS TO EXERCISES

> **NOTE** *Many exercises have multiple possible answers. You see one way to arrive at a valid answer. Don't worry too much if you've picked a different way, but make sure you understand why the author's answers work.*

Exercise 1 Solution

```
    use strict;
    use warnings;
    use Data::Dumper;

    my @first   = 1 .. 5;
    my $aref    = \@first;
    my @second = @$aref;

    print Dumper( \@first, \@second );
```

In the preceding example, the .. operator binds more tightly than the = operator, allowing you to create an assign the list without using grouping parentheses. Alternatively, you could write (remember it's the comma which creates the list):

```
    my @first   = ( 1, 2, 3, 4, 5 );
```

Exercise 2 Solution

The following code is fairly typical for Perl. Don't worry if you wrote it a different way so long as you arrived at the same numbers. However, pay particular attention to how to calculate the sum of the sales. That technique is fairly common in Perl.

```
my $sales = {
    monday    => { jim => [ 2       ], mary => [ 1, 3, 7       ] },
    tuesday   => { jim => [ 3, 8    ], mary => [ 5, 5          ] },
    wednesday => { jim => [ 7, 0    ], mary => [ 3             ] },
    thursday  => { jim => [ 4       ], mary => [ 5, 7, 2, 5, 2 ] },
```

```
        friday   => { jim => [ 1, 1, 5 ], mary => [ 2           ] },
    };
    my $friday    = $sales->{friday}{jim};
    my $num_sales = @$friday;
    my $total     = 0;
    $total       += $_ foreach @$friday;
    print "Jim had $num_sales sales, for a total of $total dollars\n";
```

Exercise 3 Solution

This one may have been tricky. You may have noticed that the qw operator uses curly braces, which are the same braces used with hash keys. However, this is not a bug. Perl is smart enough to know what you mean here.

```
my $score_for = {
    jim   => 89,
    mary  => 73,
    alice => 100,
    bob   => 83.
};

# first way
my ( $jim, $mary ) = @$score_for{ qw{jim mary} };
print "$jim $mary\n";

# second way
$jim  = $score_for->{jim};
$mary = $score_for->{mary};
print "$jim $mary\n";
```

The real problem is writing %$score_for{ ... }. Remember, when writing a slice, you use the @ symbol to show that you want to get a list of variables. That's one way to fix the issue.

The second way is to forget about using a slice and assigning the variables individually. Many programmers find this solution cleaner.

CHAPTER 7 ANSWERS TO EXERCISES

Exercise 1 Solution

The following code prints 6.4, the average of the numbers passed in:

```
sub average {
    my @numbers = @_;
    my $total   = 0;
    $total += $_ foreach @numbers;
    return $total / @numbers;
}
print average(qw< 1 5 18 3 5>);
```

Exercise 2 Solution

```perl
use Scalar::Util 'looks_like_number';
use Carp 'croak';
sub average {
    my @numbers = @_;
    my $total   = 0;
    foreach my $number (@numbers) {
        if ( not looks_like_number($number) ) {
            croak "$number doesn't look like a number";
        }
        else {
            $total += $number;
        }
    }
    return $total / @numbers;
}
print average(qw< 1 5 18 bob 3 5>);
```

Exercise 3 Solution

```perl
sub make_multiplier {
    my $number = shift;
    return sub { return shift(@_) * $number };
}
my $times_seven = make_multiplier(7);
my $times_five  = make_multiplier(5);
print 21 == $times_seven->(3) ? "yes\n" : "no\n";
print 20 == $times_five->(4)  ? "yes\n" : "no\n";
```

Exercise 4 Solution

```perl
sub sum {
    return 0 unless @_;
    my ( $head, @tail ) = @_;
    return $head + sum(@tail);
}
print sum( 1, 93, 3, 5 );
```

CHAPTER 8 ANSWERS TO EXERCISES

Exercise 1 Solution

```perl
my $social_security_re = qr/\b(\d{3})-(\d{2})-(\d{4})\b/;
# or
my $social_security_re = qr/\b(\d\d\d)-(\d\d)-(\d\d\d\d)\b/;
```

There are, of course, other solutions.

Use word boundaries at the beginning and end of the regex. If you don't, you could easily have something like this matching:

```
44444444444444-44-44444444444444
```

You don't want that, obviously.

Exercise 2 Solution

Part of the art of writing regular expressions is knowing your data. A regular expression is often crafted for a particular quick-and-dirty job. In this case, you can assume usernames are only alphabetical characters and user numbers are five-digit numbers.

```
use strict;
use warnings;
use Data::Dumper;
my $employee_numbers = <<'END_EMPLOYEES';
alice: 48472
bob:34582
# we need to fire charlie
    charlie : 45824
# denise is a new hire
denise : 34553
END_EMPLOYEES
my %employee_number_for;
while ( $employee_numbers =~ /^ \s* (\w+) \s* : \s* (\d{5}) \s* $/gmx ) {
    $employee_number_for{$1} = $2;
}
print Dumper \%employee_number_for;
```

This example looked easy, but the /g was needed to match all the employees, and the /m (multiline) is used to make the ^ and $ anchors treat each line of text as a separate string. That prints out the following:

```
$VAR1 = {
         'alice' => '48472',
         'denise' => '34553',
         'charlie' => '45824',
         'bob' => '34582'
       };
```

Exercise 3 Solution

```
my $text = <<'END';
We hired Mark in 2011-02-03. He's working on product
1034-34-345A. He is expected to finish the work on or
before 2012-12-12 because our idiot CEO thinks the world
will end.
END
```

```perl
my %month_for = (
    '01' => 'January',
    '02' => 'February',
    '03' => 'March',
    '04' => 'April',
    '05' -> 'May',
    '06' => 'June',
    '07' => 'July',
    '08' => 'August',
    '09' => 'September',
    '10' => 'October',
    '11' => 'November',
    '12' => 'December',
);
$text =~ s{\b(\d\d\d\d)-(\d\d)-(\d\d)\b}
          {sprintf "$month_for{$2} %d, %d", $3, $1}ge;
print $text;
```

And that will print out the following:

```
We hired Mark in February 3, 2011. He's working on product
1034-34-345A. He is expected to finish the work on or
before December 12, 2012 because our idiot CEO thinks the world
will end.
```

There's nothing tricky with this one, but we had to quote the hash keys because otherwise Perl would interpret those as octal numbers (see Chapter 4).

The `sprintf()` formats are also straightforward, In reality, using a module such as `DateTime` would help you validate that these are valid dates.

CHAPTER 9 ANSWERS TO EXERCISES

Exercise 1 Solution

```perl
use strict;
use warnings;
print while <>;
```

Exercise 2 Solution

```perl
use strict;
use warnings;
while (<>) {
    next if !/\S/;      # skip whitespace only lines
    next if /^\s*#/;    # skip comments
    print;
}
```

Exercise 3 Solution

```
use strict;
use warnings;
use Encode 'decode';

binmode STDOUT, ':encoding(UTF-8)';

for my $number (@ARGV) {
    $number = decode('UTF-8', $number);
    print chr($number);
}
```

After you do this correctly and have a Kannada font installed, it prints this following:

ಠ_ಠ

For a somewhat cleaner bit of code, you can write this:

```
use strict;
use warnings;
use utf8::all;
print chr for @ARGV;
```

Exercise 4 Solution

```
use strict;
use warnings;
use Encode 'decode';

binmode STDOUT, ':encoding(UTF-8)';

foreach my $word (@ARGV) {
    $word = decode('UTF-8', $word);
    my @chars = split // => $word;
    foreach my $char (@chars) {
        $char = ord $char;
        print "$char ";
    }
    print "\n";
}
```

Or more simply:

```
use strict;
use warnings;
use utf8::all;

foreach my $word (@ARGV) {
    my @chars = split // => $word;
    foreach my $char (@chars) {
```

```
        $char = ord $char;
        print "$char ";
    }
    print "\n";
}
```

Exercise 5 Solution

```
use strict;
use warnings;
use Encode 'decode';

binmode STDOUT, ':encoding(UTF-8)';

foreach my $word (@ARGV) {
    $word = decode('UTF-8', $word);
    my @chars = split // => $word;
    foreach my $char (@chars) {
        $char = ord $char;
        print "$char ";
    }
    print "\n";
}
Or more simply
use strict;
use warnings;
use utf8::all;

foreach my $word (@ARGV) {
    my @chars = split // => $word;
    foreach my $char (@chars) {
        $char = ord $char;
        print "$char ";
    }
    print "\n";
}
```

To print the Unicode code points, change the `$char = ord $char` line to this:

```
$char = "U+" . uc sprintf "%04x", ord $char;
```

CHAPTER 10 ANSWERS TO EXERCISES

Exercise 1 Solution

See `hex()` and `oct()` in Chapter 4 if you need a refresher on the `0x...` syntax. The following code is merely the hexadecimal representation of numbers:

```
my @numbers = ( 0x23, 0xAA, 0xaa, 0x01, 0xfB );
```

So a descending numeric sort is just:

```
my @sorted = sort { $b <=> $a } @numbers;
print join ', ' => @sorted;
```

And that prints:

```
251, 170, 170, 35, 1
```

Of course, you may not want to print the decimal values when the original numbers were in hexadecimal.

```
my @numbers = ( 0x23, 0xAA, 0xaa, 0x01, 0xfB );
my @sorted = sort { $b <=> $a } @numbers;
print join ', ' => map { sprintf "0x%X", $_ }  @sorted;
```

And that prints:

```
0xFB, 0xAA, 0xAA, 0x23, 0x1
```

Exercise 2 Solution

The BLOCK form looks like this:

```
my @numbers = ( 28, 49, 1000, 4, 25, 49, 529 );
my @squares = sort { $a <=> $b }
              grep { int(sqrt($_)) == sqrt($_) } @numbers;
print join ', ' => @squares;
```

The grep is taking the integer value of the square root and comparing it against the square root. For the number 9, you get 3 == 3 and that's a perfect square. However, the square root of 1000 is reduced to something like 31.6227766016838 == 31 and that is clearly not true, so 1000 is not a perfect square.

The EXPRESSION form looks like this:

```
my @squares = sort { $a <=> $b }
              grep int(sqrt($_)) == sqrt($_), @numbers;
```

It can also be written like this:

```
my @squares = sort { $a <=> $b }
              grep(int(sqrt($_)) == sqrt($_), @numbers_;
```

What happens if one of the values in the @numbers array is actually the string Get a job, hippy!? How would this change your code?

You can handle this in several ways of handling this, but one way is to realize that perfect squares must be positive integers, so the following would do the trick:

```
my @squares = sort { $a <=> $b }
              grep { /^[0-9]+$/ && ( int(sqrt($_)) == sqrt($_) ) } @numbers;
```

In other words, use the regular expression /^[0-9]+$/ to guarantee that you have only digits.

Exercise 3 Solution

One solution follows:

```
my %seen;
my @unique = grep { not $seen{$_}++ } @list;
```

This is a moderately common idiom in Perl. (Although many people just use the List::MoreUtils uniq function.) Here's how it works.

The first time that bob is encountered in grep, you have this:

```
not $seen{'bob'}++
```

You know that $seen{'bob'} must be false the first time it's encountered because there is no entry in the %seen hash, and it evaluates as this:

```
not undef
```

And that evaluates as true; allow grep to say "bob's OK and we'll pass him along." However, the ++ autoincrement operator kicks in *after* Perl has returned the value. It sees the undef value, treats it as 0 (zero) and adds 1 to it.

The second time that bob is encountered in the grep, $seen{'bob'} has the value of 1 and not 1 is 0 (zero) and that evaluates as false. Thus, grep cannot return any values after they are seen for the first time.

Exercise 4 Solution

The map and sort looks like this:

```
my @names = map  { "$_->{first_name} $_->{last_name}"  }
            sort { $a->{last_name} cmp $b->{last_name} }
            grep { $_->{years} > 1                     }
              @employees;
```

Unlike other examples, use all of sort, map, and grep. The grep filters the list before the sort because there is no point in sorting values that you will throw away (particularly if the list you sort is large). The sort, of course, comes before the map because after the map you no longer have your data structure, and it would be harder to sort on that last name.

There comes a time when you, as a Perl developer, will feel comfortable with these techniques. Here's how it might be rewritten with a for loop. Use a sort subroutine to make the sort clearer.

```
sub by_last_name { $a->{last_name} cmp $b->{last_name} }
my @names;
foreach my $employee ( sort by_last_name @employees ) {
    next if $employee->{years} <= 1;
    push @names, "$employee->{first_name} $employee->{last_name}";
}
```

It's entirely up to you (and the circumstances of your code) which method you find cleaner and easier to maintain.

CHAPTER 11 ANSWERS TO EXERCISES

Exercise 1 Solution

One way of writing this package would be:

```
package Convert::Distance::Metric;

use strict;
use warnings;

our $VERSION = '0.01';

use Exporter 'import';

our @EXPORT_OK = qw(
    kilometers_to_meters
    meters_to_kilometers
);
our %EXPORT_TAGS = ( all => \@EXPORT_OK );
use constant METERS_PER_KILOMETER => 1000;

sub meters_to_kilometers {
    my $meters = shift;
    return $meters / METERS_PER_KILOMETER;
}

sub kilometers_to_meters {
    my $kilometers = shift;
    return $kilometers * METERS_PER_KILOMETER;
}

1;
```

Don't forget that trailing 1!

Exercise 2 Solution

When you have added `Convert::Distance::Metric`, you should see a file layout like this in your `lib/` directory:

```
lib/
|  Convert/
|  |  Distance/
|  |  |--Imperial.pm
|  |  |--Metric.pm
```

Your MANIFEST should now look like this:

```
Changes
lib/Convert/Distance/Imperial.pm
lib/Convert/Distance/Metric.pm
Makefile.PL
MANIFEST                    This list of files
README
t/00-load.t
t/manifest.t
t/pod-coverage.t
t/pod.t
```

If you do not include lib/Convert/Distance/Metric.pm in your manifest, it will not be included in the distribution when you type make dist.

Exercise 3 Solution

For simplicity's sake, we're going to add the POD after a final __END__ literal.

```
__END__

=head1 NAME

Convert::Distance::Metric - Convert kilometers to meters and back

=head1 SYNOPSIS

 use Convert::Distance::Metric ":all";
 print kilometers_to_meters(7);
 print meters_to_kilometers(3800);

=head1 DESCRIPTION

This is a simple module to convert kilometers to meters and
back. It's mainly here to show how modules are built and
documented.

=head1 EXPORT

The following functions may be exported on demand. You can
export all of them with:

 use Convert::Distance::Metric ':all';

=over 4
```

```
=item * C<kilometers_to_meters>

=item * C<meters_to_kilometers>

=back

=head1 FUNCTIONS

=head2 C<kilometers_to_meters>

 my $meters = kilometers_to_meters($kilometers);

This function accepts a number representing kilometers and
returns the number of meters in that number of kilometers.

=head2 C<meters_to_kilometers>

 my $kilometers = meters_to_kilometers($meters);

This function accepts a number representing meters and returns
the number of kilometers in that number of meters.

=head1 BUGS

None known. Report bugs via e-mail to C<me@example.com>.

=head1 SEE ALSO

See the L<Convert::Distance::Imperial> modules for imperial
conversions.

=head1 AUTHOR

Curtis "Ovid" Poe C<ovid@cpan.org>

=head1 LICENSE

Copyright 2012 Curtis "Ovid" Poe.

This program is free software; you can redistribute it and/or
modify it under the terms of either: the GNU General Public
License as published by the Free Software Foundation; or the Artistic License. See
http://dev.perl.org/licenses/ for more
information.
```

Exercise 4 Solution

```
use strict;
use warnings;
use lib 'lib';
use Convert::Distance::Metric ":all";
my $kilometers = 3.5;
my $meters = kilometers_to_meters($kilometers);
```

```
print "There are $meters meters in $kilometers kilometers\n";
$kilometers = meters_to_kilometers($meters);
print "There are $kilometers kilometers in $meters meters\n";
```

Running the program should print out:

```
There are 3500 meters in 3.5 kilometers
There are 3.5 kilometers in 3500 meters
```

Exercise 5 Solution (Option)

We haven't covered testing yet, but the initial t/00-load.t looks something like this:

```
#!perl -T

use Test::More tests => 1;

BEGIN {
    use_ok( 'Convert::Distance::Imperial' )
      || print "Bail out!\n";
}
diag( "Testing Convert::Distance::Imperial
      $Convert::Distance::Imperial::VERSION,
Perl $], $^X" );
```

After you add Convert::Distance::Metric, it should look like this:

```
#!perl -T

use Test::More tests => 2;

BEGIN {
    use_ok( 'Convert::Distance::Imperial' )
      || print "Bail out!\n";
    use_ok( 'Convert::Distance::Metric' )
      || print "Bail out!\n";
}
diag( "Testing Convert::Distance::Imperial
      $Convert::Distance::Imperial::VERSION,
Perl $], $^X" );
```

Testing this with the prove utility should produce output similar to the following:

```
$ prove -lv t/00-load.t
t/00-load.t ..
1..2
ok 1 - use Convert::Distance::Imperial;
ok 2 - use Convert::Distance::Metric;
# Testing Convert::Distance::Imperial 0.01, Perl 5.010001,
/Users/ovid/perl5/perlbrew/perls/perl-5.10.1/bin/perl
ok
All tests successful.
```

```
Files=1, Tests=2,  0 wallclock secs ( 0.02 usr  0.01 sys +
  0.02 cusr  0.00 csys =  0.05 CPU)
Result: PASS
```

CHAPTER 12 ANSWERS TO EXERCISES

Exercise 1 Solution

One way of writing the Person class would be this:

```perl
package Person;

use strict;
use warnings;

use DateTime;
use Carp 'croak';

sub new {
    my ( $class, $args ) = @_;
    my $self = bless {} => $class;
    $self->_initialize($args);
    return $self;
}

sub _initialize {
    my ( $self, $args ) = @_;
    my %args      = %$args;
    my $name      = delete $args{name};
    my $birthdate = delete $args{birthdate};
    # must have at least one non-whitespace character
    unless ( $name && $name =~ /\S/ ) {
        croak "Person name must be supplied";
    }
    # trap the error if it's not an object
    unless ( eval { $birthdate->isa('DateTime') } ) {
        croak "Person birthdate must be a DateTime object";
    }
    $self->{name}     = $name;
    $self->{birthdate} = $birthdate;
}

sub name     { $_[0]->{name} }
sub birthdate { $_[0]->{birthdate} }

sub age {
    my $self = shift;
    my $duration = DateTime->now - $self->birthdate;
    return $duration->years;
}

1;
```

The `DateTime::Duration` object that is created in the `age()` method has a `years()` method (`perldoc DateTime::Duration` would have shown you this) and you can use that to figure out how many years old the person is.

You can test this with the following code:

```
use DateTime;
my $person = Person->new({
    name     => 'Bertrand Russell',
    birthdate => DateTime->new(
        year  => 1872,
        month => 5,
        day   => 18,
    ),
});
print $person->name, ' is ', $person->age, ' years old';
```

That should print; although, the age will obviously vary depending on when you run this code.

```
Bertrand Russell is 139 years old
```

Exercise 2 Solution

The problem with this code is in the `new()` constructor. We have used the one-argument form of `bless` and that automatically blesses the code into the current class. If you tried to subclass this class and you did not override the `new()` method, the object would be blessed into the superclass, not the subclass. Always use the two-argument form of `bless()`.

Exercise 3 Solution

```
my $self = bless {}, $class;
package Customer;

use strict;
use warnings;

use Carp 'croak';
use base 'Person';

sub _initialize {
    my ( $self, @args ) = @_;
    $self->SUPER::_initialize(@args);
    if ( $self->age < 18 ) {
        croak "Customers must be 18 years old or older";
    }
}

1;
```

CHAPTER 13 ANSWERS TO EXERCISES

Exercise 1 Solution

```
package User;

use Moose;
use Digest::MD5 'md5_hex';

use namespace::autoclean;

has username => ( is => 'ro', isa => 'Str', required => 1 );
has password => (
    is     => 'ro',
    isa    => 'Str',
    writer => '_set_password',
);

sub BUILD {
    my $self = shift;
    $self->_set_password(md5_hex($self->password));
}

sub password_eq {
    my ( $self, $password ) = @_;
    $password = md5_hex($password);
    return $password eq $self->password;
}

__PACKAGE__->meta->make_immutable;

1;
```

You can test the preceding code with the following snippet:

```
my $user = User->new(
    username => 'Ovid',
    password => 'Corinna',
);
print $user->dump;
print "Yes" if $user->password_eq('Corinna');
```

Exercise 2 Solution

Here's one way to write the role:

```
package Does::ToHash;

use Moose::Role;

sub to_hash {
```

```
        my $self = shift;
        my @attributes = map { $_->name }
          $self->meta->get_all_attributes;
        my %hash;
        foreach my $attribute (@attributes) {
            my $value = $self->$attribute;
            next if ref $value;
            $hash{$attribute} = $value;
        }
        return \%hash;
    }

    1;
```

And extending the User class to provide the Does::ToHash method looks like this:

```
    package User;

    use Moose;
    with 'Does::ToHash';

    use Digest::MD5 'md5_hex';
    use namespace::autoclean;

    has username => ( is => 'ro', isa => 'Str', required => 1 );
    has password => (
        is      => 'ro',
        isa     => 'Str',
        writer  => '_set_password',
    );

    sub BUILD {
        my $self = shift;
        $self->_set_password(md5_hex($self->password));
    }

    sub password_eq {
        my ( $self, $password ) = @_;
        $password = md5_hex($password);
        return $password eq $self->password;
    }

    __PACKAGE__->meta->make_immutable;

    1;
```

And if you run this test script:

```
    use Data::Dumper;
    my $user = User->new(
        username => 'Ovid',
        password => 'Corinna',
    );
    print Dumper($user->to_hash);
```

You get the following output:

```
$VAR1 = {
          'password' => '5169c96db420b1157c60ba46a6d4b43c',
          'username' => 'Ovid'
        };
```

CHAPTER 14 ANSWERS TO EXERCISES

Exercise 1 Solution

In looking at the test's @want array, you will see that the unique elements should be returned in the order they were found in the original list.

```
use Test::Most;
sub unique {
    my @array = @_;
    my %seen;
    my @unique;
    foreach my $element (@array) {
        push @unique => $element unless $seen{$element}++;
    }
    return @unique;
}
my @have = unique( 2, 3, 5, 4, 3, 5, 7 );
my @want = ( 2, 3, 5, 4, 7 );
is_deeply \@have, \@want,
  'unique() should return unique() elements in order';
done_testing;
```

And that prints out:

```
ok 1 - unique() should return unique() elements in order
1..1
```

Exercise 2 Solution

The original unique() function returned the elements in whatever order they were found in the hash keys, making them effectively random. Thus, sorting elements should be enough.

```
is_deeply [ sort @have ], [ sort @want ],
  'unique() should return unique() elements in order';
```

You don't even need to sort them numerically so long as you use the same ordering behavior for both the @have and @want arrays.

Exercise 3 Solution

There are several approaches here, but use Scalar::Util 'looks_like_number'.

```
use Test::Most;
use Carp 'croak';
use Scalar::Util 'looks_like_number';
sub reciprocal {
    my $number = shift;
    unless ( looks_like_number($number) ) {
        croak("Argument to reciprocal\(\) must be a number");
    }
    unless ($number) {
        croak("Illegal division by zero");
    }
    return 1 / $number;
}
throws_ok { reciprocal([]) }
  qr/Argument to reciprocal\(\) must be a number/,
  'Passing non-numbers to reciprocal() should fail';
diag reciprocal([]);
done_testing;
```

Exercise 4 Solution

This one is a tricky because we laid a trap for you. In the original TestsFor::TV::Episode, we had the %default_attributes hardcoded into the test method. You need to rewrite TestsFor::TV::Episode. Specifically, you'll want to pull out the hardcoded attributes into a method you can easily override.

```
package TestsFor::TV::Episode;
use Test::Most;
use base 'TestsFor';
sub attributes : Tests(14) {
    my $test               = shift;
    my %default_attributes = $test->default_attributes;
    my $class              = $test->class_to_test;
    my $episode            = $class->new(%default_attributes);
    while ( my ( $attribute, $value ) = each %default_attributes ) {
        can_ok $episode, $attribute;
        is $episode->$attribute, $value,
          "The value for '$attribute' should be correct";
    }
    my %attributes = %default_attributes;    # copy 'em
    foreach my $attribute (qw/season episode_number/) {
        $attributes{$attribute} = 0;
        throws_ok { $class->new(%attributes) }
        qr/Attribute \($attribute\) does not pass the type constraint/,
          "Setting the $attribute to a value less than zero should fail";
    }
}
sub default_attributes {
    return (
        series         => 'Firefly',
        director       => 'Marita Grabiak',
        title          => 'Jaynestown',
        genre          => 'awesome',
```

```
            season         => 1,
            episode_number => 7,
        );
    }
    1;
```

When that is done, writing the test for `TestsFor::TV::Episode::Broadcast` is simple:

```
package TestsFor::TV::Episode::Broadcast;
use Test::Most;
use DateTime;
use base 'TestsFor::TV::Episode';
sub default_attributes {
    my $test       = shift;
    my %attributes = $test->SUPER::default_attributes;
    $attributes{broadcast_date} = DateTime->new(
        year  => 2002,
        month => 10,
        day   => 8,
    );
    return %attributes;
}
sub attributes : Tests(+2) {
    my $test = shift;
    $test->SUPER::attributes;
}
1;
```

Obviously, you could easily add more tests to that, but this is a good start. Studying this example carefully and understanding why it works can give you many insights into both testing and object-oriented programming.

If you've coded all the examples from this chapter, a full run of your test suite should now look like this:

```
% prove t
t/query.t ......... ok
t/test_classes.t .. ok
t/testit.t ........ ok
All tests successful.
Files=3, Tests=59,  4 wallclock secs
Result: PASS
```

CHAPTER 15 ANSWERS TO EXERCISES

Exercise 1 Solution

First, look at the templates:

In the `templates/characters.tt`, add the following select group after the `Profession`. This enables you to choose your education.

```
<tr>
  <td>Education</td>
  <td>
    <select name="education">
      <option value="combat">Combat</option>
      <option value="medical">Medical</option>
      <option value="engineering">Engineering</option>
    </select>
  </td>
</tr>
```

In `templates/character_display.tt`, add the following line after Profession. It enables the chosen education to display.

```
<tr><td>Education</td><td>[% character.education %]</td></tr>
```

The main work is in `characters.psgi`, but it's fairly easy.

In the `generate_character()` subroutine, the `%adjustments_for` hash now looks like this:

```
my %adjustments_for = (
    profession => {
        programmer => {
            strength     => -3,
            intelligence => 8,
            health       => -2,
        },
        pilot   => { intelligence => 3 },
        redshirt => { strength     => 5 }
    },
    birthplace => {
        earth => {
            strength     => 2,
            intelligence => 0,
            health       => -2,
        },
        mars => { strength     => -5, health => 2 },
        vat  => { intelligence => 2,  health => -2 }
    },
    education => {
        combat      => { strength     => 2 },
        medical     => { health       => 2 },
        engineering => { intelligence => 2 }
    },
);
```

The `%label_for` hash now looks like this:

```
my %label_for = (
    profession => {
        pilot      => "Starship Pilot",
        programmer => "Programmer",
        redshirt   => "Doomed",
    },
```

```
        education => {
            combat      => "Combat",
            medical     => "Medical",
            engineering => "Engineering",
        },
        birthplace => {
            earth => "Earth",
            mars  => "Mars",
            vat   => "Vat 3-5LX",
        },
    );
```

Now you just need to add education to the list of attributes you iterate over:

```
        foreach my $attribute (qw/name education profession birthplace/) {
            # create character
        }
```

With that, run `plackup characters.psgi` and try it out.

Exercise 2 Solution

```
    use strict;
    use warnings;

    use WWW::Mechanize;
    use HTML::TableExtract;
    use List::Util qw/min max sum/;

    my $url  = 'http://localhost:5000/';
    my $mech = WWW::Mechanize->new;

    my %stats_for = map { $_ => [] } qw/Strength Intelligence Health/;

    for ( 1 .. 100 ) {
        $mech->get($url);
        $mech->follow_link( text_regex => qr/Please click here/ );
        $mech->submit_form(
            form_number => 1,
            fields      => {
                name       => 'Bob',
                profession => 'programmer',
                education  => 'engineering',
                birthplace => 'earth',
            },
        );

        my $te = HTML::TableExtract->new;
        $te->parse( $mech->content );

        foreach my $ts ( $te->tables ) {
            foreach my $row ( $ts->rows ) {
                if ( exists $stats_for{ $row->[0] } ) {
```

```
                    push @{ $stats_for{ $row->[0] } } => $row->[1];
                }
            }
        }
    }

    while ( my ( $stat, $values ) = each %stats_for ) {
        my $min = min @$values;
        my $max = max @$values;
        my $avg = sum(@$values)/scalar @$values;
        print "$stat:  Min ($min) Max ($max) Average ($avg)\n";
    }
```

Running this on your author's computer takes just more than a second. Running this over the web would likely take much longer. Here is the output from two sample runs:

```
Health:  Min (2) Max (23) Average (12.72)
Strength:  Min (5) Max (26) Average (15.32)
Intelligence:  Min (15) Max (39) Average (26.32)

Health:  Min (0) Max (24) Average (12.12)
Strength:  Min (4) Max (26) Average (14.79)
Intelligence:  Min (17) Max (38) Average (26.29)
```

It appears that in the second run, you generated a dead programmer. Oops.

CHAPTER 16 ANSWERS TO EXERCISES

Exercise 1 Solution

When you call prepare(), you must always call execute() before fetching results:

```
my $sth = $dbh->prepare("SELECT id, name FROM customers");
$sth->execute;
while ( my @row = $sth->fetchrow_array ) {
    print "ID: $row[0] Name: $row[1]\n";
}
```

If you find this too verbose and you don't have huge amounts of data, you can shorten this with:

```
my $customers = $dbh->selectall_arrayref($sql);
```

Exercise 2 Solution

This one is tricky and you can handle it in a few ways. If you were allowed to change the licenses table, you could switch the names of the licenses. (That would be trickier if there were more data in the licenses table.) Instead, you need to fetch all the associated IDs from both sets of data upfront and then start a transaction before making the switch. Without a transaction, if the code fails partway through (for example, if you lose the database connection), you could have serious data corruption.

You learned enough in this chapter to make this work without consulting the docs further, but you can take a quick shortcut.

This code fetches the Public Domain id and the Attribution BY CC ID. Then it fetches the media ids in separate array references, one set for the Public Domain media and one set for the Attribution BY CC media.

When you have the data, create a try/catch block and update the license IDs to their new values. (In other words, you effectively swap them.)

```
use strict;
use warnings;

use lib 'lib';
use MyDatabase 'db_handle';
use Try::Tiny;

my $pb_id = $dbh->selectall_arrayref(<<'END');
  SELECT id
    FROM licenses
   WHERE name = 'Public Domain'
END

if ( @$pb_id > 1 ) {
    die "More than one Public Domain id found";
}

my $cc_id = $dbh->selectall_arrayref(<<'END');
  SELECT id
    FROM licenses
   WHERE name = 'Attribution CC BY'
END

if ( @$cc_id > 1 ) {
    die "More than one Attribution CC BY id found";
}

my $sql    = 'SELECT id FROM media WHERE license_id = ?';
my $pb_ids = $dbh->selectcol_arrayref( $sql, undef, $pb_id->[0] );
my $cc_ids = $dbh->selectcol_arrayref( $sql, undef, $cc_id->[0] );

# now that we have all of our relevant data, time to move on:
if ( @$pb_ids && @$cc_ids ) {
    $dbh->begin_work;
    try {

        # here, we replace every id with a question mark and
        # then join the question marks.
        my $placeholders = join ',', map { '?' } @$pb_ids;
        my $rows_affected = $dbh->do(<<"END", undef, $cc_id, @$pb_ids);
        UPDATE media SET license_id = ? WHERE id IN ($placeholders)
END
```

```
            unless ( $rows_affected == @$pb_ids ) {
                my $expected = @$pb_ids;
                die "We should have changed $expected rows, not $rows_affected";
            }
            $placeholders = join ',', map { '?' } @$cc_ids;
            $rows_affected = $dbh->do( <<"END", undef, $pb_id, @$cc_ids );
            UPDATE media SET license_id = ? WHERE id IN ($placeholders)
END

            unless ( $rows_affected == @$pb_ids ) {
                my $expected = @$pb_ids;
                die "We should have changed $expected rows, not $rows_affected";
            }

            # if we got to here, we swapped them safely
            $dbh->commit;
        }
        catch {
            $dbh->rollback;
            die $_;
        };
    }
```

CHAPTER 17 ANSWERS TO EXERCISES

Exercise 1 Solution

You want to read the person's birthday from STDIN. Then, you use DateTime::Format::Strptime to parse that date into a DateTime object. Then, you can subtract that date from DateTime->now to get a DateTime::Duration object and call the years() method on it to extract the number of years since the birthday.

```
use strict;
use warnings;

use DateTime;
use DateTime::Format::Strptime;

my $datetime_formatter = DateTime::Format::Strptime->new(
    pattern   => '%Y-%m-%d',
    time_zone => 'GMT',
);

print "Enter your birthday in YYYY-MM-DD format: ";

my $birthday = <STDIN>;
chomp($birthday);

my $birthday_date = $datetime_formatter->parse_datetime($birthday)
    or die "Could not parse birthday: $birthday";

my $duration = DateTime->now - $birthday_date;
printf "You are %d years old\n" => $duration->years;
```

Exercise 2 Solution

You use `Getopt::Long` with `--birthdate` and `--age_at` command-line switches. If `--birthdate` is not supplied, prompt the user from the command line. If `--age_at` is not supplied, assume today as the end date. If the end date is before the starting date, you'll die with a useful error message.

```perl
use strict;
use warnings;

use DateTime;
use Getopt::Long;
use DateTime::Format::Strptime;

my ( $birthdate, $age_at );
GetOptions(
    'birthdate=s' => \$birthdate,
    'age_at=s'    => \$age_at,
) or die "Could not parse options";

my $name = join " " => @ARGV;
my $datetime_formatter = DateTime::Format::Strptime->new(
    pattern   => '%Y-%m-%d',
    time_zone => 'GMT',
);

unless ($birthdate) {
    print "Enter your birthday in YYYY-MM-DD format: ";
    $birthdate = <STDIN>;
    chomp($birthdate);
}

my $birthday_date = $datetime_formatter->parse_datetime($birthdate)
  or die "Could not parse birthday: $birthdate";
my $end_date = DateTime->now;

if ($age_at) {    # overwrite $end_date if we have $age_at
    $end_date = $datetime_formatter->parse_datetime($age_at)
      or die "Could not parse birthday: $age_at";
}

if ( $end_date < $birthday_date ) {
    die "End date must be on or after the birthday";
}

my $duration = $end_date - $birthday_date;
if ($name) {
    printf "$name is %d years old\n" => $duration->years;
}
else {
    printf "You are %d years old\n" => $duration->years;
}
```

Exercise 3 Solution

This one is a bit trickier and shows you that `Capture::Tiny` does the right thing, but it might be a bit hard to figure out at first. First, here's one way to write those tests:

```
use strict;
use warnings;

use Test::More;
use DateTime;
use Capture::Tiny 'capture';

my ( $stdout, $stderr, @output ) = capture {
    qx/perl age.pl --birthdate 1964-10-18 --age_at 2007-10-02 Charles Stross/;
};

is $output[0], "Charles Stross is 42 years old\n",
  'Charles Stross was 42 years old when he wrote Halting State';
( $stdout, $stderr, @output ) = capture {
    qx/perl age.pl --birthday 1967-06-20/;
};
like $stderr, qr/Unknown option: birthday/,
  'Passing an unknown option should cause the program to fail';

( $stdout, $stderr, @output ) = capture {
    open my $fh, '|-', 'perl age.pl Ovid';
    print $fh '1967-06-20';
};
like $stdout, qr/Enter your birthday in YYYY-MM-DD format:/,
  'Not entering a birthdate should prompt for our birthday';

my $today    = DateTime->now;
my $birthday = DateTime->new(
    year  => 1967,
    month => 6,
    day   => 20,
);
my $age = ( $today - $birthday )->years;

like $stdout, qr/Ovid is $age years old/,
  '... and the program should still tell use the correct age';
diag $stdout;
done_testing;
```

In your first test:

```
my ( $stdout, $stderr, @output ) = capture {
    qx/perl age.pl --birthdate 1964-10-18 --age_at 2007-10-02 Charles Stross/;
};
is $output[0], "Charles Stross is 42 years old\n",
  'Charles Stross was 42 years old when he wrote Halting State';
```

Because qx returns the program's STDOUT, it populates the @output argument in your return values. In this example, your $stdout is always empty and your $stderr remains empty if you have no errors.

Your second test shows that $stderr is gets a value when you pass a bad option:

```
( $stdout, $stderr, @output ) = capture {
    qx/perl age.pl --birthday 1967-06-20/;
};
like $stderr, qr/Unknown option: birthday/,
  'Passing an unknown option should cause the program to fail';
```

Your third test is the most interesting:

```
( $stdout, $stderr, @output ) = capture {
    open my $fh, '|-', 'perl age.pl Ovid';
    print $fh '1967-06-20';
};

like $stdout, qr/Enter your birthday in YYYY-MM-DD format:/,
  'Not entering a birthdate should prompt for our birthday';

my $today    = DateTime->now;
my $birthday = DateTime->new(
    year  => 1967,
    month => 6,
    day   => 20,
);

my $age = ( $today - $birthday )->years;
like $stdout, qr/Ovid is $age years old/,
  '... and the program should still tell use the correct age';
```

You used a piped open instead of the qx operator because you had to send some data to the program. You can then construct your own DateTime object for today to make sure that you always have the correct age in years in your test.

The entire test output should look similar to this:

```
age.t ..
ok 1 - Charles Stross was 42 years old when he wrote Halting State
ok 2 - Passing an unknown option should cause the program to fail
ok 3 - Not entering a birthdate should prompt for our birthday
ok 4 - ... and the program should still tell use the correct age
1..4
# Enter your birthday in YYYY-MM-DD format: Ovid is 44 years old
ok
All tests successful.
Files=1, Tests=4,  0 wallclock secs
Result: PASS
```

This diagnostic is in the test output:

```
# Enter your birthday in YYYY-MM-DD format: Ovid is 44 years old
```

That comes from this line of code:

```
diag $stdout;
```

Though you could determine this by reading your tests carefully, the `diag()` statement makes it clear that `Capture::Tiny` is going to return all the STDOUT into a single variable, but you can see it's on a single line without newlines. Why? If you run the `age.pl` program from the command line, you might see output like this:

```
$ perl age.pl Ovid
Enter your birthday in YYYY-MM-DD format: 1967-06-20
Ovid is 44 years old
```

So why doesn't that show up in two lines in your `$stdout` variable?

The newline that you might expect after you enter your birthday in YYYY-MM-DD format isn't present because that was actually read from the program's STDIN! Just because you can see it on the console when you ran the program from the command line doesn't mean that it's coming from that program's STDOUT. This behavior might seem confusing, but after you think about it, it's quite clear.

CHAPTER 18 ANSWERS TO EXERCISES

Exercise 1 Solution

Three potential problems may include:

➤ Commas might be embedded in quotes, breaking the split on commas.

➤ Newlines might be embedded in quotes, causing the filehandle read to return a partial column.

➤ Quotation marks are used only to quote columns with special characters and are not part of the data. The program does not remove them.

Exercise 2 Solution

You use `DateTime::Tiny` when you need only a simple data object. It can tell you the day, month, hour, and so on. It's also easy to print as a string. It's lightweight and fast; however, it does not support date comparisons or other forms of date manipulation. It can be inflated to a `DateTime` object.

The `DateTime` module is the most complete `DateTime` manipulation solution available on the CPAN. It's extremely comprehensive and flexible (including excellent handling of time zones, though those were not discussed in the chapter) and can enable you to compare date and times and do simple date math. Unfortunately, the module is large, slow to load, and often provides more functionality than a simple program might need.

Exercise 3 Solution

You should generally run Devel::NYTProf when your code runs slowly and you need to figure out why. If your code runs fast enough, running Devel::NYTProf can be interesting, but it can also service as a distraction when you have other tasks that you need to accomplish. When your program runs fast enough, you should consider leaving it alone and not falling prey to the endless tweaking to which so many programmers are prone. Further, over-optimizing your code can sometimes make it harder to read. Clean, simple code tends to be easier to maintain and often has fewer bugs than heavily optimized but obscure code.

Exercise 4 Solution

Running perlcritic -5 program.pl produces the following output:

```
Code before strictures are enabled at line 3, column 1.
  See page 429 of PBP.  (Severity: 5)
Running perlcritic -1 program.pl produces the following:
RCS keywords $Id$ not found at line 1, column 1.
  See page 441 of PBP.  (Severity: 2)
RCS keywords $Revision$, $HeadURL$, $Date$ not found at line 1, column 1.
  See page 441 of PBP.  (Severity: 2)
RCS keywords $Revision$, $Source$, $Date$ not found at line 1, column 1.
  See page 441 of PBP.  (Severity: 2)
Code not contained in explicit package at line 1, column 1.
  Violates encapsulation.  (Severity: 4)
No package-scoped "$VERSION" variable found at line 1, column 1.
  See page 404 of PBP.  (Severity: 2)
Code before strictures are enabled at line 3, column 1.
  See page 429 of PBP.  (Severity: 5)
Code before warnings are enabled at line 3, column 1.
  See page 431 of PBP.  (Severity: 4)
3 is not one of the allowed literal values (0, 1, 2).
  Use the Readonly or Const::Fast module or the "constant" pragma
  instead at line 4, column 13.
  Unnamed numeric literals make code less maintainable.  (Severity: 2)
"die" used instead of "croak" at line 9, column 6.
  See page 283 of PBP.  (Severity: 3)
Module does not end with "1;" at line 13, column 1.
  Must end with a recognizable true value.  (Severity: 4)
Always unpack @_ first at line 13, column 1.
  See page 178 of PBP.  (Severity: 4)
Subroutine "hello" does not end with "return" at line 13, column 1.
  See page 197 of PBP.  (Severity: 4)
Return value of flagged function ignored - print at line 15, column 9.
  See pages 208,278 of PBP.  (\: 1)
```

The RCS keywords violation makes little sense if you do not use external tools (such as CVS or Subversion) that support RCS keywords.

Issues such as not using strict or warnings are generally agreed to be problematic, but some of the reported issues (such as not having a package name) don't appear relevant to scripts. Others, such as die instead of croak, don't make much sense in this context.

The reported `3 is not one of the allowed literal values`, and the suggestion to replace it with a read-only constant is clearly not applicable here because you want a default value that can change.

Unpacking `@_` is almost always good advice unless this is hot code for which maximum performance is critical.

Finally, you have a curious combination of a violation for not ending the subroutine with a return statement and then ignoring the returned value. Interesting that you can get more violations reported than there are lines of code, eh?

Exercise 5 Solution

First, create a `perlcriticrc` file specifically for scripts. Save this as `perlcriticscripts`:

```
exclude = RequireRCSKeywords
[-Modules::RequireExplicitPackage]
[-Modules::RequireEndWithOne]
[-Modules::RequireVersionVar]
```

Here's one way to rewrite the program to make it pass the strictest level:

```
use strict;
use warnings;

use Getopt::Long;

sub hello {
    my ( $name, $times ) = @_;
    for ( 1 .. $times ) {
        print "$name\n";    ## no critic 'RequireCheckedSyscalls'
    }
    return;
}

my $name  = 'Nobody';
my $times = 3;              ## no critic 'ProhibitMagicNumbers'

GetOptions(
    'name=s'  => \$name,
    'times=i' => \$times,
) or die;                   ## no critic 'RequireCarping'

hello( $name, $times );
```

You can then verify this works with:

```
$ perlcritic -1 --profile perlcriticscripts my_program.pl
bad.pl source OK
```

`Perl::Critic` violations are often subjective and might not be suitable for your needs. That's OK, but make sure you understand why `Perl::Critic` warns about the issues it finds. If you don't understand the violation, you may be writing problematic code without realizing it.

CHAPTER 19 ANSWERS TO EXERCISES

Exercise 1 Solution

An object relational mapper, also known as an ORM, enables you to treat database records as objects. It can make it easy to manipulate database information without having to embed SQL in your code. They're sometimes cumbersome for reporting systems with complicated SQL that must span many tables (though `DBIx::Class` can handle this), but when you deal with many individual records, they're quite a timesaver.

Exercise 2 Solution

For this exercise, you need to choose Spanish. The Spanish text was automatically translated via Google Translate. (Your author sincerest apologies to Spanish readers for any accidental hilarity.)

Save the following template as `templates/es/letter.tt2`.

```
[% month %] [% day %], [% year %]

Estimado [% name %],

Nuestros registros indican que usted no nos debe $[% amount %].
Si usted no paga inmediatamente, nos veremos obligados romper
el [% body_party %].

Que tengas un buen día :)
Me
```

Now in `listing_19_2_letter.pl`, change the `%body_parts` hash to include an `es` entry:

```
my %body_parts = (
    en => [qw/arms legs/],
    fr => [qw/bras jambes/],
    es => [qw/brazos piernas/],
);
```

Run the program with:

```
perl listing_19_2_letter.pl --name Ovid --amount 4.50 --lang es
```

And you should see output similar to (depending on the date):

```
Junio 12, 2012
Estimado Ovid,

Nuestros registros indican que usted no nos debe $4.50.
```

```
Si usted no paga inmediatamente, nos veremos obligados romper
el brazos.

Que tengas un buen día :)
Me
```

Exercise 3 Solution

First, save the SQL to a file named `videos.sql` and just do this:

```
sqlite3 rights.db < videos.sql
```

Unfortunately, that depends on having an operating system that cooperates with that syntax. So write a Perl script to do this:

```perl
use strict;
use warnings;
use lib 'lib';
use DBI;

my $dbh = DBI->connect(
    "dbi:SQLite:dbname=rights.db",
    "",     # no username required
    "",     # no password required
    { RaiseError => 1, PrintError => 0, AutoCommit => 1 },
) or die $DBH::errstr;

my $create_videos_table = <<"SQL";
CREATE TABLE IF NOT EXISTS videos (
    id       INTEGER PRIMARY KEY,
    name     VARCHAR(255)  NOT NULL,
    url      VARCHAR(1000) NOT NULL,
    released DATETIME             NULL
);
SQL
$dbh->do($create_videos_table);

my $create_video_to_media_table = <<"SQL";
CREATE TABLE IF NOT EXISTS video_to_media (
    id       INTEGER PRIMARY KEY,
    video_id INTEGER NOT NULL,
    media_id INTEGER NOT NULL,
    FOREIGN KEY (video_id) REFERENCES videos(id)
    FOREIGN KEY (media_id) REFERENCES media(id)
);
SQL
$dbh->do($create_video_to_media_table);
```

Next, you want to create your `Rights::Schema::Result::Video` and `Rights::Schema::Result::MediaToVideo` classes and modify the `Rights::Schema::Result::Media` class. However, rather than do this manually, update your model directly with the `rights_create.pl` script:

```
perl script/rights_create.pl model Media DBIC::Schema Rights::Schema \
  create=static 'dbi:SQLite:./rights.db'
```

If you previously added your `display_name()` methods after the DO NOT MODIFY line, as explained earlier in this chapter, they remain after you have rebuilt your schema.

Edit `lib/Rights/Schema/Result/Video.pm` and add the following near the end of the module:

```
sub display_name {
    my $self = shift;
    return $self->name;
}
```

That enables `Catalyst::Plugin::AutoCRUD` to automatically display a useful name for `Videos` in the CRUD interface.

Next, create your controller:

```
perl script/rights_create.pl controller Media
```

And add these two methods, replacing the `index()` method already present in the controller:

```
sub index :Path :Args(0) {
    my ( $self, $c ) = @_;

    my $video_rs = $c->model('Media::Video')->search(
        {},     # we want all of them
        { order_by => { -asc => 'name' } },
    );
    $c->stash->{template} = 'video/all.tt';
    $c->stash->{video_rs}  = $video_rs;
}

sub video :Path :Args(1) {
    my ( $self, $c, $id ) = @_;

    my $video = $c->model('Media::Video')->find($id);
    $c->stash->{template} = 'videos/display.tt';
    $c->stash->{video}     = $video;
}
```

Finally, create a `root/videos` directory and add the following two templates:

`root/videos/all.tt`:

```
<table rules="all">
  <tr><th>Video</th><th>URL</th></tr>
[% WHILE ( video = video_rs.next ) %]
  <tr>
    <td><a href="/video/[%video.id%]">[%video.name|html%]</a></td>
    <td><a href="[% video.url %]">[% video.url | html %]</a></td>
  </tr>
[% END %]
</table>
```

`root/videos/display.tt`:

```
[% IF video %]
<table rules="all">
  <tr>
    <td>Name</td>
    <td>[% video.name |html %]</td>
  </tr>
  <tr>
    <td>URL</td>
    <td><a href="[% video.url %]">[% video.url |html %]</a></td>
  </tr>
  <tr>
    <td>Date Released</td>
    <td>[% video.released |html %]</td>
  </tr>
  [% video_to_medias_rs = video.video_to_medias_rs %]
    <td>Media</td>
  [% IF video_to_medias_rs.count %]
    <td>
      <ul>
    [% WHILE ( v2m = video_to_medias_rs.next ) %]
        <li>
          <a href="/media/[%v2m.media.id%]">[%v2m.media.name|html%]</a>
        </li>
    [% END %]
      </ul>
    </td>
  [% ELSE %]
    <td><strong>No media found</strong></td>
  [% END %]
  </tr>
</table>
[% ELSE %]
<strong>Video not found</strong>
[% END %]
```

Then restart your server. Visit `http://localhost:3000/autocrud` and add one or two videos. Then choose `Video To Media` from the drop-down menu and associate some media with your videos.

Now you can visit `http://localhost:3000/video` to see a list of all videos you added. By clicking a video, you have some basic data about that video, including all media attached to it.

In short, you should have a small, ugly, but functional application enabling you to manage rights data for your videos. When a DMCA takedown request comes along, launch the application, find the video in question, and you can send a reply with all the media you have included, with their sources and your rights to use those sources.

Feel free to play around more with this. The `Catalyst` mailing list, `http://lists.scsys.co.uk/cgi-bin/mailman/listinfo/catalyst`, is helpful and can start you on your way to creating rich, wonderful web applications.

If you feel this application is useful, consider creating a DMCA controller. For this controller, you would have a method such as:

```
sub dmca :Path :Args(1) {
    my ( $self, $c, $id ) = @_;

    my $video = $c->model('Media::Video')->find($id);
    $c->stash->{template} = 'dmca/response.tt';
    $c->stash->{video}    = $video;
}
```

The template for that controller could provide an entire DMCA takedown response for the video in question, listing all media used, their start and end times in the video, the license for each media, the date they were fetched from their respective sources, and a kind of "go away" to the originator of the DMCA request. This response would be part of a form with empty text areas for you to type extra information specific for the particular DMCA takedown request.

Imagine responding appropriately to a DMCA request with a single click of the mouse!

Have fun and congratulations on getting this far!

INDEX

Printed and bound by CPI Group (UK) Ltd, Croydon, CR0 4YY

27/10/2024

14580184-0004